Lives of
Fair and Gallant Ladies

BRANTÔME

Lives

Of

Fair and Gallant Ladies

By

The Seigneur De Brantôme

TRANSLATED FROM THE ORIGINAL

In Two Volumes

Volume I

Fredonia Books
Amsterdam, The Netherlands

Lives of Fair and Gallant Ladies

by
Seigneur De Brantome

ISBN: 1-4101-0619-5

Copyright © 2004 by Fredonia Books

Reprinted from the 1922 edition

Fredonia Books
Amsterdam, The Netherlands
http://www.fredoniabooks.com

FOREWORD

THIS very fine and accurate translation of *The Lives of Fair
and Gallant Ladies* was made by Mr. A. R. Allinson and
because of its merit must be considered one of the great English translations, equalling in every quality those of the 16th
and 17th centuries. The text of Brantôme's great work is
given practically complete in these volumes and the only modifications are based upon good taste and not on any fearful
prudery. A few of Brantôme's examples that illustrate his
points belong more in a treatise on abnormal pathology than
in a book of literary or historical interest and value, so nothing
of any value is lost by omitting them. The rare charm,
shrewd wisdom, amusing anecdote, literary merit and historical and social information will be appreciated by intelligent
readers.

The cover design used on this book was made by C. O.
Czeschka.

BRANTÔME'S HANDWRITING.
(From a fac-simile page of the manuscript
Recueil des Dames. Biblio. Nat: Mss. Nouv. fses.
No. 20-474, folio 163.)

DEDICATION

TO MONSEIGNEUR LE DUC D'ALENÇON
OF BRABANT AND COUNT OF FLANDERS

SON AND BROTHER OF OUR FRENCH KINGS

MY GRACIOUS LORD,

EEING how you have full often done me the honour at Court to converse with me in great privity of sundry jests and merry tales, the which are so familiar and ready with you they may well be said to grow apace before men's very eyes in your Lordship's mouth, so great your wit is and so keen and subtile, and your speech the same, and right eloquent to boot,—for this cause have I set me to indite these discourses, such as they be, to the best of my poor ability, to the end that in this wise some of them may please you, making the time to pass lightly and reminding you of me in your conversations, wherewith erstwhile you have honoured me as much as any gentleman of all the Court.

To you then, my Lord, do I dedicate this present book, and do beseech you fortify the same with your name and authority, till that I may find leisure to attend to discourses of a more serious content. Of such I pray you note one in especial, the which I have all but finished,

[vii]

wherein I do deduce a comparison of six great Princes and Captains that be to-day abroad in this our Christendom, to wit: the King Henri III. your brother, Your Highness' self, the King of Navarre your brother-in-law, the Duc de Guise, the Duc de Maine, and the Prince of Parma, making record for each one of you of your noblest deeds of valour and high emprize, of your excellencies and exploits, the full tale and complement whereof I do resign to others better qualified than I to indite the same.

Meanwhile, My Lord, I do beseech God to bless you always more and more in your greatness, happiness and nobility.

And I am for all time

Your very humble and very obedient subject and very loving servant.

BOURDEILLE.[1]

REGRETTING
THE DEATH OF THE DUC D'ALENÇON

I had already dedicated this second Part of my Discourses on Women to the aforesaid my Gracious Lord d'Alençon, the while he yet lived,—seeing how he oft did me the honour to be my friend and to converse very privily with me, and was ever right curious to be informed of mirthful tales. Wherefore, albeit his generous and valorous and most noble body hath fallen on the field of honour, I have not thought good for that to recall my erstwhile dedication; but I do repeat and renew the same to his illustrious ashes and noble spirit, of the valorousness whereof and of his great deeds and high achievements I do treat in their turn among those of the other great Princes and Captains. For of a truth he was indeed a great Prince and a great Captain, if such an one there was ever,—the more so considering he is dead so untimeously.

Enough of such serious themes; let us discourse a while of merrier matters.

CONTENTS

[xi]

HISTORICAL NOTE

PIERRE DE BOURDEILLE, Abbé de Brantôme et d'André, Vicomte de Bourdeille, was
born in Périgord, in 1527, in the reign of
François I. He early took up the career of
arms, serving under his friend François de Guise, Duke
of Lorraine, as his Captain, the same who was killed
before Orleans by Poltrot de Méré. Afterwards he came
up to Court, and was Gentleman of the Bedchamber under Charles IX., who showed him much favour. On the
King's death he retired to his estates, where he composed
his Works. These are: *Vies des hommes illustres et des
grands capitaines françois; Vies des grands capitaines
étrangers; Vies des dames illustres; Vies des dames
galantes; Anecdotes touchant le duel*; and *Rodomontades
et jurements des Espagnols.*—All that really concerns us
here is the *Vies des dames galantes.* It is especially from
this point of view that we propose to speak of Pierre de
Bourdeille, known almost exclusively to posterity under
the name of Brantôme. As to his Essays in the manner
of Plutarch, these do not come into our purview at all.
Besides which, I am of opinion, it is in this book that
Brantôme appears under his most characteristic aspect,
and that it is here we may best learn to know and appreciate his genius.

A gentleman of family, acknowledged and treated as kinsman by Queen Margot, wife of Henry IV., living habitually in the society of the most famous men of his time, a contemporary of Rabelais, Marot and Ronsard, a sincere but unbigoted Catholic, a man of exceptional literary endowments, Brantôme is one of the happiest representatives of the French mind in the XVIth Century.

It is the period of the Renaissance,—the days when Europe resounds with the fame of our gallant King Francis I. and his deeds of prowess in love and war, the days when Titian and Primaticcio were leaving behind on French palace walls immortal traces of their genius, when Jean Goujon was carving his admirable figures round the fountains of the Louvre and across its front, when Rabelais was uttering his stupendous guffaw, that was the Comedy of all human life, when Marot and Ronsard were writing their graceful stanzas, when the fair "Marguerite des Marguerites,"—the Queenly Pearl of Pearls,—was telling her delightful tales of love and adventure in the *Heptameron.*—Then comes the death of Francis I. His son mounts the throne. Protestantism makes serious progress in France, and Montgomery precipitates the succession of Francis II. This last wears the crown for one year only, succumbing to a fatal inflammation of the ears. Then it is Mary Stuart leaves France for ever, and with streaming eyes, as she watches the beloved shores where she has been Queen of France fade out of sight, sings sad and slow:

Adieu, plaisant pays de France!

And now we find seated on the throne of France a young Monarch of a strange, wild, unattractive exterior.

[xiv]

His eye is pale, colourless and shifty, seeming to be void of all expression. He trusts no man, and has no real assurance of his power as Sovereign; he looks long and suspiciously at those about him before speaking, rarely bestows his confidence and believes himself constantly surrounded by spies. 'Tis a nervous, timid child,—'tis Charles IX. History treats him with an extreme severity; and the "St. Bartholomew" has thrown a lurid light over this unhappy Prince's figure. He allowed the massacres on the fatal nights of the 24th and 25th of August, and even shot down the flying Protestants from his palace roof. Without going into the interminable discussions of historians as to this last alleged fact, which is as strongly denied by some authorities as it is maintained by others, I am not one of those who say hard things of Charles IX. It is more a sentiment of pity I feel for him,—this monarch who loved Brantôme and Marot, and who protected Henri IV. against Catherine de Medici. I see him surrounded by brothers whom he had learned to distrust. The Duc d'Alençon is on the spot, a legitimate object of detestation by reason of the subterranean intrigues he is for ever hatching against his person; while his other brother Henri (afterwards Henri III.), Catherine's favourite son, is in Poland, kept sedulously informed of every variation in the Prince's always feeble health, waiting impatiently for the hour when he must hurry back to France to secure the crown he covets. Then his sister's vicious outbreaks are a source of constant pain and anxiety to him; and last but not least there is his mother Catherine de Medici, an incubus that crushed out his very life-breath. He cannot forget the tortures his brother Francis suffered from his mysterious malady, and his premature death after a single year's reign.

Catherine hated Mary Stuart, his young Queen, whose only fault was to have exaggerated in herself all the frailties together with all the physical perfections of a woman; and dreadful words had been whispered with bated breath about the Queen Mother. An Italian, deprived of all power while her husband lived, insulted by a proud and beautiful favourite, yet knowing herself well fitted for command, she had brought up her children with ideas of respect and submission to her will they were never able to throw off. The ill-will she bore her daughter-in-law was the cause of all those accusations History has listened to over readily. But Charles, a nervous, affectionate child, whose natural impulses however had been chilled by his mother's influence and the indifference of his father Henri II., was thrown back on himself, and grew up timid, suspicious and morose. The frantic love of Francis for his fascinating Queen, the cold dignity of Catherine in face of slights and cruel mortifications, her bitter disappointment during her eldest son's reign, her Italian origin (held then even more than now to imply an implacable determination to avenge all injuries), her indifference to the sudden and appalling death of the young King, the insinuations of her enemies,—all combined to make a profound impression on Charles, giving a furtive and, if we may say so, a haggard bent to his character. Presently, seated on the throne of France, Huguenots and Catholics all about him, exposed to the insults and pretensions of the Guise faction on the one hand and that of Coligny on the other, dragged now this way now that between the two, yet all the while instinctively drawn toward the Catholic side by ancestral faith and his mother's counsels no less than by reasons of state, Charles signed the fatal order authorizing the Massacre of the Saint Bartholomew.

Was the young King's action justifiable or no? It is no business of ours to discuss the question here; but much may be alleged in his excuse. Again whether he did actually fire on the terrified Protestants from the Louvre is a point vehemently debated,—but one it in no way concerns us here to decide. There is no doubt however that, dating from those two terrible nights, a steady decline declared itself in his health and vitality. In no long time he died; and his brother Henri, Duke of Anjou and King of Poland, duly warned of his approaching end, arrived in hot haste to take over the crown to which he was next in succession.

This period of political and religious ferment was no less the period *par excellence* of gallantry. In its characteristics it bears considerable resemblance to the days of the Empire. At both epochs love was quick, fierce and violent. Hurry was the mark of the times. In the midst of these everlasting struggles between Huguenot and Catholic, who could be sure of to-morrow? So men made it a point to indulge no attachment that was too serious, —for them love was become a mere question of choice and quantity; while women avoided a grand passion with a fervour worthy of a better cause. If ever a deep and earnest passion does show itself, it is an exception, an anomaly; if we find a woman stabbing her faithless husband to death on catching him in the arms of another, let us not for an instant suppose 'tis the fierce stirring

[xvii]

of a loving heart which in the frenzy of its jealousy avenges the wrong it has suffered,—to die presently of sorrow and remorse, or at the least to suffer long and sorely. This act of daring,—so carefully recorded by the chroniclers of the time,—is only the effect of strong self-love cruelly wounded. But powerful as this feeling may be, it would scarcely be adequate to explain so energetic an act, if we did not remember how frequently ladies in the XVIth Century were exposed to scenes of bloodshed. The dagger and the sword were as familiar to their eyes as the needle; and Brantôme has devoted a whole Discourse,—his Fifth, to courageous dames, and seems positively to scorn weak and timid women! How opposite is this to the sentiment of the present day, where one of the charms of womanhood is held to consist in her having nothing in common with man and being for ever in need of his protection. A few isolated cases then excepted, there existed between men and women nothing better than what Chamfort has wittily defined as "l'échange de deux fantaisies et le contact de deux épidermes,"—in other words gallantry pure and simple.

This then was the atmosphere our Author breathed. His life offers nothing specially striking in the way of incident. No need for me to take him from the arms of his nurse, to follow each of his steps through life and piously close his eyes in death. He served his time without special distinction or applause at the Court of Charles IX. In all he did, he showed so modest a reserve that, but for his Works, his very existence would have remained unknown. He is not like Bussy-Rabutin, the incidents of whose wild and wicked life filled and defaced a big book, or like Tallemant, whose diary, if diary it

[xviii]

can be called, was written day by day and recounted
each day's exploits. Brantôme's life and work leave little
trace of his own personality, beyond the impression of a
genial, smiling, witty man of the world. I will be as
plain and discreet as himself, and will make no effort to
separate the Author from his book.

Brantôme possesses one of those happy, gentle, well
ordered natures, which systematically avoid every form
of excess and exaggeration. His book *Des Dames
Galantes* is from beginning to end a protest against im-
moderate passion. It is above all a work of taste. Its
seven Discourses are devoted exclusively to stories of love
and passion, yet a man must be straightlaced indeed to
feel any sort of repulsion. Another extraordinary merit!
in spite of the monotony of the subject matter, everlastingly the same, the reader's attention never flags, and
one tale read, he is irresistibly drawn on to make acquaintance with the next.

Such praise, I am aware, is very high; and especially
when we possess such masterpieces in this *genre* as the
Tales of Boccaccio, of Pietro Aretino, some of those of
Ariosto, those of Voltaire, the short stories of Tallemant
des Réaux and the indiscretions of the *Histoire amoureuse
des Gaules*. I name only the most familiar examples. Of
course all these works do not offer a complete resemblance
to the *Vies des Dames Galantes*, but they all belong to
the same race and family. I propose to say a few passing
words of each of these productions.

The most remarkable among all these chroniclers of
the frailties of the female heart is undoubtedly Boccaccio.
Pietro Aretino has done himself an irreparable wrong by
writing in such a vein that no decent man dare confess

to having read him. Ariosto is a story-teller only by the way, but then he is worthy of all imitation. The *Heptameron* is a collection of stories the chief value of which consists in a sensibility and charming grace that never fail. Tallemant tells a tale of gallantry between two daintily worded sentiments. Voltaire in this as in all departments shows an incontestable superiority of wit and *verve*. There is nothing new in La Fontaine; 'tis always the same wondrous charm, so simple in appearance, so deep in reality. As to Bussy, a man of the world and a gentleman, but vicious, spiteful and envious, his *Histoire amoureuse* is his revenge on mankind, a deliberate publication of extravagant personalities flavoured with wit.

Boccaccio, to say nothing of his striking originality, possesses other merits of the very highest order. The sorrows of unhappy love are told with genuine pathos, while lovers' wiles and the punishments they meet with at once raise a smile and provoke a resolve to profit by such valuable lessons. True Dioneo's quaint narratives are not precisely fit for ladies' ears; yet so daintily are they recounted, the most *risqué* episodes so cleverly sketched in, it is impossible to accuse them of indelicacy. An entire absence of bitterness, a genial indulgence for human weakness, a hearty admiration of women and a doctrine of genial complaisance as the only possible philosophy of life, these are the qualities that make the *Decameron* the masterpiece of this kind of composition.

Brantôme has not the same preponderating influence in literature that Boccaccio possesses, but he comes next after him. The "Lives of Gallant Ladies" are not, any more than the *Novelli*, inventions pure and simple; they

[xx]

are anecdotes, reminiscences. The great merit of these Tales of Boccaccio is the same as that of Balzac's Novels or Molière's Comedies,—to fix a character, to define a phase of manners in the life of the Author's day; in a word to create by induction and analogy a living being, hitherto unnoticed by every-day observers, but instantly recognized as lifelike. This is the true spirit of assimilation and generalisation,—the work of *genius*. Well! as for Brantôme, he is a man of talent and wit, not genius. We claim no more; genius is not so common as might be supposed, if we hearkened to all the acclamations daily raised round sundry statues,—but plaster after all, however cunningly contrived to look like bronze.

Brantôme's fame is already firmly established. To live for two centuries and a half without boring his readers; above all to be a book that scholars, men of sober learning and of literary taste, still read in these latter days, is a success worthy of some earnest thought. This chronicle of gallantry, this collection, as the Author himself describes it, of happy tricks played on each other by men and women, possesses a quite exquisite flavour of youth and freshness,—the whole told with a good-nature, a *verve*, an unconventionality, that are inexpressibly charming. You feel the characters living and breathing through the delicate, pliant style. You see the very glance of a woman's eye; you hear her ardent, or cunningly alluring, words. For such as can read with a heart unstirred, the book is a series of delicious surprises.

Strong predispositions, nay! positive prejudices, stand in the way of the proper appreciation of our Author. Such is the Puritanism of language and prudery of manners in our day, it would seem *prima facie* an impossible task to popularize Brantôme. By common agreement we speak of the *esprit français* as distinguished from the *esprit gaulois*, the latter term being used to denote a something more frank and outspoken. I heartily wish the division were a true one; for I can never forget I belong to this mighty Nineteenth Century. But for my own part, on a careful consideration of the facts, I should make a triple rather than a twofold classification. There would be the *esprit gaulois*, the *esprit français*, *not* the spirit of the age one atom, I must be allowed to observe, *and* thirdly a certain spirit of curling-irons and kid gloves and varnished boots, a sort of bastard, a cross between French and English, equally shocked at *Tristram Shandy* and the *Physiologie du Mariage* as coarse and immoral productions. *This* is our spirit, if spirit we have.

The two first types have a real and positive value; but the third is the sole and only one nowadays permitted or current as legal tender,—the others are much too outspoken. Well! I will hold my tongue, and mind my own business. An epoch is a mighty ugly customer to come to blows with. I remember Him of Galilee.

The genius of Rabelais was all instinct with this same *esprit gaulois*—a big, bold, virile spirit, breaking out in resounding guffaws, and crude, outspoken verities, equally unable and unwilling to soften down or gloss over anything, innocent of every species of periphrasis and affectation. It is genius in a merry mood rising above the petty conventionalities of speech,—often reminding us of Molière under like circumstances. Let fools be shocked, if they please; sensible men are ashamed only in presence of positive immorality and deliberate

[xxii]

vice. The *esprit gaulois* is the spirit of primitive man
going straight to its end, regardless of fetter or law.
The *esprit français* is equally natural; but then it has
acquired a certain degree of civilisation. It has less
width of scope; it has learned the little concessions men
are bound to make one another, having associated longer
with them. It has left hodden grey, and taken to the
silken doublet and cap of velvet, and rubs elbows with
men of rank. It has lost nothing of its good sense and
good temper; but it feels no longer bound in every case
to blurt its thought right out; already it leaves something to be guessed at. It is all a question of civilisation
and surroundings. But above and beyond this, it must
be allowed to be conditioned by the essential distinction
between genius and talent. The former does what it likes,
'tis lord and master; the latter is, by its very nature, a
creature of compromise.

Brantôme possesses all the *verve* and brightness of a
genuine Frenchman. All the conditions of life are highly
favourable for him; he is rich and noble, while intelligence
and wit are stamped on his very face. He wins his first
spurs under François de Guise, whose protégé he is; when
he has had enough of war, he comes to Court. There he
receives the most flattering of receptions, every Catholic
Noble extending him the hand of good fellowship. His
family connections are such, that on the very steps of the
throne is a voice ready to call him cousin, and a charming woman's lips to smile on him with favour. 'Tis a
good start; henceforth it is for his moral and intellectual
qualities to achieve the career so auspiciously begun.

As I have said already, Brantôme is the finished type
of a Frenchman of quality. Well taught and witty, brave

[xxiii]

and enterprising, capable of appreciating honesty and worth whether in thought or deed, instinctively hating tyrants and tyrannical violence, and avoiding them like the plague, blessing the happy day on which his mother gave him birth, light-hearted and sceptical, he unites in himself everything that makes life go easy. Be sure no over-bearing passion will ever disturb the serenity of his existence. He has too much good sense to let his happiness depend on the chimerical figments of the imagination, and too much real courtesy ever to reproach a woman with her frailties. The world and all its ways seem good to him. In very truth, he is not far from Pangloss's conclusion,—Pangloss, the perfect type of what a man must be so as never to suffer,—"Well! well! all is for the best in this best of possible worlds." If woman deceive, she offers so many compensations in other ways that 'tis a hundred times better to have her as she is than not at all. Men are sinners; again most true, as an abstract proposition, but if only we know how to regulate our conduct judiciously, their sinful spite will never touch us. Easy to see how, with this bent of character and these convictions, Brantôme was certain to find friendly faces wherever he went. The favourable impression his person and position had produced, his good sense completed.

The King took delight in the society of this finished gentleman with his easy and agreeable manners. In the midst of the numberless vexations he was surrounded by, one of his greatest distractions was the gay, lively conversation of this noble lord, from whom he had nothing to fear in the way of hostile speech or angry words. The Duc d'Alençon was another intimate, who putting aside for a moment his schemes of ambition, would hear and tell tales of love and intrigue, laughing the louder in proportion to the audacity and success of the trick played by the heroine. And so it was with all; the result being that Brantôme quickly acquired the repute of being the wittiest man in France. All men and all parties were on friendly terms with him. The Huguenots forgot he was a Catholic, and made an ally of him. Without religious fanaticism or personal ambition, honoured and sought after by the great, yet quite unspoiled and always simple-hearted and good-natured, equally free from prejudice and pride, he conciliated the good will of all. Throughout the whole of Brantôme's career, we never hear of his making a single enemy; and be it remembered he lived in the very hottest of the storm and stress, political and religious, of the Sixteenth Century. Let us add to complete our characterisation, a quite incalculable merit,— a discretion such as cannot be found even in the annals of Chivalry, a period indeed when lovers were only too fond of making a show of their ladies' favours. This is the one and only point where Brantôme is inconsistent with the true French type of character, mostly as eager to declare the fair inamorata's name as to appreciate the proofs of love she may have given.

Francis I. is but just dead, we must remember. His reign has been called the Renaissance, and not without good reason. Under him begins that light, graceful bearing, that elegance of manner, that politeness of address, which henceforth will make continuous advances to greater and greater refinement. Rabelais is the last expression of that old, unsoftened and unmitigated French speech, from which at a later date Matthieu Regnier will ocasionally borrow one of his picturesque phrases. In the same reign costume first becomes dainty. Men's minds grow finical like their dress; and a new mode of expression was imperatively required to match the new elegance of living. The change was effected almost without effort; 'twas a mere question of external sensibility. The body, now habituated to silk and velvet, grows more sensitive and delicate, and intellect and language follow suit. The correspondence was inevitable. So much for the mental revolution. As for the moral side, manners gained in frankness no doubt; but otherwise things were neither better nor worse than before. It has always seemed to us a strange proceeding, to take a particular period of History, as writers so often will, and declare,— 'At this epoch morals were more relaxed than ever before or since.'

Now under Francis I., and by his example, manners acquired a happy freedom, an unstudied ease, his Courtiers were sure to turn to good advantage. A King is always king of the fashion. Judging by the two celebrated lines [1] he wrote one day on a pane in one of the windows at the Castle of Chambord, Francis I., a Prince of wit and a true Frenchman, could discover no better way of punishing women for their fickleness and frivolity than that of copying their example. Every pretty woman stirred a longing to possess in the ample and facile heart of this Royal Don Juan. They were easy and happy loves,—without remorse and without bitterness, and never deformed with tears. So far did he push his rights as a Sovereign, that there is said to have been at least one instance of rivalry between him and his own

[xxvi]

son. He died, as he had lived, a lover,—and a victim to love.

Under Henri II., Diane de Poitiers is the most prominent figure on the stage; following the gallant leadership of the King's mistress, the Court continues the same mode of life and type of manners which distinguished the preceding reign.

Of the reign of Francis II., we need only speak *en passant*. During the short while he and Mary Stuart were exhausting the joys of a brief married life, there was no time for further change.

But now we come to a far more noteworthy and important period. While the Queen Mother and the Guises are silently preparing their *coup d'état;* while the Huguenots, light-hearted and unsuspecting, are dancing and making merry in the halls of the Louvre; while Catholics join them in merry feasts at the taverns then in vogue, and ladies allow no party spirit to intrude in their love affairs; while the Pré-aux-Clercs is the meeting-ground where men of honour settle their quarrels, and the happy man, the man who receives the most caressing marks of female favour, is he that has killed most, at a time like this the wits are keen and the spirit as reckless as the courage. With such a code of morals it was a difficult matter for any serious sentiment to survive. Women soon began to feel the same scorn of life that men professed. The strongest were falling day by day, and emotion and sensibility could not but be blunted. Then think of the crowd of eager candidates to seize the vacant reins of Government, and the steeple-chase existence of those days becomes intelligible and even excusable.

In all this movement Brantôme was necessarily in-

[xxvii]

volved, but he kept invariably in the back-ground, in a convenient semi-obscurity. But we must by no means assume that this prudence on the Vicomte de Bourdeille's part proceeded from any lack of energy; this would be doing him a quite undeserved injustice. He had given proofs of his courage; and Abbé as he was, his sword on hip spoke as proudly as the most doughty ruffler's. But a man of peace, he avoided provoking quarrels; he was a good Catholic, and Religion has always discountenanced the shedding of blood.

The best proof of the position he was able to win at Court is this Book of Fair and Gallant Ladies which has come down to us as its result. Amid all the gay and boisterous fêtes of the time, and the thousand lights of the Louvre, men and women both smiled graciously on our Author. His perfect discretion was perhaps his chief merit in the eyes of all these love-sick swains and garrulous young noodles. The instant a lover received an assignation from his fair one, his joy ran over in noisy fanfaronnades. A happy man is brim full of good-fellowship, and eager for a confidant. Well! if at that moment the gallant Abbé chanced to pass, what more natural than for the fortunate gentleman to seize and buttonhole him? Then he would recount his incomparable good fortune, adding a hundred piquant details, and drunk with his own babbling, enumerate one after the other the most minute particulars of his intrigue, ending by letting out the name of the husband at whose expense he had been enjoying himself. Love is so simple-minded and so charmingly selfish! Every lover seriously thinks each casual acquaintance must of course sympathise actively in his feelings. A bosom friend he must have!—no matter who, if only he can tell him, always of course under formal promise of concealment, the secret he should have kept locked in his own bosom. Nor should we look over harshly on this weakness; too much happiness, no less than too much unhappiness, will stifle the bosom that cannot throw off any of its load upon another. 'Tis the world-old story of the reeds and the secret that must be told. Self-expansion is a natural craving; without it, men grow misanthropes and die of an aneurism of the heart.

This brings us to the book of the *Dames galantes*. When eventually he retired to his estates, Brantôme took up the pen as a relief to his ennui. Among all the works he composed, this one must certainly have pleased him best, because it so exactly corresponds with his own character and ways of thought. But to write these lives of Gallant Ladies was an enterprise not without its dangers. A volume of anecdotes of the sort cannot be written without there being considerable risk in the process of falling into the coarse and commonplace vulgarities that surround such a subject. Style, wit, philosophy, gaiety, all in a degree seldom met with, were indispensable for success; yet Brantôme has succeeded. This book, of the *Vies des Dames galantes*, offers a close analogy with another celebrated study in the same *genre*, viz., Balzac's *Physiologie du mariage*. Both works deal with the same subject, the ways and wiles of women, married, widow and maid, under the varying conditions of, (1) the Sixteenth Century, and (2) the Present Day. But the mode of treatment is different; an this difference made Brantôme's task a harder one than the modern Author's. His short stories of a dozen lines, each revealing woman in one of those secret and confidential situations only open to the eye of husband or lover, might easily be displeasing, or worse still tiresome. Brantôme has avoided all these shoals and shallows. Each little tale has its own interest, always fresh and bright.

Moreover a lofty morality runs through the narratives. At first sight the word morality may seem a joke applied to such matters; but it is easy to disconcert the scoffer merely by asking him to read our Author. To support my contention, there is no need to quote any particular story or stories; all alike have their charm, and the work must be perused in its entirety to appreciate the truth of the high praise I give it. Every reader, on finally closing the book, cannot but feel a genuine enthusiasm. The delicate wit of the whole recital passes imagination. On every page we meet some physical trait or some moral remark that rivets the attention. The author puts his hand on some curiosity or perversity, and instantly stops to examine it; while at the same time the propriety of his tone allures the most sedate reader. The discussion of each point, in which the *pros* and *cons* are always balanced one against the other in the wittiest and most thorough manner, is interesting to the highest degree. In one word the book is a code and compendium of Love. All is classified, studied, analysed; each argument is supported by an appropriate anecdote,—an example,—a Life.

The mere arrangement of the contents displays consummate skill. The Author has divided his *Vies des Dames galantes* into seven Discourses, as follows:

In the First, he treats "Of ladies which do make love, and their husbands cuckolds;"

In the Second, he expatiates "On the question which doth give the more content in love, whether touching, seeing or speaking;"

In the Third, he speaks "Concerning the Beauty of a fine leg, and the virtue the same doth possess;"

In the Fourth, he discourses "Concerning old dames as fond to practise love as ever the young ones be;"

In the Fifth, he tells "How Fair and honourable ladies do love brave and valiant men, and brave men courageous women;"

In the Sixth, he teaches, "How we should never speak ill of ladies,—and of the consequences of so doing;"

In the Seventh, he asks, "Concerning married women, widows and maids—which of these be better than the other to love."

This list of subjects, displaying as it does, all the leading ideas of the book, leaves me little to add. I have no call to go into a detailed appreciation of the Work under its manifold aspects as a gallery of portraits; my task was merely to judge of its general physiognomy and explain its *raisin d'être;* and this I have attempted to do.

I will only add by way of conclusion a few words to show the especial esteem we should feel for Brantôme on this ground, that his works contain nothing to corrupt good morals. Each narrative is told simply and straightforwardly, for what it is worth. The author neither embellishes nor exaggerates. Moreover the species of corollary he clinches it with is a philosophical and physiological deduction of the happiest and most apposite kind in the great majority of instances,—some witty and

[xxxi]

ingenious remark that never offends either against good sense or good taste. If now and again the reader is tempted to shy, he should in justice put this down to the diction of the time, which had not yet adopted that tone of arrogant virtue it nowadays affects. Then there was a large number of words in former days which connoted nothing worse than something ridiculous and absurd.

Then as to beauty of language, we must go roundabout ways to reach many a point they marched straight to in old days. Brantôme at any rate is a purist of style,— one of the most striking and most correct writers I have ever read. It is a great and genuine discovery readers will make, if they do not know him already; if they do, they will be renewing acquaintance with an old friend, at once witty and delightful. In either case, 'tis a piece of luck not to be despised.

H. VIGNEAU.

LIVES OF FAIR AND GALLANT LADIES

FIRST DISCOURSE

Of Ladies which do make Love, and their Husbands cuckolds.[1]

1.

EEING 'tis the ladies have laid the foundation of all cuckoldry, and how 'tis they which do make all men cuckolds, I have thought it good to include this First Discourse in my present Book of Fair Ladies,—albeit that I shall have occasion to speak therein as much of men as of women. I know right well I am taking up a great work, and one I should never get done withal, if that I did insist on full completeness of the same. For of a truth not all the paper in the Records Office of Paris would hold in writing the half of the histories of folk in this case, whether women or men. Yet will I set down what I can; and when I can no more, I will e'en give my pen—to the devil, or mayhap to some good fellow-comrade, which shall carry on the tale.

Furthermore must I crave indulgence if in this Discourse I keep not due order and alignment, for indeed so great is the multitude of men and women so situate, and

so manifold and divers their condition, that I know not
any Commander and Master of War so skilled as that
he could range the same in proper rank and meet array.

Following therefore of mine own fantasy, will I speak
of them in such fashion as pleaseth me,—now in this
present month of April, the which bringeth round once
more the very season and open time of *cuckoos;* I mean
the cuckoos that perch on trees, for of the other sort are
to be found and seen enough and to spare in all months
and seasons of the year.

Now of this sort of cuckolds, there be many of divers
kinds, but of all sorts the worst and that which the ladies
fear above all others, doth consist of those wild, fierce,
tricky, ill-conditioned, malicious, cruel and suspicious husbands, who strike, torture and kill, some for true cause,
others for no true reason at all, so mad and furious doth
the very least suspicion in the world make them. With
such all dealings are very carefully to be shunned, both
by their wives and by the lovers of the same. Natheless
have I known ladies and their lovers which did make no
account of them; for they were just as ill-minded as the
others, and the ladies were bold and reckless, to such a
degree that if their cavaliers chanced to fail of courage,
themselves would supply them enough and to spare for
both. The more so that in proportion as any emprise
is dangerous and difficult, ought it to be undertaken in a
bold and high spirit. On the contrary I have known
other ladies of the sort who had no heart at all or ambition to adventure high endeavours; but cared for naught
but their low pleasures, even as the proverb hath it: *base
of heart as an harlot.*

Myself knew an honourable lady, and a great one, who

[4]

a good opportunity offering to have enjoyment of her
lover, when this latter did object to her the incommodity
that would ensue supposing the husband, who was not
far off, to discover it, made no more ado but left him
on the spot, deeming him no doughty lover, for that he
said nay to her urgent desire. For indeed this is what
an amorous dame, whenas the ardour and frenzy of desire
would fain be satsified, but her lover will not or cannot
content her straightway, by reason of sundry lets and
hindrances, doth hate and indignantly abominate above
all else.

Needs must we commend this lady for her doughtiness,
and many another of her kidney, who fear naught, if only
they may content their passions, albeit therein they run
more risks and dangers than any soldier or sailor doth
in the most hazardous perils of field or sea.

A Spanish dame, escorted one day by a gallant cavalier
through the rooms of the King's Palace and happening to
pass by a particular dark and secret recess, the gentleman, piquing himself on his respect for women and his
Spanish discretion, saith to her: *Señora, buen lugar, si no
fuera vuessa merced* (A good place, my lady, if it were
another than your ladyship). To this the lady merely
answered the very same words back again, *Si, buen lugar,
si no fuera vuessa merced* (Yes, Sir, a good place, if it
were another than your lordship). Thus did she imply
his cowardliness, and rebuke the same, for that he had
not taken of her in so good a place what she did wish
and desire to lose, as another and a bolder man would
have done in like case. For the which cause she did
thereupon altogether pretermit her former love for him,
and left him incontinently.

[5]

I have heard tell of a very fair and honourable lady, who did make assignation with her lover, only on condition he should not touch her (nor come to extremities at all). This the other accomplished, tarrying all night long in great ecstasy, temptation and continence; and thereat was the lady so grateful that some while after she did give him full gratification, alleging for reason that she had been fain to prove his love in accomplishing the task she had laid upon him. Wherefore she did love him much thereafter, and afforded him opportunity to do quite other feats than this one,—verily one of the hardest sort to succeed in.

Some there be will commend his discretion,—or timidity, if you had rather call it so,—others not. For myself I refer the question to such as may debate the point on this side or on that according to their several humours and predispositions.

I knew once a lady, and one of no low degree, who having made an assignation with her lover to come and stay with her one night, he hied him thither all ready, in shirt only, to do his duty. But, seeing it was in wintertide, he was so sorely a-cold on the way, that he could accomplish naught, and thought of no other thing but to get heat again. Whereat the lady did loathe the caitiff, and would have no more of him.

Another lady, discoursing of love with a gentleman, he said to her among other matters that if he were with her, he would undertake to do his devoir six times in one night, so greatly would her beauty edge him on. "You boast most high prowess," said she; "I make you assignation therefore" for such and such a night. Nor did she fail to keep tryst at the time agreed; but lo! to his undoing, he was assailed by so sad a convulsion, that he could by no means accomplish his devoir so much as once even. Whereupon the fair lady said to him, "What! are you good for naught at all? Well, then! begone out of my bed. I did never lend it you, like a bed at an inn, to take your ease forsooth therein and rest yourself. Therefore, I say, begone!" Thus did she drive him forth, and thereafter did make great mock of him, hating the recreant worse than the plague.

This last gentleman would have been happy enough, if only he had been of the complexion of the great Baraud, Protonotary and Almoner to King Francis, for whenas he lay with the Court-ladies, he would even reach the round dozen at the least, and yet next morning he would say right humbly, "I pray you, Madam, make excuse that I have not done better, but I took physic yesterday." I have myself known him of later years, when he was called Captain Baraud, a Gascon, and had quitted the lawyer's robe. He has recounted to me, at my asking, his amours, and that name by name.

As he waxed older, this masculine vigour and power somewhat failed him. Moreover he was now poor, albeit he had had good pickings, the which his prowess had gotten him; yet had he squandered it all, and was now set to compounding and distilling essences. "But verily," he would say, "if only I could now, so well as once I could in my younger days, I should be in better case, and should guide my gear better than I have done."

During the famous War of the League, an honourable gentleman, and a right brave and valiant soldier, having left the place whereof he was Governor to go to the wars, could not on his return arrive in garrison before nightfall, and so betook himself to the house of a fair and very honourable and noble widow, who straight invited him to stay the night within doors. This he gladly consented to do, for he was exceeding weary. After making him good cheer at supper, she gives him her own chamber and bed, seeing that all the other bed-chambers were dismantled by reason of the War, and their furniture,—and she had good and fair plenishing,—under lock and key. Herself meanwhile withdraws to her closet, where she had a day-bed in use.

The gentleman, after several times refusing this bed and bed-chamber, was constrained by the good lady's prayers to take it. Then so soon as he was laid down therein and asleep most soundly, lo! the lady slips in softly and lays herself down beside him in the bed without his being ware of aught all the night long, so aweary was he and heavily asleep. There lay he till broad daylight, when the lady, drawing away from him, as the sleeper began to awake, said, "You have not slept without company; for I would not yield you up the whole of my bed, so have I enjoyed the one half thereof as well as ever you have the other. You have lost a chance you will never have again."

The gentleman, cursing and railing for spite of his wasted opportunity ('twere enough to make a man hang himself), was fain to stay her and beg her over. But no such thing! On the contrary, she was sorely displeased at him for not having contented her as she would have had him do, for of a truth she had not come thither for only one poor embrace,—as the saying hath it, one embrace is only the salad of a feast. She loved the plural

[8]

number better than the singular, as do many worthy dames.

Herein they differ from a certain very fair and honourable lady I once knew, who on one occasion having made assignation with her lover to come and stay with her, in a twinkling he did accomplish three good embraces with her. But thereafter, he wishing to do a fourth and make his number yet complete, she did urge him with prayers and commands to get up and retire. He, as fresh as at first, would fain renew the combat, and doth promise he would fight furiously all that night long till dawn of day, declaring that for so little as had gone by, his vigour was in no wise diminished. But she did reply: "Be satisfied I have recognized your doughtiness and good dispositions. They are right fair and good, and at a better time and place I shall know very well how to take better advantage of them than at this present. For naught but some small illhap is lacking for you and me to be discovered. Farewell then till a better and more secure occasion, and then right freely will I put you to the great battle, and not to such a trifling encounter as this."

Many dames there be would not have shown this much prudency, but intoxicate with pleasure, seeing they had the enemy already on the field, would have had him fight till dawn of day.

The same honourable lady which I spake of before these last, was of such a gallant humour that when the caprice was on her, she had never a thought or fear of her husband, albeit he was a ready swordsman and quick at offence. Natheless hath she alway been so fortunate as that neither she nor her lovers have ever run serious risks of their lives or come near being surprised, by dint of careful posting of guards and good and watchful sentinels.

Still it behoves not ladies to trust too much to this, for one unlucky moment is all that is needed to ruin all, —as happened some while since to a certain brave and valiant gentleman [2] who was massacred on his way to see his mistress by the treachery and contrivance of the lady herself, the which her husband made her devise against him. Alas! if he had not entertained so high a presumption of his own worth and valour as he rightly did, he would have kept better guard, and would never have fallen,—more's the pity! A capital example, verily, not to trust over much to amorous dames, who to escape the cruel hand of their husbands, do play such a game as these order them, as did the lady in this case, who saved her own life,—at the sacrifice of her lover's.

Other husbands there be who kill the lady and the lover both together as I have heard it told of a very great lady whose husband was jealous of her, not for any offence he had certain knowledge of, but out of mere suspiciousness and mistaken zeal of love. He did his wife to death with poison and wasting sickness,—a grievous thing and an exceeding sad, after having first slain the lover, a good and honourable man, declaring that the sacrifice was fairer and more agreeable to kill the bull first, and the cow afterwards.

This same Prince was more cruel to his wife than he was later to one of his daughters, the which he had married to a great Prince, though not so great an one as himself was, he being indeed a monarch in all but name.

It fell out to this fickle dame to be gotten with child by another than her husband, who was at the time busied

afar in some War. Presently, having been brought to bed
of a fine child, she wist not to what Saint to make appeal,
if not to her father; so to him she did reveal all by the
mouth of a gentleman she had trust in, whom she sent to
him. No sooner had he hearkened to his confidence than
he did send and charge her husband that, for his life, he
should beware to make no essay against that of his daughter, else would he do the same against his, and make him
the poorest Prince in Christendom, the which he was well
able to accomplish. Moreover he did despatch for his
daughter a galley with a meet escort to fetch to him the
child and its nurse, and providing a good house and liveli-
hood, had the boy nourished and brought up right well.
But when after some space of time the father came to die,
thereupon the husband put her to death and so did punish
her for her faithlessness at last.

I have heard tell of another husband who did to death
the lover before the eyes of his wife, causing him to lan-
guish in long pain, to the end she might die in a martyr's
agony to see the lingering death of him she had so loved
and had held within her arms.

Yet another great nobleman did kill his wife openly
before the whole Court.[3] For the space of fifteen years
he had granted the same all liberty, and had been for long
while well aware of her ill ways, having many a time and
oft remonstrated thereat and admonished her. However
at the last a sudden caprice took him ('tis said at the
instance of a great Prince, his master), and on a certain
morning he did visit her as she still lay abed, but on the
point of rising. Then, after lying with her, and after
sporting and making much mirth together, he did give
her four or five dagger thrusts. This done, he bade a

[11]

servant finish her, and after had her laid on a litter, and carried openly before all the Court to his own house, to be there buried. He would fain have done the like to her paramours; but so would he have had overmuch on his hands, for that she had had so many they might have made a small army.

I have heard speak likewise of a certain brave and valiant Captain,[4] who conceiving some suspicion of his wife, went straight to her without more ado and strangled her himself with his own hands, in her white girdle. Thereafter he had her buried with all due honour, and himself was present at her obsequies in mourning weeds and of a very sad countenance, the which mourning he did continue for many a long day,—verily a noble satisfaction to the poor lady, as if a fine funeral could bring her to life again! Moreover he did the same by a damosel which had been in waiting on his wife and had aided and abetted her in her naughtiness. Nor yet did he die without issue by this same wife, for he had of her a gallant son, one of the bravest and foremost soldiers of his country, who by virtue of his worth and emprise did reach great honour as having served his Kings and masters right well.

I have heard likewise of a nobleman in Italy which also slew his wife, not being able to catch her gallant who had escaped into France. But it is said he slew her, not so much because of her sin,—for that he had been ware of for a long time, how she indulged in loose love and took no heed for aught else,—as in order to wed another lady of whom he was enamoured.

Now this is why it is very perilous to assail and attack an armed and defended spot,—not but that there be as many of this sort assailed and right well assailed as of unarmed and undefended ones, yea! and assailed victoriously to boot. For an example whereof, I know of one that was as well armed and championed as any in all the world. Yet, was there a certain gentleman, in sooth a most brave and valiant soldier, who was fain to hanker after the same; nay! he was not content with this, but must needs pride himself thereon and bruit his success abroad. But it was scarce any time at all before he was incontinently killed by men appointed to that end, without otherwise causing scandal, and without the lady's suffering aught therefrom. Yet was she for long while in sore fear and anguish of spirit, seeing that she was then with child and firmly believing that after her bringing to bed, the which she would full fain have seen put off for an hundred years, she would meet the like fate. But the husband showed himself a good and merciful man,— though of a truth he was one of the keenest swordsmen in all the world,—and freely pardoned her; and nothing else came of it, albeit divers of them that had been her servants were in no small affright. However the one victim paid for all. And so the lady, recognizing the goodness and graciousness of such an husband, gave but very little cause for suspicion thereafter, for that she joined herself to the ranks of the more wise and virtuous dames of that day.

It fell out very different not many years since in the Kingdom of Naples to Donna Maria d'Avalos, one of the fair Princesses of that land and married to the Prince of Venusia, who was enamoured of the Count d'Andriane, likewise one of the noble Princes of the country. So being both of them come together to enjoy their passion,

[13]

and the husband having discovered it,—by means whereof I could render an account, but the tale would be over long,—having insooth surprised them there together, had the twain of them slain by men appointed thereto. In such wise that next morning the fair and noble pair, unhappy beings, were seen lying stretched out and exposed to public view on the pavement in front of the house door, all dead and cold, in sight of all passers-by, who could not but weep and lament over their piteous lot.

Now there were kinsfolk of the said lady, thus done to death, who were exceeding grieved and greatly angered thereat, so that they were right eager to avenge the same by death and murder, as the law of that country doth allow. But for as much as she had been slain by base-born varlets and slaves who deserved not to have their hands stained with so good and noble blood, they were for making this point alone the ground of their resentment and for this seeking satisfaction from the husband, whether by way of justice or otherwise,—but not so, if he had struck the blow with his own hand. For that had been a different case, not so imperatively calling for satisfaction.

Truly an odd idea and a most foolish quibble have we here! Whereon I make appeal to our great orators and wise lawyers, that they tell me this: which act is the more monstrous, for a man to kill his wife with his own hand, the which hath so oftentimes loved and caressed her, or by that of a base-born slave? In truth there are many good arguments to be alleged on the point; but I will refrain me from adducing of them, for fear they prove over weak and silly in comparison of those of such great folk.

[14]

I have heard tell that the Viceroy, hearing of the plot that was toward, did warn the lover thereof, and the lady to boot. But their destiny would have it so; this was to be the issue, and no other, of their so delightsome loves.

This lady was daughter of Don Carlo d'Avalos, second brother of the Marquis di Pescaïra, to whom if any had played a like trick in any of his love matters wherewith I am acquaint, be sure he would have been dead this many a long day.

I once knew an husband, which coming home from abroad and having gone long without sleeping with his wife, did arrive with mind made up and glad heart to do so with her presently, and having good pleasure thereof. But arriving by night, he did hear by his little spy, how that she was accompanied by her lover in the bed. Thereupon did he straight lay hand on sword, and knocked at the door; the which being opened, he entered in resolved to kill her. After first of all hunting for the gallant, who had escaped by the window, he came near to his wife to kill her; but it so happened she was on this occasion so becomingly tricked out, so featly dressed in her night attire and her fair white shift, and so gaily decked (bear in mind she had taken all this pretty pains with herself the better to please her lover), that he had never found her so much to his taste. Then she, falling at his knees, in her shift as she was, and grovelling on the ground, did ask his forgiveness with such fair and gentle words, the which insooth she knew right well how to set forth, that raising her up and seeing her so fair and of so gracious mien, he felt his heart stir within him, and dropping his sword,—for that he had had no enjoyment for many a day and was anhungered therefor, which likely enough

[15]

did stir the lady too at nature's prompting,—he forgave
her and took and kissed her, and put her back to bed
again, and in a twinkling lay down with her, after
shutting to the door again. And the fair lady did content
him so well by her gentle ways and pretty cajoleries,—
be sure she forgat not any one of them all,—that eventually the next morning they were found better friends
than ever, and never was so much loving and caressing
between them before. As was the case likewise with King
Menelaus, that poor cuckold, the which did ever by the
space of ten or twelve years threaten his wife Helen that
he would kill her, if ever he could put hands upon her,
and even did tell her so, calling from the foot of Troy's
wall to her on the top thereof. Yet, Troy well taken,
and she fallen into his power, so ravished was he with
her beauty that he forgave her all, and did love and
fondle her in better sort than ever.

So much then for these savage husbands that from lions
turn into butterflies. But no easy thing is it for any to
get deliverance like her whose case we now tell.

A lady, young, fair and noble, in the reign of King
Francis I., married to a great Lord of France, of as
noble a house as is any to be found, did escape otherwise,
and in more pious fashion, than the last named. For,
whether it were she had given some cause for suspicion
to her husband, or that he was overtaken by a fit of distrust or sudden anger, he came at her sword in hand for
to kill her. But she bethought herself instantly to make
a vow to the glorious Virgin Mary, and to promise she
would to pay her said vow, if only she would save her life,
at her chapel of Loretto at St. Jean des Mauverets, in
the country of Anjou. And so soon as ever she had made

[16]

this vow in her own mind, lo! the said Lord did fall to
the ground, and his sword slipped from out his hand.
Then presently, rising up again as if awaking from a
dream, he did ask his wife to what Saint she had recom-
mended herself to escape out of this peril. She told him
it was to the Blessed Virgin, in her afore-named Chapel,
and how she had promised to visit the holy place.
Whereupon he said to her: "Go thither then, and fulfil
your vow,"—the which she did, and hung up there a
picture recording the story, together with sundry large
and fair votive offerings of wax, such as of yore were
customary for this purpose, the which were there to be
seen for long time after. Verily a fortunate vow, and
a right happy and unexpected escape,—as is further set
forth in the *Chronicles of Anjou*.[5]

2.

 HAVE heard say how King Francis[1] once was
fain to go to bed with a lady of his Court
whom he loved. He found her husband sword
in fist ready to kill him; but the King straightway did put his own to his throat, and did charge him,
on his life, to do him no hurt, but an if he should do him
the least ill in the world, how that he would kill him on
the spot, or else have his head cut off. So for that night
did he send him forth the house, and took his place. The
said lady was very fortunate to have found so good a
champion and protector of her person, for never after
durst the husband to say one word of complaint, and
so left her to do as she well pleased.

I have heard tell how that not this lady alone, but

[17]

many another beside, did win suchlike safeguard and protection from the King. As many folk do in War-time to save their lands, putting of the King's cognizance over their doors, even so do these ladies put the countersign of their monarchs inside and out their bodies; whereby their husbands dare not afterward say one word of reproach, who but for this would have given them incontinently to the edge of the sword.

I have known yet other ladies, favoured in this wise by kings and great princes, who did so carry their passports everywhere. Natheless were there some of them, whose husbands, albeit not daring to use cold steel to them, did yet have resort to divers poisons and secret ways of death, making pretence these were catarrhs, or apoplexy and sudden death. Verily such husbands are odious,—so to see their fair wives lying by their side, sickening and dying a slow death day after day, and do deserve death far worse than their dames. Others again do them to death between four walls, in perpetual emprisonment. Of such we have instances in sundry ancient Chronicles of France; and myself have known a great nobleman of France, the which did thus slay his wife, who was a very fair and honourable lady,—and this by judgement of the Courts, taking an infatuate delight in having by this means his cuckoldry publicly declared.

Among husbands of this mad and savage temper under cuckoldry, old men hold the first place, who distrusting their own vigour and heat of body, and bent on making sure of their wives' virtue, even when they have been so foolish as to marry young and beautiful ones, so jealous and suspicious are they of the same (as well by reason of their natural disposition as of their former doings in this sort, the which they have either done themselves of yore or seen done by others), that they lead the unhappy creatures so miserable a life that scarce could Purgatory itself be in any wise more cruel.

The Spanish proverb saith: *El diablo sabe mucho, porque es viejo,* "The devil knoweth much, because he is old"; and in like sort these old men, by reason of their age and erstwhile habitudes, know full many things. Thus are they greatly to be blamed on this point, for seeing they cannot satisfy their wives, why do they go about to marry them at all? Likewise are the women, being so fair and young, very wrong to marry old men under temptation of wealth, thinking they will enjoy the same after their death, the which they do await from hour to hour. And meanwhile do they make good cheer with young gallants whom they make friends of, for the which some of them do suffer sorely.

I have heard speak of one who, being surprised in the act, her husband, an old man, did give her a certain poison whereby she lay sick for more than a year, and grew dry as a stick. And the husband would go oft to see her, and took delight in that her sickness, and made mirth thereat, declaring she had gotten her deserts.

Yet another her husband shut her up in a room, and put her on bread and water, and very oft would he make her strip stark naked and whip her his fill, taking no pity on that fair naked flesh, and feeling no compunction thereat. And truly this is the worst of them, for seeing they be void of natural heat, and as little subject to temptation as a marble statue, no beauty doth stir their compassion, but they satiate their rage with cruel martyrdoms; whereas if that they were younger, they would

[19]

take their satisfaction on their victim's fair naked body, and so forget and forgive, as I have told of in a previous place.

This is why it is ill to marry suchlike ill-conditioned old men; for of a truth, albeit their sight is failing and coming to naught from old age, yet have they always enough to spy out and see the tricks their young wives may play them.

Even so have I heard speak of a great lady who was used to say that never a Saturday was without sun, never a beautiful woman without amours, and never an old man without his being jealous; and indeed everything goeth for the enfeeblement of his vigour.

This is why a great Prince whom I know was wont to say: that he would fain be like the lion, the which, grow he as old as he may, doth never get white; or the monkey, which, the more he performeth, the more he hath desire to perform; or the dog, for the older he waxeth, the bigger doth he become; or else the stag, forasmuch as the more aged he is, the better can he accomplish his duty, and the does will resort more willingly to him than to the younger members of the herd.

And indeed, to speak frankly, as I have heard a great personage of rank say likewise, what reason is there, or what power hath the husband so great that he may and ought to kill his wife, seeing he hath none such from God, neither by His law nor yet His holy Gospel, but only to put her away? He saith naught therein of murder, and bloodshedding, naught of death, tortures or imprisonment, of poisons or cruelties. Ah! but our Lord Jesus Christ did well admonish us that great wrong was in these fashions of doing and these murders, and that He did hardly or not at all approve thereof, whenas they brought to Him the poor woman accused of adultery, for that He might pronounce her doom and punishment. He said only to them, writing with His finger on the ground: "He that is without sin among you, let him first cast a stone at her,"—the which not one of them all durst do, feeling themselves touched to the quick by so wise and gentle a rebuke.

Our Creator was for teaching us all not to be so lightly ready to condemn folk and put them to death, even on this count, well knowing the weakness of our human Nature, and the violent errors some do commit against it. For such an one doth cause his wife to be put to death, who is more an adulterer than she, while others again often have their wives slain though innocent, being aweary of them and desiring to take other fresh ones. How many such there be! Yet doth Saint Augustine say that the adulterous man is as much to be punished as the woman.

I have heard speak of a very great Prince, and of high place in the world, who suspecting his wife of false love with a certain gallant cavalier, had him assassinated as he came forth by night from his Palace, and afterward the lady. A little while before, this latter at a Tourney that was held at Court, after fixedly gazing at her lover who did manage his horse right gracefully, said suddenly: "Great Lord! how well he doth ride!" "Yea!" was the unexpected answer, "but he rides too high an horse"; and in short time after was he poisoned by means of certain perfumes or by some draught he swallowed by way of the mouth.

I knew a Lord of a good house who did kill his wife, the which was very fair and of good family and lineage, poisoning her by her private parts, without her being ware of it, so subtle and cunningly compounded was the said poison. This did he in order to marry a great lady who before had been wife to a Prince, without the influence and protection of whose friends he was in sad case, exposed to imprisonment and danger. However as his ill-luck would have it, he did not marry her after all, but was disappointed therein and brought into very evil repute, and ill looked at by all men and honourable ladies.

I have seen high personages greatly blame our old-time Kings, such as Louis X. (le Hutin, the Obstinate) and Charles the Fair, for that they did to death their wives,—the one Marguérite, daughter of Robert Duke of Burgundy, the other Blanche, daughter of Othelin Count of Burgundy, casting up against them their adulteries. So did they have them cruelly done to death within the four walls of the Château-Gaillard, as did likewise the Comte de Foix to Jeanne d'Arthoys. Wherein was not so much guilt or such heinous crimes as they would have had men to believe; but the truth is the said monarchs were aweary of their wives, and so did bring up against them these fine charges, and after did marry others.

As in yet another case, did King Henry of England have his wife put to death and beheaded, to wit Anne Boleyn, in order to marry another, for that he was a monarch very ready to shed blood and quick to change his wives. Were it not better that they should divorce them, according to God's word, than thus cruelly cause them to be slain? But no! they must needs ever have fresh meat these folk, who are fain to sit at table apart without inviting any to share with them, or else to have new and fresh wives to bring them gear after that they have wasted that of their first spouses, or else have not gotten of these enough to satisfy them. Thus did Baldwyn,[2] second King of Jerusalem, who making it to be believed of his first wife that she had played him false, did put her away, in order to take a daughter of the Duke of Malyterne,[3] because she had a large sum of money for dowry, whereof he stood in sore need. This is to be read in the *History of the Holy Land.*[4] Truly it well becomes these Princes to alter the Law of God and invent a new one, to the end they may make away with their unhappy wives!

King Louis VII. (Le Jeune, the Young)[5] did not precisely so in regard to Leonore, duchesse d'Acquitaine, who being suspected of adultery, mayhap falsely, during his voyaging in Syria, was repudiated by him on his sole authority, without appealing to the law of other men, framed as it is and practised more by might than by right or reason. Whereby he did win greater reputation than the other Kings named above, and the name of good, while the others were called wicked, cruel and tyrannical, forasmuch as he had in his soul some traces of remorse and truth. And this forsooth is to live a Christian life! Why! the heathen Romans themselves did for the most part herein behave more Christianly; and above all sundry of their Emperors, of whom the more part were subject to be cuckolds, and their wives exceeding lustful and whorish. Yet cruel as they were, we read of many who did rid themselves of their wives more by divorces than by murders such as we that are Christians do commit.

Julius Caesar did no further hurt to his wife Pompeia, but only divorced her, who had done adultery with Publius

Clodius, a young and handsome Roman nobleman. For being madly in love with her, and she with him, he did spy out the opportunity when one day she was performing a sacrifice in her house, to which only women were admitted. So he did dress himself as a girl, for as yet had he no beard on chin, and joining in the singing and playing of instruments and so passing muster, had leisure to do that he would with his mistress. However, being presently recognized, he was driven forth and brought to trial, but by dint of bribery and influence was acquitted, and no more came of the thing.

Cicero expended his Latin in vain in a fine speech he did deliver against him. True it is that Caesar, wishful of convincing the public who would have him deem his wife innocent, did reply that he desired his bed not alone to be unstained with guilt, but free from all suspicion. This was well enough by way of so satisfying the world; but in his soul he knew right well what the thing meant, his wife being thus found with her lover. Little doubt she had given him the assignation and opportunity; for herein, when the woman doth wish and desire it, no need for the lover to trouble his head to devise means and occasions; for verily will she find more in an hour than all the rest of us men together would be able to contrive in an hundred years. As saith a certain lady of rank of mine acquaintance, who doth declare to her lover: "Only do you find means to make me *wish* to come, and never fear! I will find ways enough."

Caesar moreover knew right well the measure of these matters, for himself was a very great debauchee, and was known by the title of the *cock for all hens*. Many a husband did he make cuckold in his city, as witness the nick-

name given him by his soldiers at his Triumph in the
verse they did sing thereat: *Romani, servate uxores;
moechum adducimus calvum,*

(Romans, look well to your wives, for we bring you
the bald-headed fornicator, who will debauch 'em every
one.)

See then how that Caesar by this wise and cunning
answer he made about his wife, did shake himself free of
bearing himself the name of cuckold, the which he made
so many others to endure. But in his heart, he knew
for all that how that he was galled to the quick.

3.

CTAVIUS CAESAR [1] likewise did put away
his wife Scribonia for the sake of his own
lecherousness, without other cause, though
at the same time without doing her any other
hurt, albeit she had good excuse to make him cuckold, by
reason of an infinity of ladies that he had relations with.
Indeed before their husbands' very faces he would openly
lead them away from table at those banquets he was
used to give them; then presently, after doing his will
with them, would send them back again with hair
dishevelled and disordered, and red ears,—a sure sign
of what they had been at! Not that myself did ever
elsewhere hear tell of this last as a distinctive mark
whereby to discover such doings; a red face for a cer-
tainty have I heard so spoken of, but red ears never.
So he did gain the repute of being exceeding lecherous,
and even Mark Antony reproached him therewith; but he
was used to excuse himself, saying he did not so much

go with these ladies for mere wantonness, as thereby to discover more easily the secrets of their husbands, whom he did distrust.

I have known not a few great men and others, which have done after the same sort and have sought after ladies with this same object, wherein they have had good hap. Indeed I could name sundry which have adopted this good device; for good it is, as yielding a twofold pleasure. In this wise was Catiline's conspiracy discovered by the means of a courtesan.

The same Octavius was once seriously minded to put to death his daughter Julia, wife of Agrippa, for that she had been a notorious harlot, and had wrought great shame to him,—for verily sometimes daughters do bring more dishonour on their fathers than wives on their husbands. Still he did nothing more than banish her the country, and deprive of the use of wine and the wearing of fine clothing, compelling her to wear poor folk's dress, by way of signal punishment, as also of the society of men. And this is in sooth a sore deprivation for women of this kidney, to rob them of the two last named gratifications!

Another Emperor, and very cruel tyrant, Caligula,[2] did suspect that his wife, Livia Hostilia, had by stealth cheated him of sundry of her favours, and bestowed the same on her first husband, Caius Piso, from whom he had taken her away by force. This last was still alive, and was deemed to have received of her some pleasure and gratification of her fair body, the while the Emperor was away on a journey. Yet did he not indulge his usual cruelty toward her, but only banished her from him, two

years after he had first taken her from her husband Piso
and married her.

He did the same to Tullia Paulina, whom he had taken
from her husband Caius Memmius. He exiled her and
that was all, but in this case with the express prohibition
to have naught to do at all with the gentle art of love,
neither with any other men nor yet with her husband
—truly a cruel and rigorous order so far as the last
was concerned!

I have heard speak of a Christian Prince, and a great
one, who laid the same prohibition on a lady whom he
affected, and on her husband likewise, by no means to
touch her, so jealous was he of her favours.

Claudius,[3] son of Drusus Germanicus, merely put away
his wife Plautia Urgulanilla, for having shown herself a
most notorius harlot, and what is worse, for that he had
heard how she had made an attempt upon his life. Yet
cruel as he was, though surely these two reasons were
enough to lead him to put her to death, he was content
with divorce only.

Then again, for how long a time did he endure the wild
doings and filthy debaucheries of Valeria Messalina, his
second wife, who was not content with doing it with one
and another here and there in dissolute and abandoned
sort, but made it her regular practice to go to the
brothels to get gratification of her passions, like the biggest strumpet in all the city. So far did she go, as
Juvenal doth describe, that so soon as ever her husband
was to bed with her, she would slip lightly away from
beside him, when she saw him fast asleep and disguising
herself the best she could, would hie her to some common
brothel, where she took all she could get, and still would

retire weary rather than replete or satisfied. Nay! she did even worse. For her better contentment, and to win the repute and self-satisfaction of being a good harlot and accomplished light-o'-love, she did even ask for payment, and would tax each round and each several act, like a travelling cess-collector, to the last doit.

I have heard speak of a lady of the great world, and of no mean lineage neither, who for some while did follow the same life, and went thus to the common brothels in disguise, to make trial of this way of existence, and get gratification of her passions,—so much so that one night the town-guard, while making their rounds, did actually arrest her unwittingly. And indeed there be other ladies too which play these pranks, as is well enough known.

Boccaccio [4] in his book of "Great Folks that have been Unhappy," doth speak of this Messalina in gentle terms, and representeth her making excuse for her ill behaviour, forasmuch as she was born by nature altogether for this course of life, the day of her birth being signalized by signs in the heavens which do show in all cases an hot and fiery complexion. Her husband was ware of it, and bore long with her,—until he learned how that she was secretly married to Caius Silius, one of the handsome gallants of Rome. So seeing the matter was as good as a plot upon his life, he had her put to death on this count, though in no wise for her lechery; for this he was well accustomed to see and know, and to condone the same.

Anyone who hath seen the statue of the aforesaid Messalina found in these last days at the town of Bordeaux will readily allow she did indeed bear the true look that comported with such a life. 'Tis an antique medal, found among some ruins; and is very fine and well worthy

[28]

to be preserved to look at and carefully examine. She is a very fine woman, of a very fine, tall figure, with handsome features, and hair gracefully dressed in the old Roman fashion, and of very great stature,—all manifesting she was what History doth declare her to have been. For, by what I gather from sundry philosophers, physicians and physiognomists, big women be naturally inclined and well disposed to this thing. In truth such women are of a manly build, and so being, have share in the hot passions both of men and women, and conjoining the natures of both in one bodily frame, are thus more passionate and do possess more vigour than one alone,—even as, they say, a great and deep-laden ship doth need deep water to bear her up. Moreover, by what the learned Doctors that be expert in the mysteries of love declare, a big woman is more apt and more delightsome thereto than a small one.

The which doth mind me of a very great Prince, whom I once knew. Wishing to commend a certain woman whose favours he had enjoyed, he said in this wise: " 'Tis a most excellent harlot, as big as my lady mother." Whereon being checked at the over-reckless vivacity of his speech, he did explain how that he meant not to say she was as great a harlot as his mother, but that she was of the like stature and as tall as was his mother. For sometimes a man doth say things he intendeth in no wise to say, as sometimes on the other hand he will say, without intending, the very actual truth.

Thus we see there is better cheer with big, tall women than with little ones, were it only for the noble grace and majesty, which they do own. For in this matter are these qualities as much called for and as attractive as in other exploits and exercises,—neither more nor less for example than in horsemanship. Wherein the riding of a tall and noble charger of blood is an hundred fold more agreeable and pleasant than is that of a little pony, and doth give more enjoyment by far to the cavalier. Albeit must the same be a good rider, and carry himself well, and show much more strength and address. In similar wise must a man carry himself toward fine, tall women; for that such as be of this stature are wont to have a higher-stepping gait than others, and will full often make riders slip their stirrup, nay! even lose their saddle altogether, as I have heard some tell which have essayed to mount them. In which case do they straight make boast and great mockery, whenas they have unseated them and thrown them flat. So have I been told of a certain lady of the good town of Paris, the which, the first time her lover did stay with her, said to him frankly: "Embrace me with a will, and clip me tight to you as well as ever you can; and ride boldly, for I am high-paced, —so beware of a fall. So for your part spare me not; I am strong enough and expert enough to bear your assaults, be they as fierce as they may. For indeed, if you spare me, will I not spare you. A good ball deserveth a good return." But insooth the lady did win the match.

Thus must a man take good heed to his behaviour with suchlike bold, merry, stalwart, fleshly and well-built dames; and though truly the superabundant heat that is in them doth give great contentment, yet will they at times be overpressing by reason of their excessive passionateness. However, as the proverb saith: *There be good hinds of all sizes,* so likewise are there little, dwarf-

ish women which have action, grace and manner in these
matters coming very nigh to their taller sisters,—or
mayhap they be fain to copy them,—and as keen for the
fray as they, or even more so, (I would appeal to the
masters in these arts), just as a little horse will curvet
every whit as nimbly as a big one. This bringeth to mind
the saying of a worthy husband, who declared his wife
was like divers animals and above all like an ape, for that
when a-bed she would do naught but twist and turn and
toss about.

Sundry reminiscences have beguiled me into this digression. 'Tis time now to come back again to our original
discussion.

Another case. That cruel tyrant Nero [5] did content
himself with the mere putting away of his wife Octavia,
daughter of Claudius and Messalina, for her adultery;
and his cruelty stopped thereat.

Domitian [6] did even better, who divorced his wife Lon-
gina, because she was so fondly enamoured of a certain
comedian and buffoon named Paris, and did naught else
all day long but play the wanton with him, neglecting the
society of her husband altogether. Yet, after no long
time, did he take her back again and repented him of
the separation from her. Remember this: the said
mountebank had taught her meantime sundry tricks of
adroitness and cunning address, the which the Emperor
did hope he would have good profit of!

Pertinax [7] did show a like clemency toward his wife
Favia Sulpitiana. Not indeed that he did divorce her,
nor yet take her again, but though well knowing her to
be devoted to a singer and player of instruments of
music, and to give all her love to the same, yet made he no

complaint, but let her do her will. Meanwhile himself pursued an intrigue with one Cornificia, who was his own cousin german. Herein he did but follow the opinion of Heliogabalus, who was used to say there was naught in the world more excellent than the frequenting of one's own relations, male and female. Many there be that I wot of, which have made such exchanges and had such-like dealings, going upon the opinions of these two Princes!

So likewise did the Emperor Severus [8] take no heed of his wife's honour or dishonour, though she was a public harlot. Yet did he never think of correcting her therefor, saying only she was called Julia by her name, and that all who bare that name had from all time been fated to be mighty whores and to cuckold their husbands. In like wise do I know many ladies bearing certain names under this our Christian dispensation,—I will not say who they be for the respect I owe to our holy Religion,—the which are constantly used to be strumpets and to *lift the leg* more than other women bearing other names. Of such have been very few which have escaped this evil fate.

Well! of a truth I should never have done, were I to adduce all the infinity of examples of great ladies and Roman Emperors of yore, in whose case their husbands, though sore cajoled and albeit very cruel men, did yet refrain them from exerting their cruelty and undoubted rights and privileges against their wives, no matter how dissolute and ill-conducted these were. I ween few prudes were there in those old days, as indeed is sufficiently declared in the history of their lives, and as may be plainly discerned by careful examination of ancient portraits and medallions representing them; for indeed you may behold

in their fair faces this same lubricity manifestly and
obviously displayed by chisel and graver. Yet did their
husbands, cruel Princes as these were, pardon them, and
did put none of them to death, or but a very few. So
would it seem true that these Pagans, not knowing God,
yet were so gentle and clement toward their wives and
the human race, while the most part of our Kings, Princes,
great Lords and other Christian men, be so cruel toward
the same for a like offence.

4.

NATHELESS must we herein greatly commend
our brave and good Philip Augustus,[1] King
of France, who after having put away his wife
Angerberge, sister of Canute, King of Denmark, which was his second wife, under pretext she was
his cousin in the third degree on the side of his first wife
Ysabel, though others say he did suspect her of unfaithfulness, yet did the said King, under the weight of ecclesiastical censures, albeit he had married again elsewhere,
take her back again, and so conveyed her home behind
him on horseback, without the privity of the Diet of
Soissons, that had been summoned to decide this very
matter, but was too dilatory to come to any conclusion
thereon.

Nowadays never a one of our great men will do the
like; but the least punishment they do their wives is to
shut them up in perpetual prison, on bread and water,
poisoning them or killing them, whether by their own
hand or by legal process. If they have so great a desire
to be rid of them and marry others, as doth often happen,

[33]

why do they not divorce them and honourably separate
from them, without doing other hurt, and then ask power
of the Pope to marry another wife? For surely what
God hath joined together, man (without God's authority)
may in no wise separate. Yet have we had sundry examples thereof, and notably those of our French Kings
Charles VIII. [2] and Louis XII. [3] Whereanent I did once
hear a great Theologian discourse, namely with regard
to the late King Philip of Spain, who had married his
niece, the mother of the present King, and this by dispensation. He said thus: "Either must we outright
allow the Pope to be God's Vicegerent on earth, and so
absolutely, or else not at all. If he is, as we Catholics
are bound to believe, we must entirely confess his power
as absolute and unbounded on earth, and without limit,
and that he can tie and untie as good him seemeth. But
if we do not hold him such, well, I am sorry for them that
be in such error, but good Catholics have naught to do
with them." Wherefore hath our Holy Father authority
over dissolutions of marriage, and can allay many grave
inconveniences which come therefrom to husband and
wife, when they do ill agree together.

Certainly women are greatly blameworthy so to treat
their husbands and violate their good faith, the which
God hath so strongly charged them to observe. But yet
on the other hand hath he straitly forbid murder, and
it is highly detestable to Him, on whosesoever part it be.
Never yet hardly have I seen bloody folk and murderers,
above all of their wives, but they have paid dear for it,
and very few lovers of blood have ended well, whereas
many women that have been sinners have won the pity
of God and obtained mercy, as did the Magdalen.

[34]

In very deed these poor women are creatures more
nearly resembling the Divinity than we, because of their
beauty. For what is beautiful is more near akin to God
who is all beautiful, than the ugly, which belongeth to the
Devil.

The good Alfonzo, King of Naples, was used to say
how that beauty was a token of good and gentle manners,
as the fair flower is token of a good and fair fruit. And
insooth have I seen in my life many fair women who
were altogether good: who though they did indeed indulge
in love, did commit no evil, nor take heed for aught else
but only this pleasure, and thereto applied all their care
without a second thought.

Others again have I seen most ill-conditioned, harmful,
dangerous, cruel and exceeding spiteful, naught hindering
them from caring for love and evil-doing both together.

It may then well be asked,—why, being thus subject to
the fickle and suspicious humour of their husbands, the
which do deserve punishment ten times more in God's
eyes, why they are so sorely punished? Indeed and indeed the complexion and humour of such folk is as grievous as is the sorry task of writing of them.

I speak next of yet another such, a Lord of Dalmatia,
who having slain his wife's paramour, did compel her to
bed habitually with his dead body, stinking carrion as
it was. The end whereof was, the unhappy woman was
choked with the evil stench she did endure for several
days.

In the *Cent Nouvelles* of the Queen of Navarre will be
found the most touching and saddest tale that can be
read on this matter, the tale of that fair lady of Germany the which her husband was used to constrain to

drink ever from the skull of her dead lover, whom he had slain. This piteous sight did the Seigneur Bernage, at that day ambassador in the said country for the French King Charles VIII., see and make report thereof.

The first time ever I was in Italy, I was told, when passing through Venice, what did purport to be a true story of a certain Albanian knight, the which having surprised his wife in adultery, did kill the lover. And for spite that his wife had not been content with him, for indeed he was a gallant knight, and well fitted for Love's battles, so much so that he could engage ten or twelve times over in one night, he did contrive a strange punishment, and so did seek out carefully in all quarters a dozen stout fellows of the right lecherous sort, who had the repute of being well and vigorously built and very adroit in action. These he took and hired, and engaged the same for money. Then he did lock them in his wife's chamber, who was a very fair woman, and gave her up to them, beseeching them one and all to do their duty thoroughly, with double pay if that they did acquit themselves really well. Thus did they all go at her, one after another, and did handle her in such wise that they did kill her,—to the great pleasure of her husband, who did cast it in her teeth, when she was nigh unto death, that having loved this pleasure so much, she could now have her fill thereof. Herein he but copied what Semiramis (or rather *Thomyris*) said, as she put Cyrus' head into a vessel full of blood. A terrible death truly!

The poor lady had not so died, if only she had been of the robust complexion of a girl that was in Cæsar's camp in Gaul. Two legions did pass, 'tis said, over her body in brief space; yet at the end of all she did dance a fling, feeling no hurt thereof.

I have heard speak of a Frenchwoman, town-bred, a lady of birth and of handsome looks, who was violated in our civil wars, in a town taken by assault, by a multitude of men-at-arms. On escaping away from these, she did consult a worthy Father as to whether she had sinned greatly, first telling him her story. He said, no!—inasmuch as she had been had by force, and deflowered without her consent, but entirely misliking the thing. Whereon she did make answer: "Now God be praised, for that once in my life I have had my fill, without sinning or doing offence to God!"

A lady of good quality, having been in like wise violated at the time of the Massacre of Saint Bartholomew, and her husband being dead, she did ask of a man of knowledge and right feeling, whether she had offended God, and whether she would not be punished of His sternness, and if she had not sorely wronged the manes of her husband, who had but only quite late been slain. He answered her, that if, when she was at this work, she had taken pleasure therein, then had she surely sinned; but if she had felt but disgust at the thing, it was as if it had never been. A good and wise judgement!

I once knew well a lady who held quite other views, for she was used to say: Never did she feel so great a pleasure in these doings, as when she was half forced and all but violated as it were, and then was there much pleasure therein. The more a woman showeth herself rebellious and recalcitrant, so much the more doth the man wax ardent and push home the attack; and so having once

[37]

forced the breach, he doth use his victory more fiercely and savagely, and thereby giveth more appetite to the woman. The latter is for very delight like one half dead and swooned, or so it seemeth; but really 'tis by reason of the extreme pleasure she findeth therein. Indeed the same lady did actually say further, that oftentimes she would make these ados and show resistance to her husband, and play the prudish, capricious and scornful wife, and so put him the more on his mettle. Whereby when he did come to it, both he and she did find an hundredfold more pleasure; for many writers have noted, a woman pleaseth better who makes some little difficulties and resistances than when she lets herself straightway be taken. So in War is a victory won by force more signalised and hailed with greater delight and enthusiasm than when had for nothing, and the triumph thereof is sweeter. Yet must not the lady in all this *overdo* the part of the peevish and evil-tempered jade, else may she likely be mistaken rather for a silly whore wishful to be playing of the prude. But at such interference would she be sore offended, to go by what I am told by such dames as are most versed and apt in these matters, to the whom I do appeal. For far be it from me to give them instruction in things they do understand much better than I!

Again, I have known many greatly blame some of these callous and murderous husbands on one count in especial, namely that, if their wives be whores, themselves are the cause of it. For, as Saint Augustine saith, it is great foolishness in an husband to demand chastity of his wife, himself being all the while plunged in the slough of lecherous living; for such mode of life as he doth claim from his wife, the same he should follow himself. Moreover we do read in Holy Scripture how that it is not expedient that the husband and wife love each other so excessively, meaning by this with a wanton and lecherous love. For in that case do they set all their heart and mind on lustful pleasures, and think so much of these and give themselves up so entirely to the same, as that they do neglect the love which they owe to God. Thus have I myself seen many women who so loved their husbands, and their husbands them, and burned for them with such ardour, as that both of them did forget God's service utterly, inasmuch as the time they should have given thereto, they did devote to their lecheries and employ the whole of it therein.

Furthermore, and this is a yet worse thing, these same husbands do teach their wives a thousand lecheries. The end is that for one fire brand of lust they have in their body to begin with, they do engender an hundred, and so make them exceeding lascivious, so that being so trained and instructed, they cannot later refrain themselves from leaving their husbands to go after other swains. Whereat are their husbands in despair, and do punish their poor wives sorely. Herein they do commit great injustice, for it is only natural the wives, whenas they feel their heart stirred with satisfaction at being so well trained, should then wish to show others all they know; but the husbands would fain have them hide their science. In all this is neither sense nor reason, no more than if a good horseman should have a well-trained horse, which could go all paces, and yet should suffer no man to see the same tried or to mount on its back, but should require folk to believe it on his mere word, and take the beast without other warranty.

I have heard tell of an honourable gentleman of the great world, who having fallen deep in love with a certain fair lady, was warned by a friend of his how that he was but wasting his time, seeing she did love her husband far too well. So one day he did contrive to make an hole which looked right into their room. Then when they were together, he failed not to spy at them through this hole, whereby he did behold the greatest lubricities and lecheries, and this as much, nay! even more, on the part of the wife than of the husband. Accordingly the next day he hied him to his comrade, and detailing all the fine sight he had had, did thus say to him: " The woman is mine, I tell you, so soon as ever the husband hath started on such and such a journey; for she will never be able for long to restrain herself under the ardour which nature and art as well have given her, but must needs assuage the same. And in this wise by dint of my perseverance shall I have her."

I know yet another honourable gentleman, the which being exceedingly enamoured of a fair and honourable lady, aware she had a copy of Aretino with pictures in her closet, as her husband well knew and had seen and did allow, straightway augured therefrom that he would overcome her. And so without losing hope, did he make love to her so well, and so long and patiently, that at the last he did win the day. And hereon did he find that she had indeed learned good lessons and excellent science, whether from her husband or from others, albeit neither the one nor the other had been her first masters, but Dame Nature rather, who was a better mistress therein than all the arts. Not but what the book and good practice had helped much in the matter, as she did later confess to him.

We read in ancient Writers of a great courtesan and procuress of the days of old Rome, by name Elephantiné, [4] who did make and invent postures or *modes* of the same sort as those of Aretino, but even worse, the which the great ladies and princesses of yore, following the ways of harlotry, did study as being a very excellent book.

Also that good dame and famous whore of Cyrené in Africa, who did bear the title of *Dodecamechanos* (she of the twelve devices), because she had discovered twelve several modes whereby to make the pleasure more wanton and voluptuous.

Heliogabalus [5] was used to hire and keep in his pay, at the expense of much money and costly gifts, such men and women as did invent and bring forward new devices of this kind, the better to arouse his lecherousness. Yea! and I have heard of other such that are like him among the great folk of our own day!

But a few years since did Pope Sixtus V. cause to be hanged at Rome a Secretary which had been in the service of the Cardinal d'Este and was named Capella, for many and divers offences,—but amongst other that he had composed a book of these same fine postures, the which were figured by a great ecclesiastic whom I will not name for sake of his cloth, and by a great lady, one of the fair dames of Rome, the whole shown to the life and painted in proper form and colour. [6]

[41]

5.

 ONCE knew a Prince and a great man who did even better, for he had of a goldsmith a very fair cup made of silver gilt, by way of a masterpiece and very especial curiosity, the most high-wrought, well engraven and cunningly chiseled piece of work could anywhere be seen. And thereon were cut most featly and subtly with the graver sundry of the *postures* from Aretino, of men and women with one another; this on the lower part of the cup, and above and higher up sundry also of the divers modes of beasts.

And 'twas here I first learned (for many is the time I have seen the said cup and drunk therein, not without laughing) the way of cohabitation of the lion and lioness, the which is quite opposite to that of all other animals. This I had never known before, and as to its nature I refer me to those who are ware of the facts without my telling them. The said cup was the glory of the Prince's sideboard; for verily, as I have said, it was right fairly and richly wrought, and very pleasant to look at inside and out.

When this same Prince did give a feast to the ladies, married and single, of his Court,—and not seldom was it his habit so to invite them,—his butlers never failed, such was his strait command, to serve the company to drink in this cup. Then were such as had never afore seen it moved in divers ways, either while drinking or afterward. Some would be sore astonished, and know not what to say thereat; some would be all ashamed and the scarlet leaping to their face; some again would be whispering low to one another: "Nay! what is all this carven inside? I fear

[42]

me they be naughty pictures. I will never drink from the cup again. I must indeed be sore athirst before ever I ask for drink therefrom again?" Yet were they bound to drink from this cup, or burst with thirst; and to this end, would some shut their eyes in drinking, but the rest, who were less shamefaced, not. Such as had heard tell of the hang of it, as well matrons as maids, would be laughing the while under the rose; while such as had not, would be downright bursting with desire to do the like.

When asked what they had to laugh at and what they had seen, some would reply they had seen naught but some pictures, and for anything there was there they would make no ado about drinking another time. Others would say, "As for me, I think no ill thereof; what the eye sees or a picture shows forth doth never soil the soul." Some again would declare, "Bah! good wine is as good in this cup as in another;" and say it was as good to drink out of as any other, and did quench the thirst just the same. Then some of the ladies would be questioned, why they did not shut their eyes in drinking, to which they would make answer they were fain to see what they were drinking, for fear instead of wine it might be some drug or poison. Others would be asked which they did take the more pleasure in, seeing or drinking; whereto they would reply, "In both, of course." Some would be crying, "Oh! the quaint grotesques!" others, "Ah, ha! what be these merry mummeries we have here?" Some, "Oh! the pretty pictures!" and others, "Here be fine figures to look at!" Some, "Well, well! Master Goldsmith must needs have had good leisure to while away his time in making these gewgaws!" Others, "And you,

[43]

Sire! to think you should have taken this wondrous cup of him!" " Now feel ye not a something that doth touch you, ladies, at the sight?" They would enquire presently, to which the answer would come, " Nay! never a one of all these droll images hath had power enough to stir me!" Others again would be asked, whether they had not found the wine hot, and whether it had not warmed them finely in this wintry weather; and they would answer, " Nay! we noted no heat; for indeed our draught was cold, and did much refresh us." Some they would ask, which of all these figures they would best love to have; and they would answer they could in no wise remove them from where they were to transport them thither.

In short, an hundred thousand gibes and quips and cranks would pass thereon between the gentlefolk and ladies at table, as I have myself seen, so that it did make right merry jesting, and a very pleasant thing to see and hear. But above all, to my thinking, best and most heartsome was it to watch those innocent maids, or mayhap them that figured only to be so, and other ladies newly come to Court, striving to maintain a cold mien, with an artificial laugh on their face and lips, or else holding themselves in and playing the hypocrite, as was the way with many ladies. And mind this, though they had been a-dying of thirst, yet durst not the butlers have given them to drink in any other cup or glass. Yea! and likewise were there some ladies that sware, to put a good face on the matter, they would never, never come to these feasts again; but for all that did they in no wise fail to come again often enough, for truly the Prince was a right magnificent and dainty host. Other ladies would say, on being invited thither: "Well! I will go, but under protest we shall not be given to drink in the cup;" yet when once they were there, would they drink therein as well as ever. At the last would they aye think better of it, and make no more scruple whatever about drinking. Nay! some did even better, and turned the said images to good use in fitting time and place; and yet more than this, some did act dissolutely of set purpose to make trial of the same, for that every person of spirit would fain essay everything. So here we have the fatal effects of this cup so well dight. And hereanent must each fancy for himself all the other discourse, and thoughts and looks and words, that these ladies did indulge in and give vent to, one with another, whether in privity or in open company.

I ween this cup was of a very different sort from the one whereof M. Ronsard [1] doth speak in one of his earliest Odes, dedicated to the late King Henri, which doth thus begin:

> Comme un qui prend une couppe,
> Seul honneur de son trésor.
> Et de rang verse à la trouppe
> Du vin qui rit dedans l'or.

(As one who takes a cup, sole honour of all his treasure, and duly pours therein to the company good wine that laughs within the gold.)

However in this cup I tell of the wine laughed not at any, but rather the folk at the wine. For verily some dames did drink laughing, and others trembling with delight; and yet others would be nigh *compissoyent*,—I mean not of course just ordinary piddling, but something

[45]

more. In a word the said cup did bring dire effects with it, so touching true were these images, figures and representations.

In likewise do I remember me how once, in a gallery of the Comte de Chasteau-Villain, known as the Seigneur Adjacet, a company of ladies with their lovers having come to visit the said fair mansion, they did fall to contemplating sundry rare and beautiful pictures in the Gallery thereof. Among these they beheld a very beautiful picture, wherein were pourtrayed a number of fair ladies naked and at the bath, which did touch, and feel, and handle, and stroke, one the other, and intertwine and fondle with each other, and so enticingly and prettily and featly did show all their hidden beauties that the coldest recluse or hermit had been warmed and stirred thereat. Wherefore did a certain great lady, as I have heard it told, and indeed I do know her well, losing all restraint of herself before this picture, say to her lover, turning toward him maddened as it were at the madness of love she beheld painted; "Too long have we tarried here. Let us now straightway take coach and so to my lodging; for that no more can I hold in the ardour that is in me. Needs must away and quench it; too sore do I burn." And so she did haste away to enjoy her faithful lover.

Suchlike pictures and portrayals do bring more hurt to a weak soul than men think for. Another of the same sort there, was a Venus naked, lying on a couch and eyed by her son Cupid; another, Mars a-bed with Venus, another, a Leda with her swan. Many other there be, both there and elsewhere, that are somedel more modestly painted and better veiled than the figures of Aretino;

[46]

but all do come pretty much to one and the same, and are of the like nature with our cup whereof I have been speaking. This last had, as it were, a sort of likeness in unlikeness to the cup which Renault de Montauban found in the Castle Ariosto doth tell of, the which did openly discover unhappy husbands that were cuckolds, whereas this one was more likely to make them so. But while the one did cause somewhat too great scandal to cuckolds and their faithless wives, the other had no such effect. Nowadays is no need of these books or these pictures, for that husbands teach their wives themselves enough and to spare without them. And now for the results of suchlike husbands' schooling!

I knew an excellent Venetian printer at Paris named Messer Bernardo, a kinsman of the great Aldus Manutius of Venice [2], which did keep his shop in the Rue Saint-Jacques. The same did once tell me, and swear to it, that in less than a year he had sold more than fifty of the two volumes of Aretino [3] to very many folks, married and unmarried, as well as to women of whom he did name three very great ladies of society; but I will not repeat the names. To these he did deliver the book into their own hands, and right well bound, under oath given he would breathe never a word of it—though he did round it to me natheless. And he did tell me further how that another lady having asked him some time after, if he had not another like the one she had seen in the hands of one of the three, he had answered her: *Signora, si, e peggio* ("Yes, Madam,—and worse"); and she instantly, money on table, had bought them all at their weight in gold. Verily a frantic inquisitiveness for to send her

[47]

husband a voyage to the haven of Cornette (the Horns), near by Civita-Vecchia.

All such devices and postures are abominable in God's sight, as indeed St. Jerome saith: "Whosoever doth show himself more unrestrainedly enamoured of his wife than a husband should, is an adulteror and committeth sin. And forasmuch as sundry Doctors of the Church have spoken thereof, I will sum up the matter shortly in Latin words, seeing themselves have not thought good to say it in plain language: *Excessus,* say they, *conjugum fit, quando uxor cognoscitur ante retro stando, sedendo, in latere, et mulier super virum* (Excess between married people is committed when the wife is known before by the husband standing behind, or sitting, or sideways, or the woman on top of the man). This last posture is referred to in a little couplet I once read, and which goes as follows:

> In prato viridi monialem ludere vidi
> Cum monacho leviter, ille sub, illa super.

Other learned Doctors hold that any mode whatsoever is good, provided only that *semen ejaculetur in matricem mulieris, et quomodocunque uxor cognoscatur, si vir ejaculetur semen in matricem, non est peccatum mortale.*

These arguments are to be found in the *Summa Benedicti.* This Benedict [4] is a Doctor of the Cordeliers, who has writ most excellently of all the sins, and shown how that he hath both seen much and read widely. Anyone who will read this passage, will find therein a number of excesses which husbands do commit toward their wives. Thus he saith that *quando mulier est ita pinguis ut non possit aliter coire, non est mortale peccatum, modo vir*

ejaculetur semen in vas naturale. Whereas others again
say it were better husbands should abstain from their wives
altogether when they are with child, as do the animals,
than for them to befoul marriage with such abominations.

I knew once a famous courtesan of Rome, called "The
Greek," whom a great Lord of France had kept in that
city. After some space, she had a strong desire to visit
France, using to this end the Signor Bonvisi, a Banker
of Lyons, a native of Lucca and a very rich man, who
was her lover. Wherein having succeeded, she did make
many enquiries concerning the said gentleman and his
wife, and amongst other matters, whether mayhap she did
not cuckold him, "seeing that," she would say, "I have
so well trained her husband, and have taught him such
excellent lessons, that he having once shown them to his
wife and practised the same with her, it is not possible
but that she have desired to show the same to others also.
For insooth our trade is such an one, when it is well
learned, that a woman doth find an hundred times more
pleasure in showing and practising it with several than
with one only." Furthermore did she say that the said
lady ought of rights to make her a handsome present
and one worthy of her pains and good teaching, forasmuch as when her husband did first come to her school,
he knew naught at all, but was in these matters the most
silly, inexperienced prentice hand ever she had seen. But
now, so well had she trained him and fashioned him that
his wife must needs find him an hundred times better.
For in fact the lady, desiring to see her, went to visit
her in disguise; this the courtesan suspected, and held
all the discourse to her I have detailed,—and worse still
and more dissolute, for she was an exceeding dissolute

[49]

woman. And this is how husbands do forge the knives
to cut their own throats withal; or rather is it a question
not of throats at all, but of horns! Acting after this
sort do they pollute holy matrimony, for the which God
doth presently punish them; then must they have their
revenge on their wives, wherein are they an hundred times
more deserving of punishment than before. So am I not a
whit surprised that the same venerable Doctor did declare marriage to be in very truth but a kind of adultery,
as it were; thereby intending, when men did abuse it after
the fashion I have been discoursing of.

Thus hath marriage been forbidden our priests; for
that it is no wise meet that, just come from their wives'
bed and after polluting themselves exceedingly with them,
they should then approach an holy altar. For, by my
faith, so far as I have heard tell, some folk do wanton
more with their wives than do the very reprobates with
the harlots in brothels; for these last, fearing to catch
some ill, do not go to extremes or warm to the work
with them as do husbands with their wives. For these
be clean and can give no hurt,—that is to say the most
part of them, though truly not quite all; for myself have
known some to give it to their husbands, as also their
husbands to them.

Husbands, so abusing their wives, are much deserving
of punishment, as I have heard great and learned Doctors
say; for that they do not behave themselves modestly with
their wives in their bed, as of right they should, but
wanton with them as with concubines, whereas marriage
was instituted for necessity of procreation, and in no wise
for dissolute and lecherous pleasure. And this did the
Emperor Sejanus Commodus, otherwise called Anchus

Verus [5], well declare unto us, when he said to his wife
Calvilla, who did make complaint to him, for that he was
used to bestow on harlots and courtesans and other the
like what did of rights belong to her in her bed, and rob
her of her little enjoyments and gratifications. "Bear
with me, wife," he said to her, "that with other women
I satiate my foul passions, seeing that the name of wife
and consort is one deserving of dignity and honour, and
not one for mere pleasure and lecherousness." I have
never yet read or learned what reply his good wife the
Empress made him thereto; but little doubt can be she
was ill content with his golden saying, and did answer
him from out her heart, and in the words of the most
part, nay! of all, married women: "A fig for your dignity
and honour; pleasure for me! We thrive better on this
last than on all the other."

Nor yet must we suppose for an instant that the more
part of married men of to-day or of any other day,
which have fair wives, do speak after this wise. For indeed they do not marry and enter into wedlock, nor take
their wives, but only in order to pass their time pleasure-
ably and indulge their passion in all fashions and teach
the same merry precepts, as well for the wanton movements of their body as for the dissolute and lascivious
words of their mouth, to the end their love may be the
better awaked and stirred up thereby. Then, after having thus well instructed and debauched their minds, if
they do go astray elsewhere, lo! they are for sorely punishing them, beating and murdering and putting of them
to death.

Truly scant reasonableness is there in this, just as if
a man should have debauched a poor girl, taking her

straight from her mother's arms, and have robbed her of
her honour and maidenhood, and should then, after having his will of her, beat her and constrain her to live
quite otherwise, in entire chastity,—verily an excellent
and opportune thing to ask! Who is there would not
condemn such an one, as a man unreasonable and deserving to be made suffer? The same might justly be
said of many husbands, the which, when all is said and
done, do more debauch their wives and teach them more
precepts to lead them into lechery than ever their gallants use, for they do enjoy more time and leisure therefor than lovers can have. But presently, when they
cease their instructions, the wives most naturally do seek
a change of hand and master, being herein like a good
rider, who findeth more pleasure an hundredfold in
mounting an horse than one that is all ignorant of the
art. "And alack!" so used the courtesan we but now
spake of to say, "there is no trade in all the world that is
more cunning, nor that doth more call for constant practice, than that of Venus." Wherefore these husbands
should be warned not to give suchlike instructions to their
wives, for that they be far and away too dangerous and
harmful to the same. Or, if they needs must, and afterward find their wives playing them a knavish trick, let
them not punish them, forasmuch as it is themselves have
opened the door thereto.

Here am I constrained to make a digression to tell of a
certain married woman, fair and honourable and of good
station, whom I know, the which did give herself to an
honourable gentleman,—and that more for the jealousy
she bare toward an honourable lady whom this same
gentleman did love and keep as his paramour than for

love. Wherefore, even as he was enjoying her favour, the lady said to him: "Now at last, to my great contentment, do I triumph over you and over the love you bear to such an one." The gentleman made answer to her: "A person that is beat down, brought under and trampled on, can scarce be said to triumph greatly." The lady taketh umbrage at this reply, as touching her honour, and straightway makes answer, "You are very right," and instantly puts herself of a sudden to unseat the man, and slip away from him. Never of yore was Roman knight or warrior so quick and dexterous to mount and remount his horses at the gallop as was the lady this bout with her gallant. Then doth she handle him in this mode, saying the while, "Well then, at present I can declare truly and in good conscience I triumph over you, forasmuch as I hold you subdued under me." Verily a dame of a gay and wanton ambition, and very strange the way in which she did satisfy the same!

I have heard speak of a very fair and honourable lady of the great world, much given over to love, who yet was so arrogant and proud, and so high of heart, that when it came to it, never would she suffer her man to put her under him and humble her. For by so doing she deemed she wrought a great wrong to the nobility of her spirit, and held it a great piece of cowardice to be thus humbled and subdued, as in a triumphant conquest and enslavement; but was fain ever to guard the upper hand and pre-eminence. And one thing that did greatly help her herein was that she would never have dealings with one greater in rank than herself, for fear that, using his authority and puissance, he might succeed in giving the law to her, and so turn, twist about and trample her, just as he pleased. Rather for this work would she choose her equals and inferiors, to the which she could dictate their place and station, their order and procedure in the amorous combat, neither more nor less than doth a sergeant major to his men-at-arms on the day of battle. These orders would she in no wise have them overpass, under pain of losing what they most desire and value, in some cases her love, in others their own life. In such wise that never, standing or sitting or lying, could they prevail to return back and put upon her the smallest humiliation, submission or subservience, which she had done them. Hereanent I refer me to the words and judgement of such, men and women, as have dealt with such loves, stations and modes.

Anyway the lady we speak of could so order it, that no hurt should be done to the dignity she did affect, and no offence to her proud heart; for by what I have heard from sundry that have been familiar with her, she had powers enough to make such ordinances and regulations.

In good sooth a formidable and diverting woman's caprice, and a right curious scruple of a proud spirit. Yet was she in the right after all; for in truth is it a humiliating and painful thing to be so brought under and bent to another's will, and trod down, when one thinks of it quickly and alone, and saith to oneself, "Such an one hath put me under him and trod me underfoot,"—for underfoot it is, if not literally, at any rate in a manner of speaking, and doth amount to the same thing.

The same lady moreover would never suffer her inferiors to kiss her on the mouth, "seeing it is so," she would say, "that the touch and contact of mouth to mouth is the most delicate and precious of all contacts, whether

[54]

of the hand or other members." For this reason would she not be so approached, nor feel on her own a foul, unclean mouth, and one not meet for hers.

Now hereanent is yet another question I have known some debate: what advantage and overplus of glory hath the one, whether man or woman, over his companion, whenas they are at these amorous skirmishes and conquests?

The man on his side doth set forth the reasons given above, to wit, that the victory is much greater when as one holdeth his sweet enemy laid low beneath him, and doth subjugate, put underfoot and tame her at his ease and how he best pleaseth. For there is no Princess or great lady so high, but doth, when she is in that case, even though it were with an inferior or subordinate, suffer the law and domination which Venus hath ordained in her statutes; and for this cause glory and honour do redound therefrom to the man in very high measure.

The woman on the other hand saith: "Yes! I do confess you may well feel triumphant when you do hold me under you and put me underfoot. But if it be only a question of keeping the upper station, I likewise do sometimes take that in mere sportiveness and of a pretty caprice that assaileth me, and not of any constraint. Further, when this upperhand position doth not like me, I do make you work for me like a very serf or galley-slave, or to put it better, make you pull at the collar like a veritable waggon-horse, and there you are toiling, striving, sweating, panting, straining to perform the task and labour I choose to exact from you. Meanwhile, for me, lo! I am at my ease, and watch your efforts. Sometimes do I make merry at your expense, and take my pleasure in seeing you in such sore labour, sometimes too I compassionate you, just as pleaseth me and according as I am inclined to merriment or pity. Then after having well fulfilled my pleasure and caprice herein, I do leave my gallant there, tired, worn out, weakened and enervate, so he can do no more, and hath need of naught so much as of a good sleep and a good meal, a strong broth, a restorative, or some good soup to hearten him up. For me, for all such labours and efforts, I feel no whit the worse, but only that I have been right well served at your expense, sir gallant, and do experience no hurt; but only wish for some other to give me as much again, and to make him as much exhausted as you. And after this wise, never surrendering, but making my sweet foe surrender to me, 'tis I bear away the true victory and true glory, seeing that in a duello he that doth give in is dishonoured, and not he that doth fight on to the last dire extremity."

So have I heard this tale following told of a fair and honourable lady. One time, her husband having wakened her from a sound sleep and good rest she was enjoying, for to do the thing, when he was done, she said to him, "Well! 'tis you did it, not I." And she did clip him exceeding tight with arms, hands, feet and legs crossed over each other, saying, "I will teach you to wake me up another time," and so with might and main and right good will, pulling, pushing and shaking her husband, and who could in no wise get loose, but who lay there sweating and stewing and aweary, and was fain to cry her mercy, she did make him so exhausted, and so foredone and feeble, that he grew altogether out of breath and did swear her a sound oath how another time he would have her only at his own time, humour and desire. The tale is one better to imagine and picture to oneself than to describe in words.

Such then are the woman's arguments, with sundry other she might very well have adduced to boot. And note how the humblest strumpet can do as much to a great King or Prince, if he have gone with her,—and this is a great scorn, seeing that the blood royal is held to be the most precious can ever be. At any rate is it right carefully guarded and very expensively and preciously accommodated far more than any other man's!

This then is what the women do or say. Yet truly is it great pity a blood so precious should be polluted and contaminated so foully and unworthily. And indeed it was forbid by the law of Moses to waste the same in any wise on the ground; but it is much worse done to intermingle it in a most foul and unworthy fashion. Still 'twere too much to have them do as did a certain great Lord, of whom I have heard tell, who having in his dreams at night polluted himself among his sheets, had these buried, so scrupulous-minded was he, saying it was a babe issuing therefrom that was dead, and how that it was pity and a very great loss that this blood had not been put into his wife's womb, for then it might well be the child would have lived.

Herein might he very like have been deceived, seeing that of a thousand cohabitations the husband hath with the wife in the year, 'tis very possible, as I have above said, she will not become pregnant thereby, not once in all her life, in fact never in the case of some women which be eunuch and barren, and can never conceive. Whence hath come the error of certain misbelievers, which say that marriage was not ordained so much for the procrea-

[57]

tion of children as for pleasure. Now this is ill thought and ill said, for albeit a woman doth not grow pregnant every time a man have her, 'tis so for some purpose of God to us mysterious, and that he wills to punish in this wise both man and wife, seeing how the greatest blessing God can give us in marriage is a good offspring, and that not in mere concubinage. And many women there be that take a great delight in having it, but others not. These latter will in no wise suffer aught to enter into them, as well to avoid foisting on their husbands children that are not theirs, as to avoid the semblance of doing them wrong and making them cuckolds.

For by this name of cuckoos (or cuckolds), properly appertaining to those birds of Springtide that are so called because they do lay their eggs in other birds' nests, are men also known by antinomy,[6] when others come to lay eggs in their nest, that is in their wives' article,— which is the same thing as saying, cast their seed into them and make them children.

And this is how many wives think they are doing no wrong to their husbands in taking their fill of pleasure, provided only they do not become pregnant. Such their fine scruples of conscience! So a great lady of whom I have heard speak, was used to say to her gallant: "Take your pastime as much as ever you will, and give me pleasure; but on your life, take heed to let naught bedew me, else is it a question of life and death for you."

A like story have I heard told by the Chevalier de Sanzay of Brittany, a very honourable and gallant gentleman, who, had not death overtaken him at an early age, would have been a great seaman, having made a very good beginning of his career. And indeed he did bear the marks and signs thereof, for he had had an arm carried off by a cannon shot at a sea-fight he did engage in. As his ill luck would have it, he was taken prisoner of the Corsairs and carried off to Algiers. His master who had him as his slave, was the head Priest of the Mosque in that part, and had a very beauteous wife. This lady did fall so deep in love with the said Sanzay that she bade him come to have amorous dalliance and delight with her, saying how she would treat him very well, better than any of her other slaves. But above all else did she charge him very straitly, and on his life, or on pain of most rigorous imprisonment, not to emit in her body a single drop of his seed, forasmuch as, so she declared, she must in no wise be polluted and contaminated with Christian blood, whereby she thought she would sorely offend against the law of her people and their great Prophet Mahomet. And further she bade him, that albeit she should even order him an hundred times over to do the whole thing outright, he should do nothing of the sort, for that it would be but the exceeding pleasure wherewith she was enraptured that made her say so to him, and in no wise the will of her heart and soul.

The aforesaid Sanzay, in order to get good treatment and greater liberty, Christian as he was, did shut his eyes this once to his law. For a poor slave, hardly entreated and cruelly chained, may well forget his principles now and again. So he did obey the lady, and was so prudent and so submissive to her order, as that he did minister right well to her pleasure. Wherefore the lady did love him the better, because he was so submissive to her strait and difficult command. Even when she would cry to him: "Let go, I say; I give you full permission!" yet

[59]

would he never once do so, for he was sore afraid of being beaten as the Turks use (bastinadoed), as he did often see his comrades beaten before his eyes.

Verily a strange and sore caprice; and herein it would seem she did well prevail, both for her own soul's sake which was Turk and for the other who was Christian. But he swore to me how that never in all his life had he been in so sore a strait!

He did tell me yet another tale, the most heartsome and amusing possible, of a trick she once put upon him. But forasmuch as it is not pleasant, I will repeat it not, for dread of doing offence to modest ears.

Later was the same Sanzay ransomed by his friends, the which are folk of honour and good estate in Brittany, and related to many great persons, as to the Connétable de Sanzay, who was greatly attached to his elder brother, and did help him much toward his deliverance. Having won this, the Chevalier did come to Court, and held much discourse to M. d'Estrozze and to me of his adventures and of divers matters, and amongst other such he told us these stories.

6.

HAT are we to say now of some husbands which be not content only to procure themselves entertainment and wanton pleasure with their wives, but do give the desire therefor to others also, their companions, friends and the like? For so have I known several which do praise their wives to these, detail to them their beauties, picture to them their members and various bodily parts, recount the pleasure that they have with them, and the caresses

[60]

their wives do use towards them, make them kiss, touch
and try them, and even behold them naked.

What do such deserve? Why! that they be cuckolded
right off, as did Gyges, by the means of his ring, to Candaules,[1] King of the Lydians. For the latter, fool that
he was, having bepraised to Gyges the rare beauty of his
wife, and at the last having shown her to him stark naked,
he fell so madly in love with her that he did what seemed
him good and brought Candaules to his death and made
himself master of his Kingdom. 'Tis said the wife was
in such despite and despair at having been so shown by
her husband to another man, that she did herself constrain
Gyges to play this traitorous part, saying thus to him:
"Either must he that hath constrained and counselled you
to such a thing die by your hand, or else you, who have
looked on me in my nakedness, must die by the hand of
another." Of a surety was the said King very ill advised
so to rouse desire for a fresh dainty, so good and sweet,
which it rather behoved him to hold very specially dear
and precious.

Louis, Duke or Orleans,[2] killed at the Barbette Gate of
Paris, did the exact opposite. An arrant debaucher was
he of the ladies of the Court, and that even of the greatest
among them all. For, having once a very fair and noble
lady to bed with him, so soon as her husband came into
his bedchamber to wish him good-morrow, he did promptly
cover up the lady's head, the other's wife's that is, with
the sheet, but did uncover all the rest of her body, letting
him see her all naked and touch her at his pleasure, only
with express prohibition on his life not to take away the
linen from off the face, nor to uncover it in any wise,—a
charge he durst not contravene. Then did the Duke ask

[61]

him several times over what he thought of this fair, naked body, whereat the other was all astonished and exceeding content. At the last he did get his leave to quit the chamber, and this he did without having ever had the chance to recognize the woman for his own wife.

If only he had carefully looked over her body and examined the same, as several that I have known, he would mayhap have recognized her by sundry blemishes. Thus is it a good thing for men to go over sometimes and observe their wives' bodies.

She, after her husband was well gone, was questioned of M. d'Orléans, if she had felt any alarm or fear. I leave you to imagine what she said thereto, and all the trouble and anguish she was in by the space of a quarter of an hour, seeing all that lacked for her undoing was some little indiscretion, or the smallest disobedience her husband might have committed in lifting the sheet. 'Twas doubtless M. d'Orléans' orders, but still he would surely, on his making discovery, have straightway slain him to stay him of the vengeance he would have wrought on his wife.

And the best of it was that, being the next night to bed with his wife, he did tell her how M. d'Orléans had let him see the fairest naked woman he had ever beheld, but as to her face, that he could give no news thereof, seeing the sight of it had been forbid him. I leave you to imagine what the lady must have thought within her heart. Now of this same lady and M. d'Orléans 'tis said did spring that brave and valiant soldier, the Bastard of Orleans, the mainstay of France and scourge of England, from whom is descended the noble and generous race of the Comtes de Dunois.

However to return to our tales of husband too ready to
give others sight of their wives naked, I know one who, on
a morning, a comrade of his having gone to see him in his
chamber as he was dressing, did show him his wife quite
naked, lying all her length fast asleep, having herself
thrown her bed-clothes off her, it being very hot weather.
So he did draw aside the curtain half way, in such wise
that the rising sun shining upon her, he had leisure to
contemplate well and thoroughly at his ease, which doing
he beheld naught but what was right fair and perfect.
On all this beauty then he did feast his eyes, not indeed
as long as he would, but as long as he could; and after,
the husband and he went forth to the Palace.

The next day, the gentleman who was an ardent lover
of this same honourable lady, did report to her the sight
he had seen, and even described many things he had noted.
He said further it was the husband which did urge him
thereto, and he and no other had drawn the curtain for
him to see. The lady, out of the despite she then conceived against her husband, did let herself go, and so gave
herself to his friend on this only account,—a thing which
all his service and devotion had not before been able to
win.

I knew once a very great Lord, who, one morning, wishing to go an-hunting, and his gentlemen having come to
find him at his rising, even as they were booting him, and
he had his wife lying by him and holding him right close
to her, he did so suddenly lift the coverlet she had no time
to move away from where she rested, in such wise that
they all saw her as much as they pleased even to the half
of her body. Then with a loud laugh did the Lord cry
to these gentlemen there present: "Well, well! sirs, have

[63]

not I let you see enough and to spare of my good wife?"
But so vexed and chagrined was she at it all that she did
conceive a great grudge against him therefor, and above
all for the way she had been surprised. And it may well
be, she did pay it back to him with interest later on.

I know yet another of these great Lords, who learning
that a friend and kinsman of his was in love with his wife,
whether to make him the more envious or to make him
taste all the despite and despair he might conceive at the
thought of the other possessing so fair a woman, and he
having never so much as a chance of touching her, did
show her him one morning, when he had come to see him,
the pair being a-bed together. Yea! he did even worse,
for he did set about to embrace her before his eyes, as
though she had been altogether in a privy place. Further he kept begging of his friend to see, saying he was
doing it all to gratify him. I leave you to imagine whether
the lady did not find in such conduct of her husband excuse
to do likewise in all ways with the friend, and of good conscience, and whether he was not right well punished by
being made to bear the horns.

I have heard speak of yet another, likewise a great
Lord, who did the same with his wife before a great Prince,
his master, but, 'twas by his prayer and commandment,
for he was one that took delight in this form of gratification. Now are not such like persons blameworthy, for
that after being pandars to their own wives, they will
after be their executioners too?

It is never expedient for a man to expose his wife, any
more than his lands, countries or places. And I may cite
an example hereof which I did learn from a great Captain. It concerns the late M. de Savoye, who did dissuade

the late King of France,[3] when on his return from Poland
he was passing through Lombardy, and counselled him not
to go to Milan or enter therein, alleging that the King of
Spain might take umbrage thereat. But this was not the
real cause at all; rather was he afraid lest the King being
once there and visiting all quarters of the city, and beholding its beauty and riches and grandeur, might be
assailed by an overwhelming desire to have it again and
reconquer it by fair and honest right, as had done his
predecessors. Now this was the true reason, as a great
Prince said who knew the fact from our late King, who
for his part quite well understood what the restriction
meant. However, to be complaisant to M. de Savoye, and
to cause no offence on the part of the King of Spain, he
took his march so as to pass by the city, albeit he had
all the wish in the world to go thither, by what he did me
the honour to tell me after his return to Lyons. In this
transaction we cannot but deem M. de Savoye to have
been more of a Spaniard than a Frenchman.

I deem those husbands likewise very much to blame who
after having received their life by favour of their wives,
are so little grateful therefor, as that for any suspicion
they have of their intriguing with other men, do treat
them exceeding harshly, to the extent of making attempt
upon their lives. I have heard speak of a Lord against
whose life sundry conspirators having conspired and plot-
ted, his wife by dint of her prayers did turn them from
their purpose, and saved her husband from being assassinated. But nevertheless later on was she very ill rewarded by him and entreated most cruelly.

I have seen likewise a gentleman who, having been accused and brought to trial for very bad performance of

[65]

his duty in succouring his General in a battle, so much so
that he had left him to be killed without any help or succour at all, was nigh to be sentenced and condemned to
have his head cut off, and this notwithstanding 20,000
crowns the which he did give to save his life. Thereupon
his wife spake to a great Lord holding high place in the
world, and lay with him by permission and at the supplication of the said husband; and so what money had not
been able to do, this did her beauty and fair body effect,
and she did save him his life and liberty. Yet after he
did treat her so ill as that nothing could be worse. Of a
surety husbands of the sort, so cruel and savage, are very
pitiful creatures.

Others again have I known who did quite otherwise, for
that they have known how to show gratitude to those that
helped them, and have all their life long honoured the
good dame that had saved them from death.

There is yet another sort of cuckolds, those who are not
content to have been suspicious and difficult all their life,
but when going to leave this world and on the point of
death, are so still. Of this sort knew I one who had a very
fair and honourable lady to wife, but yet had not always
given her all to him alone. When now he was like to die,
he said to her repeatedly: "Ah! wife mine, I am going to
die! And would to God you could have kept me company,
and you and I could have gone together into the other
world! My death had not then been so hateful to me, and
I should have taken it in better part." But the lady, who
was still very fair and not more than thirty-seven years
old, was by no means fain to follow him, nor agree with
him in this. Nor yet was she willing to play the mad-
woman for his sake, as we read did Evadné, daughter of

Mars and Thebé and wife of Capaneus,[4] the which did love her husband so ardently that, he having died, so soon as ever his body was cast on the fire, she threw herself thereon all alive as she was, and was burned and consumed along with him, in her great constancy and strength of purpose, and so did accompany him in his death.

Alcestis[5] did far better yet, for having learned by an oracle that her husband Admetus, King of Thessaly, was to die presently, unless his life were redeemed by the death of some other of his friends, she did straightway devote herself to a sudden death, and so saved her husband alive.

Nowadays are no women of this kindly sort left, who are fain to go of their own pleasure into the grave before their husbands, and not survive them. No! such are no more to be found; the dams that bare them are dead, as say the horse-dealers of Paris of horses, when no more good ones are to be got.

And this is why I did account the husband, whose case I but now adduced, ill-advised to make such proposals to his wife and odious so to invite her to death, as though it had been some merry feast to invite her to. It was an arrant piece of jealousy that did make him so speak, and the despite he did feel within himself, he would presently experience yonder in the lower world, when he should see his wife, whom he had so excellently trained, in the arms of some lover of hers or some new husband.

What a strange sort of jealousy was this her husband must have been seized with for the nonce, and strange how he would keep telling her again and again how if he should recover, he would no more suffer at her hands what he had suffered aforetime! Yet, so long as he was alive and

[67]

well, he had never been attacked by the like feelings, but ever let her do at her own good pleasure.

The gallant Tancred[6] did quite otherwise, the same who in old days did so signalise his valour in the Holy War. Being at the point of death, and his wife beside him making moan, together with the Count of Tripoly, he did beg the twain when that he was dead, to wed one another, and charged his wife to obey him therein,—the which they afterward did.

Mayhap he had observed some loving dalliance betwixt them during his lifetime. For she may well have been as very a harlot as her mother, the Countess of Anjou, who after the Comte de Bretagne had had her long while, went unto Philip,[7] the King of France, who did treat her the same fashion, and had of her a bastard daughter called Cicile, whom after he did give in marriage to this same valorous Tancred, who by reason of his noble exploits did of a surety little deserve to be cuckold.

An Albanian, having been condemned in Southern lands to be hung for some offence, being in the service of the King of France, when he was to be led out to his punishment, did ask to see his wife, who was a very fair and lovable woman, and bid her farewell. Then while he was saying his farewell and in the act of kissing her, lo! he did bite her nose right off and tear it clean out of her pretty face. And the officers thereupon questioning him why he had done this horrible thing to his wife, he replied he had done it out of sheer jealousy, "seeing she is very fair, for the which after my death I wot well she will straightway be sought after and given up to some other of my comrades, for I know her to be exceeding lecherous and one to forget me without more ado. I am fain there-

[68]

fore she bear me in memory after my death, and weep and
be sorry. If she is not so for my death's sake, at least
will she be sore grieved at being disfigured, and none of
my comrades will have the pleasure of her I have had."
Verily an appalling instance of a jealous husband!

I have heard speak of others who, feeling themselves
old, failing, wounded, worn out and near to death, have
out of sheer despite and jealousy privily cut short their
mates' days, even when they have been fair and beauteous
women.

Now as to such strange humours on the part of these
cruel and tyrannic husbands which do thus put their wives
to death, I have heard the question disputed,—to wit,
whether it is permitted women, when they do perceive or
suspect the cruelty and murder their husbands are fain
to practise against them, to gain the first hand and an-
ticipate their aggressors and so save their own lives, making the others play the part first and sending these on in
front to make ready house and home in the other world.

I have heard it maintained the answer should be yes,—
that they may do so, not certainly according to God's
law, for thereby is all murder forbid, as I have said, but
by the world's way of thinking, well enough. This opinion
men base on the saying,—better 'tis to be beforehand than
behind. For no doubt everyone is bound to take heed for
his own life; and seeing God hath given it us, we must
guard it well till he shall call us away at our death.
Otherwise, knowing their death to be planned, to go head-
first into the same, and not to escape from it when they
can, is to kill their own selves,—a crime which God doth
very greatly abhor. Wherefore 'tis ever the best plan to
send them on ahead as envoys, and parry their assault, as

[69]

did Blanche d'Auverbruckt to her husband, the Sieur de Flavy, Captain of Compiègne and Governor thereof, the same who did betray the maid of Orleans, and was cause of her death and undoing. Now this lady Blanche, learning that her husband did plot to have her drowned, got beforehand with him, and by aid of his barber did smother and strangle him, for which deed our King Charles VII.[8] gave her instantly his pardon; though for the obtaining of this 'tis like the husband's treason went for much,—more indeed than any other reason. These facts are to be found in the *Chronicles of France,* and particularly in those of *Guyenne.*

The same was done by a certain Madame de la Borne, in the reign of Francis I.[9] This lady did accuse and inform against her husband for sundry follies committed and crimes, it may be monstrous crimes, he had done against her and other women. She had him thrown into prison, pleaded against him and finally got his head cut off. I have heard my grandmother tell the tale, who used to say she was of good family and a very handsome woman. Well! she at any rate did get well beforehand!

Queen Jeanne of Naples,[10] the First of that name, did the like toward the Infanta of Majorca, her third husband, whose head she did cause to be cut off for the reason I have named in the Discourse dealing with him. But it may well be she did also fear him, and was fain to be rid of him the first. Herein was she much in the right, and all women in like case, to act thus when they are suspicious of their gallants' purpose.

I have heard speak of many ladies that have bravely escaped in this fashion. Nay! I have known one, who having been found by her husband with her lover, he said

never a word to one or the other, but departed in fierce
anger, and left her there in the chamber with her lover,
sore amazed and in much despair and doubt. Still the
lady had spirit enough to declare, "He has done naught
nor said naught to me this time; but I am sore afraid he
doth bear rancour and secret spite. Now if I were only
sure he was minded to do me to death, I would take
thought how to make *him* feel death the first." Fortune
was so kind to her after some while that the husband did
die of himself. And hereof was she right glad, for never
after his discovery had he made her good cheer, no matter
what attention and consideration she showed him.

Yet another question is there in dispute as concerning
these same madmen, these furious husbands and perilous
cuckolds, to wit on which of the two they set and work
their vengeance, whether on their wives, or their wives'
lovers.

Some there be which have declared, "on the woman
only," basing their doctrine on the Italian proverb *morta
la bastia, morta la rabbia o vereno*—"when the beast is
dead, the madness, or venom, is dead." For they think,
so it would seem, to be quite cured of their hurt when
they have once killed her who caused the pain, herein
doing neither more nor less than they who have been bit
or stung by a scorpion. The most sovran remedy these
have is to take the creature, kill and crush it flat, and
put it on the bite or wound it hath made. The same are
ready to say, and do commonly say, 'tis the women who
are the more deserving of punishment. I here refer to
great ladies and of high rank, and not to humble, common and of low degree. For suchlike it is, by their lovely
charms, their confidences, their orders given and soft

[71]

words spoken, who do provoke the first skirmishes and bring on the battle, whereas the men do but follow their lead. But such as do call for war and begin it, are more deserving of blame than such as only fight in self-defence. For oftentimes men adventure themselves in the like dangerous places and on such high emprize, only when challenged by the ladies, who do signify in divers fashions their predilection. Just as we see in a great, good, well-guarded frontier town, it is exceeding difficult to attack the same unawares or surprise it, unless there be some secret undertaking among some of the inhabitants, and some that do encourage the assailants to the attempt and entice them on and give them a hand of succour.

Now, forasmuch as women are something more fragile than men, they must be forgiven, and it should be remembered how that, when once they have begun to love and set love in their hearts, they will achieve it at what cost soever, not content,—not all of them that is,—to brood over it within, and little by little waste away, and grow dried up and sickly, and spoil their beauty therefor,— which is the reason they do long to be cured of it and get pleasure therefrom, and not die *in ferret's fashion*, as the saying is.[11]

Of a surety I have known not a few fair ladies of this humour, who have been foremost to make love to the other sex, even sooner than the men, and for divers accounts,— some for that they see them handsome, brave, valiant and lovable; others to cozen them out of a sum of hard cash; others to get of them pearls and precious stones, and dresses of cloth of gold and of silver. And I have seen them take as great pains to get these things as a merchant to sell his commodities, and indeed they say the woman who takes presents, sells herself. Some again, to win Court favour; others to win the like with men of the law. Thus several fair dames I have known, who though having no right on their side, yet did get it over to them by means of their fleshly charms and bodily beauty. Yet others again, only to live delicately by the giving of their body.

Many women have I seen so enamoured of their lovers, that they would, so to speak, chase them and run amain after them, causing the world to cast scorn at them therefor.

I once knew a very fair lady so enamoured of a Lord of the great world, that whereas commonly lovers do wear the colours of their ladies, this one on the contrary would be wearing those of her gallant. I could quite well name the colours, but that would be telling over much.

I knew yet another, whose husband, having affronted her lover at a tourney which was held at Court, the while he was in the dancing-hall and was celebrating his triumph, she did out of despite dress herself in man's clothes and went to meet her lover and offer him her favours in masquerade,—for so enamoured of him was she, as that she was like to die thereof.

I knew an honourable gentleman, and one of the least spoken against at Court, who did one day manifest desire to be lover to a very fair and honourable lady, if ever there was one; but whereas she made many advances on her side, he on his stood on guard for many reasons and accounts. But the said lady, having set her love on him, and having cast the die this way at whatsoever hazard, as she did herself declare, did never cease to entice him to her by the fairest words of love that ever she could speak,

[73]

saying amongst other things: "Nay! but suffer at any
rate that I love you, if you will not love me; and look
not to my deserts, but rather to the love and passion I
do bear you,"—though in actual truth she did outbal-
ance the gentleman on the score of perfections. In this
case what could the gentleman have done but love her, as
she was very fain to love him, and serve her; then ask the
salary and reward of his service. This he had in due
course, as is but reasonable that whoever doth a favour
be paid therefor.

I could allege an infinite number of such ladies, which
do seek toward lovers rather than are sought. And I
will tell you why they have more blame than their lovers.
Once they have assailed their man, they do never leave
off till they gain their end and entice him by their alluring
looks, their charms, the pretty made-up graces they do
study to display in an hundred thousand fashions, by the
subtle bepainting of their face, if it be not beautiful, their
fine head-dresses, the rich and rare fashions of wearing
their hair, so aptly suited to their beauty, their magnificent, stately costumes, and above all by their dainty and
half-wanton words, as well as by their pretty, frolic gestures and familiarities, and lastly by gifts and presents.
So this is how men are taken: and being once taken, needs
must they take advantage of their captors. Wherefore
'tis maintained their husbands are fairly bound to wreak
their vengeance on them.

Others hold the husband should take his satisfaction of
the men, when that he can, just as one would of such as
lay siege to a town. For they it is are the first to sound
the challenge and call on the place to surrender, the first
to make reconnaissances and approaches, the first to

throw up entrenchments of gabions and raise bastions and dig trenches, the first to plant batteries and advance to the assault, and the first to open negotiations; and even so is it, they allege, with lovers. For like doughty, valiant and determined soldiers they do assault the fortress of ladies' chastity, till these, after all fashions of assault and modes of importunity have been duly observed, are constrained to make signal of capitulation and receive their pleasant foes within their fortifications. Wherein methinks they are not so blameworthy as they wauld fain make out; for indeed to be rid of an importunate beggar is very difficult without leaving somewhat of one's own behind. So have I seen many who by their long service and much perseverance have at length had their will of their mistresses, who at the first would not, so to say, have given them their *çul a baiser*, constraining them, or at any rate some of them, to this degree that out of pure pity, and tear in eye, they did give them their way. Just as at Paris a man doth very often give an alms to the beggars about an inn door more by reason of their importunity than from devotion or the love of God. The same is the case with many women, who yield rather for being over-importuned than because they are really in love—as also with great and powerful wooers, men whom they do fear and dare not refuse because of their high authority, dreading to do them a displeasure and thereafter to receive scandal and annoyance of them or a deliberate affront or great hurt and sore disparagement to their honour. For verily have I seen great mischiefs happen in suchlike conjunctions.

This is why those evil-minded husbands, which take such delight in blood and murder and evil entreatment of their wives, should not be so hasty, but ought first to make a secret inquiry into all matters, albeit such knowledge may well be grievous to them and very like to make them scratch their head for its sore itching thereat, and this even though some, wretches that they are, do give their wives all the occasion in the world to go astray.

Thus I once knew a great Prince of a foreign country, who had married a very fair and honourable lady. Yet did he very often leave her to go with another woman, which was supposed to be a famous courtesan, though others thought she was a lady of honour whom he had debauched. But not satisfied with this, when he had her to sleep with him, it was in a low-roofed chamber underneath that of his wife and underneath her bed. Then when he was fain to embrace his mistress, he was not content with the wrong he was doing his lady already, but in derision and mockery would with a half-pike knock two or three blows on the floor and shout up to his wife: "A health to you, wife mine!" This scorn and insult was repeated several days, and did so anger his wife that out of despair and desire of vengeance she did accost a very honourable gentleman one day and said to him privily: "Sir! I am fain you should have your pleasure of me; otherwise do I know of means whereby to undo you." The other, right glad of so fine an adventure, did in no wise refuse her. Wherefore, so soon as her husband had his fair leman in his arms, and she likewise her fond lover, and he would cry, "A health!" to her, then would she answer him in the same coin, crying, "And I drink to *you!*" or else, "I pledge you back, good Sir!"

These toasts and challenges and replies, so made and arranged as to suit with the acts of each, continued some

longish while, till at length the Prince, a wily and suspicious man, did suspect something. So setting a watch,
he did discover how his wife was gaily cuckolding him all
the while, and making good cheer and drinking toasts
just as well as he was, by way of retaliation and revenge.
Then having made sure it was verily so, he did quick alter
and transform his comedy into a tragedy; and having
challenged her for the last time with his toast, and she
having rendered him back his answer and as good as he
gave, he did instantly mount upstairs, and forcing and
breaking down the door, rushes in and reproaches her
for her ill-doing. But she doth make answer on her side
in this wise, "I know well I am a dead woman. So kill me
bodily; I am not afraid of death, and do welcome it
gladly, now I am avenged on you, seeing I have made you
cuckold. For you did give me great occasion thereto,
without which I had never gone astray. I had vowed all
fidelity to you, and never should I have broken my troth
for all the temptations in the whole world. Nay! you
were no wise worthy of so honest a wife as I. So kill
me straightway; but if there is any pity in your hand,
pardon, I beseech you, this poor gentleman, who of himself is no whit to blame, for I did invite him and urge
him to help me to my vengeance." The Prince, over cruel
altogether, doth ruthlessly kill the twain. But what else
should this unhappy Princess have done in view of the
indignities and insults of her husband, if not what, in
despair of any other succour in all the world, she did?
Some there be will excuse her, some accuse her; many
arguments and good reasons may be alleged thereanent
on either side.

In the *Cent Nouvelles* of the Queen of Navarre is an

almost similar tale, and a very fine one to boot, of the
Queen of Naples, who in like manner did revenge herself
on the King her husband. Yet was the end thereof not
so tragical.

7.

SO now let us have done with these demons and
mad, furious cuckolds and speak no more of
them, for that they be odious and unpleasing,
seeing I should never have finished if I should
tell of them all, and moreover the subject is neither good
nor pleasant. Let us discourse a while of kindly cuckolds,
such as are good fellows, of placable humour, men easy
to deal with and of a holy patience, well humoured and
readily appeased, that shut the eyes and are—good-
natured fools.

Now of these some are predestined of their very nature
to be so, some know how it is before they marry, to wit,
know that their ladies, widows or maids, have already gone
astray; others again know naught of it at all, but marry
them on trust, on the word of their fathers and mothers,
their family and friends.

I have known not a few which have married women and
girls of loose life, whom they well knew had been passed
in review by sundry Kings, Princes, Lords, gentlemen and
other folk. Yet for love of them, or attracted by their
goods, jewels and money that they had won at the trade
of love, have made no scruple to wed them. However I
propose here to speak only of the girls of this sort.

I have heard speak of a mistress of a very great and
sovereign Prince, who being enamoured of a certain

gentleman, and in such wise behaving herself toward him as to have received the first fruits of his love, was so desirous thereof that she did keep him a whole month in her closet, feeding him on fortifying foods, savoury soups, dainty and comforting meats, the better to distil and draw off his substance. Thus having made her first apprenticeship with him, did she continue her lessons under him so long as he lived, and under others too. Afterward she did marry at the age of forty-five years to a Lord,[1] who found naught to say against her, but rather was right proud of so rare a marriage as he had with her.

Boccaccio repeats a proverb which was current in his day to the effect that *a mouth once kissed* (others have it differently) *is never out of luck; her fortune is like the moon, and waxeth ever anew.* This proverb he doth quote in connection with a story he relates of that fair daughter of the Sultan of Egypt who did pass and repass by the weapons of nine different lovers, one after the other, at the least three thousand times in all. At long last was she delivered to the King of Garba a pure virgin, that is, 'twas so pretended, as pure as she was at the first promised to him; and he found no objection to make, but was very well pleased. The tale thereof is a right good one.

I have heard a great man declare that, with many great men, though not all it may be supposed, no heed is paid in case of women of this sort to the fact, though three or four lovers have passed them through their hands, before they make them their wives. This he said anent of a story of a great Lord who was deeply enamoured of a great lady, and one of something higher quality than himself, and she loved him back. However there fell out some hindrance that they did not wed as they did expect one with the

[79]

other. Whereupon this great nobleman, the which I have just spoken of, did straightway ask: "Did he mount the little jade, anyway?" And when he was answered, "no!" —in the other's opinion and by what men told him, "So much the worse then," he added, "for at any rate they had had so much satisfaction one of the other, and no harm would have been done!" For among the great no heed is paid to these rules and scruples of maidenhood, seeing that for these grand alliances everything must be excused. Only too delighted are they, the good husbands and gentle suckling cuckolds.

At the time when King Charles did make the circuit of his Kingdom, there was left behind in a certain good town, which I could name very well had I so wished, a female child whereof an unmarried girl of a very good house had been delivered. So the babe was given to a poor woman to nurse and rear, and there was advanced to her a sum of two hundred crowns for her pains. The said poor woman did nurse the infant and manage it so well that in fifteen years' time the girl grew up very fair, and gave herself to a life of pleasure. For never another thought had she of her mother, who in four months after wedded a very great nobleman. Ah! how many such have I known of either sex, where the like things have been, and no man suspecting aught!

I once heard tell, when I was in Spain, of a great Lord of Andalusia who had married a sister of his to another very great Lord, and who three days after the marriage was consummated, came and said to him thus: *Señor hermano, agora que soys cazado con my herman, y l'haveys bien godida solo, yo le hago aher que siendo hija, tal y tal gozaron d'ella. De lo passado no tenga cuydado, que poca*

cosa es. Dell futuro quartate, que mas y mucho a vos toca.
(My Lord and brother, now that you are married to my
sister and alone enjoy her favours, it behooves you to
know that when she was yet unwed, such and such an one
did have her. Take no heed of the past, for truly 'tis but
a small thing; but beware of the future, seeing now it doth
touch you much more close),—as much as to say that
what is done is done, and there is no need to talk about it,
but it were well to be careful of the future, for this is
more nearly concerned with a man's honour than is the
past.

Some there be are of this humour, thinking it not so ill
to be cuckold in the bud, but very ill in the flower,—and
there is some reason in this.

I have likewise heard speak of a great Lord of a foreign
land, which had a daughter who was one of the fairest
women in the world; and she being sought in marriage by
another great Lord who was well worthy of her was
bestowed on him by her father. But before ever he could
let her go forth the house, he was fain to try her himself, declaring he would not easily let go so fine a mount
and one which he had so carefully trained, without himself
having first ridden thereon, and found out how she could
go for the future. I know not whether it be true, but I
have heard say it is, and that not only he did make the
essay, but another comely and gallant gentleman to boot.
And yet did not the husband thereafter find anything
bitter, but all as sweet as sugar. He had been very hard
to please if he had otherwise, for she was one of the fairest
dames in all the world.

I have heard the like tales told of many other fathers,
and in especial of one very great nobleman, with regard to

their daughters. For herein are they said to have shown no more conscience than the Cock in Aesop's Fable. This last, when he was met by the Fox, who did threaten him and declare he purposed to kill him, did therefore proceed to rehearse all the benefits he wrought for mankind and above all else the fair and excellent poultry that came from him. To this the fox made answer, "Ha, ha!" said he, "that is just my quarrel with you, sir gallant! For so lecherous are you, you make no difficulty to tread your own daughters as readily as the other hens," and for this crime did put him to death. Verily a stern and artful judge!

I leave you then to imagine what some maids may do with their lovers,—for never yet was there a maid but had or was fain to have a lover,—and that some there be that brothers, cousins and kinsfolk have done the like with.

In our own days Ferdinand, King of Naples,[2] knew thus in wedlock his own aunt, daughter of the King of Castile, at the age of 13 or 14 years, but this was by dispensation of the Pope. Difficulties were raised at the time as to whether this ought to be or could be so given. Herein he but followed the example of Caligula, the Roman Emperor, who did debauch and have intercourse with each of his sisters, one after the other. And above and beyond all the rest, he did love exceedingly the youngest, named Drusilla, whom when only a lad he had deflowered. And later, being then married to one Lucius Cassius Longinus, a man of consular rank, he did take her from her husband, and lived with her openly, as if she had been his wife,—so much so indeed that having fallen sick on one occasion, he made her heiress of all his property, including the Empire itself. But it fell out she died, which he did

[82]

grieve for so exceedingly sore that he made proclamation to close the Courts and stay all other business, in order to constrain the people to make public mourning along with him. And for a length of time he wore his hair long and beard untrimmed for her sake; and when he was haranguing the Senate, the People or his soldiers, never swore but by the name of Drusilla.

As for his other sisters, when that he had had his fill of them, he did prostitute them and gave them up to his chief pages which he had reared up and known in very foul fashion. Still even so he had done them no outrageous ill, seeing they were accustomed thereto, and that it was a pleasant injury, as I have heard it called by some maids on being deflowered and some women who had been ravished. But over and above this, he put a thousand indignities upon them; he sent them into exile, he took from them all their rings and jewels to turn into money, having wasted and ill guided all the vast sums Tiberius had left him. Natheless did the poor girls, having after his death come back from banishment, and seeing the body of their brother ill and very meanly buried under a few clods of earth, have it disinterred and burned and duly buried as honourably as they could. Surely a good and noble deed on the part of sisters to a brother so graceless and unnatural!

The Italian, by way of excusing the illicit love of his countryman, says that *quando messer Bernardo, il buciacchio sta in colera et in sua rabbia, non riceve legge, et non perdona a nissuna dama*,—"when messer Bernardo, the young ox, stand up in anger and in his passion, he will receive no laws and spare no lady."

We can find plenty of examples amongst the Ancients of

[83]

such as have done the same. However to come back to our proper subject, I have heard a tale of one who having married a fair and honourable damsel to one of his friends, and boasting that he had given him a right good and noble mount, sound, clean and free from knots and malanders, as he put it, and that he lay the more under obligation to him therefor, he was answered by one of the company, who said aside to one of his comrades: "That is all quite true, if only she had not been mounted and ridden so young and far too soon. For it has made her a bit *foulée* in front."

But likewise I would fain ask these noble husbands whether, if such mounts had not often some fault, some little thing wrong with them, some defect or blemish, they would make the match with others who are more deserving than they, like horse-dealers who do all they can to get rid of their blemished horses, but always with those that know naught of the matter. Even so, as I have heard many a father say, 'tis a very fine riddance to be quit of a blemished daughter, or one that doth begin to be so, or seems by her looks like to be.

How many damsels of the great world I know who have not carried their maidenhood to the couch of Hymen, but who have for all that been well instructed of their mothers, or other their kinswomen and friends, right cunning pimps as they are, to make a good show at this first assault. Divers are the means and contrivances they do resort to with artful subtleties, to make their husbands think it well and convince them never a breach has been made before. The most part resort to the making of a desperate resistance and defence at this point of attack, and do fight obstinately to the last extremity. Whereof there are some

husbands much delighted, for they do firmly believe they
have had all the honour and made the first conquest, like
right determined and intrepid soldiers. Then next morning they have fine tales to tell, how they have strutted it
like little cocks or cockerels that have eat much millet-
seed in the evening, making many boasts to their comrades and friends, and even mayhap to the very men who
have been the first to invade the fortress, unwittingly to
them. Whereat these do laugh their fill in their sleeves,
and with the women their mistresses, and boast they did
their part well too, and gave the damsels as good as they
got.

Some suspicious husbands there be however who hold all
this resistance as of bad augury, and take no satisfaction
in seeing them so recalcitrant. Like one I know who
asked his wife why did she thus play the prude and make
difficulties, and if she disdained him so much as all that;
but she thinking to make excuse and put off the fault on
something else than disdain, told him 'twas because she
was afraid he would hurt her. To this he retorted, "Now
have you given proof positive, for no hurt can be known
without having been first suffered." But she was wily,
and denied, saying she had heard tell of it by some of her
companions who had been married, and had so advised
her. And, "Hum! fine advice truly and fine words!" was
all he could say.

Another remedy these women recommend is this,—next
morning after their wedlock to show their linen stained
with drops of blood, the which the poor girls shed in the
cruel work of their deflowering. So is it done in Spain,
where they do publicly display from the window the afore-

said linen, crying aloud, "Virgen la tenemos,"—"we hold her for a maid."

Likewise of a surety I have heard say that at Viterbo [3] this custom is similarly observed. Moreover, seeing such damsels as have previously affronted the battle cannot make this display of their own blood, they have devised the plan, as I have heard say, and as several young courtesans at Rome have themselves assured me, the better to sell their maidenhood, of staining the said linen with pigeon's blood, which is the most meet of all for the purpose. So next morning the husband doth see the blood and doth feel a great satisfaction thereof, and doth believe firmly 'tis the virginal blood of his wife. He thinks himself a gallant and happy man, but he is sore deceived all the while.

Hereanent will I repeat the following merry tale of a gentleman who had his string tied in a knot the first night of his wedlock; but the bride, who was not one of the very fair and high-born sort, fearing he would be sore enraged thereat, did not fail, by advice of her good comrades, matrons, kinswomen and good friends, to have the bit of linen stained as usual. But the mischief for her was that the husband was so sore tied that he could do naught at all, albeit she thought no harm to make him a very enticing display and deck herself for the assault as well as ever she could, and lie conveniently without playing the prude or making any show of reluctance or deviltry. At least so the lookers-on, hid near by according to custom, did report; and indeed she did so the better to conceal the loss of her maidenhood elsewhere. But for all the red linen, he had really done naught whatever.

At night, by established custom, the midnight repast

having been carried in, there was as usual a worthy guest
ready to advise that in the customary wedding scramble
they should filch away the sheet, which they did find finely
stained with blood. This was instantly displayed and all
in attendance were assured by loud cries she was no longer
a maid, and here was the evidence her virgin membrane
had been deforced and ruptured. The husband, who was
quite certain he had done naught, but who nevertheless
was fain to pose as a brave and valiant champion, remained sore astounded and wot not what this stained
sheet might mean. Only after sufficient pondering, he
did begin to suspect some knavish, cunning harlot's trick,
yet never breathed a word.

The bride and her confidantes were likewise sore
troubled and astounded for that the husband had so
missed fire, and that their business was not turning out
better. Nothing however was suffered to appear till after
a week's time, when lo! the husband found his knot untied,
and did straight let fly with might and main. Whereat
being right glad and remembering naught else, he went
forth and published to all the company how in all good
conscience he had now given proof of his prowess and
made his wife a true wife and a proper married woman;
but did confess that up till then he had been seized with
absolute impotence to do aught. Hereupon those present
at the time did hold diverse discourse, and cast much
blame and scorn on the bride, whom all had deemed a
wife by her stained linen. Thus did she bring scandal
on herself,—albeit she was not properly speaking an
altogether cause thereof, but rather her husband, who
by feebleness, slackness and lack of vigour did spoil his
own wedding.

[87]

Again, there are some husbands that do know at their
first night as to the maidenhood of their wives, whether
they have won it or no, by the signs they find. So one that
I know, who did marry a wife in second wedlock; but the
wife was for making him believe her first husband had never
touched her, by reason of his impotence, and that she was
virgin and a maid, as much as before being married at all.
Yet did he find her of such ample capacity that he exclaimed, "What ho! are *you* the maid of Marolles, so tight
and small as they told me you were?" So he had just to
take it as it was, and make the best of it. For if her first
husband had never touched her, as was quite true, yet
many another man had.

8.

UT what are we to say of some mothers who,
seeing the impotence of their sons-in-law, or
that they have the string knotted or some
other defect, are procuresses to their own
daughters. Thus to win their jointures, they get them
to yield to others, and often to become with child by
them, to the end they may have offspring to inherit after
the death of the father.

I know one such who was ready enough to give this
counsel to her daughter, and indeed spared no effort to
bring it about, but the misfortune for her was that never
could she have a child at all. Also I know a husband who,
not being able to do aught to his wife, did yield his place to
a big lackey he had, a handsome lad, to lie with his wife
and deflower her as she slept, and in this way save his

honour. But she did discover the trick and the lackey had no success. For which cause they had a long suit at law, and finally were separated.

King Henry of Castile[1] did the like, who as Fulgosius[2] relates, seeing he could make no children with his wife, did call in the help of a handsome young gentleman of his Court to make them for him. The which he did; and for his pains the King gave him great estates and advanced him in all honours, distinctions and dignities. Little doubt the wife was grateful to him therefor, and did find the arrangement much to her liking. This is what I call an accommodating cuckold!

As to these "knotted strings" spoken of above, there was lately a law process thereanent in the Court of the Parliament of Paris, between the Sieur de Bray, High Treasurer, and his wife, to whom he could do naught, suffering as he did from this or other like defect, for which the wife, once well married, did call him to account. It was ordered by the Court that they should be visited, the two of them, by great doctors expert in these matters. The husband did choose his, and the wife hers. And hereon was writ a right merry sonnet at the Court, the which a great lady read over to me herself, and gave me, whenas I was dining with her. 'Twas said a lady had writ it, though others said a man. Here it is:

SONNET

Entre les médecins renommés à Paris
En sçavoir, en espreuve, en science, en doctrine,
Pour juger l'imparfait de la coupe androgine,
Par de Bray et sa femme ont esté sept choisis,

[89]

De Bray a eu pour lui les trois de moindre prix,
Le Court, l'Endormy, Piétre: et sa femme plus fine,
Les quatre plus experts en l'art de médecine,
Le Grand, le Gros, Duret et Vigoureux a pris.

On peut par là juger qui des deux gaignera,
Et si le Grand du Court victorieux sera,
Vigoureux d'Endormy, le Gros, Duret, de Piètre.

Et de Bray n'ayant point ces deux de son costé,
Estant tant imparfait que mari le peut estre,
A faute de bon droict en sera débouté.

(Among all the great doctors of Paris, famed for
knowledge, skill, science and learning, seven were chosen
out by de Bray and his wife, to judge of the defect in the
cup of man and wife.—De Bray has on his side the three
of lesser price, Le Court, l'Endormy, Piètre (Drs. Short,
Sleepy, Puny); his wife has been cleverer and taken Le
Grand, Le Gros, Duret and Vigoureux (Drs. Tall, Stout,
Hardy and Vigorous).—From this it may be guessed
which of the pair will gain the day, and if Le Grand will
give a good account of Le Court, Vigoureaux, of Endormy, Le Gros and Duret of Piètre.—So de Bray not
having these two on his side, and being as ill-dowered as a
husband can well be, for lack of a good case will surely
be nonsuited.)

I have heard speak of another husband, who did hold
his new-made wife in his arms the first night; and she
was so ravished with delight and pleasure that quite forgetting herself she could not refrain from a slight turning
and twisting and mobile action of the body, such as new
wed wives are scarce wont to make. At this he said naught

[90]

else, but only, "Ha, ha! I know now," and went on his way to the end. These be our cuckolds *in embryo*, of the which I could tell thousands of tales, but I should never have done. And the worst thing I see in them is when they wed cow and calf at once, as the saying is, and take them when already great with child. Like one I know, who had married a very fair and honourable damsel, by the favour and wish of their Prince and feudal Lord, who was much attached to the said gentleman and had made the marriage. But at the end of a week it became known she was with child, and she did actually publish it abroad, the better to play her part. The Prince, who had always suspected some love-making between her and another, said to her, "My lady! I have carefully writ down on my tablets the day and hour of your marriage; when folk shall set these against the time of your bringing to bed, you will have bitter shame!" But she at this word only blushed a little, and did naught else thereanent, but only kept ever the mien and bearing of a *donna da ben* (virtuous lady).

Then again there are some daughters which do so fear their father and mother they had rather lose the life out of their bodies than their maidenhood, dreading their parents an hundred times more than their husbands.

I have heard speak of a very fair and honourable damsel, who being sore tempted by her lover to take her pleasure of his love, did answer "under this cloak of marriage which doth cover all, we will take our joy with a right good will."

Another, being eagerly sought after by a great nobleman, she said to him, "Petition our Prince and put some pressure on him, that he wed me soon to him that is now

[91]

my suitor, and let me quickly make good my marriage that he hath promised me. The day after my wedding, if we meet not one another, why! the bargain is off!"

I know a lady who was wooed to love but four days before her bridal by a gentleman, and kinsman of her husband; yet six days after he did enjoy his will,—at any rate he did make boast to the effect. Nor was it hard to believe, for they did show such familiarity the one to the other, you would have said they had been brought up together all their lives. Moreover he did even tell sundry signs and marks she had on her body, and further that they did continue their merry sport long while after. The gentleman always declared the familiarity that did afford them opportunity to come so far was, that in order to carry out a masquerade they did change clothes with one another. He took the dress of his mistress and she that of her admirer, whereat the husband did nothing but laugh, though some there were did find occasion to blame them and think ill of the thing.

There was made a song about it at Court,—of a husband who was married o' Tuesday and cuckolded o' Thursday, a fair rate of progress in sooth!

What shall we say of another damsel who was long while wooed by a gentleman of a good house and rich, but for all that niggardly and not worthy of her? So being hard pressed at the instance of her family to marry him, she made answer she had liever die than marry him, and that he should be spoken thereof to her or to her kinsfolk. For, she declared, if they did force her to marry him, she would only make him cuckold. But for all that it behooved to go by that road, for so was she constrained by the urgency of all the great folk, men and women, who had influence and authority over her, as well as by her kinsfolks' orders.

On the eve of her bridal, her husband seeing her all sad and pensive, asked her what ailed her; and she did answer him angrily, "You would never believe me, and be persuaded to leave off your pursuit of me. You know what I have always said, that if ever I were so unfortunate as to become your wife, I would make you cuckold. And I swear I will do so, and keep my word to you." She was in no wise dainty about saying the same before sundry of her lady companions and male admirers. Afterward rest assured she was as good as her word, and did show him she was a good and true woman, for that she kept her promise faithfully!

I leave you to judge whether she is to be blamed, for a man once warned should be twice careful, and she did plainly tell him the ill plight he would fall into. So why would he not take heed? But indeed he thought little enough of what she said.

These maids which thus let themselves go astray straightway after being married, but do as the Italian proverb saith: *Che la vacca, ché é stata molto tempo ligata, corre più ché quella ché ha havuto sempre piana libertá,*—"The cow that hath been long tied up, runs more wild than one that hath ever had her full liberty." Thus did the first wife of Baldwyn, King of Jerusalem, whom I have spoken of before, who having been forced to take the veil by her husband, brake from the cloister and escaped out, and making now for Constantinople, behaved herself in such wanton wise as that she did bestow her favours on all wayfarers by that road, whether going or coming, as well men-at-arms as pilgrims to Jerusalem,

[93]

without heed to her Royal rank. But the reason was the long fast she had had therefrom during her imprisonment.

I might easily name many other such. Well! they are a good sort of cuckolds these, as are likewise those others which suffer their wives' unfaithfulness, when these be fair and much sought after for their beauty, and abandon them to it, in order to win favour for themselves, and draw profit and wealth therefrom. Many such are to be seen at the Courts of great Kings and Princes, the which do get good advantage thereby; for from poor men as they were aforetime, whether from pledging of their goods, or by some process of law, or mayhap through the cost of warlike expeditions, they be brought low, are they straight raised up again and enriched greatly by way of their good wives' *trou*. Yet do they find no diminution whatever in that same place, but rather augmentation!

Herein was the case different with a very fair lady I have heard tell of, for that she had lost the half of her affair by misadventure, her husband having, so they said, given her the pox which had eaten it away for her.

Truly the favours and benefits of the great may well shake the most chaste hearts, and are cause of many and many a cuckoldry. And hereanent I have heard the tale related of a foreign Prince [3] who was appointed General by his Sovereign Prince and master of a great expedition of War he had ordered to be made, and left his wife behind, one of the fairest ladies in all Christendom, at his Master's Court. But this last did set to and make suit to her to such effect that he very soon shook and laid low her resolve, and had his will so far that he did get her with child.

The husband, returning at the end of twelve or thirteen

months, doth find her in this state, and though sore
grieved and very wroth against her, durst not ask her
the how and why of it. 'Twas for her, and very adroit
she was, to frame her excuses, and a certain brother-in-
law of hers to help her out. And this-like was the plea
she made out: " 'Tis the issue of your campaign that
is cause of this, which hath been taken so ill by your
Master,—for indeed he did gain little profit thereby. So
sorely have you been blamed in your absence for that you
did not carry out his behests better, that had not your
Lord set his love on me, you had verily been undone;
and so to save you from undoing, I have e'en suffered
myself to be undone. Your honour is as much concerned
as mine own, and more, and for your advancement I
have not spared the most precious thing I possess.
Reflect then if I have done so ill as you might say at first;
for without me, your life, your honour and favour would
all have been risked. You are in better case than ever,
while the matter is not so public that the stain to your
repute be too manifest. Wherefore, I beseech you to
excuse and forgive me for that I have done."

The brother-in-law, who was of the best at a specious
tale, and who mayhap had somewhat to do with the lady's
condition, added thereto yet other good and weighty
words, so that at the last all ended well. Thus was peace
made, and the twain were of better accord than ever living together in all freedom and good fellowship. Yet,
or so have I heard tell, did the Prince their master, the
which had done the wrong and had made all the difficulty,
never esteem him so highly as he had done aforetime, for
having taken the thing so mildly. Never after did he
deem him a man of such high-souled honour as he had

thought him previously, though in his heart of hearts
he was right glad the poor lady had not to suffer for the
pleasure she had given him. I have known sundry, both
men and women, ready to excuse the lady in question,
and to hold she did well so to suffer her own undoing
in order to save her husband and set him back again in
his Sovereign's favour.

Ah! how many examples are to be found to match this;
as that of a great lady who did save her husband's life,
the which had been condemned to death in full Court,
having been convicted of great peculations and malversa-
tions in his government and office. For which thing the
husband did after love her well all his life.

I have heard speak again of a great Lord, who had been
condemned to have his head cut off; but lo! he being
already set on the scaffold, his pardon did arrive, the
which his daughter, one of the fairest of women,[4] had
obtained. Whereon, being come down off the scaffold,
he did say this word, and naught else at all: "God save
my girl's good *motte*, which hath saved my life!"

Saint Augustine doth express a doubt whether a certain
citizen of Antioch, a Christian, did sin, when to acquit him
of a heavy sum of money for the which he was in strict
confinement, he gave his wife leave to lie with a gentleman
of greath wealth, who undertook to free him from his
debt.

If such is the opinion of Saint Augustine, what would
he not allow to many women, widows and maids, who to
redeem their fathers, kinsmen, yea! sometimes their husbands themselves, do surrender their gentle body under
stress of many and sundry trials that fall to their lot, as
imprisonment, enslavement, peril to life itself, assaults

[96]

and takings of cities, and in a word an host of other the like incommodities. Nay! sometimes to gain over captains and soldiers, to cause them to fight stubbornly and hold their ground, or to sustain a siege or retake a place,—I could recount an hundred instances,—they will go the length of fearlessly prostituting their chastity to gain their ends. What evil report or scandal can come to them for this? None surely, but rather much glory and advantage.

Who then will deny it to be a good thing on occasion to be cuckold, forasmuch as a man may draw therefrom such advantages in the way of life saved and favour regained, of honour, dignities and riches? How many do I know in like case; and have heard speak of many more which have been advanced by the beauty and bodies of their wives!

I wish not to offend any, but I will take upon me to say this much, that I have it from not a few, both men and women, how ladies have served their mates right well, and how the merits of some of them have not availed them near so much as their wives'.

I know a great lady of much adroit skill who got the Order of St. Michael bestowed on her husband, he being at that time the only one that had it along with the two greatest Princes of Christendom. She would oft tell him, and say out the same before everybody,—for indeed she was of merry demeanour and excellent company: "Ha, ha! my friend, you might have sweated yourself many a long day before you got this pretty bauble to hang at your neck!"

I have heard speak of a great man, in the days of King Francis, who having received the Order, and being fain to make boast thereof one day before M. de la Chastaigneraie, my uncle, did say to him: "Ah! how glad would you be to have this Order hanging at your neck like me!" My uncle, who was ready of tongue and high of hand and hot-tempered, if ever man was, straight replied: "I had rather be dead than have it by the way you had it by!" The other answered never a word, for he knew the man he had to deal with.

I have heard the story told of a great Lord, whose wife had begged for him the patent appointing him to one of the great offices of his district and did bring it to him in his house, his Prince having bestowed it upon him only by favour of his wife. But he would in no wise accept it, forasmuch as he was aware his wife had tarried three months with the Prince in high favour, and not without suspicions of something worse. Herein he did manifest the same nobility of spirit he had shown all his life; yet at the last he did take it, after having done a thing I had rather not name.

And this is how fair ladies have made as many knights as battles, and more,—the which I would name, knowing their names as well as another, were it not I desired to avoid speaking ill of any, or making scandal. And if they have given them these honours, they have brought them much riches as well.

I know one who was but a poor devil when he first brought his wife to Court, the which was a very beautiful woman. And lo! in less than two years they were in good ease and become very rich folk.

9.

ELL! we must needs think highly of these ladies which do thus raise their husbands in wealth and position, and make them cuckolds not without compensation. Even as men say of Marguerite de Namur, who was so foolish as to bind herself and give all ever she could to Louis, Duke of Orleans, one who was so great and puissant a Lord already, and brother to the King. To this end she did get from her husband whatever she could, till at the last he became a poor man, and was forced to sell his Earldom of Blois to the said M. d'Orléans. And this latter, —to think of it!—did pay him therefore in the very same coin and goods the man's infatuate wife had given him. Foolish indeed she was, for that she was giving to one greater than herself. And to think that he did laugh at the pair of them, for in good sooth he was the very man so to do, so fickle was he and inconstant in love.

I know a great lady who, having fallen deep in love with a gentleman of the Court, did accordingly suffer him to have his joy of her. And not being able to give him money, seeing her husband ever kept his hoard hid like a priest, did give him the greater part of her precious stones, the which did mount up to a value of thirty thousand crowns. Whence men said at Court he might well begin to build now, since he had plenty of stones laid up and stored away. Soon afterward, being come into a great inheritance and having put her hand on some twenty thousand crowns, she scarce kept any thereof, but her lover did enjoy the greater part. And 'twas said that if this inheritance had not fallen in to her, not

[99]

knowing what else she could give him, she would have given him the very clothes off her body down to her shift itself. Wherein are suchlike scamps and scorners greatly to blame so to set about it and distil and draw off all the substance of these poor creatures, so hot-headed and infatuate with passion and caprice. For their purse, being so oft visited, cannot stay always swelled out and at its full capacity, like the purse in front, which is ever in the same condition, and ever ready for whosoever wills to fish therein, without the captives that have entered and come forth again of the same finding a word to say against it. This worthy gentleman, whom I spoke of as so well stocked with stones, came some time after to die. Then did all his effects, as is the way at Paris, come to be cried and sold at public auction, and so were in this wise reckoned up and known by many persons as having belonged to the lady, not without bitter and deep shame to the same.

There was a great Prince who loving a very honourable lady, did purchase a dozen diamond studs, brilliants of the first water and admirably set, with their Egyptian letters and hieroglyphics, containing a secret and cabalistic meaning, the which he did make a present of to his mistress. But she after looking at the same attentively, said to him that at present she found no need of hieroglyphic lettering, forasmuch as the writings were already done and accomplished between them twain, even as they had been between the gentleman and the fair lady spoken of just above.

I knew once a lady who was forever saying to her husband, how she had rather make him criminal than cuckold. But truly the two words are something equivo-

cal, and mayhap more or less of both of these fine qualities
mated together in her and in her husband.

Yet I have known well plenty of fair ladies that have
not done so at all. Rather have they kept the purse of
their crown-pieces far tighter drawn than that of their
fair body. For, albeit very great ladies, never would
they be giving but a ring or two, a few favours and such
other little compliments, muffs or scarfs, to wear for
love of them to enhance their repute.

Yet have I known one very great lady [1] which was
exceeding free and generous herein, for the least of her
scarfs and the favours she was used to give her lovers
was worth five hundred crowns, a thousand crowns, or
even three, whereon was such abundance of embroidery,
and pearls, and cyphers, and cabalistic letters and pretty
conceits, nothing in all this world ever was richer and
rarer to look on. And she was right; for so her gifts,
once made, were not hid away in chests or in purses, like
those of many other dames, but were displayed before all
men. For she deemed that her friends did manifest their
worth looking at them and showing them as tokens of her
regard, whereas such presents when made in coin did
smack rather of common women that give money to their
bullies than of high-born and honourable ladies. Sometimes again she would give beautiful rings of rich jewel-
work, forasmuch as favours and scarfs are not ordinarily
worn, but only on some great and high emprise, whereas
a ring on the finger keeps better company and more constant with the wearer.

Though, verily, a gentle and noble-hearted knight
should be of this generous complexion that he had rather
serve his lady for the beauties which do make her shine

[101]

resplendent than for all the shining gold and silver she may have.

For myself, I can boast of having served in my day honourable ladies, and those of no low estate. But truly if I had been willing to take all they gave me and extract from their generosity all I might have had, why, I should be a richer man to-day, whether in goods or money or plenishing, than I am by a good thirty thousand crowns; yet have I alway been content to make evident my love rather by my generosity than by my avariciousness.

Without doubt there is good reason for it, that inasmuch as the man doth put somewhat of his own into the purse the woman hath, the woman should likewise put something of hers in the man's. Yet herein must due proportion be kept; for just as the man cannot cast in and give as much of his into the woman's purse as she would fain have, so is the man bound in fairness not to draw from that of the woman all he would. The law of give and take must needs be observed and proper measure kept.

I have moreover before now seen many gentlemen lose the love of their mistresses by reason of the importunity of their demands and their inordinate rapacity. For these, seeing them such beggars and so eager to have their pay, have quietly broke off the connexion and left them in the lurch, and that notwithstanding the excellent service rendered.

Wherefore it is that every noble-minded lover were better to be guilty of greed for his lady's body than for her money; because supposing the lady to be over generous of her goods, the husband finding his property lessening

[102]

apace, is more angered thereat ten times over than at a thousand largesses she may have made of her person.

Further, some cuckolds there be that are made such in the way of revenge. I mean that often men who have a grudge against some great Lord or gentleman or other person, from the which they have received injuries and affronts, do avenge their wrongs on them by making love to their wives, whom they do debauch and make fine cuckolds of their enemies.

I knew once a great Prince who had suffered from sundry attempts at rebellion on the part of one of his subjects, a great Lord, yet was all unable to revenge himself, seeing the offender did all he could to escape him, so that the Prince could never lay hands on him. However, his wife having one day come to Court to solicit her husband's pardon and the better ordering of his case, the Prince did appoint with her to meet him to confer thereof in a garden and a chamber adjoining it. But it was really to talk of love to her, wherein he won his triumph on the spot, without much ado, for she was of very accommodating character. Nor did he content himself with having her in his proper person, but did likewise prostitute her to others, down to the very footmen of the chambers. And in this wise would the Prince declare he did feel himself well revenged on his unfaithful subject, having so debauched his wife and crowned his head with a good coronal of horns. Albeit but a subject, he had been fain to play petty king and sovereign; but instead of winning a regal crown of fleurs-de-lis, he had gotten himself a fine one of horns![2]

This same Prince did a like thing in another case at the instigation of his mother, for he did debauch a Princess

that was a maid, well knowing she was to wed a certain
Prince who had done him displeasure and sore troubled
his brother's government. Thus he did deflower her and
had his will of her finely; yet after two months was she
delivered to the poor Prince as a virgin and to be his
wife. The revenge herefor was of the mildest,—pending
other action that did ensue later, of a harsh and violent
enough sort.[3]

I knew once a very honourable gentleman who, being
lover of a fair lady and one of good belongings, did ask
her for the recompense of his long love and courtship;
but she answered frankly, she would not give him so much
as a single doit's worth, seeing she was quite assured he
loved her not for this, and bare her not such fond affection for her beauty's sake, as he alleged. His wish was
rather, by having his will of her, to avenge himself on her
husband, who had done him some displeasure; wherefore
he was fain to win this consolation to his pride and to
feel for the future he had had the upper hand. But the
gentleman, assuring her of the contrary, continued to
court her humbly for more than two years longer, and this
so faithfully and with such passion, that at the last she
did show such ample and full gratitude that she did grant
him all she had before refused, declaring that had she not,
at the first beginning of their courtship, supposed some
idea of vengeance intended to be in his mind, she would
immediately have made him as happy a man as she now
did at the end, for that her natural bent was to love and
prefer him. Note how the lady was able wisely to command her passion so that love did never carry her away
to do what all the while she did most desire, for that she

[104]

wished to be loved for her own sake and not merely as a means to a man's vengeance on another.

The late M. du Gua, one of the truly gallant and perfect gentlemen of the world in every way, did invite me to the Court one day to dine with him. He had brought together a dozen of the most learned men of the Court, amongst others the Lord Bishop of Dol,[4] of the house of Espinay in Brittany, MM. de Ronsard, de Baïf, Des Portes, d'Aubigny (the last two are still living, and could contradict me, if I lie), and others whose names I forget. Amongst them all was no man of the sword but only M. du Gua and myself. The discourse during dinner turned on love, and the commodities and incommodities, pleasures and displeasures, good and ill, it brought in its train. After each guest had declared his opinion on the one side or the other, himself did conclude that the sovereign good of its gratification lay in this vengeance it made possible, and prayed each of all these great personages to make a *quatrain* thereon impromptu. This they all did, and I would I had them to insert here; but his Lordship of Dol, whose words were true gold, whether spoke or writ, did bear off the prize.

And doubtless M. du Gua had good reason to maintain this view, as against two great Lords of my acquaintance, whom he did cause to wear the horns for the hatred he bare them. Their wives were very fair women, so in this case he did win double pleasures, satisfaction of his vengeance and gratification of his passions. Many other folk have so revenged themselves and taken delight herein, and accordingly have shared in the same opinion.

Moreover I have known many fair and honourable ladies, who did say and affirm that, when their husbands

[105]

had maltreated or bullied them, rated or censured them, beat them or otherwise ill-used and outraged them, their greatest joy and delight was to give them a pair of horns, and in the act, to think of them, and scoff and mock and make fun of them with their paramours, going so far as to declare they did hereby have a greater access of appetite and sure delight of pleasure than could well be described.

I have heard speak of a fair and honourable lady who, being asked once if ever she had made her husband cuckold, did make answer, "Nay! why should I have made him so, seeing he hath never beat nor even threatened me?" As though implying that, if he had done either one or the other, her champion that she had in front would very soon have revenged her.

And speaking of wit and mockery, I once knew a very honourable and fair lady who, being in these gentle transports of pleasure, did chance by dint of her wild caresses to break an earring she had in the shape of a cornucopia, which was but of black glass, such as were worn in those days. Whereupon she cried instantly to her lover, "Look you, how provident Dame Nature is; I have broken one horn, but here I am making a dozen others for my poor cuckold of a husband, to bedeck him withal some fine feast-day, if he so will."

Another, having left her husband a-bed and asleep, went to see her lover before lying down herself. Then asked he her where her husband was, and she did reply, "He is keeping his bed, guarding his cuckoo's nest for fear another come to lay therein. But 'tis not with his bed, nor his sheets, nor his nest you have to do, but with me,

[106]

who am come to see you. I have left him there as sentinel, though truly he is but a sleepy one."

Talking of sentinels, I have heard a tale told of a certain gentleman of consideration, whom I well knew, who one day coming to words with a very honourable lady, whom also I knew, he did ask her, by way of insult, if she had ever gone on pilgrimage to Saint Mathurin.[5] "Oh, yes!" she replied, "but I could never get into the Church, for so full and so well occupied was it with cuckolds, they would never suffer me to enter. And you, who were one of the foremost, were mounted on the steeple, to act sentinel and warn the others."

I could tell a thousand other such tales, but I should never have done. Yet do I hope to find room for some of them in some corner or other of my book.

10.

OME cuckolds there be which are good-natured and which of their own impulse do invite themselves to this feast of cuckoldry. Thus I have known some who would say to their wives, "Such and such an one is in love with you; I know him well, and he often cometh to visit us, but 'tis for love of you, my pretty. Give him good welcome; he can do us much pleasure, his acquaintance may advantage us greatly."

Others again will say to their wives' admirers, "My wife is in love with you, and right fond of you. Come and see her, you will give her pleasure; you can chat and hold discourse together, and pass the time agreeably." So do they invite folk to feast at their expense. As did the

[107]

Emperor Hadrian,[1] who being one time in Britain (as we read in his Life), carrying on War there, did receive sundry warnings, how that his wife, the Empress Sabina, was making unbridled love with a number of gallant Roman noblemen. As fate would have it, she had writ and despatched a letter from Rome to a certain young Roman gentleman who was with the Emperor in Britain, complaining that he had forgot her, and took no more account of her, and that it must needs be he had some intrigue in that region and that some affected little wanton had caught him in the lakes of her beauty. This letter fell by chance into the Emperor's hands; and when the nobleman in question did some days after ask leave of absence under colour of wishing to go to Rome immediately for family affairs of his own, Hadrian said to him in mocking wise, "Well, well! young sir, go there,—and boldly, for the Empress, my wife, is expecting you in all affection." But the Roman hearing this, and finding the Emperor had discovered his secret and might likely play him some ill turn, started the very next night, without saying by your leave or with your leave, and took refuge in Ireland.

Still he had no need to be greatly afraid for all this. Indeed the Emperor himself would often say, being regaled continually with tales of the extravagant love affairs of his wife, "Why, certainly, were I not Emperor, I should have long ago rid me of my wife; but I desire not to show an evil example." As much as to say, it matters not to the great to be in this case, so long as they let it not be known publicly. And what a fate for great men,— one which truly some of them have consented to, though not for the same reason! So we see this good Emperor suffering himself complacently to be made cuckold.

Another good Emperor, Marcus Aurelius,[2] who had as wife Faustina, a downright harlot, replied on being advised to put her away, "If we give her up, we are bound also to give up her dowry, which is the Empire." And who would not be cuckold like him for such a prize, or even a less one?

His son, Antonius Verus, surnamed Commodus, though he grew up very cruel, yet held the like language to such as advised him to have the said Faustina, his mother, put to death. So madly in love was she and so hot after a gladiator that she could never be cured of the fierce malady, till at last they bethought them to kill the rascally gladiator and make her drink his blood.

Many and many a husband hath done and doth the same as the good Marcus Aurelius, for they do fear to kill their wives, whores though they be, for dread of losing the great fortunes they have of them, and had rather be rich cuckolds on these easy terms than cruel villains.

Heavens! how many of the sort have I known, who were forever inviting their kinsmen and friends and comrades to come and visit their wives, going so far as to make banquets for them, the better to attract them. Then, when they were there, they would leave them alone with the lady in bedchamber or closet, and so away, with the words, "I leave my wife in your care."

One I knew, a nobleman of the great world, of such behaviour you would have said his whole happiness did rest in this only, to be cuckolded. He seemed to make it his study to give opportunities therefor, and especially never forgot to say this first word, "My wife is in love with you; do you love her as well as she loves you, I wonder?" Many a time when he saw his wife with her admirer, he would carry off the company from the room to take a walk, leaving the twain of them together, so giving them good leisure to discuss their loves. And if by any chance he had to return of a sudden into the room, from the very bottom step of the stairs he would begin shouting aloud, calling after someone, spitting or coughing, to the end he might not catch the lovers in the act. For commonly, even though one know of them and suspect their coming, these peeps and surprises are scarce pleasant whether to the one party or the other.

This same Lord was having a fine mansion built one time, and the master mason having asked whether he would not have the cornices *horn*-amented, he made answer, "I don't know what *horn*amentation means. Go and ask my wife who understands the thing, and knows geometry; and whatever she tells you to do, do it."

Still worse was it with one I know of, who one day selling one of his estates to a purchaser for fifty thousand crowns, did take forty-five thousand of the sum in gold and silver, and in lieu of the remaining five accepted a unicorn's horn. Huge laughter amid them that knew him; "Ha, ha!" they said, "as if he had not enough horns at home already, that he must fit in this one to boot."

I knew a very great Lord, a brave and gallant man, who did greet a certain honourable gentleman and profess himself his very good servant, yet adding with a smile these words, "My dear Sir, I know not what you have done to my wife, but she is so much in love with you that day and night she doth nothing but speak to me of you, and is forever singing your praises. For all answer I tell her I have known you longer than she hath, and am well aware of your worth and deserts, which are great." Who more astonished than this same gentleman? for he had but just taken in this lady on his arm to Vespers, which the Queen was attending, and that was all. However, he at once regained his countenance and replied, "Sir! I am your wife's most humble servant, and deeply grateful for the good opinion she hath of me, and do greatly respect her. Yet do I not make love to her," he went on in a merry tone. "All I do is to pay her my court, herein following the good advice yourself gave me quite lately, seeing she hath much influence with my mistress, whom I may be enabled to wed by her help, and therefore do hope she will give me her assistance."

The Prince had no suspicion and did naught but laugh and admonish the gentleman to court his wife more assiduously than ever. This he did, being right glad under this pretext to be lover to so fair a lady and so great a Princess, who soon made him forget his other mistress he had been fain to wed, and scarce to think of her again, except to find her a convenient mask to dissemble and cover up the whole thing withal. Even so could the Prince not help but feel some pangs of jealousy when one day he did see the said gentleman in the Queen's chamber wearing on his arm a ribband of Spanish scarlet, which had just been brought to Court as a fine novelty, and which he did touch and handle as he talked with him; then going to find his wife who was by the Queen's bedside, lo! he saw she had one that was its very match, which he did likewise touch and handle and proved it to be like it in all respects and part of the same piece as the other. Yet did he breathe never a word, nor take any steps in the matter. And

[111]

indeed in such intrigues it is very needful to cover up
their fires with such cinders of discretion and good counsel as that they may never be discovered; for very oft
such discovery of the scandal will anger husbands far
more against their wives than when the same is done, but
all in secret,—herein illustrating the proverb, *Si non
caste, tamen caute*,—"If not with virtue, at any rate with
prudence."

What terrible scandals and great incommodities have
I seen in my time arise from the indiscretions of ladies
and their lovers! Yet would the husbands have cared
naught at all about the thing, if only they had done their
doings *sotto coperte* (under cover, under the rose), as
the saying is, and the matter had never seen the light.

I knew one dame who was all for manifesting quite
openly her loves and preferences, which she did indulge as
if she had had no husband at all, and had been her own
mistress entirely, refusing to listen to the counsels of her
friends and lovers, who did remonstrate with her and
point out the inconveniences she was exposing herself to.
And of these she did later reap a sore harvest!

This lady did otherwise than many worthy dames have
done at all times, who have gaily enjoyed love and lived a
merry life, yet have never given much evidence thereof to
the world, except mayhap some small suspicions, that
could scarce have revealed the truth even to the most
clear-sighted. For they would address their lovers in
public so dexterously, and deal with them so adroitly, that
neither husbands nor spies, all their life long, could ever
get aught to bite at. And when their favourites departed
on some journey, or came to die, they would dissemble

and conceal their grief so cunningly that none ever discovered aught.

I knew a fair and honourable lady, who the day a certain great Lord, her lover, died, did appear in the Queen's chamber with a countenance as gay and smiling as the day before. Some did think highly of her for such discretion, deeming she did so for fear of doing the King displeasure and angering him, for that he liked not the man deceased. Others blamed her, attributing this bearing rather to the lack of true love, wherein 'twas said she was but poorly furnished, like all women who lead the life she did.

I knew on the other hand two fair and honourable ladies, who having lost their lovers in a misadventure of war, did make great sorrow and lamentation, and did make manifest their mourning by their dusky weeds, and eke holy-water vessels and sprinklers of gold engraven with figures, and death's-heads, and all kinds of trophies of dissolution, in their trinkets, jewels and bracelets which they wear. All this did bring much scandal upon them and was greatly to their hurt; though their husbands did take no special heed thereof.

This is how these ladies do themselves hurt by the making public their amours; these we may rightly praise and esteem for their constancy, though not for their discretion, for on this last count what they do is much to their disadvantage.

And if ladies so doing are blameworthy, there be many likewise among their lovers which do deserve reprimand quite as much as they. For they will ever be putting on looks as they were half dead, like she-goats in kid, and a most languorous mien, making eyes and casting ap-

[113]

pealing glances, indulging in passionate gestures and love-
sick sighs in company, openly bedecking themselves with
their ladies' colours,—in a word giving way to so many
silly indiscretions that a blind man could scarce fail to
note them. Some of them moreover do the like more in
pretence than in reality, desiring to let all the Court
understand they are in love in an high quarter, and are
happy in their amours. Whereas, God wot, it may well
be the ladies would not give them so much as one poor
farthing in alms, to save their repute for deeds of charity!

I do know well a certain nobleman and great Lord, who
desiring to satisfy the world he was the lover of a fair
and honourable lady that I know of, had his little mule
held in front of her door, with a couple of his lackeys and
pages. As it fell out, M. d'Estrozze and myself did pass
that way, and beheld this mystery of the mule and the
man's pages and lackeys. He asked instantly where was
their master, and they replied he was within, in the lady's
house. Hereupon M. d'Estrozze burst out a-laughing,
and turning to me, said he would wager his life he was
not there at all. And in a moment after he posted his
page as sentinel to watch if the pretended lover should
come forth; then quickly we hied us to the Queen's chamber, where we found our man,—not without some laughter
betwixt him and me.

Then towards evening we went to greet him, and pretending to quarrel with him, did ask him where he was at
such and such an hour of the afternoon, and how that he
could not deceive us, as we had seen his mule and his
pages before the said lady's door. But the fellow, making as though he were vexed we had seen so much and were
for this cause attacking him for carrying out an intrigue

in this high quarter, did confess he was there in very truth. At the same time he besought us not to breathe a word; else should we bring him into sore trouble, and the poor lady would incur scandal and the displeasure of her husband. And this we did faithfully promise him,— laughing all the while heartily and making mock at him, albeit he was a nobleman of no small rank and quality, and declaring we would not speak of the thing, and never a syllable pass our lips.

Finally after some days during which he did continue his trick with the mule too often for our patience, we did discover our artfulness to him, and attacked him with right good will and in good company. This made him desist for very shame, and indeed the lady did know of it by this time through our information, and had the mule and the pages watched one day and incontinently driven away from her door like beggars in front of an inn. Nay! we did even better, for we told the tale to the husband, and that in such merry wise he found it right diverting and laughed heartily at the thing, saying he had no fear this fellow would make him cuckold, and that if ever he should find the said mule and pages stationed at his door, he would have the gates opened and invite them inside, to the end they might be more at ease and sheltered from heat, cold or rain. Not but what others all the whole while were cuckolding him soundly enough. And this is how this noble Lord was fain, at the expense of an honourable lady and her repute, to exalt himself, without any heed to the scandal he might cause thereby.

I knew another nobleman who did bring sore scandal on a very fair and honourable lady by his behaviour. He had for some while been in love with her, and did urge her to grant him the little tit-bit reserved for her husband's mouth, but she did refuse him flatly. At last, after several refusals, he said to her, as if in despair, "Well, if you won't, why, you won't; but I give you my oath I will ruin your honour and repute." And to this end he bethought him to make many comings and goings in secret, yet not so secret but that he made himself seen of set purpose by sundry eyes, and let himself be noted by day and by night frequenting the house where she dwelt. Then he would be ever vaunting and boasting under the rose of his pretended successes, and in company seeking out the lady with more familiarity than he had any call to do, and among his comrades swaggering as the happy lover, and this all in mere pretence. The end was that one night having slipped in very late into the said lady's bedchamber, all muffled in his cloak and hiding from the folk of the house, and after playing sundry of his stealthy tricks, he was suspected by the seneschal of the household, who had a watch set. And though they could not find him, yet did the husband beat his wife and give her several buffets; but later, urged thereto by the seneschal, who said it was not punishment enough, did stab her and kill her; and readily won his pardon therefor from the King. A sad pity truly for the poor lady, who was very fair and beauteous. Afterward the nobleman, which had been cause of all the mischief, did not fare far or well, but was killed in a passage of war, by God's good will, for having so unjustly robbed an honourable lady of her good name and her life.

11.

O tell the truth as to this example and a host of others I have seen, there are some ladies which do themselves great wrong, and which are the true cause of the scandal and dishonour they incur. For 'tis themselves that do provoke the first skirmishes and purposely draw the gallants to them, from the beginning lavishing on them the fondest caresses, favours and familiarities, raising their hopes by all sorts of gentle wiles and flattering words. Yet when it cometh to the point, they will refuse outright, in such wise that the honourable gentlemen which had promised themselves many a pleasant treat of their person, fall into anger and despair and quit them with harsh words. So they depart abusing them and giving them out for the biggest strumpets in all the world, and make out an hundredfold worse tale of their demerits than is really deserved.

And this is why an honourable lady should never set herself to draw a gallant to her, and suffer him to be her servant, if she will not satisfy him at the last according to his deserts and loving service. It behooves her to realize this, unless she would be undone, even when she hath to do with an honourable and gallant man; else from the first beginning, when he doth first accost her, and she sees it is with this end so much desired in view, that he pay his vows to her, but she feeleth no desire to gratify him herein, she should give him his dismissal at the very threshold. For indeed, to speak quite candidly, any woman that doth suffer a lover to court her, doth lay herself under such obligation that she cannot withdraw

[117]

afterward from the fight. She is bound to come to it sooner or later, long though the coming may sometimes be.

There be some dames, however, whose joy is to be served for nothing, but only for the light of their bright eyes. They say they love to be served and courted, that this is their great happiness, and not to come to the final act at all. Their pleasure, they declare, doth lie in wishing for it, not in actually performing of it. I have known many ladies which have told me this. Yet can they never stop there; for if once they do begin wishing for it, without shadow of doubt they will some day come to the doing of it as well. For this is the law of love, that when once a woman doth wish or hope, or but dream of wishing and desiring a man for herself, the thing is done. If only the man know it, and steadily follow up his fair assailant, he will surely have leg or wing, fur or feathers, as they say.

In this wise then are poor husbands made cuckold by such thoughts on the part of ladies, who are ready to wish forsooth, but not to do. For truly, without suspecting it, they will of their own fault be burned in the candle, or at the fire they have themselves built. Like poor simple shepherdesses, which to warm themselves in the fields as they watch their sheep and lambs, do kindle a little fire, without thought of any harm or ill to follow. But they give no heed to the chance their little fire may set so great an one ablaze as will burn up a whole country-side of plains and woods.

'Twere well if such ladies would take example, to teach them wisdom, of the Comtesse d'Escaldasor, a very fair lady dwelling at Pavia, to whom M. de Lescu, afterward known as the Maréchal de Foix, was paying court. He was then a student at Pavia, and was called the Protonotary de Foix, seeing he was destined for the Church, though afterward he did quit the long robe to adopt the profession of arms. And he might well love her, seeing at that day she bare the bell for beauty over all the ladies of Lombardy. So seeing herself hotly pressed by him, yet not wishing to rudely disoblige him or dismiss him roughly, for he was a near kinsman of the renowned Gaston de Foix, at whose fame all Italy trembled in those days, the Countess on a day of high festivity and state at Pavia, whereat all the fairest ladies of the city and neighbourhood were gathered and many noble gentlemen, did appear, the fairest of them all, superbly attired in a robe of sky blue, all trimmed and bespangled over all its length and breadth with torches and butterflies fluttering round them and burning themselves in their flame. The whole was in broidery of gold and silver, for truly the embroiderers of Milan have ever surpassed those of all the rest of the world, and won the lady the general repute of being the best adorned of all the company there present.

Then the Protonotary, leading her out to the dance, was moved to ask her what might be the meaning of the designs on her robe, strongly suspecting there lay beneath some hidden signification unfavourable to him. She made answer in these words, "Sir, I have had my robe fashioned thus, just as soldiers and horsemen do with their horses when they are wild and vicious, and kick and fling out their heels. For they do fix on their crupper a big silver bell, to the end that this signal may warn their comrades, when they are riding in a close press of company, to take heed of the vicious kicker, lest he do them an injury. In like wise by my fluttering butterflies, burning themselves in these torches, I do warn those honour-

[119]

able gentlemen which do me the favour of loving me and admiring my beauty, not to come too nigh, nor to desire aught else, but only the sight of me. For they will gain nothing thereby, but only like the butterflies,—to long, and burn, and get no satisfaction."

The story is writ in the *Emblems* of Paulus Jovius.[1] In this fashion did she warn her lover to take heed for himself in time. I know not whether or no he did come more nigh, or what he did. But later, being wounded to the death at the battle of Pavia, and taken prisoner, he begged to be carried to the house of this same Countess at Pavia, where he was very well received and tended by her. In three days' time he died there, to the great sorrow of the lady, as I did hear the story told me by M. de Monluc, one time we were together in the trenches at Rochelle. It was night and we were talking together, when I related to him the tale of the robe and its device; on this he assured me he had seen the said Countess, who was very fair, and did love the Maréchal well, and how he had been most honourably entreated of her. For the rest he knew not if ever they had gone further at all. This example should be warning enough for many of the ladies the which I have spoken of above.

Then again, there be cuckolds which are so righteous they have their wives preached to and admonished by good and religious men, with a view to their conversion and reform. And these, with forced tears and words of pretended sorrow, do make many vows, promising mountains and marvels of repentance, and never, never to do the like again. But their oaths do scarce endure an instant, for truly the vows and tears of suchlike dames are of just so much weight as are the oaths and adjurations of lovers.

So have I seen and known well a certain lady to the which a great Prince, her Sovereign, did offer the affront of commissioning appointing a Cordelier monk, as from himself and coming from the Court, to go find her husband, who was spending his vacation on his estate, to warn the same of his wife's reckless loves and the ill report current of the wrong she was doing him, and to say how, for the respect due to his position and office, he was sending him timely news thereof, to the end he might correct this sinful soul. The husband was greatly astounded and moved at such a message and kindly warning; yet did take no overt action, except only to thank his Prince and assure him he would see to the matter. Yet on his return he did make no difference for the worse in his treatment of his wife; for truly what would he have gained thereby? Once a woman hath taken to these courses, naught will alter her, like a posthorse which is grown so thoroughly used to go at the gallop that he can in no wise learn to go any other gait whatsoever.

Alas! how oft have we seen honourable ladies which, having been surprised at these tricks, and thereupon chid and beaten, yea! and admonished by every prayer and remonstrance not to return to the like course, do promise, protest and swear they will behave them chastely, yet do presently illustrate the proverb, *passato il periglio, gabbato il santo* (the danger past, the Saint is mocked), and return again with all the more zest to the game of love. Nay! many have we seen, which themselves feeling some worm of remorse gnawing their soul, have of their proper act made holy and right solemn vows of reformation, yet have never kept them, but presently have repented of their repentance, as M. du Bellay doth say of penitent coürtesans :[2]

> Mère d'amour, suivant mes premiers vœux,
> Dessous tes lois remettre je me veux,
> Dont je voudrois n'estre jamais sortie;
> Et me repens de m'estre repentie.

(Mother of love, returning to my earlier vows, I am fain to put me again beneath thy laws, which I would I had never deserted; lo! I repent me of my penitence.)

Such women declare 'tis exceeding hard to give up forever so sweet a habit and fond custom, seeing their time is so short in this brief sojourn they make in this world.

To confirm what I here say I would readily appeal to many a fair maid, which hath repented in youth and taken the veil and become a nun. If such were asked on her faith and conscience what she did really desire, many a time, I know, she would say, "Ah! would the high convent walls were broken down, that I might straight be free again!"

Wherefore husbands need never think to reduce their wives to order again, after once these have made the first breach in their honour, or that they can aught else but only give them the rein, merely recommending discretion and all possible avoidance of scandal. For truly we may apply all the remedies of love which ever Ovid taught, and an host of other subtle remedies that others have invented, yea! and those puissant ones of François Rabelais,[3] which he did teach to the venerable Panurge, yet will none of them all avail. But 'twere best of all to follow the advice given in the refrain of an old song of King Francis' time, which saith,

Qui voudroit garder qu'une femme
N'aille du tout à l'abandon,
Il faudroit la fermer dans une pipe,
Et en jouir par le bondon.

(If a man would make sure of his wife never going to the
bad at all, he had best shut her up in a cask, and enjoy her
through the bung-hole.)

In the reign of the late King Henri of France there
was a certain jeweller which did import and expose for
sale at the great Fair of St. Germains a round dozen of
a certain contrivance for confining women's affairs.[4]
These were made of iron and were worn like a belt, joining underneath and locking with a key, and were so cunningly framed that the woman, once confined therein,
could never find opportunity for the pleasures of love,
there being only a few little tiny holes in the thing for
empissoyent through.

'Tis said that five or six jealous husbands were found
ready to buy one, wherewith they did confine their wives
in such wise they might well say, "Good-bye, good times
for ever and aye!" Yet was there one wife who bethought her to apply to a locksmith very cunning in his
art. So, when she had shown him the said contrivance,
her husband being away in the country, he did so well use
his ingenuity that he forged a false key therefor, so that
the good lady could open and shut the thing at any time,
whenever she would. The husband did never suspect or
say a word, while the wife took her fill of the best of all
pleasures, in spite of the jealous fool and silly cuckold
her husband, who did imagine all the time he was living
free of all apprehension of such a fate. But truly the

[123]

naughty locksmith, which made the false key, quite spoiled his game; yea! and did even better, by what they say, for he was the first who tasted the dainty, and cuckolded him. Nor was this so extraordinary, for did not Venus, which was the fairest woman and harlot in all the world, mate with Vulcan, ironworker and locksmith, the which was exceeding mean-looking, foul, lame and hideous.

They say, moreover, that there were a number of gallant and honourable gentlemen of the Court which did threaten the jeweller that if ever again he should have aught to do with bringing such villainies with him, he would be killed. They bade him never come back again, and made him throw all the others that were left into the draught-house; and since then no more has been heard of such contrivances. And this was wisely done; for truly 'twas as good, or as bad, as destroying one half of mankind, so to hinder the engendering of posterity by dint of such confining, locking up and imprisoning of nature,—an abominable and hateful wrong to human productiveness.

Some there be which do give their wives into the hands of eunuchs to guard their honour, a thing which the Emperor Alexander Severus did strongly reprobate, harshly bidding them never have dealings with Roman ladies. But they were soon recalled again. Not indeed that these could ever beget children or the women conceive of them; yet can they afford some slight feeling and superficial taste of minor pleasures, giving some colourable imitation of the complete and perfect bliss. Of this many husbands do take very little account, declaring that their main grievance in the adultery of their wives had naught at all to do with what they got given them, but that it vexed them sore to have to rear and bring up and recognise as heirs children they had never begotten.

Indeed but for this, there is nothing they would have made less ado about. Thus have I known not a few husbands, who when they did find the lovers, who had made their wives children, to be easy and good-natured, and ready to give freely and keep them, took no more account of the thing at all, or even advised their wives to beg of them and crave some allowance to keep the little one they had had of them.

So have I heard tell of a great lady, which was the mother of Villeconnin, natural son of Francis I. The same did beseech the King to give or assign her some little property, before he died, for the child he had begot,— and this he did. He made over for this end two hundred thousand crowns in bank, which did profit him well and ran on ever growing, what with interest and re-investment, in such wise that it became a great sum and he did spend money with such magnificence and seemed in such good case and ample funds at Court that all were astonished thereat. And all thought he enjoyed the favours of some mysterious lady. None believed her his mother, but, seeing he never went about without her, it was universally supposed the great expenditure he made did come from his connexion with her. Yet it was not so at all, for she was really his mother; though few people were ware of it. Nor was anything known for sure of his lineage or birth, except that he eventually died at Constantinople, and that his inheritance as King's bastard was given to the Maréchal de Retz, who was keen and cunning enough to have discovered this little secret which he was able to turn to his profit, and did verify the bastardy which had been so long hid. Thus he did win the gift of this inheritance over the head of M. de Teligny, who had been constituted heir of the aforesaid Villeconnin.

Other folk, however, declared that the said lady had had the child by another than the King, and had so enriched him out of her own fortune. But M. de Retz did scrutinize and search among the banks so carefully that he did find the money and the original securities of King Francis. For all this some still held the child to have been the son of another Prince not so high as the King, or some one else of inferior rank, maintaining that for the purpose of covering up and concealing the whole thing and yet providing the child a maintenance, 'twas no bad device to lay it all to his Majesty's account, as indeed hath been done in other instances.

This much I do firmly believe, that there be many women in the world, nay! even in France, which if only they thought they could bring children into existence at this rate, would right readily suffer Kings and great Princes to mount on their bellies. But in very fact they ofttimes so mount without any grand regale following. Then are the poor ladies sore deceived and disappointed, for when they do consent to give themselves to suchlike great personages, 'tis only to have the *galardon* (guerdon, recompense), as folk say in Spanish.

Now as to such putative and doubtful children, a question doth arise open to much dispute, to wit whether they ought to succeed to their father's and mother's goods, some maintaining 'tis a great sin for women to make them so succeed. Some authorities have declared the woman should surely reveal the thing to the husband and tell him the whole truth, and this is the opinion held by the well-known "Subtle Doctor." Others on the contrary hold this opinion to be bad, because the woman would then be defaming herself by revealing it, and this she is in no wise bound to do; for good repute is a more precious possession than riches, saith Solomon.

'Tis better then for the goods to be taken, even unjustly, by the child than that the mother's good name be lost, for as a proverb hath it, "A good name is better than a golden girdle." Now the Theologians hold a maxim to the effect that when two opposite precepts and commands are binding on us, the less must give way to the greater. But the command to guard one's repute is greater and more stringent than that which orders to restore another's goods; and so must be preferred before it.

Nay! more, if the wife do reveal this to her husband, she doth thereby put herself in danger of being actually killed at his hands; but it is straitly forbid for any to compass their own death.

12.

EITHER is it allowed a woman to kill herself for dread of being violated, or after being so; else would she be doing a mortal sin. Wherefore is it better for her to suffer herself to be ravished, if that she can in no wise by fight or crying out avoid the same, than to kill herself. For the violation of the body is not sin, except with the consent of the will. Hence the reply which Saint Lucy did make to the tyrant who threatened to have her taken to the brothel. "If

you have me forced," she said, "why! my chastity will receive a double crown."

For this cause Lucretia hath been found to blame by some. True it is Saint Sabina and Saint Sophronia, along with other Christian virgins, who did take their own lives rather than fall into the hands of barbarians, are excused by our doctors and fathers of the Church, which say they did so by special prompting of the Holy Spirit. By this same prompting, after the taking of Cyprus, a certain Cypriote damsel, lately made Christian, seeing herself being carried off as a slave with many another lady of her sort, to be the prey of Turks, did secretly fire the powder magazine in the galley, so that in an instant all was burned up and consumed along with her, saying, "So please God, our bodies will never be polluted and ravished by these foul Turks and Saracens!" Or 'tis possible, God knows, it had already been polluted and she was fain to do penance therefor,—unless indeed the fact was her master had refrained from touching her, to the end he might make more money by selling her a maid, seeing men are desirous in those lands, as indeed in all other lands, to taste a fresh and untainted morsel.

However, to return to the noble custodians of these poor women,—the eunuchs. These, as I have said, are not utterly unable to do adultery with them and make their husbands cuckold, excepting always the engendering of children.

I knew two women in France which did deliberately set their love on two gentlemen who were castrate, to the end they might not become with child; yet did they find pleasure therein, and free from all fear of scandal. But there have been husbands in Turkey and Barbary so jealous,

[128]

that having discovered this deceit, they have determined
to castrate their wretched slaves altogether and entirely,
and cut the whole concern clean off. Now, by what those
say who have had experience of Turkey, not two out of
the dozen escape of those on whom they do practise this
cruelty, and do not die therefrom. Them that do survive, they do cherish and make much of, as true, certain
and chaste guardians of their wives' chastity and sure
guarantors of their honour.

We Christians on our part do not practise suchlike
abominable and too utterly horrible cruelties; but instead
of these castrated slaves, we give our women old men of
sixty for guardians. This for instance is done in Spain,
even at the Court of the Queens of that country, where
I have seen them as custodians of the maids of honour
and Court ladies. Yet, God knows, there be old men more
dangerous for ruining maids and wives than any young
ones, and an hundred times more hot, ingenious and per-
severing to gain over and corrupt the same.

I do not believe such men, for all they be hoary headed
and white bearded, are more sure guardians at all than
younger men, nor old women neither. Thus an aged
Spanish duenna once, taking out her maids and passing
by a great hall and seeing men's members painted up on
the wall in lifelike portrayal, only exaggerated and out
of all proportion, did remark, *Mira que tan bravos no los
pintan estos hombres, como quien no los conociese* (Look
how brave men those be, and how ill they have painted
them, like one who has never seen the things). Then all
her maids did turn toward her, and noted what she said,
except one, of my acquaintance, who acting the *ingénue*,
did ask one of her companions what birds those were;

for some of them were depicted with wings. And the other made answer, they were birds of Barbary, more beautiful in reality than even as depicted. God only knows if she had ever seen any such; but she had to make what pretence she could.

Many husbands are sore deceived, and often, in their duennas. For they think, provided only their women-kind are in the charge of some old woman, whom both parties do call mother as a title of respect, that they must needs be well safeguarded in front. Yet none are more easy than such guardians to be bribed and won over; for being as they are, avaricious of their very nature, they are ready to take gold from any quarter to sell their prisoners.

Others again cannot be forever on the watch over their young charges, who themselves are always wide awake and on the alert, especially when they be in love; for truly most of their time the old dames will be asleep in the chimney-corner, while before their very face the husbands will be a-cuckolding, without their heeding or knowing aught about it.

I knew once a lady which did it before her duenna's very eyes, in such cunning wise she never perceived anything wrong. Another did the like in her own husband's presence and all but under his eyes, the while he was playing at primero.

Then other aged dames will be feeble of foot, and cannot follow up their ladies at a round pace, so that by the time they do reach the extremity of a walk or a wood or a room, the young ones have whipped their little present into their pocket, without the old duenna having observed what was a-doing, or seen aught whatever, being slow of foot and dim of sight. Again there be yet other dames of the sort which, themselves having plied the trade of old, do think it pity to see the young fast, and are so good-natured to them, they will of their own accord open the way for their charges, yea! and provoke them to follow in the same, and help them all they can. Thus Aretino saith how the greatest of pleasures for a woman that hath travelled that road, and her highest satisfaction, is ever to make another do likewise.

And this is why, when a man doth crave the aid of a good minister for his amours, he will alway apply and address himself to an old procuress rather than to a young woman. So I do remember a certain very gallant gentleman, which did mislike sorely, and did forbid it expressly, that his wife should ever frequent the company of old women, as being much too dangerous society,— but with younger women she might go as much as she pleased. And for this course he would adduce many excellent reasons, the which I will leave to men of apter discourse than I to detail in full.

And this is why a certain Lord of the great world I know of did entrust his wife, of whom he was very jealous, to a lady, a cousin of his own, but unmarried, to be her *surveillante*. This office she did zealously perform, albeit for her own part she did copy the half only of the character of the gardener's dog, seeing he doth never eat the cabbage out of his master's garden, nor yet will suffer other to do so; but this lady would eat readily enough, but would never suffer her cousin. Yet was the other forever filching some dainty bit, without her noting it, cunning as she was,—or mayhap she did but make pretence not to see.

[131]

I could right easily adduce an host of devices which poor jealous cuckolds do employ to confine, constrain, curb and keep in their wives, that they kick not over the traces. But it is of mighty little use for them either to try these ancient means they have heard tell of, or to invent new ones; they but lose their labour. For once women have gotten this naughty worm of love in their heads, they will ever be sending their poor husbands to keep house with Guillot the Pensive. And hereof do I hope to discourse further in a chapter I have already half writ, on the ruses and stratagems of women in this matter, the which I do compare with the ambuscades and stratagems of soldiers in war. But the finest device of all, the most sure and eke the kindest preventive a jealous husband can apply to his wife, is ever to let her go her way in full liberty, as I have heard a very gallant married man declare, for that it is the woman's nature the more she is forbid a thing, so much the more to long for the same; and this is especially true in love, where the appetite doth grow far hotter by forbidding than by letting things take their course.

Then is there another sort of cuckolds, as to whom doth arise the following question, to wit,—whether if a man hath had full enjoyment of a woman during the lifetime of her cuckold husband, and this latter die, and the lover do afterward marry the widow in second nuptials, he ought to wear the name and title of cuckold,—a case I have heard debated in regard to several, and these great men.

Some there be do say he cannot be cuckold, because it is himself did have the doing of it, and no one else did make him so but only himself, and the horns were made by him and no other. Yet are there many armourors that do make swords whereby themselves are killed, or do kill each other.

Others again say he is really cuckold, but only *in embryo.* For this they do allege many reasons, but seeing the process is yet undecided, I leave it to be pleaded before the first audience that will listen to the case.

The same may be said concerning a very great lady, and a married one, which did break her marriage vow fourteen years agone with the lover who doth keep to her still, and since that day hath been ever awaiting and longing for her husband's death. But the devil is in it if he hath ever yet contrived to die to meet her wishes! So that she might well say, "Cursed be the husband and mate, which hath lived longer than I desired!" Sicknesses and calamities of body he hath had galore, but never fatal. In fact our King, the last Henri, having bestowed the inheritance in the fine and rich estate the said cuckold husband had of him on a very honourable and brave gentleman, would ofttimes say, "Two persons there be at my Court which are thinking it long till so and so die, one for his estate's sake and the other to wed her lover. But both one and the other have been sore deluded up to now."

See how wise and foreseeing God is, not to send folk what they wish, when it is evil. However, I have been told that for some while past this pair are in ill accord, and have now burned their promise of future marriage and broke the agreement,—to the huge despite of the lady and joy of the prospective husband, seeing he did in no wise desire to go on longer and wait forever for the death of the other. This last was alway making a mock of folk, continually giving alarms, as that he was just

[133]

about to die; yet in the end he hath survived his would-be
supplanter. An instance surely of God's punishment,
for a marriage so made is a thing all but unheard of; and
indeed 'tis a great sin, and an odious, to contract and
agree upon a second marriage, the first being still exist-
ent in its entirety.

I had rather have one, also a great lady, albeit not so
great as the other I have just spoke of, who being sought
of a nobleman in marriage, did wed him, not for the love
she bare him, but because she saw him sickly, thin and
worn, and in constant ill-health, and as the doctors told
her he would not outlive the year, even after having known
this fair lady several times abed. Wherefore she did
expect his death very soon, and did make all dispositions
after his demise as to his goods and property, fine plenishing and great wealth, which he did bring her by marriage;
for he was a nobleman of much riches and very well-to-do.
But she was finely cheated; for he liveth still a sturdy
wight, and in better fettle an hundred times than before
he married her; since then the lady herself is dead. They
say the aforesaid nobleman was used to feign to be sickly
and ailing to the end that, knowing as he did the lady to
be exceeding avaricious, she might wed him in the hope
of getting so rich an inheritance. Yet did God above
dispose it all quite contrariwise, and made the she-goat
feed where she had been tied, in spite of herself.

Now what shall we say of such men as do wed with
harlots and courtesans, that are very famous, as is commonly done in France, but still more in Spain and Italy,
where men are persuaded they are winning God's mercy
for good deeds, *por librar un' anima christiana del in-*

[134]

fierno,—"for delivering a Christian soul from hell," as
they say, and setting it in the right way.

I have undoubtedly seen some men maintain this opinion and doctrine, that if they did marry them for this
good and religious object, they ought in no wise to be
ranked as cuckolds. For surely what is done for the
honour of God should not be made a matter of shame.
This, of course, provided that their wives, once started
afresh in the right way, do not leave it again and return
to the other. So have I seen some of these women in the
two countries named which did sin no more after being
married, but others that could never reform, and went
back to trip and stumble in the old ditch.

The first time ever I was in Italy, I fell in love with a
very beautiful courtesan of Rome, who was called Faustina. But seeing I had no great wealth, and she was of
a very high price, from ten to twelve crowns a night, I
was constrained to content me with words and looks only.
After some time I paid a second visit to the same city,
and being now better furnished with money, I went to
visit her at her lodging by the introduction of another
lady, and did find her married to a man of the law, though
still established in her old quarters. She did welcome me
affectionately, and recounted me the good fortune of her
marriage, repudiating altogether the follies of her previous life, to the which she had said farewell forever. I
did then show her an handful of good French crowns, for
indeed I was dying of love for her worse than ever. She
was tempted at the sight and did grant me that I longed
for, saying how in concluding marriage, she had claimed
and agreed with her husband for her entire liberty,—
without scandal, however, or concealment, and only at the

[135]

price of a large sum,—to the end the pair of them might live in affluence. She was therefore to be had only by wealthy men; and to them he would yield very willingly, but not to petty customers at all. Truly here was a husband cuckold out and out, in bud and blossom too.

I have heard speak of a lady of the great world who, in concluding marriage, did desire and stipulate that her husband should leave her at Court to follow the pursuit of love, reserving herself alway the use of her forest of dead-wood or common faggot at her own good pleasure. However, in return, she was to give him every month a thousand francs for his little indulgences of every day. In fact the one thought was to have a merry life of it.

Thus it is, such women as have been free, cannot easily refrain, but will e'en burst the strait bars of the doors imprisoning them, however strong these be and well guarded, wherever gold doth clink and glitter. Witness the beauteous daughter of King Acrisius (Danaë), who all confined and imprisoned in her great tower as she was, yet did feel the persuasive drops of Jupiter's fair rain of gold, and admit the same.

Ah! how hard it is, a gallant gentleman of my acquaintance used to say, to safeguard a woman which is fair, ambitious, greedy and covetous of being bravely attired, and richly dressed, gaily decked out and well appointed, so that she lay not *cul en terre*,—no matter how well armed, as they say, her fort be, and however brave and valiant a man her husband be, and albeit he doth carry a good sword to defend her withal.

I have known so many of these same brave and valiant folk which have all gone this road. And truly 'tis great pity to see these honourable and brave men come to this,

and that, after so many gallant victories won by them,
so many notable conquests over their enemies and noble
combats decided by their valour, they should yet be
forced to carry horns intermingled among the fair flowers
and leaves of the crowns of triumph they wear,—horns
which do altogether spoil the effect thereof. Yet do they
think far more of their high ambitions and noble combats, their honourable emprises and valiant exploits, than
of safeguarding their wives and throwing light on their
dark places. And this is how, without more ado, they do
come to the city of Cuckoldland and the conquest of the
same. Yet is it a sore pity. For instance, I once knew
a very brave and valiant gentleman, bearing a very high
name and title, who was one day proudly telling over his
valiant deeds and conquests, when a very honourable and
noble gentleman, his comrade and friend, who was present, did say, "Yes! there he is telling us of all his won-
derful conquests; but truly to master his own wife's affair
is the greatest of all he hath ever won, or ever will!"

Many others have I known, who no matter what grace,
majesty and proud carriage they might show, yet did
every one display that look of the cuckold which doth
spoil all the rest. For truly this look and defect cannot
ever be hid or dissembled; no confidence of bearing and
gesture whatsoever can hinder its being known and evidently noted. And for myself, never have I seen any
one of these folk in all my life but did have their own distinctive marks, gestures, postures, looks and defects,—
excepting only one I knew once, in whom the most keen-
sighted could have found naught to observe or take hold
of, without knowing his wife as well; such an easy grace,

[137]

pleasant manners, and honourable, dignified deportment were his.

I would earnestly beg ladies which have husbands so perfect not to play them such tricks and put such affronts on them. But then they might in their turn retort upon me, "Nay! tell us where are to be found these perfect husbands, such as was the man whose example you have just quoted to us?"

Verily, ladies, you are right; for that all men cannot be Scipios and Cæsars. I hold, therefore, that herein ye must e'en follow your fancies. For indeed, speaking of the Cæsars, the most gallant of mankind have all gone this road, and the most virtuous and perfect, as I have said above and as we do read of that enlightened Emperor Trajan,[2] whose perfections, however, could not hinder his wife Plotina from yielding herself up entirely to the good pleasure of Hadrian, which was Emperor afterward. From her did this last win great advantages, profits and aggrandisement, so much so that she was the chief cause of his advancement. Nor was he in any wise ungrateful, after he had come to greatness, for he did love her and ever honour her right well. And after her death he did make such mourning and felt such sadness that at the last he did altogether lose all wish to eat and drink for a while, and was forced to tarry in Narbonese Gaul, where he had heard the sad tidings, three or four months, during which time he writ to the Senate ordering them to stablish Plotina in the number of the Goddesses, and did command that at her funeral sacrifices, exceeding rich and sumptuous, should be offered. Meantime he did employ his leisure in building and raising up, to her honour and memory, a very beautiful temple near

[138]

Nemausus, now called Nimes, adorned with most fair and rich marbles and porphyries, with other gawds.

See then how in matters of love and its satisfaction, naught at all can be laid down for certain. For truly Cupid the God thereof is blind, as doth clearly appear in sundry women, which having husbands as handsome and honourable and accomplished as can anywhere be seen, yet do fall in love with other men as ill-favoured and foul as mortals may be.

I have seen many cases that did force one to ask this question: Which is the more whorish dame, she that hath a right handsome and honourable husband, yet taketh an ill-favoured lover, one that is evil-tempered and quite unlike her husband; or she which hath an ill-favoured and ill-conditioned husband, and doth take a handsome, agreeable lover, and yet ceaseth not to love and fondly caress her husband, as if he were the prince of men for beauty, —as myself have seen many a woman do?

Of a surety the common voice doth declare that she which, having an handsome husband, yet doth leave the same to love an ill-favoured lover is a very great whore, —just as a person is surely a foul glutton which doth quit good food to eat of bad. So when a woman doth quit an handsome piece to take up with an ill-favoured, it hath all the semblance of her doing this out of sheer lecherousness, seeing there is naught more licentious and more fitted to satisfy licentiousness than an ugly man, with a savour more after the fashion of a stinking, filthy and lascivious goat than of a proper man. And in very deed handsome and honourable men are something more delicate and less apt to satiate an excessive and unbridled

[139]

wantonness than is a coarse, bearded, lewd fellow, some big ramping countrified satyr.

Others maintain that the woman which doth love a handsome lover and an ill-favoured husband, and doth caress them both, is at the least as great a whore as the other, for that she is fain to lose naught whatever of her ordinary diet and sustenance.

Such women are like them that travel in foreign lands, yea! and in France to boot, which being arrived at night at the inn to supper, do never forget to claim of mine host the wheeler's measure. Yea! and the fellow must needs have it too, albeit he should be full of good liquor to the throat already.

So will these dames, when night comes, never be without their "wheeler's measure,"—as was the way with one I knew well, who yet had a husband that was a right good performer. Natheless are they fain to increase and redouble their pleasure by any means they may, liking to have the lover for the day, which doth show up his beauty and so make the lady more eager for the fray, and give her more delight and satisfaction by reason of the good daylight. But the worthy husband with his ill-favoured face is kept for nighttime; for truly, as they say all cats are grey at night, and provided the lady have satisfaction of her appetites, she recks naught whether her mate is ill or well favoured.

Indeed, as I learn from sundry, when one is in these ecstasies of amorous pleasure, neither man nor woman reck aught of any other thing or thought whatever, but only what they are at for the instant; albeit on the other hand I have it on good authority how many dames have persuaded their lovers that, when they were at it with their husbands, they would ever give their thoughts to their lovers, and not reck at all of their husbands, in order to get the greater pleasure therefrom. So likewise have I heard husbands declare that when with their wives, they would be alway thinking of their mistresses with the like object. But these be disagreeable subjects!

Natural philosophers have told me that none but the present object of passion can possibly dominate them at this crisis, and in no wise the absent; and give many reasons for their opinion. However I am not philosopher enough nor sufficiently learned to contradict them; and besides sundry of their reasons are filthy ones, and I would fain ever preserve decency. But for these predilections for all-favoured loves, I have seen many such in my day that have astonished me an hundred times over.

Returning once from a journey in a foreign land,—I will not give the name, for fear men should recognise whereof I speak,—and discoursing with a noble lady of the great world, I chanced to speak of another great lady and Princess, the which I had seen in those parts; whereupon she did ask me as to this latter's love affairs. So I told her the name of the personage whom she held favourite, one that was neither handsome nor of graceful presence, and of very low degree. Her reply was, "Verily she doth herself great wrong, and eke plays love a sorry trick, seeing she is so fair and honourable a lady, as all men hold."

And the said lady was surely right in the language she held, for that herself did act accordingly, and gainsaid not her opinions. For she had a worthy and honourable lover, whom she cherished right well. And when all is said, a fair lady will be doing no harm in loving, if only she will choose a worthy object of her love, nor wronging her husband neither,—if for no other reason, at least for the sake of their descendants. This, seeing there be husbands that are so ill-favoured, so stupid, senseless and silly, so graceless and cowardly, so poor spirited and good for naught, that their wives, having children of them and like them, might as well have none at all. And indeed myself have known many ladies, which have borne children to suchlike husbands, and these have been all of them just like their fathers; yet afterward, when they have e'en borrowed one or two from their lovers, these have surpassed their supposed fathers, their brothers and sisters in all things whatsoever.

Some, moreover, among philosophers which have treated of this matter, have always maintained how that children thus borrowed by stealth, or stolen, if you will, thus engendered under the rose, and on the spur of the moment, are ever far more gallant, and recall more the merry fashion wherein they are used to be created, nimbly and cleverly, than such as are begot in bed, heavily, dully, ponderously, at leisure, their parents more than half asleep the while, giving never a thought but of brutish satisfaction to the pleasure in hand.

In like wise have I heard them that have charge of the stud-farms of kings and great lords say how they have many a time seen better foals got stealthily by their dams than others bred with every precaution by the masters of the stud, and from stallions specially chosen and assigned thereto. And so it is with human beings.

How many cases have I seen where ladies have borne handsomer and braver and more excellent children than they would have done, if the putative fathers had really begotten them,—mere calves and brute beasts as they would then have been.

A good reason why women are well advised to seek the help and commodity of good and handsome stallions, to the end they may produce good offspring. Yet I have seen on the other hand some which had handsome husbands, but did nevertheless call in the aid of ill-favoured lovers and base stallions, which did beget ugly and evil-conditioned descendants.

This indeed is one of the most signal commodities and incommodities of the state of cuckoldry.

I once knew a great lady of society which had an exceeding ill-favoured and ill-bred husband; and of four girls and two boys she had, there were only two good for aught, being children of her lover, while the others, coming of her scrub of a husband,—I had all but said her screech-owl of a husband, for truly he had all the look of one,—were but poor misbegotten creatures.

Now herein doth it behoove ladies to be very well advised and cunning withal, for as a rule children do resemble their fathers, and whenas they do not so, bring grave suspicion on their mothers' honour. So have I seen in my life many fair ladies possessed of this craze, to have it said and thought of all the world that their children do altogether resemble their father and not themselves, though really they are not the least like them. For to say so is the greatest pleasure one can do them, seeing there is then presumption they have not borrowed them from any other, however opposite the truth may really be.

One time I was present at a great assemblage of the Court, whereat folk were discussing the portraits of two daughters of a certain very great Queen. Each stated his opinion as to whom they did resemble, in such wise that all, men and women, declared they took altogether after the mother. But I, being a most humble servant and admirer of the mother, did hold the other side, and maintained stoutly they took entirely after the father, and that if only they had known and seen the same as intimately as I had, they would grant me it was so. Whereupon the Queen's sister did thank me for my words, and was exceeding grateful to me, seeing there were sundry persons, which did say what they did, of set purpose, to raise suspicion of her going astray in love,—the more that there *was* something of dust in her flute, as the saying is. Thus did my judgement as to the children's likeness to their father put all right again. Wherefore in this matter, whosoever shall love a lady and shall be looking upon children of her blood and bone, let him alway declare these do take after the father altogether, whether it be so or no.

True they will do no hurt, if they maintain the children take a little after the mother, as was said by a gentleman of the Court, a chief friend of mine, speaking in company of two gentlemen, brothers and high favourites with the King. Being asked which they were like, the father or mother, he did make answer that the one which was cold was like the father, and the other, which was hot, the mother. By this quip giving a pretty stroke at the mother, who was of a somewhat hot complexion. And as a matter of fact these two children did partake of these two several humours, the hot and the cold.

There is yet another sort of cuckolds, they which are made such by reason of the scorn they show their wives. Thus I have known several who, though having fair and honourable dames to wife, did take no account of them, but would ever scorn and disdain them. These being sharp of wit and full of spirit, and of good family to boot, seeing themselves so disdained, did proceed to pay them back in their own coin. Quick was there fine love making, and quick the accomplishment of the same; for as saith the Italian and Neapolitan catch, *amor non si vince con altro che con sdegno*—"love si mastered by scorn, and scorn only."

For so a fair and honourable lady, and one that doth know herself such and taketh pride therein, seeing her husband treating her with mere disdain, though she should bear him the fondest wifely love in the world, and albeit they should preach and put before her all the commands of the law to love and honour him, yet if she have the least spark of spirit, will she leave him in the lurch and take a lover elsewhere to help her in her little needs, and choose her out some private pleasure of her own.

I knew once two ladies of the Court, that were sisters-in-law. Of these the one had married an husband which was high in favour, a courtier and an adroit one. Yet did he not make such account of his wife as it behooved, seeing the birth she was of, but would speak to her before company as she were a mere savage, and treat her very roughly. This behaviour she did endure patiently for a while, till at length the husband did fall something out of favour. Then noting her opportunity and taking it cleverly as it came, having indeed waited for a good one, she straightway paid him back the scorn he had put on her, lightly and gaily making the poor man cuckold. And her sister did likewise, following her example. This last had been wed when very young and of tender years, so that her husband took no great heed of her, deeming her a mere chit and child, and did not love her as he should. But she coming to a riper time of life, and finding out she had a heart and was fair to look on, did soon pay him back in his own coin, and so made him a present of a fine pair of horns by way of interest on his past neglect.

Another time I knew a great Lord, which having taken two courtesans into favour, whereof one was a Moorish woman, to be his delight and joy of heart, did make no account of his wife, albeit she did seek to him with all due respect, and all the wifely love and reverence ever she could. Yet could he never look upon her with a favourable eye, or cherish her with a good grace, and of an hundred nights he would hardly bestow twain on her. What must she do then, the poor girl, after so many indignities, but what she did,—choose another vacant bed, and couple with another better half, and so take that she was fain of?

At least she had been justified, if the husband had been like another I know of, who was of a like humour, and being pressed by his wife, a very fair lady and one that did take her joy elsewhere than at home, did tell her frankly: "Well! well! take your pleasures abroad; I give you full leave. Do on your part what you please with another; I leave you in perfect liberty. Only make no trouble about my amours, and suffer me to do as I like. I will never hinder your pleasures and satisfaction; so do not you hinder mine." So, each independent of the other, the twain did go forth on their merry way, one to right, the other to left, without a thought or care for one another; a good and happy life truly!

No less should I commend a certain old man I knew

once, who being impotent, sickly and gouty, did say thus
one fine day to his wife, who was very fair, seeing clearly
he could not satisfy her as she was fain to be dealt with:
"I know right well, my pretty, how that my impotence
accords ill with your heartsome years. This may well
make me odious to you, and render it impossible to you
to be my loving wife, as if I could to you the regular
offices a strong, robust husband should. So I have
thought good to suffer you and grant you full freedom
to love some other, and borrow one that may satisfy you
better than I can. But above all, I pray you choose out
one that is discreet and modest, and will in no wise bring
scandal on you, nor on me neither. And may he make
you a pair of fine lads, the which I will love and rear as
my own, in such wise that all men shall think them our
own true and lawful offspring. And this is the more
possible, seeing I have still in me some show of vigour and
strength, and appearance enough of bodily manhood to
make folk suppose them mine."

I leave you to suppose whether the fair girl was glad
to receive this agreeable little homily, and free leave to
enjoy such pleasing liberty. This she did turn to such
good account that in a twinkling she did people the house
with two or three fine infants, wherein the husband, inasmuch as he did touch her at times and sleep with her,
might deem he had some share, and did actually think so,
and the neighbours and every one. In such wise were
both husband and wife well pleased, and had good prog-
eny, to boot.

Here again is another sort of cuckolds, they which are
made so by reason of an amiable opinion certain women
hold, to wit that there is no thing nobler and more lawful

and more commendable than Charity. And by Charity they say they mean not merely giving to the poor who have need of succour and assistance from the wealth and abundance of the rich, but likewise helping to assuage the flames of poor languishing lovers that one sees consuming with the fire of an ardent passion. "For of a truth," they declare, "what can be more charitable than to restore life to one we see dying, and to quite refresh again the man thus consuming away?" So says that brave Paladin, the Seigneur de Montauban, upholding the fair Genevra in Ariosto, who doth maintain that of rights the woman should die, which robs her lover of life, and not she who gives it him.

This did he say of a maid, and if it be true of a maid, then much more are suchlike deeds of Charity commendable in wives even more than in maids, seeing these have not their purses untied and open yet like married women, —the which, or at any rate some among them, have these same exceeding ample and well adapted to enlarge their charities!

Which doth remind me of a tale of a very fair lady of the Court, who did attire herself for a Candlemas-tide all in a dress of white damask, with all else white to match, so that naught that day did look fairer or more white. Then did the lady's lover win over one of her companions, which likewise was a very fair lady, but somewhat older and better skilled in speech, and well fitted to intercede for him. So, whenas they all three were looking at a very fine picture, wherein was depicted Charity clad all in white with a white veil, this last did say to her friend: "You do wear this day the same dress as Charity here; but seeing you do resemble her in attire, you should be like her too as concerneth your lover, there being no other thing more commendable than good pity and sweet charity, in whatsoever way it be showed forth, provided always it be with good will to help one's neighbour. Therefore be charitable; but if you have the fear of your husband and the sanctity of wedlock before your eyes, why! 'tis a vain superstition we women should never entertain, seeing how nature hath given us good things in divers sorts, not to use the same niggardly, like some vile miserly hag with her treasure hoard, but rather to distribute them generously to poor suffering mortals and men in dire straits. True it is our chastity doth resemble a treasure, which it behooves us be niggard of on base occasions; but for high and noble ones, we should dispense thereof liberally and without stint. In like wise ought we to deal with our chastity, the which we must yield up generously to folk of merit and desert, and ill-fortune to boot, but refuse to such as be vile, worthless, and such as do not stand in need. As for our husbands, truly these be fine idols, for us never to pay our vows and candles to any but them only, and never to visit other handsome images! For 'tis to God alone we do owe absolute and unbroken allegiance, and to no man."

Now this discourse was in no wise displeasing to the lady, and did much advantage the lover, who by help of a little perseverance, did presently reap the benefit thereof. Yet are Charity sermons of the sort right dangerous for the unhappy husbands. I have heard tell (I know not whether it be true, so I will not say for certain it is so), how at the beginning when the Huguenots did first establish their religion, and they would be holding their preachings at night and in secret places, for fear of being surprised, sought out and punished, whenas one day they were thus in the Rue St. Jacques at Paris, in the days of King Henri II., certain great ladies resorting thither to receive this Charity, were all but caught in the act. After the Minister had done his sermon, at the end thereof he did recommend them to be charitable; whereupon without more ado they did extinguish the lights, and on the spot each man and woman did exercise the same towards his or her brother or sister in Christ, dispensing it one to the other according to the good will and ability of each. But this I dare not assert right out, though I have been assured 'tis a true thing. Yet on the contrary 'tis very possible the whole is a mere lie and imposture.

At any rate I know this much well, how at Poitiers there dwelt at that time a certain advocate's wife, known by the name of the fair Gotterelle, whom myself have seen, which was one of the most beautiful women of her day, of the most charming grace and shape, and one of the most desirable dames in all the town at that time. Wherefore was every man fain to be making eyes at the same, and laying of his heart at her feet. She was one day at the end of sermon time handled by a round dozen of student lads, one after the other, whether in the Consistory or under some pent-house, or as I have heard some say, under a gallows in the Old Market,—at any rate without her having made one single outcry or refusal. Rather, asking only the text of the sermon for password, she did welcome them one after other right courteously, as her true brothers in Christ. This gentle alms-giving she did long continue afterward towards them, yet would she never bestow one farthing's worth on any Papist.

Yet were there sundry of that faith which, borrowing of
the Huguenot comrades the word and the jargon of their
meeting-house, did enjoy her favours. Others again
would resort to the sermonizing expressly for this cause,
and pretend to be converted, to learn the secret and so
have pleasure of this beauteous dame. I was then at
Poitiers as a student lad, and several good comrades of
mine, who had their share of her favour, did assure me
of the fact, and swear to it; moreover the general bruit
in the place did confirm the same. Verily a delectable
and charitable deed to do, and a right conscientious lady
thus to make choice and preference of her fellow religionists!

Yet another form of Charity is there, which is oft times
practised towards poor prisoners who are shut up in
dungeons and robbed of all enjoyments with women. On
such do the gaolers' wives and women that have charge
over them, or châtelaines who have prisoners of war in
their Castle, take pity and give them share of their love
out of very charity and mercifulness. Thus did a certain
Roman courtesan say once to her daughter, of whom a
gallant was deeply enamoured, but she would never bestow on him so much as a farthing's worth: *E dagli, al
manco por misericordia*,—"Well, well! do him charity then
for pity's sake."

Thus do these gaolers' wives, noble châtelaines and
others, treat their prisoners, the which, captive and unhappy though they be, yet cease not for that to feel the
prickings of the flesh, as much as ever they did in their
best days. As saith the old proverb, "Longing cometh
of lacking," so even in the straw and on the hard ground,

my lord Priapus will still be lifting his head, as well as on the best and softest bed in all the world.

Hence it cometh that beggars and prisoners, in their lazar-houses and prisons, are just as wanton as Kings, Princes and great folk in their rich Palaces and on their royal and dainty couches.

To confirm what I say, I will instance a tale that Captain Beaulieu, Captain of the King's Galleys, of whom I have before spoke once and again, did tell me. He was in the service of the late Grand Prior of France, a member of the house of Lorraine, who was much attached to him. Going one time to take his patron on board at Malta in a frigate, he was taken by the Sicilian galleys, and carried prisoner to the Castel-à-mare at Palermo, where he was shut up in an exceeding narrow, dark and wretched dungeon, and very ill entreated by the space of three months. By good hap the Governor of the Castle, who was a Spaniard, had two very fair daughters, who hearing him complaining and making moan, did one day ask leave of their father to visit him, for the honour of the good God; and this he did freely give them permission to do. And seeing the Captain was of a surety a right gallant gentleman, and as ready-tongued as most, he was able so to win them over at this, the very first visit, that they did gain their father's leave for him to quit his wretched dungeon and to be put in a seemly enough chamber and receive better treatment. Nor was this all, for they did crave and get permission to come and see him freely every day and converse with him.

And this did fall out so well that presently both the twain of them were in love with him, albeit he was not

[152]

handsome to look upon, and they very fair ladies. And
so, without a thought of the chance of more rigorous
imprisonment or even death, but rather tempted by such
opportunities, he did set himself to the enjoyment of the
two girls with good will and hearty appetite. And these
pleasures did continue without any scandal, for so fortunate was he in this conquest of his for the space of eight
whole months, that no scandal did ever hap all that time,
and no ill, inconvenience, nor any surprise or discovery
at all. For indeed the two sisters had so good an understanding between them and did so generously lend a hand
to each other and so obligingly play sentinel to one another, that no ill hap did ever occur. And he sware to
me, being my very intimate friend as he was, that never
in his days of greatest liberty had he enjoyed so excellent
entertainment or felt keener ardour or better appetite
for it than in the said prison,—which truly was a right
good prison for him, albeit folk say no prison can be
good. And this happy time did continue for the space
of eight months, till the truce was made betwixt the
Emperor and Henri II., King of France, whereby all prisoners did leave their dungeons and were released. He
sware that never was he more grieved than at quitting
this good prison of his, but was exceeding sorry to leave
these fair maids, with whom he was in such high favour,
and who did express all possible regrets at his departing.

I did ask him if ever he apprehended ill consequences,
if he were discovered. To which he made reply, he most
certainly did, yet was not afeared thereof. For at the
worst they would but have put him to death, and he had
rather have died than go back to his first dungeon.
Moreover he was afraid, if he had failed to gratify these

honourable maids, seeing they sought to him so eagerly,
that they would have conceived so sore a despite and disdain against him, that he would have gotten some worse
treatment even than afore. Wherefore, close shutting his
eyes to all consequences, he did adventure boldly on this
merry emprise.

Many another adventure of the sort is related in our
land of France, as of the Duc d'Arschot, who when a
prisoner in the Bois de Vincennes, did escape by the help
of an honourable lady; the which lady however was like
to have suffered sore for it, seeing 'twas a matter of the
King's service. And indeed suchlike deeds of charity
are blameworthy, if they do touch the general weal,
though very good and commendable, when only the individual is concerned, and the lover's life and his mistress's
only endangered. In this there is scant hurt.

I could instance many fine examples pertinent to this
matter, if I were desirous of writing a separate discourse
thereon,—and insooth 'twould be by no means an un-
amusing subject. However I will but quote the following
one, and no other beside, for the sake of telling a pleasant and classic tale.

We read in Livy how, after the Romans had utterly
destroyed the town of Capua, certain inhabitants of that
city did come to Rome to represent their unhappy state
to the Senate, and beseech the Fathers to have pity on
them. The matter was debated and amongst others
which did pronounce an opinion was M. Atilius Regulus,
who did maintain they should show no mercy whatever.
"For he could in no wise discover," he declared, "any single Capuan, since the revolting of their city, who could
be said to have displayed the least atom of friendliness

or affection for the Roman State, except only two honourable women,"—the one Vestia Oppia, an Atellane, from
the city of Atella, domiciled at Capua at the time, and the
other, one Faucula Cluvia, both of whom had been aforetime ladies of pleasure and courtesans, plying their trade
publicly in that city. The one had let never a day pass
without offering up prayers and sacrifices for the success
and victory of the Roman People, while the other had
deserved well for having by stealth succoured with victuals
the poor prisoners of war, dying of hunger and misery.

Verily good and pious deeds of Charity these! But
hereanent, a noble gentleman, an honourable lady and
myself reading of this passage of Livy together one day,
we did suddenly exclaim one to the other, how seeing
these two honourable dames had gone thus far and had
performed such good and pious offices, that doubtless they
had gone on to yet others, and had bestowed on the poor
prisoners the charity of their fair bodies. For indeed in
former days they had distributed these same alms to other
folk, being then courtesans, or mayhap being so still.
Still the book doth not say so, but leaveth this point in
doubt; yet may we guess how 'twas. But even granting
they had of yore plied this trade, but had now left it off
for some space, yet might they very well have taken it up
again, nothing being more easy and facile to do. Then
likely enough they did recognise and once again receive
some of the good lovers of their former acquaintance, and
were now ready to return once more somewhat on their
old courses. Or again 'tis quite likely that among the
prisoners, they may have seen some, hitherto unknown and
which they had never set eyes on but this once, and found
the same handsome, brave, valiant and well-liking gal-

lants, that did well deserve all their charity, and so could they do no otherwise than grant them full enjoyment of their good favours.

Thus, in whatsoever way it came about, did these honourable ladies well earn the courtesy which the Roman Commonwealth showed them, making them to recover all their goods, and assuring them the peaceable enjoyment of the same for all time. Nay! more, they did make known to them how they might ask what they would, and they should have their request. And to speak candidly, if Titus Livy had not been so reticent and unduly constrained by shamefacedness and overmodesty, he might very well have spoke right out about these ladies, and said plainly they did not grudge the favour of their fair bodies. So would this passage of History have been yet more excellent and entertaining to peruse, had he not thus docked his narrative, and left sticking at his penpoint the best part of the tale. Such was the discourse we three did hold thereon at the time.

13.

ING JOHN of France,[1] when a prisoner in England, did in like-wise receive many marks of favour from the Countess of Salisbury, and such pleasant ones that, not being able to forget the same and the titbits she bestowed on him, he did return once more to see her again, as she had made him swear and promise he would do.

Other ladies there be which are complaisant herein up to a certain point of conscience and charity. Of this sort was one which would never suffer her lover, sleep

with her as oft as he might, to kiss her the least in the
world on the lips, giving as her reason that 'twas her
mouth had made the oath of faith and fealty to her
husband, and she would fain not foul the same by way
of the very mouth that hade made and taken it. But as
for that of the body, the which had said never a word and
promised naught, this she did let him do with at his good
pleasure, and made no scruple to yield to her lover, seeing
it is not in the competence of the upper part to pledge
itself for the lower, any more than for the lower for the
upper. For that the custom of Law doth say that none
can bind himself for another without the consent and
word of either party, nor one only for the whole.

Another most conscientious and scrupulous dame, when
granting her friend enjoyment of her, would always take
the upper station and bring her man under her, never
abating one jot of this rule. For, by observing the same
straitly and regularly, she would say, if her husband or
any other did ask whether such an one had done to her,
that she could deny even on oath, and assuredly protest,
without sinning against God, that never had he done so
with her. This oath she did so emphatically make as to
quite satisfy her husband and others by dint of her confident swearing in answer to their questions. So did they
credit her in what she alleged, "yet had never the wit,"
she would say, "to demand if ever she had taken the
upper part herself; by the which question they would
have brought much scorn on me," she said, "and sore
trouble of mind."

Methinks I have before now spoke of this point; yet
cannot a man always remember everything. Moreover it

[157]

doth better accord with the matter here in hand than with other, as it seemeth me.

Commonly ladies of this sort are great liars, and speak never a word of truth. For so trained are they and broken in to lying,—and truly if they do otherwise, they are fools, and come but to ill,—to their husbands and lovers anent these matters and these changes of love, and so used to swearing they never give themselves to any but them only, that when they come to deal with other matters of consequence, of business or argument, they never do aught but lie, and no man can believe a thing they say.

Other women again I have both known and heard speak of, which would never grant their favours to their lovers but when they were with child, to the end they might not conceive. Wherein they did make great scruple so as not to falsely give their husbands a fruit that was not really theirs, and nourish, feed and bring up the same as their own. I have already spoke on this subject. However, being once pregnant, they would deem they were doing the husband no wrong nor making him cuckold by prostituting themselves.

Very like, some were used to do thus for the same reasons as moved Julia, the Emperor Augustus' daughter and wife of Agrippa, who in her time was a notorious harlot, whereat was her father more sore angered than her husband. Once being asked if that she were not afeared of being made pregnant by her lovers, and her husband noting it and being very wroth with her, she made answer: "Nay! I take good heed in this, for I do receive no man and take never a passenger in my ship, but when it is laden and carrying full cargo."

Now here we have yet another sort of cuckolds; and these same are true martyrs, they which have wives as ugly as devils in hell, who nevertheless are fain to take their share in tasting the sweets of love just as much as their fairer sisters, though these last properly do deserve this privilege alone according to the proverb: "Handsome men to the gallows, fair dames to the brothel." [2] Yet do these ugly coal-wenches play the gay woman like the rest. And they must needs be forgiven; for are they not women too, and with a like nature and complexion, only not so fair seeming. I have seen very plain women, at any rate in their youth, which did rate themselves just as highly as fairer dames, deeming that a woman is valued at just the worth she doth put upon herself and will sell herself for. Even as at a good market all sorts of wares are sold and pledged, some at a high, some at a lower rate, according to the amount of business a-doing, and the time at which one cometh to market after others, and according to the good or bad price one doth find ruling there. For, as folk say, a man goeth always to the best market, and albeit the stuff be not of the best, the price will depend on the skill of the market-man and market-woman.

So is it with plain women, of whom I have seen some that, by my troth, were as hot and lustful and as well inclined for love as the fairest, and would put themselves on the market and be as fain as any to get a good price and full value.

But the worst thing I find in them is this, that whereas the dealers make offers to the fairest, these others do make offers to the dealers and beg them to take and accept of their goods, the which they are ready to give

[159]

them for nothing or at a very low price. Nay! they
go further still; for most often they do give them money
to taste of their lecherousness and be debauched of them.
Now look at the pity of it! for in payment of such debauching no little sum of money is needed,—so much so
that it doth cost more than the person is worth. And
yet is the poor husband no less degraded and made cuckold by a plain wife, whose fare is much harder to digest
than a beautiful woman's. To say nothing of a man's
having to lie by his side a devil of hell, in place of a
beauteous angel.

Wherefore I have heard many gallant men say they
had rather have a beautiful woman, and one something
whorish, than a plain woman, though the most chaste in
all the world. For in a foul dame is to be found naught
but wretchedness and displeasure; in a fair one is abundance of all pleasure and good happiness,—as some folk
maintain. For myself I refer me to such as have trod
this roadway and path.

I have heard some men say sometimes, that for husbands it is no such grand thing for them to have their
wives chaste. For then are these so boastful of the fact,
I mean those women that do possess this most uncommon
gift, that you might almost declare them fain to dominate not alone their husbands, but the very world itself
and the stars of heaven! Nay! they seem to think, judging from their pride of chastity, that God doth owe them
some special return therefor. Yet are they greatly deceived; for I have heard learned Doctors say, how that
God doth more love a poor sinful woman, repentant and
contrite, as in the case of the Magdalene, than a prideful
and haughty dame, which doth suppose she hath surely

won Paradise, without any need for the pity and merciful judgment of God.

I have heard tell of a lady so boastful by reason of her chastity that she did come so to look down upon her husband, that when asked if she had lain with him, "No!" she would reply, "but he hath lain with me." So proud a dame was she! I leave you to imagine how these same silly, boastful, virtuous wives do chide their poor husbands, even though they may have naught really to reproach them with. So in especial do such wives as are chaste and rich likewise. A wife that is at once virtuous and wealthy in her own right, will ever be playing the disdainful, haughty, proud and bold lady towards her husband, so that by reason of the over high value she doth set on her chastity and her well guarded front, she cannot refrain her from putting on the airs of an empress and chiding her husband on his committing the smallest fault, as I have seen sundry do, and above all on his ill way of life. If he gamble, or be wasteful or extravagant, mightily doth she protest and storm, making her home to seem rather a hell upon earth than an honourable household. Then if he need to sell aught of his property to meet the cost of a journey to Court or to the wars, or of his lawsuits, necessities or minor follies and frivolous expenses, never a word must he speak thereof. For such an empire hath the wife assumed over him, resting it on the strong foundation of her virtue, that her husband must needs refer all to her judgment, as Juvenal well says in one of his Satires:

> ". . . Animus uxoris si deditus uni,
> Nil unquam invita donabis conjuge; vendes,
> Hac obstante, nihil haec, si nolit, emetur." [3]

[161]

These lines of the poet show plainly that the ancient
Roman dames were in this matter of an humour much
akin to that of many ladies of our own day. On the
contrary, when a wife is something whorish, she will show
herself far more acommodating, more yielding, docile and
timid, of a much gentler and more agreeable disposition,
more humble and ready to do aught her husband may
desire, and more complaisant to him in all things. So
have I seen some such which durst never scold or cry
out, nor show themselves cross-gained, for fear the husband should confront them with their fault and throw
their adultery in their face, and make them to feel the
consequences thereof at the cost of their life itself. Then
if the gallant fellow is fain to sell some property of theirs,
lo! their names are writ to the contract before ever the
husband have time to say the word. Many of this sort
have I seen. In one word they do what their husbands
please.

Well! are these then so sorely hurt to be made cuckold
of such fair dames, and to win of them such fine goods
and advantages as these,—to say naught of the fine,
delightsome pleasure they do enjoy in wantoning with
suchlike beauteous women, and swimming, so to speak,
with them in a beautiful, clear stream instead of a foul
and repulsive slough? And since a man must die, as a
certain great Captain I know used to say, is it not far
better for it to be by a fine fresh sword, bright, clear,
shining and keen-edged, than by an old blade, all rusted
and ill burnished, one calling for more emery than all
the sword-cutlers of Paris together could furnish?

And what I say of young women that are plain, I say
the like of some old women, the which are fain to be

[162]

debauched and be kept clean and bright by use, just as much as the fairest in all the world. Elsewhere do I give a special Discourse to this subject (the Fifth Discourse, following). And this is the worst of it: when their husbands cannot fulfil the duty, then the rogues will be calling in substitutes, being every bit as passionate as younger women, or even more so. So have I seen some that neither at the beginning nor the middle of life are ready to be excited, but only at the end. And rightly do men say that in these matters the end is more fierce than the two other ages, the beginning and the middle,— so far as wishing goes. For very often strength and competence are then lacking, a thing that doth vex them sore,—as saith the old proverb: 'Tis great grief and pain, when a backside hath right good will, but power is a-wanting.

So are there always some of these poor old wretches, which do admit their lovers gratis, like a muleteer on his beast, and do distribute their largess at the expense of their two purses; but 'tis the money purse only makes these find the other, the body's purse, good and narrow. Thus we say that liberality is more to be esteemed in all matters than avarice and niggardliness, except only with women, who, the more liberal they are, the less are they esteemed, but the avaricious and niggard all the more for being so.

This was what a great Lord did say one time of two great ladies, sisters, whom I know of, whereof the one was niggard of her honour, but liberal of her purse and expenditure, the other exceeding chary of her purse and money, but very liberal of her person.

Next there is yet another sort of cuckolds, one that of

[163]

a surety is utterly abominable and hateful before God
and man alike, they who, enamoured of some handsome
Adonis, do abandon their wives to men of this kind in
order to enjoy their favour in return.

The first time ever I was in Italy, I did hear of an
example of this at Ferrara, the tale being told me of
one who, captivated by a certain handsome youth, did
persuade his wife to accord her favours to the said young
man, who was in love with her, and to appoint a day and
consent to do all he should bid her. The lady was willing
enough, for truly she did desire no better venison to
regale herself withal than this. At length was the day
fixed, and the hour being come when the young lover and
the lady were at their pleasant game and entertainment,
lo! the husband, who was hid near at hand, according
to the compact betwixt him and his wife, did rush in.
So catching them in the very act, he did put his dagger
to the lover's throat, deeming him worthy of death for
such offence, in accordance with the laws of Italy, which
herein be something more rigorous than in France. So
was he constrained to grant the husband what he did
desire, and they made exchange one with the other. The
young man did prostitute himself and the husband did
abandon his wife to the young man. Thus was the husband cuckold after an exceeding foul fashion.

I have heard tell of a lady, which being desperately
in love with an honourable gentleman whom she had taken
for lover and chief favourite, and this latter fearing the
husband would do him or her some ill turn, did comfort
him, saying, "Nay! have no fear, for he would in no
wise dare do aught, for dread I should accuse him of
having wished to practice the backdoor Venus, which

[164]

might well bring about his death, if I were to breathe the
least word thereof and denounce him to justice. But in
this way I do hold him in check and in terror, so that
for fear of my accusation, he dares not say one word
to me."

Without a doubt such accusation would have involved
the poor husband in naught less than peril of his life;
for the legists declare that this act is punishable for the
mere wish to commit the same. But mayhap the lady
did never mean to let out the word altogether, and would
not have gone so far as this without reconsidering her
intent.

I have been told how in one of these latter years a
young French gentleman, a handsome gallant that had
been seen many a day at Court, being gone to Rome
for instruction in manly exercises, like others his contemporaries, was in that city regarded with so favourable
an eye, and did meet with such great admiration of his
beauty, as well of men as of women, that folk were ready
almost to force him to their will. And so whenever they
were aware of his going to Mass or other place of public
assemblage, they would never fail, either men or women,
to be there likewise for to see him. Nay, more, several
husbands did suffer their wives to give him love assignations in their houses, to the end that being come thither
and then surprised, they might effect an exchange, the
one of his wife, the other of him. For which cause he was
advised never to yield to the love and wishes of these
ladies, seeing the whole matter had been contrived and
arranged merely to entrap him. And herein he did show
himself wise and did set his honour and good conscience
above all such detestable pleasures, winning thereby a

[165]

high and worthy repute. Yet at the last his squire did kill him. Divers reasons are given therefor. At any rate 'twas a sore pity, for that he was a very honourable young man, of good station, and one that did promise well of his nature as well by reason of his noble actions as of the fine and noble character he did manifest herein. For indeed, as I have heard a very gallant man of my time say, and as is most true, never yet was *bougre* or catamite a brave, valiant and generous man but only the great Julius Cæsar, seeing that by divine permission and ordinance all such abominable folk are brought low and reduced to shame. And this doth make me wonder how sundry, whom I have seen stained by this horrid vice, have yet prospered under heaven in high good fortune; yet doth God wait for them, and at the last we shall surely see them meet their proper fate.

How many women there be in the world, which if they were examined by midwives and doctors and expert surgeons, would be found no more virgin one way than another, and which could at any moment bring action against their husbands. Yet do they dissimulate it and dare not discover the matter, for fear of bringing scandal on themselves and their husbands, or perhaps because they do find therein some greater pleasure than we can suppose. Or it may be for the purpose I have above named,—to keep their husbands in such subjection, if they do make love in other quarters, which indeed some husbands do on these terms allow them to do. Yet are none of these reasons really sufficient to account for the thing.

The *Summa Benedicti* saith: If the husband chooseth thus to take his part contrary to the order of nature, he commits a mortal sin; and if he maintain that he may dispose of his own wife as he please, he doth fall into a detestable and foul heresy of sundry Jews and evil Rabbis, which are cited as saying thus, *duabus mulieribus apud synagogam conquestis se fuisse a viris suis cognitu sodomitico cognitas, responsum est ab illis Rabinis: virum esse uxoris dominum, proinde posse uti ejus utcumque libuerit, non aliter quam qui piscem emit: ille enim, tam anterioribus quam posterioribus partibus, ad arbitrium vesci posse.*

This have I quoted only in Latin, forasmuch as it soundeth ill to honourable and modest ears. Abominable wretches that they be,—thus to desert a fair, pure and lawful habit, to adopt instead one that is foul, dirty, filthy and forbid, and disgraceful to boot.

But if the man will take the woman so, it is lawful for her to separate from him, if there is no other means to cure him. And yet, it is stated again, such women as fear God ought never to consent thereto, but rather cry out for help, regardless of the scandal which might so arise, and of dishonour and the fear of death; for 'tis better, saith the law, to die than to consent to evil. The same book doth say another thing which I deem very strange: that whatsoever way a husband know his wife, provided she may conceive thereby, herein is no mortal sin, but only a venial one. Nor do these same smack at all of marital purity, albeit, as I have before said, it may be permissible in case of pregnant women, as well as such as have a strong and unpleasant breath, whether from the mouth or nose. Thus have I known and heard speak of several women to kiss whom and scent their breath was as bad as smelling at a sewer; or to put it another way, I

[167]

have heard it said of a certain great lady, a very great one indeed I mean, that once one of her ladies declared her breath stank more than a backhouse. These are the very words she used.

I would say more of this, but in truth I have a horror of speaking thereof at all. It hath vexed me to have said so much as I have; but 'tis needful sometimes to lay open public vices in order to reform the same.

14.

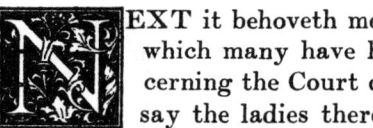EXT it behoveth me to mention an ill opinion which many have held and do still hold concerning the Court of our French Kings. Men say the ladies thereof, both maids and wives, do oft times trip, indeed do so customarily. But in this are they very much deceived, for truly there be amongst these very chaste, honourable and virtuous women, nay! even more than elsewhere. Virtue doth reside there just as much, or more than in other places,—a fact we should duly prize, for that it can readily be put to proof.

Je n'alléguerai que ce seul exemple de Mme. la grande-duchesse de Florence d'aujourd'hui, de la maison de Lorraine, laquelle étant arrivée á Florence le soir que le grand-duc l'épousa, et qu'il voulut aller coucher avec elle pour la dépuceler, il la fit avant pisser dans un bel urinoir de cristal, le plus beau et le plus clair qu'il put, et en ayant vu l'urine, il la consulta avec son médecin, qui était un très grand et très savant et expert personnage, pour savoir de lui, par cette inspection, si elle était pucelle oui ou non. Le médecin l'ayant bien fixement et doctement inspectée, il trouva qu'elle était telle comme

quand sortit du ventre de sa mère, et qu'il y allât hardi-
ment, et qu'il n'y trouverait point le chemin nullement
ouvert, frayé ni battu; ce qu'il fit, et en trouva la vérité
telle et puis.

Then next morning, in amaze, he did exclaim thus:
"Lo and behold, a miracle,—that the girl should thus
have come forth a virgin from yonder Court of France!"
Truly a curious investigation, and a strange opinion!
I know not if the tale be true, but it hath been confidently
affirmed to me as being so.

A fine repute for our Court. But indeed 'tis no long
while since men generally held that all the ladies of the
Court and of Paris city were not so virtuous of their
body as they of the open countryside, and such as never
left their homes. There have been men known so scrupulous they would never wed with girls or women which had
travelled far afield, and seen the world, be it ever so little.
Thus in our native Guyenne, in the days of my youth, I
have heard not a few gallant gentlemen say this and seen
them swear to the same, that they would never wed girl
or woman which should ever have gone forth of the Port
de Pille, to journey away toward France. Poor silly
creatures surely herein, albeit wise and gallant men
enough in other matters, to suppose that cuckoldry did
never abide in their own houses, at their hearths and in
their closets and bedchambers, just as readily,—or mayhap more so, seeing the easy opportunities,—as in the
Royal Palaces and the great Royal towns! For could
not lovers well enough come thither to suborn, win over,
court and undo their wives for them, when they were
themselves away at Court, at the wars, or the chase,
attending their law business or on their journeyings

[169]

abroad? This they would never understand, but were so
simple as to think men would never dare to say one word
of love to their ladies, but speak only of their households,
gardens, hunting and hawking parties. And so by such
blindness and rash confidence they did get themselves
cuckolded even more freely than elsewhere; for there is no
spot where a fair and clever woman, and an honourable
and gallant man, cannot find room and convenience for
love-making. Poor fools and idiots that they were! could
they not realize how that Venus hath no fixed and special
place of abode, as of old in Cyprus, at Paphos and
Amathos, and see that she doth dwell everywhere, yea!
even in the very herdsmen's cots and the lowly lap of
shepherdesses the most simple seeming?

Since some while now have they begun to abandon
these silly prejudices. For, having observed that in all
parts was risk of this same unhappy cuckoldry, they
have of late taken wives wherever they have pleased or
been able. Nay! they have gone yet further; for they
have sent them or taken them with them to Court, to let
their beauty be manifest and have full appreciation, and
so strike envy to the heart of all and sundry,—as if for
the very end of getting themselves a set of horns!

Others again do nowadays send their wives, or take
the same along with them, to plead and influence by their
solicitations their suits at law; whereof some really and
truly have no law business at all, but do make pretense
they have. Or else, if they really have some case toward,
they will wilfully prolong the same, the better to prolong
their amours. Nay! sometimes husbands will actually
leave their wives on duty at the Courts, in the galleries
and great Hall thereof, and so away to their own homes,

deeming these will better do their business for them, and
they will win their cause better so. And in truth I do
know of several which have so won them, more by the
dexterity and delights of their wives' fore parts than by
any claim of justice on their side. And so many a time
will the wives be gotten with child at this game, and then
to avoid scandal,—drugs having failed of their efficacy
to preserve them therefrom,—will speedily hie away home
to their husbands, feigning they are going thither to look
up titles or documents of the which they stand in need,
or to institute some enquiry, or else that 'tis to await
Martinmas and the re-opening of the Courts, and that
being unable in vacation time to make any progress
in their suit, they are fain to have a bout of the male and
see their households again and husbands. And so they
do in sooth, but they were well in child, ere ever they
began!

I appeal to many a learned judge and presiding mag-
istrate as to the fine tit-bits these same have enjoyed
from time to time of country gentlemen's wives.

'Tis no long while since a very fair, great and honourable lady, which myself have known, going in this wise
to forward her case at the Paris Courts, one seeing it
did say, "Why! what doth she think to do? She will
surely lose, for she hath no great claim of right and
justice." But, tell me, doth not her right and justice
lie in the beauty of her fore part, even as Cæsar did bear
his on the pommel and point of his sword?

Thus are country gentlemen cuckolded by the men of
the Law, in revenge for the cuckoldries they themselves
commit on judges' and magistrates' good ladies. And indeed some of these last I have seen who have been a fair

[171]

match, when all charms were displayed, for many wives and daughters of Lords, Knights and high-born gentlemen of the Court and other such.

I knew once a great lady, which had been very fair, but years had worn out her beauty. Having a law case at Paris, and seeing her beauty was no more meet to help her to forward and win her process, she did take with her a certain neighbour of hers, a young and pretty woman. And to this end she did supply her with a good sum of money, as much as ten thousand crowns; and so what she could not herself do, willing as she would have been, in this she did find her advantage, and the young lady to boot, and both the twain were well pleased.

'Tis no long while since I saw a mother take thither one of her daughters, albeit she was a married woman, to help her forward her case, having no other business there at all. And truly she is a very fair lady, and well worth a man's while to listen to.

However 'tis high time I should make an end in this my grand discourse concerning cuckoldry. For at the last would my long periods, tossed to and fro in these deep waters and mighty torrents, be clean drowned; and I should never have done, or have wit enough to get me out of the thing, no more than out of that Labyrinth of yore, though I should have the longest and strongest thread was ever in this world for guide and safe conduct.

Finally I will conclude by saying this, that if we are the cause of many ills, and do give torments, martyrdoms and evil times to the poor cuckolds, still we do verily pay for the same through the nose, as the saying is, and are mulcted in a triple interest. For verily the more part of them that do them wrong and make unlawful love, the more part of the same gallants, do endure quite as great ills as they inflict, seeing all the jealousies they are liable to, not less from their rivals in the pursuit than from the husbands themselves. Then consider the anxieties and caprices they have to put up with, the risks they run of danger and death, of maiming and wounds, of affronts, insults, quarrels, terrors, pains and penalties of every kind. Think how they must needs endure cold and wet, wind and heat. I say naught here of pox and chancres, all the plagues and diseases they incur at this game, as much with high-born dames as with those of low degree. Thus it is that many and many a time they buy right dear what is granted them, and the game is truly not worth the candle.

Yea! many such have we seen perish miserably, at the very time they were set forth on their way to conquer a whole kingdom. Witness M. de Bussi, the paragon of his day, and many another.

Of such I could cite an host more; but I will leave them unnamed, to the end I may have done, only admonishing lovers and advising them to practise the Italian proverb which saith, *Che molto guadagna chi putana perde!* (He who loseth an harlot, gaineth much).

Amé, Count of Savoy, was often used to say:

> En jeu d'armes et d'amours
> Pour une joye cent doulours.
> ("In the sport of arms and of love,
> for one joy an hundred dolours.")

using this quaint old word, the better to make out his rhyme. Another saying of his was, that love and anger had this point of great unlikeness one with the other,

[173]

that whereas anger doth pass away soon and very readily from the person affected, love doth so only with the extreme of difficulty.

And this is why we should guard well against love of this sort for that it doth cost us quite as much as it is worth, and doth often lead to great ill fortunes. And to speak the real truth, the more part of patient and contented cuckolds have an hundred fold better time, if only they have the wit to recognise their position and come to an agreement with their wives, than have the active agents. Yea! and many an one have I seen, though his horns were in question, would make mock at us and laugh at all the humours and pretty speeches of us gallants in converse of love with the wife. The same again when we had perchance to do with wily dames, who do make an understanding with their husbands and so sell us. So I knew once a very brave and honourable gentleman, who had long loved a certain fair and honourable lady and had had of her the enjoyment he had been fain of for so long. But one day having observed that the husband and she were making merry at some peculiarity of his, he did take the thing in such dudgeon that he did leave her, and for good; for taking a long journey for to divert his thoughts, he did never speak to the lady again, so he told me. And truly suchlike wily, cunning and fickle dames must be guarded against, as they were savage beasts; for to content and appease their husbands, they will quit their old lovers, and thereafter again take other ones, being in no wise able to do without them altogether.

So too I have known a very honourable and great lady, which yet had this ill fortune with her, that of five or six lovers I have seen her have in my day, all died one after the other, not without sore grief on her part therefor. Wherefore did men say of her how that she was Sejanus' horse, seeing all they which did mount her did die, and scarce ever survived. Yet had she this good in her and this merit, that whosoever it may have been, she was never known to change or abandon any of her good friends and lovers while yet living, for to take others instead. Only when they did come to die, she was ever eager to have a new mount, to the end she might not go a-foot. Moreover, as the lawyers themselves maintain, 'tis allowed to adopt any protector one may choose for one's estate and lands, whenas they are deprived of their first master. Such constancy in this fair lady was much to be commended; but albeit *she* was so far firm in her good faith, yet have there ever been an host of other dames that have been far from so constant.

Besides, to speak candidly, 'tis never advisable to grow old in one and the same spot, and no man of spirit ever doth so. A man must be a bold adventurer and ever be turning him this way and that, just as much in love as in war and in other matters. For verily if a sailor do trust to but one anchor in his ship, if he drag this, he is very likely to lose his vessel, especially if it be in an exposed place and in a storm, where squalls and tempestuous waves are more like to occur than in a calm and in harbour.

And in what more dangerous and exposed waters could a man adventure himself and sail forth than in making love to one fair lady only? For though of herself she may not have been wily and cunning at the beginning, yet we men do soon make her so and sharpen her wits by the many strange tricks we play with her, whereby we

[175]

do often hurt ourselves, by making her able to carry the war into our own country, having fashioned and trained her thereto. So is it better far, as a certain gallant gentleman was used to say, to wed some fair and honourable dame, albeit with the risk of having a touch of the horns and suffering this misfortune of cuckoldry that is common to so many, rather than to endure so many hardships and perils in the making of other folks cuckold.

However this is all contrary to the opinion expressed by M. du Gua, to whom one day I did make a proposition on the part of a certain great lady which had begged me so to do, to marry him. But he did make this answer only, that heretofore he had ever deemed me one of his best friends, but that now I did make him think himself deceived in this, by my holding such language to him, trying to hunt him into the very thing he most did hate, that is to get him to marry and be cuckolded, in lieu of his making other men so. He did further say he could always wed plenty of women every year, speaking of marriage as an hidden prostitution of a man's repute and liberty, ordained by a specious law. Moreover that the worst of it was, this, as myself also do see and have noted to be the case, that the more part, nay! all, of them that have thus taken delight in making other folks cuckold, when themselves come to wed, infallibly do they fall into the married, I mean the cuckolded, state. Never yet have I known it fall out otherwise, according to the word, "As thou shalt do to others, so shall it be done unto you."

Before making an end, I will say yet one word more,—how that I have seen a dispute raised that is still undecided, to wit, in which provinces and regions of our Christendom and Europe there be most cuckolds and

[176]

harlots? Men declare that in Italy the ladies are exceedingly hot, and for that cause very whorish, as saith M. de
Bèze[1] in a Latin Epigram, to the effect that where the
sun is hot and doth shine with most power, there doth
it the most heat women, inditing a verse thus conceived;

Credible est ignes multiplicare suos.

('Tis to believed he doth there multiply their fires.)

Spain is in the like case, though it lie more to the Westward; yet doth the sun there warm fair ladies as well as
ever it can in the East.

Flemish, Swiss, German, English and Scotch women,
albeit they dwell more to the Northward and inhabit cold
regions, share no less in this same natural heat; and indeed
I have known them as hot as dames of any other land.

The Greeks have good reason to be so, for that they
are well to the Eastward. So in Italy men do pray for
Greca in letto,—or "a Greek bedfellow." And in sooth
they do possess many attractive points and merits, as is
but to be expected, seeing in times of old they were the
delight of all the world, and have taught many a secret
to the ladies of Italy and Spain, from ancient times even
to the present day,—so much so that these do well nigh
surpass their teachers, whether ancient or modern. And
verily was not the Queen and Empress of all harlots,
which was Venus, a Greek?

As for my fair countrywomen of France, in old days
they were notoriously very coarse and unrefined, contenting themselves with doing of it in a coarse, rude fashion.
But, beginning some fifty years since, they have borrowed
so much and learned from other nations so many gentle
ways, pretty tricks, charms and attractions, fine clothes,

[177]

wanton looks, or else themselves have so well studied to
fashion themselves therein, that we are bound to say that
they do now surpass all other women in every way. So,
as I have heard even men of foreign nations admit, they
are better worth a man's having than any others, not to
mention that naughty words in French are more naughty,
better sounding and more rousing, than in any other
tongue.

Over and above all this, that excellent liberty we have
in France, a thing more to be esteemed than aught else,
doth surely make our women more desirable and lovable,
more easy of access and more amenable, than they of any
other nation. Again adultery is not so constantly punished as in other lands, by the good wisdom of our noble
Councils and French law-makers, which seeing abuses to
arise by reason of such harsh punishments, have something checked the same, and corrected the rigorous laws
of a former day, passed by men which herein did allow
themselves full license of merry disport, but deprived
women altogether of the same privilege. Thus was it not
allowed to an innocent woman to accuse her husband of
adultery, by any laws imperial or canon, as Cajetan doth
assure us. But truly cunning men did make this rule for
the reasons named in the following Italian verses:

> Perche, di quel che Natura concede
> Cel' vieti tu, dura legge d'honore.
> Ella à noi liberal large ne diede
> Com' agli altri animai legge d'amore.
> Ma l'huomo fraudulento, e senza fede,
> Che fu legislator di quest' errore,
> Vendendo nostre forze e buona schiena,
> Copri la sua debolezza con la pena.

[178]

("Oh! over harsh law of honour, why dost thou forbid the thing that Nature urges us to do? She grants us, as to all animals, the enjoyment of love abundantly and liberally. But the base deceiver, man, knowing only too well the vigour of our loins, has established this mistaken law, so to conceal the weakness of the sexes.")

In a word, 'tis good to love in this land of France. I appeal to our authentic doctors in this science, and even to our courtesans, which will be more apt than I to elaborate subtle details thereanent. And to tell the very truth: harlots are there in all lands, and cuckolds the same, as myself can surely testify, for that I have seen all the countries I have named, and others to boot. Chastity abideth not in one quarter of the earth more than another.

15.

OW will I further ask this one question only, and never another, one which mayhap hath never yet been enquired into of any, or possibly even thought of,—to wit, whether two ladies that be in love one with the other, as hath been seen aforetime, and is often seen nowadays, sleeping together in one bed, and doing what is called *donna con donna*, imitating in fact that learned poetess Sappho, of Lesbos, whether these can commit adultery, and between them make their husbands cuckold.

Of a surety do they commit this crime, if we are to believe Martial in Epigram CXIX of his First Book. Therein doth he introduce and speak of a woman by name Bassa, a tribad, reproaching the same greatly in that men were never seen to visit her, in such wise that folk deemed her a second Lucretia for chasteness. But presently she came to be discovered, for that she was observed to be constantly welcoming at her house beautiful women and girls; and 'twas found that she herself did serve these and counterfeit a man. And the poet, to describe this, doth use the words, *geminos committere cunnos*. And further on, protesting against the thing, he doth signify the riddle and give it out to be guessed and imagined, in this Latin line:

Hic, ubi vir non est, ut sit adulterium,

"a strange thing," that is, "that where no man is, yet is adultery done."

I knew once a courtesan of Rome, old and wily if ever there was one, that was named Isabella de Luna, a Spanish woman, which did take in this sort of friendship another courtesan named Pandora. This latter was eventually married to a butler in the Cardinal d'Armaignac's household, but without abandoning her first calling. Now this same Isabella did keep her, and extravagant and ill-ordered as she was in speech, I have oft times heard her say how that she did cause her to give her husbands more horns than all the wild fellows she had ever had. I know not in what sense she did intend this, unless she did follow the meaning of the Epigram of Martial just referred to.

'Tis said how that Sappho the Lesbian was a very high mistress in this art, and that in after times the Lesbian dames have copied her therein, and continued the practice to the present day. So Lucian saith: such is the charac-

ter of the Lesbian women, which will not suffer men at all.
Now such women as love this practice will not suffer men,
but devote themselves to other women and are called
tribads, a Greek word derived, as I have learned of the
Greeks, from τρίδω, τρίδειν, that is to say *fricare*. These
tribads are called in Latin *fricatrices*, and in French the
same, that is women who do the way of *donne con donne*,
as it is still found at the present day.

Juvenal again speaks of these women, when he saith:

> . . . frictum Grissantis adorat

talking of such a tribad, who adored and loved the embraces of one Grissas.

The excellent and diverting Lucian hath a chapter on
this subject, and saith therein how that women do come
mutually together. Moreover this name of tribad, which
doth elsewhere occur but rarely as applied to these
women, is freely employed by him throughout, and he
saith that the female sex must needs be like the notorious
Philaenis, who was used to parody the actions of manly
love. At the same time he doth add, 'tis better far for
a woman to be given up to a lustful affection for playing
the male, than it is for a man to be womanish; so utterly
lacking in all courage and nobility of character doth
such an one show himself. Thus the woman, according to
this, which doth counterfeit the man, may well be reputed
to be more valorous and courageous than another, as in
truth I have known some such to be, as well in body as
in spirit.

En un autre endroit, Lucien introduit deux dames devi-
santes de cet amour; et une demande à l'autre si une telle
avait été amoureuse d'elle, et si elle avait couché avec elle,

et ce qu'elle lui avait fait. L'autre répondit librement: "Premièrement, elle me baisa ainsi que font les hommes, non pas seulement en joignant les lèvres, mais en ouvrant aussi la bouche, cela s'entend en pigeonne, la langue en bouche; et, encore qu'elle n'eût point le membre viril et qu'elle fût semblable à nous autres, si est-ce qu'elle disait avoir de coeur, l'affection et tout le reste víril; et puis je l'embrassai comme un homme, et elle me le faisait, me baisait et allentait (je n'entends point bien ce mot), et me semblait qu'elle y prit plaisir outre mesure, et cohabita d'une certain Jaçon beaucoup plus agréable que d'un homme." Voila ce qu'en dit Lucien.

Well, by what I have heard say, there be in many regions and lands plenty of such dames and Lesbian devotees,—in France, in Italy, in Spain, Turkey, Greece and other places. And wherever the women are kept secluded, and have not their entire liberty, this practice doth greatly prevail.

The Turkish women go to the baths more for this than for any other reason, and are greatly devoted thereto. Even the courtesans, which have men at their wish and at all times, still do employ this habit, seeking out the one the other, as I have heard of sundry doing in Italy and in Spain. In my native France women of the sort are common enough; yet it is said to be no long time since they first began to meddle therewith, in fact that the fashion was imported from Italy by a certain lady of quality, whom I will not name.

Several others have I known which have given account of the same manner of loves, amongst whom I have heard tell of a noble lady of the great world, who was superlatively given this way, and who did love many

[182]

ladies, courting the same and serving them as men are
wont. So would she take them and keep them at bed and
board, and give them whatever they would. Her husband
was right glad and well content thereat, as were many
other husbands I have known, all of whom were right glad
their wives did follow after this sort of affection rather
than that of men, deeming them to be thus less wild.
But indeed I think they were much deceived; for by what
I have heard said, this is but an apprenticeship, to come
later to the greater one with men.

How many of these Lesbian dames have I seen who,
for all their customs and habits, yet fail not at the last
to go after men! Even Sappho herself, the mistress of
them all, did she not end by loving her fond, favourite
Phaon, for whose sake she died? For after all, as I have
heard many fair ladies declare, there is nothing like men.
All these other things do but serve them but in the lack of
men. And if they but find a chance and opportunity
free from scandal, they will straight quit their comrades
and go throw their arms round some good man's neck.

I have known in my time two very fair and honourable
damsels of a noble house, cousins of one another, which
having been used to lie together in one bed for the space
of three years, did grow so well accustomed to this,
that at the last getting the idea the said pleasure was
but a meagre and imperfect one compared with that to
be had with men, they did determine to try the latter,
and soon became downright harlots. And this was the
answer a very honourable damsel I knew did once make to
her lover, when he asked her if she did never follow this
way with her lady friend,—"No, no!" she replied, "I like
men too well."

[183]

I have heard of an honourable gentleman who, desiring one day at Court to seek in marriage a certain very honourable damsel, did consult one of her kinswomen thereon. She told him frankly he would but be wasting his time; for, as she did herself tell me, such and such a lady, naming her, ('twas one I had already heard talk of) will never suffer her to marry. Instantly I did recognize the hang of it, for I was well aware how she did keep this damsel at bed and board, and did guard her carefully. The gentleman did thank the said cousin for her good advice and warning, not without a merry gibe or two at herself the while, saying she did herein put in a word or two for herself as well as for the other, for that she did take her little pleasures now and again under the rose. But this she did stoutly deny to me.

This doth remind me of certain women which do thus and actually love these friends so dearly they would not share them for all the wealth in the world, neither with Prince nor great noble, with comrade or friend. They are as jealous of them as a beggarman of his drinking barrel; yet even he will offer this to any that would drink. But this lady was fain to keep the damsel all to herself, without giving one scrap to others.

'Tis said how that weasels are touched with this sort of love, and delight female with female to unite and dwell together. And so in hieroglyphic signs, women loving one another with this kind of affection were represented of yore by weasels. I have heard tell of a lady which was used always to keep some of these animals, for that she did take pleasure in watching her little pets together.

Voici un autre point, c'est que ces amours féminines se

[184]

traitent en deux façons, les unes par fricarelles, et par, comme dit ce poète, *geminos committere connos.*

Cette façon n'apporte point de dommage, ce disent aucuns, comme quand on s'aide d'instruments façonnés de . . ., mais qu'on a voulu appeler des g. . . .

J'ai ouï conter q'un grand prince, se doutant de deux dames de sa cour qui s'en aidaient, leur fit faire le guet si bien qu'il les surprit, tellement que l'une se trouva saisie et accommodée d'un gros entre les jambes, si gentiment attaché avec de petites bandelettes à l'entour du corps qu'il semblait un membre naturel. Elle en fut si surprise qu'elle n'eut loisir de l'ôter; tellement que ce prince la contraignit de lui montrer comment elles deux se le faisaient.

On dit que plusieurs femmes en sont mortes, pour engendrer en leurs matrices des apostumes faites par mouvements et frottements point naturels.

J'en sais bien quelques-unes de ce nombre, dont ç'a été grand dommage, car c'étaient de très belles et honnêtes dames et demoiselles, qu'il eût bien mieux valu qu'elles eussent eu compagnie de quelques honnêtes gentilhommes, qui pour cela ne les font mourir, mais vivre et ressusciter, ainsi que j'espère le dire ailleurs; et même que pour la guérison de tel mal, comme j'ai ouï conter à aucuns chirurgiens, qu'il n'y a rien de plus propre que de les faire bien nettoyer làdedans par ces membres naturels des hommes, qui sont meilleurs que des pessaires qu'usent les médecins et chirurgiens, avec des eaux à ce composées; et toutefois il y a plusieurs femmes, nonobstant les inconvénients qu'elles en voient arriver souvent, si faut-il qu'elles en aient de ces engins contrefaits.

—J'ai ouï faire un conte, moi étant lors à la Cour, que la reine mère ayant fait commandement de visiter un jour

[185]

les chambres et coffres de tous ceux qui étaient logés dans le Louvre, sans épargner dames et filles, pour voir s'il n'y avait point d'armes cachées et même des pistolets, durant nos troubles, il y en eut une qui fut trouvée saisie dans son coffre par le capitaine des gardes, non point de pistolets, mais de quatre gros g. . . . gentiment façonnés, qui donnèrent bien de la risée au monde, et à elle bien de l'étonnement.

Je connais la demoiselle : je crois qu'elle vit encore ; mais elle n'eut jamais bon visage. Tels instruments enfin sont très dangereux. Je ferai encore ce conte de deux dames de la cour qui s'entr'aimaient si fort et étaient si chaudes à leur métier, qu'en quelque endroit qu'elles fussent ne s'en pouvaient garder ni abstenir que pour le moins ne fissent quelques signes d'amourettes ou de baiser ; qui les scandalisaient si fort et donnaient à penser beaucoup aux hommes. Il y en avait une veuve, et l'autre mariée ; et comme la mariée, un jour d'une grande magnificence, se fut fort bien parée et habillée d'une robe de toile d'argent, ainsi que leur maîtresse était allée à vêpres, elles entrèrent dans son cabinet, et sur sa chaise percée se mirent à faire leur fricarelle si rudement et si impétueusement qu'elle en rompit sous elles, et la dame mariée qui faisait le dessous tomba avec sa belle robe de toile d'argent à la renverse tout à plat sur l'ordure du bassin, si bien qu'elle se gâta et souilla si fort qu'elle ne sut que faire que s'essuyer le mieux qu'elle put, se trousser, et s'en aller en grande hâte changer de robe dans sa chambre, non sans pourtant avoir été aperçue et bien sentie à la trace, tant elle puait : dont il en fut ri assez par aucuns qui en surent le conte ; même leur maîtresse le sut, qui s'en aidait comme elle, et en rit son saoul. Aussi il fallait bien que cette ardeur les maît-

[186]

risât fort, que de n'attendre un lieu et un temps à propos, sans se scandaliser.

Still excuse may be made for maids and widows for loving these frivolous and empty pleasures, preferring to devote themselves to these than to go with men and come to dishonour, or else to lose their pains altogether, as some have done and do every day. Moreover they deem they do not so much offend God, and are not such great harlots, as if they had to do with the men, maintaining there is a great difference betwixt throwing water in a vessel and merely watering about it and round the rim. However I refer me to them; I am neither their judge nor their husband. These last may find it ill, but generally I have never seen any but were right glad their wives should be companionable with their lady friends. And in very deed this is a very different thing from that with men, and, let Martial say what he please, this alone will make no man cuckold. 'Tis no Gospel text, this word of a foolish poet. In this at any rate he saith true, that 'tis much better for a woman to be masculine and a very Amazon and lewd after this fashion, than for a man to be feminine, like Sardanapalus or Heliogabalus, and many another their fellows in sin. For the more manlike she is, the braver is she. But concerning all this, I must refer me to the decision of wiser heads.

Monsieur du Gua and I were reading one day in a little Italian book, called the *Book of Beauty*, writ in the form of a dialogue by the Signor Angelo Firenzuola, a Florentine, and fell upon a passage wherein he saith that women were originally made by Jupiter and created of such nature that some are set to love men, but others the beauty of one another. But of these last, some purely

[187]

and holily, and as an example of this the author doth
cite the very illustrious Marguerite of Austria, which
did love the fair Laodamia Fortenguerre, but others
again wantonly and lasciviously, like Sappho the Lesbian, and in our own time at Rome the famous courtesan
Cecilia of Venice. Now this sort do of their nature hate
to marry, and fly the conversation of men all ever they
can.

Hereupon did Monsieur du Gua criticise the author,
saying 'twas a falsehood that the said fair lady, Marguerite of Austria, did love the other fair dame of a
pure and holy love. For seeing she had taken up her
rather than others which might well be equally fair and
virtuous as she, 'twas to be supposed it was to use her for
her pleasures, neither more nor less than other women
that do the like. Only to cover up her naughtiness, she
did say and publish abroad how that her love for her
was a pure and holy love, as we see many of her fellows
do, which do dissemble their lewdness with suchlike words.

This was what Monsieur du Gua did remark thereanent; and if any man doth wish to discuss the matter
farther, well! he is at liberty to do so.

This same fair Marguerite was the fairest Princess
was ever in all Christendom in her day. Now beauty and
beauty will ever feel mutual love of one sort or another,
but wanton love more often than the other. She was
married three times, having at her first wedlock espoused
King Charles VIII. of France, secondly John, son of the
King of Aragon, and thirdly the Duke of Savoy, surnamed the Handsome. And men spake of them as
the handsomest pair and fairest couple of the time in
all the world. However the Princess did have little

[188]

profit of this union, for that he died very young, and at the height of his beauty, for the which she had very deep sorrow and regret, and for that cause would never marry again.

She it was had that fair church [2] built which lyeth near Bourg en Bresse, one of the most beautiful and noble edifices in Christendom. She was aunt to the Emperor Charles, and did greatly help her nephew; for she was ever eager to allay all differences, as she and the Queen Regent did at the treaty of Cambrai, whereunto both of them did assemble and met together there. And I have heard tell from old folk, men and women, how it was a beauteous sight there to see these two great Princesses together.

Cornelius Agrippa hath writ a brief Treatise on the virtue of women, and all in panegyric of this same Marguerite. The book is a right good one, as it could not but be on so fair a subject, and considering its author, who was a very notable personage.

I have heard a tale of a certain great lady, a Princess, which among all her maids of honour did love one above all and more than the rest. At first were folk greatly surprised at this, for there were plenty of others did surpass her in all respects. But eventually 'twas discovered she was a hermaphrodite.

I have heard a certain great lady also named as being hermaphrodite. She hath a virile member, but very tiny; yet hath she more of the woman's complexion, and I know, by having seen her, she is very fair. I have heard sundry famous doctors say they have seen plenty such.

Well, this is all I shall say on the subject of this Chapter, one I could have made a thousand times longer

[189]

than I have done, having matter so ample and lengthy, that if all the cuckold husbands and their wives that do make them so, were to hold hands, and form a ring, I verily believe this would be great enough to surround and encircle a good half of the globe.

In the days of the late King Francis an old song was current, which I have heard a very honourable and venerable dame repeat, to the following effect:

> Mais quand viendra la saison
> Que les cocus s'assembleront,
> Le mien ira devant, qui portera la bannière;
> Les autres suivront après, le vostre sera au derrière.
> La procession en sera grande,
> L'on verra une très longue bande.

(But when the season shall come that the cuckolds shall muster, then mine shall march in front, and shall bear the banner; the rest shall follow after, while yours shall bring up the rear. A grand sight will the procession of them be,—a long, long train!)

Yet would I not inveigh over much against honourable and modest wives, which have borne themselves virtuously and faithfully in the fealty sacredly sworn to their husbands; and I do hope anon to write a separate chapter to their praise, and give the lie to Master Jean de Meung.[3] Now this poet in his *Roman de la Rose* did write these words: Toutes vous autres femmes . . .

> Estes ou fustes,
> D'effet ou de volonté, putes.

(Ye women every one are, or have been, mere whores, if not in deed, then in desire.)

By these verses he did incur such ill will on the part of the Court ladies of that day, that by a plot sanctioned

of the Queen and with her privity, these did undertake
one day to whip the poet, and did strip him stark naked.
But as all stood ready to strike, he did beseech them
that at any rate the greatest whore of all should begin
first. Then each for very shame durst not strike first;
and in this wise he did escape the whip. Myself have
seen the story represented in an old tapestry among the
ancient furnishings of the Louvre.

16.

O less do I admire a certain Preacher, who one
day preaching to a worthy company, and tak-
ing occasion to reprove the habits of some
women and of their husbands which did en-
dure to be cuckolded of them, did of a sudden set to and
shout out: "Yes, I know them well, I can see them, and I
am going to throw these two stones at the heads of the
biggest cuckolds in the assembly." Then as he did make
pretence to throw them, there was never a man in all the
congregation but did duck his head, or put up his cloak,
or his cape, or his arm, before his face, for to ward off the
blow. But the divine, rebuking them, cried, "Did I not
tell you? I did suppose there might be two or three cuckolds in my congregation; but lo! by what I see, there is
never a man but is one."

Still, let these wild talkers say what they will, there be
many very chaste and honourable women, who if they had
to give battle to their opposites, would gain the day, not
for their numbers but their virtue, which doth resist and
easily subdue its contrary.

Moreover when the aforenamed Jean de Meung doth

blame those women which are "whores, in desire," meseems he ought rather to commend and extol such to the skies, seeing that if they do burn so ardently in their body and spirit, yet put no wrong in practice, they do herein manifest their virtue, and the firmness and nobility of their heart. For they do choose rather to burn and consume away in their own fire and flame of desire, like that rare and wondrous bird the phœnix, than forfeit and stain their honour. Herein they do resemble the white ermine, which had rather die than foul itself,—'tis the device of a very great lady I knew at one time, yet but ill carried out by her,—seeing how, it being in their power to apply the remedy, yet do they so nobly refrain, and seeing there is no greater virtue nor no nobler victory than to master and subdue one's own nature. Hereanent we have a very excellent story in the *Cent Nouvelles* of the Queen of Navarre, concerning that honourable lady of Pampeluna, who albeit in her heart and of desire a whore, and burning for the love of the handsome and noble M. d'Avannes, did choose rather to die in her heat of longing than seek her remedy, as she did find means to inform him in her dying words.

Most unfairly and unjustly then did this same fair and honourable lady bring to pass her own death; and, as I did hear an honourable gentleman and lady say, when discoursing on this passage, the thing was not void of offence against God, seeing she could have saved herself from death. But to so bring it on herself and precipitate it, this is rightly called suicide. And there be many of her kidney which by reason of this great continence and abstinence from the pleasures of love, do bring about their own death, both for body and spirit.

[192]

I have it from a very great physician,—and I fancy he hath given a like lesson and instruction to several honourable dames,—that the human body can scarce ever be well, unless all the parts and members thereof, from the greatest to the least, do all of them and in due accord perform those offices and functions which wise nature hath appointed them for their proper health. All must make one harmony together, like a concert of music, it being in no wise right that while some of the said parts and members are active, others be out of work. So in a commonweal must all officers, artisans, workmen and others, do their several tasks unanimously, without idling and without throwing their work the one on the other, if it is to go well and the body politic to continue healthy and entire. And so is it likewise with the human body.

Suchlike fair ladies, whores in spirit but chaste in body, do verily deserve everlasting praises. Not so they which are cold as marble, dull, slack, and stirless as a rock, and have naught of the flesh about them or any atom of feeling—though such are scarce ever really to be found. These be neither fair nor sought after of men, and may be described in the Latin poet's words,

. . . Casta quam nemo rogavit,

(Chaste, seeing no man ever solicited her favours.)

As to this, I do know a great lady, who was used to say to sundry of her companions that were fair of face, "Truly God hath done me a great grace in that he hath not made me fair like you. For then should I have loved like you, and been an harlot even as you are." Wherefore the more should men commend such women as are fair and yet chaste, seeing what their natural bent is.

[193]

Very often too are we deceived in such women. For some of them there be which, to see them so full of airs and graces, so rueful and pitiful of mien, so cold and discreet in bearing, and so straitlaced and modest in their words and severe costume, a man might well take for regular Saints and most prudish dames. Yet are the same inwardly and of heart's desire, and eke outwardly in very deed, downright fine harlots.

Others again we see which by their pleasant ways and merry words, their free gestures and worldly, modish dress, might well be deemed of dissolute manners and ready to give themselves at a moment's notice. Yet of their body will these same be highly correct and respectable dames,—in the world's eye. As to their secret life, we can only guess at the truth, so well is it hid away.

Of these things I could bring forward many and many an example, that myself have seen and heard of; but I will content me with one which Livy doth cite, and Boccaccio in even better terms, of a certain fair Roman dame, by name Claudia Quinta. This lady did ever appear abroad more than all the other Roman ladies in showy and something immodest dress, and by her gay and free bearing did seem more worldly than was meet, and so won a very ill name as touching her honour. Yet when the great day came for the welcoming to the city of the goddess Cybelé, she was cleared of all ill repute. For she had the especial honour, above all other women, to receive the image of the goddess out of the ship, to handle and convey the same to the town. At this were all men astonished, for it had been declared that the best man and the best woman of the city alone were worthy of this office. Note how folk may be deceived in women. One is bound

[194]

to know them well first, and well examine them, before judging them, one sort as much as the other.

So must I, before making an end of this subject, name yet another virtue and property cuckoldry doth contain. This I have of a very honourable and fair lady of a good house, into whose closet being one day entered in, I did find her in the very act of finishing the inditing of a Tale with her own hand. This Tale she did show me very freely, for I was one of her close friends, and she kept no secrets from me. She was very witty and ready of words, and right well endowed for love. Now the opening of the tale was after this wise:

"It doth seem," she saith, "how that among other good properties cuckoldry may bring with it, is the good and excellent knowledge won thereby as to how the wit is right pleasantly exercised for the pleasure and content of human nature. For this it is which doth watch and invent and fashion the needful artifices to succeed, whereas mere nature doth only furnish the desire and sensual appetite. And this may be hid by many ruses and cunning devices that are practised in the trade of love, which doth give horns to poor mankind. For 'tis needful to cajole a jealous, suspicious and angry husband; 'tis needful to cajole and blind the eyes of those that be most ready to suspect evil, and to turn aside the most curious from knowledge of the truth. 'Tis needful to inspire belief in good faith just where is naught but fraud, and frankness where is naught but dissimulation. In a word so many be the difficulties must be overcome to ensure success, these do far exceed what natural endowment can reach. The wit must be given full play, which doth furnish forth pleasure, and maketh more horns than ever

the body doth, which strictly speaking implanteth and
fixeth the same."

Such were the very words of the said fair lady's discourse, without any change whatsoever, which she doth
make at the beginning of her story, that she writ herself.
However she did disguise the thing under other names;
and so, following out the loves of the Lord and lady she
hath to do with, and to reach an end and proper perfection, she doth allege that the appearance of love is but
one of satisfaction and content. 'Tis altogether without
form until the entire gratification and possession of the
same, and many a time folk deem they have arrived at
this extreme, when really they are far enough from their
desire. Then for all recompense remaineth naught but
the time lost, a cause for bitter regrets. These last words
do deserve to be carefully noted and well weighed, for
they do hit the mark and afford matter for serious
thought. Still there is no other thing but the actual enjoyment in love whether for man or woman to prevent all
regrets for the past time. And for this cause the said
honourable lady did give assignation to her lover in a
wood, whither oft times she would betake her to walk in a
very fair avenue, at the entrance whereof she did leave
her women, and so went forward to find him under a fine,
spreading, shady chestnut. For it was in summer-tide.
"In the which retreat," to go on with the lady's tale in
her own words, "there is no doubt what life the twain did
lead for a space, and what a fine altar they did raise up
to the poor husband in the Temple of Ceraton (Temple
of Horns), albeit they were not in the island of Delos,
the which fane was made all of horns,—doubtless founded
by some gay and gallant fellow of yore."

[196]

This is the way the lady did make a mock of her husband, as well in her writings as also in her pleasures and in very deed. Note well all she saith, for her words do carry weight, being pronounced and writ down by so clever and honourable a dame.

The Tale in truth is right excellent, and I would gladly have copied the same and inserted it in this place. But alas! 'tis too long, for the discourse and negotiations before coming to the end they did, are finely expressed and eke lengthy. First she doth reproach her lover, who was ever praising her extravagantly, how that 'twas the effect rather of native and fresh passion in him than of any especial merit in her, albeit she was one of the fairest and most honourable ladies of the time. Then, for to combat this opinion, the lover must needs give great proofs of his love, the which are right well specified and depicted in the said Tale. Afterward, being now in accord, the pair do exhibit all sorts of ruses, trickeries and love cajoleries, both against the husband and against other folk,—all which be of a surety very excellent and very wittily conceived.

I did beseech the lady to give me a copy of the Tale. This she did very readily, and would have none copy it but herself, for fear of indiscretion; the which copy I do hold as one of my most precious possessions.

Now this lady was very right in assigning this virtue and good property to cuckoldry. For before devoting herself to love, she was not clever at all. But later, having once taken it in hand, she did become one of the most witty and clever women in all France, as well in this province as in others. And in truth she is by no means the only one I have seen which hath got good training by the

[197]

handling of love. For I have known an host of dames which were most silly and awkward at their first beginning; yet had the same not tarried a year at the school of Cupid and his lady mother Venus before they came forth thereof right clever and accomplished adepts in all ways. And for myself I have never yet seen an harlot but was right clever and well able to hold her own.

Now will I ask yet this one question more,—in which season of the year are the most cuckolds made, and which is the most meet for love, and to shake the virtue of a woman, whether wife or maid? Without a doubt common consent hath it there is never a time for this like the Spring, the which doth awaken body and spirit, both put to sleep by the wearisome, melancholic winter-tide. Seeing all birds and beasts do rejoice at this season's coming, and all betake them to love, surely mankind, which have yet stronger feelings and promptings, will experience the same even more, and womenfolk above all others,— an opinion maintained by many philosophers and wise physicians. For truly women do then entertain a greater heat and lovingness than at any other season,—as I have heard sundry fair and honourable dames say, and in especial a certain great lady, that did never miss, so sure as Spring-tide came round, to be more touched and pricked of these feelings than at any other period whatsoever. She was used to say she did feel the fresh grass springing, and did crave after the same like as mare and colts do, and she must needs taste thereof, or she should grow pined and thin. And this she did, I do assure you, and at the season did wax more lustful than ever. Thus three or four new intrigues that I have seen her enter on in her life, all these she did commence in Spring,—and not with-

[198]

out reason; for of all the months in the year, April and May be the most surely consecrate and devoted to Venus, at the which times fair ladies do set them, more than afore, to pet their bodies and deck them out daintily, to arrange their hair in wanton wise and don light raiment. And it may well be said how that these new changes in dress and ways do all aim at one and the same thing, to wit lasciviousness, and to people the earth with cuckoos a-walking about thereon, to match the winged ones that the air of heaven doth produce in these same months of April and May.

Further, 'tis not to be supposed but that fair dames, maids and widows alike, whenas they do behold in their walks abroad in their forests and woods, their warrens, parks, meadows, gardens, shrubberies and other pleasaunces, beasts and birds all a-making love together and sporting in wanton wise, should feel strange prickings in their flesh, which do make them fain to apply instant remedy for the smart. And this is just one of the persuasive and moving things that a many lovers are wont to say one to the other, when they see their mates lacking heat and flame and zest; for then do they upbraid them, pointing to the example of beasts and birds, the which whether wild or tame, as sparrows and house-pigeons, are ever at some wanton sport, ever engendering and conceiving, all nature at the work of reproduction, down to the very trees and plants. Now this is what a fair Spanish lady found one day to say to a cavalier who was over cold or over respectful: *Sa, gentil cavallero, mira como los amores de todas suertes se tratan y triumfan en este verano, y V. S. quada flaco y abatido,* that is to say, "See, Sir cavalier, how every sort of love doth prevail and triumph in this Spring-time; yet all the while you are slack and crest-fallen."

Spring-time ended doth give place to Summer, which cometh after, bringing its hot days with it. And seeing one heat doth provoke another, fair dames do thereby double theirs; and truly no refreshment can so well assuage the same as a *bain chaud et trouble de sperme venerig.* 'Tis in no wise contrary to sense for an ill to be medicined by its contrary, as like is medicined by like. For albeit a woman should bathe her every day, and every day plunge in the clearest fountain of a whole countryside, yet do this naught avail, nor yet the lightest garments ever she can don, for to give her refreshing coolness, though she tuck them up as short as she please, without ever a petticoat, as many do in hot weather. And this is just the worst of it; for in such costume are they drawn to look at themselves, and take delight in their own beauty, and pore over their own charms in the fair sunlight, and thus beholding their bodies so fair, white, smooth, plump and in good case, do of a sudden feel the heat of concupiscence and sore temptation. But indeed of such martyrs of continence mighty few have ever been known; and silly fools would they have been, had it been otherwise. And so they lie there in their fine beds, unable to endure coverlet or sheet, but tucking up their very shifts to display themselves half naked; then at daybreak, as the rising sun doth shine in on them and they come to contemplate their bodies more closely still and at their ease on all sides and in every part, they grow exceeding fain after their lovers and fondly wait their coming. And so, should these by any hap arrive at this moment, lo! they are right welcome, and very soon clipped in their

[200]

arms and close embraced. "For then," say they, "is the very best embracement and enjoyment of any hour of day or night."

None the less is there an old proverb which saith: "June and July, mouth wet and body dry;" and to these may be added the month of August likewise. The same is true also of men, who are in a parlous state when they do get overheated at these seasons, and in especial when the dog-star is in the ascendant,—a thing they should beware of. But if they *will* burn at their own candle, well! so much the worse for them! Women run no such risk, for that every month, and every season, every time and every planet, are good for them.

Then again the good summer fruits appear, that seem as if they must refresh these worthy dames. Some I have noted to eat little of these, others much. Yet for all this, scarce any change is seen in their heat, whether they eat much or little, whether they refrain altogether or eat thereof freely. For the worst of it is that, if there be sundry fruits which have power to refresh, there are many others that have just as powerful a heating effect,—to the which the ladies do most often resort, as also to sundry simples that be of their nature good and pleasant to eat in soups and salads, as for example asparagus, artichokes, morels, truffles, mushrooms, and pumpkins. Then there be sundry newfangled viands which the cooks, at their orders, do well know how to contrive and accommodate at once to their gourmandise and their wanton desires, and which doctors likewise are cunning in ordering them. But if only some wise gallant, expert in these mysteries, would undertake to complete this poor account of mine, he might well fulfil the task far better than I can.

After all these fine dainties, look to yourselves, that's all, poor lovers and husbands! Verily if you be not well prepared, you are very like to be disgraced, and find the fair ones have left you for pastures new.

Nor is this all; for to these new fruits, and herbs of garden and field, must be added great rich pasties, an invention of late times, compounded of great store of pistachio nuts, pine-seeds and other inflammatory drugs of the apothecary's store, the which Summer doth produce and give in greater abundance than Winter and the other seasons. Moreover in Summer time is there usually a greater slaughter of cockerels and young cocks; whereas in Winter 'tis rather the grown birds, that are not so good or so fitting for this as the young ones, these last being hotter, more ardent and more wanton than the other sort. Here is one, amongst many, of the good pleasures and conveniences that Summer-tide doth afford for lovers.

Now these pasties compounded in this wise of dainty trifles, of young cocks and the tips of artichokes and truffles, or other heating viands, are much used by many ladies, by what I hear said. And these same ladies, when they are eating thereof and a-fishing in the platter, putting their hand into the mess or plunging a fork therein, will bring out and clap in their mouth now an artichoke or a truffle, now a pistachio-nut or a cockscomb or other morsel, and at any of these will cry out with a look of sad disappointment, "Bah! a blank." But when they come across one of the dear cock's crests, and find these under their teeth, lo! they do exclaim, "A prize, by'r lady!" and laugh gaily. 'Tis like at the lottery in Italy;

and a man might deem they had drawn a real prize and won some rich and precious jewel.

Well! they surely owe good thanks to these same good little cockerels, which Summer doth produce,—as doth the first half of Autumn likewise, the which season I put along with Summer. The same time of each year doth give us many other sorts of fruits and small fowl that are an hundred times more hot than those of Winter-tide or the second half of Autumn, the near neighbour of chill Winter. True this is reckoned part of the season of Autumn; yet can we not gather therein all these excellent simples at their best nor aught else as in the hot time of the year. Yet doth Winter ever endeavour to supply what it may,— for instance those good thistles which do engender an excellent heat and concupiscence, whether raw or cooked, including the little hot field thistles, on the which asses live and thrive and are vigorous love-makers. These Summer doth harden and dry up, whereas Winter doth make the same tender and delicate. Exceeding good salads are made of these,—a new invented delicacy.

Furthermore, and beside all these things, so many other serviceable drugs are sought out by apothecaries, dealers and perfumers, that naught is overlooked, whether for these same pasties or for soups. And of a surety good justification may be found by women for this keeping up and maintaining of the heat in Winter time all ever they can. "For," say they, "just as we are careful to maintain the heat of the outside of the body by heavy clothing and thick furs, why shall we not do the same for the inside?" The men say on their side, "Nay! what availeth it thus to add heat to heat, like putting silk on silk, contrary to the Canons, seeing of their own selves they be

[203]

hot enough already, and that at whatsoever hour we are fain to assail them, they be always ready by their natural complexion, without resort to any artificial aid at all?" What would you have? Mayhap 'tis that they fear their hot and boiling blood will lose strength and ebb in their veins, and grow chill and icy, and if it be not kept hot, like that of an hermit that liveth on roots alone.

Well! well! let them have their way. 'Tis all good for merry gallants; for women being so constantly in ardour, at the smallest assailment of love upon them, lo! they are taken at once, and the poor husbands cuckold and horned like satyrs! Nay! sometimes they will go still further, these worthy dames, for that they do sometimes share their good pasties, broths and soups with their lovers out of compassion, to the end these may be more doughty and not find themselves overexhausted when it cometh to work, and so themselves may enjoy more exciting and abundant pleasure. Likewise will they give them receipts to have dishes compounded privately in their own kitchens. But herein have some been sore deceived and disappointed. Thus a certain gallant gentleman I have heard tell of, having in this wise taken his special soup and coming all cock-a-whoop to accost his mistress, did threat her how that he would give it her soundly, telling her he had taken his soup and eat his pasty. She did merely answer him, "Well! you shall prove your worth; at present I know naught about it." Presently, when they were now in each other's arms and at work, these dainties did but serve him poorly. Whereon the lady did declare that either his cook had compounded them ill, or had been niggardly of the drugs and ingredients needed, or else he had not made all due preparation before taking his sovran medi-

cine, or mayhap his body was for that while ill disposed
to take it and feel the proper effects thereof. Thus did
she make mock of the poor man.

Still 'tis to be remembered all simples and all drugs, all
viands and all medicines, are not suitable for all alike.
With some they will operate, while others do but draw
blank. Moreover I have known women which, eating of
these viands, when 'twas cast up to them how they would
surely by this means have extraordinary and excessive enjoyment, could yet declare, and affirm the same on oath,
that such diet did never cause them any temptation of any
sort whatever. But God wot, they must herein surely
have been playing the pretended prude!

Now as to the claims of Winter, ladies that do champion this season, maintain that for soups and hot viands,
they do know as good receipts for to make these every
whit as good in Winter time as at any other part of the
year. They do possess ample experience, and do declare
this season very meet for love-making. True it is Winter is dim and dark, close, quiet, retired and secret, yet
so must love be, and be performed in secret, in some retired and darkling spot,—whether in a closet apart, or
in a chimney corner near a good fire, the which doth engender, by keeping close thereto and for a considerable
while, as much good heat as ever the Summer can provoke. Then how it is in the dimly lit space betwixt bed
and wall, where the eyes of the company, provided they
be near the fire a-warming of themselves, do but hardly
penetrate, or else seated on chests or beds in remote cor-
ners, so to enjoy dalliance. For seeing man and maid
pressing the one to the other, folk deem 'tis but because
of the cold and to keep them warm. Yet in this wise are

[205]

fine things done, when the lights are far withdrawn on a distant table or sideboard.

Besides, which is best, Summer or Winter, when one is in bed? 'Tis the greatest delight in all the world for lovers, man and maid, to cling together and kiss close, to entwine one with other, for fear of the nipping cold, and this not for a brief space but for a long while, and so right pleasantly warm each other,—all this without feeling aught at all of the excessive heat Summer doth provoke, and that extreme of sweating that doth sore hinder the carrying out of love. For truly in Summer time, instead of embracing tight and pressing together and squeezing close, a pair must needs hold loosely and much apart. Then Winter is best in this, say the ladies, according to the doctors: men are more meet for love, more ardent and devoted thereto, in Winter than in Summer.

I knew once in former days a very great Princess, who was possessed of much wit, and both spake and wrote better than most. One day she did set herself to compose verses in favour and praise of Winter, and the meetness of that season for love. By this we may conceive herself had found it highly favourable and fitting for the same. These stanzas were very well composed, and I had them long preserved in my study. Would I had valued them more, and could find them now, to give the same here, to the end men might read therein and mark the great merits of Wintertide and the good properties and meetness for love of that season.

I knew another very high-born lady, and one of the fairest women in all the world, which being new widowed, and making pretence she cared not, in view of her new weeds and state of widowhood, to go of evenings after

[206]

supper either to visit the Court, or the dance, or the Queen's *couchée*, and was fain not to seem worldly-minded, did never leave her chamber, but suffering all and sundry of her attendants, male and female, to hie them to the dance, and her son and every soul about her, or even actually sending them thither, would retire to her secret chamber. And thither her lover of old, well treated, loved and favoured of her in her married life, would presently arrive. Or else, having supped with her, he would stay on and never leave her, sitting out a certain brother-in-law, who was much by way of guarding the fair lady from ill. So there would they practise and renew their former loves, and indulge in new ones preparatory to a second wedlock, the which was duly accomplished the following Summer. Well! by all I can see after duly considering the circumstances, I do believe no other season could have been so favourable for their projects as Winter was, as indeed I did overhear one of her dainty, intriguing maids also declare.

So now, to draw to an end, I do maintain and declare: that all seasons be meet for love, when they be chosen suitably, and so as to accord with the caprice of the men and women which do adopt the same. For just as War, that is Mars' pastime, is made at all seasons and times, and just as the God doth give his victories as it pleaseth him, and according as he doth find his fighting men well armed and of good spirit to offer battle, so doth Venus in like wise, according as she doth find her bands of lovers, men and maids, well disposed for the fray. Indeed the seasons have scarce aught to do therewith, and which of them is taken and which chosen doth make but little difference. Nor yet do their simples, or fruits, their drugs,

[207]

or drug-dealers, nor any artifice or device that women do resort to, much avail them, whether to augment their heat, or to refresh and cool the same.

For indeed, as to this last, I do know a great lady, whose mother, from her childhood up, seeing her of a complexion so hot and lecherous that it was like to take her one fine day straight on the road to the brothel, did make her use sorrel-juice constantly by the space of thirty years regularly at all her meals, whether with her meat or in her soups and broths, or to drink great two-handled bowls full thereof unmixed with other viands; in one word every sauce she did taste was sorrel-juice, sorrel-juice, everlastingly. Yet were these mysterious and cooling devices all in vain, for she ended by becoming a right famous and most arrant harlot,—one that had never need of those pasties I have spoke of above to give her heat of body, seeing she had enough and to spare of her own. Yet is this lady as greedy as any to eat of these same dishes!

Well! I must needs make an end, albeit I could have said much more and alleged many more good reasons and instances. But we must not be for ever gnawing contentedly at the same bone; and I would fain hand over my pen to another and better writer than myself, to argue out the merits of the divers seasons. I will only name the wish and longing a worthy Spanish dame did once express. The same did wish and desire it to be Winter when her love time should be, and her lover a fire, to the end that when she should come to warm herself at him and be rid of the bitter cold she should feel, he might enjoy the delight of warming her, and she of absorbing his heat as she did get warm. Moreover she would so have oppor-

[208]

tunity of displaying and exposing herself to him often and at her ease, that he might enjoy the sight of her lovely limbs hid before under her linen and skirts, as to warm herself the more thoroughly, and keep up her other, internal, fire and heat of concupiscence.

Next she did wish for Spring to come, and her lover to be a garden full of flowers, with the which she might deck her head and her beautiful throat and bosom, yea! and roll her lovely body among them between the sheets.

Likewise she did oftimes wish it to be Summer, and her lover a clear fountain or glittering stream, for to receive her in his fair, fresh waters, when she should go to bathe therein and take sport, and so fully and completely to let him see, touch over and over again, each of her lovely, wanton limbs.

Finally she did desire it to be Autumn, for him to return once more to his proper shape, and she to be a woman and her lover a man, that both might in that season have wit, sense and reason to contemplate and remember over all the by-gone happiness, and so live in these delightsome memories and reveries of the past, and inquire and discourse betwixt them which season had been most meet and pleasant for their loves.

In such wise was this lady used to apportion and adjudge the seasons. Wherein I do refer me to the decision of better informed writers than myself to say which of the four was like to be in its qualities most delightful and agreeable to the twain.

Now for good and all I do make an end of this present subject. If any will know further thereof and learn more of the divers humours of cuckolds, let him study an old song which was made at Court some fifteen or sixteen years agone, concerning cuckolds, whereof this is the burden:

Un cocu meine l'autre, et tousjours sont en peine;
Un cocu meine l'autre.

(One cuckoo maketh many, and all are in sorry case; one cuckoo many maketh.)

I beg all honourable ladies which shall read any of my tales in this chapter, if byhap they do pay any heed to the same, to forgive me and if they be somewhat highly spiced, for that I could scarce have disguised them in more modest fashion, seeing the sauce such must needs have. And I will say further I could well have cited others still more extravagant and diverting, were it not that, finding it impossible to cover the same with any veil of decent modesty, I was afeared to offend such honourable ladies as shall be at the pains and do me the honour to read my books. Now will I add but one thing further, to wit, that these tales which I have here set down are no petty stories of market-town and village gossip, but do come from high and worthy sources, and deal not with common and humble personages. I have cared not to have aught to do but only with great and high subjects, albeit I have dealt with such discreetly; and as I name no names, I think I have well avoided all scandal and cause of offence.

Femmes, qui transformez vos marys en oyseaux,
Ne vous en lassez point, la forme en est très-belle;
Car, si vous les laissez en leurs premières peaux,
Ilz voudront vous tenir toujours en curatelle,

> Et comme hommes voudront user de leur puissance;
> Au lieu qu'estant oyseaux, ne vous feront d'offense.

(Ladies fair, which do transform your husbands into birds, weary not of the task, the shape they so take is a right convenient one. For if you do leave them in their first skins, they will for ever keep you under watch and ward, and manlike will fain to use their power over you; whereas being birds, they will do you no offence.)

Another Song:

> Ceux qui voudront blasmer les femmes amiables
> Qui font secrètement leurs bons marys cornards,
> Les blasment à grand tort, et ne sont que bavards;
> Car elles font l'aumosne et sont fort charitables.
> En gardant bien la loy à l'aumosne donner,
> Ne faut en hypocrit la trompette sonner.

(They that will be blaming well meaning wives which do in secret give their husbands horns, these do much wrong by their reproaches, and are but vain babblers; for indeed such dames are but giving alms and showing good charity. They do well observe the Christian law of almsgiving,—never, like the hypocrites, sound the trumpet to proclaim your good deeds!)

An old Rhyme on the Game of Love,—found by the Author among some old papers:

> Le jeu d'amours, où jeunesse s'esbat,
> A un tablier se peut accomparer.
> Sur un tablier les dames on abat;
> Puis il convient le trictrac préparer,
> Et en celui ne faut que se parer.
> Plusieurs font Jean. N'est-ce pas jeu honneste,

[211]

Qui par nature un joueur admoneste
Passer le temps de cœur joyeusement?
Mais en défaut de trouver la raye nette,
Il s'en ensuit un grand jeu de torment.

(The game of love, whereat youth takes its delight, may be likened to a chess-board. On a chess-board we lay down the pieces,—*dames,* ladies; then 'tis the time to marshal our men, and herein we have but to make the best game we can. Many play the masterful king; and is it not merely fair play, and an abomination of dame Nature, that a man should make his game in hearty, joyous wise? But should he fail to find a sound queen (quean), why! his game is like to end in woeful pain and sorrow.[1])

SECOND DISCOURSE

On the question which doth give the more content in love, whether touching, seeing or speaking.

INTRODUCTION

HIS is a question as concerning love that might well deserve a more profound and deeper writer to solve than I, to wit: which doth afford the more contentment in the fruition of love, whether contact or attouchment, speech, or sight. Mr. Pasquier,[1] a great authority of a surety in jurisprudence the which is his especial profession, as well as in the polite and humane sciences, doth give a disquisition thereon in his letters, the which he hath left us in writing. Yet hath he been by far too brief, and seeing how distinguished a man he is, he should not in this matter have shown himself so niggard of his wise words as he hath been. For if only he had seen good to enlarge somewhat thereon, and frankly to declare what he might well have told us, his letter which he hath indited on this point had been an hundred times more delightsome and agreeable.

He doth base his main discourse on sundry ancient rhymes of the Comte Thibaut de Champagne,[2] the which verses I have never set eyes on, save only the small fragment that M. Pasquier doth quote in his letter. This same good and gallant Knight of yore doth, I conceive, write exceeding well,—not certainly in such good set terms as do our gallant poets of to-day, but still with excellent good sense and sound reason. Moreover he had a right beauteous and worthy subject, to wit the fair Queen Blanche of Castille, mother of Saint-Louis, of whom he was not little enamoured, but indeed most deeply, and had taken her for his mistress. But in this what blame or what reproach for the said Queen? Though she had been the most prudent and virtuous of women, yet could she in any wise hinder the world from loving her and burning at the fire of her beauty and high qualities, seeing it is the nature of all merit and high perfection to provoke love? The whole secret is not to yield blindly to the will of the lover.

This is why we must not deem it strange, or blame this fair Queen, if that she was too fondly loved, and that during her reign and sovereignty there did prevail in France sore divisions and seditions and much civil strife. For, as I have heard said by a very great personage, seditions be oft stirred up as much for intrigues of love as by embroilments of State; and in the days of our fathers was current an old saw, which said that: All the world went mad after the merry-hearted Queen.

I know not for sure of which Queen this word was said; but it may well be 'twas pronounced by this same Comte Thibaut, who very like, either because he was treated ill of her as concerning that he was fain of, or that his love was scorned altogether, or another preferred before him, did conceive in his heart such a disgust and discontent as did urge him to his ruin in the wars and troubles of the time.

[214]

So doth it often fall out when a fair and high-born Queen or Princess or great lady doth set her to govern a State, that every man doth love to serve her, and to honour and pay respect to her, as well for the good happiness of being agreeable to her and high in her favour, as to the end he may boast him of governing and ruling the State along with her, and drawing profit therefrom. I could allege many examples, but I had liever refrain.

Be this as it may, this Comte Thibaut did find inducement in the fair subject I have named to write excellent verses, and mayhap to pose the question which M. Pasquier doth cite for us. To this latter I do refer the curious reader, and do say naught here of rhymes good or ill; for 'twould be pure waste of words so to do. 'Twill be enough for me at this present to declare what I think thereanent, whether of mine own judgment or of that of other more experienced lovers than I.

1.

OF THE SENSE OF TOUCH IN LOVE

NOW as to touch, it must be allowed that touching is very delightsome, for that the perfection of love is to enjoy the delight thereof, and the said enjoyment cannot be had without touching. For even as hunger and thirst can in no wise be assuaged or appeased except by eating and drinking, so too doth not love pass by dint either of seeing or hearing only, but by touching, kissing and the practice of Venus' rites. To this did that witty coxcomb Diogenes the Cynic allude facetiously, yet somewhat nastily, when he said he only wished he could relieve his hunger by rubbing his belly, even as *frottant la verge* he did appease the paroxysm of desire. I would fain have put this in plainer words, but 'tis a thing must needs be passed over trippingly. He was something like that lover of Lamia, who having been too extravagantly fleeced by her to be able to enjoy her love any more, could not or would not consent to lose the pleasure of her. Wherefore he did devise this plan: he would think of her, and so thinking corrupt himself, and in this fashion enjoy her in imagination. But she hearing of this, did summon him before the Judge to render her satisfaction and payment for his enjoyment. Whereupon the Judge did order that he should but *show* her the money, whose sound and tinkle would be payment enough, and she would so enjoy the gold in imagination just as the other in dreams and fancy had had the gratification of *his* desire.

True, many other sorts of love may be alleged against what I say, the which the old philosophers do feign; but for these I do refer me to these same philosophers and the like subtle persons who will fain be discussing such points. In any case forasmuch as the fruit of mere earthly love is no other thing but enjoyment thereof, it must needs be deemed to be rightly attained only by dint of touching and kissing. So likewise have many held this pleasure to be but thin and poor, apart from seeing and speaking; whereof we have a good example in the *Cent Nouvelles* of the Queen of Navarre. An honourable gentleman, having several separate times enjoyed the favours of a certain honourable lady, at night time and disguised with a small hand-mask, (for regular masks as now used were not yet employed), in a dark, ill-lighted gallery or pas-

sage, albeit he was right well assured by the sense of
touch there was nothing here but what was good, tasty
and exquisite, yet was not content, but was fain to know
with whom he had to do. Wherefore one day as he was
a-kissing her and did hold her in his arms, he did make
a mark with chalk on the back of her gown, which was of
black velvet; and then in the evening after supper, (for
their assignations were at a certain fixed hour), as the
ladies were coming into the ball-room, he did place himself behind the door. Thus noting them attentively as
they passed in, he saw his own fair one enter with the
chalk mark on her shoulder; and lo! it was such an one as
he would never have dreamed of, for in mien and face and
words she might have been taken for the very Wisdom
of Solomon, and by that name the Queen was wont to
describe her.

Who then was thunderstruck? Who but the gentleman,
by reason of his great good fortune, thus loved of a
woman which he had deemed least like so to yield of all the
ladies of the Court? True it is he was fain to go further,
and not stop at this; for he did much desire to discover all,
and know wherefore she was so set on hiding herself from
him, and would lief have herself thus served under cover
and by stealth. But she, crafty and wily as she was, did
deny and re-deny everything, to the renunciation of her
share in Paradise and the damnation of her immortal
soul,—as is the way of women, when we will throw in their
faces love secrets they had rather not have known, albeit
we be certain of the fact, and they be otherwise most
truthtelling.

She grew angry at his persistence; and in this way did
the gentleman lose his good fortune. For good it was of

[217]

a surety, seeing the lady was a great lady and well worth winning. Moreover as she was for playing the sugared, chaste, demure prude, herein he might well have found double pleasure,—part for the sensual enjoyment of so sweet, good and delicate a morsel, part that of gazing at her oft times in company, with her demure, coy mien, her cold and modest look and her conversation all chaste, strict and precise, thinking the while in his own mind of her wanton ways, her gay abandonment and naughtiness whenas they two were alone together.

Thus we see the said gentleman was much at fault to have asked her any questions. Rather should he have steadily pursued his pleasure and eaten his meat in quiet, just as tasty without candle at all as if illuminated by all the lights of a festal chamber. Still he had a right to know who she was! and in a way his inquisitiveness was praiseworthy, seeing, as the Tale doth declare, he was afeared he had to do with some kind of demon. For devils of the sort love to change shape and take the form of women for to have intercourse with men, and do so deceive them sore. However, as I have heard sundry skilled in magic arts declare, such do find it more easy to take on the shape and countenance of a woman than to imitate her speech.

And this is why the said gentleman was right in wishing to see and know with whom he had to do; and by what he said himself, 'twas her refraining altogether from speech that did cause him more apprehension than what he saw, and did set him on thinking of the Devil. And herein he but showed a proper fear of God.

But surely, after having discovered all the truth, he should have said never a word. But, nay! another will say to this, friendship and love be not perfect but when openly declared of heart and mouth; and for this cause the gentleman would fain have told her his passion. Anyhow he did gain naught thereby; but rather lost all. Moreover by any who had known the real honour of this gentleman, he will be excused, for he was in no wise so cold or so discreet as naturally to play this game and display such overcaution; and by what I have heard my mother say, which was in the service of the Queen of Navarre, and did know sundry secrets concerning the *Nouvelles*, and was one of the devisers of this work, the hero of the Tale was my own uncle, the late M. de la Chastaigneraie, a man of a rough, ready and somewhat fickle disposition.

The Tale is so disguised however as to carefully hide who it was; for in reality the said mine Uncle was never in the service of the great Princess, the mistress of the lady in question, though he was in that of the King, her brother. And so he did continue, for he was much loved both of the King and the Princess. As for the lady, I will by no means tell her name; but she was a widow and lady in waiting to a very great Princess, and one that was better at showing the part of a prude than of a Court lady.

I have heard tell of another Court lady under our late Sovereigns, and one I do know by acquaintance, who being enamoured of a very honourable gentleman of the Court, was fain to imitate the way of love adopted by the aforenamed lady. But every time she did return from her assignation and rendez-vous, she would betake her to her chamber and there have herself examined by one of her maids or chamberwomen on all sides, to make sure she was not marked; by the which means she did guard her-

[219]

self from being discovered and recognized. Nor was she ever marked until the ninth time of meeting, when the mark was at once discovered and noted by her women. Wherefore, for dread of being brought to shame and falling into disgrace, she did break it all off, and never after returned to the tryst.

It had been better worth her while, it may be suggested, to have let her lover make these marks at his good pleasure, and then, directly they were made, have unmade and rubbed out the same. In this way she would have had double pleasure,—first of the amorous delight enjoyed, and secondly that of making mock of her man, who was so keen to discover his philosopher's stone, to wit to find out and recognize her, yet could never succeed.

I have heard tell of another in the days of King Francis in connection with that handsome Squire, Gruffy by name, which was a squire of the Stable under the said King, and died at Naples in the suite of M. de Lantric on his journey thither. The dame in question was a very great lady of the Court and did fall deep in love with him; for indeed he was exceedingly handsome, and was commonly known by no other title than *the handsome Gruffy*. I have seen the man's portrait, which doth certainly show him to have been so.

She did secretly summon one day her valet of the chamber, in whom she had trust, but yet a man unknown to most by sight, into her closet. This man she did charge to go tell Gruffy, the messenger being handsomely dressed to seem to be one of her gentlemen, that a very honourable and fair lady did send him greeting, and that she was so smit with love for him she did greatly desire his acquaintance,—more than that of any man at court. Yet must it

[220]

be under this condition that for nothing in all the wide world must he see her or discover who she was. But at the hour of retiring, and when every member of the Court should be abed, he would come for him and meet him at a certain spot he would indicate, and from whence he would lead him to the chamber of his lady. However there was yet a further condition, to wit that he was to muffle his eyes in a fair white kerchief, like a trumpet led into an enemy's city at a truce, to the end he might not see nor recognize the place and chamber wither he was to lead him, and that he was to hold him by the hands all the time to hinder him from undoing the said kerchief. For such were the conditions his mistress had ordered him to offer, to the end she might not be known of him before a certain fixed and given time which he did name and appoint to him. All which being so, he was to ponder it over and decide at leisure whether he would agree to the said conditions, and was to let the messenger know his answer the next day. For he said he would come for him then at a certain place he did name; but above all he must be alone. And he said he would take him on so good an errand he would never regret having gone on the same.

Truly an agreeable assignation, but conjoined with strange conditions! I like no less that of a Spanish lady, which did summon one to a meeting, but with the charge he should bring with him thither three S.S.S., which were to signify *sabio, solo, segreto*, "prudent, alone and secret." The other did assure her he would come, but that she should adorn and furnish herself with three F.F.F., that is she must not be *fea, flaca* nor *fria*, "ill-favoured, slack nor cold."

To return to Gruffy's story,—the go-between now left

[221]

him, having delivered his message. Who so embarrassed and full of thought as he? Indeed, he had much cause for thought, whether it were not a trick played him by some enemy at Court, to bring him into trouble,—his death mayhap or at least the King's displeasure. He pondered too what lady it could be, tall, short or of middle stature, well or ill favoured,—which last did most trouble him, though truly all cats be grey at night time, they say, and all spots alike in the dark. However, after confiding the matter to one of his intimate comrades, he did resolve to try the risk, deeming that to win the love of a great lady, which he did conclude her to be, he must suffer no fear or apprehension to stay him. Wherefore the next night, when the King, the Queen and her ladies, all the gentlemen and ladies of the Court, were retired to bed, he made no fail to be at the spot the messenger had appointed him. The latter in likewise soon came for him there with a companion to help him keep guard, if the other were followed neither by page, lackey nor gentleman. The instant he saw him, he said this only, "Come, Sir! the lady waits you." Then in a moment he bound his eyes, and did conduct him through dark, narrow places and unknown passages, in such wise that the other told him frankly he had no notion whither he was taking him. Thus did he introduce him to the lady's chamber, which was so dim and dark he could see or distinguish naught therein, no more than in an oven.

Well, there he did find the lady smelling right sweet and richly perfumed, the which made him hope for some dainty treat. Whereupon the valet did straightway make him disrobe, and himself aided him; and next led him by the hand, after taking off the kerchief from his face, to the lady's bed, who was awaiting him with right good will. Then did he lay himself down beside her, and began to caress her, in the which he found naught but what was good and delicious, as well her skin as her linen and magnificent bed, which he did explore with his hands. So with right merry cheer did he spend his night with the fair lady. I have heard her name, but will not repeat it. In a word he was well and thoroughly satisfied at all points; and recognized how he was excellently well lodged for the night. The only thing that troubled him, he said, was that he could never draw one single word out of her. She took good heed of this, seeing he was used oft times to speak with her by day, as with other Court ladies, and so would have known her voice directly. Yet at the same time, of frolickings and fondlings, handlings and caresses, and every sort of love shows and wantonness, she was most lavish; and he did find his entertainment much to his mind.

Next morning at break of day the messenger did not fail to come and wake him, make him get up, and dress him, then bind eyes as before, lead him back to the spot whence he had taken him, and commend him to God till his next return, which he promised should be soon. Nor did he omit to ask him if he had lied at all, and if he were not glad to have trusted him, and whether he thought he had showed himself a good quartermaster, and had found him good harbourage.

The handsome Gruffy, after thanking him an hundred times, bade him farewell, saying he would always be ready to come back again for such good entertainment, and would be very willing to return when he pleased. This did he, and the merry doings continued a whole month, at the end of which time it behoved Gruffy to depart on his

Naples journey. So he took leave of his mistress and bade her adieu with much regret, yet without drawing one single word from her lips, but only sighs and the tears which he did note to flow from her eyes. The end was he did finally leave her without in the least recognizing her or discovering who she was.

Since then 'tis said this lady did practice the same way of life with two or three others in similar fashion, in this manner taking her enjoyment. And some declared she was fain to adopt this crafty device, because that she was very niggardly, and in this wise did spare her substance, and was not liable to make gifts to her lovers. For in truth is every great lady bound by her honour to give, be it much or little, whether money or rings or jewels or it may be richly wrought favours. In this way the gallant dame was able to afford her person disport, yet spare her purse, merely by never revealing who she was; and by this means could incur no reproof in relation to either of her purses, whether the natural or the artificial, as she did never let her identity be known. A sorry humour truly for a high-born dame to indulge!

Some will doubtless find her method good, while others will blame her, and others again deem her a very astute person. Certain folk will esteem her an excellent manager and a wise, but for myself I do refer me to others better qualified to form a good judgement thereon than I. At any rate she can in no wise incur such severe censure as that notorious Queen which did dwell in the Hôtel de Nesle at Paris.[1] This wicked woman did keep watch on the passers-by, and such as liked her for their looks and pleased her best, whatsoever sort of folk they were, she would have summoned to her side. Then after having gotten of them what she would, she did have them cast down from the Tower, the which is yet standing, into the water beneath, and so drowned them.[2]

I cannot say for sure if this be a true tale. At any rate the common folk, at least the most of them at Paris, do declare it is. And so familiar is the tale, that if one but point to the Tower, and ask about it, they will of their own accord recount the story.

Well, let us quit these unholy loves, which be nothing better than sheer monstrosities. The better part of our ladies of to-day do abhor such, as they are surely right to do, preferring to have free and frank intercourse with their lovers and not to deal with them as though they were of stone or marble. Rather, having well and carefully chosen them, they know well how to be bravely and generously served and loved of them. Then when they have thoroughly tried their fidelity and loyalty, they do give themselves up to an ardent love with them, and take their pleasure with the same not masked, nor silent, nor dumb, nor yet in the darkness of night and mystery. Nay! but in the free and open light of day they do suffer them to see, touch, taste and kiss their fair bodies, entertaining them the while with fine, lecherous discourse, merry, naughty words and wanton conversation. Yet sometimes will they have recourse to masks; for there be ladies which are at times constrained to wear them when a-doing of it, whether it be on account of sun-burn they do so, for fear of spoiling their complexion, or for other causes. Or they may use them to the end that, if they do get too hot in the work, and are suddenly surprised, their red cheeks may escape note, and the disorder of their countenances. I

have known such cases. But the mask doth hide all, and
so they befool the world.

2.

OF THE POWER OF SPEECH IN LOVE

HAVE heard many fair ladies and cavaliers
which have practised love declare how that,
but for sight and speech, they had rather be
like brute beasts, that following a mere natural appetite of the senses, have no thought of love or
affection, but only to satisfy their sensual rage and
animal heat.

Likewise have I heard many lords and gallants which
have lain with high-born ladies say, that they have ever
found these an hundred times more lascivious and outspoken in words than common women and the like. Herein
do they show much art, seeing it is impossible for a man,
be he as vigorous as he may, to be alway hard at the collar
and in full work. So when the lover cometh to lie still
and relax his efforts, he doth find it so pleasant and so
appetizing whenas his lady doth entertain him with
naughty tales and words of wit and wantonness, that
Venus, no matter how soundly put to sleep for the time
being, is of a sudden waked up again. Nay! more, many
ladies, conversing with their lovers in company, whether
in the apartments of Queens and Princesses or elsewhere,
will strangely lure them on, for that they will be saying
such lascivious and enticing words to them that both men
and women will be just as wanton as in a bed together.

Yet all the while we that be onlookers will deem their conversation to be of quite other matters.

This again is the reason why Mark Antony did so love Cleopatra and preferred her before his own wife Octavia, who was an hundred times more beautiful and lovable than the Egyptian Queen. But this Cleopatra was mistress of such happy phrases and such witty conversation, with such wanton ways and seductive graces, that Antony did forget all else for love of her.

Plutarch doth assure us, speaking of sundry quips and tricks of tongue she was used to make such pretty play withal, that Mark Antony, when he would fain imitate her, was in his bearing (albeit he was only too anxious to play the gallant lover) like naught so much as a common soldier or rough man-at-arms, as compared with her and her brilliant ways of talk.

Pliny doth relate a story of her which I think excellent, and so I will repeat the same here in brief. One day, being in one of her wildest moods, she was attired most enticingly and to great advantage, and especially did wear on her head a garland of divers blossoms most suitable to provoke wanton imaginings. Well, as they sat at table, and Mark Antony was fain to drink, she did amuse him with pleasant discourse, and meanwhile all the time she spake, she kept plucking out one by one fair flowers from her garland (but they were really strewed over every one with poisonous essences), and tossing the same from time to time into the cup Antony held ready to drink from. Presently when she had ended her discourse and Mark Antony was on the point of lifting the goblet to his lips to drink, Cleopatra doth stay him suddenly with her hand, and having stationed some slave or con-

[227]

demned criminal ready to hand, she did call this fellow
to her and made them give him the draught Mark Antony
was about to swallow. On drinking this he fell down dead;
and she turning to Antony, said, "And if I did not love
you as I do, I should e'en now have been rid of you;
yea! and would gladly have had it so, only that I see
plainly I cannot live without you." These words and this
device were well fitted to confirm Mark Antony in his
passion, and to make him even more submissive before his
charmer's feet.

In such ways did her cleverness of tongue serve Cleopatra, whom all the Historians do describe as having been
exceedingly ready of speech. Mark Antony was used
never to call her anything but "the Queen," by way of
greater distinction. So he did write to Octavius Cæsar,
previous to the time when they were declared open enemies:
"What hath changed you," he writes, "concerning my loving the Queen? She is my wife. Is it but now I have
begun the connection? You fondle Drusilla, Tortalé,
Leontiphé and a dozen others; what reck you on whom
you do bestow your favour, when the caprice seizeth
you?"

In this letter Mark Antony was for extolling his own
constancy, and reproaching the other's changeableness,
for loving so many women at once, while himself did love
only the Queen. And I only wonder Octavius did not love
her too after Antony's death. It may well be he had his
pleasure when he had her come alone to his chamber, and
he there beheld her beauty and heard her address him; or
mayhap he found her not so fair as he had thought, or
scorned her for some other reason, and did wish to make
his triumph of her at Rome and show her in his public

procession. But this indignity she did forestall by her
self-inflicted death.

There can be no doubt, to return to our first point,
that when a woman is fain after love, or is once well
engaged therein, no orator in all the world can talk better
than she. Consider how Sophonisba hath been described
to us by Livy, Appian and other writers, and how eloquent
she did show herself in Massinissa's case, when she did
come to him for to win over and claim his love, and later
again when it behooved to swallowed the fatal poison. In
short, every woman, to be well loved, is bound to possess
good powers of speech; and in very deed there be few
known which cannot speak well and have not words
enough to move heaven and earth, yea! though this were
fast frozen in mid winter.

Above all must they have this gift which devote themselves to love. If they can say naught, why! they be so
savourless, the morsel they give us hath neither taste nor
flavour. Now when M. du Bellay, speaking of his mistress
and declaring her ways, in the words,

> De la vertu je sçavois deviser,
> Et je sçavois tellement éguiser,
> Que rien qu'honneur ne sortait de ma bouche;
> Sage au parler et folastre à la couche.

(Of virtue I knew how to discourse, and hold such fair language, naught but honour did issue from my mouth; modest in
speech, and wanton a-bed.)

doth describe her as "modest in speech, and wanton
a-bed," [1] this means of course in speaking before company
and in general converse. Yet when that she is alone and

[229]

in private with her lover, every gallant dame is ready enough to be free of her speech and to say what she chooseth, the better to provoke his passion.

I have heard tales told by sundry that have enjoyed fair and high-born ladies, or that have been curious to listen to such talking with others a-bed, how that these were every whit as free and bold in their discourse as any courtesans they had ever known. And this is a noteworthy fact that, accustomed as they were so to entertain their husbands or lovers with lecherous and wanton words, phrases and discourse, and even freely to name the most secret parts of their bodies, and this without any disguisement, yet when the same ladies be set to polite converse, they do never go astray and not one of all these naughty words doth ever issue from their lips. Well, we can only say they are right well skilled in self-command and the art of dissimulation; for no other thing is there which is so frisky and tricksome as a lady's tongue or an harlot's.

So I once knew a very fair and honourable lady of the great world, who one day discoursing with an honourable gentleman of the Court concerning military events in the civil wars of the time, did say to him: "I have heard say the King hath had every spot in all that countryside broke down." Now when she did say "every spot, what she meant to say was every bridge" (pont); but, being just come from her husband, or mayhap thinking of her lover, she still had the other word fresh in her mouth. And this same slip of the tongue did mightily stir up the gentleman for her. Another lady I knew, talking with a certain great lady and one better born than herself, and praising and extolling her beauty, did presently say thus to her, "Nay! Madam, what I tell you, is not to *futter* you," meaning to say, *flatter* you, and did afterward correct herself. The fact is her mind was full of futtering and such like.

In short, lively speech hath a very great efficacy in the game of love; and where it is lacking, the pleasure is incomplete. So in very truth a fair body, if it have not a fair mind to match, is more like a mere image of itself or idol than a true human body. However fair it may be, it must needs be seconded by a fair mind likewise, if it is to be really loved; and if this be not so by nature, it must be so fashioned by art.

The courtesans of Rome do make great mock of the gentlewomen of the same city, which are not trained in witty speech like themselves, and do say of them that *chiavano come cani, ma che sono quiete della bocca come sassi*, that is, "they yield them like bitches, but are dumb of mouth like sticks and stones."

And this is why I have known many honourable gentlemen which have declined the acquaintance of ladies, and very fair ladies I tell you, because that they were simpletons, without soul, wit or conversation, and have quitted them for good and all, saying they would as soon have to do with a beautiful statue of fair white marble, like that Athenian youth which did love a statue, and went so far as to take his pleasure thereof. And for the same reason strangers that do travel in foreign lands do seldom care to love foreign women, nor are at all apt to take a fancy to them. For they understand not what they say, and their words in no wise touch their hearts. I speak of course of such as know not their language. And if they *do* go with them, 'tis but to satisfy nature, and quench the

[231]

mere brute flame of lust, and then *andar in barca* ("away to the ship"), as said an Italian who had come ashore one day at Marseilles on his way to Spain, and enquired a place where women were to be found. He was directed to a spot where a wedding feast was being held. So when a lady came up to accost him and engage him in conversation, he said to her only, *V. S. mi perdona, non voglio parlare, voglio solamente chiavare, e poi me n'andar in barca,* —"Pardon me, Madam; I want not to talk, but only to do, and then away again to the ship."

A Frenchman doth find no great pleasure with a German, Swiss, Flemish, English, Scotch, Slavonian, or other foreign woman, albeit she should chatter with the best, if he understand her not. But he taketh great delight with his French mistress, or with an Italian or Spanish woman, for generally speaking the most part of Frenchmen of our day, at any rate such as have seen the world a little, can speak or understand these languages. And God wot, it matters not if he be skilled and meet for love, for whosoever shall have to do with a Frenchwoman, an Italian, Spanish or Greek, and she be quick of tongue, he must needs frankly own he is fairly catched and conquered.

In former times this our French tongue was not so excellent and rich a language as nowadays it is; whereas for many a long year the Italian, Spanish and Greek have been so. And I will freely own I have scarce ever seen a lady of these nations, if she have but practised a little the profession of love, but hath a very good gift of speech. I do refer me to them that have dealt with such women. Certain it is, a fair lady, if endowed with fair and witty words, doth afford double contentment.

3.

OF THE POWER OF SIGHT IN LOVE

I

TO speak next of the power of sight. Without a doubt, seeing the eyes be the first part to join combat in love, it must be allowed that these do give a very great contentment, whenas they are the means to our beholding something fair and rare in beauty. And by my faith! what thing is there in all the world a man may see fairer than a fair woman, whether clothed and handsomely tricked out, or naked? If clothed, then 'tis only the face you see naked; but even so, when a fair body, of a beauteous shape, with fine carriage and graceful port, stately look and proud mien, is presented to our view in all its charms, what fairer and more delightsome display can there be in all the world? Then again, when you come to enjoy a fair lady, thus fully dressed and magnificently attired, the desire and enjoyment of her are doubled, albeit a man doth see only the face, while all the other parts of the body are hid. For indeed 'tis a hard matter to enjoy a great lady according to all the conveniences one might desire, unless it were in a chamber apart at full leisure and in a secret place, to do what one best liketh. So spied upon is such an one of all observers!

And this is why a certain great lady I have heard speak of, if ever she did meet her lover conveniently, and out of sight of other folk and fear of surprise, would always seize the occasion at once, to content her wishes as

[233]

promptly and shortly as ever she could. And indeed she did say to him one day, "They were fools, those good ladies of former days, which being fain of over refinement in their love pleasure, would shut themselves up in their closets or other privy places, and there would so draw out their sports and pastimes that presently they would be discovered and their shame made public. Nowadays must we seize opportunity whenever it cometh, with the briefest delay possible, like a city no sooner assailed than invested and straightway captured. And in this wise we do best avoid the chance of scandal."

And I ween the lady was quite right; for such men as have practised love, have ever held this a sound maxim that there is naught to be compared with a woman in her clothes. Again when you reflect how a man doth brave, rumple, squeeze and make light of his lady's finery, and how he doth work ruin and loss to the grand cloth of gold and web of silver, to tinsel and silken stuffs, pearls and precious stones, 'tis plain how his ardour and satisfaction be increased manifold,—far more than with some simple shepherdess or other woman of like quality, be she as fair as she may.

And why of yore was Venus found so fair and so desirable, if not that with all her beauty she was alway gracefully attired likewise, and generally scented, that she did ever smell sweet an hundred paces away? For it hath ever been held of all how that perfumes be a great incitement to love.

This is the reason why the Empresses and great dames of Rome did make much usage of these perfumes, as do likewise our great ladies of France,—and above all those of Spain and Italy, which from the oldest times have been

more curious and more exquisite in luxury than Frenchwomen, as well in perfumes as in costumes and magnificent
attire, whereof the fair ones of France have since borrowed the patterns and copied the dainty workmanship.
Moreover the others, Italian and Spanish, had learned the
same from old models and ancient statues of Roman ladies,
the which are to be seen among sundry other antiquities
yet extant in Spain and Italy; the which, if any man will
regard them carefully, will be found very perfect in mode
of hair-dressing and fashion of robes, and very meet to
incite love. On the contrary, at this present day our
ladies of France do surpass all others. 'Tis to the Queen
of Navarre [1] they do owe thanks for this great improvement.

Wherefore is it good and desirable to have to do with
suchlike fair ladies so well appointed, so richly tricked out
and in such stately wise. So have I heard many courtiers,
my comrades, declare, as we did discourse together on
these matters,

*De sorte que j'ai ouï dire à aucuns courtisans, mes com-
pagnons, ainsi que nous devisions ensemble, qu'ils les aimaient mieux ainsi que désacoutrées et couchées neus entre
deux linceuls, et dans un lit le plus enrichi de broderie
que l'on sut faire.*

*D'autres disaient qu'il n'y avait que le naturel, sans
aucun fard ni artifice, comme un grand prince que je
sais, lequel pourtant faisait coucher ses courtisanes ou
dames dans des draps de taffetas noir bien tendus, toutes
nues, afin que leur blancheur et délicatesse de chair parut
bien mieux parmi ce noir et donnât plus d'ébat.* [2]

There can be no real doubt the fairest sight of any in
the whole world would be that of a beautiful woman, all

complete and perfect in her loveliness; but such an one
is ill to find. Thus do we find it recorded of Zeuxis, the
famous painter, how that being asked by sundry honourable ladies and damsels of his acquaintance to make them
a portrait of the fair Helen of Troy and depict her to
them as beautiful as folk say she was, he was loath to
refuse their prayer. But, before painting the portrait,
he did gaze at them all and each steadfastly, and choosing
from one or the other whatever he did find in each severally
most beautiful, he did make out the portrait of these fragments brought together and combined, and by this means
did portray Helen so beautiful no exception could be taken
to any feature. This portrait did stir the admiration of
all, but above all of them which had by their several beauties and separate features helped to create the same no
less thans Zeuxis himself had with his brush. Now this was
as good as saying that in one Helen 'twas impossible to
find all perfections of beauty combined, albeit she may
have been most exceeding fair above all women.

Be this as it may, the Spaniard saith that to make a
woman all perfect, complete and absolute in loveliness,
she must needs have thirty several beauties,[3] the which a
Spanish lady did once enumerate to me at Toledo, a city
where be very fair and charming women, and well instructed to boot. The thirty then are as followeth:

(Translated, for the reader's better comprehension:)
Three things white: skin, teeth and hands.
Three black: eyes, brows and lids.
Three red: lips, cheeks and nails.
Three long: body, hair and hands.
Three short: teeth, ears and feet.

[236]

Three wide: chest or bosom, forehead and space betwixt the eyes.

Three narrow: mouth (upper and lower), girth or waist, and ankle.

Three big and thick: arm, thigh and calf.

Three long and fine: fingers, hair and lips.

Three small and delicate: breasts, nose and head.

Making thirty in all.

'Tis not inconceivable nor impossible but that all these beauties should be united all together in one and the same fair lady; but in that case she must needs be framed in the mould of absolute perfection. For indeed to see them all so combined, without there being a single one to carp at and find at fault is scarce possible. I do refer me to such as have seen beautiful women, or will see such anon, and who would fain be heedful in noting the same and appraising them, what they shall say of them. But though they be not complete and perfectly beautiful in all these points, yet will a beautiful woman alway be beautiful, an if she have but the half, and those the chief ones, of the parts and features I have named. For truly I have seen many which had more than the half, and were exceeding fair and very lovable. Just as a wood seemeth ever beautiful in Spring-tide, even though it be not filled with all the little pretty shrubs one might wish for. Yet are there plenty of fine, tall, spreading trees, which by their abundance may very well hide the lack of other smaller vegetation.

M. de Ronsard must pardon me, if he will. Never did his mistress, whom he hath represented as so very beautiful, really attain such perfection, nor any other lady he ever saw in his day or did describe. He calleth her his fair Cassandra, and sure I am she *was* fair, but he hath disguised her under a fictitious name. And the same is equally true of his Marie, who never bore other name but that, as it is of the first mentioned. Still it is allowed to poets and painters to say and do what pleaseth them,— for instance you will find in the *Orlando Furioso* wondrous fair beauties portrayed by Ariosto, those of Alcina and of many another fair one.

All this is well enough; but as I have heard a great personage of my acquaintance say, never could plain nature make so fair and perfect a woman as the keen and subtile imagination of some eloquent poet might featly describe, or the pencil and brush of some inspired painter represent. No matter! a man's eyes are ever satisfied to see a beautiful woman of fair, clear-complexioned and well-featured face. Yea! and though it be somewhat brown of hue, 'tis all one; the brunette is as good as the blonde many a time, as the Spanish girl hath it, *Aunque io sia morisca, no soy de menos preciar*,—"Brown though I be, I am not to be scorned for that." So the fair Marfisa *era brunetta alquanto*—"was something brown of face." Still must not the brown overset the white too much! Again, a beautiful countenance must be borne by a body fashioned and built to correspond. This doth hold good of little as well as big, but tall stature will ever take first place.

Well, as to seeking out suchlike exquisite points of beauty as I have just spoke of, and as poets have of old depicted, this we may very well dispense with, and find pleasure enough in our common and everyday beauties. Not that I would say common in any ill sense, for verily we have some so rare that, by my faith! they be better far

[238]

than all those which your fantastic poets, and whimsical painters, and lyrical extollers of female charms could ever delineate.

Alas! the worst of it is this. Whenas we do see suchlike fair beauties and gracious countenances, we do admire and long for the fair bodies to match, for the love of the pretty faces. But lo! in some cases, when these come to be revealed and brought to light, we do lose all appetite therefor. They be so ugly, spoiled, blotched, disfigured and hideous, they do give the lie direct to the face. This is one of the ways we men are oft sore taken in.

Hereof we have a good example in a certain gentleman of the Island of Majorca, by name Raymond Lulle,[4] of a very good, wealthy and ancient family. This nobleman by reason of his high birth, his valour and merit, was appointed in the prime of his years to the governorship of the said island. While in this office, as will oft happen to Governors of provinces and cities, he did grow enamoured of a beautiful lady of the island, one of the most accomplished, beautiful and ready-witted women of those parts. Long and eagerly did he court her; and at length, seeing he was ever demanding the reward of his exertions, the lady after refusing as long as ever she could, did one day give him an assignation. This he did not fail to keep, nor did she; but presently appeared thereat, more beautiful than ever and more richly apparelled. Then just as he thought the gates of Paradise were opening for him, lo! she stepped forward and did show him her breast and bosom all covered over with a dozen plasters, and tearing these off one after other and angrily tossing them to the ground, did exhibit a horrid cancer to him. So with tears in her eyes, she did rehearse all her wretch-

[239]

edness and her affection to him, and asked him,—was there then such mighty cause why he should be so much enamoured of her, making him so sad and dismal a discourse, that he did presently leave her, all overcome with ruth for the grief of this fair lady. Then later, after making supplication to God for her restoration to health, he did give up his office, and turned hermit.

Afterward, on returning from the Holy Wars, to the which he had vowed himself, he went to study at Paris under Arnaldus de Villanova, a learned philosopher; then after finishing his course there, he did withdraw into England, where the King of that day did welcome him with all the good will in the world for the sake of his deep learning, and seeing he did transmute sundry ingots and bars of iron, copper and tin, scorning the common, trivial fashion of transmuting lead and iron into gold. For he knew how more than one of his contemporaries could do this much as well as he, whereas he had skill to do both this and the other as well. But he was fain to perform a feat above the capacity of the rest of alchemists.

I have this tale from a gallant gentleman, which told me himself had it of the jurisconsult Oldrade. This author doth speak of Raymond Lulle in the Commentary he made on the Code *De Falsa Moneta* ("On False Coining"). Likewise he had it, so he said, on the authority of Carolus Bovillus,[5] a native of Picardy, who hath writ in Latin a life of this same Raymond Lulle.

This is how he did rid himself of his craving for the love of this fair lady. Other men, 'tis very like, had done differently, and would not have ceased to love, but shutting their eyes would e'en have taken what they did desire of her. This he might well enough have done, had he been so minded, seeing the part he did aim at was in no wise touched by any such disease.

I knew once a gentleman and a widow lady of the great world, which were not so scrupulous. For though the lady was afflicted with a great and foul cancer of the breast, yet he did not hesitate to wed her, nor she to take him, contrary to her mother's advice.

I knew likewise a very honourable gentleman, and a great friend of mine, who told me that one time being at Rome, he did chance to love a certain Spanish lady, one of the fairest was ever seen in that city. Now when he did go with her, she would never suffer him to see her, nor ever to touch her, but only with her clothes on. For, if ever he was for touching her, she would cry out in Spanish, *Ah! no me tocays, hareis me quosquillas*, that is to say, "Nay! do not touch me; you tickle me." But one morning, passing by her house and finding the door open, he goes boldly in. So having entered, without meeting either domestic, page or any living soul, he did penetrate to her bedchamber, and there found her so fast asleep he had leisure to behold and examine her at his ease, for that it was very hot weather. And he declared he did never see aught so fair as was her body, excepting only that he did discover how that, while the one thigh was fair, white, smooth and well-shapen, the other was all dried up, withered and shrunken, so that it looked no bigger than a young child's arm. Who so astonished as my friend? Who yet did not much compassionate her, and never after returned to visit her, nor had any subsequent dealings with her.

Many ladies there be which are not indeed thus shrunken by disease, yet are so thin, scraggy, withered and fleshless

[241]

they can show naught but the mere skeleton of a woman.
Thus did I know one, a very great lady, of whom the
Bishop of Sisteron,[6] one of the wittiest men at Court, did
by way of jest and gibe declare that it were better to
sleep with a rat-trap of brass-wire than with her. In a
like strain did another gentleman of the Court, when we
were rallying him on having dealings with a certain great
lady, reply, "Nay! but you are all wrong, for indeed I
do love good flesh too well, and she hath naught but
bones." Yet to look at these two ladies, so fair and
beauteous of face, you would have supposed them both
most fleshy and right dainty morsels.

A very high-born Prince of the great world did chance
once to be in love with two very fair ladies at one and the
same time, as doth often happen to the great, which do
love change and variety. The one was exceeding fair,
the other a brunette, but both the twain right handsome
and most lovable women. So one day as he came away
from visiting the dark one, her fair rival being jealous
did say to him: "Ah, ha! so you've been flying for crow!"
Whereto the Prince did make answer, something angered
and ruffled at the word: "And when I am with you, my
lady, what am I flying for then?" The lady straight
made answer: "Why! for a phœnix, to be sure!" But the
Prince, who had as ready a tongue as most, did retort:
"Nay! say rather for a bird of Paradise, the which hath
ever more feathers than flesh"; casting up at her by this
word how that she was rather thin and meagre. The fact
is she was too young a thing to be very fat, stoutness
commonly coming only upon such women as are getting
on in years, at the time when they do begin to lay on
flesh and get bigger in limbs and all bodily parts.

[242]

A certain gentleman did make a good reply to a great
Lord I wot of. Both had handsome wives. The great
Lord in question found the gentleman much to his taste,
and most enticing. So one day he said to him, "Sir! I
must e'en sleep with your wife." To this the gentleman,
without a thought, for he was very ready of tongue, did
answer, "I am willing enough, but on condition I sleep
with yours." The Lord replied, "Why! what would you
be at? I tell you, mine is so thin, you would not find her
to your taste at all." To this the gentleman did retort,
"Yea! by my faith! *je la larderai si menu que je la rendrai
de bon gout.*"

Many women there be whose pretty, chubby faces make
men fain to enjoy them yet when they do come to it,
they find them so fleshless the pleasure and temptation be
right soon done away. Among other defects, we do often
find the *gridiron* form, as it called, the bones so prominent
and fleshless they do press and chafe a man as sorely as
though he had a mule's packsaddle on him. To remedy
this, there be some dames are used to employ little cushions
or pads, very soft and very delicately made, to bear the
brunt and avoid chafing. I have heard speak of many
which have used these in such wise that lovers not in
the secret, when they do come to them, find naught but
what is good to touch, and are quite persuaded 'tis their
mistress's natural plumpness. For above the satin, they
will wear thin, loose, white muslin. In this way the lover
would leave the lady well pleased and satisfied, and himself deem her a right good mistress.

Other women again there be which have the skin all
veined and marked like marble, or like mosaic work, dap-
pled like a fawn's coat, itchy and subject to sores and

[243]

farcies; in a word so foul and disfigured the sight thereof is very far from pleasant.

I have heard speak of a certain great lady, and I have known her myself and do know her still, who is all shaggy and hairy over the chest, stomach, shoulders and all down the spine, like a savage. I leave you to imagine the effect. The proverb hath it, no person thus hairy is ever rich or wanton; but verily in this case the lady is both the one and the other, I can assure you, and is well able to win admirers, to please their eye and gain their love.

Others' skin is like goose flesh or like a feathered starling, all rugged and cross-grained, and black as the devil. Others are blessed with great dangling bosoms, hanging down worse than a cow's giving its calf milk. Very sure am I these be not the fair breasts of Helen, who one day desiring to present to the Temple of Diana an elegant cup in fulfilment of a vow, and employing a goldsmith to make it for her, did cause him to model the same on one of her lovely breasts. He did make the goblet of white gold and in such wise that folk knew not which to admire the most, the cup itself or its resemblance to the beautiful bosom which he had taken for his pattern. It looked so round and sweet and plump, the copy only made men the more to desire the real thing. Pliny doth make especial mention thereof, in the place where he treateth of the existence of white gold. 'Tis very strange, but of white gold was this goblet made.

But who, I should like to know, would care to model golden cups on the great ugly breasts I speak of and have seen. We should be bound to give the goldsmith a big supply of gold, and then all our expense would but end in laughter and mockery, when we should cry, "Look! see

[244]

our cup wrought on the model of so and so's breasts."
Indeed they would not so much be like drinking cups at
all as those great wooden puncheons, round and big-bel-
lied, we see used for feeding swine withal.

Others there be the nipples of whose breasts are for all
the world like a rotten pear. Others again whose bodies
are all rough and wrinkled, that you would take them for
old leathern game-bags, such as troopers and innkeepers
carry. This cometh to women which have borne children,
but who have not been properly seen to by the midwives.
On the contrary there be others which have the same sweet
and smooth and polished, and their bosom as plump and
pretty as if they were still maids.

*   *   *   *   *   *   *

Other women there be have their parts so pale and
wan you would say they had the fever. Such do resemble
some drunkards, which though they do drink more
wine than a sucking pig, are yet always as pale as
the dead. Wherefore do men call them traitors to their
wine, as in contrast with such tipplers as are rosy-faced.
In like fashion women that are pale in this region might
very well be spoke of as traitors to Venus, were it not for
the proverb which saith, "a pale whore and a red-faced
scamp." Be this as it may, there is no doubt their being
pale and wan is not agreeable to see; and is very far from
resembling that of one of the fairest ladies of our time,
and one that doth hold high rank (and myself have seen
her), who they used to say did commonly sport three fine
colours all together, to wit scarlet, white and black.
For her mouth was brilliant and as red as coral, her hair
pretty and curly and as black as ebony. So should it
ever be, for indeed this is one of the chiefest beauties of

[245]

a woman. Then the skin was white as alabaster, and was finely shadowed by this dark hair. A fair sight in truth!

I have heard Madame de Fontaine-Chalandray, known as *the fair Torcy*, relate how that her Mistress, Queen Eleanor, being robed and dressed, did appear a very beauteous Princess, and indeed there be many which have seen her looking so at our King's Court, and of a good noble figure. But being stripped, she did seem a very giantess in body, so long was it and big; whereas going lower down, she seemed but a dwarf, so short and small were her thighs and legs and all those parts.

Another great lady I have heard speak of was just the opposite. For whereas in body she looked a dwarf, so short and diminutive was it, for the rest down below she was a perfect giantess or colossus, so big, long and high-forked were her thighs and legs, though at the same time well-proportioned and fleshy.

There be many husbands and lovers among us Christians which do desire to be in all respects different from the Turks, which last take no pleasure in looking at women closely, because they say, as I have stated above, they have no shape. We Christians on the other hand do find, 'tis said, great contentment in regarding them carefully and do delight in such. Nay! not only do men enjoy seeing them, but likewise in kissing, and many ladies have shown their lovers the way. Thus a Spanish lady did reply to her lover on his quitting her one day with the words, *Bezo las manos y los pies, Señora; Senor, en el medio esta la mejore stacion.*

Other women have their thighs so ill proportioned, so unattractive looking and so badly made that they deserve not to be regarded or desired at all; and the same is true of their legs, which in some be so stout and heavy you would say the thick part thereof was a rabbit's belly when it is with young. In others again they be so thin and tiny and so like a stork's shanks, you might well deem them flute pipes rather than a woman's thighs and legs. What the rest is like, I will e'en leave you to imagine!

If I were to detail all the other beauties and deformities women are subject to, truly I should never have done. Now all I do say hereanent, or might say, is never of low-born or common women, but always of high-born, or at least well-born, ladies, which by their fairness of face do set the world on fire, but what of their person is hid doth but ill correspond.

<h2 style="text-align:center">2.</h2>

T is no long while agone since in a certain district of Guyenne a married dame, of very good station and descent, had a strange adventure. As she was overlooking her children's studies, lo! their tutor, by some madness or frenzy of the brain, or maybe from a fierce access of love that did suddenly master him, did take a sword belonging to her husband and which lay on the bed, and did assail her so furiously as that he did transpierce her two thighs and her two labia from the one part to the other. Whereof she did after all but die, and would have right out but for the help of an excellent surgeon. She might well say of her poor body how that it had been in two divers wars and assailed in two different ways. The sight thereof afterward was, I imagine, scarce agreeable, seeing it was so scarred and its *wings* so torn. I say *wings*, for while

the Greeks do call these labia *hymenaea,* the Latins name
the same *alae* (wings), the moderns *labia,* or lips, and
sundry other names. For truly there is no beast or bird,
be it falcon, raw and untrained, like that of our young
girls, or hawk, whether haggard or well practised, as of
our married women and widows, that doth go more nimbly
or hath the wing so active.

Other women, for dread of colds and catarrhs, do
smother themselves in bed with cape and mufflers about
the head, till upon my word they do look more like old
witches than young women. Yet once out of bed, they
are as smart as dolls. Others again be all rouged and
painted up like images, fine enough by day; but a-nights
the paint is off, and they are as ugly as sin.

It were well to examine suchlike dames before loving,
marrying and enjoying the same, as Octavius Caesar was
used to do. For along with his friends he did have sundry
great ladies and Roman matrons stripped naked, and
even vigins of marriageable age, and did examine them
from head to foot, as if they had been slave-women and
purchased serfs. The said examination was carried out by
a certain horse-jockey or dealer by name Toranus, and
according as this man did approve and find them to his
liking, and unspoiled, would the Emperor take his pleasure with them.

This is precisely what the Turks do in their slave-mar-
ket at Constantinople and other great towns, when they
buy slaves, whether male or female.

Well! I will say no more of all this; indeed methinks I
have already said over much. So this is how we be sore
deceived in many sights we at the first imagine and believe
very admirable. But if we be thus deceived in some good

ladies, no less are we edified and well satisfied in other
some, the which are so fair and sweet and clean, so fresh
and plump, so lovable and desirable, in one word so perfect in all their bodily parts, that after them all sights in
this world are but mean and empty. Whence it cometh
there be men, which at such a sight do so lose their wits
they must at once to work. Moreover 'tis often the case
that such fair dames do find pleasure in showing their
persons and do make no difficulty so to do, knowing themselves as they do without spot or blemish, to the end they
may the better rouse temptation and concupiscence in
our manly bosoms.

One day when we were together at the siege of La Rochelle, the late unfortunate Duc de Guise,[1] which did me
the honour to hold me in affection, did come and show
me some tables he had just filched from Monsieur the
King's brother,[2] our General in that enterprise, from out
the pocket of his breeches, and said thus: "Monsieur
hath done me a displeasure and mocked me concerning
my love for a certain lady. Well I would fain now take
my revenge; look at these tables of his, and read what I
have writ therein." With this he did hand me the tables,
and I saw writ therein in his hand these four verses following, which he had just made up,—only that the word
was set down outright in the first line:

> Si vous ne m'avez congeue,
> Il n'a pas tenu à moy;
> Car vous m'avez bien vue nue,
> Et vous ay monstré de quoy.

(If you have not known me, this is no fault of mine. For
indeed you have seen me naked, and I have shown you all you
need.)

After, he did tell me the lady's name, an unmarried
girl to say truth, which I did already suspect. I said I
was greatly surprised the Prince had never touched or
known her, seeing his opportunities had been very ample,
and he was credited by common report with being her
lover. But he did answer, 'twas not so, and that it was
solely by his own fault. To which I replied, "Then it
must needs, my Lord, have been, either that at the time he
was so weary and so sated in other quarters he was unable
to bear the brunt, or else that he was so entranced with
the contemplation of her naked charms that he did give
never a thought to the active part."—"Well! it may be,"
the Prince answered, "he was good to do it; but anyhow
this time he failed to take his opportunity. So I am
having my fun of him, and I am going to put his tables
back in his pocket, which he will presently examine, as is
his wont, and must needs read what I have writ. And so
I have my revenge." This he did, and never after did they
twain meet without having a good laugh over it, and a
merry passage of arms. For at that period was great
friendship and intimacy betwixt these two, though after
so strangely altered.

A lady of the great world, or to speak strictly a young
maid, was held in much love and close intimacy by a certain great Princess. The latter was one time in her bed,
resting, as was her wont, when a gentleman did come to
see the damsel, one which was deep in love with her, albeit
he had naught at all but his love to aid his suit. Then
the fair lady, being so well loved and on such intimate
terms with her Mistress the Princess, did come to her as
she lay, and nimbly, without any warning whatsoever, did
suddenly drag away all the coverings from off her, in

such wise that the gentleman, by no means slow to use his eyes, did instantly cast them on her, and beheld, as he did tell me the tale afterward, the fairest sight ever he saw or is like to see,—her beautiful body, and all her lovely, white, exquisite person, that did make him think he was gazing on the beauties of Paradise. But this scarce lasted an instant; for the moment the bed-clothes were thrown off, the lady did snatch back the same, the girl having meanwhile run off. Yet as luck would have it, the more the fair lady did struggle to pull back the coverings, the more she did display her charms. This in no wise spoiled the sight and the pleasure the gentleman had therein, who you may be sure did not put himself about to help her,—he had been a fool so to do. However, presently in one way or another she did get her coverings over her again as before, chiding her favourite, but gently withal, and telling her she should pay for her pranks. The damsel, who had slipped away a little out of her reach, did only reply, "Madam, you did play me a trick a while agone; forgive me if that I have paid you back in your own coin." And so saying, through the chamber-door and away! But peace was not long a-making.

Meanwhile the gentleman was so content with what he had seen, and so full of ecstasy, delight and satisfaction, I have heard him declare an hundred times over he did wish for naught else his life long but only to live and dream of this fair sight day by day. And in sooth he was right for to judge by the fair face that is without a rival and the beauteous bosom that hath so ravished mankind, there must indeed have been yet more exquisite dainties. And he did affirm that among these charms, the

[251]

said lady did possess the finest figure, and the best developed, ever he did set eyes on. And it may well be so, for she was of a very rich and opulent figure, and this must needs be one of the chief of all a woman's beauties, and like a frontier fortress, one of the most necessary and indispensable.

When the said gentleman had told me all his tale, I could only bid him, "Live on, my friend, live on; with this divine sight to dream on and this happy contemplation, you should never die. And heaven grant me before I die, at least to see so fair a spectacle!"

The said gentleman did surely owe an eternal debt of gratitude to the damsel, and did ever after honour and love her with all his heart. And he did woo her right eagerly as lover, yet married her not at the last; for another suitor, richer than he, did carry her off, for truly 'tis the way of all women to run after the solid good things of life.

Sights like this be fair and right pleasant; yet must we beware they work not harm, as the view of the beauteous Diana in her nakedness did to poor Acteon, or yet another I am about to tell of.

A great King did in his day love fondly a very beautiful, honourable and great lady, a widow, so that men did esteem him bewitched of her charms. For little did he reck of other women, or even of his wife, except only now and again, for this fair lady did always have the pick of the flowers of his garden. This did sorely grieve the Queen, for she knew herself as fair and lovable, as well deserving of loyal service and as worthy to enjoy such dainty morsels as the other. All this did both anger and surprise her much; wherefore having made her moan to a great lady which was her chief favourite, she did plot with her and contrive if there were no way whereby she might e'en spy through some peep-hole the game her husband and the lady should play together. And accordingly she did contrive to make sundry holes in the ceiling of the said lady's chamber, for to see it all and the life they twain should lead with one another. So they did set them to view the sight; yet beheld naught but what was fair to see, for they did behold only a most beauteous, white and delicately made woman, tender and sweet, half muffled in her shift, entertaining of her lover with pretty, dainty caresses and most tricksome pranks, and her lover performing the like to her. Then presently the twain would lie and frolic together on the thick, soft carpet which was by the bed-side, so to escape the heat and the better to enjoy the cool. For it was then at the hottest of the year; and myself have also known another very great Prince which was used to take his amusement with his wife in this fashion, to avoid the heat brought on by the great warmth of the summer season, as himself did declare.

The unhappy Queen then, having seen and observed it all, did of very despite set to and weep, sob, sigh and make sore moan, thinking, and saying too, how that her husband did never the like with her, nor ever went through suchlike amorous follies as she had seen him perform with his mistress.

The other lady, which was with her, did what she could for to comfort her, and chided her for making so sad a moan, saying what was true enough, that as she had been so curious as to spy out such doings, she could scarce have expected else. To this the Queen did make no other

[253]

answer but only this, "Alas! yes, I was wilful, and fain to
see a thing I should never have beheld, for verily the sight
thereof did hurt me very sore!" Natheless did she find
some comfort anon and resolution of mind, and did leave
off sorrowing.

I have heard yet another story of an honourable
lady who when a girl was whipped by her mother
twice every day, not that she had done aught wrong, but
because, as she supposed, her mother did find a pleasure
in seeing her so wriggle.

I have heard even a worse thing of a great Lord and
Prince, more than eighty years agone, how that before
going to cohabit with his wife, he was used to have himself whipped, not being able to be moved nor to do anything without this ridiculous remedy. I should greatly
like some competent physician to tell me the reason
hereof.

That great and distinguished author, Pico della Mirandola,[3] doth declare himself to have seen a gallant of his
day, who the more he was thrashed with heavy blows of a
stirrup-leather, the more was he thereby fierce after wom-
en. Never was he so valiant with them as after he had
been so leathered, though when it was once well done, he
was as fierce as any man. Truly here be some strange
and terrible caprices! At any rate to see others whipped
is a more agreeable sort of humour than this last!

3.

HEN I was at Milan, I was one day told a diverting tale,—how the late Marquis de Pescaire,[1] dead no long while agone, erst Viceroy of Sicily, did fall deeply in love with a very fair lady. And so one morning, believing her husband was gone abroad, he set forth to visit her, finding her still a-bed; but in conversation with her, he did win naught else but only to see her, gaze at her under the clothes at his leisure, and touch her with his hand. While this was a-doing, lo! the husband did appear, a man which was not of the high consideration of the Marquis in any respect, and did surprise them in such sort that the Marquis had no time to get back his glove, the which was lost some way or another among the sheets, as doth frequently happen. Presently, after exchanging a few words with him, he did leave the chamber, conducted to the door by the husband. The latter on returning did, as chance would have it, discover the Marquis's glove lost among the sheets, the lady not having noticed the same. This he did take and lock up, and after, putting on a cold demeanour toward his wife, did long remain without sleeping with her or touching her at all. Wherefore one day she being alone in her chamber, did set hand to pen and write this quatrain following:

Vigna era, vigna son.
Era podata, or piu non son;
E non so per qual cagion
Non mi poda il mio patron.

[255]

So leaving these verses writ out on the table, anon the husband came and saw the lines; and so taketh pen and doth thus reply:

> Vigna eri, vigna sei,
> Eri podata, e piu non sei.
> Per la granfa del leon,
> Non ti poda il tuo patron.

These he did leave likewise on the table. The whole was carried to the Marquis, who made answer:

> A la vigna chez voi dite
> Io fui, e qui restai;
> Alzai il pampano; guardai la vite;
> Ma, se Dio m'ajuti, non toccai.

This in turn was shown to the husband, who satisfied with so honourable a reply and fair apology, did take his vine to him again, and did cultivate the same as industriously as heretofore; and never were husband and wife happier together.

I will now translate the verses from the Italian, that all may follow the sense:

"I was a vine, and am so still. I was well cultivated; but am so no more. And I know not for what cause my master doth not now cultivate me as before."

ANSWER:

"A vine thou wert, and art so still; thou wert well cultivated, and art so no more. Because of the lion's claw, for this cause thy master doth not now cultivate thee as before."

ANSWER OF THE MARQUIS:

"The vine you both do speak of I visited 'tis true, and tarried a space. I lifted the cluster, and looked at the grape; but, so God help me, touched not at all."

By the "lion's claw" the husband meaneth to signify the glove he had found lost between the sheets.

A good husband this, which did not take umbrage overmuch, and putting away his suspicions, did thus forgive his wife. And there is no doubt there be ladies which do take such a delight in themselves they do love to see themselves naked and gaze at their own beauty, in such wise that they are filled with ravishment beholding themselves so lovely, like Narcissus. What then, I ask, is it like we men should do, whenas we do see and gaze at the same?

Mariamné, the wife of Herod,[2] a fair and honourable lady, when that one day her husband was fain to sleep with her at full midday, and see openly all her charms, did refuse flatly, so Josephus doth record. Nor did he insist on his rights as a husband, as did a great Lord I knew once with his wife, one of the fairest of the fair, whom he did enjoy thus in open day, and did strip her stark naked, she protesting stoutly the while. After, he did send her women to her to dress her again, who did find her all in tears and filled with shame. Other dames on the contrary there be which do make no set scruples of the sort at making display of their beauty and showing themselves thus, the better to stir their lovers' passion and caprice, and draw them the more fondly to them. Yet will they in no wise suffer them to enjoy their most precious favour. Some indeed, ill liking to halt on so

[257]

pleasant a road, soon go further; but others there be,—I have heard tell of not a few such,—which have long time entertained their lovers with such fair sights, and no more.

Happy they which have patience so to bide their time, without yielding overmuch to temptation. Yet must the man be fair bewitched of virtue who seeing a beautiful woman, doth give his eyes no gratification. So was Alexander the Great used to say at whiles to his friends how that the Persian maids did much hurt the eyes of such as did gaze at them. And for this cause, when he held prisoners the daughters of King Darius, he would never greet them but with downcast eyes, and likewise as seldom as ever he could, for fear he should have been overcome by the excellence of their beauty.

Not in those times only, but likewise in our own days, among all the women of the East, the Persian fair ones do bear the bell and prize of beauty, and fine proportion of bodily parts, and natural charm, as well as of becoming grace and fitness in dress and foot-gear—and above all others, they of the ancient and royal city of Shiraz.[3] These last be so commended for their beauty, fair skin, civility of manners and sweet grace, that the Moors do say in an old and well-known proverb, how that their Prophet Mahomet would never go to Shiraz, for fear, had he once set eyes on its lovely women, his soul after death would never have entered Paradise. Travellers which have been to that city and writ thereof, do say the same. And herein observe the hypocrisy of that same dissolute and rascal Prophet and his pretended continence; as if it were not to be found writ down, as Belon doth tell us, in an Arab work entitled "Of the Good Customs of Ma-

homet," extolling the Prophet's corporeal vigour, how
that he was used to boast of working and satisfying all
his eleven wives which he had in a single hour, one after
the other. To the deuce with the rascally fellow! Let us
speak no more of him. When all is said and done, I had
as lief never have named him at all!

I have heard this question raised concerning the behaviour of Alexander which I have described above and
that of Scipio Africanus,—to wit which of the twain did
merit the greater praise of continency?

Alexander, distrusting the strength of his chasteness,
did refuse even to look at the fair Persian maids. Scipio,
after the taking of New Carthage, did look at the beautiful Spanish girl his soldiers brought him and offered
him as his share of the booty, which maid was so excellent
in beauty and of so fair a time of life and flower of age,
that wheresoever she did pass, she would brighten and
charm the eyes of all that did behold her, and eke of Scipio
himself. But he, after greeting her right courteously,
did make inquiry of what city of Spain she was and of
her family.

Then was he informed, among other things, how that
she was betrothed to a young man, Alucius by name,
Prince of the Celtiberians, to whom he did give her up and
to her father and mother, without ever laying a hand on
her. By which conduct he did lay the said lady, her relations and her betrothed, under such obligation that they
did ever after show themselves most well affectioned to
the city of Rome and the Commonwealth.

Yet who knoweth but in her secret soul this fair damsel had not rather have been assailed first of all by Scipio,
—who, remember, was young, handsome, brave, valiant

[259]

and victorious? It may well be that if some bosom friend, male or female of the girl's had asked her on her faith and conscience whether she had not wished it so, I leave it to the reader to suppose what she would have answered, and if at the least she would not have made some little sign or gesture signifying what her real wish had been. For think how the climate of her country and that westering sun of Spain might well have made her hot and keen for love, as it hath many another fair lady of that land, as fair and gracious as she, in our own day, as myself have seen many an one. It can scarce be doubted then, if this fair and honourable maid had but been asked and courted of the young and handsome Scipio, but she would have taken him at the word, yea! even on the altar of her heathen gods!

Herein hath Scipio doubtless been commended highly of some for his noble gift of continence. Yet hath he been no less blamed of others; for wherein may a brave and valorous gallant better show forth the generosity of his heart towards a fair and honourable lady than by manifesting to her in deeds that he doth prize her beauty and highly admire it. Better this than treating her with that cold respect, that modesty and discretion, the which I have heard many good gentlemen and honest ladies call rather by the name of silliness and want of spirit than of virtue? Nay, verily! 'tis not such qualities at all a beautiful and worthy dame doth love in her heart of hearts, but rather good love and service that is prudent, discreet and secret. In one word, as an honourable lady did one day exclaim a-reading of this tale, Scipio was a fool, valiant and noble captain as he was, to go out of his way so to bind folk to him under obligation and to the Roman side by any such silly ways, when he might have done it just as well by other means more convenient. Beside, 'twas booty of War, whereof a man may take his joy and triumph as legitimately as of any other thing whatsoever in the world, or more so.

The great First Founder of Rome did not so, on occasion of the rape of the fair Sabine women, toward her which fell to his share. Rather he did to her according to his good pleasure, and paid her no cold respect whatever. This she did relish well enough and felt no grievance, neither she nor her companions, which did very soon make accord with their new husbands and ravishers. The women for their part did make no complaint like their fathers and mothers, which did rouse a fierce war of reprisals.

True it is, folk be of different sorts, and there be women *and* women. Some are loth to yield to any stranger in this sort, herein more resembling the wife of King Ortiagon, one of the Galatian monarchs of Asia Minor. She was of a perfect beauty, and being taken captive on the Kings' defeat by a Roman Centurion and solicited in her honour, she did stand firm in refusal, having a horror of yielding herself to him, a man of so low and base a station compared with herself. Wherefore he did have her by force and violence, whom the fortune and chance of War had given him by right of conquest to make his slave of. But 'twas no long while before he did repent him, and meet with vengeance for this offence; for the Queen, having promised him a great ransom for her liberty, and both being come to the appointed place for him to receive the money, she did have him slain, as he was a-counting of the gold, and did carry away it and his head to her

[261]

husband. To this last she did confess freely how that
the Roman had indeed violated her chastity, but that she
had taken her vengeance of him therefor in this fashion,—
the which her husband did approve and did highly honour
her for her behaviour. And from that day forth, said the
history, she did faithfully keep her honour unsullied to
the last day of her life with all scrupulousness and serious-
ness. Anyway she did enjoy this good treat, albeit it did
come from a low-born fellow.

Lucretia did otherwise, for she tasted not the pleasure
at all, albeit solicited by a gallant King. Herein was she
doubly a fool, first not to gratify him on the spot and
readily enough, and secondly to kill herself.

To return once more to Scipio, 'twould seem he knew
not yet the ways of War concerning booty and pillage.
For by what I learn of a great Captain of our troops,
there is no such dainty morsel for loot as a woman taken
in War. The same good soldier did make much mock
of sundry others his comrades, which were used to insist
above all things, at assaults and surprises of towns, on
the saving of the women's honour, as well as on divers
other occasions and rencontres. This is sheer folly, seeing women do always love men of arms more than any
others, and the very roughness of these doth give them the
better appetite. So who can find aught to blame? The
pleasure is theirs; their honour and their husbands' is
in no way fouled; and where is the mighty harm and ruin?
And yet another point,—they do oft by this means save
their husbands' goods and lives,—as did Eunoé, wife of
Bogud or Bocchus, King of Mauretania, to whom Cæsar
did give great possessions and to her husband likewise,
not so much, we may well believe, for having followed his

side, as Juba, King of Bithynia did that of Pompey, as
because she was a beautiful woman, and Cæsar did have
the enjoyment of her pleasant favours.

Many other excellent conveniences are there and advantages of these loves I must needs pass over. Yet, this same
great Captain would exclaim, in spite of them all would
other commanders, his comrades and fellows, obeying silly,
old-fashioned laws of War, be fain to preserve the honour
of women. But surely 'twere more meet first to find out in
secrecy and confidence their real wishes, and then decide
what to do. Or mayhap they be of the complexion of our
friend Scipio, who was worse than the gardener's dog,
which, as I have before said, will neither himself eat the
cabbages in the garden, nor yet let other folk taste of
them. This is the way he did treat the unhappy Massinissa, who had so oft times risked his life for him and
for the Roman People, and so sore laboured, sweated and
endeavoured, for to gain him glory and victory. Yet after
all he did refuse him the fair Queen Sophonisba and did
rob him of her, seeing he had chose her for his chiefest
and most precious spoil. He did take her from him to
send her to Rome, there to live out the rest of her days as
a wretched slave,—if Massinissa had not found a remedy
to save her from this fate. The Conqueror's glory had
been fairer and nobler, if she had appeared at Rome as a
glorious and stately Queen, and wife of Massinissa, so
that folk would have said, as they saw her go by: "Look!
one of the fair vestiges of Scipio's conquests." Surely
true glory doth lie much rather in the display of great
and noble things than of mean and degraded.

In fine, Scipio, in all this discussion, was shown to have
committed grievous faults, whether because he was an

[263]

enemy of the whole female sex, or as having been altogether impotent to satisfy its wishes. And yet 'tis said that in his later years he did engage in a love intrigue with one of his wife's maids,—the which the latter did very patiently endure, for reasons that might easily be alleged to account for the said complaisancy.

4.

OWEVER, to return from the digression I have just been indulging in and come back into the direct course of my argument, I do declare as my last word in this discourse, that nothing in all the wide world is so fair to see and look upon as a beautiful woman splendidly attired or else daintily disrobed and laid upon a fair bed, provided always she be sound and sweet, without blemish, blot or defect, as I have afore said.

King Francis I. was used to say, no gentleman, howsoever magnificent, could in any better wise receive a great Lord, howsoever mighty and high-born, at his mansion or castle, than by offering to his view on his first arrival a beautiful woman, a fine horse and a handsome hound. For by casting his gaze now on the one, now on the other and presently on the third, he would never be a-weary in that house, having there the three things most pleasant to look upon and admire, and so exercising his eyes right agreeably.

Queen Isabelle of Castile was wont to say, there were four things did give her very great pleasure to behold: *Hombre d'armas en campo, obisbo puesto en pontifical, linda dama en la cama, y ladron en la horca,*—"A man of arms in the field, a Bishop in his pontificals, a fair lady in her bed, and a thief on the gallows."

I have heard the late Cardinal de Lorraine, a short while since deceased, relate how on the occasion of his going to Rome to the Court of Pope Paul IV., to break off the truce made with the Emperor, he did pass through Venice, where he was very honourably received, we cannot doubt, seeing he was so high in the favour of so high and puissant a King. The most noble and magnificent Senate of that city did set forth in a body to meet him. Presently, passing up the Grand Canal, where every window of all the houses was crowded with all the fairest ladies of the place, who had assembled thither to see the state entry, there was a certain great man of the highest rank which did discourse to him on the business of the State, and spake at length of great matters. But after a while, seeing the Cardinal was for ever casting his eyes and fixing them on all these beautiful dames, he said to him in his native Venetian dialect: "My Lord Cardinal, I think you heed me not, and you are right enough. For surely 'tis much more pleasure and diversion to watch these fair ladies at the windows and take delight of their beauty than to listen to the talk of a peevish old man like me, even though he should be talking of some great achievement and success to redound to your advantage." On this the Cardinal, who had no lack of ready wit and memory, did repeat to him word for word all he had said, leaving the good old man excellently well pleased with him, and full of wonder and esteem, seeing that for all his feasting of his eyes on the fair ladies of Venice, he had neither forgot nor neglected aught of all he had said to him.

Any man which hath seen the Court of our French

Kings, Francis I., Henri II., and other Sovereigns his
sons, will freely allow, whosoever he be and though he
have seen all the world, he hath never beheld aught so fair
and admirable as the ladies which did frequent their
Court and that of the Queens and Princesses, their wives,
mothers and sisters. Yet a still fairer sight would he
have seen, say some, if only the grandsire of Master Gon-
nin had yet been alive, who by dint of his contrivances,
illusions, witchcrafts and enchantments could have shown
the same all undressed and stript naked, as they say he
did once in a private company at the behest of King
Francis. For indeed he was a man very expert and subtile
in his art of sorcery; whose grandson, the which we have
ourselves seen, knew naught at all in this sort to be compared with him.

This sight I ween would be as agreeable and diverting as
was of yore that of the Egyptian women at Alexandria, on
occasion of the reception and welcoming of their great
god Apis, to greet whom they were used to go forth in
great state, and lifting their gowns, bodices and shifts, and
tucking up the same as high as ever they could, did show
the god themselves right out. If any will see the tale, let
him read Alexander ab Alexandro, in the 6th book of his
Dies Joviales. I think such a sight must indeed have
been a right agreeable one, for in those days the ladies
of Alexandria were exceeding fair, as they are still to
this day.

Doubtless the old and ugly women did in like wise; but
there! what matter? The eye should never strain but
after what is fair and comely, and avoid the foul and
unlovely all it may.

In Switzerland, men and women do meet promiscuously

[266]

in the baths, hot and cold, without doing any dishonest
deed, but are satisfied with putting a linen cloth in front
of them. If this be pretty loose, well! we may see something, mayhap agreeable or mayhap not, according as
our companion is fair or foul.

Before ending this part of my discourse, I will add yet
one word more. Just think again to what sore temptations were exposed the young lords, knights and nobles,
plebeians and other men of Rome, and what delectation of
the eye they did enjoy in ancient times on the day when
was kept the feast of Flora at Rome. This Flora, 'tis
said, was the most engaging and successful courtesan
that did ever practise harlotry at Rome, or in any other
city. And what did yet more recommend her herein was
the fact she was of a good house and noble lineage; for
dames of such high sort do naturally please the more,
and to go with such doth afford greater gratification.

Thus the lady Flora had this excellence and advantage
over Laïs, seeing the latter would give herself to any like
a common strumpet, but Flora to great folk only. And
indeed she had this writing put up at the entering in of
her door, "Kings, Princes, Dictators, Consuls, Censors,
Pontifices, Quæstors, Ambassadors, and other the like
great Lords, enter; but no other."

Laïs did ever ask payment beforehand, but Flora never,
saying she did act so with great folk to the end they might
likewise act by her as great and illustrious men should, and
also that a woman of much beauty and high lineage will
ever be esteemed as she doth value herself. So would she
take naught but what was freely given her, declaring
every gentle dame should do pleasure to her lover for

love's sake, and not for avarice, for that all things have their price save and except true love alone.

In a word, she did in her day so excellently and sweetly practise love, and did win her such gallant lovers, that whenever she did quit her lodging now and again to walk abroad in the city, there was talk of her enough to last a month, as well for her beauty, her fair and rich attire, her gallant bearing and engaging mien, as for the ample suite of courtiers and lovers and great lords which went with her, and did follow and attend her like veritable slaves,—an honour she did take with no ill grace. And ambassadors from foreign lands, when they did return to their own country, would ever find more delight in tales of the beauty and wondrous excellence of the divine Flora than in describing the greatness of the Roman State. And above all would they extol her generosity, a thing contrary to the common bias of suchlike dames; but then she was out of the common altogether, seeing she was of noble origin.

Eventually she did die so rich and opulent that the worth of her money, furniture and jewels were enough to rebuild the walls of Rome, and furthermore to free the State of debt. She did make the Roman People her heir in chief; and in memory thereof was erected at Rome a very sumptuous Temple, which was called from her name the Florianum.

The first Festival ever the Emperor Galba did celebrate was that of the fond Flora, at the which 'twas allowed all Roman men and women to do every sort of debauchery, dissoluteness, abomination and extravagance they chose and could imagine. Indeed *she* was deemed the most re-

ligious and most gallant dame, which on that day did best
play the dissolute, debauched and abandoned wanton.

Think of it! Never a *fiscaigne* ('tis a lascivious dance
the loose women and Moorish slave-girls dance on Sun-
days at Malta publicly in the open square), nor saraband
did come near these Floralia for naughtiness; and never
a movement or wanton posture or provocative gesture or
lascivious twist and twirl did these Roman dames omit.
Nay! the more dissolute and extravagant the figures she
did devise, the more gallant and gay was deemed the performer; for the Romans did hold this creed that the more
wanton and lecherous the gesture and carriage wherewith
a woman did approach the Temple of this goddess, the
more like was she to win the same charms and opulence
Flora herself had enjoyed.

Verily a fine creed, and a fine mode of solemnizing a
festival! but remember they were but Pagans. Well! little
doubt there was never a sort of naughtiness they did fail
to bethink them of, and that for long beforehand these
worthy dames would be a-studying of their lessons, just
as our own countrywomen will set to work to learn a ballet,
and would devote all their heart and soul to these things.
Then the young men, and the old ones too, would be no
less eager to look on and behold their quaint grimacings
and wanton tricks. If such a show could be held in our
days, folks would be right glad to profit by the same in
every sense; and to be present at such a sight, the public
would verily crowd itself to death!

Further details let each imagine for himself; I leave
the task to our merry gallants. Let any that is fain,
read Suetonius, as also Pausanias in Greek and Manilius in
Latin, in the books they have writ concerning illustrious,

[269]

amorous and famous ladies, and he will learn the whole in full.

This one more story, and then an end. We read how the Lacedæmonians set forth once to lay siege to Messené; but the Messenians were beforehand with them. For they did sally out upon the enemy, some of them, whilst the rest did make all haste and away to Lacedæmon, thinking to surprise their town and pillage it, while the Spartans were occupied before Messené. They were however valorously repelled and driven off by the women which had been left behind. Hearing of their design, the Lacedæmonians did turn about and make their way back toward their own city. But from a long way off they did make out their women all armed, who had already driven off the enemy whose attack on the city they had dreaded. Then did the said women straightway inform them of all, and relate their victory,—the news whereof did so delight them they did set to on the spot to kiss, fondle and caress the victors. In such wise that, forgetting all shame and without even waiting to take off their harness, neither men nor women, they did gallantly do the thing with them on the very spot where they had met them first. Then were things to be seen not usual in War, and a right pleasant rattle and tinkle of arms and armour and the like to make itself heard. In memory whereof they did have built a temple and statue to the goddess Venus, under the title of the *Armed Venus*, unlike all other images of the goddess, which do always represent her naked. A merry tale of a merry encounter, and a happy idea to depict Venus armed, and call her by that title!

'Tis no uncommon sight among men of arms, especially at the taking of towns by assault, to see soldiers fully

armed enjoying women, having neither the time nor patience to disarm before satisfying their lust and appetite,
so fierce and eager are they. But to see soldier and
woman both armed in cohabitation together is a thing
seldom seen.

Well, well! enough! we must needs make an end,—
albeit I could have filled out this discourse to more ample
length by not a few other examples, had I not feared to
seem over wanton, and incur an ill repute of naughtiness.

However, after so much praise of fair ladies, I do feel
me bound to repeat the words of a Spaniard, who one
day wishing ill to a woman, did describe her in very proper
terms to me thus:

*Señor, vieja es como la lampada azeytunada d'iglesia, y
de hechura del armario, larga y desvayada, el color y gesto
como mascara mal pintada, el talle como una campana o
mola de el andar y vision d'una antigua fantasma de la
noche, que tanto tuviese encontrar-la de noche, como ver
una mandragora. Iesus! Iesus! Dios me libre de su mal
encuentro! No se contenta de tener en su casa por hues-
ped al provisor del obispo, ni se contenta con la demasiada
conversacion del vicario ni del guardian, ni de la amistad
antigua del dean, sino que agora de nuevo ha tomado al
que pide para las animas del purgatorio, para acabar su
negra vida;*—"Sir! look at her! She is like an old, greasy
Church lamp. Form and shape are those of a great
aumry, all mis-shapen and ill made; complexion and features like a badly drawn mask; figure as shapely as a
monastery bell or a great millstone. Her face is like
an old idol; her look and gait like an antic ghost that
walks by night. I should be as sore afraid to meet her
in the dark as to face a horrid mandrake. The good

[271]

Jesus keep me from such an encounter! The Bishop's
Ordinary is her constant guest, but she is not satisfied;
the garrulous Vicar and the good old Dean are her oldest
friends, but she is not content. She must needs entangle
now the Pardoner for poor souls in Purgatory, to complete the infamy of her black and odious life."

Observe how the Spaniard, which hath so well described
the thirty beauties of a fair lady (have I not quoted them
above, in this same Discourse?), can, when he so wills,
abuse the sex with the like gusto.

THIRD DISCOURSE

Concerning the beauty of a fine leg, and the virtue the same doth possess.

1.

AMONG many and sundry beauties the which I have at divers times known us courtiers to praise, and which are right well adapted to attract love, one of the highest esteemed is a fine leg on a fine woman. Many fair ladies have I known take great pride therein, and use great pains to have and to keep the same beautiful. Amongst others I have heard tell of a noble Princess of the great world, and one that I did myself know, which did cherish one of her ladies above all the rest, and did favour her beyond all, for this only because she could draw on her mistress' hose so close and tight, and arrange them so cleverly to fit the leg, and fasten the garter so prettily,—better than any other. For this only reason she gat great preferment at her hands, and even did win considerable wealth. Now in view of all this care she took to keep her leg in such good trim, we may be very sure 'twas not to hide the same under her petticoats or under skirts or frock, but to make display thereof at whiles with fine drawers of cloth of gold and silver, or other the like rich stuff, very prettily and daintily made, which she did commonly wear. For verily a woman taketh not such pleasure in her body without being fain to give others a share also in the sight, yea! and the enjoyment thereof.

Moreover this lady could not make excuse, saying 'twas all done to pleasure her husband, as the most part of women, and even of old women, will ever declare, whenas they do make themselves so seductive and gay, though they be quite elderly; for she was a widow. True it is in her husband's lifetime she had done the same, and would not leave off the habit afterward, merely because she had lost him.

I have known many fair and honourable ladies, both wives and maids, which are no less painstaking thus to keep their fine legs in well cared for, seemly and attractive guise. And very right they be so to do; for truly there is more wanton seduction doth lie therein than you would readily suppose.

I have heard speak of a very great lady, of the days of King Francis, and a right fair dame, who having broken a leg and had the same set, did after find 'twas ill done, and the limb was left all twisted. So stout of heart was she, that she did make the bone-setter break it afresh, for to restore it to its right shape as before, and make it as fine and straight as ever. Hereat a certain lady did express no little surprise; but another fair lady, and a well experienced one, did answer thus and said, "Ah! I see plainly you know not what amorous virtue a fine leg hath in it."

I knew in former days a very fair and honourable damsel of the great world, who being much in love with a great Lord, for to attract him to her and by way of trying some good device to win him to her,—a design wherein she could never succeed, one day being in a wooded avenue and seeing him approach, did make a pretense as though her garter were coming down. So withdrawing a little on one side, she did lift up her leg, and began to pull up her stocking and re-adjust her garter. The great lord did note it all well, and found her leg an exceeding fine one. Indeed he did lose his head so completely that this sight of her did work more effect on him than ever her face had done, for he did think to himself how that two such fine columns must needs support a very fine building. And later he did admit as much to his mistress, who afterward did with him as she would. A noteworthy device truly, and a pretty bit of love practice!

I have heard speak likewise of a fair and honourable lady, and one especially witty and of a gay good humour, who one day, when her chamber valet was a-drawing on of her hose, did ask him if this did not put him in heat, temptation and concupiscence;[1] nay! she put it yet more plainly, and said the plain word right out. The valet, thinking to please and for the respect he bare his mistress, did answer her, No!—At this she did of a sudden lift her hand and gave him a sound cuff on the head, crying out, "Begone with you! you shall never serve me more. You are a simpleton, and I do give you notice from this day."

There be many young ladies' valets nowadays which be not so self-restrained at the rising of their mistresses from bed and in the dressing of them and putting on of their footgear. Moreover many a gentleman would have found it hard to act thus, seeing so fair a treat spread out before his eyes.

[275]

'Tis not only in our own day men have esteemed the
beauty of fine legs and pretty feet (for 'tis one and the
same thing; but in the time of the old Romans likewise
we do read how Lucius Vitellius, father of the Emperor
Vitellius, being very sore smit with love for Messalina
and desiring to be in favour with her husband by her
means, did one day beseech her to do him the honour of
granting him a boon. The Empress asked him, "What
boon?"—" 'Tis this, Madam," he replied, "that you be
pleased one day to suffer me to take off your shoes."
Messalina, who was ever full of courtesy for her subjects,
could not refuse him this favour. Then he, after remov-
ing her shoes, did keep one of them, and bore the same
always about with him betwixt his shirt and his skin, kissing it as oft as ever he had opportunity, in this wise
worshipping his lady's pretty feet in the guise of her
slippers, forasmuch as he could not have at his disposal
the foot itself nor the fine leg appertaining thereto.

Then you have that English Lord in the *Cent Nouvelles*
of the Queen of Navarre, which did in like wise wear his
mistress' glove by his side, and that so richly adorned.
Again I have known many gentlemen which, before
donning of their silk stockings, would beg their fair ladies
and mistresses to try on the same and wear them the
first a week or ten days, more or less; after which themselves would wear them in great respect and high content
of mind and body.

I knew once a Lord of the great world, who being at
sea with a very great lady and one of the fairest of
womankind, had the happiness, seeing he was travelling
with her through his country and as her women were
all ill of seasickness and so in very ill case to serve her,

[276]

to be obliged to put her to bed with his own hands every night and get her up in the morning. But in so doing and in putting on of her footgear and taking off the same, he did grow so much enamoured as to be well nigh desperate, albeit she was his near kinswoman. For verily the temptation herein was too exceeding great, and there doth not exist the man so mortified in spirit but he is something moved by the same.

We do read of the wife of Nero, Poppæa Sabina, which was the favourite of all his wives and mistresses, how that, beside being the most lavish of women in all sorts of superfluities, ornaments, embellishments, gawds and costly weeds, she did wear shoes and slippers all of pure gold. This luxury was not like to make her hide her foot and leg from Nero, her cuckold mate; nor yet did he enjoy the sole delight and pleasure of the sight, for there was many another lover had the same privilege. Well might she display this extravagance for herself, seeing she was used to have her horses' hoofs, which did draw her chariot, shod with shoes of silver.

Saint Jerome doth reprove in very severe terms a lady of his time which was over careful of the beauty of her leg, using these exact words: "With her little brown boot, well fitting and well polished, she doth decoy young men, and the tinkle of her shoe-buckles is a snare unto them." No doubt this was some dainty fashion of footgear in vogue in those days, that was over luxurious and ill becoming to modest women. The wearing of foot-gear of the sort is to this present day in use among Turkish ladies, and those the best-born and most virtuous.

I have seen the question raised and discussed which is the more seductive and alluring, the naked leg, or the leg

[277]

covered and stockinged? Many hold there is naught like the natural article, when 'tis well made and perfectly turned, according to the points of beauty enumerated by the Spaniard I did quote from a little above, and is white, fair and smooth, and appropriately displayed in a fine bed. For if it be otherwise and a lady were fain to show her leg all bare in walking and so on, and with shoes on her feet, albeit she should be the most magnificently dressed out possible, yet would she never be deemed becomingly apparelled. Nor would she really and truly look so fair as one that should be properly equipped with pretty hose of coloured silk or else of white thread, such as be made at Florence for summer wear, and which I have often seen our ladies wearing in former times, before the great vogue we do now see of silk stockings. But the hose must ever be drawn close and stretched as tight as a drum and so fastened with clasps or otherwise, according to the preference and good pleasure of the wearer. Further must the foot be fitted with a pretty white shoe, or a slipper of black velvet or velvet of some other colour, or else a neat little high-heeled shoe, cut to perfection, such as I have seen a certain very noble lady of the great world wear, of such sort that naught could well be better or more dainty.

Wherein again the beauty of the foot must be considered. If this be too large, 'tis not pretty; but an if it be too tiny, it doth give a naughty hint and ill notion of its wearer. Rather it should be of a middling size, as I have seen sundry which have been exceeding appetizing, above all when their owners did thrust the same half in, half out, and just show them beneath their petticoat, and make them shift and quiver in little tricksome, wanton movements, being shod with a pretty little high-heeled shoe, thinly soled, or else a white slipper, pointed, not square-toed in front; but the white is the most daintiest. But these little high-heeled shoes and pumps be for big, tall women, not for the short and dwarfish ones, which do have their great horse-shoes with soles two feet thick. One had as lief as these see a giant's club on the swing, or a fool's bawble.

Another thing a woman should beware of is the disguising her sex and dressing herself as a boy, whether for a masquerade or for any other occasion. For so attired, though she have the finest leg in the world, yet doth she look ill-shapen in that part, seeing all things have their proper setting and suitable array. Thus in falsifying of their sex, they do altogether disfigure their beauty and natural grace.

This is why 'tis not becoming for a woman to dress as a boy for to display her charms to the more advantage, —unless indeed it be merely to don a dainty, gallant cap with the Guelf or Ghibelline feather stuck therein, or perched above the brow, in such wise to be distinctively neither male nor female, after the fashion our ladies have of late adopted. Yet even this doth not suit all women equally well; the face must be saucy and of just the right expression to carry it off, as we have seen in the case of our Queen Marguerite of Navarre. Her it did suit so well that, seeing her face only when she was so bedecked, no man could tell which sex she came the nearer to, whether she more looked the handsome boy or the beautiful woman she really was.

This doth remind me of another lady of the great world, and one I knew, which wishing to imitate the same

[279]

mode when about twenty-five years of age, and altogether
over tall and big statured, a great masculine looking
woman and but lately come to Court, and thinking to
play the gallant dame, did one day appear so attired
in the ball-room. Nor did she fail to be much stared at
and rallied not a little on her costume. Even the King
himself did pronounce his judgement thereon, for indeed
he was one of the wittiest men in his realm, and declared
she did resemble a mountebank's wench, or still better
one of those painted figures of women that are imported
from Flanders and set up in front of the chimney-pieces
in inns and taverns with German flutes at their lips. In
fact he went so far as to have her told that if she did
appear any more in that dress and get-up, he would order
her to bring her flute with her for to play a merry greeting to the noble company withal and divert them with
her music. Such cruel sport did he make of her, as well
because the said head-gear did so ill suit her as for a
grudge he had against her husband.

So we see such masquerading doth not suit all ladies
alike. For when this same Queen of Navarre, the fairest
woman in all the world, was pleased to adopt a further
disguise beyond the cap, she did never appear so fair
as she really was, nor ever would have. And indeed what
shape could she have taken more beauteous than her own,
seeing there is none better she could have borrowed from
any in all the world? And if she had chose to show her
leg, the which I have heard sundry of her women describe
as the finest and best ever known, otherwise than in its
proper form, and appearing well and fitly stockinged and
shod below her fine clothes, never would it have been
deemed so handsome as it was. Thus with a due regard

to surroundings doth it behove fair ladies to show and
make display of their beauties.

2.

I HAVE read in a Spanish book entitled *El
Viage del Principe,* or "The Prince's Voyage," to wit that which the King of Spain [1]
did make in his Province of the Low Coun-
tries, in the time of the Emperor Charles his father, how
among other fine receptions he did meet with among his
rich and wealthy cities of those parts, was one of the
Queen of Hungary in the fair city of Bains, which did
give rise to a proverb, *Mas brava que las fiestas de Bains,*
—"Finer than the festivities of Bains."

Among other magnificent shows was this. During the
siege of a sham castle that was erected, and besieged in
form as a place of war, (a description of the same is
given elsewhere in my Works), she did one day give an
entertainment, notable among all others, to the Emperor
her good brother, the Queen Eleanor her sister, the King
her nephew, and all the Lords, nights and ladies of the
Court. Toward the end of the show did appear a lady,
accompanied by six Oreads, or mountain nymphs, clad
in the antique mode, in the costume of nymphs of the
Virgin Huntress, all attired in cloth of silver and green
and crescents on their brow all beset with diamonds in
such wise that they seemed to imitate the brilliancy of the
moon, and carrying each her bow and arrow in hand,
and rich quivers at their side, their shoes in like wise of
cloth of silver, well fitting and well put on so as that they
could not be better. And so caparisoned they did enter

[281]

the great hall, leading their dogs after them, and did present to the Emperor and laid on the table before him all sorts of game in pasties, the which they had taken in their hunting.

Thereafter did come Pales, the goddess of shepherds, with six nymphs of the meadows, clad all in white of cloth of silver, with furniture of the same on their heads all beset with pearls, wearing likewise hosen of the same material with white slippers; and these did bring all sorts of milk confections, and laid the same before the Emperor.

Then for the third band, came the goddess Pomona, with her Naïads, or water nymphs, which did bring the last offering of fruits. And this goddess was the daughter of Donna Beatrix Pacecho, Comtesse d'Autremont, lady-in-waiting of Queen Eleanor, a child at that time of some nine years old. She it is that is now wife of the Admiral de Chastillon, he having wedded her as his second wife. This pretty maid and goddess did bring in, she and her companions, all sorts of fruits such as could be found at that season, for it was Summer time, the richest and rarest procurable, and did present the same to the Emperor with a set speech so eloquent, so fine and pronounced with so sweet a grace that she did win the great love and admiration of the Emperor and all the company there assembled, her youth being taken in account, that from that day forward 'twas foretold of all that she would be what she is to-day, a fair, wise, honourable, virtuous, clever and witty lady.

She was similarly attired as a nymph like the rest of her companions, all being clad in cloth of silver and white, with hosen and shoes of the same, and their heads decked with much wealth of jewels. But these were all

emeralds this time, to represent in part the colour of
the fruit they did offer. And besides the gift of fruit, she
did make one to the Emperor and the King of Spain of
a Tree of Victory all enamelled in green, the boughs laden
with great pearls and precious stones, right rich to behold and of inestimable worth; also to the Queen Eleanor
a fan, with a mirror in the mid thereof, the whole garnished with jewels of great price.

Verily this Princess and Queen of Hungary did show
right well that she was an honourable lady in all points,
and that her address and tact was as admirable as was
her skill in the art of war. And indeed, by all I have
heard said, the Emperor her brother did feel no little
content and comfort to have so honourable a sister and
so worthy of him.

Now have I laid myself open to blame and might fairly
enough be asked why I have made this digression in the
course of my Discourse. 'Tis to point out how that all
these maids that did represent these characters had been
chose out and selected as being the fairest among all the
suite of the Queens of France and of Hungary and of
Madame de Lorraine,—being Frenchwomen, Italians,
Flemish, German and Lorrainers. In all the number was
no defect of beauty; and God knoweth if the Queen of
Hungary had been painstaking and exact to choose such
as were fairest and most graceful.

Madame de Fontaine-Chalandry, who is yet alive, could
give us good assurance of this, who was at the time
maid of honour of the Queen Eleanor, and one of the
fairest. She was known also by the name of "the fair
Torcy," and hath told me the tale of all these doings.
And I have it for sure both of her and from other

quarters too how that all the lords, gentlemen and knights of that Court did take their diversion in looking at and examining fine legs, limbs and pretty little feet of these ladies. For attired thus as nymphs, they were dressed in short gowns, and could make a very engaging display, more enticing even than their pretty faces, which admirers could see every day, whereas 'twas not so with their other beauties. And so sundry courtiers did grow more enamoured by the sight and display of these same fine legs, than ever of their pretty faces, seeing that atop of such fine columns there be commonly found fine cornices with their friezes, fine architraves, and rich capitals, smoothly polished and curiously carved.

So must I be allowed yet another digression, and to say my say as I please, now we be upon the subject of shows and suchlike representations. Almost at the same moment as these noble festivities were a-doing in the Low Countries, and above all at Bains, on occasion of the reception of the King of Spain, was made the state entry of King Henri, on his way back from visiting his province of Piedmont and his garrisons there, into Lyons, which was of a surety one of the finest and most triumphant ever known, as I have heard honourable ladies and gentlemen of the Court declare, which were there at the time.

Well! if this show and representation of Diana and her hunt was found admirable at these Royal festivities of the Queen of Hungary, another was contrived at Lyons which was different again and still more lifelike. For as the King was marching along, and just about to reach a grand obelisk of Classic fashion, on the right hand of his way he did actually find a meadow by the side of the high road surrounded by a wall something

[284]

more than six feet high, and the said meadow within filled up with earth to the same height. This had been regularly filled up with trees of moderate growth, planted in between with thick undergrowth and many shrubs and smaller brushwood, as well as with a good supply of fruit trees. In this miniature forest did disport them many little stags all alive, and fawns and roebuck, though of course tame ones. Presently his Majesty did hear sundry hunting-horns and trumpets sound softly; and thereupon instantly did behold through the aforesaid wood Diana a-hunting with her companions and forest maids, holding in her hand a richly dight Turkish bow, and her quiver hanging at her side, attired in the costume of a nymph, after the fashion the remains of Antiquity do yet show us. Her body was clad in a short doublet with six great round scallops of black cloth of gold, strewn with silver stars, the sleeves and body of crimson satin with borderings of gold, tucked up to mid thigh, displaying her fine limb and pretty leg, and her sandals of the antique shape, set with pearls embedded in embroideries. Her hair was interlaced with heavy strings of rich pearls, with wealth of precious stones and jewels of price; while above the brow a little silver crescent was set, blazing with tiny little diamonds. For gold would not have been so well, nor so true a representation of the natural crescent, which is clear and silvery.

Her companions were accoutred in divers sorts of costumes of lustring striped with gold, both wide and narrow stripes, always in the antique mode, as well as sundry other colours of an antique sort, varied and intermingled as well for curiousness of effect as for gaiety of appearance. Hosen and shoes were of satin; their heads decked

[285]

out in like wise in the character of nymphs, with many pearls and precious stones.

Some were leading in leash sleuth-hounds, small greyhounds, spaniels and other dogs by cords of silk white and black, the King's colours which he bare for the love of a lady named Diana whom he loved; others did go along with and encourage the running dogs, that were in full cry. Others again did carry little darts of hard wood, the point gilded, and having pretty little hanging tassels of black and white silk, and hunting-horns and trumpets mounted in gold and silver hanging in bandoleers with cords of thread of silver and black silk.

And so soon as ever they did perceive the King, a lion did sally forth of the wood, which was tamed and trained long before for this, and did throw himself at the feet of the said goddess, giving her welcome. So she, seeing him so mansuete and gentle, did take him by a great rope of silver cord and black silk, and on the instant did present the same to the King. Thus coming forward with the lion to the edge of the wall of the meadow bordering the road, and within a pace or so of his Majesty, she did make offer to him of the beast in a rhymed stanza, of the sort composed in those days, yet not so ill wrought either or ill sounding. And according to this rhyme, the which she did pronounce with a very good grace and sweetness, under the guise of the lion so gentle and well behaved she did offer him his town of Lyons, now all gentle, well behaved and brought under to his laws and orders.

All this being said and done with a very sweet grace, Diana and all her companions did make him an humble reverence; whereupon having looked at them all with a

[286]

favourable eye and greeted them graciously, signifying
he had found their hunting shows right agreeable and
thanking them heartily, he did so part from them and
went on his way to his entry into the city. Now observe
that this same Diana and all her nymphs were the most
highly thought on and fairest wives, widows and maids
of Lyons, where is no lack of such, which did play their
mystery so well and in such engaging sort that the most
part of the Princes, Lords, gentlemen and courtiers were
exceedingly delighted thereat. I leave you to judge
whether they had not good cause so to be.

Madame de Valentinois, known as Diane de Poitiers,
the King's mistress, in whose name this hunting was made,
was not less well content, and did like well all her life
long the good town of Lyons. And indeed she was their
neighbour, by reason of the Duchy of Valentinois which
is quite close to that place.

Well! as we are on the subject of the pleasure to be
derived from the sight of a fine leg, we may be assured,
as I have heard say, that not the King only, but all these
Court gallants, did find a marvellous great pleasure in
contemplating and gazing at those of these fair nymphs,
so gaily attired and high kilted as that they did give as
much,—or more,—temptation to ascend to a yet higher
level, as admiration and reason to approve so pretty and
pleasantly contrived a divertisement.

However, to quit our digression and return to the
point at which we left our main subject, I mention how
we have seen played at our Court and represented by our
Queens right graceful ballets, and especially by the Queen
Mother; yet as a rule, for us courtiers we would be ever
casting our eyes on the feet and legs of the ladies which

[287]

did take part in them, and did find by far our greatest
pleasure in seeing them display their legs so agreeably,
and so move and twinkle their feet so nimbly as that
naught could be better. For their petticoats and frocks
were much shorter than usual, though not so much so
as in the nypmhs' costume, nor so high as they should
have been and as was desired of many. Yet did our eyes
fasten somewhat on those parts, and especially when they
were dancing the quick step, which making the skirts to
flutter up, would generally show something or other pleasant to look at,—a sight that I have seen several find
altogether too much for them, so that they did lose all
self-control over themselves.

The fair ladies of Sienna, at the first beginning of the
revolt of their city and republic, did form three companies of the most beautiful and greatest ladies were in
that town. Each company did mount to a thousand, so
as the whole was three thousand strong. One company
was clad in violet lustring, one in white, and one in red,
all being attired as nymphs with very short skirts, in such
wise that they did make full display of fine limbs and
legs. In this wise they did pass in review before all their
fellow townsmen as well as before his Grace the Cardinal
of Ferrara and M. de Termes, Lieutenants General of our
French King Henri, all firmly resolved and determined to
die for the Republic and for France, and all ready to give
a hand to the work of fortifying the said city. Indeed
all and each did carry a fascine ready on shoulder; and
did rouse by their gallantry the admiration of all. This
tale I do set down in another place, where I am speaking
of high-spirited women; for truly 'tis one of the finest
exploits was ever done by gallant dames.

For the present I will content me with saying how I have heard it told by many gentlemen and soldiers, both French and foreign, and especially by sundry of that town, that never aught finer was seen, seeing they were all great ladies and of the chiefest families of that place, and each fairer than another, for 'tis well known that beauty is far from lacking in that city, but is very general therein. But if it were a fine sight to behold their handsome faces, 'twas no less so to see and gaze upon their handsome limbs and fine legs, with their pretty hosen and shoes well fitting and well put on, as the dames of those parts know right well how to do. Then they did all wear their gowns very short, in the guise of nymphs, that they might march the easier,—the which was enough to tempt and warm up the most chilliest and mortified of mankind. And what did most pleasure the onlookers was this, that whereas they might any day see their faces, they could not so behold these fine and handsome legs of theirs. He was no fool which did devise this same mode and costume of nymphs, for it doth readily afford many fine sights and agreeable spectacles. The skirts be cut very short, and are divided up the side to boot, as we do yet see it represented in the fine Roman antiques, which doth still more flatter the wantonness of the eye.

But in our own day, with the fair ladies of Chios, matrons and maids, what and how is it they be so attractive? Why! truly 'tis their beauty and their charms of face and figure,—but also their superb fashions of dress, and above all their very short gowns, which do make full display of their dainty, well shod feet.

This doth remind me how one time at Court a lady of very tall and imposing figure, looking at a magnificent

[289]

and noble hunting piece in tapestry, wherein Diana and all her band of virgin huntresses were very naturally represented, and all by the fashion of their dress did show their pretty feet and fine legs, did chance to have with her one of her companions, which was of very low and small stature, and who was likewise diverting herself along with the other in examining the said tapestry. To her she did say thus: "Ha! ha! little one, if all we women did dress after that fashion, you would be in a bad way and would lose all advantage, for your great high-heeled shoes would betray you; and you would never have such grace in your walk, nor such charm in showing of your leg, as we that are tall and stately. You would have to keep close and scarce show at all. Give thanks then to the days we live in and the long gowns we wear, which be so favourable to you, and do hide your legs so conveniently. For indeed with your great high-heeled shoes a foot tall, these be more like a cudgel than a woman's leg. If a man had never a weapon to fight withal, he would but have to cut off a leg and grasp it by the end where your foot is shod and encased in your high shoes, and he would have a beautiful club for the fiercest encounter."

This lady was very right in what she said, for truly the prettiest leg in the world, if it be so imprisoned in these great, heavy, high-heeled shoes, doth lose its beauty altogether, seeing this great club foot doth cause too great a deformity for anything; for if a pretty foot well shod and dainty goeth not with the leg, all is of no avail. Now these dames which do adopt these great, heavy, lumbering high-heeled shoes think no doubt to embellish and better their figures and thereby appear more

[290]

beautiful and be the more loved; but on the other hand they do worsen their fine leg and foot, which be surely in their natural beauty worth as much as a fine tall figure that is but a sham.

Similarly in time of yore, a pretty foot did carry with is so much of wanton fascination, that many prudish minded and chaste Roman ladies, or at the least such as did feign to be so,—and even in our own day some do the like in Italy in imitation of antique morals,—do as much scruple about showing this part in public as their faces, hiding it under their flowing gowns all ever they can, so that none may see it; and in walking do go so prudishly, discreetly and carefully as that it never passeth out from under their robe.

This is well enough for such as are trained in prudish bearing and respectability, and are for never offering temptation; we must say this much for them. Yet I ween, an if they had their free choice, they would make display enough both of foot and leg, and of other things to boot. Beside, they do consent to show the same to their husbands, for all their hypocrisy and petty scruples about being dames of position and respectability. However I but relate the fact as it is.

I do know of a certain gentleman, a very gallant and honourable man, which only by having seen at Rheims at the Consecration of the late King, the lovely leg, in a white silk stocking, of a great and very fair lady, a widow and of tall stature, from underneath those scaffolds they erect for ladies to see the ceremony from, did fall so deep in love with her as that he grew well nigh desperate with passion. Thus what her handsome face had failed to effect, this her fine development of leg did

[291]

bring about; though truly the said lady did deserve by the beauty of all her person to drive an honourable gentleman to his death. And I have known other men too of the like humour.

At any rate for final word will I say this, and I have known the same to be held as an incontrovertible maxim by many gallant courtiers, my comrades, that the display of a fine leg and pretty foot is a thing most dangerously apt to fascinate wanton eyes to love; and I wonder much that some of our many good writers, whether poets or others, have never writ the praises thereof, as they have of other parts of fair ladies' bodies. For myself, I would have writ more on this subject, but that I was afeared, if I did overmuch belaud these parts of the person, I should be reproached as scarce enough heeding the rest. Beside I have perforce to treat of other matters, and may not tarry too long over one.

Wherefore I do now make an end with this little word of advice: "For God's sake, Ladies, be not so careful to make you seem of taller stature and other than you are; but rather look to the beauty of your legs, the which be so fair and fine, at any rate with some of you. But ye do mar the charm of them with those monstrous high-heeled boots and huge horse-shoes ye do wear. Doubtless ye do need such; but by having the same of such exaggerated size, ye do disgust folk far more than ye imagine."

I have said my say. Whosoever will, may bepraise the other beauties of woman, as sundry of our poets have done; but I maintain, a fine leg, a limb well shapen and a pretty foot, do exercise no small fascination and power in the realm of Love.

[292]

FOURTH DISCOURSE

*Concerning old dames as fond to practise love as
ever the young ones be.*

1.

 I HAVE spoke afore of old dames which be fain to play the wanton; yet do I further append this discourse here. So by way of commencement, I will say how one day myself being at the Court of Spain and conversing with a very honourable and fair lady, but withal something advanced in age, I did hear her pronounce these words: *Que ningunas damas lindas, o alo menos pocas, se hazen viejas de la cinta hasta abaxo,* "that never a fair lady, or at the least very few such, are old from the waist downwards." On my asking her in what sense she did mean this, whether 'twas the beauty of person from waist down that did never diminish in any wise by reason of age, or the desire and appetite of concupiscence that did not at all fail or grow chilled in these parts, she did make answer she intended both the one and the other. "For indeed," she went on, "as to the prickings of the flesh, no cure is there for these you must know, but death only; albeit old age would seem to be an obstacle thereto. Yet doth every beautiful woman ever fondly love her own self, and in so loving, 'tis not for her own, but some other's sake; and is in

[293]

no wise like Narcissus, the which, so foolish was the youth, himself lover and beloved, did think scorn of all other affections."

A beautiful woman hath naught of this humour about her. So have I heard it related of a very fair lady, which after first loving herself and taking much joy of her own beauty alone and by herself, and in her bed stripping of herself quite naked, and so looking at her own person, and admiring and contemplating the same, did curse her hard fate to be vowed to one sole husband that was not worthy to enjoy so fair a body, holding him to be in no wise her equal in merit. At the last was she so fired by such contemplations and sights and longings as that she did bid a long farewell to her virtue and her marriage vow, and did practise new love with a new lover.

This is how a woman's beauty doth kindle and inflame her, constraining her to have resort to such, whether husbands or lovers, as may satisfy her desire; while 'tis always the nature of one love to lead to another. Wherefore being thus fair and sought after of some admirer, and if she disdain not to answer to his passion, she is at once in the snare. So Laïs, the famous courtesan, was used to declare, that so soon as ever a woman doth open her mouth to make a gentle reply to her friend, lo! her heart is flown, and the door opened straightway.

Moreover no fair and honourable woman doth ever refuse any good praise that men render her; and once she is gratified and doth suffer such commendation of her beauty, grace and gentle ways, the which we courtiers be ever wont to make by way of first assault of love, though it may be some while a-doing, yet in the long run we do always win the place.

Further, it is a true thing that no beautiful woman, having once made essay of the game of love, doth ever unlearn the same, and for ever after is the sport right pleasant and delightsome to her. Just as when a man hath grown accustomed to good living, 'tis exceeding disagreeable to discontinue the same; and as this is better for the health, the more a man is got on in years, (as the doctors declare), so the more a woman advanceth in age, all the more is she greedy after the good cheer she is accustomed to. This daintiness is nowise forgot or remitted because of the weight of years, but more like by some long sickness, (so the faculty tell us), or other accident; and albeit disinclination may be experienced for some while, yet will the taste for such good things be renewed anon.

'Tis said, again, how that all activities do decrease and diminish by reason of age, which doth rob folk of the strength to properly exercise the same,—except only that of Venus, the which is carried out very luxuriously, without sore trouble or much exertion, in a soft, comfortable bed, and altogether at ease. I do speak now of the woman, and not of the man, to the share of which latter falleth all the labour and task-work in this province. A man then, once deprived of this pleasure, doth easily and early abstain from further indulgence,—albeit sometimes it may be in spite of himself; whereas a woman, be she of what age she will, doth take to her, like a furnace, and burn up, all stuff that cometh her way. Nay! even though a dame should be so aged as to look but ill, and find herself in no such good case as in her younger years, yet she may by dint of money find means to get gallant cavaliers at the current rate, and good ones too, as I have heard say. All commodities that cost dear do sore vex the purse,—(this goes counter to Heliogabalus' opinion, who the dearer he did buy his viands, the better he thought them),—except only the commodities of Love, the which be the more agreeable in proportion as they cost more, by reason of the great desire felt to get good value of the bargain and thoroughly enjoy the article purchased. So the poor talent one hath, is made to do triple service, or even hundredfold service, if that may any way be.

This is what a certain Spanish courtesan meant by her word to two brave gentlemen which did pick a quarrel together over her, and sallying forth to her house, did take sword in hand and fall to a-fighting. But she putting head out of window, did cry out to them: *Señores, mis amores se ganan con oron y plata, non con hierro,*—"Nay! Sirs, my love is won with gold and silver, not with iron."

All love well purchased is well and good. Many a lady and many a cavalier which have done such traffic could tell us so much. But to allege here examples of ladies,—and there be many such,—which have burned as hot in their old age as ever in youth, and have satisfied, or to put it better, have kept up, their fires with second husbands and new lovers, would be for me now a waste of labour, seeing I have elsewhere given many such. Yet will I bring forward one or two here also, for my subject doth require it and is suitable to such matters.

I have heard speak of a great lady, one that was as well talked about as any of her day, which one day seeing a young gentleman with very white hands, did ask him what he was used to do to have them so. To this he made answer, by way of jape and jest, that so oft as ever he could,

[296]

he would be a-rubbing of them with the spirit of love. "Ah! well," she replied, " 'tis my bad luck then; for more than sixty years have I been washing myself therewith, and I'm just as bad as the day I began. Yet do I bathe so every day."

I have heard speak of a lady of pretty advanced age, who wishing to marry again, did one day ask a physician's advice, basing her reasons for so doing on the fact that she was exceeding full of all sorts of evil humours, which had assailed and ever afflicted her since she was a widow. Yet had this never so happed in the lifetime of her husband, seeing that by dint of the constant exercises they did perform together, the said humours were consumed. The physician, who was a merry fellow, and willing enough to please her herein, did counsel her to marry again, and in this fashion to chase away the humours from her, saying 'twas better far to be happy than sad. The lady did put this advice in practise, and found it answer very well, indeed, superannuated as she was. This was, I mean, with a new husband and lover,—which did love her at least as much for the sake of her good money as for any pleasure he gat of her. Though of a surety there be many quite old dames, with whom as much enjoyment is to be had as with younger women; nay! 'tis sometimes greater and better with such, by reason of their understanding the art and science of love better, and so the more stimulating their lovers' taste therefor.

The courtesans of Rome and of Italy generally, when they are verging toward ripe years, do maintain this maxim, that *una galina vecchia fa miglior brodo che un' altra,*—"an old hen doth make better broth than any other."

The Latin poet Horace doth make mention of an old woman, which did so stir and toss about when she came to bed, and move her so violently and restlessly, that she would set not alone the bed but the whole house a-trembling. A gallant old dame in sooth! Now the Latins do name suchlike agitation and wanton movement *subare a sue.*

We do read of the Emperor Caligula, that of all his women which he had, he did love best Cæsonia, and this not so much by reason of her beauty, nor because she was in the flower of age, for indeed she was by then well on in years, but on account of her exceeding lustfulness and the wantonness that was in her, as well as the good pains she did take in the exercise thereof, and the experience her age, and long practise had taught her, herein leaving all the other women in the lurch, albeit handsomer and younger than herself. He was used to take her commonly to the wars with him, clad and armed like a man, and riding in manlike wise side by side with him, going so far even as often times to show her to his comrades all naked, and make her exhibit to them her feats of suppleness.

Thus are we bound to allow that age had in no wise diminished the lady's beauty, seeing how greatly the Emperor was attached to her. Natheless, with all this fond love he did bear her, very oft whenas he was a-kissing and touching her fair neck, he could not hinder himself, so bloody-minded was he, from saying: "Ah! the beautiful neck it is; yet 'tis in my power at will to have it cut." Alas and alas! the poor woman was slain along with her husband with a sword thrust through the body by a Centurion, and her daughter broken and dashed to

[298]

death against a wall,—the which could never have been but
for the ill deeds of her father.[1]

We read further of Julia, step-mother of the Emperor
Caracalla,[2] how that one day being as it were by inad-
vertence half naked, she did expose one-half of her body
to his eyes; whereupon he said these words, "Ha, ha! but
I could relish it well enough, an if it were allowed me!"
She answered straightway, "So please you, know you not
you are Emperor, and therefore make laws instead of obeying them?" On hearing these words and seeing her readiness, he did marry her and couple with her.

A reply of pretty much the same import was given to one
of our last three French Kings, whose name I will not
mention. Being enamoured and fallen deep in love with
a very fair and honourable lady, after having made the
earlier advances and preliminaries of his suit to her, did
one day cause his pleasure to be conveyed to her more
at length by an honourable and very judicious and adroit
gentleman I know by name and repute. So he, conveying
to her the Sovereign's little missive, did use all his elo-
quence to persuade her to consent. But she, no fool at
this game, did defend herself the best she could by many
excellent reasons the which she well knew how to allege,
without forgetting the chiefest, her honour,—that mighty,
or rather mighty small, treasure. At the last, the gentleman after much disputing and many protestations, did ask
her finally what she did desire he should tell the King.
Then she, after some moments of reflection, did suddenly,
as if brought to bay, pronounce these words following:
"What are you to tell him?" she cried, "why! what else
but this? tell him I know well enough that no refusal was
ever advantageous to any, man or woman, which doth

[299]

make such to his King and Sovereign; and that very oft a Prince, exerting the power he hath, will rather give the orders and taking a thing than go on begging and praying for it." Not ill content with this reply, the gentleman doth straightway bear it to the King; who taking time by the fore-lock, doth hie him to the lady in her chamber, and without any over great effort or resistance doth have his will. The reply was at once witty, and showed her good will to pleasure her King. Albeit men say 'tis never well to have sport or dealings with the King, yet must we except this particular game, wherefrom never was ill advantage gotten, if only the woman do behave her prudently and faithfully.

To return to the afore named Julia, step-mother of the Emperor, she must need have been a very harlot to love and take for husband one which had on her own bosom slain some while before their own proper son; [3] verily she was a base harlot and of base heart. Still 'twas a grand thing to be Empress, and for such an honour all else is forgot. This Julia was greatly loved of her husband, albeit she was well advanced in years. Yet had she lost naught of her beauty; but was very fair and very ready-witted, as those her words do witness, which did make yet greater the bed of her greatness.

2.

ILIPPO MARIA, Third Duke of Milan,[1] did wed as second wife Beatrix, widow of the late deceased Facino Cane,[2] being then an old woman. But she did bring him for marriage portion four hundred thousand crowns, without reckoning other furnishings, rings and jewelry, which did amount to a great sum, and quite wiped out all thought of her age. Yet spite of all, she did fall under her husband's suspicions of having gone to play the wanton elsewhere, and for this suspicion was done to death of him. You see how little did old age destroy her taste for the games of love. We must e'en suppose the great practice she had had thereof had but given her the desire for more and more.

Constance, Queen of Sicily,[3] who from her youth up and near all her days, had been vestal and never budged forth of a cloister-cell, but lived there in life-long chastity, getting her freedom to come out in the world at last at the age of fifty, though in no wise fair and quite decrepit, yet was fain to taste the joys of the flesh and marry. She did grow pregnant of a child at the age of fifty-two, and did desire to be brought to bed publicly in the open meadows about Palermo, having had a tent or pavilion set up there on purpose, to the end folk might have never a doubt but the fruit of her body was verily to hand. And this was one of the greatest miracles ever seen since the days of Saint Elizabeth. Natheless the *History of Naples*[4] doth affirm 'twas reputed a supposititious child. At any rate he did grow up a great man for all that; but indeed these, and the greater part of valiant men,

[301]

are just the folk that be often bastards, as a high-born friend of mine did one day remark to me.

I knew once an Abbess of Tarascon, sister of Madame d'Usez, of the noble house of Tallard,⁵ which did leave off her religious habit and quit her convent at over fifty years of age, and did wed the great Chanay we have seen play so gamesome a part at Court.

Many other women of religion have done the like, whether in wedlock or otherwise, for to taste the joys of the flesh, and this at a very ripe age. If such as these do so, what are we to expect our everyday dames to do, which have been broken in thereto from their tenderest years? Is age like to hinder them from now and again tasting and eating tit-bits, the customary enjoyment whereof they have so long been used to? Else what would become of so many good strengthening soups and cunningly compounded broths, so much ambergris and other warming and comfortable drugs for to warm and comfort their stomach now grown old and chilly? For 'tis not open to doubt but that such like decoctions, while they do recreate and keep sound their weakly stomachs, do likewise perform another function on the sly, in giving them more heat of body, and rousing some degree of passionate warmth. This is sure and certain,—without appealing to the opinion of physicians, to whom however I do refer me as to the matter.

And another and yet greater advantage for them is this. Being now aged and coming nigh on to their fifty years, they need feel no more fear of getting with child, and so have full, plenary and most ample freedom to enjoy and make up all arrears of those pleasures which mayhap some of them have not dared take hitherto for dread of the consequences. So it is that there be many which do give more rein to their amours when got to the wrong side of fifty than when still on the right. Not a few ladies both of the highest and less exalted rank have I heard tell of as being of this complexion, so much so that I have known or heard of several that have many a time and oft longed for their fifty years to have come and gone, to hinder them of conceiving and suffer them to do it the more freely without risk or scandal of any sort. Nay! why *should* they refrain them on the approach of old age? Indeed you might well say that after death itself there be women which yet feel some movement and pricking of the flesh. This bringeth me to another tale I must needs tell.

I had in former days a younger brother called Captain Bourdeille, one of the bravest and most valiant captains of his time. I am bound to say thus much of him, albeit he was my brother, without going too far in my panegyric of him. The same is proved by the fights he fought both in battle and in the lists; for indeed he was of all gentlemen of France the one that had most skill of arms, so that in Piedmont he was known as one of the Rodomonts of those parts. He was slain at the assault of Hedin, the last time that place was retaken.

He was intended by his father and mother for a life of letters; and with this view was sent at the age of eighteen into Italy to study. He did take up his abode at Ferrara, for the reason that Madame Renée de France, Duchess of Ferrara, was much attached to my mother, and did keep him in that city to pursue his studies, for there was an University there. However, seeing he was

[303]

fitted neither by birth nor disposition for this sort of
life, he did study scarce at all, but did rather amuse himself with the delights of love and courtship. In fact he
did fall deep in love with a certain French lady, a widow,
which was in the service of the Duchess, known as Mlle. de
La Roche (or de La Mothe) and did have much pleasure
with her, each loving the other exceeding well, till at the
last my brother, being recalled home again by his father,
who saw he was ill fitted for letters, was reluctantly constrained to return.

The lady, loving him greatly, and greatly fearing it
might turn out ill with him, for she was much of Luther's
way of thinking, who was then widely followed, did beg
my brother to take her with him to France and to the
Court of Marguerite, Queen of Navarre,⁶ in whose service she had been, and who had given her to Madame
Renée, when she was married and went to live in Italy.
My brother, who was young and quite heedless, was only
too glad of such excellent company, and did willingly
escort her to Paris, where the Queen was then residing.
This last was right glad to behold her, for of all women
she was the wittiest and most ready of tongue, and was
a handsome widow to boot and perfect in all accomplishments.

My brother, after having tarried some days with my
grandmother and my mother, who was then performing
her Court service, did presently go home to see his father.
After some while, sickening utterly of letters, and seeing
himself in no wise fitted for their pursuit, he doth quit
that career altogether and away to the wars in Piedmont and Parma, where he did win much honour. So
he did serve in these wars by the space of five or six

[304]

months without returning home. At the end of this time he went to see his mother, who was at the time at Court with the Queen of Navarre; the Queen was then holding Court at Pau, and my brother did make his reverence to her as she was returning from Vespers. Being one of the best natured Princesses was ever in this world, she did receive him right graciously, and taking him by the hand, did walk with him up and down the Church for an hour or twain, asking him news of the wars in Piedmont and Italy and of many other matters. To all this my brother did make answer so well that she was very well satisfied (for indeed he was as ready of tongue as any of his time) as well with his wit as with his person,— for he was a most handsome man, and of the age then of twenty-four. At the last, after long discourse with him, for 'twas ever the nature and complexion of the said noble Princess in no wise to scorn good talk and the conversation of good and honourable folk, gliding from subject to subject and still walking up and down the while, she did quietly bring my brother right over the tomb of Mlle. de La Roche, which had died three months before, and there staid him. Presently taking his hand, she said thus; "Cousin mine" (she called him so, seeing that a daughter of Albret had married into our house of Bourdeille; but for all that I do keep no greater state than another, nor suffer my ambition to run away with me), "cannot you feel something move down below under your feet?"—"Why! no, Madame," he did reply.— "Nay! take heed and mark carefully, cousin," she did resume.—But my brother only made answer, "Madame, I *have* taken heed, but I can feel nothing moving. The stone I tread on is firm enough."—"Well, well! I must

tell you then," the Queen went on, without keeping him
longer in suspense, "that you are standing above the
tomb and the body of poor Mlle. de La Roche, whom
erst you did love so fondly; she is interred beneath this
spot. Now seeing that our souls do possess feeling after
our death, how can we doubt that this excellent creature,
dead but lately, was moved so soon as ever you came over
her? And if you did not mark it by reason of the gross-
ness of the tomb, no doubt for this cause was she the
more stirred and moved in herself. Now forasmuch as
'tis a right pious office to have memory of the dead, and
specially of them we have loved, I do beseech you give her
a *Pater noster* and an *Ave Maria* and a *de Profundis*
to boot, and sprinkle her resting place with holy water;
so shall you win the name of a very faithful lover and a
good Christian. And to this end will I now leave you,"
and so quits him and hies her away. My brother, (who
is since dead), failed not to perform what she had said,
and then went to see her again; whereupon she did
somewhat take him to task and rally him, for she was
familiar with folk,—in a good sense that is,—and had
graceful skill in gentle mockery.

Such then was the view this Princess did hold, but more
by way of witty conceit and gentle sentiment than from
actual belief, as I think.

These gentle words of the Princess do further remind
me of an epitaph over a courtesan that is buried at the
Church of our Lady of the People (del Popolo) at Rome,
which doth read thus: *Quaesco, viator, ne me diutius
calcatam amplius calces,* "To him that passeth by: 'I
have been kicked and spurned enough in my lifetime;
spurn me no more.'" The Latin expression hath more

grace than the English equivalent. I do put the thing down here more by way of a jest than anything else.

Well, to draw to an end, no need to be astonished that the Spanish lady named above did hold the maxim she did enunciate good of all such fair ladies as have been greatly loved of others, and have loved, and do love, themselves, and do take delight in being praised, albeit they may have but little left of their by-gone beauty. But yet 'tis ever the chiefest pleasure you can give them, and the one they do love the most, whenas you tell them they are still the same, and are in no wise changed or aged, and above all those of them which grow not old from the waist downwards.

I have heard speak of a very fair and honourable lady which one day did say thus to her lover: "I know not whether for the future old age will bring me increasing inconvenience and incapacity,"—she was fifty-five years old; "but, God be thanked, I did never do myself pleasure so well as I do now, nor ever took greater joy therein. Whether this do last out and continue till my extremest old age or no, I have no fault to find, nor complaint to make of my days gone by."

Now as concerning love and concupiscence, I have both here and elsewhere adduced examples enough, without dwelling longer on this subject. Let us now consider a while the maxim as concerning this special beauty of fair ladies, how that it doth not diminish by reason of old age.

For sure, the aforesaid Spanish lady did allege many good reasons and seemly comparisons, likening these fair ladies to fine old buildings of yore whose ruins do yet remain superb and imposing. So amid the noble antiqui-

[307]

ties of Rome do we see the ruins of palaces, superb relics of Collosseum and Thermæ, which to this day do plainly show what they once were, and do inspire all beholders with wonder and awe, their mere ruins being wondrous and surprising. Nay, more! on these same ruins men do still build right noble edifices, proving that the foundations be better and finer than fresh new ones. So very often in their constructions, the which our good architects and masons do undertake, if that they find some old ruins and ancient foundations, straightway do they build on these, and that in preference to laying new ones.

Likewise have I seen good galleys and ships built and reconstructed on old hulls and old keels, the which had long lain in harbour doing nothing; and these were every whit as good and sound as others which the ship-carpenters did frame and build all new, and of new timber fresh from the forest.

Furthermore, our Spanish lady was used to say,—do we not many a time see the summits of high towers carried away, overthrown and disfigured by winds, storms and lightning, while the base doth remain safe and sound? For 'tis ever against such lofty points that storms do spend their fury. The sea winds moreover do corrode and eat away the upper stones of a building and do wear them hollow more than those at the bottom, seeing these be not so much exposed as the ones higher up.

In like wise many fair ladies do lose the brilliancy and beauty of their pretty faces by various accidents whether of cold or heat, of sun and moon, and the like, as well as, more's the pity, by reason of various cosmetics, the which they do apply to them, thinking so to heighten their charms, but really and truly spoiling all their beauty thereby. Whereas in other parts, they do apply no other preparation but only nature's method, feeling therefore neither cold, nor rain, nor wind, neither sun nor moon, none of which do affect them at all.

If heat do inconvenience them, they know many means to gain relief and coolness; as likewise they can guard against cold in plenty of ways. So many inconveniences and injuries must needs be warded off from a woman's beauty of face, but few or none from that which lieth elsewhere. Wherefore we should never conclude, because a woman's countenance is spoiled, that she is all foredone all over, and that naught doth remain of fine and good, and that 'tis useless to build on that foundation.

I have heard a tale told of a certain great lady, which had been exceeding fair and much devoted to love. One of her old lovers having lost sight of her for the space of four years, through some journey he did undertake, on returning from the same did find her sadly changed from the fair countenance he had known erstwhile, the which did so disappoint him and chill his ardour as that he did no more care to board her nor to renew with her again the pleasure of former days. She did recognize him readily enough, did endeavour all she could to get him to come and see her. Accordingly to this end she did one day counterfeit sickness, and when he had come to visit her by daylight did thus say to him: "I know well enough, Sir! you do scorn me for my poor face so changed by age; but come, look you, and see if there be aught changed there. If my face has deceived you, at any rate there is no deception about that." So the gentleman examining her and finding her as fair and sound as ever, did straight recover appetite and did enjoy the flesh he had thought

[309]

to be spoiled. "Now this is the way, Sir," said the lady, "you men are deceived! Another time, give no credence to the lies our false faces tell; for indeed the rest of our bodies doth by no means always match them. This is the lesson I would have you learn."

Another lady of the like sort, being thus sorely changed of her fair face, was in such great anger and despite against the same, that she would never more look at it in her mirror, saying 'twas unworthy of so much honour. So she had her head always dressed by her maids; and to make up, would ever look at the other parts of herself only and gaze at these, taking as much pride and delight therein as she had aforetime done in her beautiful face.

I have heard speak of another lady, who whenever she did lie by daylight with her lover, was used to cover her face with a fair white kerchief of fine Holland web, for fear lest, if he should look in her face, the upper works might chill and stay his affection, and move him to mere disgust; for indeed below was naught to chide at, but all was as fine as ever. This doth remind me of yet another very honourable lady I have heard tell of, who did make a diverting and witty reply. Her husband one day asking her why her hair in one place was not grown white and hoary like that of her head, "Ah, yes," she did exclaim, "the wretch it is! It hath done all the folly, yet doth it feel naught, nor experience any ill consequences. Many and many a time hath it made my head to suffer; whereas it doth ever remain unchanged, in the same good estate and vigour, and keepeth the same complexion, and above all the same natural heat, and the same appetite and sound health. But how far otherwise it is with my other parts,

[310]

which do endure aches and pains for it, and my hair which
hath long ago grown white and hoary."

And she had good reason so to speak; for truly this
doth engender in women many ills, and gout and other
sicknesses. Moreover for being over hot at it, so the
doctors say, do they grow prematurely hoary-headed.
Thus we see fair ladies do never grow old in some parts,
either in one fashion or the other.

I have heard many men relate,—men which have followed women freely, even going with courtesans,—how
that they have scarce ever seen pretty women get old in
certain parts, did always keep all their former beauty, and
good will and hearty disposition to boot as good as aforetime. Nay, more! I have heard not a few husbands declare
they did find their *old women* (so they called them) as fair
and fine as ever, and as full of desire and wantonness,
beauty and good will, discovering no change at all but of
face, and were as fain to love them as ever they were in
their young days.

In fine, how many men there be which do love old
women for many reasons better than young! Just as there
be many which do love old horses best, whether for a good
day's work, or for the riding-school and display,—such
animals as have been so well drilled in their youth as that
you will have never a fault to find with them when grown
old. Right well trained have they been, and have never
after forgot their pretty cunning.

I have myself seen in our Royal stables a horse they
called *Quadragant*, first broke in the time of King Henri.
He was over two and twenty years old; but aged as he was,
he yet went very well, and had forgot naught of his exercises. He could still give his King, and all which did see

[311]

him go through his paces, great and real pleasure. I have seen the like done by a tall charger called *Gonzago*, from the stud-farm of Mantua, and which was of the same age as *Quadragant*.

I have likewise seen that magnificent and well-known black, which had been set to stallion's work. Signor Antonio, who had charge of the Royal stud, did show him me at Meung,[7] one day I did pass that way, making him do the two strides and a leap, and the round step,—both which he did execute as well as the day M. de Carnavallet had first trained him,—for he was his horse. The late M. de Longueville was fain to hire him of his master for three thousand livres; however King Charles would not have it, but took him for himself, recompensing the owner in another way. A whole host of others I could easily name; but I should never have done, and so do refer me to those worthy squires which have seen so many of the sort.

Our late King Henri, at the camp of Amiens, had chose for his mount on the day of battle an horse called *le Bay de la Paix*, a very fine and strong charger, and aged. But he died of fever in the camp of Amiens; so the most expert farriers did declare, but 'twas deemed a strange thing to have happed.

The late Duc de Guise did send to his stud-farm of Esclairon[8] for the bay *Sanson*, which was there serving the mares as stallion, to be his mount at the battle of Dreux, where he did carry him excellently.

In his first wars the late Prince did take from the stud at Mun two and twenty horses, which were there as stallions, to serve him in his campaigns; and did divide the same among the different lords which were with him, after reserving his own share. Whereof the gallant Avaret did have a charger which the great Constable had given to King Henri, and which was called *le Compère* (Old Gossip). Aged as he was, never was seen a better mount; his master did prove him in some good tough rencontres, and he did carry him right well. Captain Bourdet gat the Arab, on whose back our late King Henri was wounded and slain, a horse the late M. de Savoie had given him, called *le Malheureux* (the Unlucky). This was his name when he was presented to the King, and verily 'twas one of very ill omen to him. Never in his youth was he near so good as he was in his old age; though 'tis true his master, which was one of the most gallant gentlemen of France, did show him ever to the best advantage. In a word, of all these stallions, was not one that age did hinder from serving his master well, and his Prince and country. Indeed there be some old horses that will never give up; hence 'tis well said, no good horse doth ever become a mere hack.

3.

F such sort be many fair dames, which in their old age be every whit as good as other women in their youth, and do give as great pleasure, from their having been in their time thoroughly well taught and trained. And be sure such lessons are not easily forgot. Then again the best of it is these be always most liberal and generous in giving, so as to keep in hand their cavalier and riders, which do get more money and demand an higher salary to bestride an old mount than a young one. 'Tis just the opposite with squires and real horsemen, which do never care so much

to mount broke horses as young ones that be yet to break. However this is but reasonable after all.

There is a question I have seen debated on the subject of women of years, to wit: which doth bring the greater glory, to love a woman of years and have the enjoyment of her, or to so do with a young one. Not a few have I heard pronounce for the older woman. For they would maintain that the foolishness and heat which be in youth are of themselves debauched enough already and right easy to undo; whereas the prudence and coldness that would seem natural to age cannot but with difficulty be led astray. And so they which do succeed in corrupting such win the higher repute.

In like wise was the famous courtesan Laïs used to boast and glorify herself greatly of the fact that the philosophers did come so oft to visit her and learn in her school, more than of all the young and giddy folks which did frequent her society. So also Flora was ever proud to see great and dignified Roman senators arrive at her door, rather than young and foolish gallants. Thus methinks 'tis great glory to vanquish and overcome the wise prudence which should be in persons of ripe age, so far as pleasure and satisfaction go.

I do refer me to such men as have made experiment hereof, of the which sundry have told me how that a trained mount is ever more agreeable than a wild colt and one that doth not so much as know the trot. Furthermore, what pleasure and what greatest delight may not a man enjoy in mind, whenas he doth behold enter a ballroom, or one of the Queen's apartments, or a Church, or other place crowded with company, a lady of ripe years and dignity, *de alta guisa* (of lofty carriage) as they say

[314]

in Italian, and above all a lady of honour to the Queen or some Princess, or the governess of some King's daughter, young queen or great princess, or mayhap mother of the maids of honour, one that is chose out and set in this high and sober office by reason of her modest and seemly carriage? You shall see her assuming all the part of the prudish, chaste and virtuous dame, while everybody doth of course suppose her so, by reason of her years; then what joy, when a man doth think in his heart, or e'en say it out to some trusty comrade and confidant of his, "Look at her yonder, with her solemn ways, her staid and cold and scornful mien! To see her, would you not deem butter would not melt in her mouth? Yet, alack-a-day! never a weathercock in all the wide world doth so shift and whirl so swift and nimbly as doth she."

For myself, I do verily believe the man which hath known this joy and can so say, is right well content at heart. Ha! ha! but I have known a many such dames in this world, which did counterfeit to be most modest, prudish and censorious duennas, yet were exceeding dissolute and lecherous when they did come to it. Yea! and they would be put on their backs far more than most young damsels, which, by reason of their too much inexperience, be afraid of the gentle strife! So do they say there is naught so good as old vixens for hunting abroad and getting food for their cubs to eat.

We read how of old days several Roman Emperors did take their pleasure in the debauching and having their will of suchlike high-born ladies of honour and repute, as well for the pleasure and contentment to be had therein,—and in good sooth there is more with such than with women of inferior sort,—as for sake of the glory and honour they

did arrogate to themselves for having so debauched and
bested them. So in like wise have I known in my own time
not a few great Lords, Princes and Noblemen, which have
found great boast and great content at heart, by reason
of having done the same.

Julius Cæsar and Octavius, his successor, were exceeding
ardent after such sort of conquests, as I have alleged before; and after them Caligula, who summoning to his
feasts the most illustrious Roman ladies together with
their husbands, would gaze steadfastly at the same and
examine them minutely, nay! would actually put out his
hand and lift their faces up, if by chance any of them
did hang their heads as conscious of being dames of
honour and repute,—though truly other some were fain
but to counterfeit this modesty, and play the shamefaced
prude. But verily there cannot have been a many genuine
prudes in the days of these dissolute Emperors; yet must
they needs make the pretense, albeit nothing more. Else
had the game not been worth the playing; and I have
myself in our day seen many a fair lady do the like.

Afterward such of them as did hit the worthy Emperor's
taste, these he would take aside openly and from their very
husbands' side, and leading them from the hall would escort
them to a privy chamber, where he would take his pleasure
of them to his full content. This done he would lead them
back to sit down once more in their place; and then before
all the company would proceed to commend their beauties
and special hidden charms that were in them, specifying
these same separately and severally. And any which had
any blemishes, faults or defects of beauty, these he would
by no means let off in silence, but was used always to

describe and declare the same openly, without disguising or concealing aught.

Nero was even yet worse than this, being so curious as that he did examine his own mother's dead body, gazing steadfastly upon the same and handling all her limbs and parts, commending some and abusing others.

I have heard the same thing told of sundry great Lords of Christian days, which have had this same strange curiosity toward their dead mothers.

Nor was this all with the said Caligula; for he was used to retail all their movements, their naughty ways and tricks, and the modes and fashions they did follow in their doing of it, and in special of any which had been modest and prudish, or which had made pretense to be so at table. For verily if a-bed they were fain to do the like, there is small doubt but the cruel tyrant did menace them with death, unless they would do all his pleasure for his full content, and so constrained them by the terror of execution. Then after would he speak despitefully of them to his heart's content, to the sore shame and general mockery of the poor dames, who thinking to be accounted chaste and modest as ever women can be, and to play the hypocrite and counterfeit *donne da ben* (virtuous ladies), were utterly and entirely revealed in their true colours and made known as mere harlots and wanton wenches. And truly this was no bad business so to discover them in a character they did never wish to be known. And better still, 'twas always, as I have said, great ladies that were so entreated, such as wives of consuls, dictators, prætors, quæstors, senators, censors, knights, and others of the highest estate and dignity, as we might say in our own days and Christian lands, mighty Queens, (which yet are not to be compared with Consuls' wives, seeing these were paramount over all men), Princesses of greater and less puissance, Duchesses, Marchionesses, and Countesses, great and small, Baronesses, Knights' dames, and the like ladies of rank and rich estate. And truly there is no doubt at all but that many Christian Emperors and Kings, if they had the power to do the like of the Emperor Caligula toward ladies of such quality, would avail themselves thereof. But then they be Christians, which have the fear of God before their eyes, his holy ordinances, their own conscience and honour, and the ill-repute of their fellows, to say naught of the ladies' husbands, to whose generous spirit suchlike tyranny would be unendurable. Wherein of a surety our Christian Kings be deserving of high esteem and commendation, thus to win the love of fair ladies rather by dint of gentleness and loving arts than by brute force and harsh rigour,— and the conquest so gained is by far a nobler one.

I have heard speak of two great Princes [1] which have taken exceeding pleasure in thus discovering their ladies' beauties, charms and especial graces, as well as their deformities, blemishes and defects, together with their little ways, privy movements and wanton wiles,—not however in public, as did Caligula, but in privity, with their close and particular friends. Truly a sad fashion to entreat the pretty persons of these poor ladies. Thinking to do well and sport agreeably for to pleasure their husbands, they be but scorned therefor and made a laughing-stock.

Well, to return to our former comparison,—just as we do see beautiful buildings based on better foundations and of better stone and material some than others, and for this cause endure longer in their glory and beauty,

[318]

even so there be some dames of bodies so well complexioned and fairly fashioned, and endowed with so fine a beauty, as that time doth in no wise so prevail over them as with others, nor seem to undermine their comeliness at all.

We read in history how that Artaxerxes,[2] among all the wives he had, did love the most Astacia, which was a woman of very ripe age, yet still most beautiful, and had been the mistress of his late brother Darius. His son did fall so deep in love with her, so exceeding fair was she in spite of years, that he did demand to share her with his father, in the same way as his share of the Kingdom. But the father, angered by this and jealous at the notion of another sharing with him this dainty morsel, did make her Priestess of the Sun, forasmuch as in Persia women which hold this estate must vow themselves to absolute chastity.

We read again in the History of Naples how Ladislas, a Hungarian and King of Naples, did besiege in Taranto the Duchess Marie, widow of Rammondelo de Balzo, and after sundry assaults and feats of arms, did take her by arrangement with her children, and wed her, albeit she was of ripe years, yet exceeding fair to look upon, and carried her with him to Naples. She was thereafter known as Queen Marie and fondly loved and cherished of the King.

Myself once saw the fair Duchesse de Valentinois (Diane de Poitiers) at the age of seventy, as fair of face, as fresh-looking and lovable as at thirty; and verily she was well loved and courted by one of the greatest and most gallant Kings in all the world. I may tell her age frankly, without wrong to the beauty of this fair lady, seeing whenever a lady is loved of a great King, 'tis sure sign perfection

[319]

doth abundantly reside in her, and make her dear to him. And surely that beauty which is given of heaven should never be spared in favour of heaven's demigods.

I saw this lady, six months before she died, still so very fair I can imagine no heart so flinty as not to have been stirred thereby, and though a while before she had broke a leg on the stony pavement of Orleans, riding and sitting her horse as lightly and cleverly as she had ever done. But the horse slipped and fell under her; and for this broken limb, and all the pains and sufferings she did endure, one would have thought her fair face must have been changed. But nothing of the sort, for her beauty, grace, majesty and gallant mien were just what they had ever been. And above all, she did possess an extraordinary whiteness of skin, without any recourse had to paint; only 'tis said that every morning she did employ certain washes compounded of spring water and sundry drugs, the which I cannot name like good doctors or cunning apothecaries can. I do believe that if this fair lady had lived yet another hundred years, she would never have aged, whether in face, so excellently framed was it, or in body, the parts covered and concealed that is, of such excellent temper and good condition was this. The pity is earth should ever cover these beauteous forms!

Likewise myself have seen the Marquise de Rothelin,[3] mother of the Dowager Princess de Condé and the late deceased M. de Longueville, in no wise diminished of her beauty by time or age, but keeping the fresh flower of her youth as aforetime, except only that her face did grow something redder toward the end. Yet did her beautiful eyes, that were unmatched in all the world, and which her

[320]

daughter hath inherited, never alter, but were to the last as meet to wound hearts as ever.

Another I have seen in like case was Madame de la Bourdaisière,[4] afterward by a second marriage wife to the Maréchal d'Aumont. This lady in her later days was so fair to look on you would have said she was in her early youth still, and her five daughters, all beautiful women, did in no wise eclipse her. And readily enough, if the choice had been to make, would a man have left the daughters to take the mother in preference; yet had she borne a number of children. And truly of all women she did most take heed of her good looks, for she was a mortal enemy of the night damp and moonlight, and did avoid these all ever she could. The ordinary use of paint for the face, practised by so many ladies, was quite unknown to her.

I have also seen, and this is a more striking instance still, Madame de Mareuil, mother of the Marquise de Mézières and grandmother of the Princess-Dauphin, at the age of an hundred, at which she died, looking as fresh and upright, as alert, healthy and comely as at fifty. She had been a very handsome woman in her younger days.

Her daughter, the Marquise de Mézières named above, was of like sort and died in the like good case, but she was twenty years younger when this took place, and her figure had shrunk somewhat. She was aunt of Mme. de Bourdeille, my elder brother's wife, and did bring him the like excellent qualities. For albeit she have passed her fifty-third year and hath had fourteen children, one may truthfully say this,—and others which see her are of better judgment than I, and do assure me of the fact,—that the

[321]

four daughters she hath by her side do look like her own sisters. So do we often see winter fruits, and relics of the past season, match those of Summer itself, and keep their sweetness, and be as fine and savour as these, and even more.

The Amirale de Brion too, and her daughter, Mme. de Barbézieux,[5] did continue very handsome women to quite old age.

I have been told of late how that the fair Paule de Toulouse,[6] so renowned of old days, is yet as beautiful as ever, though she is now eighty-four, and no change is to be seen, whether in her fine, tall figure or her beautiful face.

Another I have seen is the Présidente de Conte, of Bordeaux, of equal age and equal beauty, in all ways most lovable and desirable; and indeed she was a woman of many perfections. Many other such could I name, but I should never have done.

A young Spanish knight speaking of love to a lady of advanced age, but still handsome, she did make him this answer: *A mis completas desta manera me habla V. M.?* "How can you speak so to my complines?"—meaning to signify by complines her age and the decline of her best days, and the approach of night. The knight did reply: *Sus completas valen mas, y son mas graciosas que las horas de prima de qualquier otra dama,* "Your complines are better worth, and more fair and delectable than the hours of prime of any other lady." A very pretty conceit surely!

Another speaking in like wise of love to a lady of ripe years, and she making objection to him of her withered beauty,—which yet was not over and above so,—did thus

[322]

answer her: *A las visperas se conoce la fiesta,*—"at vespers
is the feast at its best."

4.

E have yet among us to this day Madame de
Nemours, of yore in the April of her beauty
the wonder of the world, which doth still defy
all devastating time. I may truly say of her,
as may all that have seen her with me, that she was erst
the fairest dame, in her blooming days, in all Christendom. I did see her one day dance, as I have told elsewhere, with the Queen of Scots, they twain all alone together and without any other ladies to bear them company, by way of a caprice, so that all such, men and
women, as did behold them knew not to which to adjudge
the palm of beauty. Verily, as one said at the time, you
would have thought them those two suns which we read in
Pliny to have once appeared together in the sky, to dazzle
the world. Madame de Nemours, at that time Madame
de Guise, did show the more luxurious figure; and if it be
allowed me so to say without offence to the Queen of
Scots, she had the more imposing and apparent dignity
of port, albeit she was not a Queen like the other. But
then she was grand-daughter of that great King,[1] the
father of his people, whom she did resemble in many of her
features, as I have seen him portrayed in the gallery of
the Queen of Navarre, showing in every look the great
monarch he was.

I think I was the first which did call her by this name of
Grand-daughter of the great King, Father of his People.
This was at Lyons, time when the King did return out of

Poland; and often would I call her so, and she did me the honour to deem it well, and like it at my hands. She was in very deed a true grand-daughter of that great King, and especially in goodness of heart and beauty. For she was ever very good-hearted, and few or none are to be found that she ever did ill or displeasure to, while many did win great advantage in the time of her favour, that is to say in the time of her late husband, Monsieur de Guise, which did enjoy high consideration in France. Thus were there two very noble perfections united in this lady, goodness and beauty, and both of these hath she right well maintained to this present day, and by their means hath married two most honourable husbands, and two that few or none at all could have been found to match. And indeed, and if another could be found of like sort and worthy of her, and if she did wish for a third, she might well enjoy one more, so fair is she yet.

And 'tis a fact that in Italy folk do hold the ladies of Ferrara for good and tasty morsels,—whence hath come the saying, *potta ferraresa*, just as they say, *cazzo mantuano* (a Mantua verge). As to this, when once a great Lord of that country was making court to a great and beauteous Princess of France, and they were all commending him at Court for his excellent merits, valiance and the high qualities which did make him deserving of her favours, there was one, the late M. d'Au,[2] Captain of the Scottish Guards, which did come nearer the point than any with these words, "Nay! you do forget the chief of all, his *cazzo mantuano* to wit."

I did once hear a like speech, how when the Duke of Mantua, which was nicknamed the *Gobin* (Hunchback), because he was excessively hunchbacked, was desirous of

[324]

wedding the sister of the Emperor Maximilian, the lady was told that he was so sadly deformed. But she only made answer, as 'tis said: *Non importa purche la campana habbia qualche diffetto, ma ch' el sonaglio sia buono* ("No matter if the bell have some flaw, provided the clapper be good"),—meaning thereby this same *cazzo mantuano*. Some indeed aver she did never say the thing at all, seeing she was too modest and well brought up; but at any rate others did say it for her.

But to return to this same Princess of Ferrara, I did see her at the marriage of the late M. de Joyeuse appear clad in a mantle of the Italian fashion, the sleeves drawn back half way up the arms in the Siennese mode. But there was no lady there which could outshine her, and no man but said: "This fair Princess cannot make herself any fairer, so fair is she already. And 'tis easy to judge by her beauteous face that she hath other hidden beauties of great charm and parts which are not seen. Just as by looking at the noble façade of a fine building, 'tis easy to judge that within there be fair chambers, antechambers and closets, fair alcoves and privy places." In many another spot likewise hath she displayed her beauty, and no long while since, in this autumn of her days, and especially in Spain at the marriage of Monsieur and Madame de Savoie, in such wise that the admiration of her and her charms did remain graven in that land for all time. And if my pen had wings of power and range enough to raise her to the skies, right gladly would I devote it to the task; but 'tis too weak for such emprise. Yet will I speak of her again later. No doubt is there but this Princess was a very beautiful woman in her Springtide,

[325]

her Summer and Autumn, yea! and is still in her Winter, albeit she hath had many griefs and many children.

The worst of it is that the Italians, scorning a woman which hath had a number of children, do call such an one *scrofa*, that is to say a "sow." But surely they which do bear handsome, gallant and noble sons, as did this Princess, are praiseworthy, and do in no wise merit this ugly name, but rather that of heaven's favourites.

I will only add this remark: What a strange and wondrous inconsistency is here, that the thing of all others most fickle and inconsistent doth offer such resistance to time, to wit a pretty woman! 'Tis not I which do say this; sorry should I be to do so. For truly I do esteem highly the constancy of many of the sex, nor are all inconstant. 'Tis from another I borrow the remark.

I would gladly adduce the names of ladies of other lands, as well as of our own, that have still been fair in their Autumn and Winter; but for this while I will mention two only in this class.

One is the good Queen Elizabeth of England, the which is reigning at this day, and who they tell me is as fair as ever. If this be true, I do hold her for a very fair and beauteous Princess; for myself have seen her in her Summertide and in her Autumn season. As for her Winter, she doth now approach near the same, if she be not there already; for 'tis long ago I did see her, and the first time ever I saw her, I know what age they did give her then. I do believe what hath kept her so long in her prime of beauty is that she hath never been wed, nor borne the burden of marriage, the which is a very grievous one, above all when a woman hath many children. The said Queen is deserving of all praise on all accounts, were it not for the death of that gallant, beautiful and peerless Princess, the Queen of Scots, the which hath sore stained her good repute.

5.

HE second foreign Princess I shall name is the Marquise de Gouast, Donna Maria of Aragon, which lady myself have seen still very beautiful in her final season. And I will show this in an account, the which I will abridge all ever I can.

After the death of King Henri[1] of France, one month later died also Pope Paul IV.,[2] Caraffa, and it became needful for the election of a new Pope that all the Cardinals should meet together. Amongst others there came from France the Cardinal de Guise, and did fare to Rome by sea with the King's galleys, whereof the General was François de Lorraine, Grand Prior of France, brother of the said Cardinal, who did convoy him, as a good brother should, with a fleet of sixteen galleys. And they did make such good speed and with so fine a wind astern, as that they did arrive in two days and two nights at Civita Vecchia, and from there presently to Rome. But being come thither, the Grand Prior seeing they were not yet ready to proceed to the new election (and as a fact it was yet three months more a-doing), and that accordingly his brother could not at present return, and his galleys were but lying idle in port meantime, he did determine to go on to Naples to see that town and spend his leisure there.

So on his arrival, the Viceroy, at that time the Duke of Alcala, did receive him as if he had been a King. But

[327]

before his actual arrival he did salute the town with a very fine salvo of artillery which did last a great while; and the same honour was repaid him by the town and its forts, so as you would have said the very heavens were strangely thundering during the said cannonade. And keeping his galleys in line of battle and review order, and at some distance to seaward, he did despatch in a skiff M. de l'Estrange, a gentleman of Languedoc, a very discreet and honourable man, and one which could speak very gracefully, to the Viceroy, to the end he might not startle him, and to ask his leave (seeing that albeit we were at peace and on the best of terms we did come with all the terrors of war) to enter the harbour, for to see the town and visit the sepulchres of his ancestors which were there interred, and cast holy water upon them and make a prayer.

This the Viceroy did accord very readily. Then did the Grand Prior advance and renew the salvo with as fine and furious a cannonade as before, both with the main-deck guns and his sixteen galleys and other pieces of ordnance and with arquebus fire, in such wise that all his fleet was a mass of flame. So did he make entry most proudly to the mole, with standards and pennants flying, and dressed with flags of crimson silk, and his own of damask, and with all the galley-slaves clad in crimson velvet, and the soldiers of his body-guard the same, and wearing short cloaks covered with silver broidery. The commander of these was Captain Geoffroy, a Provençal and a brave and gallant soldier. Altogether our French galleys were found of all right fine, swift and well careened and above all the "Ship Royal," to the which never a fault

[328]

could be found; for indeed this Prince was in all ways
exceeding magnificent and right liberal.

So being come to the mole in this gallant array, he did
there land and all we his suite with him, at a spot where
the Viceroy had commanded to have ready horses and
coaches for to receive us and carry us to the town. And
truly we did there find an hundred steeds,—coursers, jennets, Spaniards, barbs and other horses, each finer than
the other, with saddle-cloths of velvet all wrought with
broidery, some silver and some gold. He that would ride
a-horse did so, and he that preferred to go in a coach,
found one ready, for there were a score there of the finest
and richest, excellently horsed and drawn by the finest
cattle ever seen. There too stood many great Princes
and Lords, as well of the Kingdom of Naples as of Spain,
which did welcome the Grand Prior most honourably on
behalf of the Viceroy. On landing he did mount a Spanish horse, the finest I have seen for many a long day,
which the Viceroy did after present to him; and did manage him right well, and make him perform some brilliant
curvets, as was much spoke of at the time. The Prince,
who was a very good horseman, as good indeed as he was
a seaman, did make a very fine show thus mounted; and he
did display his horse's paces to the best advantage, and
in most graceful style, seeing he was one of the handsomest Princes of his day, and one of the most pleasant
and accomplished, and of a fine, tall and active figure,—
which is a rare thing with suchlike great personages.
Thus was he conducted by all these Lords and many
another noble gentleman to the Viceroy's Palace, where
this last did await him and paid him all possible honour,
and lodged him in his own house, and did feast him most

sumptuously, both him and all his band. This he was well able to do, seeing he did profit him by twenty thousand crowns through this journey. We were, I daresay, a couple of hundred gentlemen that were with him, Captain of galleys and others, and were lodged with most of the great Lords of the city, and that most sumptuously.

First thing in the morning, on coming out from our chambers, we did find attendants so well appointed as that they would present themselves instantly to ask what we were fain to do, and whither we would go to take our pleasure. And if we did call for horses or coaches, in a moment, our wish was no sooner expressed than satisfied. So they would away at once to seek whatever mount we did crave, and all these so fine, rich and magnificent as might have contented a King; and then off on our way to take our day's pleasure, in such wise as each did prefer. In very fact were we well nigh spoiled by excess of enjoyment and all delights in that fair city; nor can we say there was any lack of such, for indeed I have never seen a town better supplied therewith in every sort. One alone was wanting, to wit the familiar converse, frank and free, with ladies of honour and repute,—for of others there was enough and to spare. But the defect was well and wisely remedied for the time being by the complaisance of this same Marquise de Gouast, in whose honour is the present discourse writ. For she, being a right courteous lady and full of all honourable feeling, and well fitting the nobility of her house, having heard the high repute of the Grand Prior for all the perfections that were in him, and having seen him pass through the city on horseback and recognized his worth, as is meet between folk of high station toward one another, with the magnanimity she did ever show in all things, did send one day a very honourable and well mannered gentleman of her attendance to greet the Prince from her, charging him to say, that if her sex and the custom of the country had suffered her to visit him, she would right gladly have come very readily to offer him her best services, as all the great Lords of the Kingdom had done. But she did beg him to take the will for the deed, offering him the use of her houses, castles and her best service in all things.

The Grand Prior, who was courtesy itself, did thank her most heartily, as was but meet; and did send word how that he would come to kiss her hands straightway after dinner. And this he did not fail to do, accompanied by all of us gentlemen which were with him in his suite. We did find the Marquise in her guest hall along with her two daughters, Donna Antonina and Donna Hieronima,—or was it Donna Joanna? for indeed I cannot say for sure, it having now slipped my memory,—as well as many other fair dames and damsels, so richly apparelled and of such a charming grace as that I have never, outside our own Court of France and that of Spain, seen elsewhere a more beauteous band of fair ladies.

Then did the Marquise salute the Grand Prior in the French fashion and did welcome him with every mark of honour; and he did return the same, even yet more humbly,—*con mas gran sosiego* (with the very greatest respect), as they say in Spanish. Their discourse was for the present of mere commonplaces; while the rest of us, such as could speak Italian or Spanish, did accost the other ladies, whom we did find most honourable and gallant, and of very pleasing conversation.

On our departure, the Marquise, having learned from

the Grand Prior that he did purpose to make a stay of a fortnight in the place, said thus to him: "Sir, if at any time you know not what to do and are in lack of pastime, your coming hither will ever do me much honour, and you shall be most welcome, as it were at the house of your own lady mother; and I beg you to use the same precisely as though it were your own, neither more nor less. I have the good fortune to be loved and visited by honourable and fair dames of this Kingdom and city as much as any lady therein; and seeing your youth and merit do set you to love the conversation of honourable ladies, I will beseech them to resort hither yet more frequently than they do use, to bear you company and all the fair and noble gentlefolk which be with you. Here stand my two daughters, the which I will direct, albeit they are not so well accomplished as they should be, to bear you company after the French fashion, to wit to laugh, dance, play and talk freely, modestly and honourably, even as you do at the Court of France. And I would gladly enough offer myself for one; only 'twould be very irksome to a young Prince, handsome and gallant like yourself, to have to entertain an old woman, worn out, tiresome and unlovable such as I. For verily and indeed youth and age do scarce accord well together."

These words the Grand Prior did straightway take objection to, assuring her that old age had gat no hold at all upon her, and that he would never hear of any such thing, but that her Autumn did overpass all the Spring-tides and Summers that were in that hall. And truly she did still seem a very handsome and very lovable woman, yea! even more than her two daughters, pretty and young as these were. Yet was she then very nigh sixty good years old. This little speech of the Prince did much pleasure the Marquise, as we could easily see by her laughing face and all her words and ways.

We did leave her house exceeding delighted with the lady,—and above all the Grand Prior himself, who had instantly fallen in love with her, as he did inform us. Little doubt then but this fair and honourable lady, and her fair band of attendant dames, did draw the Grand Prior to resort every day to her house; for indeed if we went not there after dinner, we did so in the evening. The Prince did take for mistress her eldest daughter, albeit he did better love the mother; but 'twas done *per adumbrar la cosa*,—"to veil the matter."

Tiltings at the ring were held in plenty, whereat the Grand Prior did bear away the prize, as well as many ballets and dances. In a word, the gay society he did enjoy was the cause of this, that whereas he had purposed to tarry but a fortnight, we were there for a good six weeks. Nor were we in any wise irked thereby, for we had likewise gotten us mistresses no less than our General. Nay! we had certainly remained longer still, had not a courier come from the King, bringing him news of the breaking out of the war in Spain. For this cause he had to weigh anchor and carry his galleys from the Eastern shore to the Western, though in fact they did not cross over till eight months later.

So had we to take leave of all these delightsome pleasures, and quit the good and gracious town of Naples; and truly 'twas not without great sadness and many regrets to our General and all of us, but we were right sorry to leave a place where we had been so happy.

At the end of some six years, or mayhap longer, when

[333]

we were on our way to the succour of Malta, I was again at Naples and did make enquiry if the aforesaid fair lady were yet alive. I was told yes! and that she was in that town. Instantly I made a point of going to see her; and was immediately recognized by an old seneschal of her house, which did away to tell his mistress that I was fain to kiss her hands. She, remembering my name of Bourdeille, did summon me up to her chamber to see her. I found her keeping her bed, by reason of a slight rash she had on one of her cheeks. She did make me, I swear, a right excellent welcome. I did find her very little changed, and still so handsome a woman she might well have made any man commit a mortal sin, whether in will or deed.

She did ask me eagerly for news of my late General the Grand Prior, and lovingly, and how he had died; and saying she had been told how that he had been poisoned, did curse an hundred times over the wretch that had done the deed. I told her 'twas not so, and bade her disabuse her fancy of any such idea, informing her how he had died really of a treacherous and secret pleurisy he had caught at the battle of Dreux, where he had fought like a Cæsar all day long. But at evening, after the last charge, being greatly heated by fight and a-sweat, and then withdrawing on a night of the most bitter hard frost, he was chilled to the bone. He did conceal his sickness, and died of it a month or six weeks afterward.

She did manifest, both by words and manner, her deep regret for him. And note now, two or three years before this, he had despatched two galleys on a freebooting expedition under the charge of Captain Beaulieu, one of the Lieutenants of his galleys. He had adopted the flag of the Queen of Scots, one which had never been seen or known in the Eastern seas, and which did cause folk much amaze; for 'twas out of the question to take that of France, because of the alliance with the Turks. Now the Grand Prior had given orders to the said Captain Beaulieu to land at Naples and pay a visit on his behalf to the Marquise de Gouast and her daughters, to which three ladies he did send by his hand an host of presents, all the little novelties then in vogue at the Court and Palace, in Paris and in France generally. Indeed this same noble Grand Prior was ever the soul of generosity and magnificence. This task Captain Beaulieu did not fail to perform, and did present all his master's gifts; himself was most excellently received, and rewarded by a fine present for his mission.

The Marquise did feel such obligation for these gifts and for that he had continued to remember her, that she did tell me again and again how gratified she had been and how she had loved him yet more than afore for his goodness. Again for love of him, she did a graceful courtesy to a gentleman of Gascony, which was at that time an officer in the galleys of the Grand Prior. This gentleman was left behind, when we set sail, sick unto death. But so kind was fortune to him, that addressing himself to the said lady in his adversity, he was so well succoured of her that his life was saved. She did take him in her household, and did serve him so well, as that a Captaincy falling vacant in one of her Castles, she did bestow the same on him, and procured him to marry a rich wife to boot.

None of the rest of us were aware what had become of the poor gentleman, and we deemed him dead. But lo! at the time of this latter voyage to Malta, there was amongst us a gentleman, younger brother of him I spake of, which did one day in heedless talk tell me of the main occasion for his going abroad. This he said was to seek news of a brother of his that had formerly been in the service of the Grand Prior, and had tarried behind sick at Naples more than six years before and had never been heard of since. Then did I bethink me, and presently did make enquiry for news of him of the folk belonging to the Marquise. These told me of his good fortune, and I did at once inform the younger brother. The latter did thank me very heartily, and accompanied me to pay his respects to the said lady, who did take him into great favour also, and went to visit him at his lodging.

Truly a pretty gratitude and remembrance of a friendship of old days,—which remembrance she did still cherish, as I have said. For she did make me even better cheer than before, and did entertain me with tales of the old happy time and many other subjects,—all which did make me to find her company very pleasant and agreeable. For she was of a good intelligence and bright wit, and an excellent talker.

She did beseech me an hundred times over to take no other lodging or meal but with her; but to this I would never consent, it not being my nature ever to be importunate or self-seeking. But I did use to go and visit her every day for the seven or eight days we did tarry there, and I was always most welcome, and her chamber ever open to me without any difficulty.

When at last I bade her adieu, she did give me letters of recommendation to her son, the Marquis de Pescaïre, General at that time in the Spanish army. Besides which, she did make me promise that on my return I would come to see her, and take up my lodging in no other house but hers.

However so great was my ill luck that the galleys which did carry us did land us only at Terracina, from whence we hied to Rome, and I was unable to retrace my steps. Moreover I was fain at that time to join the wars in Hungary; but being at Venice, we did learn the death of the great Sultan Soliman. 'Twas there I did curse my luck an hundred times over, for that I had not anyhow returned to Naples, where I should have passed my time to advantage. Indeed it may well be, that by favour of my lady the Marquise I should there have found some good fortune, whether by marriage or otherwise. For she did certainly do me the honour to like me well.

I suppose my evil destiny willed it not so, but was determined to take me back again to France to be for ever unfortunate there. In this hath dame Fortune never showed me a favourable countenance, except only so far as appearances go and a fair repute as a good and gallant man of worth and honour. Yet goods and rank have I never gotten like sundry of my comrades,—and even some of our lower estate, men I have known which would have deemed themselves happy if I had but spoke to them in a courtyard, or King's or Queen's apartment, or in hall, though only aside and over the shoulder. Yet today I do see these same fellows advanced and grown exceeding big with the rapidity of pumpkins,—though indeed I do make but light of them and hold them no greater than myself and would not defer to any of them by so much as the length of my nail.

Well, well! I may herein apply to myself the word which our Redeemer Jesus Christ did pronounce out of his own mouth, "a prophet hath no honour in his own country." Mayhap had I served foreign Princes as well as I have done mine own, and sought adventure among them as I have among those of our land, I should now be more laden with wealth and dignities than I actually am with years and vexations. Patience! if 'tis my Fate hath spun it so, I do curse the jade; if 'tis my Princes be to blame, I do give them to all the devils, an if they be not there already!

This doth end my account of this most honourable lady. She is dead, with an excellent repute as having been a right fair noble dame and having left behind her a good and generous line, as the Marquis eldest son, Don Juan, Don Carlos, Don Cæsar d'Avalos, all which myself have seen and have spoke of them elsewhere. The daughters no less have followed in their brothers' steps. And herewith I do terminate the main thread of my principal Discourse.

NOTES AND APPENDICES

BIBLIOGRAPHY

(This list is simply a selection from the many editions of the works of Brantôme in French and German. There are also texts in Spanish and Italian. A complete bibliography would fill many pages and would not be essential to the present text.)

EDITIONS

—Leyde, 1666, chez Sambix le jeune, 2 vol. in-12. Le titre portait. *"Vies des dames galantes."*

—Leyde, 1666, chez Jean de la Tourterelle, 2 vol. in-12. Le titre portait. *"Mémoires de messire Pierre de Bourdeille, seigneur de Brantôme, contenans les vies des dames galantes de son temps."*

—Leyde, 1722, chez Jean de la Tourterelle, 2 vol. in-12. Titre rouge et noir. Même titre que dans l'édition précédente et mêmes fautes.

—Londres, 1739, Wood et S. Palmer, 2 vol. in-12, titre rouge et noir. *"Mémoires de messire Pierre de Bourdeille, seigneur de Brantôme, contenant les vies des dames galantes de son temps."* Édition copiée sur les précédentes.

—La Haye, 1740, 15 vol. in-12. Cette édition est de Le Duchat, Lancelot et Prosper Marchand, et les remarques critiques ont servi aux éditions postérieures.

—Londres, 1779, aux dépens du libraire, 15 vol. in-8º. *"Œuvres du seigneur de Brantôme, nouvelle édition considérablement augmentée, accompagnée de remarques historiques et critiques et distribuée, dans un meilleur ordre."* Les *Dames galantes* occupent les tomes III et IV.

—Paris, 1822, Foucault, 8 vol. in-8º. *"Œuvres complétes*

*du seigneur de Brantôme, accompagnées de remarques his-
toriques et critiques. Nouvelle édition collationnée sur les
manuscrits de la Bibliothèque du Roi."* (Monmerqué). Les
Dames galantes occupent le VIIe vol.

—Paris, 1834, Ledoux, 2 vol. in-8°. *"Les Dames galantes,
par le seigneur de Brantôme, nouvelle édition avec une préface
de M. Ph. Chasles."* Édition qui a beaucop et mal profité
de l'édition précédente.

—Paris, 1841-1869, Garnier frères, 1 vol. in-18. Édition
populaire plusieurs fois réimprimée et faite d'après l'édition
de 1740.

—Paris, 1857, A. Delahays, 1 vol. in-12. *"Œuvres de
Brantôme, nouvelle édition revue d'après les meilleurs textes,
avec une préface historique et critique par H. Vigneau. Vies
des Dames galantes."* Édition faite d'après les éditions an-
téricures. Les notes sont bonnes.

Il a été fait une nouvelle édition de ce travail en 1857,
chez Delahays, en in-18.

—Paris, 1876, Renouard, libraire de la Société de l'histoire
de France. *"Œuvres complètes de Pierre de Bourdeille,
seigneur de Brantôme, publiées d'après les manuscrits, avec
variantes et fragments inédits, pour la Société de l'histoire de
France, par Ludovic Lalanne. Tome neuvième. Des Dames"*
(suite). Un gros vol. in-8 de 743 pages, titre non compris.

Cette édition est la première qui indique les sources aux-
quelles Brantôme a puisé ses historiettes. M. Lalanne n'a
laissé aucunp assage sans une explication tojours courte et
toujours substantielle.

—L'Œuvre du Seigneur de Brantôme. *"Vie des Dames galantes."* Introduction and notes by B. de Villeneuve. Paris,
1913.

—*Les Dames galantes.* Publiées d'apres les manuscrits
de la Bibliothèque Nationale, par Henri Bouchot. 2 vols.
E. Flammarion. Paris. (A very fine edition.)

—Brantôme: *Das Leben der Galanten Damen.* (Dionysos-Bücherei). Introduction by George Harsdörfer. 2 vols. Berlin. (The best German edition.)

—Brantôme: *Lives of Fair and Gallant Ladies.* Translated from the original by A. R. Allinson. 2 vols. Paris. Carrington. 1902.

BRANTÔME: By Arthur Tilley

Like Montaigne, Brantôme pretended to be careless of literary fame, but in reality took every pains to secure it; like Montaigne he loved digressions, *gaillardes escapades,* from his main theme; like Montaigne he has drawn for us, though in his case unconsciously, a portrait of himself; like Montaigne he was curious of information, fond of travel and books. But these points of similarity are after all superficial; the difference is fundamental. While Montaigne tested the world and society by the light of his shrewd common sense, Brantôme accepted them without question or reflexion. Montaigne was essentially a thinker, Brantôme was merely a reporter; Montaigne was a moralist, for Brantôme the word morality had no meaning. Montaigne criticised his age, Brantôme reflected it. That indeed is Brantôme's chief value, that he reflects his age like a mirror, but it must be added that he reflects chiefly its more trivial, not to say its more scandalous side. He is the Suetonius of the French Renaissance.

Pierre de Bourdeille, "reverend father in God, abbe de Brantôme," belonged to a noble and ancient family of Perigord. The precise date of his birth is uncertain, but it must be placed somewhere between 1539 and 1542. He spent his childhood with his grandmother, Louise de Vivonne, wife of the seneschal of Poitou, at the court of Margaret of Navarre, and after studying first at Paris and then at Poitiers, travelled for more than a year in Italy, returning to France at the beginning of 1560, when he made his first appearance at the court. Though he already held other benefices besides the abbey from which he took his title, he was not in orders. The next fourteen years were spent by him either in fighting on the Catholic side in the religious wars, or in attendance at the court, or in travel. In 1574 his military career came to an end, for his duties as gentleman of the chamber, to which post he had been appointed in 1568, kept him at court, frivolous, idle, and discontented. At last the refusal of Henry III. to bestow on him the promised post of governor of Perigord filled him with such fury that he determined to enter the service of Spain. But a fall from his horse, which kept him in bed for four years (1583-1587), saved him from being a renegade to his country and turned him into a man of letters.

For it was during this forced inactivity, apparently in 1584, that he began his literary labours, which he continued for the next thirty years, most of which he spent on his estate. He died in 1614, leaving a will of portentous length, in which, among other things, he charged his heirs to have his works printed *en belle et grand lettre et grand volume.* The charge was neglected, and it was not till 1665-1666 that an incomplete and defective edition was published at Leyden, in the Elzevir form. Previous to this, however, several copies had been made of his manuscripts, and Le Laboureur in his edition of Castelnau's Memoirs, published in 1659, had printed long extracts.

Brantôme was a disappointed man when he wrote his memoirs. He had been an assiduous courtier for a quarter of a century and had gained nothing by it, while he had seen men whose merits he believed to be inferior to his rise to wealth and honour. But though he had the love of frivolity and the moral indifference of a true courtier, he had not his pliability. "He was violent," says Le Laboureur, "difficult to live with and of a too unforgiving spirit." Perhaps the best thing that can be said in his favour is that among his most intimate friends were two of the most virtuous characters of their time, Téligny, the son-in-law of Coligny, and Téligny's brother-in-law, François de la Noue. Among his other friends were Louis de Berenger, seigneur du Guast, who was assassinated by order of Marguerite de Valois, and above all Filippo Strozzi, the son of Piero Strozzi, who was his friend for over twenty years, and who exercised over him considerable influence.

The names by which Brantôme's writings are generally known are not those which he himself gave them. Thus the titles *Dames illustres* and *Dames galantes* are an invention of the Leyden publisher for the *Premier et Second livre des Dames*. The other main division of his writings, *Hommes*, consisted in Brantôme's manuscript of two volumes, the first containing the *Grands capitaines*, French and Spanish, and the second *Les couronnels, Discours sur les duels, Rodomontades espagnoles*, and a separate account of La Noue. His original manuscript was completed while Margaret was still the wife of Henry IV., that is to say before November, 1599, but some time after her divorce he made a carefully revised copy. It is upon this copy that the text of M. Lalanne's edition is based for the first five volumes.

Regarded strictly as biographies Brantôme's lives have slender merit, for the majority give one little or no idea of the character of the persons treated. He is at least successful with those who had in them elements of real greatness, such as Coligny and Condé. Even the long life of François de Guise, though it contains some interesting and valuable information, throws little light on Guise himself. But he gives us good superficial portraits of Charles IX., Catharine de Medici, and the Constable de Montmorency, while several of the minor lives, such as Brissac and his brother Cosse, Matignon, and Mary of Hungary, are not only amusing but hit off the characters with considerable success. One of the most entertaining is the unfinished account of his father. On the other hand the account of Margaret of Valois, though it contains some interesting details, is too ecstatic in its open-

[347]

mouthed admiration to have any value as a biography. The conclusion of the account of Monluc may be quoted not only for its reference to Monluc's conversational powers, but as throwing light on Brantôme's own character.

Much of the interest of Brantôme's book is to be found in his numerous digressions, for which he is constantly apologizing. Thus in the middle of the account of Montmorency we have a laudatory sketch of Michel de l'Hospital, in that of Tavannes a digression on the order of St. Michael, in that of Bellegarde an account of his own treatment by Henry III. The digressions are frequently made occasions for amusing stories, which, like Montaigne's, are distinguished from such as Bouchet and Beroalde de Verville collected, in that they generally illustrate some trait of human character.

Like Montaigne again, Brantôme copies freely and without acknowledgment from books. Whole pages are taken from *Le loyal serviteur,* stories are borrowed from Rabelais, Des Periers, and the *Heptameron,* as well as from most of the writers dealt with in the last chapter. But Brantôme, unlike Montaigne, tries to conceal his thefts by judicious alterations, or by pretending that he heard the story himself, or even that he was a witness of the event related. *J'ai ouy conter* and *J'ai vu* are frequently in his mouth. He was doubtless chiefly influenced in these endeavours to conceal his borrowings by the same form of vanity as Montaigne, the desire to be regarded, not as a man of letters, but as a gentleman who amused himself by putting down his reminiscences on paper. It is for this reason that he tries to give a negligent and conversational air to his style. The result is that he is often ungrammatical and sometimes obscure. Yet his style, at any rate in the eyes of a foreigner, has considerable merit, and chiefly from its power of vivid presentment. For Brantôme, like other Gascons, like Montaigne and Monluc and Henry IV., saw things vividly and can make his readers see them. He has a store of expressive words and phrases such as *un peu hommasse* (of Mary of Hungary). A noticeable feature of his style is his love of Italian and Spanish words, reflecting in this, as in other features, the prevailing fashion of the Court.

Brantôme's keen enjoyment of the world pageantry was seldom disturbed by inconvenient reflexion. His only quarrel with society was that the ruling powers were blind to his own merits. He thought the duel, even in the treacherous and bloodthirsty fashion in which it was then carried on, an excellent institution, and at the end of his account of Coligny he inserts an elaborate disquisition on the material benefits which the religious wars had conferred on France. All classes had profited, nobles, clergy, magistrates, merchants, artisans.

And all this is said in sober earnest, without a suspicion of irony. One might at any rate give Brantôme credit for originality had he not told us at the outset that this was the substance of a conversation which he overheard at Court between two great persons, one a soldier and the other a statesman, and both excellent Catholics. Brantôme was the echo as well as the mirror of the Court.

Brantôme's glowing panegyric on Margaret of Valois induced that virtuous princess to write her memoirs, partly in order to supplement his account of her, partly to correct a few errors into which he had fallen. It is to Brantôme accordinly that her memoirs are addressed. They were written about the year 1597 in the château of Usson in Auvergne, where she had resided, nominally as a prisoner, since 1587.

[From *The Literature of the French Renaissance*, Vol. II. 1904.]

APPENDIX—B

BRANTÔME: By George Saintsbury

The complement and counterpart of this moralising[1] on human business and pleasure is necessarily to be found in chronicles of that business and that pleasure as actually pursued. In these the sixteenth century is extraordinarily rich. Correspondence had hardly yet attained the importance in French literature which it afterwards acquired, but professed history and, still more, personal memoirs were largely written. The name of Brantôme has been chosen as the central and representative name of this section of writers, because he is on the whole the most original and certainly the most famous of them. His work, moreover, has more than one point of resemblance to that of the great contemporary author (Montaigne) with whom he is linked at the head of this chapter. Brantôme neither wrote actual history nor directly personal memoirs, but desultory biographical essays, forming a curious and perhaps designed pendant to the desultory moral essays of his neighbour Montaigne. Around him rank many writers, some historians pure and simple, some memoir-writers pure and simple, of whom not a few approach him in literary genius, and surpass him in correctness and finish of style, while almost all exceed him in whatever advantage may be derived from uniformity of plan, and from regard to the decencies of literature.

Pierre de Bourdeille (s) (who derived the name by which he is, and indeed was during his lifetime, generally known from an abbacy given to him by Henri II. when he was still a boy) was born about 1540, in the province of Perigord, but

[1] Referring to Montaigne's *Essays.*

[351]

the exact date and place of his birth have not been ascertained. He was the third son of François, Comte de Bourdeilles, and his mother, Anne de Vivonne de la Chataigneraie, was the sister of the famous duelist whose encounter with Jarnac his nephew has described in a well-known passage. In the court of Marguerite d'Angouleme, the literary nursery of so great a part of the talent of France at this time, he passed his early youth, went to school at Paris and at Poitiers, and was made Abbé de Brantôme at the age of sixteen. He was thus sufficiently provided for, and he never took any orders, but was a courtier and a soldier throughout the whole of his active life. Indeed almost the first use he made of his benefice was to equip himself and a respectable suite for a journey into Italy, where he served under the Marechal de Brissac. He accompanied Mary Stuart to Scotland, served in the Spanish army in Africa, volunteered for the relief of Malta from the Turks, and again for the expedition destined to assist Hungary against Soliman, and in other ways led the life of a knight-errant. The religious wars in his own country gave him plenty of employment; but in the reigns of Charles IX. and Henri III. he was more particularly attached to the suite of the queen dowager and her daughter Marguerite. He was, however, somewhat disappointed in his hopes of recompense; and after hesitating for a time between the Royalists, the Leaguers, and the Spaniards, he left the court, retired into private life, and began to write memoirs, partly in consequence of a severe accident. He seems to have begun to write about 1594, and he lived for twenty years longer, dying on the 15th of July, 1614.

The form of Brantôme's works is, as has been said, peculiar. They are usually divided into two parts, dealing respectively with men and women. The first part in its turn consists of many subdivisions, the chief of which is made up of the *Vies des Grand Capitaines Etrangers et Français,* while others consist of separate disquisitions or essays, *Des Rodomontades*

Espagnoles, "On some Duels and Challenges in France" and elsewhere, "On certain Retreats, and how they are sometimes better than Battles," etc. Of the part which is devoted to women the chief portion is the celebrated *Dames Galantes,* which is preceded by a series of *Vies des Dames Illustres,* matching the *Grands Capitaines. The Dames Galantes* is subdivided into eight discourses, with titles which smack of Montaigne. These discourses are, however, in reality little but a congerie of anecdotes, often scandalous enough. Besides these, his principal works, Brantôme left divers *Opuscula,* some of which are definitely literary, dealing chiefly with Lucan. None of his works were published in his lifetime, nor did any appear in print until 1659. Meanwhile manuscript copies had, as usual, been multiplied, with the result, also usual, that the text was much falsified and mutilated.

The great merit of Brantôme lies in the extraordinary vividness of his powers of literary presentment. His style is careless, though it is probable that the carelessness is not unstudied. But his irregular, brightly coloured, and easily flowing manner represents, as hardly any age has ever been represented, the characteristics of the great society of his time. It is needless to say that the morals of that time were utterly corrupt, but Brantôme accepts them with a placid complacency which is almost innocent. No writer, perhaps, has ever put things more disgraceful on paper; but no writer has ever written of such things in such a perfectly natural manner. Brantôme was in his way a hero-worshipper, though his heroes and heroines were sometimes oddly coupled. Bayard and Marguerite de Valois represent his ideals, and a good knight or a beautiful lady *de par le monde* can do no wrong. This unquestioning acceptance of, and belief in, the moral standards of his own society give a genuineness and a freshness to his work which are very rare in literature. Few writers, again, have had the knack of hitting off character,

[353]

superficially it is true, yet with sufficient distinction, which Brantôme has. There is something individual about all the innumerable characters who move across his stage, and something thoroughly human about all, even the anonymous men and women, who appear for a moment as the actors in some too frequently discreditable scene. With all this there is a considerable vein of moralising in Brantôme which serves to throw up the relief of his actual narratives. He has sometimes been compared to Pepys, but, except in point of garrulity and of readiness to set down on paper anything that came into their heads, there is little likeness between the two. Brantôme was emphatically an *ecrivain* (unscholarly and Italianised as his phrase sometimes appears, if judged by the standards of a severer age), and some of the best passages from his works are among the most striking examples of French prose.

[From *A Short History of French Literature*. 6th Ed. Oxford. 1901.]

NOTES TO VOLUME I

HISTORICAL NOTE

P. V: The Duc d'Alençon was later called the Duc d'Anjou. He died at Château-Thierry, on Sunday, June 10, 1584, from dysentery, which had almost reduced him to a shadow. Nevers, in his *Mémoires* (Vol. I, p. 91), maintains that he was poisoned by a maid of one of his mistresses. According to L'Estoile's account, the Duke was given a magnificent funeral in Paris. He was by no means handsome; his pimpled and deformed nose earned for him an epigram during his expedition in Flanders:

> Flamands, ne soyez estonnez
> Si à François voyez deux nez:
> Car par droit, raison et usage,
> Faut deux nez à double visage.

P. VIII: Pierre de Bourdeille, Seigneur de l'Abbaye de Brantôme. Was born in Périgord, 1527; died 1614. Of an old and distinguished family. Served his apprenticeship to war under the famous Captain François de Guise. Later Gentleman of the Chamber to two French Kings in succession, Charles IX. and Henri III., being high in favour with the latter; Chamberlain to the Duc d'Alençon. As soldier or traveller visited most parts of Europe; intimate with many of the most famous men of his day, including the poet Ronsard. Some time after the death of Charles IX. he retired (disappointed apparently by a diminution of Court favour, and suffering from the results of a serious accident due to a fall from his horse) to his estates in Guyenne, where he employed his leisure in the composition of a number of voluminous works based on reminiscences of the active period of his life.

These are:

Vies des Hommes illustres et grands Capitaines français,
Vies des Grands Capitaines étrangers,
Vies des Dames illustres,
Vies des Dames galantes,
Anecdotes touchant des Duels,
Rodomontades et Jurements espagnols,
and sundry fragments.

P. XXII:

> Souvent femme varie,
> Bien fol qui s'y fie!

(Woman is changing ever; fool the man who trusts her!)

P. 3: The word which Molière popularized does not date from that time; it was used much earlier, and in the thirteenth century we see a man pay a fine of twenty ounces of gold for calling an unfortunate husband *coucou* (cuckold). (*Usatica regni Majorici, Anno* 1248.) About the middle of the fifteenth century, in a letter of remission to a guilty fellow, we find this curious remark: *"Cogul,* which is the same (in the vernacular) as *coulz* or *couppault,* is one of the vilest insults to be thrust at a married man." At times the word *coux* was used:

> Suis-je mis en la confrairie
> Saint Arnoul le seignenur des Coux.

But it was just about the fifteenth century that the confusion appeared between this word and the bird of April (cuckoo); the word *coucou* (cuckoo), which had been explained by a fable, merely imitated the cry, whereas the word *cocu* (cuckold) had been derived from the early Low Latin *cugus.* "Couquou, thus named after its manner of singing and because it is famed for laying its eggs in the nests of other birds; so, inconsistently, he is called a *cocu* (cuckold) in whose nest another man comes." (Bouchet, *Serées.*) There is also a play by Passerat on the metamorphosis of a cuckoo which is worth mentioning. (Bib. Nat., manuscrit français, 22565, f° 24 v°.)

P. 4: In the present work the Author constantly uses the words *belle et honneste* (fair and honourable) to describe such and such a lady, of whom at the same time he speaks as being an unmitigated whore. But when he adds, as he does sometimes, *vertueuse* (virtuous) to *belle et honneste,* he implies by this that the lady was chaste and modest, and raised no talk about herself.

P. 7: The prothonotary Baraud was one of those churchmen of whom Brantôme says elsewhere: "It was customary at the time that prothonotaries, even those of good families, should scarcely be learned, but give themselves up to pleasure," etc.

P. 10: Cosimo de Medici, who had his wife Eleonora de Toledo poisoned. The daughter of whom Brantôme speaks was Isabella,

[356]

whom he married to Paolo Orsini, the Duke of Bracciano. But Cosimo had too marked an affection for this daughter; although she was married, he insisted that she live in Florence and remain with him. Vasari, who painted for the Medici one of the arches of the Palazzo Vecchio, one day surprised the father and the daughter, and recounts the strange adventure which he witnessed. After the death of Cosimo, Paolo Orsini called Isabella to his apartment, and there, according to Litta, "with a rope around her neck coldly strangled her on the night of July 16, 1576, in the act of consummating the marriage." (Medici, t, IV, tavola xiv.) That unhappy woman was one of the most marvellous of her time: beautiful, cultured, musical, she had all the brilliant advantages of the mind and of the body. Meanwhile, she had had as a lover Troilo Orsini, who was attached to her husband as a bodyguard, and who was assassinated in France, where he had retired.

P. 10: Louis de Clermont de Bussy d'Amboise was born towards the middle of the XVIth Century, and took an active part in the Massacre of Saint Bartholomew. On that occasion, profiting by the confusion, he murdered his kinsman Antoine de Clermont, with whom he was at law for the possession of the Marquisat de Renel. Having obtained from his patron the Duc d'Anjou the governorship of the Castle of Angers, he made himself the terror of the countryside. Letters of his addressed to the wife of the Comte de Montsoreau, whom he was endeavouring to seduce, having fallen into Charles IX.'s hands, were by him shown to the husband. The latter forced his wife to write a reply to her lover appointing a rendezvous. On his appearing there, Montsoreau and a band of armed men fell upon and despatched him (1579). The comment of the historian de Thou is in these words: "The entire Province was overjoyed at Bussy's death, while the Duke of Anjou himself was not sorry to be rid of him." [Transl.]

P. 11: René de Villequier, Baron de Clairvaux, murdered his first wife, Françoise de la Marck, in cold blood, in 1577 at the Castle of Poitiers, where the Court was residing. He killed at the same time a young girl who was holding a mirror before her mistress at the moment. According to some authorities he acted on the suggestion of the king, Henri III. At any rate he got off with absolute impunity, and within a very short time after was decorated by his Sovereign with the Order of the St. Esprit. [Transl.]

P. 12: Sampietro, the famous soldier of fortune, and commander

[357]

of the Italian troops under the French Kings Francis I. and Henri II., was born near Ajaccio in Corsica in 1501. He was of humble birth, but his many brilliant feats of war made him celebrated throughout Europe. He actually strangled his wife,—Vanina, a lady of good family, but not in consequence of such misconduct on her part as Brantôme represents. The real circumstances were as follows. Sampietro having attempted to raise his Corsican compatriots in revolt against the Genoese, he was imprisoned and all but put to death by the latter. This roused in him so implacable a hatred of the Genoese State, that on learning that his wife during his absence at Constantinople had condescended to implore his pardon from the Genoese, he deliberately put her to death in the way described. He was himself eventually murdered, being treacherously stabbed in the back by his Lieutenant and friend Vitelli at the instigation of his Genoese enemies. [Transl.]

P. 12: This is another allusion to Paolo Orsini, Duke of Bracciano, who could not overtake Troilo Orsini, and killed Isabella that he might marry Vittoria Accoramboni, whose husband he had assassinated. (Litta, Orsini, t, VII, tav. XXIX.)

P. 15: The Avalos family originally came from Spain, and gave Italy the Marquis de Pescaire, one of the greatest captains of the sixteenth century. It is of him that Brantôme speaks as the *viceroy*. Maria d'Avalos was married to Carlos Gesualdo, prince of Venousse, and was the niece of this Marquis de Pescaire and of Del Guasto, whom Brantôme describes as "dameret" (foppish) to such a degree that he perfumed the saddles of his horses. He was the one who lost the battle of Cérisoles in 1544.

P. 16: Iliad, Bk. III, —

P. 16: Paul de Caussade de Saint-Mégrin, favorite of the king, was killed on leaving the Louvre by a band of assassins led by Mayenne. He was the lover of Catherine de Clèves, Duchess de Guise. Henri IV., then king of Navarre, who had good reasons not to like favorites, says apropos of this: "I am thankful to the Duc de Guise for refusing to tolerate that a bed favorite like Saint-Mégrin should make him a cuckold. This treatment ought to be meted out to all the little court gallants who try to approach the princesses with the aim of making love to them."

P. 17: Françoise de Saillon, married to Jacques de Rohan. She was saved by a miracle, says Jean Bourdigné's chronicle, in 1526.

[358]

P. 17: Brantôme refers to Françoise de Foix, Chateaubriant's lady, regarding whom an old pamphlet of 1606 says as follows: "She could do what she desired, and she desired many things that she ought not to at all. During her lifetime, her husband was ever afflicted and tormented." (Factum pour M. le connestable contre Madame de Guise, 1606.) That is also the opinion of Gaillard in his *Histoire de Françoise I*er, t. VII, p. 179, in the 1769 edition, who sees in this passage an allusion to Mme. de Chateaubriant.

P. 17: Jean de Bourdigné, author of *Histoire agrégative des Annales et Chroniques d'Anjou et du Maine* (Angers, 1529, fol.), was born at Angers. He was a priest and Canon of the Cathedral of his native town. The book is very rare; as a history it is almost worthless, being full of the wildest fables.

P. 17: Francis I. king of France, 1515–1547.

P. 21: Philip II. had his wife Isabelle de Valois poisoned; he suspected her of adultery with Don Carlos, his son of a former marriage.

P. 22: Louis X., surnamed le Hutin, had caused his wife Marguerite de Bourgogne to be strangled at the Château-Gaillard. She had been imprisoned there in 1314. As to Gaston II., of Foix, outraged by the life of debauch Jeanne d'Artois (his mother) led, he obtained from Philippe de Valois an order of internment in 1331.

P. 22: Anne Boleyn, who was the cause of the Anglican schism. The king had had her beheaded because of her infidelity and married Jane Seymour. As to the charge of which Brantôme speaks, Henry VIII. was so keen on that matter that he had caused Catherine Howard to be beheaded because he had not been quite convinced of her virginity.

P. 23: Baldwyn II., cousin and successor of the first Baldwyn, king of Jerusalem, brother of Godfrey de Bouillon, reigned from 1119 to 1131. Brantôme is mistaken here. Baldwyn II. had married Morphie, daughter of Prince de Mélitine; but he had not been formerly married. Does he wish to speak of Baudoin I*re*, who repudiated the daughter of the Prince d'Arménie and then Adéle de Monferrat? (Cf. Guillaume de Tyr, liv. II, c. xv.)

P. 23: Read *Melitene;* this is how the Ancients named this town,

[359]

the modern name of which is *Meletin,* in Latin *Malatia;* in Armenia, on the Euphrates.

P. 23: *History of the Holy Land;* by William of Tyre.

P. 23: Louis VII. succeeded his father, Louis le Gros, on the throne of France 1137, and died 1180. His wife, whom he divorced soon after his return from the Holy Land, whither she had accompanied him, was Eleanore of Guienne. This divorce was very painful to Louis VII., surnamed le Jeune, because he had to give up the duchy of Aquitaine and cast off the beautiful equestrian seal which he had had engraved for himself in his rank as duke.

P. 24: Suetonius, *Cæsar,* Chap. VI. Brantôme is thinking of Clodius; but Cicero never made the speech in question.

P. 24: Brantôme (Lalanne edition, t. VIII, p. 198) repeats this anecdote without giving further details.

P. 25: Fulvia. (Sallust, Chap. XXIII.)

P. 25: Octavius (Augustus), first Roman Emperor, was the son of C. Octavius, by Atia, a daughter of Julia, the sister of Julius Cæsar. He was therefore the grand-nephew of the latter, the founder of the Empire and virtual, though not nominal, first Emperor. He married Livia after his divorce of Scribonia.

P. 26: Caligula, the third Roman Emperor, A. D. 37-41. His name was Caius Cæsar, Caligula being properly only a friendly nickname, "Little Boots," bestowed on him as a boy by the soldiers in his father, Germanicus' camp in Germany, where he was brought up. He was inordinately cruel and licentious and madly extravagant. Eventually murdered.

P. 26: Brantôme does not appear to know very well the persons he is speaking of here: Hostilla is Orestilla; Tullia is Lollia; Herculalina is Urgulanilla.

P. 27: Claudius, the fourth Roman Emperor, A.D. 41-54. The notorious Messalina was his third wife. For a lurid picture of her immoralities see Juvenal's famous Sixth Satire.

P. 28: Giovanni Boccaccio, the author of the Decameron, was born at Paris in 1313, being the (illegitimate) son of a wealthy merchant of Florence. He died 1375 at Certaldo, a village near Florence, the original seat of the family.

P. 28: Does the following *chanson* refer to the same woman?

> On void Simonne
> Proumener aux bordeaux
> Matin, soir, nonne,
> Avec ses macquereaux.
> (Bib. Nat., ms. français 22565, f° 41 v°.)

P. 28: This is indeed one of the most curious passages of the book, and I am glad to remove one of Lalanne's doubts. Brantôme is really talking of a statue, an antique piece which was found July 21, 1594, in a field near the Saint-Martin priory. It had been admirably conserved. Unfortunately, Louis XIV. having claimed it later, it was placed on a barge which sank in the Garonne, and was never recovered. (O'Reilly, History of Bordeaux, 1863, Vol. II.) The statue is described as having had one breast uncovered and curled hair, a description that agrees only partly with Visconti's type (*Iconographie romaine*, t. II., planche 28), in which Messalina is not décolleté and carries her son. Was the Bordeaux statue indeed a Messalina?

P. 31: Brantôme is mistaken; Nero caused Octavia to be killed. (See Suetonius, *Nero*, Chap. XXXV.)

P. 31: Nero, fifth Roman Emperor, A. D. 54-63.

P. 31: Domitian succeeded his father Titus on the Imperial throne; reigned from A. D. 81 to 96.

P. 31: Pertinax, a man of peasant birth, but who had carved out for himself a distinguished career as soldier and administrator, was elected Emperor by the Prætorian Guards on the murder of Commodus, A. D. 193. Himself murdered after a two months' reign.

P. 32: Septimius Severus, Emperor from A.D. 193 to 211. He was a great general and conducted successful campaigns in Britain, where he died,—at York.

P. 33: Philippe Auguste, King of France 1180-1223. Philip Augustus repudiated Ingeburga after twenty-eight days of marriage, and married Agnes de Méranie. The censure of the church induced the king to discard the second marriage and return to Ingeburga (1201). The latter was reputed to have a secret vice which greatly angered the king.

P. 34: Marguerite, daughter of the Archduke Maximilian, whom Charles VIII. rejected in order to marry Anne of Brittany (1491). Louis XII. turned away Jeanne in order to marry the widow of Charles VIII.

P. 34: Charles VIII., 1483-1498, of the House of Valois.

P. 34: Louis XII., successor of the last named, reigned 1498-1515, the immediate predecessor of Francis I.

P. 35: Alfonso V., king of Aragon, who left maxims which were collected by Antonio Beccadelli, surnamed Panormita.

P. 35: Twenty-second tale. M. de Bernage was equerry of King Charles VIII. and the lord of Civray, near Chenonceaux.

P. 36: It is not Semiramis, but Thomyris, who, according to Justin (Bk. I.) and Herodotus (Bk. II.), thrust the head of Cyrus into a vat of blood. Xenophon says, on the contrary, that Cyrus died a natural death.

P. 40: Albert de Gondy, Duke de Retz, was reputed as a practitioner of Aretino's principles. His wife, Claudine Catherine de Clermont, deserved, perhaps wrongfully, to occupy a place in the pamphlet entitled: "Bibliothèque de Mme. de Montpensier."

P. 41: Elephantis is referred to by Martial and Suetonius as the writer of amatory works—"molles Elephantidos libelli," but nothing is known of her otherwise. She was probably a Greek, not a Roman.

P. 41: Heliogabalus, or Elagabalus, Emperor from A. D. 218 to 222. Born at Emesa, and originally high-priest of Elagabalus the Syrian Sun-god. After a very short reign marked by every sort of extravagant folly, he was succeeded by Alexander Severus.

[362]

P. 41: The Cardinal de Lorraine, Cardinal du Perron, and others, had been already represented in the same way along with Catherine de Medici, Mary Stuart and the Duchesse de Guise, in two paintings mentioned in the *Légende du Cardinal de Lorraine*, fol. 24, and in the *Réveille-Matin des Français*, pp. 11 and 123.

P. 42: I agree with Lalanne that this prince was no other than the Duke d'Alençon. As to the fable of the coupling of the lions, it came from an error of Aristotle, which was repeated by most naturalists until the eighteenth century.

P. 45: Ronsard the poet was born 1524, being the son of Louis de Ronsard, sieur de la Poissonnière, an officer in the household of King Francis I., and died 1586. He enjoyed an immense reputation in his lifetime, and was the favourite poet of Mary Queen of Scots. Her lover, the unfortunate Chastelard, read his *Hymne de la mort* on the scaffold, and refused any other book or confessor to prepare him for death. Originator and leading member of the famous *Pleïade* of Poets.

P. 46: He was a Florentine, Luigi di Ghiaceti, who had grown rich by negotiating the taxes with the king. He married the beautiful Mlle. d'Atri, and to please her he had bought for 400,000 francs the estate of Chateauvilain. Mme. de Chateauvilain was a model of virtue, if Brantôme is to be believed; but we wonder, fully agreeing with the author of the notes to the *Journal de Henri III.*, where this lady could have acquired her virtue—was it at the court or at her husband's estate? Besides this gallery of pictures which is mentioned here, Louis Adjecet (the French form for Luigi Ghiaceti) had mistresses with whom he indulged in the low appetites of rich upstarts. He was killed in 1593 by an officer; and his wife withdrew to Langres, where she lived with her children.

P. 47: Ariosto, *Orlando furioso*, canto XLII., stanza 98.

> Ecco un donzello a chi l'ufficio tocca
> Por su la mensa un bel nappo d'or fino . . .

P. 47: Very likely Bernardin Turissan. Brantôme is perhaps referring to the *Ragionamento della Nanna*, printed in Paris in 1584, without the name of the publisher. The *peggio* must have been one of those infamous Italian books which the noblemen of the court wrangled over. The *Nanna* was well known at the French court (see *Le Divorce satyrique*, t. I. of the *Journal de Henri III.*, 1720 edition, p. 190).

P. 47: Bernardino Turisan, who used as his sign the well-known mark of the Manutii, his kinsmen.

P. 47: Pietro Aretino was born at Arezzo in Tuscany in 1492. The natural son of a plain gentleman he became the companion and protégé of Princes, and their unscrupulous and adroit flatterer. Friend of Michael Angelo and Titian. His works are full of learning and wit,—and obscenity.

P. 48: This book, entitled *La Somme des péchés et les remèdes d'iceux* (Compendium of all Sins, and the Remedies of the same), printed at Lyons, by Charles Pesnot c. 1584, 4to, and several times since, was compiled by Jean Benedict, a Cordelier monk of Brittany. He has filled it with filth and foulness as full as did the Jesuit Sanchez his treatise *De Matrimonio* (on Marriage). It is a singular fact that a work so indecent should have been none the less dedicated to the Holy Virgin. As we see from the text, Brantôme and his fellows quite well understood how to turn such works to their advantage and find fresh stories of lubricity in their pages.

P. 49: This Bonvisi, a Lyons banker, had had as receiver Field Marshal de Retz, the son of a Gondi, who had become a bankrupt in Lyons. (Notes of the Confession de Sancy, 1720 edition, t. II., p. 244.)

P. 51: L. Aurelius Commodus (not Sejanus), Emperor A. D. 180–192, was the son of the Emperor Marcus Aurelius and Faustina. Annius Verus was his brother, and received the appellation of *Cæsar* along with his elder brother in 166.

P. 58: *Antonomasia*, properly.

P. 60: The Sanzays were a family of Poitou who had settled in Brittany. René de Sanzay, head of the family at the time in question, had four sons: René, Christophe, Claude, and Charles. René continued the line. Claude was his lieutenant in 1569, as colonel of his forces. Charles married and died only in 1646 (?). Christophe, the second son, was a prothonotary. It seems that Brantôme had Claude in mind. Moreover, the constable of Montmorency having died in 1568 and Claude having been a lieutenant of his brother in 1569, we may conjecture that the adventure of which Brantôme speaks had happened to him previously, for the constable is concerned with his ransom. (Bib. Nat., Cabinet des titres, art. Sanzay.)

P. 61: Cicero, *De officis*, Bk. IV., Chap. ix.

P. 61: The second son of Charles V.; he was assassinated at the Gate of Barbette, at the end of Rue Vieille-du-Temple, in 1407, by the orders of Jean Sans peur. He had had for a long time adulterous relations with his sister-in-law Isabeau de Bavière. The woman in question here was Marie d'Enghien, wife of Aubert de Cany and mother of the Bâtard d'Orléans. This anecdote has inspired several story-tellers, such as Bandello, Strappardo, Malespini, etc. See also the first of the *Cents Nouvelles nouvelles*.

P. 61: "Candaules was the last Heracleid king of Lydia. According to the account of Herodotus, he was extremely proud of his wife's beauty, and insisted on exhibiting her unveiled charms, but without her knowledge, to Gyges, his favourite officer. Gyges was seen by the queen, as he was stealing from her chamber, and the next day she summoned him before her, intent on vengeance, and bade him choose whether he would undergo the punishment of death himself, or would consent to murder Candaules and receive the kingdom together with her hand. He chose the latter alternative, and became the founder of the dynasty of the Mermnadæ, about B. C. 715."

P. 62: Jean Dunois, comte d'Orléans et de Longueville, Grand Chamberlain of France, was his natural son by Mariette d'Enghien, wife of Aubert de Cany-Dunois, and is famous in history under the name of the Bastard of Orleans. Born at Paris 1402; died 1468. Distinguished himself at the sieges of Montargis and Orleans (where he was seconded by Jeanne d'Arc) and in many other encounters. The gallant champion of Charles VII. and the great enemy of the English.

P. 65. Henri III., 1574-1589, last king of the House of Valois; succeeded Charles IX.

P. 65: Emmanuel Philibert, Duke of Savoy, surnamed *Tête de fer*. He had married Marguerite, sister of Henri II. It was during this journey that the Duchess Marguerite tried to obtain from her nephew Henri III. the retrocession of several fortresses which France still held. (Litta, t. VI., tav. xiv.)

[365]

P. 66: Sainte-Soline abandoned Strozzi at the battle of the Iles Ter Tercères.

P. 67. Capaneus was one of the mythical seven heroes who marched from Argos against Thebes (Aeschylus, *Septem contra Thebas*). "During the siege, he was presumptuous enough to say, that even the fire of Zeus should not prevent his scaling the walls of the city; but when she saw his body was burning, his wife Euadné leaped into the flames and destroyed herself."

P. 67: Alcestis was a daughter of Pelias, and the wife of Admetus, King of Pheræ in Thessaly. According to the legend, Apollo having induced the Fates to promise Admetus deliverance from death, if at the hour of his decease his father, mother or wife would die for him, Alcestis sacrificed herself for her husband's sake. But Heracles brought her back again from the underworld, and "all ended well." The story is the subject of Euripides' beautiful play of *Alcestis*.

P. 68: Tancred, one of the chief heroes of the First Crusade, was the son of Odo the Good, of Sicily. Date of his birth is uncertain; he died 1112. Type of the gallant soldier and adventurer and the "very perfect, gentle knight."

P. 68: Philippe I.—1060-1108.

P. 68: See Guillaume de Tyr, liv. XI., who tells this anecdote about Tancrède. Bertrade d'Anjou, the wife of Foulques, had been carried off by Philip I., to whom she bore, among other children, Cécile, who married Tancrède.

P. 68: Compare this Albanian savagery with the story of Councillor Jean Lavoix, who lived with the wife of an attorney named Boulanger. The wife having decided to discontinue that liaison, the Councillor grew so furious that he caused her to be slashed and disfigured, although he could not get her nose cut off. He was pardoned after having paid his judges. The following song was written about him:

> Chasteauvillain, Poisle et Levois,
> Seront jugez tous d'une voix
> Par un arrest aussi leger
> Que fust celluy de Saint-Leger.
> Car le malheur est tel en France
> Que tout se juge par la finance.
>
> (Bib. Nat., ms. français, 22563, f° 101.)

P. 70: See the *Annales d'Aquitaine*, f° 140 v°.—Jeanne de Montal, married to Charles d'Aubusson, lord of La Borne. This Charles had had a liaison with the prioress of Blessac, who bore him four children. He was tried for theft and robbery in the convents of his vicinity, and hanged, February 23, 1533. (Anselme, t. V., p. 335.) A genealogy by Pierre Robert states precisely what Brantôme records here.

P. 70: See Brantôme in the Lalanne edition, t. VIII., p. 148. There must be some mistake here. Jacques d'Aragon, the titular king of Majorca, died in an expedition in 1375, according to the *Art de verifier les dates*.

P. 70: Charles VII. (surnamed the Victorious), crowned at Poitiers 1422, consecrated at Rheims 1429; died 1461, the King for whom Jeanne d'Arc fought against the Burgundians and English, and who really owed his crown to her.

P. 70: Francis I., 1515-1547.

P. 70: Jeanne I., Queen of Naples, 1353-1381, daughter of Charles Duke of Calabria and grand-daughter of the wise King Robert of Naples.

P. 72: The proverb says, the ferret. It should be the ermine, which animal is said to allow itself to be caught rather than soil itself.

P. 72: The opinion that the female ferret would die if it did not find a male to satisfy her during the mating season was still held by naturalists at the beginning of the nineteenth century. Lalanne is mistaken about the ermine, which, on the contrary, dies of the slightest contamination:

> Et moi, je suis si délicate
> Qu'une tache me fait mourir.
> (Florian, *Fables*, liv. III., fab. xiii.)

P. 78: Nouvelle III.

P. 78: Unhappy husbands were classified as follows:

> Celluy qui, marié, par sa femme est coqu
> Et (qui) pas ne le sçait, d'une corne est cornu.

[367]

Deux en a cestui-là qui peut dissimuler;
Qui le voit et le souffre, icelluy trois en porte;
Et quatre cestui-là qui meine pour culler
Chez lui des poursuivans. Cil qui en toute sorte
Dit qu'il n'est de ceux-là, et en sa femme croid,
Cinq cornes pour certain sur le front on lui void.
                              (Bib. Nat., ms. français 22565, f° 41.)

P. 79: It was the marriage of Marguerite of France, the Duchess de Savoie, to Emmanuel Philibert, the Duke de Savoie, which caused the army to grumble.

P. 79: Boccaccio, Seventh tale of the second day.

P. 79: Brantôme alludes here most likely to Marguerite of France, sister of Henri II., who was 45 when she married the Duke of Savoy.

P. 80: Mlle. de Limeuil was the mistress of the Prince de Condé. During the journey of the court at Lyons, in July, 1564, she was confined in the cabinet of the queen mother, who was so furious that she had her locked up in a Franciscan monastery at Auxonne. But the *Confession de Sancy* and several authors of that time differ from Brantôme in saying that the child was a son and not a daughter, and died immediately after birth. The Huguenots wrote verses about the adventure; but the young lady nevertheless married an Italian, Scipion Sardini, for whom she soon forgot the Prince de Condé. Mlle. de Limeuil called herself Isabelle de La Tour de Turenne, and was Dame de Limeuil.

P. 81: Cosimo I, Duke of Tuscany. Besides, Pope Alexander VI. was also in a somewhat similar situation.

P. 82: Ferdinand II., King of Naples, 1495-96. Died prematurely at the age of 26. Ferdinand II. married the sister of his father, the daughter of the king of Naples and not of Castile.

P. 86: An ancient city of Italy. At the fort of Monte Cimino, in the Campagna 40 miles NN W. of Rome.

P. 86: *La Nanna* by Aretino, in the chapter on married women, tells of similar practices of deception regarding the virtue of newly married women.

[368]

P. 89: Henry IV. of Castile, 1454-1474, a feeble and dissipated Prince, was a brother of Isabelle of Castile. The young man chosen was not a nobleman, but simply an Antinous of negligible origin whom the king created Duke d'Albuquerque. A child, Jeanne, was born of this complacent match, but she did not reign. Castile preferred Henri III.'s sister, Isabelle.

P. 89: Fulgosius (Battista Fregose), born at Genoa 1440, of a family famous in Genoese history, and for a time Doge of his native City. His chief Work, *Factorum et Dictorum Memorabilium libri IX.* (Memorable Deeds and Words, 9 bks.), has been more than once reprinted. This particular statement is to be found in ch. 3. of Bk. IX.

P. 91: We have here, perhaps, a discreet allusion to Henri IV.'s passion for Mlle. de Tignonville, who had been unmanageable until she married. (See the *Confession de Sancy,* and t. II., p. 128, of the *Journal de Henri III.*)

P. 94: François de Lorraine, Duc de Guise, who was killed by Poltrot.

P. 96: The famous Diane de Poitiers, eldest daughter of Jean de Poitiers, Seigneur de St. Vallier, belonging to one of the most ancient families in Dauphiné, was born 1499. At the age of 13 she was married to Louis de Brèze, Comte de Maulevrier, Grand Seneschal of Normandy. She became a widow in 1531. The story of François I. having pardoned her father at the price of her honour, as told by Brantôme and others, is apparently apocryphal. It was not till after the death of her husband, to whom she was faithful and whose name she honoured, that she became the mistress of François I. She was as renowned for her wit and charms of mind as for her beauty. Died 1566.

P. 96: M. de Saint-Vallier, father of Diane de Poitiers. It is not known whether he uttered the word, but his pardon came in time. The headsman had already begged his pardon, according to custom, for killing him, and was about to cut his head off when a clerk, Mathieu Delot, rose and read the royal letter which commuted the capital sentence to imprisonment. The letter is dated February 17, 1523. (Ms. Saint-Germain, 1556, f° 74.)

P. 97: Duke d'Etampes, chevalier of the order and governor of

[369]

Brittany, an obliging and kind husband.—François de Vivonne, lord
of La Chasteigneraie, was among the least meek-minded of the court.
Princess de La Roche-sur-Yon having stupidly asked him one day
for a domestic favor, he called her "a little muddy princess," which
afforded King Francis I. no little laughter. He was killed by Jarnac
in a famous duel.

P. 98: An allusion to the demon who threw to the ground the
archangel Saint Michael, and who was represented on the collar of
the order. It is rather difficult to know of which lady Brantôme
is speaking here: the collar of Saint Michael had been given to so
many people that it was called "the collar for all animals." (Castelnau, *Mémoires*, I., p. 363.)

P. 99: Where did Brantôme get this story? Gui de Châtillon had
expended on banquets the greater part of his fortune and sold his
county to Louis d'Orléans; the latter was merely seventeen at the
time. It is difficult to admit that he could have carried on a liaison
with a woman so ripe in years. After the death of Gui, Marguerite
married an officer of the Duke d'Orléans.

P. 101: Apparently Queen Marguerite de Valois. Marguerite de
Valois, sister of François I., was born at Angouleme in 1492. Married in 1509 to Charles 4th Duc d'Alençon, who died (1525) soon
after the disastrous battle of Pavia, at which François I. was taken
prisoner. In 1527 she married Henri d'Albret, king of Navarre. She
was a Princess of many talents and accomplishments, and the delight
of her brother François I., who called her his *Mignonne*, and his
Marguerite des Marguerites; Du Bellay and Clément Marot were
both members of her literary coterie. Authoress of the famous
Heptameron, or *Nouvelles de la Reine de Navarre*, composed in
imitation of Boccaccio's *Decameron*. Died 1549.

P. 101: This is also an allusion to Queen Marguerite. Martigues,
one of her lovers, had received from her a scarf and a little dog which
he wore at the tournaments.

P. 103: Henri III., who had a short-lived affair with Catherine
Charlotte de La Tremoille, the wife of Prince de Condé. But the
victory was too easy; the princess was quite corrupt. Later on,
the king prostituted her with one of his pages, with whom she conspired to poison her husband. The plot failed. When brought before
the Court, she was pardoned; but a servant named Brilland was torn

[370]

apart by four horses. It was also Henri III. who had debauched Marie de Clèves, the first wife of the same Prince de Condé.

P. 103: May very well refer to Henri de Lorraine, Duc de Guise, assassinated at Blois.

P. 103: Most probably refers to Marguerite de Valois, the king of Navarre, the Duc d'Anjou and the St. Bartholomew.

P. 105: Louis de Béranger du Guasi, one of Henri III.'s favorites, assassinated in 1575 by M. de Viteaux. His epitaph is in the *Manuscrit français* 22565, f° 901° (Bibliotheque Nationale). Brantôme, who boasts of being a swordsman, forgets that D'Aubigné was also one.

P. 105: A small town of Brittany (Dep. Ille-et-Vilaine), 14 miles from St. Mâlo. Has a cathedral of 12th and 13th centuries; the bishopric was suppressed in 1790.

P. 107: To take a journey to Saint-Mathurin was a proverbial expression which meant that a person was mad. Henri Estienne says that this is a purely imaginary saint; be that as it may, he was credited with curing madmen, and the satirical songs of the time are full of allusions to that healing power. (See *Journal de Henri III*, 1720 edition, t. II., pp. 307 and 308.)

P. 108: Lalanne proves by a passage from Spartianus that this anecdote is apocryphal, or that at least Brantôme has embellished it for his own needs. (*Dames*, tom. IX., p. 116.)

P. 108: Hadrian (P. Aelius Hadrianus), 14th in the series of Roman Emperors, A. D. 117-138, succeeded his guardian and kinsman Trajan. His wife, Sabina, here mentioned, was a grand-daughter of Trajan's sister Marciana.

P. 109: Marcus Aurelius Antoninus ("The Philosopher") succeeded Antonius Pius as Emperor in A. D. 168. Died 180. His wife Faustina (as profligate a woman as Messalina herself) was daughter of Pius. Author of the famous *Meditations*. His son Commodus, who succeeded him as Emperor, was a complete contrast in character to his father, being vicious, weak, cruel and dissolute.

P. 109: Another embellished passage. Faustine had died before

[371]

Antoninus Commodus was emperor. Moreover, she was only washed (*sublevare,* says the text) with the blood of the gladiator. (J. Capitolin, *Marc-Antoine le Philosophe,* Chap. xix.)

P. 113: A discreet and veiled allusion to the amours of Marguerite de Valois and of the Duchess de Nevers with La Môle and Coconas. Implicated in the affair of Field Marshals de Cossé and de Montmorency, La Môle, a Provençal nobleman, and Coconas, a Piedmontese, were beheaded on the square of Grève towards the end of April, 1574, and not killed in battle as Brantôme tries to insinuate. The two princesses, mad with despair, transported the bodies in their carriages to the place of burial, at Montmartre, and kept the heads, which they had had embalmed. (*Mémoires de Nevers,* I., p. 75, and *Le Divorce satirique.*)

P. 114: It is Philippe Strozzi, Field Marshal of France, who was born at Venice. Made lieutenant of the naval army in 1579 in order to further the pretensions of Antonio of Portugal, he was defeated, July 28, 1583, and put to death in cold blood by Santa Cruz, his rival. (*Vie et mort . . . de Philippe Strozzi.* Paris, Guil. Lenoir, 1608.)

P. 119: Thomas de Foix, lord of L'Escu or Lescun, was the brother of Mme. de Chateaubriant, mistress of François Ier. He was captured at Pavia and carried, mortally wounded, to the home of the lady of whom Brantôme speaks. It was he who, by the surrender of Cremona in 1522, caused France to lose Italy. (Guicciardini, t. III., p. 473, Fribourg edition, 1775.)

P. 120: Paolo Jovio, *Dialogo delle imprese militari ed amorose,* 1559, p. 13.

P. 120: Blaise de Montluc, author of the *Commentaires,* a diabolical Gascon, made Field Marshal of France in 1574. The siege of La Rôchelle, which is here mentioned, took place in 1573. For details on this personage, see the De Ruble edition of the *Commentaires,* 1854-74, 5 vols.

P. 120: Paulus Jovius (Paolo Giovio), Historian, was a native of Como; born 1483, died 1552.

P. 122: In his *Contre-Repentie* (fol. 444, A. of his *Works,* 1576). Joachim du Bellay, the poet, was born about 1524 at Lire in Anjou, of a noble and distinguished family of that Province. After an unfortunate youth, his talents ensured him a welcome at the Court of François I. and his sister Marguerite de Valois, where he spent some years. Died young, after a life of ill health, in 1560.

P. 122: Francis Rabelais was born about 1483 at Chinon in Touraine, where his father was an apothecary. After a stormy youth and some years spent as a Monk in more than one Monastery of more than one Order, and later wandering the country as a vagabond secular priest, he was admitted Doctor in the Faculty of Medicine at Montpellier. Countless stories of his pranks and adventures are told, many no doubt mythical. He visited Rome as well as most parts of France in the course of his life. He died Curé of Meudon, about 1553.

P. 123: Chastity-belts of this sort were already in use at Venice at the time.

P. 123: There is in the Hennin collection of prints at the Bibliothèque Nationale (t. III., f° 64) a satirical print representing what Brantôme relates here. A lady returns to her husband the key; but behind the bed, the lover, hidden by a duenna, receives from the latter a key similar to the husband's. This instrument of jealousy was the *cingulum pudicitiæ* of the Romans, the "Florentine lock" of the sixteenth century. Henri Aldegraver also engraved on the sheath of a dagger a lady who is adorned with a lock of this kind. (Bartsch, *Peintre-Graveur*, VIII., p. 437.) These refinements in jealousy as well as the refinements in debauchery (of which Brantôme will speak later) were of Italian origin. (See on this subject *La Description de l'Ile des Hermaphrodites*, Cologne, 1724, p. 43.)

P. 124: Lampride, *Alexandre Sévère*, Chap. XXII.

P. 125: Nicolas d'Estouteville, lord of Villeconnin, and not Villecouvin, nobleman of the Chambre, died in Constantinople in February, 1567. He had gone to Turkey to forget a disappointment in love or in politics. Here is his epitaph:

> Le preux Villeconin en la fleur de ses ans, 5
> Hélas! a delaissé nos esbatz si plaisans,
> Laissant au temple sainct de la digne Memoire
> Son labeur, son renom, son honneur et sa gloire.

P. 127: Dr. Subtil, surname of J. Scott or Duns.

P. 128: Saint Sophronie.

P. 128: See De Thou liv. XLIX. There were, at the court of France, other women who had escaped from Cyprus and who scarcely resembled this heroine. Témoin de la Dayelle, of whom Brantôme speaks in the *Dames illustres*, in the chapter on the Medicis. (*Journal de Henri III.*, 1720 edition, t. II., p. 142.)

P. 132: Guillot le Songeur is, according to Lalanne, Don Guilan el Cuidador of the *Amadis de Gaule*.

P. 132: "Guillot le Songeur," a name applied to any Pensive man,— from the knight Julian le Pensif, one of the characters of the *Amadis of Gaul*.

P. 136: Danae, daughter of Acrisius, King of Argos, who confined her in brazen tower, where Jupiter obtained access in the form of a golden shower.

P. 137: An allusion to Duke Henri de Guise. His wife Catherine de Clèves had, in addition to her "bed lovers," many other intrigues. (See the *Confession de Sancy*, Chap. VIII., notes.)

P. 138: Trajan (M. Ulpius Trajanus), Emperor A. D. 98-117. His wife Plotina, here mentioned, was a woman of extraordinary merits and virtues, according to the statements of all writers, with one exception, who speak of her. She persuaded her husband to adopt Hadrian who became his successor; but Dion Cassius is the only author who says a word as to her intercourse with the latter having been of a criminal character, and such a thing is utterly opposed to all we know of her character.

P. 141: This refers very likely to Brantôme's voyage to Scotland. He had accompanied Queen Mary Stuart in August, 1561, at the time of her departure from France. Riccio, who was the favorite of "low rank," had arrived one year later; but Brantôme, who is relating something which happened a long time before, is not precise: he is unquestionably responding to a request of Queen Catherine.

P. 144: In this passage, where Brantôme cleverly avows his wiles as a courtier, he refers to the Queen of Spain, Elizabeth, the wife of Philip II. The sister of the princess was Marguerite, Queen of Navarre. The two young infantas, whose portraits are examined in detail, were: the first, Isabella Claire Eugenie (later married to Albert of Austria), who became a nun towards the end of her life; the other, Catherine, married Charles Emmanuel de Savoie in 1585. It is difficult to-day to see the resemblance of the two princesses to their father, in spite of the great number of portraits of all these personages; in fact, we can say that they were scarcely more beautiful than their mother. (Cf. the beautiful portrait in crayon of Queen Elizabeth at the Bibliothèque Nationale, Estampes Na 21, f° 69.)

P. 144: The two Joyeuses: M. du Bouchage, and a gay companion.

P. 145: Marguerite de Lorraine, married to Anne (Duke) de Joyeuse, the favorite. of Henri III. The sister-in-law of whom Brantôme speaks could be neither Mme. du Bouchage nor Mme. de Mercoeur, who were spared by the cruelest pamphleteers; he undoubtedly refers to Henriette, Duchess de Montpensier.

P. 146: François de Vendôme, vidam of Chartres? (See *Fæneste*, 1729 edition, p. 345.)

P. 148: Ariosto, *Orlando furioso*, canto V., stanza 57:

> Io non credo, signor, che ti sia nova
> La legge nostra . . .

P. 149: How can Brantôme, who had friends in the Huguenot camp, deliberately relate such absurd tales?

P. 150: There is a close likeness between this woman and the Godard de Blois, a Huguenot, who was hanged for adultery in the year 1563.

P. 152: At that period several persons bore the name of Beaulieu. Brantôme may have in mind Captain Beaulieu, who held Vincennes for the Ligue in 1594. (Chron. Novenn. III., liv. VII.) The chief prior was Charles de Lorraine, son of the Duke de Guise.

P. 154: The Comtesse de Senizon was accused of having contrived his escape, and brought to book for it.

P. 155: According to his habit, Brantôme disfigures what he quotes. Vesta Oppia alone has the right to the name of "good

[375]

woman"; Cluvia was a profession-courtesan. (Cf. Livy, XXVI., Chap. xxxiii.)

P. 156: This more human reason is probably truer than the one generally given of Jean's chivalrous conduct regarding his pledge.

P. 156: Jean (surnamed le Bon), King of France, 1350-1364. Taken prisoner by Edward the Black Prince at the battle of Poitiers.

P. 159: Proverb marking the small connection that often exists between gifts of body and good qualities of mind and character.

P. 164: The quotation as given in the text is mutilated and the words transposed. It should read:

> "Si tibi simplicitas uxoria, deditus uni
> Est animus:......................
> ....
> Nil unquam invita donabis conjuge: vendes
> Hac obstante nihil; nihil, haec si nolit, emetur."
> JUVENAL, Sat. VI, 205 sqq.

that is to say, "If you are attached solely and entirely to your wife, . . . you will not be able to give a thing away, or sell or buy a thing, without her consent."

P. 164: They used to say of those Italian infamies: *"In Spagna, gli preti; in Francia, i grandi; in Italia, tutti quanti."*

P. 164: Why not let Boccaccio have the responsibility of this baseness? (Decameron, Vth day, Xth story.)

P. 168: Christine de Lorraine, daughter of Duke Charles, married to Ferdinand I. de Medici. This young princess had arrived in Italy adorned in her rich French gowns, which she soon cast off in favor of Italian fashions. This concession quickly made her a favorite. It was at the wedding of Christine that the first Italian operas were performed. (Litta, *Medici di Firenze*, IV., tav. xv.)

P. 171: Brantôme is very likely thinking of Princess de Condé, whom Pisani brought before the Parliament, which acquitted her.

P. 174-175: Probably an allusion to Mme. de Simiers and not to Marguerite de Valois, as Lalanne thinks. More tenacious if not more constant than the princess, Louise de Vitry, Lady de Simiers, lost successively Charles d'Humières at Ham, Admiral de Villars at Dourlens, and the Duke de Guise, whom she deeply loved and who gave her so little in return; this does not include Count de Radan, who died at Issoire, and others of less importance. When she reached old age, old Desportes alone remained for her. He had been her first lover, a poet, whom she had forgotten among her warriors; but it was much too late for both of them.

P. 175: Brantôme is mistaken; it is Seius and not Séjanus.

P. 177: Théodore de Bèze, the Reformer; born at Vézelais, in the Nivernais, 1519. Author, scholar, jurist and theologian. Died 1595.

P. 178: All the satirical authors agree in charging Catherine de'Medici with this radical change of the old French manners. It would be juster to think also of the civil wars in Italy, which were not without influence upon the looseness of the armies, and, therefore, upon the whole of France.

P. 179: It is the 91st epigram of Bk. I.

P. 180: Isabella de Luna, a famous courtesan mentioned by Bandello.

P. 180: Cardinal d'Armagnac was Georges, born in 1502, who was successively ambassador in Italy and archbishop of Toulouse, and finally archbishop of Evignon.

P. 181: Quotation badly understood. *Crissantis,* in the Latin verse, is a participle and not a proper noun. (Cf. Juvenal, sat. iv.)

P. 181: *Filènes,* from *Philenus,* a courtesan in Lucian.

P. 181: The line should read,

Ipsa Medullinæ frictum crissantis adorat.

P. 184: Brantôme seems to speak of himself; yet he might merely have played the side rôle of confidant in the comedy.

P. 187: Brantôme refers to the *Dialogue de la beauté des dames.* Marguerite d'Autriche is not (as he says) the Duchess de Savoie, who died in 1530, but the natural daughter of the Emperor; she married Alessandro de'Medici, and later Ottavio Farnese.

P. 189: The famous Church of Brou, at Bourg, was built in 1511-86 by the beautiful Marguerite of Austria, wife of Philobert II., le Beau, Duke of Savoy, in fulfilment of a vow made by Marguerite of Bourbon, her mother-in-law. It contains the magnificent tombs of Marguerite herself, her husband and mother-in-law. Celebrated in a well-known poem, "The Church of Brou," of Matthew Arnold.

P. 190: Jean de Meung, the poet (nicknamed Clopinel on account of his lameness), was born at the small town of Meung-sur-Loire in the middle of the XIIIth Century. Died at Paris somewhere about 1320. His famous *Roman de la Rose* was a continuation of an earlier work of the same name by Guillaume de Lorris, completed and published in its final form by Jean de Meung.

P. 192: Twenty-sixth Tale. It is Lord d'Avesnes, Gabriel d'Albret.

P. 194: Claudia Quinta (Livy XXIX, 14).

P. 196: Plutarch, Œuvres mêlées, LXXVII, t. II., p. 167, in the 1808 edition.

P. 200: The vogue of drawers dated from about 1577; three years later the hoop was in great favor and served to do away with the petticoat. Brantôme probably means that the lady discards the petticoat and wears the hoop over the drawers.

P. 212: The pun on *raynette* and *raye nette* cannot be reproduced in English.

P. 213: Etienne Pasquier, the great lawyer and opponent of the Jesuits, was born at Paris, 1529; died 1615.

P. 213: Thibaut, sixth of the name, Comte de Champagne et Brie, subsequently King of Navarre, was born 1201. Surnamed *Faiseur de Chansons* from his poetic achievements. Brought up at the Court of Philippe-Auguste. The whole romance of his love for Queen Blanche of Castille is apparently apocryphal; it rests almost entirely on statements of one (English) historian, Matthew Paris. She was 16 years older than he, and is never once mentioned in his poems.

P. 213: E. Pasquier, *Œuvres*, 1723, t. II, p. 38. "Which of the two," says Pasquier, "brings more satisfaction to a lover—to feel and touch his love without speaking to her, or to see and speak to her without touching her?" In the dialogue between Thibaut de Champagne and Count de Soissons, Thibaut preferred to speak.

P. 215: Brantôme aims here at Queen Catherine de'Medici and her favorites.

P. 215: *Cf.* Plutarch, De Stoicorum repugnantiis, c. xxi.

P. 216: *Id.*, Demetrius, cap. xxvii. Brantôme is mistaken; the woman in question was Thônis.

P. 216: Eighteenth Tale.

P. 216: The "wheel of the nose" was a sort of "mask beard" that women wore in cold weather; it was attached to the hood below the eyes.

P. 220: It was François de Compeys, lord of Gruffy, who sold his estate in 1518 in order to expatriate himself.

P. 221: It is not three but four S's that the perfect lover must carry with him, according to Luis Barabona (*Lagrimas de Angelica,* canto IV.), and these four S's mean:

SABIO, SOLO, SOLICITO ET SEGRETO.

These initial letters were much in vogue in Spain during the sixteenth century.

P. 224: This story was popular in Paris; it was amplified and embellished into a drama and ascribed to Marguerite de Bourgogne. Was it not Isabeau de Bavière?

P. 224: Isabeau, or Isabelle, de Bavière, wife of the half imbecile Charles VI. of France, and daughter of Stephen II., Duke of Bavaria, was born 1371; died 1435. Among countless other intrigues was one with the Duc d'Orléans, her husband's brother. One of her lovers, Louis de Boisbourdon, was thrown into the Seine in a leather sack inscribed *Laissez passer la justice du roi.* The famous story of the Tour de Nesles seems mythical.

[379]

P. 225: See under *Buridan*, in Bayle's *Dict. Critique.* Compare also Villon, in his Ballade of the *Dames des Temps Jadis* (Fair Dames of Yore):

> Semblablement où est la reine,
> Qui commanda que Buridan
> Fust jeté en un sac en Seine?

(Likewise where is the Queen, who commanded Buridan to be cast in a sack into the Seine?)

P. 227: Plutarch, Anthony, Chap. xxxii.

P. 229: Livy, lib. XXX., cap. xv. Appien, *De Rebus punicis,* XXVII.

P. 229: Joachim du Bellay, *Œuvres poétiques,* 1597.

P. 229: *La Vieille Courtisane* ("The Old Courtesan"), fol. 449. B. of the *Œuvres poét.* of Joachim du Bellay, edition of 1597.

P. 230: This pun is difficult to explain.

P. 231: Lucian, *Amours,* XV.

P. 235: Marguerite, wife of Henri IV., whose elegance drew from the old Queen Catherine this remark: "No matter where you may go, the court will take the fashion from you, and not you from the court."
(Brantôme, *Elogé de la reine Marguerite.*)

P. 235: Brantôme alludes to the Duke d'Anjou.

P. 235: Jeanne de Navarre, wife of Philippe le Bel, King of France, daughter and sole heiress of Henri I. of Navarre, was born 1272, died 1305 at the early age of 33. She was a beautiful and accomplished Princess, and the tales told by some historians reflecting on her character are apparently quite without foundation.

P. 235: The *Divorce satyrique* attributes this contrivance to Queen Marguerite, who adopted it to make her husband, the King of Navarre, more deeply enamoured and more naughty.

P. 236: These are taken from an old French book entitled: *De la louange et beauté des Dames* ("Of the Praise and Beauty of Ladies"). François Corniger has put the same into 18 Latin lines. Vencentio Calmeta has rendered them also into Italian verse, commencing with the words: *Dolce Flaminia.*

P. 236: Pliny speaks of this Helen of Zeuxis.

P. 237: Ronsard, *Œuvres,* 1584 edition, p. 112. It is a poem addressed to the famous painter Clouet, according to Janet, in which the poet sings the praises of his fair lady. This poem has more than one point in common with the present chapter of the *Dames.*

P. 238: Marot had arranged this Spanish proverb into a quatrain, and at the time of the Ligue it was applied to the Infanta of Spain:

> Pourtant, si je suis brunette,
> Amy, n'en prenez esmoy,
> Car autant aymer souhaitte
> Qu'une plus blanche que moy.

P. 239: Raymond Lulle was a native of Majorca, and lived towards the end of the thirteenth century: he was reputed to be a magician. The story that Brantôme tells was taken from the *Opuscula* by Charles Bovelles, fol. XXXIV. of the in-4° edition of 1521. The famous Raimond Lulle (generally known in England as Raimond Lully), philosopher and schoolman, was celebrated throughout the Middle Ages for his logic and his commentary on Aristotle, and above all for his art of Memory, or Ars Lulliana. He was born at Palma, the capital of Majorca, in 1235. He travelled in various countries, and died (1315) in Africa after suffering great hardships, having gone there as a missionary.

P. 240: Or Charles de Bouvelles. His life of Raymond Lulle is a quarto, printed at Paris, and published by Ascencius. It is dated 3rd of the Nones of December, 1511. Several other works by the same author are extant.

P. 240: Arnauld de Villeneuve, a famous alchemist of the end of the thirteenth century; he died in a shipwreck, in 1313.

P. 240: Oldrade, a jurist, was born at Lodi in the thirteenth century. His *Codex de falsa moneta* is not known.

P. 242: Sisteron, in the Department of the Basses-Alpes, on the Durance. Seat of a Bishopric from the 4th Century down to 1770.

P. 242: Aimeric de Rochechouart (1545-1582) was the bishop of Sisteron; he succeeded his uncle Albin de Rochechouart. As to the "very great lady," that applies to one of a dozen princesses.

P. 244: Pliny, XXXIII., cap. iv. Brantôme is mistaken about the temple.

P. 246: Claude Blosset, lady of Torcy, the daughter of Jean Blosset and of Anne de Cugnac. She married Louis de Montberon (in 1553), Baron de Fontaines and Chalandray, first gentleman of the king's bed-chamber. The beautiful Torcy, as she was called, had been presented to Queen Eleonor by Mme. de Canaples, the enemy of Mme. d'Etampes.

P. 246: Hubert Thomas, *Annales de vita Friderici II. Palatini* (Francfort, 1624), gives no idea of this exaggeration of Queen Eleonor's bust, who was promised to Frederick Palatine.

P. 248: Suetonius, *Octavius Augustus*, cap. lxix.

P. 249: Henri de Lorraine, Duc de Guise, nicknamed *le Balafré*, born 1550. Murdered by the King's (Henri III.) orders at Blois in 1588.

P. 249: Duc d'Anjou, afterwards Henri III.

P. 250: The personages in question are probably Bussy d'Amboise and Marguerite de Valois.

P. 252: The king was Henri II., and the grand widow lady the Duchess de Valentinois. They thought it was due to a charm.

P. 254: Pico della Mirandola, *Opera omnia*, t. II., liv. III., chap. xxii., in the 1517 edition.

P. 254: Pico della Mirandola, one of the greatest of all the brilliant scholars of the Renaissance, and so famous for the precocity and versatility of his talents, was born 1463. After completing his studies at Bologna and elsewhere, he visited Rome, where he publicly exhibited a hundred propositions *De omni re scribili*, which he undertook to defend against all comers. The maturity of his powers he devoted to the study of religion and the Platonic philosophy. He died 1494, on the day of Charles VIII.'s entry into Florence.

P. 255: Ferdinando Francesco Avalos, Marquis de Pescaire, of a well-known Neapolitan family, began his career as a soldier in 1512 at the battle of Ravenna. Distinguished himself by the capture of Milan (1521) and numerous other brilliant feats of arms. Took an important part in the battle of Pavia, where François I. of France was taken prisoner. Wounded in that battle, and died in the same year, 1525. His wife was the celebrated Vittoria Colonna.

P. 257: Josephus, *The Antiquities of the Jews*, Bk. XV., Chap. vii. Herod the Great; died B. C. 4. He put to death his wife Mariamné, as well as her grandfather and his own sons by her.

P. 258: Shiraz, a town of Persia, capital of the Province of Fars, famous for its roses, wine and nightingales, sung by the Persian poets Hafiz and Saadi.

P. 258: Plutarch, *Alexander,* Chap. XXXIX.

P. 258: It is in his *Observations de plusieurs singularités* (Paris, 1554) that Belon reports this fact. (Liv. III., chap. x., p. 179.)

P. 261: The usual form is Ortiagon. The woman is the beautiful Queen Chiomara. (*Cf.* Livy, XXXVIII., cap. xxiv., and Boccaccio, *De claris mulieribus,* LXXIV.) Chiomara, wife of Ortiagon, King of Galatia, was taken prisoner by the Romans when Cn. Manlius Vulso invaded Galatia, B. C. 189. The story is told by Polybius (XXII., 21).

P. 262: Suetonius, *Cæsar,* LII.

P. 263: Livy, XXX., cap. xv.

P. 263: Plutarch, *Cato the Elder.* Brantôme attributes the anecdote to Scipion.

P. 265: Charles de Lorraine, Cardinal de Guise, known as Cardinal de Lorraine, died in 1574. He played an important rôle at the Council of Trente. Brantôme refers to the truce of Vaucelles between Henri II. and the Emperor, which Cardinal Caraffa had succeeded in breaking in 1556. This passage had evidently been written before 1588, the year of the death of another Cardinal de Guise, the brother of Balafré.

P. 265: The beautiful Venitians are described by Vecellio as wearing exquisite gowns on holidays. (See Vecellio, *Habiti antichi*, Venice, 1590.)

P. 266: This passage is not in the *Dies geniales* by Alessandro, but in Herodotus, II., chap. ix.

P. 267: What Brantôme says of Flora is not true. The woman in question was not called Flora, but Acca Taruntia.

P. 269: Pausanius, Suetonius, and Manilius have not written special works on women. Brantôme is no doubt referring to the anecdotes that are found in their works.

P. 273: This princess was Catherine de'Medeci.

P. 275: The same story has been told of Mademoiselle, cousin german of Louis XIV., with this addition that she was in the habit of giving any of her pages who were tempted by her charms a few louis to enable them to satisfy their passion elsewhere.

P. 276: Suetonius, *Vitellius,* cap. ii.: "Messalina petit ut sibi pedes præberet excalceandos." Brantôme prefers to quote in his own manner.

P. 276: LVIIth Tale.

P. 276: Undoubtedly the grand prior François de Lorraine, who accompanied Mary Stuart to Scotland; however, D'Aumale and Remé d'Elbeuf also accompanied her.

P. 281: Philip II., of Spain, son of Charles the Fifth, born 1527; died 1588. The husband of Queen Mary of England.

P. 282: Béatrix Pacheco was lady of honor to Eleonor d'Autriche prior to 1544 with several other Spanish ladies; she became Countess d'Entremont through her marriage with Sébastien d'Entremont. Her daughter, the woman in question here, was Jacqueline, the second wife of Admiral de Coligny, against whom the enemies of her husband turned; she was not, however, beyond reproach.

P. 284: The description which follows was textually taken by Brantôme from account printed at Lyons, in 1549, entitled: "La magnificence de la superbe et triomphante entrée de la noble et antique cité de Lyon faicte au très-chrestien Roy de France Henry deuxiesme."

P. 286: Brazilian wood, known before the discovery of America. *Brésil* is a common noun here.

P. 287: The king's visit to Lyons took place September 18, 1548.

P. 288: La *volte* was a dance that had come from Italy in which the gentleman, after having made his partner turn two or three times, raised her from the floor in order to make her cut a caper in the air. This is the caper of which Brantôme is speaking.

P. 288: Paul de Labarthe, lord of Thermes, Field Marshal of France, died in 1562. (Montluc, Ruble edition, t. II., p. 55.)

P. 289: Scio (Chios) was the only island in the Orient where the women wore short dresses.

P. 298: Suetonius, *Caligula*, XXV. "Cæsonia was first the mistress and afterwards the wife of the Emperor Caligula. She was neither handsome nor young when Caligula fell in love with her; but she was a woman of the greatest licentiousness . . . At the time he was married to Lollia Paulina, whom, however, he divorced in order to marry Cæsonia, who was with child by him, A. D. 38. . . . Cæsonia contrived to preserve the attachment of her imperial husband down to the end of his life; but she is said to have effected this by love-potions, which she gave him to drink, and to which some persons attributed the unsettled state of Caligula's mental powers during the latter years of his life. Cæsonia and her daughter (Julia Drusilla) were put to death on the same day that Caligula was murdered, A. D. 41."

P. 299: The Emperor Caracalla (M. Aurelius Antoninus) was the son of the Emperor Septimus Severus and was born at Lyons, at the time his father was Governor of Gallia Lugdunensis. Caracalla (like Caligula) is really only a nickname, derived from the long Gaulish cloak which he adopted and made fashionable. Reigned from Severus' death at York in 211 to his own assassination in 217. His brother Geta was at first associated with him in the Empire. Him he murdered, and is said to have suffered remorse for the act to the end of his life,—remorse from which he sought distraction in every kind of extravagant folly and reckless cruelty.

P. 299: Spartianus, *Caracalla*, Chap. x.

P. 300: This son was Geta.

P. 301: Béatrix was the daughter of Count Guillaume de Tenda; to her second husband, Phillipe Marie Visconti, she brought all the wealth of her first husband, Facino Cane. In spite of her ripe years, Béatrix was suspected of adultery with Michel Orombelli, and Phillipe Marie had them both killed. As a matter of fact this was a convenient way of appropriating Facino Cane's wealth.

P. 301: Collenuccio, liv. IV., anno 1194.

P. 301: Filippo Maria Visconti; born 1391, died 1447. Last Duke of Milan of the house of Visconti, the sovereignty passing at his death to the Sforzas.

P. 301: Facino (Bonifacio) Cane, the famous *condottiere* and despot of Alessandria, was born of a noble family about 1360. The principality he eventually acquired in N. Italy embraced, besides Alessandria, Pavia, Vercelli, Tortona, Varese, and all the shores of the Lago Maggiore. Died 1412.

P. 301: Mother of Frederick II.

P. 301: Pandolfo Collenuccio, famous as author, historian and juris-consult towards the end of the XIVth century. Born at Pesaro, where he spent most of his life, and where he was executed (1500) by order of Giovanni Sforza, in consequence of his intrigues with Cæsar Borgia, who was anxious to acquire the sovereignty of that city.

P. 302: Daughter of Bernardin de Clermont, Vicomte de Tallard.

P. 302: Brantôme undoubtedly aims here at Marguerite de Clermont.

P. 303: Jean de Bourdeille.

P. 303: Renée, daughter of Louis XII., married to the Duke of Ferraro. She was ungainly but very learned.

P. 304: Marguerite d'Angoulème.

P. 312: Meung-sur-Loire, dep. Loiret, on right bank of the Loire, eleven miles below Orléans.

P. 312: Eclaron, dép. Maute-Marne.

P. 312: Leonor, Duke de Longueville.

P. 312: François de Lorraine, Duke de Guise.

P. 313: Louis I., Prince de Condé.

P. 313: Captain Averet, died at Orléans in 1562.

P. 313: *Compère* was the name King Henri II. gave the Constable de Montmorency.

P. 316: *Octavius* is translated *Octavie* by Brantôme. *Cf.* Suetonius, *Caligula*, XXXVI., and *Octavius Augustus*, LXIX.

P. 316: Suetonius, *Nero*, XXXIV.

P. 318: Brantôme undoubtedly refers to Henri III. and to the Duke d'Alençon, his brother.

P. 319: Plutarch names this woman *Aspasia* and makes her a priestess of Diana. *Cf. Artaxerxes-Mnemon*, Chap. XXVI.

P. 319: Collenuccio, liv. V., p. 208.

P. 319: Artaxerxes I. (Longimanus), King of Persia for forty years, B. C. 465 to 425; he succeeded his father Xerxes, having put to death his brother Darius.

[387]

P. 320:   Wife of François d'Orléans.

P. 320:   Diane died at the age of 66, April 22, 1566; she was born in 1499.

P. 320:   Jacqueline de Rohan-Gié, married to François d'Orléans, Marquis de Rothelin.

P. 321:   François Robertet, widow of Jean Babou, whose second husband was Field Marshal d'Aumont.

P. 321:   Catherine de Clermont, wife of Guy de Mareuil, grandmother of the Duke du Montpensier, François, surnamed the *Prince-Dauphin*.

P. 321:   Gabrielle de Mareuil, married to Nicolas d'Anjou, Marquis de Mézières.

P. 321:   Jacqueline or Jacquette de Montberon.

P. 321:   Françoise Robertet, widow of Jean Babon de la Bourdaisière.

P. 322:   Paule Viguier, baronne de Fontenille.

P. 322:   Françoise de Longwi.

P. 322:   The praise of this Toulousean beauty is to be found in the very rare opuscule by G. Minot, *De la beauté*, 1587.

P. 323:   Anne d'Este. She was not exempt from the faults of a corrupt court.

P. 323:   This journey occurred in 1574.

P. 323:   Louis XII.

P. 324:   Jean d'O, seigneur de Maillebois.

P. 324:   It is not François Gonzagne, but Guillaume Gonzagne, his brother and successor to the duchy of Mantoue, born in 1538, died in 1587.

[388]

NOTES AND APPENDICES

P. 325: He returns here to the Duchess de Guise.

P. 326: At the wedding of Charles Emmanuel, married to Catherine, daughter of Philip II. of Spain.

P. 327: Marie d'Aragon, wedded to Alphonse d'Avalos, Marquis del Guasto or Vasto.

P. 327: Henri II., son of Francis I., and husband of Catherine de Medici. Born 1518. Came to throne in 1547; accidentally killed in a tourney by Montgommeri 1559.

P. 327: Paul IV. (of the illustrious Neapolitan family of Caraffa) was raised to the chair of St. Peter in 1558; died 1559.

P. 327: This viceroy was Don Perafan, Duke d'Alcala, who entered Naples June 12, 1559.

P. 328: Claude de Lestrange?

P. 331: Brantôme's memory fails him. Of the two daughters of the Marquess, Béatrix, the first married Count de Potenza; the other, Prince de Sulmone.

P. 336: His son was François Ferdinand, Viceroy of Sicily, died in 1571.

P. 337: Soliman II.

END OF VOLUME ONE.

Lives of
Fair and Gallant Ladies

Marguerite of Valois

From an old engraving.

Lives

Of

Fair and Gallant Ladies

By

The Seigneur De Brantôme

TRANSLATED FROM THE ORIGINAL

———

Volume II

———

Fredonia Books
Amsterdam, The Netherlands

CONTENTS

INTRODUCTION

HE Mondragola of Machiavelli, which reflects Italian morals at the time of the Renaissance, is well known. Lafontaine has later made use of this motif in one of his humorous stories. In the fourth chapter Liguro arrays in battle order an officer, a valet and a doctor, for a humorous love expedition. Liguro says: "In the right corner we shall place Callimaque; I shall place myself in the extreme left corner, and the doctor in the middle. He will be called St. Cuckold."

An interlocutor: "Who is this Saint?"

"The greatest Saint of France."

This question and the answer given are delicious. Brantôme might have made this witticism even in his time. Perhaps he merely did not write it down, for after all he could not make too extensive use of his favorite play with the word "cocu."

"The cuckold, the greatest Saint of France"; this might have been the motto of the "Dames Galantes." Philarete Chasles would have denied this, of course. He always maintained that Gaul was pure and chaste, and that if France was full of vice, it had merely been infected by neighboring peoples. But this worthy academician was well informed merely regarding Italian influence. He was extremely unaware of the existence of the cuckold in the sixteenth century. He even asserts in the strongest terms (in his preface to the edition of 1834) that all of this had not been so serious; the courtiers had merely desired to be immoral in an elegant fashion. He even calls Brantôme "un fanfaron de licence," a braggart of vice. Indeed he would feel unhappy if he could not reassure us: "Quand il se plonge dans les impuretes, c'est, croyez-moi, pure fanfaronnade de viee." Who would not smile at this worthy academician who has remained so unfamiliar with the history of his kings? His "believe me" sounds very well. But the best is yet to come. The book of the "Dames Galantes" was by no means to be considered merely a frivolous collection of scandalous anecdotes, but a "curious historical document."

There will probably always be a difference of opinion regarding Brantôme's position in the history of civilization. It will probably be impossible to change the judgments of the ordinary superficial reader. But we do not wish to dispose of Brantôme as simply as that. It is very easy for a Puritan to condemn him. But we must seek to form a fairer judgment. Now in order to overcome this difficulty, it is, of course, very tempting simply to proclaim his importance for the history of civilization and to put him on the market as such. This would not be wrong, but this method has been used altogether too freely, both properly and improperly. Besides, Brantôme is too good to be labelled in this manner. He does not need it either, he is of sufficient historical importance even without its being pointed out. The question now arises: From what point of view are we then to comprehend Brantôme? We could answer, from the time in which he lived. But that, speaking in such general terms, is a commonplace. It is not quite correct either. For in spite of the opinions of the educated we must clearly distinguish between Brantôme as an author and Brantôme as a man—and we shall hear more of this bold anarchistic personality, who almost throws his chamberlain's key back at the king. This is another striking case where the author must by no means be identified with his book. These events might have passed through another person's mind; they would have remained the same nevertheless. For Brantôme did not originate them, he merely chronicled them. Now it usually happens that things are attributed to an author of which he is entirely innocent (does not Society make an author pay for his confessions in book-form?). He is even charged with a crime when he merely reports such events. The responsibility which Brantôme must bear for his writings is greatly to be limited. And if our educated old maids simply refuse to be reconciled with his share we need merely tell them that this share is completely neutralized by his own personal life.

Brantôme undoubtedly considered himself an historian. That was a pardonable error. There is a great difference of opinion regarding the historical value of his reports, the most general opinion being that Brantôme's accuracy is in no way to be relied upon, and that he was more a chronicler and a writer of memoirs. To be sure, Brantôme cannot prove the historical accuracy of every statement he makes. Who would be able to give an exact account of this kaleidoscope of details? But the significance, the symbolic value is there.

In order to substantiate this sharp distinction between the book of Fair and Gallant Ladies and the supposed character of its author, I must be permitted to describe France of the sixteenth century. Various essayists have said that this period had been quite tame and pure in morals, that Brantôme had merely invented and exaggerated these stories. But when they began to cite examples, it became evident that their opinion was like a snake biting its own tail. Their examples proved the very opposite of their views.

Brantôme's book could only have been written at the time of the last of the Valois. These dissolute kings furnished material for his book. Very few of these exploits can be charged to his own account, and even these he relates in an impersonal manner. Most of them he either witnessed or they were related to him, largely by the kings themselves. No matter in what connection one may read the history of the second half of the sixteenth century, the dissolute, licentious and immoral Valois are always mentioned. The kings corrupted this period to such an extent that Brantôme would have had to be a Heliogabalus in order to make his own contributions felt.

[ix]

At the beginning of this period we meet with the influence of the Italian Renaissance. Through the crusades of Charles VIII., France came into close contact with it. These kings conducted long wars for the possession of Milan, Genoa, Siena and Naples. A dream of the South induced the French to cross the Alps, and every campaign was followed by a new flood of Italian culture. If at the beginning of the sixteenth century France was not yet the Capital of grand manners, it approached this condition with giant strides during the reign of Francis I. For now there was added an invasion of Spanish culture. Next to Rome, Madrid had the greatest influence upon Paris. Francis I., this chivalrous king (1515-1547), introduced a flourishing court life. He induced Italian artists such as Leonardo and Cellini to come to Blois and try to introduce the grand Spanish manners into his own court. For a time France still seemed to be an imitation of Italy, but a poor one. With the preponderance of the Spanish influence the Etiquette of Society approached its perfection.

Francis I. therefore brought knighthood into flower. He considered a nobleman the foremost representative of the people and prized chivalry more than anything else. The court surrendered itself to a life of gaiety and frivolity; even at this period the keeping of mistresses became almost an official institution. "I have heard of the king's wish," Brantôme relates, "that the noblemen of his court should not be without a lady of their heart and if they did not do as he wished he considered them simpletons without taste. But he frequently asked the others the name of their mistresses and promised to help and to speak for them. Such was his kindness and intimacy." Francis I. is responsible for this saying: "A court without women is like a year without a spring, like a spring without roses." To be sure, there was also another side to this court life. There were serious financial troubles, corruption in administration and sale of offices. The Italian architects who constructed the magnificent buildings of Saint

Germain, Chantilly, Chambord and Chenonceaux were by no means inexpensive. Great interest was also taken in literary things. A more refined French was developed at this period. In Blois a library, Chambre de Librarye, was established. All of the Valois had great talent in composing poetic epistles, songs and stories, not merely Marguerite of Navarre, the sister of Francis I., who following the example of her brother was a patroness of the arts. To be sure, mention is also made of the "terrifying immorality" in Pau, even though this may not have been so bad. Brantôme is already connected with this court life in Pau. His grandmother, Louise of Daillon, Seneschal of Poitiers, was one of the most intimate ladies-in-waiting of the Queen of Navarre. His mother, Anne of Bourdeille, is even introduced in several stories of the *Heptameron.* She is called Ennasuite, and his father Francis of Bourdeille appears as Simontaut. Life in the Louvre became more and more lax. Francis I., this royal Don Juan, is even said to have been a rival of his son, without our knowing, however, whether this refers to Catherine of Medici or to Diana of Poitiers. Another version of the story makes Henri II. a rival of his father for the favor of Diana of Poitiers. But the well known revenge of that deceived nobleman which caused the death of Francis I. was entirely unnecessary. It is said that the king had been intentionally infected. He could not be healed and died of this disease. At any rate, his body was completely poisoned by venereal ulcers, when he died. This physical degeneration was a terrible heritage which he left to his son, Henri II. (1547-1550).

The latter had in the meantime married Catherine of Medici. Italian depravities now crossed the Alps in even greater numbers. She was followed by a large number of astrologers, dancers, singers, conjurors and musicians who were like a plague of locusts. She thus accelerated the cultural process, she steeped the court of Henri II. as well as that of his three sons in the spirit of Italy and Spain. (The numerous citations of Brantôme indicate the frequency and closeness of relations at this time between France and Spain, the classical country of chivalry.) But her greed for power was always greater than her sensual desires. Though of imposing exterior, she was not beautiful, rather robust, ardently devoted to hunting, and masculine also in the quantity of food she consumed. She talked extremely well and made use of her literary skill in her diplomatic correspondence, which is estimated at about 6,000 letters. She was not, however, spared the great humiliation of sharing the bed and board of her royal husband with Madame de Valentinois, Diana of Poitiers, the mistress of Henri II. In this difficult position with an ignorant and narrow-minded husband who was moreover completely dominated by his favorites, she maintained a very wise attitude. Catherine of Medici was, of course, an intriguing woman who later tried to carry out her most secret purposes in the midst of her own celebrations.

Henri II. had four sons and a daughter, who were born to him by Catherine of Medici after ten years of sterility. In them the tragic fate of the last of the Valois was fulfilled. One after the other mounts the throne which is devoid of any happiness. The last of them is consumed when he has barely reached it. The blood of the Valois would have died out completely but for its continuation in the Bourbons through Marguerite, the last of the Valois, who with her bewitching beauty infatuated men and as the first wife of Henri IV. filled the world with the reports of her scandalous life. There is tragedy in the fact that the book of Fair and Gallant Ladies was dedicated to Alençon, the last and youngest of the Valois. Of these four sons each was more depraved than the other; they furnished the material for Brantôme's story. The book of Fair and Gallant Ladies, therefore, also seals the end of the race.

The line began with Francis II. He mounted the throne when he was a boy of sixteen. He was as weak mentally as he was physically. He died in 1560, less than a year later, "as a result of an ulcer in the head." Then Catherine of

Medici was Regent for ten years. In 1571 the next son, Charles, was old enough to mount the throne. He was twenty-two years old, tall and thin, weak on his legs, with a stooping position and sickly pale complexion. Thus he was painted by François Clouet, called Janet, a famous painting which is now in possession of the Duke of Aumale. While a young prince, he received the very best education. His teachers were Amyot and Henri Estienne, with whom he read Plotin, Plato, Virgil, Cicero, Tacitus, Polybius and Machiavelli. Amyot's translation of Plutarch's Lives delighted the entire court. "The princesses of the House of France," Brantôme relates, "together with their ladies-in-waiting and maids-of-honor, took the greatest pleasure in the sayings of the Greeks and Romans which have been preserved by sweet Plutarch." Thus literature came into its own even in this court life. But they did not merely do homage to the old classical literature, all of them were also versed in the art of the sonnet, and were able to rhyme graceful love songs as well as Ronsard. Charles IX. himself wrote poetry and translated the Odes of Horace into French. His effeminate nature, at one moment given to humiliating excesses and in the next consumed by pangs of conscience, was fond of graceful and frivolous poetry. But there was also some good in this movement. Whereas the French language had been officially designated in 1539 as the Language of Law, to be used also in lectures, Charles IX. now gave his consent in 1570 for the founding of a Society to develop and purify the language. But even in this respect the honest de Thou denounced "this depraved age" and spoke of "the poisoning of women by immoral songs." This worthy man himself wrote Latin, of course. A time of disorder was now approaching, the revolts of the Huguenots were sweeping through France. But these very disorders and dangers encouraged a certain bold carelessness and recklessness. Murder was slinking through the streets. It was the year of St. Bartholomew's Eve. The Duke of Anjou himself relates that he feared to be stabbed by his own brother king, Charles

[xiii]

IX., and later when he himself mounted the throne his brother Alençon was in conspiracy against him. The Mignons and the Rodomonts, the coxcombs and braggarts, were increasing at this depraved court. Soon it was able seriously to compete with Madrid and Naples. Indeed the people down there now began to look up to France as the centre of fashion. Brantôme was the first to recognize this and he was glad of it. Indeed he even encouraged it. Even at that time the Frenchman wished to be superior to all other people.

The king was completely broken by the results of St. Bartholomew's Eve. His mind wandered back and forth. He became gloomy and vehement, had terrible hallucinations, and heard the spirits of the dead in the air. By superhuman exertions he tried to drown his conscience and procure sleep. He was constantly hunting, remaining in the saddle continuously from twelve to fourteen hours and often three days in succession. When he did not hunt he fenced or played ball or stood for three to four hours at the blacksmith's anvil swinging an enormous hammer. Finally, consumption forced him to stay in bed. But even now he passed his time by writing about his favorite occupation, he was composing the *Livre du Roy Charles,* a dissertation on natural history and the deer hunt. When he reached the twenty-ninth chapter death overtook him. This fragment deserves praise, it was well thought out and not badly written.

It is always unpleasant to say of a king that he had more talent to be an author than a king. It is unfortunate but true that the Valois were a literary race. But France itself in 1577 was in a sorry state. Everywhere there were ruins of destroyed villages and castles. There were enormous stretches of uncultivated land and cattle-raising was greatly diminished. There were many loafing vagabonds accustomed to war and robbery who were a danger to the traveller and the farmer. Every province, every city, almost every house was divided against itself.

Francis of Alençon, the fourth of these brothers, who felt

[xiv]

himself coming of age, the last of the Valois, had already begun his agitation. Charles IX. despised him and suspected his secret intrigues. His other brother, Henri, had to watch his every step in order to feel secure.

Henri III. (1574-1589), formerly Henri of Anjou, was barely twenty-five years old when his strength was exhausted. But his greed of power which had already made him king of the Polish throne was still undiminished. He was the most elegant, the most graceful and the most tasteful of the Valois. It was therefore only to be expected that he would introduce new forms of stricter etiquette. D'Aubigne relates that he was a good judge of the arts, and that he was "one of the most eloquent men of his age." He was always on the search for poetry to gratify his erotic impulses. A life of revelry and pleasure now began in the palace. Immorality is the mildest reproach of his contemporary chroniclers. Although well educated and a friend of the Sciences, of Poetry and the Arts, as well as gifted by nature with a good mind, he was nevertheless very frivolous, indifferent, physically and mentally indolent. He almost despised hunting as much as the conscientious discharge of government affairs. He greatly preferred to be in the society of women, himself dressed in a feminine fashion, with two or three rings in each ear. He usually knew what was right and proper, but his desires, conveniences and other secondary matters prevented him from doing it. He discharged all the more serious and efficient men and surrounded himself with insignificant coxcombs, the so-called Mignons, with whom he dallied and adorned himself, and to whom he surrendered the government of the state. These conceited young men, who were without any redeeming merit, simply led a gay life at the court. In his History of France (I, 265), Ranke relates: "He surrounded himself with young people of pleasing appearance who tried to outdo him in cleanliness of dress and neatness of appearance. To be a favorite, a Mignon, was not a question of momentary approval but a kind of permanent position." Assassinations were daily occurrences. D'Aubigne severely criticized the terrifying conditions in the court and public life in general. A chronicler says: "At that time anything was permitted except to say and do what was right and proper." This frivolous, scandalous court consumed enormous sums of money. Such a miserable wretch as Henri III. required for his personal pleasures an annual sum of 1,000,000 gold thalers, which is equivalent to about $10,000,000 in present values, and yet the entire state had to get along with 6,000,000 thalers. For this was all that could be squeezed out of the country. Ranke says (page 269): "In a diary of this period, the violent means of obtaining money and the squandering of the same by the favorites are related side by side, and it shows the disagreeable impression that these things made." Then there was also the contrast between his religious and his worldly life. At one time he would steep his feelings in orgies, then again he would parade them in processions. He was entirely capable of suddenly changing the gayest raiment for sackcloth and ashes. He would take off his jewel-covered belt and put on another covered with skulls. And in order that Satan might not be lacking, the criminal court ("chambre ardente") which was established at Blois had plenty of work to do during his reign. It was also evident that he would never have any children with his sickly wife.

This same Henry III. while still Duke of Orleans tried to gain the favor of Brantôme, who was then twenty-four years old, and when he entered upon his reign appointed him his chamberlain. This appointment took place in 1574. At the same time, however, Francis of Alençon sought his favor. Subsequently Brantôme entered into very intimate relations with him.

Alençon is described to us as being small though well built but with coarse, crude features, with the temper and irritability of a woman and even greater cowardliness, likewise unreliable, ambitious and greedy. He was a very vain, frivolous person without political or religious convictions. From his youth up he was weak and sickly. His brother Henri despised and hated him and kept him a barely concealed prisoner as long as he could. Then Alençon revolted, gathered armies, founded a new Ultra-Royal party and moved on Paris. He even wished at one time to have his mother removed from the court, who was still carrying on her intrigues throughout the entire kingdom. They were obliged to negotiate with him and he succeeded in extorting an indemnity which was almost equal to a royal authority. He received five duchies and four earldoms and his court had the power of passing death sentences. He had a guard and a corps of pages in expensive liveries and conducted a brilliant court. We must try and picture him as Ranke describes him, "small and stocky, of an obstinate bearing, bushy black hair over his ugly pock-marked face, which, however, was brightened by a fiery eye."

The book of Fair and Gallant Ladies is dedicated to Alençon, but he did not see it any more. Brantôme, however, must have begun it while he was still living. Alençon died in 1584 at the age of thirty-one.

Five years later Henri III. was stabbed by Jacques Clement. Thus the race of Henri III., which was apparently so fruitful, had withered in his sons. The remaining sister, who was inferior according to the Salic Law, was also extremely immoral.

Her husband, Henry IV., entered a country that was completely exhausted. The state debt at the time he entered upon his reign clearly showed the spirit of the previous governments. In 1560 the state debt was 43,000,000 livres. At the end of the century it had risen to 300,000,000. The Valois sold titles and dignities to the rich, squeezed them besides and were finally capable of mortgaging anything they could lay their hands upon. In 1595 Henri IV. remarked in Blois that "the majority of the farms and almost all the villages were uninhabited and empty." This mounting of the state debt clearly indicates the extent of the depravity of the court. During the reign of Charles IX. and Henri III., that

[xvii]

is between 1570-1590, the dissoluteness reached its height and this made it possible for Brantôme to collect such a large number of stories and anecdotes. Catherine of Medici, who outlived her race by a year and whose influence continued during this entire period, does not seem to have been a saint herself. But the last three of the Valois were the worst, the most frivolous and lascivious of them all. It was during their reign that the rule of mistresses was at its height in the Louvre and the royal castles which furnished Brantôme with his inexhaustible material. Such were the Valois.

This is the background of Brantôme's life. We should like to know more about him. He has written about many generals and important women of his age, but there are only fragments regarding himself.

The family Bourdeille is one of the most important in Perigord. Like other old races they sought to trace their ancestors back into the times of Gaul and Rome. Charlemagne is said to have founded the Abbey Brantôme.

Brantôme's father was the "first page of the royal litter." His son speaks of him as "un homme scabreaux, haut a la main et mauvais garcon." His mother, a born Châtaigneraie, was lady-in-waiting of the Queen of Navarre. Pierre was probably also born in Navarre, but nothing is known as to the exact day of birth. Former biographers simply copied, one from the other, that he had died in 1614 at the age of eighty-seven. This would make 1528 the year of his birth. But now it is well known that Brantôme spent the first years of his life in Navarre. Queen Marguerite died in 1549 and Brantôme later writes of his sojourn at her court: "Moy estant petit garcon en sa court." Various methods of calculation seem to indicate that he was born in 1540.

After the death of the Queen of Navarre—this is also a matter of record—Brantôme went to Paris to take up his studies. From Paris, where he probably also was a companion of the *enfants sanssouci,* he went to Poitiers to continue them. There in 1555, while still "a young student," he became acquainted with the beautiful Gotterelle, who is said to have had illicit relations with the Huguenot students. When he had completed his studies in 1556 he as the youngest son had to enter the church. He also received his share of the Abbey Brantôme from Henri II. as a reward for the heroisms of his older brother. This young abbot was about sixteen years old. His signature and his title in family documents in this period are very amusing: "Révérend père en Dieu abbè de Brantôme." As an abbot he had no ecclesiastical duties. He was his own pastor, could go to war, get married and do as he pleased. But nevertheless, this ecclesiastical position did not suit him, and so he raised 500 gold thalers by selling wood from his forests with which he fitted himself out and then went off to Italy at the age of eighteen: "Portant L'coquebuse a meche et un beau fourniment de Milan, monte sur une haquenee de cent ecus et menant toujours six on sept gentils hommes, armes et montes de meme, et bien en point sur bons courtands."

He simply went off wherever there was war. In Piedmont he was shot in the face by an arrow which almost deprived him of his sight. There he was lying in Portofino in these marvellously beautiful foothills along the Genoese coast, and there he was strangely healed: "Une fort belle dame de la ma jettait dans les yeux du lait de ses beaux et blancs tetins" (*Vies des Capitaines français*, Ch. IV, 499). Then he went to Naples with François de Guise. He himself describes his reception by the Duke of Alcala. Here he also became acquainted with Madame de Guast, die Marquise del Vasto.

In 1560 he left Italy and took up the administration of his estates which heretofore had been in the hands of his oldest brother, Andre. He joined the court in Amboise, where Francis II. was conducting tournaments. At the same time the House of Guise took notice of him. In recollection of his uncle, La Châtaigneraie, he was offered high protection at the court of Lorraine. From this time on he was at the court for over thirty years. At first he accompanied the Duke of Guise to his castle. Then after the death of Francis II. he accompanied his widow, Mary Stuart, to England in August, 1561, and heard her final farewell to France.

Although Brantôme could not say enough in praise of the princes of Lorraine, the Guises, he did not go over to their side. Once at a later period when he was deeply embittered he allowed himself to be carried away by them. At the outbreak of the civil wars, Brantôme, of course, sided with the court. He also participated in the battle of Dreux. If there happened to be no war in France he would fight somewhere abroad. In 1564 he entered into closer relations with the court of the Duke of Orleans (later Henri III.). He became one of his noblemen and received 600 livres annually. (The receipts are still in existence.) In the same year he also took part in an expedition against the Berbers on the Coast of Morocco. We find him in Lisbon and in Madrid, where he was highly honored by the courts. When Sultan Soliman attacked Malta, Brantôme also hurried thither. He returned by way of Naples and again presented himself to the Marquise de Guast. He thought that at last he had found his fortune but he felt constrained to continue his journey. He later denounces this episode in the most vehement terms. "Toujours trottant, traversant et vagabondant le monde." He was on his way to a new war in Hungary, but when he arrived in Venice he heard that it was not worth while. He returned by way of Milan and Turin, where he gave the impression of being greatly impoverished, but he was too proud to accept the purse of the Duchess of Savoy.

In the meantime, the Huguenots had forced the king to make greater and greater concessions. Prince Condé and Admiral Coligny had the upper hand. The Huguenots, who heard that Brantôme had reasons to be displeased with the king, tried to induce him to commit treason. But Brantôme remained firm. He was given the title Captain ("Maître de camp") of two companies even though he only had one—but that is typical of the French. This company (enseigne) was under his command in the Battle of St. Venis (1567). In the following year, 1568, Charles IX. engaged him as a paid chamberlain. After the Battle of Jarnac in the following year he was seized by a fever, as a result of which he had to spend almost a year on his estates in order to recover.

As soon as he was well again he wished to go off to war somewhere. He complained that it had been impossible for him to participate in the Battle of Lepanto. His friend, Strozzi, was now getting ready an expedition to Peru, which was to recompense him. But some misunderstanding caused his separation from Strozzi shortly afterwards. The preparations for this expedition had, however, kept him away from St. Bartholomew's Eve, even though later he cursed them for personal reasons.

Brantôme was not religious. He cannot be considered a good judge in affairs of the Huguenots, for he was more than neutral in religious matters. He took an indifferent attitude towards the League. For as a secular priest, he had the very best reasons for being neither in favor of the League nor of the Huguenots. He speaks with great respect of Coligny. They frequently met and the admiral was always friendly. Brantôme disapproved of the Massacre of St. Bartholomew's Eve and considered it entirely reprehensible and purposeless. This good warrior would have greatly preferred to have seen these restless spirits engaged in a foreign war. He says of this bloody eve: "Mort malheurse lu puis-je bien appeller pour toute la France." To be sure, in the following year he was present at the Siege of La Rochelle, the White City.

He was at the court when Charles IX. died. He accompanied the corpse from Notre Dame to St. Denis and then entered the services of Henri III., who finally bestowed some favors upon the brothers Bourdeille and gave them the Bishopric of Perigneux.

Then this restless soul was driven to approach Alençon,

[xxi]

the youngest of the Valois. Bussy d'Amboise, the foremost nobleman of Alençon, was his friend. Alençon overwhelmed him with kindness and Brantôme had to beg the angry king's pardon for his defection.

But now an event occurred which almost drove Brantôme into open rebellion. In 1582 his oldest brother died. The Abbey had belonged to both of them, but his brother had appointed his own heir and the king was helpless against this. Brantôme became very angry because he was not the heir. "Je ne suis qu'un ver de terre," he writes. He now desired that the king should at least give his share of the Abbey to his nephew, but he was unsuccessful in this as well. Aubeterre became Seneschal and Governor of Perigord. This fault-finder could not control his anger: "Un matin, second jour de premier de l'an . . . je luy en fis ma plainte; il m'en fit des excuses, bien qu'il fust mon roy. Je ne luy respondis autre chose sinon: Eh bien, Sire, vous ne m'avez donne se coup grand subject de vous faire jainais service comme j'ay faict." And so he ran off "fort despit." As he left the Louvre he noticed that the golden chamberlain's key was still hanging on his belt; he tore it off and threw it into the Seine, so great was his anger.

(When Aubeterre died in 1593 these posts were returned to the family Bourdeille.)

(Other reasons which angered Brantôme were less serious. Thus he could not bear Montaigne because the latter was of more recent nobility. He himself has shown that a man of the sword could very well take up the pen to pass the time. But he could not understand that the opposite might happen, and a sword given to a man of the pen. He was appointed a knight in the Order of St. Michael. But this did not satisfy his ambition very much when he looked around and saw that he had to share this distinction with many other men. He wished to have it limited to the nobility of the sword. Now his neighbor, Michel de Montaigne, received the same order. Brantôme writes regarding this: "We have seen councillors

[xxii]

leave the courts of justice, put down their robe and their four-cornered hat and take up a sword. Immediately the king bestowed the distinction upon them without their ever having gone to war. This has happened to Monsieur de Montaigne, who would have done better to remain at his trade and continue to write his essays rather than exchange his pen for a sword which was not nearly so becoming.")

Henri II. pardoned him his unmannerly behavior, but the king's rooms were closed to him. Then the Duke of Alençon wished to gain his allegiance and appointed him chamberlain, thereby rewarding him for the intimate relationship which had existed between them ever since 1579. The duke was the leader of the dissatisfied and so this fault-finder was quite welcome to him. The book of Fair and Gallant Ladies is the direct result of the conversations at the Court of Alençon, for we hear that Brantôme soon wrote a few discourses which he dedicated to the prince. Brantôme sold himself to Alençon, which is almost to be taken literally. Then Alençon died. Brantôme's hopes were now completely crushed.

What was he to do now? He was angry at the king. His boundless anger almost blinded him. Then the Guises approached him and tried to induce him to swear allegiance to the enemies of the Valois. He was quite ready to do this and was at the point of committing high treason, for the King of Spain was behind the Guises, to whom he swore allegiance. But the outbreak of the war of the Huguenots, which resulted in a temporary depreciation of all estates, prevented him from carrying out his plans immediately. He could not sell anything, and without money life in Spain was impossible. But this new state of affairs gave him new energy and new life. He walked about with "sprightly vigor." He later described his feelings in the *Capitaines français* (Ch. IV, 108): "Possible que, si je fusse venu an bout de vies attantes et propositions, J'eusse faut plus de mal a ma patrie que jamais n'a faict renegat d'Alger a'la sienne, dont J'en fusse este mandict a perpetuite, possible de Dieu et des hommes."

Then a horse that he was about to mount, shied, rose up and fell, rolling over him, so that all his ribs were broken. He was confined to his bed for almost four years; crippled and lame, without being able to move because of pain.

When he was able to rise again the new order of things was in full progress, and when the iron hand of Henri IV., this cunning Navarrese and secret Huguenot, swept over France, the old court life also disappeared. Brantôme was sickly and when the old Queen-mother Medici also died (1590) he buried himself completely in his abbey and took no interest henceforth in the events of his time.

"Chaffoureur du papier"—this might be the motto of his further life. Alas, writing was also such a resignation for Brantôme, otherwise he would not have heaped such abuse upon it. But we must not imagine that his literary talent only developed after his unfortunate fall. Naturally he made quite different and more extensive use of it under these conditions than he otherwise would have done. Stirring up his old memories became more and more a means of mastering the sterile life of that period. Literature is a product of impoverished life. It is the opium intoxication of memory, the conjuring up of bygone events. The death-shadowed eyes of Alençon had seen the first fragments of the book of Fair and Gallant Ladies. The *Rondomontades Espagnoles* must have been finished in 1590, for he offered them to the Queen of Navarre in the Castle of Usson in Auvergne. But beginning in 1590 there was a conscious exchange of the sword for the pen. He knew himself well. On his bed of pain the recollections of his varied life, his sufferings and the complaints of his thwarted ambitions became a longed-for distraction. He died July 15, 1614, and was buried in the Chapel of Richemond.

His manuscripts had a strange fate. They were the principal care of his last will and testament. This in itself is a monument to his pride. "J'ai bien de l'ambition," he writes,

"je la veux encore monstrer apres ma mort." He had decided elements of greatness. The books in his library were
to remain together, "set up in the castle and not to be scat-
tered hither and thither or loaned to anyone." He wished to
have the library preserved "in eternal commemoration of himself." He was particularly interested in having his works
published. He pretended to be a knight, and a nobleman, and
yet he prized most highly these six volumes beautifully bound
in blue, green and black velvet. His books, furthermore, were
not to be published with a pseudonym, but his own name was
to be openly printed on the title-page. He does not wish
to be deprived of his labors and his fame. He gave the strict-
est instructions to his heirs, but he was constantly forced to
make additions to the will, because his executors died. He
outlived too many of them and had made his will too early.
The instructions regarding the printing of his books are very
amusing: "Pour les faire imprimer mieux a ma fantaisie,
. . . y'ordonne et veux, que l'on prenne sur ma lotate heredite
l'argent qu 'en pouvra valoir la dite impression, et qui ne se
pouvra certes monter a beaucoup, cur j'ay veu force impri-
meurs . . . que s'ils ont mis une foys la veue, en donneront
plusoost pour les imprimer qu'ils n'en voudraient recepvoir;
car ils en impriment plusierus gratis que no valent pas les
mieux. Je m'en puys bien vanter, mesmes que je les ay
monstrez au moins en partie, a aueuns qui les ont voulu
imprimer sans rien. . . . Mais je n'ay voulu qu ils fussent
imprimez durant mon vivant. Surtout, je veux que la dicte
impression en soit en belle et gross lettre, et grand colume,
pour mieux paroistre. . . ." The typographical directions
are quite modern. The execution of the will finally came into
the hands of his niece, the Countess of Duretal, but on account
of the offence that these books might give, she hesitated to
carry out the last will of her uncle. Then his later heirs
refused to have the books published, and locked the manuscripts in the library. In the course of time, however, copies
came into circulation, more and more copies were made, and

one of them found its way into the office of a printer. A fragment was smuggled into the memoirs of Castelnau and was printed with them in 1659. A better edition was now not far off. In 1665 and 1666 the first edition was published in Leyden by Jean Sambix. It comprised nine volumes in Elzevir. This very incomplete and unreliable edition was printed from a copy. Speculating printers now made a number of reprints. A large number of manuscripts were now in circulation which were named according to the copyists. In the 17th and 18th centuries these books were invariably printed from copies. The edition of 1822, *Oeuvres completes du seigneur de Brantôme* (Paris: Foucault), was the first to go back to the original manuscripts in possession of the family Bourdeille. Monmergue edited it. The manuscript of the book of Fair and Gallant Ladies was in the possession of the Baroness James Rothschild as late as 1903. After her death in the beginning of 1904, it came into possession of the National Library in Paris, which now has all of Brantôme's manuscripts, and also plans to publish a critical revised edition of his collected works.

The two books, *Vies des Dames illustres* and *Vies des Dames galantes,* were originally called by Brantôme Premier and Second Livre des Dames. The new titles were invented by publishers speculating on the taste of the times, which from 1660-1670 greatly preferred the words illustre and galante. The best subsequent edition of the Fair and Gallant Ladies is that printed by Abel Ledoux in Paris, 1834, which was edited by Philarete Chasles, who also supplied an introduction and notes. On the other hand, the critical edition of his collected works in 1822 still contains the best information regarding Brantôme himself, and the remarks by the editor Monmergue are very excellent and far superior to the opinions which Philarete Chasles expresses, poetic as they may be. The crayon-drawings and copper-cuts of Famous and Gallant Ladies of the sixteenth century contained in Bouchot's book, *Les femmes de Brantôme,* are very good; Bouchot's text, however, is merely a re-hash of Brantôme himself. Neither must one over-estimate his reflections regarding the author of the Fair and Gallant Ladies.

There is a great difference between the two Livres des Dames. What is an advantage in the one is a disadvantage in the other. Undoubtedly Brantôme's genius is best expressed in the *Dames Galantes*. In this book the large number of symbolical anecdotes is the best method of narration. In the other they are more or less unimportant. Of course, Brantôme could not escape the questionable historical methods of that period, but shares these faults with all of his contemporaries. Besides, he was too good an author to be an excellent historian. The devil take the historical connection, as long as the story is a good one.

The courtier Brantôme sees all of history from the perspective of boudoir-wit. Therefore his portraits of famous ladies of his age are mere mosaics of haphazard observations and opinions. He is a naïve story-teller and therefore his ideas are seldom coherent. The value of his biographical portraits consists in the fact that they are influenced by his manner of writing, that they are the result of scandal and gossip which he heard in the Louvre, or of conversations in the saddle or in the trenches. He always preserves a respectful attitude and restrains himself from spicing things too freely. He did not allow himself to become a purveyor of malicious gossip, he took great care not to offend his high connections by unbridled speech, but his book lost interest on that account.

If we wish to do justice to Brantôme as the author of Fair and Gallant Ladies, we must try and picture his position in his age and in his society. It is not to be understood that he suddenly invented all of these stories during his long illness. Let us try and follow the origin of these memoirs. At that time the most primitive conceptions of literary work in general prevailed. The actual writing down of the stories was the least. An author laboriously working out his stories was ridiculous. The idea and the actual creative work came long before the moment when the author sat down to write. None of Brantôme's stories originated in his abbey, but in Madrid, in Naples, in Malta before La Rochelle, in the Louvre, in Blois and in Alençon. Writing down a story was a reproduction of what had already been created, of what had been formed and reformed in frequent retelling and polished to perfection. The culture of the court was of great aid to him in his style, but his own style was nevertheless far superior.

For decades Brantôme was a nobleman of his royal masters. He was constantly present at the court and participated in all of the major and minor events of its daily life, in quarrels and celebrations. He was a courtier. He was entirely at home in the halls and chambers of the Louvre, but even though he stopped to chat with the idle courtiers in the halls of the Louvre he never lowered himself to their level. He could be extremely boisterous, yet inwardly he was reserved and observant. He was the very opposite of the noisy, impetuous Bussy-Rabutin. His intelligence and his wisdom made him a source of danger among the chamberlains. His was a dual nature, he was at the same time cynical and religious, disrespectful and enthusiastic, refined and brutal, at the same time abbot, warrior and courtier. Like Bernhard Palissy he ridiculed the astrologers, yet he was subject to the superstitions of his age. His temperament showed that his cradle had not been far from the banks of the Garonne, near the Gascogne. There was combined with his bold, optimistic, adventurous and restless spirit, with his chivalrous ideas and prejudices, a boundless vanity. A contemporary said of him: "He was as boastful as Cellini." Indeed he believed himself far superior to his class, he not only boasted of himself and his family, but also of his most insignificant deeds. He was irreconcilable in hate, and even admonished his heirs to revenge him. His royal masters he treated with respect tempered by irony. As a contemporary or Rabelais, Marot and Ronsard, he was an

[xxviii]

excellent speaker. If Rabelais had a Gallic mind then Brantôme's was French. His cheerful and lively conversation was pleasing to all. He had a reputation of being a brilliant man. But he was also known as a discreet person. Alençon, who was a splendid story-teller himself and liked to hear love stories more than anything else, preferred conversation with him to anyone. His naïveté and originality made friends for him everywhere. He had a brave and noble nature and was proud of being a Frenchman, he was the personified *gentilhomme français*.

And thus his book originated. He must have taken up his pen quite spontaneously one day. Now from the great variety of his own experiences at court and in war, he poured forth a remarkable wealth of peculiar and interesting features which his memory had preserved. It is a book of the love-life during the reign of the Valois. These stories were not invented, but they were anecdotes and reports taken from real life. He was able to evade the danger of boredom. There is style even in his most impudent indiscretions. He only stopped at mere obscenities. On the other hand, he never hesitated to be cynical. As this age was fond of strong expressions, a puritanical language was out of the question. Not until the reign of Louis XIV. did the language become more polite. Neither was Brantôme a Puritan, how could he have been? But he had character. He took pleasure in everything which was a manifestation of human energy. He loved passion and the power to do good or evil. (To be sure he also had some splendid things to say against immoderacy and vehemence of passions. So he was a fit companion of the Medici and the Valois.)

There is not much composition in his books. His attention wandered from one story to the other. Boccaccio, the foremost story-teller of this period, is more logical. An academical critic says of Brantôme: "He reports without choice what is good and bad, what is noble and abominable, the good not without warmth, but the bad with indestructible cheerfulness." There is neither order nor method in his writing. He passes on abruptly, without motif, without transition. A courtier, unfamiliar with the rules of the school, he himself confesses (in the *Rodomontades Espagnoles*): "Son pen de profession du scavoir et de l'art de bien dire, et remet aux meux disans la belle disposition de paroles eloquentes." Because of the variety his stories have unusual charm. In these numerous anecdotes the graceful indecencies of the ladies-in-waiting at the court of the Valois are described as if they had happened openly. His reports of the illicit relations are rendered in a charming style. Even though his sketches and pictures are modelled entirely on the life at the courts, nevertheless he adds two personal elements: an amusing smile and a remarkable literary talent. The following may even have been the case. In the beginning Brantôme may have taken an entirely neutral attitude towards the material at hand, but took no greater personal interest in them than he would, say, in memoirs. But when we can tell a story well, then we also take pleasure in our ability. We permeate the story with our own enjoyment, and in a flash it turns out to be pleasure in the thing itself. The light of our soul glows upon them and then the things themselves look like gold. Brantôme rarely breaks through his reserve. He usually keeps his own opinions regarding these grand ladies and gentlemen in the background, he leaves it to the competent "grands discoureurs" to judge these things. To be sure, if one wished to get information regarding the court of Henri II. and Catherine of Medici, one ought not exactly to read Brantôme, who creates the impression as if the court were a model of a moral institution. "Sa compaignie et sa court estait un vray paradis du monde et escole de toute honnestate, de virtu, l'ornement de la France," he once says somewhere in the *Dames illustres* (page 64). On the other hand, L'Etorle in May, 1577, gives us a report of a banquet given by the Queen-mother in Chenonceaux: "Les femmes les plus belles et honnestes de la cour, estant a moitie nues et ayant, les cheveux epars comme espou-

sees, fuient employees a faire le service." Other contemporaries likewise report a great deal of the immorality prevailing at the court. Thus we have curious reports regarding
the pregnancy of Limeuil, who had her birth-throes in the
queen's wardrobe in Lyon (1564), the father being the Prince
of Conde. Likewise, Johanna d'Albret warns her son, later
Henri IV., against the corruption of the court. When she
later visited him in Paris she was horrified at the immorality
at the court of her daughter-in-law, later Queen Margot, who
lived in the "most depraved and dissolute society." (Brantôme pretended that he was a relative of hers, and pronounced
a panegyric upon her in his Rodomontades which was
answered in her memoirs dedicated to him.) He did not feel
it his mission to be a Savonarola. To his great regret this
"culture" came home to him in his own family. He had more
and more cause to be dissatisfied with his youngest sister,
Madeleine. The wicked life of this lady-in-waiting filled
him with fury. He paid her her share and drove her from
the house.

Certain Puritans among the historians find fault with Brantôme for having uncovered the "abominations" at the courts
of the Valois. His vanity may have led him to make many
modifications in the events, but most of these are probably
due to his desire to be entertaining. In his dedication to the
Rodomontades Espagnoles he addresses Queen Margot as
follows: "Bien vous dirai-je, que ce que j'escrits est plein
de verite; de ce que j'ay veu, je l'asseure, di ce que j'ay scen
et appris d'autray, si on m'a trompe je n'en puis mais si tiens-
je pourtant beaucoup de choses de personnages et de livres
tres-veritables et dignes de foy." Nevertheless, his method
was very primitive. In his descriptions of personalities, he
had a thread on which he could string up his recollections, so
that there was at least some consistency. In the book of
Fair and Gallant Ladies the individual fact is of less importance and has more of symbolic value. They are pictures of
the time composed of a confusing multitude of anecdotes.

[xxxi]

Perhaps the subject-matter required this bizarre method. The *Heptameron* of Marguerite of Navarre was altogether too precise. Brantôme was a man of the sword and a courtier, but a courtier who occasionally liked to put his hand on his sword in between his witticisms. In this state of mind, he was an excellent story-teller, and his anecdotes and stories therefore also have the actuality and the vigorous composition of naïvely related stories.

The book of Fair and Gallant Ladies still contains much of historical value. Almost all the old noble races are mentioned; there is information regarding Navarre, Parma, Florence, Rome and Toulouse. The Huguenots likewise appear, and St. Bartholomew's Eve (1572), which was far back, still sheds its gloom over these pages. The trenches before La Rochelle play an important part; Brantôme always fought against the Huguenots. Perhaps this was the reason why he was no longer in favor with the Bourbon Henri IV. However, one cannot charge him with animosity. Perhaps the frank and open methods of reforming had affected him. Without taking interest in religious quarrels, he probably also hated the monks and priests. Thus one would be inclined to say to the Puritans who condemn Brantôme: If one may speak of guilt and responsibility, then it is his age which must bear them. Brantôme merely chronicled the morals of his times. The material was furnished to him, he merely wrote it down. He is no more responsible for his book, than an editor of a newspaper for the report of a raid or a bomb attack. Ranke once said regarding the times of Henri II.: "If one wishes to know the thoughts and opinions of France at that period, one must read Rabelais" (History of France, Ch. I, 133). Whoever wishes to become familiar with the age of Charles IX. and Henri III. must read Brantôme.

GEORG HARSDÖRFER.

(Translated from the German.)

LIVES OF FAIR AND GALLANT LADIES

FIFTH DISCOURSE

Telling how fair and honourable ladies do love brave and valiant men, and brave men courageous women.

1.

T hath ever been the case that fair and honourable ladies have loved brave and valiant men, albeit by natural bent they be cowardly and timid creatures. But such a virtue doth valour possess with them, as that they do grow altogether enamoured thereof. What else is this but to constrain their exact opposite to love them, and this spite of their own natural complexion? And for an instance of this truth, Venus, which in ancient days was the goddess of Beauty, and of all gentle and courteous bearing, being fain, there in the skies and at the Court of Jupiter, to choose her some fair and handsome lover and so make cuckold her worthy husband Vulcan, did set her choice on never a one of the pretty young gallants, those dapper, curled darlings, whereof were so many to hand, but did select and fall deep in love with the god Mars, god of armies and warlike prowess,—and this albeit he was all foul and a-sweat with the wars he had but just come from, and all besmirched with dust and as filthy as might

[3]

be, more smacking of the soldier in the field than the gallant at Court. Nay! worse still, very oft mayhap all bloody, as returning from battle, he would so lie with her, without any sort of cleansing of himself or scenting of his person.

Again, the fair and high-born Penthesilea, Queen of the Amazons, having learned of fame concerning the valour and prowess of the doughty Hector, and his wondrous feats of arms which he did before Troy against the Greeks, did at the mere report of all this grow so fondly enamoured of the hero, that being fain to have so valiant a knight for father of her children, her daughters to wit which should succeed to her kingdom, she did hie her forth to seek him at Troy. There beholding him, and contemplating and admiring his puissance, she did all ever she could to find favour with him, not less by the brave deeds of war she wrought than by her beauty, the which was exceeding rare. And never did Hector make sally upon his foes but she would be at his side, and was always as well to the front as Hector himself in the mêlée, wherever the fight was hottest. In such wise that 'tis said she did several times accomplish such deeds of daring and so stir the Trojan's wonder as that he would stop short as if astonished in the midst of the fiercest combats, and so withdraw somewhat on one side, the better to see and admire this most valiant Queen doing such gallant deeds.

Thereafter, we leave the world to suppose what was the issue of their love, and if they did put the same in practise; and truly the result could not long be doubtful. But any way, their pleasure was to be of no great duration for the Queen, the better to delight her lover, did so constantly rush forth to confront all hazards, that she

[4]

was slain at last in one of the fiercest and fellest encounters. Others however say she did never see Hector
at all, but that he was dead before her arrival. So coming on the scene and learning his death, she did thereupon fall into so great grief and such sadness to have lost
the goodly sight she had so fondly desired and had come
from so far a land to seek, that she did start forth to meet
a voluntary death in the bloodiest battles of the war;
and so she died, having no further cause to live, now she
had failed of beholding the gallant being she had chosen
as best of all and had loved the most.[1]

The like was done by Thalestris, another Queen of the
Amazons, who did traverse a great country and cover I
know not how many leagues for to visit Alexander the
Great, and asking it of him as a favour, or as but a fair
exchange of courtesy, did lie with him in order that she
might have issue by him of so noble and generous a blood,
having heard him so high rated of all men. This boon
did Alexander very gladly grant her; and verily he must
needs have been sore spoiled and sick of women if he had
done otherwise, for the said Queen was as beautiful as she
was valiant. Quintus Curtius, Orosius and Justin do affirm moreover that she did thus visit Alexander with
three hundred ladies in her suite, all bearing arms,
and all so fair apparelled and of such a beauteous
grace as that naught could surpass the same. So
attended, she did make her reverence before the King,
who did welcome her with the highest marks of honour.
And she did tarry thirteen days and thirteen nights with
him, submitting herself in all ways to his good will and
pleasure. At the same time she did frankly tell him how
that if she had a daughter by him, she would guard her as

[5]

a most priceless treasure; but an if she had a son, that she would send him back to the King, by reason of the abhorrence she bear to the male sex, in the matter of holding rule and exercising any command among them, in accordance with the laws introduced in their companies after they had slain their husbands.

Herein need we have no doubt whatever but that the rest of the ladies and attendant dames did after a like manner, and had themselves covered by the different captains and men of war of the said King Alexander. For they were bound in this matter to follow their mistress' example.

So too the fair maiden Camilla, at once beautiful and noble-hearted, and one which did serve her mistress Diana right faithfully in the woodlands and forests on her hunting parties, having heard the bruit of Turnus' valiance, and how he had to do with another valiant warrior, to wit Aeneas, which did press him sore, did choose her side. Then did she seek out her favourite and join him, but with three very honourable and fair ladies beside for her comrades, the which she had taken for her close friends and trusty confidantes,—and for tribads too mayhap, and for mutual naughtiness. And so did she hold these same in honour and use them on all occasions, as Virgil doth describe in his *Æneid*. And they were called the one Armia, a virgin and a valiant maid, another Tullia, and the third Tarpeia, which was skilled to wield the pike and dart, and that in two divers fashions, be it understood,— all three being daughters of Italy.

Thus then did Camilla arrive with her beauteous little band (as they say "little and good") for to seek out Turnus, with whom she did perform sundry excellent feats

[6]

of arms; and did sally forth so oft and join battle with the doughty Trojans that she was presently slain, to the very sore grief of Turnus, who did regard her most highly, as well for her beauty as for the good succour she brought. In such wise did these fair and courageous dames seek out brave and valiant heroes, succouring the same in their ways and encounters.

What else was it did fill the breast of poor Dido with the flame of so ardent a love, what but the valiance she did feel to be in her Aeneas,—if we are to credit Virgil? For she had begged him to tell her of his wars, and the ruin and destruction of Troy, and he had gratified her wish,— albeit to his own great grief, to renew the memory of such sorrows, and in his discourse had dwelt by the way on his own valiant achievements. And Dido having well marked all these and pondered them in her breast, and presently declaring of her love to her sister Anna, the chiefest and most pregnant of the words she said to her were these and no other: "Ah! sister mine, what a guest is this which hath come to my Court! Oh! the noble way he hath with him, and how his very carriage doth announce him a brave and most valiant warrior, in deed and in spirit! I do firmly believe him to be the offspring of some race of gods; for churlish hearts are ever cowardly of their very nature." Such were Dido's words; and I think she did come to love him so, quite as much because she was herself brave and generous-hearted, and that her instinct did push her to love her fellow, as to win help and service of him in case of need. But the wretch did deceive and desert her in pitiful wise,—an ill deed he should never have done to so honourable a lady, which had given him

[7]

her heart and her love, to him, I say, that was but a stranger and an outlaw.

Boccaccio in his book of *Famous Folk which have been Unfortunate,*[2] doth tell a tale of a certain Duchess of Forli, named Romilda, who having lost husband and lands and goods, all which Caucan, King of the Avarese, had robbed her of, was constrained to take refuge with her children in her castle of Forli, and was therein besieged by him. But one day when he did approach near the walls to make a reconnaissance, Romilda who was on the top of a tower, saw him and did long and carefully observe him. Then seeing him so handsome, being in the flower of his age, mounted on a fine horse and clad in a magnificent suit of mail, and knowing how he was used to do many doughty deeds of war, and that he did never spare himself any more than the least of his soldiers, she did incontinently fall deeply enamoured of the man, and quitting to mourn for her husband and all care for her castle and the siege thereof, did send him word by a messenger that, if he would have her in marriage, she would yield him up the place on the day their wedding should be celebrated.

King Caucan took her at her word. Accordingly the day agreed upon being come, lo! she doth deck herself most stately as a duchess should in her finest and most magnificent attire, which did make her yet fairer still to look on, exceeding fair as she was by nature. So having come to the King's camp for to consummate the marriage, this last, to the end he might not be blamed as not having kept his word, did spend all that night in satisfying the enamoured duchess's desires. But the next morning, on rising, he did have a dozen Averese soldiers of his called,

[8]

such as he deemed to be the strongest and most stalwart fellows, and gave Romilda into their hands, to take their pleasure of her one after other. These did have her for all a night long so oft as ever they could. But then, when day was come again, Caucan having summoned her before him, and after sternly upbraiding her for her wantonness and heaping many insults upon her, did have her impaled through her belly, of which cruel treatment she did presently die. Truly a savage and barbarous act, so to mishandle a fair and honourable lady, instead of displaying gratitude, rewarding her and treating her with all possible courtesy, for the good opinion she had showed of his generosity, valour and noble courage, and her love for him therefor! And of this must fair ladies sometimes have good heed; for of these valiant men of war there be some which have so grown accustomed to killing and slashing and savagely plying the steel, that now and again it doth take their humour to exercise the like barbarity on women. Yet are not all of this complexion, but rather, when honourable ladies do them this honour to love them and hold their valour in high esteem, they do leave behind in camp their fury and fierce passions, and in court and ladies' chambers do fit themselves to the practise of all gentleness and kindness and fair courtesy.

Bandello in his *Tragic Histories* [3] doth relate one, the finest story I have ever read, of a certain Duchess of Savoy, who one day coming forth from her good town of Turin, did hear a Spanish woman, a pilgrim on her road to Loretto to perform a vow, cry out and admire her beauty and loudly declare, how that if only so fair and perfect a lady were wedded to her brother, the Señor de Mendoza, which was himself so handsome, brave and valiant, folk

[9]

might well say in all lands that now the finest and handsomest couple in all the world were mated together. The
Duchess who did very well understand the Spanish tongue,
having graven these words in her breast and pondered
them over in her heart, did anon begin to grave love in
the same place likewise. In such wise that by this report
of his merits she did fall so passionately in love with the
Señor de Mendoza as that she did never slacken till she
had planned a pretended pilgrimage to St. James of Com-
postella, for to see the man for whom she had so suddenly
been smit with love. So having journeyed to Spain, and
taken the road passing by the house of de Mendoza, she
had time and leisure to content and satisfy her eyes with
a good sight of the fair object she had chosen. For the
Señor de Mendoza's sister, which was in the Duchess'
train, had advised her brother of so distinguished and fair
a visitor's coming. Wherefore he did not fail to go forth
to meet her in gallant array, and mounted on a noble
Spanish horse, and this with so fine a grace as that the
Duchess could not but be assured of the truth of the fair
report which had been given her, and did admire him
greatly, as well for his handsome person as for his noble
carriage, which did plainly manifest the valiance that was
in him. This she did esteem even more highly than all his
other merits, accomplishments and perfections, presaging
even at that date how she would one day mayhap have need
of his valour,—as truly in after times he did excellently
serve her under the false accusation which Count Pancalier
brought against her chastity. Natheless, though she did
find him brave and courageous as a man of arms, yet for
the nonce was he a recreant in love; for he did show himself so cold and respectful toward her as to try never an

assault of amorous words, the very thing she did most desire, and for which she had undertook her journey. Wherefore, in sore despite at so chilling a respect, or to speak plainly such recreancy in love, she did part from him on the morrow, not near so well content as she had come.

Thus we see how true 'tis that ladies do sometimes love men no less which are bold in love than they which be brave in arms,—not that they would have them brazen and over-bold, impudent and self-satisfied, as I have known some to be. But in this matter must they keep ever the *via media*.

I have known not a few which have lost many a good fortune with women by reason of such over-respectfulness, whereof I could tell some excellent stories, were I not afeared of wandering too far from the proper subject of my Discourse. But I hope to give them in a separate place; so I will only tell the following one here.

I have heard tell in former days of a lady, and one of the fairest in all the world, who having in the like fashion heard a certain Prince given out by repute for brave and valiant, and that he had already in his young days done and performed great exploits of war, and in especial won two great and signal victories against his foes,[4] did conceive a strong desire to see him; and to this end did make a journey to the province wherein he was then tarrying, under some pretext or other that I need not name. Well! at last she did set forth; and presently,—for what is not possible to a brave and loving heart?—she doth gain sight of him and can contemplate him at her ease, for he did come out a long distance to meet her, and doth now receive her with all possible honour and respect, as was

[11]

meet for so great, fair and noble-hearted a Princess. Nay! the respect was e'en *too* great, some do say; for the same thing happened as with the Señor de Mendoza and the Duchess of Savoy, and such excessive respectfulness did but engender the like despite and dissatisfaction. At any rate she did part from him by no means so well satisfied as she had come. It may well be he would but have wasted his time without her yielding one whit to his wishes; but at the least the attempt would not have been ill, but rather becoming to a gallant man, and folk would have esteemed him the better therefor.

Why! what is the use of a bold and generous spirit, if it show not itself in all things, as well in love as in war? For love and arms be comrades, and do go side by side with a single heart, as saith the Latin poet: "Every lover is a man of war, and Cupid hath his camp and arms no less than Mars." Ronsard hath writ a fine sonnet hereanent in the first book of his "Amours."

2.

OWEVER to return to the fainness women do display to see and love great-hearted and valiant men,—I have heard it told of the Queen of England, Elizabeth, the same which is yet reigning at this hour, how that one day being at table, entertaining at supper the Grand Prior of France, a nobleman of the house of Lorraine, and M. d'Anville, now M. de Montmorency and Constable of France, the table discourse having fallen among divers other matters on the merits of the late King Henri II. of France, she did commend that Prince most highly, for that he was

so brave, and to use her own word so *martial* a monarch, as he had manifested plainly in all his doings. For which cause she had resolved, an if he had not died so early, to go visit him in his Kingdom, and had actually had her galleys prepared and made ready for to cross over into France, and so the twain clasp hands and pledge their faith and peaceable intent. "In fact 'twas one of my strongest wishes to see this hero. I scarce think he would have refused me, for," she did declare, "my humour is to love men of courage. And I do sore begrudge death his having snatched away so gallant a King, at any rate before I had looked on his face."

This same Queen, some while after, having heard great renown of the Duc de Nemours for the high qualities and valour that were in him, was most eager to enquire news of him from the late deceased M. de Rendan [1] at the time when King Francis II did send him to Scotland to conclude a peace under the walls of Leith,[2] which was then besieged by the English. And so soon as he had told the Queen at length all the particulars of that nobleman's high and noble deeds and merits and points of gallantry, M. de Rendan, who was no less understanding in matters of love than of arms, did note in her and in her countenance a certain sparkle of love or at the least liking, as well as in her words a very strong desire to see him. Wherefore, fain not to stay her in so excellent a path, he did what he could to find out from her whether, if the Duke should come to see her, he would be welcome and well received. She did assure him this would certainly be so, from which he did conclude they might very well come to be wed.

Presently being returned to the Court of France from

[13]

off his embassy, he did report all the discourse to the King and M. de Nemours. Whereupon the former did command and urge M. de Nemours to agree to the thing. This he did with very great alacrity, if he could come into so fine a Kingdom by the means of so fair, so virtuous and noble a Queen.

As a result the irons were soon in the fire. With the good means the King did put in his hands, the Duke did presently make very great and magnificent preparations and equipments, both of raiment, horses and arms, and in fact of all costly and beautiful things, without omitting aught needful (for myself did see all this) to go and appear before this fair Princess, above all forgetting not to carry thither with him all the flower of the young nobility of the Court. Indeed Greffier, the Court fool, remarking thereupon did say 'twas wondrous how all the gay *pease blossom* of the land was going overseas, pointing by this his jape at the wild young bloods of the French Court.

Meantime M. de Lignerolles, a gentleman of much adroitness and skill, and at that time an high favourite with M. de Nemours, his master, was despatched to the said fair Princess, and anon returned bearing a most gentle answer and one very meet to content him, and cause him to press on and further hasten his journey. And I remember me the marriage was held at Court to be as good as made. Yet did we observe how all of a sudden the voyage in question was broke off short and never made, and this in spite of a very great expenditure thereon, now all vain and useless.

Myself could say as well as any man in France what 'twas did lead to this rupture; yet will I remark thus much only in passing:—It may well be other loves did

[14]

more move his heart, and held him more firm a captive. For truly he was so accomplished in all ways and so skilful in arms and all good exercises, as that ladies did vie with each other in running after him. So I have seen some of the most high-spirited and virtuous women which were ready enough to break their fast of chastity for him.

We have, in the *Cent Nouvelles* of Queen Marguerite of Navarre, a very excellent tale of that lady of Milan, which having given assignation to the late M. de Bonnivet, since that day Admiral of France, one night, did charge her chamber-women to stand with drawn swords in hand and to make a disturbance on the steps, just as he should be ready to go to bed. This they did to great effect, following therein their mistress' orders, which for her part did feign to be terrified and sore afraid, crying out 'twas her husband's brothers which had noted something amiss, and that she was undone, and that he should hide under the bed or behind the arras. But M. de Bonnivet, without the least panic, taking his cloak round the one arm and his sword in the other hand, said only: "Well, well! where be they, these doughty brothers, which would fright me or do me hurt? Soon as they shall see me, they will not so much as dare look at the point of my sword." So saying, he did throw open the door and sally forth, but as he was for charging down the steps, lo! he did find only the women and their silly noise, which were sore scared at sight of him and began to scream and confess the whole truth. M. de Bonnivet, seeing what was toward, did straight leave the jades, commending them to the devil, and hying him back to the bedchamber, shutteth to the door behind him. Thus did he betake him to his lady once more, which did then fall a-laughing and

[15]

a-kissing of him, confessing how 'twas naught but a trick of her contriving, and declaring, an if he had played the poltroon and had not shown his valiance, whereof he had the repute, that he should never have lain with her. But seeing he had proved him so bold and confident of heart, she did therefore kiss him and frankly welcome him to her bed. And all night long 'twere better not to enquire too close what they did; for indeed she was one of the fairest women in all Milan, and one with whom he had had much pains to win her over.

I once knew a gallant gentleman, who one day being at Rome to bed with a pretty Roman lady, in her husband's absence, was alarmed in like wise; for she did cause one of her waiting women to come in hot haste to warn him the husband was hunting round. The lady, pretending sore amazement, did beseech the gentleman to hide in a closet, else she was undone. "No, no!" my friend made answer, "I would not do that for all the world; but an if he come, why! I will kill him." With this he did spring to grasp his sword; but the lady only fell a-laughing, and did confess how she had arranged it all of set purpose to prove him, to see what he would do, if her husband did threat him with hurt, and whether he would make a good defence of his mistress.

I likewise knew a very fair lady, who did quit outright a lover she had, because she deemed him a coward; and did change him for another, which did in no way resemble him, but was feared and dreaded exceedingly for his powers of fence, being one of the best swordsmen to be found in those days.

I have heard a tale told at Court by the old gossips, of a lady which was at Court, mistress of the late M. de

[16]

Lorge,[8] that good soldier and in his younger days one of
the bravest and most renowned captains of foot men
of his time. She having heard so much praise given to
his valour, was fain, one day that King Francis the First
was showing a fight of lions at his Court, to prove him
whether he was so brave as folk made out. Wherefore
she did drop one of her gloves in the lions' den, whenas
they were at their fiercest; and with that did pray M. de
Lorge to go get it for her, an if his love of her were as
great as he was forever saying. He without any show
of surprise, doth take his cloak on fist and his sword in
the other hand, and so boldly forth among the lions for
to recover the glove. In this emprise was fortune so
favourable to him, that seeing he did all through show a
good front and kept the point of his sword boldly presented to the lions, these did not dare attack him. So
after picking up the glove, he did return toward his mistress and gave it back to her; for the which she and
all the company there present did esteem him very highly.
But 'tis said that out of sheer despite at such treatment,
M. de Lorge did quit her for ever, forasmuch as she had
thought good to make her pastime of him and his valiance
in this fashion. Nay! more, they say he did throw the
glove in her face, out of mere despite; for he had rather
an hundred times she had bid him go break up a whole
battalion of foot soldiery, a matter he was duly trained
to undertake, than thus to fight beasts, a contest where
glory is scarce to be gained. At any rate suchlike trials
of men's courage be neither good nor honourable, and
they that do provoke the same are much to be blamed.

I like as little another trick which a certain lady did
play her lover. For when he was offering her his service,

assuring her there was never a thing, be it as perilous as it might, he would not do for her, she taking him at his word, did reply, "Well! an if you love me so much, and be as courageous as you say, stab yourself with your dagger in the arm for the love of me." The other, who was dying for love of her, did straight draw his weapon, ready to give himself the blow. However I did hold his arm and took the dagger from him, remonstrating and saying he would be a great fool to go about it in any such fashion to prove his love and courage. I will not name the lady; but the gentleman concerned was the late deceased M. de Clermont-Tallard the elder, which fell at the battle of Montcontour, one of the bravest and most valiant gentlemen of France, as he did show by his death, when in command of a company of men-at-arms,—a man I did love and honour greatly.

I have heard say a like thing did once happen to the late M. de Genlis, the same which fell in Germany, leading the Huguenot troops in the third of our wars of Religion. For crossing the Seine one day in front of the Louvre with his mistress, she did let fall her handkerchief, which was a rich and beautiful one, into the water on purpose, and told him to leap into the river to recover the same. He, knowing not how to swim but like a stone, was fain to be excused; but she upbraiding him and saying he was a recreant lover, and no brave man, without a word more he did throw himself headlong into the stream, and thinking to get the handkerchief, would assuredly have been drowned, had he not been promptly rescued by a boat.

Myself believe that suchlike women, by such trials, do desire in this wise gracefully to be rid of their lovers, which mayhap do weary them. 'Twere much better did they give them good favours once for all and pray them, for the love they bear them, to carry these forth to honourable and perilous places in the wars, and so prove their valour. Thus would they push them on to greater prowess, rather than make them perform the follies I have just spoke of, and of which I could recount an infinity of instances.

This doth remind me, how that, whenas we were advancing to lay siege to Rouen in the first war of Religion, Mademoiselle de Piennes, one of the honourable damsels of the Court, being in doubt as to whether the late M. de Gergeay was valiant enough to have killed, himself alone and man to man, the late deceased Baron d'Ingrande, which was one of the most valiant gentlemen of the Court, did for to prove his valiance, give him a favour,—a scarf which he did affix to his head harness. Then, on occasion of the making a reconnaissance of the Fort of St. Catherine, he did charge so boldly and valiantly on a troop of horse which had sallied forth of the city, that bravely fighting he did receive a pistol shot in the head, whereof he did fall stark dead on the spot. In this wise was the said damsel fully satisfied of his valour, and had he not been thus killed, seeing he had fought so well, she would have wedded him; but doubting somewhat his courage, and deeming he had slain the aforesaid Baron unfairly, for so she did suspect, she was fain, as she said, to make this visible trial of him. And verily, although there be many men naturally courageous, yet do the ladies push the same on to greater prowess; while if they be cold and cowardly, they do move them to some gallantry and warm them up to some show of fight.

We have an excellent example hereof in the beautiful

[19]

Agnes Sorel,[4] who seeing the King of France Charles
VII.[5] deep in love with her, and recking of naught but to
pleasure her, and slack and cowardly take no heed for his
kingdom, did say to him one day, how that when she was
a child, an astrologer had predicted she would be loved
and served of one of the most valiant and courageous
kings of Christendom. Accordingly, whenas the King
did her the honour to love her, she did think he was the
valorous monarch which had been predicted for her; but
seeing him so slack, with so little care of his proper business, she did plainly perceive she was deceived in this, and
that the courageous King intended was not he at all, but
the King of England,[6] which did perform such fine feats
of war, and did take so many of his fairest cities from
under his very nose. "Wherefore," she said to her lover,
"I am away to find him, for of a surety 'tis he the astrologer did intend." These words did so sorely prick the
King's heart, as that he fell a-weeping; and thencefor-
ward, plucking up spirit and quitting his hunting and
his gardens, he did take the bit in his teeth,—and this to
such good effect that by dint of good hap and his own
valiance he did drive the English forth of his Kingdom
altogether.

Bertrand du Guesclin [7] having wedded his wife Madame
Tiphaine, did set himself all to pleasure her and so did
neglect the management of the War, he who had been so
forward therein afore, and had won him such praise and
glory. But she did upbraid him with this remonstrance,
how that before their marriage folk did speak of naught
but him and his gallant deeds, but henceforth she might
well be reproached for the discontinuance of her husband's fair deeds and good repute. This she said was a

very great disgrace to her and him, that he had now
grown such a stay-at-home; and did never cease her chiding, till she had roused in him his erstwhile spirit, and
sent him back to the wars, where he did even doughtier
deeds than aforetime.

Thus do we see how this honourable lady did not love
so much her night's pleasures as she did value the honour
of her husband. And of a surety our wives themselves,
though they do find us near by their side, yet an if we be
not brave and valiant, will never really love us nor keep
us by them of good and willing heart; whereas when we
be returned from the wars and have done some fine and
noble exploit, then they do verily and indeed love us and
embrace of right good will, and themselves find the enjoyment most precious.

The fourth daughter of the Comte de Provence, father-
in-law of St. Louis, and herself wife to Charles, Count of
Anjou, brother of the said King, being sore vexed, high-
spirited and ambitious Princess as she was, at being but
plain Countess of Anjou and Provence, and because she
alone of her three sisters, of whom two were Queens and
the third Empress, did bear no better title than that my
Lady and Countess, did never cease till she had prayed,
beseeched and importuned her husband to conquer and
get some Kingdom for himself. And they did contrive
so well as that they were chose of Pope Urban to be King
and Queen of the Two Sicilies; and they did away, the
twain of them, to Rome with thirty galleys to be crowned
by his Holiness, with all state and splendour, King and
Queen of Jerusalem and Naples, which dominion he did
win afterward, no less by his victorious arms than by the
aid his wife afforded him, selling all her rings and jewels

for to provide the expenses of the war. So thereafter did they twain reign long and not unpeaceably in the fine kingdoms they had gotten.

Long years after, one of their grand-daughters, issue of them and theirs, Ysabeau de Lorraine to wit, without help of her husband René, did carry out a like emprise. For while her husband was prisoner in the hands of Charles, Duke of Burgundy, she being a Princess of a wise prudence and high heart and courage, the Kingdom of Sicily and Naples having meantime fallen to them in due succession, did assemble an army of thirty thousand men. This she did lead forth in person, and so conquer all the Kingdom and take possession of Naples.

3.

 COULD name an host of ladies which have in suchlike ways done great and good service to their husbands, and how being high of heart and ambition they have pushed on and encouraged their mates to court fortune, and to win goods and grandeur and much wealth. And truly 'tis the most noble and most honourable fashion of getting of such things, thus at the sword's point.

I have known many men in this our land of France and at our Courts, which really more by the urging of their wives than by any will of their own, have undertaken and accomplished gallant exploits.

Many women on the other hand have I known, which thinking only of their own good pleasures, have stood in their husbands' way and kept the same ever by their side, hindering them of doing noble deeds, unwilling to have them find amusement in aught else but in contenting them at the game of Venus, so keen were they after this sport. I could tell many a tale hereof, but I should be going too far astray from my subject, which is a worthier one for sure, seeing it doth handle virtue, than the other, which hath to do with vice. 'Tis more pleasant by far to hear tell of such ladies as have pushed on their men to noble deeds. Nor do I speak solely of married women, but of many others beside, which by dint of one little favour bestowed, have made their lovers to do many a fine thing they had never done else. For what a satisfaction is theirs! what incitement and warming of heart is greater than when at the wars a man doth think how he is well loved of his mistress, and if only he do some fine thing for the love of her, what kind looks and pretty ways, what fair glances, what kissings, delights and joys, he may hope after to receive of her?

Scipio amongst other rebukes he did administer to Massinissa, when, all but bloody yet from battle, he did wed Sophonisba, said to him: how that 'twas ill-becoming to think of ladies and the love of ladies, when at the wars. He must pardon me here, an if he will; but for my own part, I ween there is no such great contentment, nor one that giveth more courage and emulation to do nobly than they. I have travelled in that country myself in old days. And not only I, but all such, I do firmly believe, as take the field and fight, do find the same; and to them I make appeal. I am sure they be all of my opinion, be they who they may, and that whenas they are embarked on some good warlike emprise, and presently find themselves in the heat of battle and press of the foe, their heart doth swell within them as they think on their ladies, the

[23]

favours they do carry of them, and the caresses and gentle welcome they will receive of the same after the war is done, if they but escape,—and if they come to die, the sore grief they will feel for love of them and thought of their end. In a word, for the love of their ladies and fond thoughts of them, all emprises be facile and easy, the sternest fights be but merry tourneys to them, and death itself a triumph.

I do remember me how at the battle of Dreux the late M. des Bordes, a brave and gentle knight if ever there was one in his day, being Lieutenant under M. de Nevers, known at the first as the Comte d'Eu, a most excellent Prince and soldier, when he had to charge to break up a battalion of foot which was marching straight on the advanced guard where was the late M. de Guise the Great, and the signal to charge was given, the said Des Bordes, mounted on a grey barb, doth start forward instantly, adorned and garnished with a very fine favour his mistress had given him (I will not name her, but she was one of the fair and honourable damsels and great ladies of the Court), and as he gave rein, he did cry: "Ha! I am away to fight valiantly for the love of my mistress, or to die for her!" And this boast he failed not to fulfil; for after piercing the six first ranks, he fell at the seventh, borne down to earth. Now tell me if this lady had not well used her favour, and if she had aught to reproach her with for having bestowed it on him!

M. de Bussi again was a young soldier which did as great honour to his mistresses' favours as any man of his time, yea! and the favours of some I know of, which did merit more stricken fields and deeds of daring and good sword thrusts than did ever the fair Angelica of the

Paladins and Knights of yore, whether Christian or Sara-
cen. Yet have I heard him often declare that in all the
single combats and wars and general rencounters (for he
hath fought in many such) where he hath ever been engaged, 'twas not so much for the service of his Prince
nor yet for love of success as for the sole honour and
glory of contenting his lady love. He was surely right
in this, for verily all the success in the world and all its
ambitions be little worth in comparison of the love and
kindness of a fair and honourable lady and mistress.

And why else have so many brave Knights errant of the
Round Table and so many valorous Paladins of France
in olden time undertaken so many wars and far journeyings, and gone forth on such gallant emprises, if not
for the love of the fair ladies they did serve or were fain
to serve? I do appeal to our Paladins of France, our
Rolands, Renauds, Ogiers, our Olivers, Yvons and Rich-
ards, and an host of others. And truly 'twas a good
time and a lucky; for if they did accomplish some gallant
deed for love of their ladies, these same fair ladies, in
no wise ingrate, knew well how to reward them, whenas
they hied them back to meet them, or mayhap would give
them tryst there, in the forests and woodlands, or near
some fair fountain or amid the green meadows. And is
not this the guerdon of his doughtiness a soldier most
doth crave of his lady love?

Well! it yet remains to ask, why women do so love
these men of valiance? First, as I did say at the beginning, valour hath in it a certain force and overmastering
power to make itself loved of its opposite. Then beside, there is a kind of natural inclination doth exist,
constraining women to love great-heartedness, which to be

sure is an hundred times more lovable than cowardice,—
even as virtue is alway more to be desired than vice.

Some ladies there be which do love men thus gifted with
valour, because they imagine that just as they be brave
and expert at arms and in the trade of War, they must
be the same at that of Love.

And this rule doth hold really good with some. 'Twas
fulfilled for instance by Cæsar, that champion of the
world, and many another gallant soldier I have known,
though I name no names. And such lovers do possess
a very different sort of vigour and charm from rustics
and folk of any other profession but that of arms, so
much so that one push of these same gallants is worth
four of ordinary folk. When I say this, I do mean in
the eyes of women moderately lustful, not of such as be
inordinately so, for the mere number is what pleaseth
this latter sort. But if this rule doth hold good sometimes in some of these warlike fellows, and according to
the humour of some women, it doth fail in others; for
some of these valiant soldiers there be so broken down
by the burden of their harness and the heavy tasks of
war, that they have no strength left when they have to
come to this gentle game of love, in such wise that they
cannot content their ladies,—of whom some (and many
are of such complexion), had liever have one good work-
man at Venus' trade, fresh and ground to a good point,
than four of these sons of Mars, thus broken-winged.

I have known many of the sex of this sort and this
humour; for after all, they say, the great thing is to pass
one's time merrily, and get the quintessence of enjoyment
out of it, without any special choice of persons. A good
man of war is good, and a fine sight on the field of bat-

tle; but an if he can do naught a-bed, they declare, a good stout lackey, in good case and practice, is every whit as worth having as a handsome and valiant gentleman,— tired out.

I do refer me to such dames as have made trial thereof, and do so every day; for the gallant soldier's loins, be he as brave and valiant as he may, being broken and chafed of the harness they have so long carried on them, cannot afford the needful supply, as other men do, which have never borne hardship or fatigue.

Other ladies there be which do love brave men, whether it be for husbands or for lovers, to the end these may show good fight and so better defend their honour and chastity, if any detractors should be fain to befoul these with ill words. Several such I have seen at Court, where I knew in former days a very great and a very fair lady [1] whose name I had rather not give, who being much subject to evil tongues, did quit a lover, and a very favourite one, she had, seeing him backward to come to blows and pick a quarrel and fight it out, to take another [2] instead which was a mettlesome wight, a brave and valiant soul, which would gallantly bear his lady's honour on the point of his sword, without ever a man daring to touch the same in any wise.

Many ladies have I known in my time of this humour, wishful always to have a brave gallant for their escort and defence. This no doubt is a good and very useful thing oftentimes for them; but then they must take good heed not to stumble or let their heart change toward them, once they have submitted to their domination. For if these fellows do note the least in the world of their pranks and fickle changes, they do lead them a fine life and rebuke

[27]

them in terrible wise, both them and their new gallants, if ever they change. Of this I have seen not a few examples in the course of my life.

Thus do we see how suchlike women, those that will fain have at command suchlike brave and mettlesome lovers, must needs themselves be brave and very faithful in their dealings with the same, or at any rate so secret in their intrigues as that they may never be discovered. Unless indeed they do compass the thing by some arrangement, as do the Italian and Roman courtesans, who are fain ever to have a *bravo* (this is the name they give him) to defend and keep them in countenance; but 'tis always part of the bargain that they shall have other favoured swains as well, and the bravo shall never say one word.

This is mighty well for the courtesans of Rome and their bravos, but not for the gallant gentlemen of France and other lands. But an if an honourable dame is ready to keep herself in all firmness and constancy, her lover is bound to spare his life in no way for to maintain and defend her honour, if she do run the very smallest risk of hurt, whether to her life or her reputation, or of some ill word of scandal. So have I seen at our own Court several which have made evil tattlers to hold their tongues at a moment's notice, when these had started some detraction of their ladies or mistresses. For by devoir of knighthood and its laws we be bound to serve as their champions in any trouble, as did the brave Renaud for the fair Ginevra in Scotland,[3] the Señor de Mendoza for the beautiful Duchess I have spoke of above, and the Seigneur de Carouge for his own wedded wife in the days of King Charles VI., as we do read in our Chronicles. I could quote an host of other instances, as well of old as of mod-

[28]

ern times, to say naught of those I have witnessed at our own Court; but I should never have done.

Other ladies I have known which have quitted cowardly fellows, albeit these were very rich, to love and wed gentlemen that did possess naught at all but sword and cloak, so to say. But then they were valorous and greathearted, and had hopes, by dint of their valiance and bravery, to attain to rank and high estate. Though truly 'tis not the bravest that do most oft win these prizes; but they do rather suffer sore wrong, while many a time we behold the cowardly and fainthearted succeed instead. Yet be this as it may, such fortune doth never become these so well as it doth the men of valour.

But there, I should never get me done, were I to recount at length the divers causes and reasons why women do so love men of high heart and courage. I am quite sure, were I set on amplifying this Discourse with all the host of reasons and examples I might, I could make a whole book of it alone. However, as I wish not to tarry over one subject only, so much as to deal with various and divers matters, I will be satisfied to have said what I have said,—albeit sundry will likely blame me, how that such and such a point was surely worthy of being enriched by more instances and a string of prolix reasons, which themselves could very well supply, exclaiming, "Why! he hath clean forgot this; he hath clean forgot that." I know my subject well enough for all that; and mayhap I know more instances than ever they could adduce, and more startling and private. But I prefer not to divulge them all, and not to give the names.

This is why I do hold my tongue. Yet, before making an end, I will add this further word by the way. Just

as ladies do love men which be valiant and bold under
arms, so likewise do they love such as be of like sort in
love; and the man which is cowardly and over and above
respectful toward them, will never win their good favour.
Not that they would have them so overweening, bold and
presumptuous, as that they should by main force lay
them on the floor; but rather they desire in them a certain hardy modesty, or perhaps better a certain modest
hardihood.   For while themselves are not exactly wantons,
and will neither solicit a man nor yet actually offer their
favours, yet do they know well how to rouse the appetites
and passions, and prettily allure to the skirmish in such
wise that he which doth not take occasion by the forelock
and join encounter, and that without the least awe of
rank and greatness, without a scruple of conscience or
a fear or any sort of hesitation, he verily is a fool and
a spiritless poltroon, and one which doth merit to be forever abandoned of kind fortune.

I have heard of two honourable gentlemen and comrades, for the which two very honourable ladies, and of by
no means humble quality, made tryst one day at Paris
to go walking in a garden.   Being come thither, each
lady did separate apart one from the other, each alone
with her own cavalier, each in a several alley of the garden, that was so close covered in with a fair trellis of
boughs as that daylight could really scarce penetrate
there at all, and the coolness of the place was very grateful.   Now one of the twain was a bold man, and well
knowing how the party had been made for something else
than merely to walk and take the air, and judging by
his lady's face, which he saw to be all a-fire, that she had
longings to taste other fare than the muscatels that hung

on the trellis, as also by her hot, wanton and wild speech, he did promptly seize on so fair an opportunity. So catching hold of her without the least ceremony, he did lay her on a little couch that was there made of turf and clods of earth, and did very pleasantly work his will of her, without her ever uttering a word but only: "Heavens! Sir, what are you at? Surely you be the maddest and strangest fellow ever was! If anyone comes, whatever will they say? Great heavens! get out!" But the gentleman, without disturbing himself, did so well continue what he had begun that he did finish, and she to boot, with such content as that after taking three or four turns up and down the alley, they did presently start afresh. Anon, coming forth into another, open, alley, they did see in another part of the garden the other pair, who were walking about together just as they had left them at first. Whereupon the lady, well content, did say to the gentleman in the like condition, "I verily believe so and so hath played the silly prude, and hath given his lady no other entertainment but only words, fine speeches and promenading."

Afterward when all four were come together, the two ladies did fall to asking one another how it had fared with each. Then the one which was well content did reply she was exceeding well, indeed she was; indeed for the nonce she could scarce be better. The other, which was ill content, did declare for her part she had had to do with the biggest fool and most coward lover she had ever seen; and all the time the two gentlemen could see them laughing together as they walked and crying out: "Oh! the silly fool! the shamefaced poltroon and coward!" At this the successful gallant said to his companion: "Hark

to our ladies, which do cry out at you, and mock you sore.
You will find you have overplayed the prude and coxcomb
this bout." So much he did allow; but there was no more
time to remedy his error, for opportunity gave him no
other handle to seize her by. Natheless, now recognizing
his mistake, after some while he did repair the same by
certain other means which I could tell, an if I would.

Again I knew once two great Lords, brothers, both of
them highly bred and highly accomplished gentlemen
which did love two ladies, but the one of these was of much
higher quality and more account than the other in all
respects. Now being entered both into the chamber of
this great lady, who for the time being was keeping her
bed, each did withdraw apart for to entertain his mistress. The one did converse with the high-born dame
with every possible respect and humble salutation and
kissing of hands, with words of honour and stately compliment, without making ever an attempt to come near
and try to force the place. The other brother, without
any ceremony of words or fine phrases, did take his fair
one to a recessed window, and incontinently making free
with her (for he was very strong), he did soon show her
'twas not his way to love *à l'espagnole*, with eyes and
tricks of face and words, but in the genuine fashion and
proper mode every true lover should desire. Presently
having finished his task, he doth quit the chamber; but as
he goes, saith to his brother, loud enough for his lady
to hear the words: "Do you as I have done, brother
mine; else you do naught at all. Be you as brave and
hardy as you will elsewhere, yet if you show not your
hardihood here and now, you are disgraced; for here is
no place of ceremony and respect, but one where you do

[32]

see your lady before you, which doth but wait your attack." So with this he did leave his brother, which yet for that while did refrain him and put it off to another time. But for this the lady did by no means esteem him more highly, whether it was she did put it down to an over chilliness in love, or a lack of courage, or a defect of bodily vigour. And still he had shown prowess enough elsewhere, both in war and love.

The late deceased Queen Mother did one day cause to be played, for a Shrove Tuesday interlude, at Paris at the Hôtel de Reims, a very excellent Comedy which Cornelio Fiasco, Captain of the Royal Galleys, had devised. All the Court was present, both men and ladies, and many folk beside of the city. Amongst other matters, was shown a young man which had laid hid a whole night long in a very fair lady's bedchamber, yet had never laid finger on her. Telling this hap to his friend, the latter asketh him: *Ch'avete fatto?* (What did you do?), to which the other maketh answer: *Niente* (Nothing). On hearing this, his friend doth exclaim: *Ah! poltronazzo, senza cuore! non havete fatto niente! che maldita sia la tua poltronneria!*—"Oh! poltroon and spiritless! you did nothing! a curse on your poltroonery then!"

The same evening after the playing of this Comedy, as we were assembled in the Queen's chamber, and were discoursing of the said play, I did ask a very fair and honourable lady, whose name I will not give, what were the finest points she had noted and observed in the Comedy, and which had most pleased her. She told me quite simply and frankly: The best point I noted was when his friend did make answer to the young man called Lucio, who had told him *che non haveva fatto niente* (that he had

[33]

done nothing) in this wise, *Ah poltronazzo! non havete fatto niente! che maldita sia la tua poltronneria!*—"Oh! you poltroon! you did nothing! a curse be on your poltroonery!"

So you see how this fair lady which did talk with me was in agreement with the friend in reprobating his poltroonery, and that she did in no wise approve of him for having been so slack and unenterprising. Thereafter she and I did more openly discourse together of the mistakes men make by not seizing opportunity and taking advantage of the wind when it bloweth fair, as doth the good mariner.

This bringeth me to yet another tale, which I am fain, diverting and droll as it is, to mingle among the more serious ones. Well, then! I have heard it told by an honourable gentleman and a good friend of mine own, how a lady of his native place, having often shown great familiarities and special favour to one of her chamber lackeys, which did only need time and opportunity to come to a point, the said lackey, neither a prude nor a fool, finding his mistress one morning half asleep and lying on her bed, turned over away from the wall, tempted by such a display of beauty and a posture making it so easy and convenient, she being at the very edge of the bed, he did come up softly, and alongside the lady. She turning her head saw 'twas her lackey, which she was fain of; and just as she was, her place occupied and all, without withdrawing or moving one whit, and neither resisting nor trying in the very least to shake off the hold he had of her, did only say to him, turning round her head only and holding still for fear of losing him, "Ho! ho! Mister prude, and what hath made you so bold as to do this?" The lackey did

answer with all proper respect, "Madam, shall I leave?"——
"That's not what I said, Mister prude," the lady replied,
"I ask you, what made you so bold as to put yourself
there?" But the other did ever come back to the same
question, "Madam, shall I stop? if you wish, I will go
out,"—and she to repeating again and again, "That is
not what I say, not what I say, Mister prude!" In fact,
the pair of them did make these same replies and repeti-
tions three or four times over,—which did please the lady
far better than if she had ordered her gallant to stop,
when he did ask her. Thus it did serve her well to stick
to her first question without ever a variation, and the
lover in his reply and the repetition thereof. And in this
wise did they continue to lie together for long after, the
same rubric being always repeated as an accompaniment.
For 'tis, as men say, the first batch only, and the first
measure of wine, that costs dear.

A good lackey and an enterprising! To such bold
fellows we must needs say in the words of the Italian
proverb, *A bravo cazzo mai non manca favor.*

Well, from all this you learn how that there be many
men which are brave, bold and valiant, as well in arms as
in love; others which be so in arms, but not in love; others
again, which be so in love and not in arms. Of this last
sort was that rascally Paris, who indeed had hardihood
and valiance enough to carry off Helen from her poor
cuckold of a husband Menelaus, but not to do battle with
him before Troy town.

Moreover this is why the ladies love not old men, nor
such as be too far advanced in years, seeing such be very
timid in love and shamefaced at asking favours. This is
not because they have not concupiscence and desires as

[35]

great as young men, or even greater, but because they have not the powers to match. And this is what a Spanish lady meant, which said once: how that old men did much resemble persons who, whenas they do behold kings in their magnificence, domination and authority, do covet exceedingly to be like them, yet would they never dare to make any attempt against them to dispossess them of their kingdoms and seize their place. She was used further to say, *Y a penas es nacido el deseo, cuando se muere luego,*—"Scarce is the desire born, but it dies straightway." Thus old men, when they do see fair objects of attack, dare not take action, *porque los viejos naturalmente son temerosos; y amor y temor no se caben en un saco,*—"for that old men are naturally timid; and love and fear do never go well in one pack." And indeed they are quite right; for they have arms neither for offence nor defence, like young folks, which have youth and beauty on their side. So verily, as saith the poet: naught is unbecoming to youth, do what it will; and as another hath it: two sorry sights,—an old man-at-arms and an old lover.

4.

ELL! enough hath been said on this subject; so I do here make an end and speak no more thereof. Only will I add somewhat on another point, one that is appertinent and belonging as it were to this, to wit: how just as fair ladies do love brave men, and such as be valorous and greathearted, in like wise do men love women brave of heart and noble-spirited. And as noble-spirited and courageous men be ever more lovable and admirable than others,

so is the like true of illustrious, noble-hearted and
courageous dames,—not that I would have these perform
the deeds of men, nor yet arm and accoutre them like a
man,—as I have seen and known, as well as heard tell
of, some which would mount a-horse-back like a man,
carry their pistol at saddle-bow, shoot off the same, and
generally fight like a man.

I could name one famous instance at any rate of a lady
which did all this during the recent Wars of the League.
But truly suchlike disguisement is an outrage to the sex.
Besides its being neither becoming nor suitable, 'tis not
lawful, and doth bring more harm and ill repute than
many do suppose. Thus it did work great hurt to the
gentle Maid of Orleans, who at her trial was sore calumni-
ated on this very account, and this was in part cause of
her sore and piteous downfall and death. Wherefore such
masqueradings do like me not, nor stir me to any great
admiration. Yet do I approve and much esteem a fair
dame which doth make manifest her courageous and
valiant spirit, being in adversity and downright need, by
brave, womanly acts that do show a man's heart and courage. Without borrowing examples from the noble-
hearted dames of Rome and of Sparta of yore, the which
have excelled herein all other women in the world, there
be others plain enough to be seen before our very eyes;
and I do choose rather to adduce such modern instances
belonging to our own day.

The first example I shall give, and in my eyes the finest
I know of is that of those fair, honourable and doughty
dames of Sienna, at the time of the revolt of their city
against the intolerable yoke of the Imperialists (Ghibel-
lines). For after the dispositions had been fixed for the

[37]

defence, the women of the city, being set aside therein as not apt for war like the men, were fain to make a display of their mettle, and show how that they could do something else than only ply their female tasks of day and night. So, to bear their part of the work of defence, they did divide them into three bands or companies; and one St. Anthony's day, in the month of January, they did appear in public led by three of the fairest ladies, and the greatest and best born, of all the city, in the Great Square of that town (and it is a very noble one), with their drums and ensigns.

The first was the Signora Forteguerra, clad in violet, her ensign of the same colour and all her company in like array, her banner bearing this device: *Pur che sia il vero* (Let the truth prevail). Now all these ladies were dressed in the guise of nymphs, with short skirts which did best discover and display the fine leg beneath. The second was the Signora Piccolomini, clad in scarlet, and her company and ensign the same, with a white cross and this device: *Pur che no l'habbia tutto* (Let him not have it all). The third was the Signora Livia Fausta, clad all in white, and her company in white and a white ensign, whereon was a palm, and for device: *Pur che l'habbia* (Let him have it, then!).

Round about and in the train of these three, which did seem very goddesses, were a good three thousand other women, both gentlewomen, citizens' wives and others, all fair to look upon, and all duly clad in their proper dress and livery, whether of satin, taffety, damask, or other silken stuff, and each and all firm resolved to live or die for freedom. Moreover each did carry a fascine on her shoulder for a fort which was a-building, while all cried

[38]

out together, *France, France!* With this spectacle, so
rare and delightsome an one, the Cardinal of Ferrara and
M. de Termes, the French King's Lieutenants, were so
ravished, as that they did find no other pleasure but only
in watching, admiring and commending these same fair
and honourable ladies. And of a truth I have heard
many say, both men and women, which were there present, that never was seen so fine a sight. And God knoweth, beautiful women be not lacking in this city of Sienna,
and that in abundance, and without picking and choosing.

The men of the city, which of their own wishes were
greatly set on winning their freedom, were yet more encouraged to the same by this noble display, unwilling to
fall below the women in zeal. In such wise that all did
vie with one another, Lords, gentlemen, citizens, trades-
folk, artizans, rich and poor alike, and all did flock to
the fort to imitate the example of these fair, virtuous
and honourable dames. So all in much emulation,—and
not laymen alone, but churchmen to boot,—did join in
pushing on the good work. Then, on returning back
from the fort, the men on one side, and the women likewise ranged in battle array in the great square before
the Palace of the Signoria, they did advance one after
other, and company after company, to salute the image of
the Blessed Virgin, patroness of the city, singing the while
sundry hymns and canticles in her honour, to airs so soft
and with so gracious an harmony that, part of pleasure,
part of pity, tears 'gan fall from the eyes of all the people
present. These after receiving the benediction of the
most reverend Cardinal of Ferrara, did withdraw, each
to their own abode,—all the whole folk, men and women

[39]

alike, with fixed resolve to do their duty yet better for the future.

This sacred ceremony of these ladies doth remind me (but without making comparison 'twixt the two) of a heathen one, yet goodly withal, which was performed at Rome at the period of the Punic Wars, as we do read in the Historian Livy. 'Twas a solemn progress and procession made by three times nine, which is twenty-seven, young and pretty Roman maids, all of them virgins, clad in longish frocks, of which history doth not however tell us the colours. These dainty maids, their solemn march and procession completed, did then make halt at a certain spot, where they proceeded to dance a measure before the assembled people, passing from hand to hand a cord or ribband, ranged all in order one after other, and stepping a round, accommodating the motion and twinkling of their feet to the cadence of the tune and the song they sang the while. It was a right pretty sight to see, no less for the beauty of the maids than for their sweet grace, their dainty way of dancing and the adroit tripping of their feet, the which is one of the chiefest charms of a maid, when she is skilled to move and guide the same daintily and well.

I have oft pictured to myself the measure they did so dance; and it hath brought to my mind one I have seen performed in my young days by the girls of mine own countryside, called the "garter." In this, the village girls, giving and taking the garter from hand to hand, would pass and re-pass these above their heads, then entangle and interlace the same between their legs, leaping nimbly over them, then unwinding them and slipping free with little, dainty bounds,—all this while keeping rank

[40]

one after other, without once losing cadence with the song or instrument of music which led the measure, in such wise that the thing was a mighty pretty thing to see. For the little leaps and bounds they gave, the interlacing and slipping free again, the wielding of the garter and the graceful carriage of the girls, did all provoke so dainty a smack of naughtiness, as that I do marvel much the said dance hath never been practised at Court in these days of ours. Pleasant 'tis to see the dainty drawers, and the fine leg freely exhibited in this dance, and which lass hath the best fitting shoe and the most alluring mien. But truly it can be better appreciated by the eye than described in words.

But to return to our ladies of Sienna. Ah! fair and valiant dames, you should surely never die,—you nor your glory, which will be for ever immortal. So too another fair and gentle maid of your city, who during its siege, seeing one night her brother kept a prisoner by sickness in his bed and in very ill case to go on guard, doth leave him there a-bed and slipping quietly away from his side, doth take his arms and accoutrements, and so, a very perfect likeness of her brother, maketh appearance with the watch. Nor was she discovered, but by favour of the night was really taken for him she did represent. A gentle act, in truth! for albeit she had donned a man's dress and arms, yet was it not to make a constant habit thereof, but for the nonce only to do a good office for her brother. And indeed 'tis said no love is like that of brother and sister, and further that in a good cause no risk should be spared to show a gentle intrepidity of heart, in whatsoever place it be.

I ween the corporal of the guard which was then in

command of the squad in which was this fair girl, when
he wist of her act, was sore vexed he had not better recognized her, so to have published abroad her merit on the
spot, or mayhap to have relieved her of standing sentry,
or else merely to have taken his pleasure in gazing on her
beauty and grace, and her military bearing; for no doubt
at all she did study in all things to counterfeit a soldier's
mien.

Of a surety so fine a deed could scarce be overpraised,
and above all when the occasion was so excellent, and the
thing carried out for a brother's sake. The like was done
by the gentle Richardet, in the Romance, but for different
purpose, when after hearing one evening his sister
Bramante discourse of the beauties of the fair Princess
of Spain, and of her own love and vain desires after her,
he did take her accoutrements and fine frock, after she
was to bed, and so disguiseth himself in the likeness of his
sister,—the which he could readily accomplish, so like
they were in face and beauty. Then presently, under this
feigned form he did win from the said lovely Princess what
was denied his sister by reason of her sex. Whereof, however, great hurt had come to him, but for the favour of
Roger, who taking him for his mistress Bramante, did
save him scatheless of death.[1]

Now as to the ladies of Sienna, I have heard it of M. de
La Chapelle des Ursins, which was at that time in Italy,
and did make report of this their gallant exploit to our
late King Henri II. of France, how that this monarch
did find the same so noble, that with tears in his eyes he
took an oath, an if one day God should grant him peace
or truce with the Emperor, he would hie him with his
galleys across the Tuscan sea, and so to Sienna, to see

this city so well affected to him and his party, and thank the citizens for their good will and gallantry, and above all to behold these fair and honourable ladies and give them especial thanks.

I am sure he would not have failed so to do, for he did highly honour the said good and noble dames. Accordinly he did write them, addressing chiefly the three chief leaders, letters the most gracious possible, full of thanks and compliments, the which did pleasure them greatly and animate their courage to yet an higher pitch.

Alas! the truce came right enough some while after; but meantime the city had been taken, as I have described elsewhere. Truly 'twas an irreparable loss to France to be deprived of so noble and affectionate an ally, which mindful and conscious of the ties of its ancient origin, was always fain to join us and take place in our ranks. For they say these gallant Siennese be sprung from that people of France which in Gaul they did call the Senones in old times, now known as the folk of Sens. Moreover they do retain to this day somewhat of the humour of us Frenchmen; they do very much wear their heart on their sleeve, as the saying is, and be quick, sudden and keen like us. The Siennese ladies likewise have much of those pretty ways and charming manners and graceful familiarities which be the especial mark of Frenchwomen.

I have read in an old Chronicle, which I have cited elsewhere, how King Charles VIII., on his Naples journey, when he did come to Sienna, was there welcomed with so magnificent and so triumphal an entry, as that it did surpass all the others he received in all Italy. They did even go so far by way of showing greater respect and as a sign of humbleness, as to take all the city gates from

[43]

off their hinges and lay the same flat on the ground; and so long as he did tarry there, the gates were thus left open and unguarded to all that came and went, then after, on his departure, set up again as before.

I leave you to imagine if the King, and all his Court and army, had not ample and sufficient cause to love and honour this city (as indeed he did always), and to say all possible good thereof. In fact their stay there was exceeding agreeable to him and to all, and 'twas forbid under penalty of death to offer any sort of insult, as truly not the very smallest did ever occur. Ah! gallant folk of Sienna, may ye live for ever! Would to heaven ye were still ours in all else, as it may well be, ye are yet in heart and soul! For the overrule of a King of France is far gentler than that of a Duke of Florence; and besides this, the kinship of blood can never go for naught. If only we were as near neighbours as we be actually remote from each other, we might very like be found at one in will and deed.

In like wise the chiefest ladies of Pavia, at the siege of that town by King Francis I. of France, following the lead and example of the noble Countess Hippolita de Malespina, their generalissima, did set them to carrying of the earth-baskets, shifting soil and repairing the breaches in their walls, vying with the soldiery in their activity.

Conduct like that of the Siennese dames I have just told of, myself did behold on the part of certain ladies of La Rochelle,[2] at the siege of their town. And I remember me how on the first Sunday of Lent during the siege, the King's brother, our General, did summon M. de la Noue to come before him on his parole, and speak with

him and give account of the negotiations he had charged
him withal on behalf of the said city,—all the tale whereof
is long and most curious, as I do hope elsewhere to describe
the same. M. de la Noue failed not to appear, to which
end M. d'Estrozze was given as an hostage on the town,
and truce was made for that day and for the next following.

This truce once concluded, there did appear immediately, as on our side we too did show us outside our
trenches, many of the towns-folk on the ramparts and
walls. And notable over all were seen an hundred or so
of noble ladies and citizens' wives and daughters, the
greatest, richest and fairest of all the town, all clad in
white, the dress, which did cover head as well as body,
being all of fine white Holland linen, that 'twas a very
fair sight to see. And they had adopted this dress by
reason of the fortification of the ramparts at which they
were at work, whether carrying of the earth-baskets or
moving the soil. Now other garments would have soon
grown foul, but these white ones had but to be sent to the
wash, and all was well again; beside, with this white costume were they more readily distinguished among the
rest. For our part we were much delighted to behold these
fair ladies, and I do assure you many of us did find more
divertisement herein than in aught else. Nor were they
the least chary of giving us a sight of them, for they did
line the edge of the rampart, standing in a most gracious
and agreeable attitude, so as they were well worth our
looking at and longing after.

We were right curious to learn what ladies they were.
The towns-folk did inform us they were a company of
ladies so sworn and banded together, and so attired for

the work at the fortifications and for the performing
of suchlike services to their native city. And of a truth
did they do good service, even to the more virile and stalwart of them bearing arms. Yea! I have heard it told
of one, how, for having oft repulsed her foes with a pike,
she doth to this day keep the same carefully as 'twere a
sacred relic, so that she would not part with it nor sell
it for much money, so dear a home treasure doth she
hold it.

I have heard the tale told by sundry old Knights Commanders of Rhodes, and have even read the same in an
old book, how that, when Rhodes was besieged by Sultan
Soliman, the fair dames and damsels of that place did in
no wise spare their fair faces and tender and delicate
bodies, for to bear their full share of the hardships and
fatigues of the siege, but would even come forward many
a time at the most hot and dangerous attacks, and gallantly second the knights and soldiery to bear up against
the same. Ah! fair Rhodian maids, your name and fame
is for all time; and ill did you deserve to be now fallen
under the rule of infidel barbarians! In the reign of our
good King Francis I., the town of Saint-Riquier in
Picardy was attempted and assailed by a Flemish gentleman, named Domrin, Ensign of M. du Ru, accompanied
by two hundred men at arms and two thousand foot folk,
beside some artillery. Inside the place were but an hundred foot men, the which was far too few for defence.
It had for sure been captured, but that the women of the
town did appear on the walls with arms in hand, boiling
water and oil and stones, and did gallantly repulse the
foe, albeit these did exert every effort to gain an entry.
Furthermore two of the said brave ladies did wrest a pair

of standards from the hands of the enemy, and bore them from the walls into the town, the end of all being that the besiegers were constrained to abandon the breach they had made and the walls altogether, and make off and retire. The fame of this exploit did spread through all France, Flanders and Burgundy; while King Francis, passing by the place some time after, was fain to see the women concerned, and did praise and thank them for their deed.

The ladies of Péronne [3] did in like gallant wise, when that town was besieged by the Comte de Nassau, and did aid the brave soldiers which were in the place in the same fashion as their sisters of Saint-Riquier, for which they were esteemed, commended and thanked of their sovereign.

The women of Sancerre [4] again, in the late civil wars and during the siege of their town, were admired and praised for the noble deeds they did at that time in all sorts.

Also, during the War of the League, the dames of Vitré [5] did acquit them right well in similar wise at the besieging of the town by M. de Mercueur. The women there be very fair and always right daintily put on, and have ever been so from old time; yet did they not spare their beauty for to show themselves manlike and courageous. And surely all manly and brave-hearted deeds, at such a time of need, are as highly to be esteemed in women as in men.

Of the same gallant sort were of yore the women of Carthage, who whenas they beheld their husbands, brothers, kinsfolk and the soldiery generally cease shooting at the foe, for lack of strings to their bows, these being all worn out by dint of shooting all through the long and terrible siege, and for the same cause no longer being able to provide them with hemp, or flax, or silk, or aught else wherewithal to make bow-strings, did resolve to cut off their lovely tresses and fair, yellow locks, not sparing this beauteous honour of their heads and chief adornment of their beauty. Nay! with their own fair hands, so white and delicate, they did twist and wind the same and make it into bow-strings to supply the men of war. And I leave you to imagine with what high courage and mettle these would now stretch and bend their bows, shoot their arrows and fight the foe, bearing as they did such fine favours of the ladies.

We read in the History of Naples [6] how that great Captain Sforza, serving under the orders of Queen Jeanne II., having been taken prisoner by the Queen's husband, James, and set in strict confinement and having some taste of the strappado, would without a doubt ere much longer have had his head cut off, but that his sister did fly to arms and straight take the field. She made so good a fight, she in her own person, as that she did capture four of the chiefest Neapolitan gentlemen, and this done, sent to tell the King that whatsoever treatment he should deal to her brother, the same would she meet out to his friends. The end was, he was constrained to make peace and deliver him up safe and sound. Ah! brave and gallant-hearted sister, rising so superior to her sex's weakness!

I do know of certain sisters and kinswomen, who if but they had dared a like deed, some while agone, might mayhap have saved alive a gallant brother of theirs, which

was undone for lack of help and timely succour of the
sort.

5.

OW am I fain to have done with the consideration of these warlike and great-hearted dames
in general, and to speak of some particular
instances of the same. And as the fairest
example Antiquity hath to show us, I will adduce the
gallant Zenobia [1] only, to answer for all. This Queen,
after the death of her husband, was too wise to waste
her time, like so many others in like case, in mere lamentation and vain regrets, but did grasp the reins of his
empire in the name of her children, and make war against
the Romans and their Emperor Aurelian,[2] at that time
reigning at Rome. Much trouble did she give these foes
for eight long years, till at the last coming to a pitched
battle with his legions, she was vanquished therein and
taken prisoner and brought before the Emperor. On his
asking her how she had had the hardihood to make war
against the Emperors of Rome, she did answer only this:
"Verily! I do well recognise that you are Emperor, seeing
that you have vanquished me."

So great content had he of his victory, and so proud
thereof was he and exalted, that he was fain to hold a
triumph over her. So with an exceeding great pomp and
magnificence did she walk before his triumphal car, right
gorgeously put on and adorned with much wealth of
pearls and precious stones, superb jewels and great
chains of gold, wherewith she was bound about the body
and by the hands and feet, in sign of being captive and

[49]

slave of her conqueror. And so it was that by reason
of the heavy weight of her jewels and chains she was constrained to make sundry pauses and to rest her again and
again on this march of triumph. A fine thing, of a
surety, and an admirable, that all vanquished and prisoner as she was, she could yet give the law to her triumphant conqueror, and thus make him tarry and wait her
pleasure till that she had recovered breath! A great instance too of good feeling and honest courtesy on the
part of the Emperor, so to allow her breathing space
and rest, and to suffer her weakness, rather than unduly
to constrain or press her to hurry more than she well
could. So that one doth scarce know which to commend
the more, the honourable courtesy of the Emperor, or the
Queen's way of acting,—who it may well be, did play
this part of set purpose, not so much forced thereto
by her actual weakness of body and weariness, as for to
make some show of pride and prove to all how she would
and could gather this little sprig of respect in the evening of her fortunes no less than she had done in the
morning-tide of the same, and let them see how the Emperor did grant her this much privilege, to wait on her
slow steps and lingering progress.

Much was the Queen gazed at and admired by men and
women alike, not a few of which last had been but too
glad to resemble so fair an apparition. For truly she
was one of the most lovely of women, by what is said
of the historians of these events. She was of a very fine,
tall and opulent figure, say they, her carriage right noble,
and her grace and dignity to match; furthermore her
face very beautiful and exceeding pleasing, her eyes dark
and piercing. Beside her other beauties, these writers do

give her fine and very white teeth, a keen wit and a
modest bearing, a sincere and at need a kind and merciful
heart. Her speech was eloquent and spoke with a fine
clear voice; moreover she was used always to express her
ideas and wishes herself to her soldiers, and would many a
time harangue the same publicly.

I ween he did so show her to best advantage, thus
richly and gracefully attired in women's weeds, no less
than when she was armed in all points as the Warrior
Queen. For sex doth always count for much; and we may
rightly suppose the Emperor was fain to display her at
his triumph only under guise of her own fair sex, wherein
she would seem most beauteous and agreeable to the pop-
ulace in all the perfection of her charms. Furthermore,
'tis to be supposed, so lovely as she was, the Emperor
had tasted and enjoyed her loveliness, and was yet in the
enjoyment thereof. So albeit he had vanquished her in
one fashion, yet had she,—or he, if you prefer it so, for
the two be as one in this,—won the victory in another.

Mine own wonder is, that seeing the said Zenobia was
so beautiful, the Emperor did not take her and keep
her for one of his mistresses; or else that she did not
open and establish by his permission, or the Senate's, a
shop or market of love and harlotry, as did the fair
Flora in the same city, for to win wealth and store up
much gear and goods, by the toil of her body and shaking
of her bed. For to such a market had surely resorted
all the greatest men of Rome, one vying with other in
eagerness; seeing there is no contentment 'twould seem, or
satisfaction in all the world like that of a man's taking his
will of a Royal or Princely person, and enjoying of a fair
Queen, or Princess or a high-born Lady. As to this I

do appeal to such men as have embarked on these voyages, and made such good traffic there. Now in this fashion would Queen Zenobia have soon grown rich out of the purse of these great folks, as did Flora, which did receive no others in her place of commerce. Had it not been far better for her to make of her life a scene of merry-making and magnificence, of money getting and compliments, than to have fallen into that need and extremity of poverty she did come to? For she was constrained to gain her bread a-spinning among common work-women, and would have died of hunger, but that the Senate, taking pity of her in view of her former greatness, did decree her a pension for her maintenance, and some trifling lands and possessions, which were for long after known as "Zenobia's Lands." For indeed and indeed is poverty a sore evil; and whosoever can avoid the same, no matter what transformation be taken to that end, doth well and right, as one I wot of was used to declare.

Thus we see how Zenobia did not carry her high courage to the end of her career, as she should,—and as folk should ever persist in every course of action to the last. 'Tis said she had had a triumphal car constructed, the most magnificent ever seen in Rome, to the end she might, as she was often used to say in her days of high prosperity and glorying, hold triumph therein at Rome. For her ambition was to conquer and subdue the Roman Empire! Alas! for her presumption; for it did all fall out quite otherwise, and the Emperor having won the day, did take her car for himself, and use it in his own triumph, while she did march a-foot, and did make as much triumph and ceremonial over her as if he had vanquished a puissant King,—and more. Yet be sure, a victory won

over a woman, be it gained how it may, is no very great
or famous exploit!

After a like fashion did Augustus long to triumph
over Cleopatra; but he got no success in this. She did
forestall him in good time, and in the same way which
Aemilius Paulus did signify in what he said to Perseus,[8]
when in his captivity he did beseech him to have pity on
him, answering him he should have seen to that beforehand, meaning that he ought to have killed himself.

I have heard say that our late King Henri II. did
long for no other thing so sore as to be able to take
prisoner the Queen of Hungary, and this not to treat her
ill, albeit she had given him many causes of offence by her
devastations of his territory, but only to have the glory
of holding this great Princess captive, and to see what
bearing and countenance she would show in her prison,
and if she would then be so gallant and proud-spirited
as at the head of her armies. For in truth there is
naught else so fine and gallant as such a fair, brave and
high-born lady, when she hath will and courage as had
this same Princess, which did much delight in the name
the Spanish soldiers had given her; for just as they did
call her brother the Emperor *el padre de los soldados,*
"the father of the soldiers," so did they entitle her
la madre, "the mother," of the same. So in old days,
in the times of the Romans, was Victoria or Victorina
known in her armies by the name of "the mother of the
camp." Of a surety, an if a great and beautiful lady
do undertake an exploit of war, she doth contribute much
to its success and giveth much encouragement and spirit
to her folk, as myself have seen in the case of our own
Queen Mother, Catherine de Medici, which did often visit

[53]

our armies, and so doing did greatly animate their courage and rouse their ardour. The same is done at this present by her grand-daughter, the Infanta⁴ in Flanders, which doth take the lead of her army, and show herself a valorous chief of her fighting men,—so much so that without her and her noble and delightful presence, Flanders could never have been retained, as all men allow. And never did even the Queen of Hungary herself, her grand-aunt, make so fair a show of beauty, valour, great-heartedness and graceful bearing.

In our histories of France we do read of how much avail was the presence of the noble-hearted Comtesse de Montfort,⁵ when shut up and besieged in Hennebon. For albeit her men were brave and valiant, and had quit themselves in battle and withstood the enemy's assaults as well as ever any folk could, yet did they at the last begin to lose heart and talk of surrendering. But she did harangue them so eloquently, and did re-animate their courage with such good and intrepid words, inspiriting them so finely and so well, as that they did hold out till the succour, so long and eagerly desired, did arrive, and the siege was raised. Nay! she did better still; for whenas the enemy were set on the attack and were all busied therewith, seeing their tents to be all left empty and unprotected, she did make a sally, mounted on a good horse and with fifty good horses to follow her. In this wise doth she surprise the camp and set it a-fire, the result being that Charles de Blois, deeming himself to be betrayed, did straight abandon the assault. On this subject, I will add yet another little tale:

During the late Wars of the League, the Prince de Condé, since deceased, being at Saint-Jean, did send to demand of Madame de Bourdeille,[6] then a widow of the age of forty, and a very handsome woman, six or seven of the wealthiest tenants of her estate, the which had taken refuge in her castle of Mathas at her side. She did refuse him outright, declaring she would never betray nor give up these unhappy folk, who had put themselves under her protection and trusted to her honour for their safety. On this he did summon her for the last time, informing her that unless she would deliver them up to him, he would teach her better obedience. She did make reply to this (for myself was with her by way of rendering help) that, seeing he knew not himself how to obey, she did find it very strange he should wish to make others do so, and that so soon as he should have obeyed his King's orders, she would obey him. For the rest, she did declare that for all his threats, she was afraid neither of his cannon nor of his siege, and how that she was descended from the far-famed Comtesse de Montfort, from whom her folk had inherited the place, and herself too, and therewith some share of her gallantry. Further that she was determined to defend the same so well as that he should never take it, and that she should win no less fame herein than her ancestress, the aforesaid Countess, had done at Hennebon. The Prince did ponder long over this reply, and did delay some days' space, without further threatening her. Yet, had he not presently died, he would assuredly have laid siege to her castle; but in that case was she right well prepared in heart, resolution, men and gear, to receive him warmly, and I do think he would have gotten a shameful rebuff.

Machiavelli, in his book *On the Art of War*, doth relate how that Catherine, Countess of Forli, was besieged in that her good town fortress by Cæsar Borgia, aided by the French army, which did make a most gallant resistance to him, yet at the last was taken. The cause of its loss was this, that the said strong town was over full of fortresses and strongholds, for folk to retire from the one to the other; so much so that Borgia having made his approaches, the Signor Giovanni de Casale (whom the said Countess had chose for her helper and protector), did abandon the breach to withdraw into his strongholds. Through the which error, Borgia did force an entrance and took the place. And so, saith the author, these errors did much wrong the high-hearted courage and re-pute of the said gallant Countess, which had withstood an army the King of Naples and the Duke of Milan had not dared to face; and albeit the issue was unfortunate, yet did she win the honour she so well deserved, and for this exploit many rhymes and verses were writ in Italy in her honour. This passage is one well worthy the at-tention of all such as have to do with the fortifying of places of strength, and do set them to build therein great numbers of castles, strongholds, fortresses and citadels.

To return to our proper subject, we have had in times past many Princesses and high-born ladies in this our land of France, which have given excellent marks of their prowess. As did Paule, daughter of the Comte de Penth-ièvre, who was besieged in Roye by the Comte de Charo-lais, and did there show herself so gallant and great-hearted as that, on the town being taken, the Count did grant her very good conditions, and had her conducted in safety to Compiègne, not suffering any hurt to be done her. So greatly did he honour her for her valour,—and this albeit he felt deep resentment against her husband,

whom he held guilty of having tried to work his death
by black arts and sundry evil devices of images and
candles.

Richilda,[7] only daughter and heiress of Mons in Hainault, and wife of Baldwyn the Sixth, Count of Flanders,
did make all efforts against Robert the Frisian, her
brother-in-law, appointed guardian of the children of
Flanders, for to take away from him the duty and administration of the same, and have it assigned to herself.
To which end she did take up arms with the help of
Philip, King of France, and hazarded two battles[8] against
Count Robert. In the first she was taken prisoner, as
was likewise her foe, the said Count Robert, but afterward were the twain given back in exchange one of the
other. A second battle followed, which she lost, her son
Arnulphe being slain therein, and was driven back to
Mons.

Ysabel of France, daughter of King Philippe le Bel,
and wife of Edward II.[9] of England, and Duke of
Guienne, was ill looked on of the King her husband,
through the intrigues of Hugh le Despenser, whereby she
was constrained to withdraw to France with her son
Edward. Afterward she did return to England with the
Chevalier de Hainault, her kinsman, and an army which
she did lead thither, and by means of which she did presently take her husband prisoner. Him she did deliver
up into the hands of men which did soon bring about his
death; a fate that overtook herself likewise, for by reason
of her loves with a certain Lord Mortimer, she was confined by her own son in a castle, and there ended her
days. She it was that did afford the English pretext
to quarrel with France to the sore hurt of the same.

[57]

Yet surely we have here a piece of base ingratitude on her son's part, who all forgetful of great benefit received, did so cruelly treat his mother for so small a fault. Small I call it, for that 'twas but natural, and an easy thing, that after dealing long with men of arms, and grown so accustomed to go in manly guise with them amid armies and tents and camps, she should do the like also a-bed.

This is a thing oft times seen to happen. For example I do refer me to our Queen Léonor, Duchess of Guienne, which did accompany her husband over seas and to the Holy Wars. By dint of much frequenting of men at arms and troopers and such folk, she did come to derogate very gravely from her honour,—so far as that she did have dealings even with the Saracens. For the which the King her husband did put her away, a thing that cost us very dear. We can but suppose she was fain to try whether these worthy foes were as gallant champions in a lady's chamber as in the open field, and that mayhap 'twas her humour to ever love valiant wights, and that one valiance doth ever attract another, as virtue doth to virtue. For verily he saith most true, which doth declare virtue to be like the lightning, that pierceth through all things.

The said Queen Léonor was not the only lady which did accompany her husband to these same Holy Wars. But both before her day, and with her, and after her, no few other Princesses and great ladies did along with their lords take the cross,—not that they did therefore cross their legs, but did rather open these and stretch them right wide, in such wise that while some did remain there for good and all, others came back from the wars most

finished harlots. So under pretext of visiting the Holy
Sepulchre, amid all that press of arms they did much
amorous wantoning; for verily, as I have observed afore,
arms and love do well accord together, so close and con-
gruous is the sympathy betwixt these twain.

Suchlike dames ought surely to be esteemed, loved and
treated like men,—not as the Amazons did of old, which
proclaiming themselves daughters of Mars, did rid them
of their husbands, pretending marriage was sheer slavery;
yet desire enough and to spare had they to go with other
men, for to have daughters of them, but killing all the
male children.

Jo. Nauclerus, in his *Cosmography*, relates how, in the
year of Christ 1123, after the death of Tibussa, Queen
of the Bohemians, she who did first close in the town of
Prague with walls, and who did very greatly abhor the
power and domination of men, there was one of her damsels, by name Valasca, which did so well gain over the
maids and matrons of that land by her fair and alluring
promises of liberty, and did so thoroughly disgust and
set them against their servitude to manfolk, as that they
did slay each her man, one her husband, another her
brother, another her kinsman or next neighbour, and so
in less than no time were mistresses of the realm. Then
having taken their husbands' harness of war, they did
make such good use thereof, and grew so valiant and
skilled in arms, fighting after the Amazon fashion, as
that they soon gat them several victories. Yet were they
presently, by the conduct and cunning wiles of one Primis-
laus, husband of Tibussa, a man she had raised up from
low and humble state, routed entirely and put to death.
This was sure God Almighty's vengeance for so heinous

[59]

an act and dread attempt, no less indeed than to destroy the human race itself.

6.

HUS did these Amazonian dames find no other fashion of showing forth their gallant spirit for fine, bold and manly exploits but only by these cruel deeds we have named. On the contrary, how many Empresses, Queens, Princesses and other high-born Ladies, have done the like by means of noble acts, both in the governance and management of their dominions, and in other excellent ways, whereof the Histories be so full that I need not recount the same. For the desire of holding sway, of reigning and ruling, doth lodge within women's breasts no less than in men's, and they be just as eager after domination as the other sex.

Well! now I am about to speak of one that was unsullied of this ambition, to wit Vittoria Colonna,[1] wife of the Marquis de Pescaire. I have read of this lady in a Spanish book, how that whenas the said Marquis did hearken to the fine offers made him by Hieronimo Mouron on the Pope's behalf (as I have said in a previous passage) of the Kingdom of Naples, if only he would enter into the league with him, she being informed of the matter by her husband himself, who did never hide aught from her of his privy affairs, neither small nor great, did write to him (for she had an excellent gift of language), and bade him remember his ancient valour and virtue, the which had given him such glory and high repute, as that these did exceed the fame and fortune of the greatest

[60]

Kings of the earth. She then went on: *non con grandeza de los reynos, de Estados ny de hermosos titulos, sino con fè illustre y clara virtud, se alcançava la honra, la qual con loor siempre vivo, legava a los descendientes; y que no havia ningun grado tan alto que no fuese vencido de una trahicion y mala fe. Que por esto, ningun deseo tenia de ser muger de rey, queriendo antes ser muger de tal capitan, que no solamente en guerra con valorosa mano, mas en paz con gran honra de animo no vencido, havia sabido vencer reyes, y grandissimos prncipes, y capitanes, y darlos a triunfos, y imperiarlos,*—"not by the greatness of Kingdoms and of vast Dominions, nor yet of high and sounding titles, but by fair faith and unsullied virtue, is honour won,—the virtue that with ever living praise doth go down to all descendants. And there is never a rank so exalted but it were undone and spoiled by treason wrought and good faith broke. For such a prize she had no wish to be a King's wife, but had rather be a simple Captain's such as he, which not alone in war by his valiant arm, but in peace likewise with the honour of an unbroken spirit, had been strong to vanquish Kings, great Princes and mighty Captains, to triumph over the same and master them." High courage and virtue and truth did all mark this lady's words; for truly to reign by ill faith is a very evil and sorry thing, but to give the law to Kings and kingdoms by honesty and worth a right noble one.

Fulvia, wife of Publius Clodius, and in second wedlock that of Mark Antony, finding but small amusement in her household tasks, did set herself to higher business, to manage affairs of State that is, till she did win herself the repute of ruling the Rulers of Rome. And indeed

Cleopatra did owe her some gratitude and obligation for having so well trained and disciplined Mark Antony to obey and bend him under the laws of submission.

We read moreover of that great French Prince Charles Martel, which in his day would never take nor bear the title of King, as 'twas within his power to do, but liked better to govern Kings and give orders to the same.

However let us speak of some of our own country-women. We had, in our War of the League, Madame de Montpensier, sister of the late Duc de Guise, who was a great Stateswoman, and did contribute much, as well by the subtile inventions of her fine spirit as by the labour of her hands, to build up the said league. And after the same had been now well established, playing one day at cards (for she doth well love this pastime) and taking the first deal, on their telling her she should well shuffle the cards, she did answer before all the company: "I have shuffled the cards so well, as that they could not be better shuffled or combined together." This would all have turned out well, if only her friends had lived; on whose unhappy end however, without losing heart at all at such a loss, she did set herself to avenge them. And having heard the news when in Paris, she doth not shut herself in her chamber to indulge her grief, as most other women would have done, but cometh forth of her house with her brother's children, and holding these by the hand, doth take them up and down the city, making public mourning of her bereavement before the citizens, rousing the same by her tears and piteous cries and sad words which she did utter to all, to take up arms and rise in fierce protest, and insult the King's[1] house and picture, as we have seen done, and I do hope to relate

[62]

in his life, and deny all fealty to him, swearing rank
rebellion to his authority, all which did presently result
in his murder. As to which 'tis well enough known what
persons, men and women, did counsel the same, and are
properly guilty thereof. Of a surety no sister's heart,
losing such brothers, could well digest such deadly venom
without vengeance of this foul murder.

I have heard it related how after she had thus put the
good folk of Paris in so great a state of animosity and
dissatisfaction, she did set her forth to ask of the Duke
of Parma his help toward her vengeance. So thither she
maketh her way, but by such long and heavy stages as
that her coach horses were left so wearied out and
foundered, stranded in the mire somewhere in the very
midst of Picardy, that they could not go another step
either forward or backward, nor put one foot before
another. As chance would have it, there did pass that
way a very honourable gentleman of that countryside,
which was a Protestant, and who, albeit she was disguised both as to name and in dress, did recognize her
well enough. But yet, ignoring all the hurts she had
wrought against his fellows in religion, and the hatred
she bare them, with frank and full courtesy, he did thus
accost her: "Madam, I know you well, and am your most
humble servant. I find you in ill case, and beg you, an
if you will, come to my house, which is close at hand,
to dry your clothes and rest you. I will afford you every
convenience I can to the very best of my ability. Have
no fear; for though I be of the reformed faith, which
you do hate so sore in us, I would fain not leave you
without offering you a courtesy you do stand much in
need of." This fair offer she did in no wise refuse, but

[63]

did accept very readily; then after that he had provided
her with such things as were needful, she doth take the
road again, he conducting her on her way two leagues,
though all the while she did keep secret from him the
purport of her journey. Later on in the course of the
war, by what I have heard, she did repay her debt to the
said gentleman by many acts of courtesy done him.

Many have wondered at her trusting of herself to him,
being Huguenot as he was. But there! necessity hath no
law; and beside, she did see him so honourable seeming,
and heard him speak so honestly and frankly, that she
could not but believe him disposed to deal fairly with her.

As for Madame de Nemours, her mother, who was
thrown into prison after the murder of her noble son's
children, there can be little doubt of the despair and
desolation she was left in by so intolerable a loss; and
albeit till that day she had ever shown herself of a gentle
and cold humour, and one that did need good and sufficient cause to rouse her, she did now spew forth a
thousand insults against the King, and cast in his teeth
a thousand curses and execrations, going so far (for
verily what deed or word could ever match the vehemence
of such a loss and bitter sorrow?) as always to speak of
him by no other name but this, *that Tyrant*. Later,
being come somewhat to herself, she would say: "Alas!
what say I,—Tyrant? Nay! nay! I will not call him so,
but a most good and clement King, if only he will kill me
as he hath killed my children, to take me out of the
wretchedness wherein I am, and remove me to the blessedness of God's heaven!" Later again, softening still further her words and bitter cries, and finding some surcease
of sorrow, she would say naught else but only, "Ah! my

[64]

children! my poor children!"—repeating these same
words over and over again with floods of tears, that
'twould have melted an heart of stone. Alas! she might
well lament and deplore them so sore, being so good and
great hearted, so virtuous and so valorous, as they were,
but above all the noble Duc de Guise, a worthy eldest
son and true paragon of all valour and true-heartedness.
Moreover she did love her children so fondly, that one
day as I was discoursing with a noble lady of the Court
of the said Madame de Nemours, she told me how that
Princess was the happiest in all the world, for sundry
reasons which she did give me,—except only in one thing,
which was that she did love her children over much; for
that she did love them with such excess of fondness as
that the common anxiety she had of their safety and the
fear some ill should happen them, did cloud all her
happiness, making her to live always in inquietude and
alarm for their sake. I leave you then, reader, to imagine
how grievous was the sorrow, bitterness and pain she
did feel at the death of these twain, and how lively the
terror for the other, which was away in the neighbourhood of Lyons, as well as for the Duke her husband,
then a prisoner. For of his imprisonment she had never
a suspicion, as herself did declare, nor of his death
neither, as I have said above.

When she was removed from the Castle of Blois to be
conveyed to that of Amboise for straiter confinement
therein, just as she had passed the gate, she did turn
her round and lifted her head toward the figure of King
Louis XII., her grandfather, which is there carven in
stone above the door, on horseback and with a very
noble mien and warlike bearing. So she, tarrying there

a little space and gazing thereon, said in a loud voice before a great number of folk which had come together, with a fine bold look which did never desert her: "An if he which is there pourtrayed were alive, he would never suffer his granddaughter thus to be carried away prisoner, and treated as she is this day." Then with these words, she did go on her way, without further remonstrance. Understand this, that in her heart she was invoking and making appeal to the manes of that her great-hearted ancestor, to avenge her of the injustice of her imprisonment. Herein she acted precisely as did certain of the conspirators for Cæsar's death, which as they were about to strike their blow, did turn them toward the statue of Pompey, and did inwardly invoke and make appeal to the shade of his valiant arm, so puissant of old, to conduct the emprise they were set on to a successful issue. It may well be the invocation of this Princess may have something aided and advanced the death of the King which had so outraged her. A lady of high heart and spirit which doth thus brood over vengeance to come is no little to be dreaded.

I do remember me how, when her late husband, the Duc de Guise, did get the stroke whereof he died, she was at the time in his camp, having come thither some days previously to visit the same. So soon as ever he did come into his quarters wounded, she did advance to meet him as far as the door of his lodging all tearful and despairing, and after saluting him, did suddenly cry out: "Can it be that the wretch which hath struck this blow and he that hath set him on (signifying her suspicion of the Admiral de Coligny) should go unpunished? Oh God! an if thou art just, as thou must needs

be, avenge this deed; or else........," but stopping at
this word, she did not end her sentence, for that her
noble husband did interrupt her, saying: "Nay! dear
heart, defy not God. An if 'tis He which hath sent me
this for my sins, His will be done, and we should glorify
him therefor. But an if it come from other, seeing vengeance is His alone, He will surely exact the penalty
without you." Natheless, when he was dead, did she so
fiercely follow up her revenge, as that the murderer was
torn to pieces of four horses, while the supposed author
of the crime was assassinated after the lapse of some
years, as I will tell in its proper place. This was due to
the instruction she did give her son, as myself have seen,
and the counsel and persuasion she did feed him withal
from his tenderest years, till at the last final and complete
vengeance was accomplished.

7.

HE counsel and appeal of great-hearted wives
and loving mothers be of no small avail in
such matters. As to this, I do remember me
how, when King Charles IX. was making his
Royal progress about his Kingdom, and was now at
Bordeaux, the Baron de Bournazel was put in prison,
a very brave and honourable gentleman of Gascony, for
having slain another gentleman of his own neighbourhood,
named La Tour,—and, so 'twas said, by dint of much
traitorous subtlety. The widow did so eagerly press for
his punishment, as that care was taken the news should
reach the King's and Queen's chambers, that they were
about to cut off the said Baron's head. Hereon did the

gentlemen and ladies of the Court of a sudden bestir
themselves, and much effort was made to save his life.
Twice over were the King and Queen besought to grant
his pardon. The High Chancellor did set him strongly
against this, saying justice must needs be done; whereas
the King was much in favour of mercy, for that he was
a young man, and asked for naught better than to save
his life, as he was one of the gallants frequenting the
Court, and M. de Cipierre[1] was keen in urging the same
course. Yet was the hour of execution now drawing nigh,
without aught being done,—to the astonishment of everybody.

Hereupon did M. de Nemours intervene, which loved
the unhappy Baron, who had followed him gallantly on
sundry fields of battle. The Duke went and threw himself at the Queen's feet, and did earnestly beseech her
to give the poor gentleman his life, begging and praying so hard and pressing her so with his words as that
the favour was e'en given him at the last. Then on the
instant was sent a Captain of the Guard, which went and
sought the man out and took him from the prison, just
as he was being led forth to his doom. Thus was he
saved, but in such fearful circumstances that a look of
terror did remain ever after imprinted on his features,
and he could never thereafter regain his colour, as myself
have seen. I have heard tell how the same thing did
happen to M. de Saint-Vallier, which did have a fine
escape by the interest of M. de Bourbon.

Meantime however the widow was not idle, but did
come next day to intercept the King as he was going to
Mass, and did throw herself at his feet. She did present
him her son, which might be three or four years old,

saying thus: "At the least, Sire, as you have given pardon
to this child's murderer, I do beseech you grant the same
to him now at this moment, for the time when he shall
be grown up and shall have taken his vengeance and
slain that wretch." And from that time onward, by what
I have heard said, the mother would come every morning
to awake her child; and showing him the bloody shirt his
father had on when he was killed, would repeat to him
three times over: "Mark this token, well, and bear well
in mind, when you be grown up, to avenge this wrong;
else do I disinherit you." A bitter spirit of revenge
truly!

Myself when I was in Spain, did hear the tale how
Antonio Roques, one of the most brave and valiant, cunning, cautious and skilful, famous and withal most courteous, bandits ever was in all Spain ('tis a matter of
common knowledge), did in his early years desire to enter
religion and be ordained priest. But the day being now
come when he was to sing his first mass, just as he was
coming forth from the vestry and was stepping with great
ceremony toward the High Altar of his parish Church
duly robed and accoutred to do his office, and chalice in
hand, he did hear his mother saying to him as he passed
her: *Ah! vellaco, vellaco, mejor seria de vengar la muerte
de tu padre, que de cantar misa,*—"Ah! wretch and mis-
creant that you are! 'twere better far to avenge your
father's death than to be singing Mass." This word did
so touch him at heart, as that he doth coldly turn him
about in mid progress, and back to the vestry, where he
doth unrobe him, pretending his heart had failed him
from indisposition, and that it should be for another
time. Then off to the mountains to join the brigands,

[69]

among whom he doth presently win such esteem and renown that he was chose their chief; there he doth many
crimes and thefts, and avengeth his father's death, which
had been killed, some said, of a comrade, though others
declared him a victim of the King's justice. This tale
was told me by one that was a bandit himself, and had
been under his orders in former days. This man did bepraise him to the third heaven; and true it is the Emperor
Charles could never do him any hurt.

But to return once more to Madame de Nemours, the
King did keep her in prison scarce any time, whereof was
M. d'Escars in part the cause. He did soon release her,
for to send her on a mission to the Ducs du Maine and
de Nemours, and other Princes members of the League,
bearing to all words of peace and oblivion of all past
grievances:—dead men were dead, and there an end; best
be good friends as aforetime. In fact, the King did take
an oath of her, that she would faithfully perform this
said embassy. Accordingly on her arrival, at first accost
'twas naught but tears and lamentations and regrets for
all their losses; then anon did she make report of her
instructions, whereto M. du Maine did reply, asking her
if this were her own advice. She answered simply: "I
have not come hither, my son, to advise you, but only to
repeat to you the message I am charged withal and bidden
give you. 'Tis for you to think whether you have sufficient cause to do so, and if your duty points that way.
As to what I tell you, your heart and your conscience
should give you the best advice. For myself, I do but
discharge a commission I have promised to fulfil." Natheless, under the rose, she knew well enough how to stir the
fire, which did long burn so fierce.

Many folks have wondered greatly, how the King, that was so wise and one of the most adroit men of his Kingdom, came to employ this lady for such an office, having so sorely injured her that she could have had neither heart nor feeling if she had taken therein the very least pains in the world; but there, she did simply make mock of him and his instructions. Report said at the time this was the fine advice of the Maréchal de Retz, who did give a like piece of counsel to King Charles, namely to send M. de la Noue into the town of La Rochelle, for to persuade the inhabitants to peace and their proper duty and allegiance. The better to accredit him to them, he did permit him to play the eager partisan on their side and on his own, to fight desperately for them, and give them counsel and advice against the King,—but all under this condition that when his services should be claimed by the King or the King's brother, which was his Lieutenant General, and he ordered to leave the place, he would obey. This he did and all else, making fierce enough war, and finally quitting the place; yet meanwhile he did so confirm his folk and sharpen their spirit, and did give them such excellent lessons and so greatly encouraged them, as that for that time they did cut our beards to rights for us. Many would have it, there was no subtlety in all this; but I did see it all with mine own eyes, and I do hope to give full account of these doings elsewhere. At any rate this was all the said Maréchal did avail his King and country; one that 'twere more natural surely to hold a charlatan and swindler than a good counsellor and a Marshal of France.

I will tell one other little word of the aforesaid Duchesse de Nemours. I have heard it said that at the time they

[71]

were framing the famous League, and she would be examining the papers and the lists of the towns which did join it, not yet seeing Paris figuring therein, she would ever say to her son: "All this is naught, my son; we must have Paris to boot. If you have not Paris, you have done naught; wherefore, ho! for Paris city." And never a word but Paris, Paris, was always in her mouth; and the end of it all was the barricades that were seen afterward.

8.

IN this we see how a brave heart doth ever fly at the highest game. And this doth again remind me of a little tale I have read in a Spanish Romance called *la Conquista de Navarra*, "The Conquest of Navarre."[1] This Kingdom having been taken and usurped from King John of Navarre by the King of Aragon, Louis XII. did send an army under M. de la Palice to win it back. Our King did send word to the Queen, Donna Catherine, by M. de la Palice which did bring her the news, that she should come to the Court of France and there tarry with his Queen Anne, while that the King, her husband, along with M de la Palice was making essay to recover the Kingdom. The Queen did make him this gallant answer: "How now, Sir! I did suppose the King your master had sent you hither for to carry me with you to my Kingdom and set me again at Pampeluna, and for me to accompany you thither, as my mind was made up to do and my preparations made. Yet now you bid me go stay at the Court of France? Truly a poor hope and ill augury for me! I see plainly

I shall never set foot in mine own land again." And even as she did presage, the thing fell out.

It was told and commanded the Duchess de Valentinois, on the approach of the death of King Henri II., when his health was now despaired of, to retire to her mansion in Paris, and go no more into his chamber,—to the end she might not disturb him in his pious meditations, and no less on account of the hostility certain did bear her. Then when she had so withdrawn, they did send to her again to demand sundry rings and jewels, which did belong to the Crown and which she must give back. At this she did on a sudden ask the worthy spokesman: "Why! is the King dead then?"—"No! Madam," replied the other, "but it can scarce be long first."—"As long as there is one breath of life left in his body, I would have my enemies to know I fear them not a whit, and that I will never obey them, so long as he shall be alive. My courage is still invincible. But when he is dead, I care not to live on after him, and all the vexations you could inflict on me would be but kindness compared with the bitterness of my loss. So, whether my King be quick or dead, I fear not mine enemies at all."

Herein did this fair lady show great spirit, and a true heart. Yet she did not die, 'twill be objected of some, as she did say she would. True! yet did she not fail to experience some threatenings of death; beside, she did better to choose rather to live than to die, for to show her enemies she was no wise afeared of them. Having erst seen them shake and tremble before her, she would fain escape doing the same before them, and did wish to show so good a face and confident look to them as that they never durst do her any displeasure. Nay! more than this;

within two years' space they did seek to her more than ever, and renewed their friendship with her, as I did myself see. And this is the way with great lords and ladies, which have little solid continuance in their friendships, and in their differences do readily make it up again, like thieves at a fair, and the same with all their loves and hatreds. This we smaller folks do never do; for either we must needs fight, avenge and die, or else make up the quarrel by way of punctilious, minutely ordered and carefully arranged terms of agreement. So in this we do play the better part.

We cannot but admire this lady's conduct and behaviour; and truly these high-born dames which have to do with affairs of State, do commonly act in a grander way than the ordinary run of women. And this is why our late King Henri III., last deceased, and the Queen, his mother, did by no means love such ladies of their Court as did much trouble their wits with matters of State and put their nose therein and did concern them to speak of other matters near touching the government of the Kingdom. 'Twas as if, their Majesties were used to declare, they had some great part therein and might be heirs of the same, or just as if they had given the sweat of their bodies and force of their hands to its management and maintenance, like men; whereas, for a mere pastime, talking at the fireside, sitting comfortably in their chairs or lying on their pillows, or their daybeds, they would discourse at their ease of the world at large and the state of the Country, as if they did arrange it all. On this point a certain great lady of fashion, whom I will not name, did one time make a shrewd reply, who taking on her to say out all her say on occasion of the first meeting of the

Estates at Blois, their Majesties did cause a slight reprimand to be given her, telling her she should attend to
the affairs of her own house and her prayers to God.
To this being something too free in her speech, she did
answer thus: "In days of yore when Princes, Kings and
great Lords did take the cross and hie them over-seas, to
do so noble exploits in the Holy Land, insooth 'twas allowed us women only to fast and pray, make orisons and
vows, that God might give them a successful journey and
a safe return. But nowadays that we do see them do
naught better than ourselves, 'tis surely allowed us to
speak of all matters; for as to praying God for them,
why should we do so, seeing they do no more heroic deeds
than ourselves?"

This speech was for sure too bold and outspoken, and
indeed it came very nigh to costing her dear. She had all
the difficulty in the world to win pardon and excuse, which
she had to ask for right humbly; and had it not been for
a certain private reason I could tell, and if I would, she
had received dire pains and penalties therefor, and very
signal punishment.

'Tis not always well to speak out a sharp saying such
as this, when it cometh to the lips. Myself have seen not
a few folk which could in no wise govern their wit in this
sort, but were more untamed than a Barbary charger.
Finding a good shrewd gibe in their mouth, out they must
spit it, without sparing relations, friends or superiors.
Many such I have known at our own Court of France,
where they were well called *Marquis et Marquises de belle-
bouche*, "Lords and Ladies of Frank Speech;" but many
and many a time did their frank speech bring them in sore
trouble.

[75]

9.

AVING thus described the brave and gallant bearing of sundry ladies on sundry noble occasions of their life, I am fain now to give some examples of the like high qualities displayed at their death. Without borrowing any instance of Antiquity, I will merely adduce that of the late deceased Queen Regent [1] mother of our noble King Francis I. In her day this Princess, as I have heard many of mine acquaintance say, both men and women, was a very fair lady, and very gay and gallant to boot, which she did continue to be even in her declining years. And for this cause, when folk did talk to her of death, she did exceedingly mislike such discourse, not excepting preachers which did hold forth on this subject in their sermons. "As if," she would cry, "we did not all of us know well enough we must one day die. The fact is, these preachers, whenas they can find naught further to say in their sermons, and be at the end of their powers of invention, like other simple folk, do take refuge in this theme of death." The late Queen of Navarre, her daughter, did no less than her mother detest these same harpings on death and sermonizings on mortality.

Well, being now come near her fated end, and lying on her deathbed, three days before that event, she did see her chamber at night all lit up by a brilliant gleam shining in through the window. She did hereupon chide her bedchamber women, which were sitting up with her, asking them for why they did make so big and bright a fire. But they did answer, that there was but a small

[76]

fire burning, and that 'twas the moon which did shine
so bright and cause the illumination. "Why!" she did
exclaim, "there is no moon at this time of the month; it
hath no business to be shining now." And of a sudden,
bidding open her curtain, she did behold a comet, which
shone right on her bed. "Ah, look!" she cried, "yonder
is a sign which doth not appear for persons of common
quality. God doth show it forth only for us great lords
and ladies. Shut the window again; 'tis a comet, announc-
ing my death; we must prepare therefor." So next morning, having sent to seek her confessor, she did perform
all the duty of a good Christian, albeit the physicians did
assure her she was not yet come to this. "Had I not
seen the sign of my death," she said, "I should believe you,
for indeed I do not feel me so far gone," and thereon did
describe to them all the appearance of the comet. Finally,
three days later, leaving all concerns of this world, she did
pass away.

I cannot but believe but that great ladies, and such as
be young, beautiful and high-born, do feel greater and
more sore regret to leave this world than other women.
Yet will I now name some such, which have made light
of death, and have met the same with a good heart, though
for the moment the announcement thereof was exceeding
bitter and hateful to them. The late Comtesse de La
Rochefoucault, of the house of Roye, in my opinion and
that of many beside, one of the fairest and most charming
women in all France, when her minister (for she was of the
Reformed Faith, as everybody is aware) did warn her she
must think no more of worldly things, and that her hour
was now come, that she must presently away to God
which was calling her, and leave all worldly vanities,

which were naught as compared with the blessedness of heaven, she said to him thus: "This is all very well, Sir Minister, to say to women which have no great contentment and pleasure in this world, and which have one foot in the grave already; but to me, that am no more than in the bloom of mine age and my delight in this world and my beauty, your sentence is exceeding bitter. And albeit I have more cause to hug myself in this world than in any other, and much reason to regret dying, yet would I fain show you my high courage herein, and do assure you I take my death with as good will as the most common, abject, low, foul old crone that ever was in this world." So presently, she did set her to sing psalms with much pious devotion, and so died.

Madame d'Espernon, of the house of Candale, was attacked of so sudden and deadly a malady as that she was carried off in less than a week. Before her death, she did essay all remedies which might cure her, imploring the help of men and of God in most fervent prayers, as well as of all her friends, and her retainers male and female, taking it very hard that she was to die so young. But when they did reason with her and inform her she must verily and indeed quit this world, and that no remedy was of any avail: "Is it true?" she said; "leave me alone then, I will make up my mind to bear it bravely." These were the exact words she used. Then lifting up her two soft, white arms, and laying her two hands one against the other, with an open look and a confident spirit, she made her ready to wait death with all patience, and to leave this world, which she did proceed to abjure in very pious and Christian terms. Thus did she die as a devout and good Christian should, at the age of twenty-six, being

one of the handsomest and most charming women of her
time.

'Tis not right, they say, to praise one's own belongings;
on the other hand what is at once good and true should not
be kept hid. This is why I am fain in this place to commend
Madame d'Aubeterre,[2] mine own niece and daughter of my
elder brother, who as all they that have seen her at Court
or elsewhere will go with me in saying, was one of the
fairest and most perfect ladies you could see, as well in
body as in mind. The former did plainly and externally
show forth its excellence in her handsome and charming
face, her graceful figure, and all her sweet mien and bearing; while for the mind, 'twas divinely gifted and ignorant
of naught it were meet to know. Her discourse was very
fit, simple and unadorned, and did flow right smoothly and
agreeably from her lips, whether in serious converse or in
merry interchange of wit. No woman have I ever seen
which, in my opinion, did more resemble our Queen Marguerite of France, as well in her general air as in her special charms; and I did once hear the Queen Mother say
the same. To say this is by itself commendation enough,
so I will add no more; none which have ever seen her,
will, I am well assured, give me the lie as to this. Of a
sudden it befell this lady to be attacked by a malady,
which the physicians did fail to recognize rightly, merely
wasting their Latin in the attempt. Herself, however, did
believe she had been poisoned; though I will not say in
what quarter. Still God will avenge all, and mayhap
the guilty in this matter will yet be punished. She did
all she could in the way of remedies,—though not, she
did declare, because she was afeared of dying. For since
her husband's death, she had lost all fear of this, albeit

[79]

he was for sure in no wise her equal in merit, nor deserving of her or of the tender tears her fair eyes did shed after his death. Yet would she have been right glad to live on a while longer for the love of her daughter, the which she was leaving a tender slip of a girl. This last was a good and excellent reason, while regrets for an husband that was both foolish and vexatious are surely but vain and idle.

Thus she, seeing now no remedy was of avail, and feeling her own pulse, which she did herself try and find to be galloping fast (for she had understanding of all such matters), two days before she died, did send to summon her daughter,[3] and did make her a very good and pious exhortation, such as no other mother mayhap that I know of could have made a finer one or one better expressed,—at once instructing her how to live in this world and how to win the grace of God in the next; this ended, she did give her her blessing, bidding her no more trouble with her tears the sweet easefulness and repose she was about to enjoy with God. Presently she did ask for her mirror, and looking at herself very fixedly therein, did exclaim, "Ah! traitor face, that doth in no wise declare my sickness (for indeed 'twas as fair to look on as ever), thou art yet unchanged; but very soon death, which is drawing nigh, will have the better of thy beauty, which shall rot away and be devoured of worms." Moreover she had put the most part of her rings on her fingers; and gazing on these, and her hand withal, which was very well shaped: "Lo! a vanity I have much loved in days gone-by; yet now I do quit the same willingly, to bedeck me in the other world with another much fairer adornment."

Then seeing her sisters weeping their eyes out at her bedside, she did comfort them, exhorting them to take in

[80]

good part, as she did, what God was pleased to send her, and saying that as they had always loved each other so well, they should not grieve at that which did bring her only joy and contentment. She did further tell them that the fond friendship she had ever borne them should be eternal, beseeching them to return her the like, and above all to extend it to her child. Presently seeing them but weep the harder at this, she said once more: "Sisters mine, an if ye do love me, why do ye not rejoice with me over the exchange I make of a wretched life for one most happy? My soul, wearied of so many troubles, doth long to be free, and to be in blessed rest with Jesus Christ my Saviour. Yet you would fain have it still tied to this miserable body, which is but its prison, not its domicile. I do beseech you, therefore, my sisters, torment yourselves no more."

Many other the like words did she prefer, so pious and Christian as that there is never a Divine, however great could have uttered better or more blessed,—all which I do pass over. In especial she did often ask to see Madame de Bourdeille, her mother, whom she had prayed her sisters to send fetch, and kept saying to them: "Oh! sisters, is not Madame de Bourdeille coming yet? Oh! how slow your couriers be! they be really not fit to ride post and make special speed." Her mother did at last arrive, but never saw her alive, for she had died an hour before.

She did ask earnestly too for me, whom she ever spake of as her dear uncle, and did send us her last farewell. She did beg them to have her body opened after death, a thing she had always strongly abhorred, to the end, as she said to her sisters, that the cause of her death being more evidently discovered, this should enable them and her

[81]

daughter the better to take precautions and so preserve
their lives. "For I must admit," she said, "a suspicion
that I was poisoned five years agone along with mine uncle
de Brantôme and my sister the Comtesse de Durtal; but
I did get the biggest piece. Yet would I willingly charge
no one with such a crime, for fear it should prove a false
accusation and my soul be weighted with the guilt thereof,
—my soul which I do earnestly desire may be free of all
blame, rancour, ill-will and sinfulness, that it may fly
straight to God its Creator."

I should never have done, if I were to repeat all; for
her discourse was full and long, and such as did show no
sign at all of an outwearied body or a weak and failing
spirit. As to this, there was a certain gentleman, her
neighbour, a witty talker and one she had loved to converse and jest withal, who did present himself and to whom
she said: "Ha, ha! good friend! needs must give in this
fall, tongue and sword and all. So, fare you well!"

Her physician and her sisters did wish her to take some
cordial medicine or other; but she begged them not to give
it her, "for these would merely," she said, "be helping
to prolong my pain and put off my final rest." So she did
ask them to leave her alone; and was again and again
heard to say: "Dear God! how gentle sweet is death!
who had ever dreamed it could be so?" Then, little by
little, yielding up her spirit very softly, she did close her
eyes, without making any of those hideous and fearsome
signs that death doth show in many at the supreme
moment.

Madame de Bourdeille, her mother, was not long in
following her. For the melancholy she did conceive at the
death of this her noble daughter did carry her off in

eighteen months, after a sickness lasting seven months, at
one time giving cause for good hope of recovery, at another seeming desperate. But from the very first, herself
did declare she would never get the better of it, in no
wise fearing death, and never praying God to grant
her life and health, but only patience in her sufferings
and above that He would send her a peaceful death, and
one neither painful nor long drawn out. And so it befell;
for while we deemed her only fainted, she did give up her
soul so gently as that she was never seen to move either
foot or arm or limb, nor give any fearful and hideous
look; but casting a glance around with eyes that were as
fair as ever, she passed away, remaining as beautiful in
death as she had been when alive and in the plenitude of
her charms.

A sore pity, verily, of her and of all fair ladies that die
so in the bloom of their years! Only I do believe this, that
Heaven, not content with those fair lights which from the
creation of the world do adorn its vault, is fain, beside
these, to have yet other new stars to still illumine us, as
erst they did when alive, with their beauteous eyes.

Another example, and then an end:
You have seen in these last days the case of Madame de
Balagny, true sister in all ways of the gallant Bussy.
When Cambrai was besieged, she did all ever she could,
of her brave and noble heart, to prevent its being taken;
but after having in vain exhausted herself in every sort
of defensive means she could contrive, and seeing now
'twas all over and the town already in the enemy's power,
and the citadel soon to go the same road, unable to endure
the smart and heart's pang of evacuating her Principality

(for her husband and herself had gotten themselves to be
called Prince and Princess of Cambrai and Cambrésis,—
a title sundry nations did find odious and much too presumptuous, seeing their rank was but that of plain
gentlefolk), did die of grief and so perished at the post
of honour. Some say she did die by her own hand, an act
deemed however more Pagan than Christian. Be this as it
may, she deserveth but praise for her gallantry and
bravery in all this, and for the rebuke she did administer
her husband at the time of her death, when she thus said
to him: "How can you endure, Balagny, to live on after
your most dismal fall of Fortune, to be a spectacle and
laughing stock to all the world, which will point the finger
of scorn at you, thus falling from great glory whereto
you had been elevated to the low place I see awaiting you,
and if you follow not my example? Learn then of me
to die nobly, and not survive your misfortunes and disgrace." 'Tis a grand thing thus to see a woman teaching
us how to live,—and how to die. Yet would he neither
obey nor believe her; but at the end of seven or eight
months, quick fogetting the memory of this gallant lady,
he did re-wed with the sister of Madame de Monceaux,[4] no
doubt a fair and honourable damosel,—manifesting to all
and sundry how that to keep alive was his one thing
needful, be it on what terms it may.

Of a surety life is good and sweet; natheless is a noble
death greatly to be commended, such as was this lady's,
who dying as she did of grief, doth appear of a contrary
complexion to that of some women, which are said to be of
an opposite nature to men, for that they do die of joy and
in joy.

10.

F this sort of death I will allege only the instance of Mlle. de Limueil, the elder, which did die at Court, being one of the Queen's maids of honour. All through her sickness, whereof she died, her tongue did never leave off wagging, but she did talk continuously; for she was a very great chatterbox, a sayer of very witty and telling scoffs, and a very fine woman withal. When the hour of her death was come, she did summon her chamber valet to her; for each maid of honour hath her own. He was called Julian, and did play excellently on the violin. "Julian," saith she to him, "come take your violin and go on playing me the *Défaite des Suisses* (Switzers' Rout)[1] till I be dead, and play it as well as ever you can; and when you come to the words, *Tout est perdu* ("All is lost"), play the passage over four or five times as pathetically as you may." This the other did, while she joined in with her voice; and when 'twas come to *Tout est perdue*, she did repeat it over twice. Then turning to the other side of the bed, she cried to her friends: "Yes! all is lost this bout, and for good and all," and so died. Truly a death we may call gay and pleasant! This tale I have of two of her companions, persons of credit, who saw the mystery played out.

If then there be women which do die of joy and in joyous wise, no less are men to be found which have done the like. Thus we read of that great Pope, Leo X., how he did die of joy and delight, when he beheld us French-men driven out altogether from the State of Milan; so sore a hate he bare us!

The late Grand Prior, M. de Lorraine, did one time conceive the wish to send a pair of his Galleys on an expedition to the Levant under the command of Captain Beaulieu, one of his Lieutenants, of the which I have spoke somewhat in another place. Beaulieu went readily enough, being a brave and valiant sailor. When he was toward the Archipelago, he did fall in with a great Venetian ship, well armed and well found, which he set him to fire upon. But the ship did return his salute to some purpose; for at the first volley she did carry clean away two of his banks of oars, galley-slaves and all. Amongst other sore wounded was his Lieutenant, a man named Captain Panier ("Basket") and a good fellow enough, which had time to cry out this word only before he died: "Good-bye baskets all, the harvest is done,"—a merry and a pleasant jest to enliven his death withal! The end was, M. de Beaulieu had to retire, this big ship proving beyond his power to overcome.

The first year King Charles IX. was King, at the time of the July edict when he was yet residing in the Faubourg St. Germain, we did see the hanging of a certain gallows-bird in that quarter, which had stolen six silver goblets from the kitchen of the Prince de La Roche-sur-Yonne. So soon as he was on the ladder, he did beg the hangman to grant him a little space for a dying speech, and did take up his parable, remonstrating with the folk and telling them he was unjustly put to death, "for never," said he, "have I practised my thievings on the poor, on beggars and the vulgar herd, but only on Princes and great Lords, which be greater thieves than we, and do rob us every day of their lives; and 'tis a good deed to recover again of these folk what they do rob and filch from us." Much more diverting nonsense of the sort he did utter, the which 'twere but wasted time to repeat. Presently the priest which was with him at the top of the ladder, turning to the people, as we see done, did call upon them: "Good sirs! this poor criminal doth recommend himself to your prayers; we will say all together for him and his soul's peace a *Pater noster* and an *Ave Maria*, and will sing a *Salve*." Then just as the folk were answering, the said poor criminal did drop his head, and fixing his eyes on the priest, did start bellowing like a calf, and making mock of the priest in the most absurd fashion; then lending him a kick, did send him flying from the top of the ladder to the bottom, so big a leap that he brake a leg. "Ah, ha! Sir priest!" cried the fellow, "God's truth, I knew I should shift you. Well! you've got your gruel now, my fine fellow." Hearing him groan, he did set up a loud and hearty guffaw; then this ended, did jump off the ladder of his own motion and set himself a-swinging into space. I dare swear the Court did laugh merrily at the trick, albeit the poor priest had done himself a serious hurt. A death, in good sooth, that can scarce be called grave and melancholy!

The late deceased M. d'Estampes had a fool called Colin, a very diverting fellow. When his death was now nigh, his master did enquire how Colin was doing. They told him, "But poorly, my Lord; he is going to die, for he will take nothing."—"Come now," said M. d'Estampes, who was at the moment at table, "take him this soup, and tell him, an if he will not take somewhat for love of me, I will never love him more, for they inform me he will take naught." The message was delivered to Colin, who, death already 'twixt the teeth of him, did make answer, "And who be they which have told my Lord I would take naught?" Then being surrounded by a countless cloud of flies (for 'twas summer time), he began to hunt them with his hand, as we see pages and lackeys and children do, a-trying to catch them; and having taken two with one swoop, he cried, making a funny gesture more readily imagined than described, "Go tell my Lord," said he, "what I have taken for love of him, and that now I'm away to the kingdom of the flies," and so saying and turning him round to the other side of the bed, the merry rascal did expire.

As to this, I have heard sundry philosophers declare that folk do very often at the moment of death remember them of those things they have the most loved in life, and tell of these; so gentlemen, soldiers, sportsmen, artisans, all in fact, very near, according to their former occupation, do say some word thereof when a-dying. This is a fact often noted no less in past time than at the present day.

Women in like wise do often out with a similar rigmarole,—whores just as much as honest dames. So have I heard speak of a certain lady, of very good quality too, which on her death-bed did exult to spit out all about her divers intrigues, naughtinesses and past pleasures, to such purpose that she told more thereof than ever folk had known before, albeit she had always been suspected as a desperate wanton. This revelation she may have made, either in a dream possibly, or else because truth, that can never be hid, did constrain her thereto, or mayhap because she was fain so to discharge her conscience. Anyhow, she did actually, with clear conscience and true repentance, confess and ask forgiveness for her sins, detail-

[88]

ing them each and all, dotting i's and crossing t's, till all
was as clear as day. Verily, a curious thing, she should
have found leisure at that supreme hour so to be sweeping
her conscience clean of such a muckheap of scandal,—
and with such careful particularity.

Another good lady I have heard of which was so apt
to dream every night, as that she would tell out by night
everything she did by day, in such wise that she did bring
sore suspicion of herself on her husband's part, who did
presently set himself to listen to her talking and prattling
and pay heed to her dreams, whereby an ill fate did later
on befall her.

'Tis no long while since a gentleman of the great world,
belonging to a province I will not name, did the same
thing on his death-bed, publishing abroad his loves and
lecheries, and specifying the ladies, wives and maids,
which he had had to do with, and in what places, and how
and under what circumstances. All this he did confess
loud out, asking God's pardon therefor before everybody.
This last did worse than the woman just mentioned, for
whereas she did bring disrepute on herself only, he did
blacken several fair ladies' good name. A fine pair of
gallants truly!

'Tis said that misers, both male and female, have likewise this trick of thinking much, in the hour of death,
on their hoard of crowns, forever talking of the same.
Some forty years agone there was a certain lady of Morte-
mar, one of the richest ladies in all Poitou and one of the
most moneyed, which afterward when she came to die had
never a thought for aught but her crowns that were in her
closet. All the time of her sickness, she would rise from
her bed twenty times a day to go visit her treasure. At

the last, when she was now very nigh her end and the priest was exhorting her to think of the life eternal, she would make no other reply nor say any other word but only this: "Give me my gown; the villains are robbing me." Her one thought was to rise and visit her strong-room, as she did sore strive to do, but the effort was beyond the poor lady. And so she died.

I have let myself toward the end wander a little away from the first intention of my present Discourse; but we should bear in mind that after preaching and tragedy, farce ever cometh next. With this word, I make an end.

SIXTH DISCOURSE

Of how we should never speak ill of ladies, and of the consequences of so doing.

1.

NE point there is to be noted in these fair and honourable dames which do indulge in love, to wit that whatsoever freedom they do allow themselves, they will never willingly suffer offence or scandal to be said of them by others, and if any do say ill of them, they know very well how to avenge the affront sooner or later. In a word, they be ready enough to do the thing, but unwilling it should be spoken about. And in very sooth 'tis not well done to bring ill repute on an honourable lady, nor to divulge on her; for indeed what have a number of other folks to do with it, an if they *do* please their senses and their lovers' to boot?

The Courts of our French Kings, and amongst others, those of later years in especial, have been greatly given to blazon abroad the faults of these worthy dames; and I have known the days when was never a gallant about the Palace but did discover some falsehood to tell against the ladies, or at least find some true though scandalous tale to repeat. All this is very blameworthy; for a man ought never to offend the honour of fair ladies, and least of all great ladies. And I do say this as well to such as do reap enjoyment of ladies' favour, as to them which cannot taste the venison, and for this cause do decry the same.

The Courts of our later Kings have, I repeat it, been overmuch given to this scandal-mongering and tale-bearing,—herein differing widely from those of earlier Sovereigns, their predecessors, alway excepting that of Louis XI., that seasoned reprobate. Of him 'tis said that most times he would eat at a common table, in open Hall, with many gentlemen of his privy household and others withal; and whoever could tell him the best and most lecherous story of light women and their doings, this man was best welcomed and made most of. Himself, too, showed no scruple to do the like, for he was exceeding inquisitive and loved to be informed of all secrets; then having found these out, he would often divulge the same to companions, and that publicly.[1] This was indeed a very grave scandal. He had a most ill opinion of women, and an entire disbelief in their chastity. After inviting the King of England to Paris on a visit of good fellowship, and being taken at his word by that Prince, he did straight repent him, and invented an *alibi* to break off the engagement. "Holy Christ!" he said on this occasion, "I don't want him coming here. He would certainly find some little smart, dainty minx, that he would fall over head and ears in love with, who would tempt him to stay longer and come oftener than I should at all like."

Natheless of his wife [2] he had a very high opinion, who was a very modest and virtuous lady; and truly she had need be so, for else, being a distrustful and suspicious

[92]

Prince if ever there was one, he would very soon have treated her like the rest. And when he died, he did charge his son to love and honour his mother well, but not to be ruled of her,—"not that she was not both wise and chaste," he declared, "but that she was more Burgundian than French." And indeed he did never really love her but to have an heir of her; and when he had gotten this, he made scarce nay account of her more. He kept her at the Castle of Amboise like a plain Gentlewoman in very scanty state and as ill-dressed as any young country girl. There he would leave her with few attendants to say her prayers, while himself was away travelling and taking his pleasure elsewhere. I leave you to imagine, such being the opinion the King held of women, and such his delight in speaking ill of them, how they were maltreated by every evil tongue at Court. Not that he did otherwise wish them ill for so taking their pleasure, nor that he desired to stop their amusements at all, as I have seen some fain to do; but his chiefest joy was to gird at them, the effect being that these poor ladies, weighed down under such a load of detraction, were often hindered from kicking of their heels so freely as they would else have liked to do. Yet did harlotry much prevail in his day; for the King himself did greatly help to establish and keep up the same with the gentlemen of his Court. Then was the only question, who could make the merriest mock thereat, whether in public or in privity, and who could tell the merriest tales of the ladies' wantonings and *wriggles* (this was his phrase) and general naughtiness. True it is the names of great ladies were left unmentioned, such being censured only by guess-work and appearances; and I ween they had a better time than some I have seen in the days of

[93]

the late King, which did torment and chide and bully them most strangely. Such is the account I have heard of that good monarch, Louis XI., from divers old stagers.

At any rate his son, King Charles VIII., which did succeed him, was not of this complexion; for 'tis reported of him now that he was the most reticent and fair-speaking monarch was even seen, and did never offend man or woman by the very smallest ill word. I leave you then to think of the fair ladies of his reign, and all merry lovers of the sex, did not have good times in those days. And indeed he did love them right well and faithfully,—in fact too well; for returning back from his Naples expedition triumphant and victorious, he did find such excessive diversion in loving and fondling the same, and pleasuring them with so many delights at Lyons, in the way of tournaments and tourneys which he did hold for love of them, that clean forgetting his partisans which he had left in that Kingdom, he did leave these to perish,—and towns and kingdom and castles to boot, which yet held out, and were stretching forth hands of supplication to him to send them succour. 'Tis said moreover that overmuch devotion to the ladies was the cause of his death, for by reason of a too reckless abandonment to these pleasures, he did, being of a very weakly frame of body, so enervate and undermine his health as that this behaviour did no little contribute to his death.

Our good King Louis XII. was very respectful toward the ladies; for as I have said in another place, he would ever pardon all stage-players, as well as scholars and clerks of the Palace in their guilds, no matter who they did make free to speak of, excepting the Queen his wife, and her ladies and damosels,—albeit he was a merry gallant in his day and did love fair women as well as other folk. Herein he did take after his grand-father, Duke Louis of Orleans,—though not in this latter's ill tongue and inordinate conceit and boastfulness. And truly this defect did cost him his life, for one day having boasted loud out at a banquet whereat Duke John of Burgundy, his cousin, was present, how that he had in his private closet portraits of all the fairest ladies he had enjoyed, as chance would have it, Duke John himself did enter this same closet. The very first lady whose picture he beheld there, and the first sight that met his eyes, was his own most noble lady wife, which was at that day held in high esteem for her beauty. She was called Marguerite, daughter of Albert of Bavaria, Count of Hainault and Zealand. Who was amazed then? who but the worthy husband? Fancy him muttering low down to himself, "Ha, ha! I see it all!" However, making no outcry about the flea that really bit him, he did hide it all, though hatching vengeance, be sure, for a later day, and so picked a quarrel with him as to his regency and administration of the Kingdom. Thus putting off his grievance on this cause and not on any matter of his wife at all, he had the Duke assassinated at the Porte Barbette of Paris. Then presently his first wife being now dead (we may suspect by poison), and right soon after, he did wed in the second place the daughter of Louis, third Duke of Bourbon. Mayhap this bargain was no better than his first; for truly with folks which be meet for horns, change bed-chamber and quarters as they may, they will ever encounter the same.

The Duke in this matter did very wisely, so to avenge him of his adultery without setting tongues a-wagging of his concerns or his wife's, and 'twas a judicious piece of dissimulation on his part. Indeed I have heard a very great nobleman and soldier say, how that there be three things a wise man ought never to make public, an if he be wronged therein. Rather should he hold his tongue on the matter, or better still invent some other pretext to fight upon and get his revenge,—unless that is the thing was so clear and manifest, and so public to many persons, as that he could not possibly put off his action onto any other motive but the true one.

The first is, when 'tis brought up against a man that he is cuckold and his wife unfaithful; another, when he is taxed with buggery and sodomy; the third, when 'tis stated of him that he is a coward, and that he hath basely run away from a fight or a battle. All three charges be most shameful, when a man's name is mentioned in connection therewith; so he doth fight the accusation, and will sometimes suppose he can well clear himself and prove his name to have been falsely smirched. But the matter being thus made public, doth cause only the greater scandal; and the more 'tis stirred, the more doth it stink, exactly as vile stench waxeth worse, the more it is disturbed. And this is why 'tis always best, if a man can with honour, to hold his tongue, and contrive and invent some new motive to account for his punishment of the old offence; for such like grievances should ever be ignored so far as may be, and never brought into court, or made subjects of discussion or contention. Many examples could I bring of this truth; but 'twould be over irksome to me, and would unduly lengthen out my Discourse.

So we see Duke John was very wise and prudent thus to dissimulate and hide his horns, and on quite other grounds

[96]

take his revenge on his cousin, which had shamed him. Else had he been made mock of, and his name blazoned abroad. No doubt dread of such mockery and scandal did touch him as nigh at heart as ever his ambition, and made him act like the wise and experienced man of the world he was.

Now, however, to return from the digression which hath delayed me, our King Francis I., who was a good lover of fair ladies, and that in spite of the opinion he did express, as I have said elsewhere, how that they were fickle and inconstant creatures, would never have the same ill spoke of at his Court, and was always most anxious they should be held in all high respect and honour. I have heard it related how that one time, when he was spending his Lent at Meudon near Paris, there was one of the gentlemen in his service there named the Sieur de Brizam-bourg, of Saintogne. As this gentleman was serving the King with meat, he having a dispensation to eat thereof, his master bade him carry the rest, as we see sometimes done at Court, to the ladies of the privy company, whose names I had rather not give, for fear of offence. The gentleman in question did take upon him to say, among his comrades and others of the Court, how that these ladies not content with eating of raw meat in Lent, were now eating cooked as well,—and their belly full. The ladies hearing of it, did promptly make complaint to the King, which thereupon was filled with so great an anger, as that he did instantly command the archers of the Palace guard to take the man and hang him out of hand. By lucky chance the poor gentleman had wind of what was a-foot from one of his friends, and so fled and escaped in the nick of time. But an if he had been caught, he would

[97]

most certainly have been hanged, albeit he was a man of good quality, so sore was the King seen to be wroth that time, and little like to go back on his word. I have this anecdote of a person of honour and credibility which was present; and at the time the King did say right out, that any man which should offend the honour of ladies, the same should be hanged without benefit of clergy.

A little while before, Pope Farnese being come to Nice, and the King paying him his respects in state with all his Court and Lords and Ladies, there were some of these last, and not the least fair of the company, which did go to the Pope for to kiss his slipper. Whereupon a gentleman did take on him to say they had gone to beg his Holiness for a dispensation to taste of raw flesh without sin or shame, whenever and as much as ever they might desire. The King got to know thereof; and well it was for the gentleman he did fly smartly, else had he been hanged, as well for the veneration due to the Pope as for the respect proper to fair ladies.

2.

HESE gentlemen were not so happy in their speeches and interviews as was once the late deceased M. d'Albanie. The time when Pope Clement did visit Marseilles to celebrate the marriage of his niece with M. d'Orleans, there were three widow ladies, of fair face and honourable birth, which by reason of the pains, vexations and griefs they suffered from the absence of their late husbands and of those pleasures that were no more, had come so low, and grown so thin, weak and sickly, as that they did beseech M. d'Al-

banie, their kinsman, who did possess a good share of the
Pope's favour, to ask of him dispensation for the three of
them to eat meat on prohibited days. This the said Duke
did promise them to do, and to that end did one day bring
them on a friendly footing to the Pope's lodging. Meantime he had warned the King of what was a-foot, telling
him he would afford him some sport. So having put him
up to the game, and the three ladies being on their knees
before his Holiness, M. d'Albanie took the word first,
saying in a low tone and in Italian, so that the ladies did
not catch his words: "Holy Father, see here before you
three widow ladies, fair to look on and very well born.
These same for the respect they bear toward their dead
husbands and the love they have for the children they have
borne to these, will not for aught in all the world marry
again and so wrong their husbands and children. But
whereas they be sometimes sore tempted by the pricks of
the flesh, they do therefore humbly beseech your Holiness
for leave to go with men without marriage, whenever and
wherever they shall find them under the said temptation."
—"What say you, cousin?" cried the Pope. "Why!
'twould be against God's own commandments, wherefrom
I can give no dispensation." "Well! the ladies are here
before you, Holy Father, and if it please you to hear them
say their say." At this one of the three, taking the word,
said: "Holy Father! we have besought M. d'Albanie to
make you our very humble petition for us three poor
women, and to represent to your Holiness our frailty and
our weakly complexion."—"Nay! my daughters," replied
the Pope, "but your petition is in no wise reasonable, for
the thing would be clean against God's commandments."
Then the widows, still quite ignorant of what M. d'Albanie

[99]

had told the Pope, made answer: "At the least, Holy Father, may it please you give us leave three times a week, without scandal to our name."—"What!" exclaimed the Pope, "give you leave to commit *il peccato di lussuria* (the sin of lasciviousness?). I should damn mine own soul; I cannot do it!" Hereupon the three ladies, perceiving at last 'twas a case of scampishness and knavery, and that M. d'Albanie had played a trick on them, declared, " 'Tis not of that we speak, Holy Father; we but ask permission to eat meat on prohibited days."—Hearing these words, the Duc d'Albanie told them, "Nay! I thought 'twas live flesh you meant, ladies!" The Pope was quick to understand the knavery put on them, and said with a dawning smile, "You have put these noble ladies to the blush, my cousin; the Queen will be angered when she doth hear of it." The Queen did hear of it anon, but made no ado, and found the tale diverting. The King likewise did afterward make good mirth thereof with the Pope; while the Holy Father himself, after giving them his benediction, did grant them the dispensation they craved, and dismissed them well content.

I have been given the names of the three ladies concerned, namely: Madame de Chasteau-Briant or Madame de Canaples, Madame de Chastillon and the Baillive de Caen, all three very honourable ladies. I have the tale from sundry old frequenters of the Court.

Madame d'Uzès [1] did yet better, at the time when Pope Paul III. came to Nice to visit King Francis. She was then Madame du Bellay, and a lady which hath from her youth up always had merry ways and spake many a witty word. One day, prostrating herself at his Holiness' feet, she did make three supplications to him: first, that he grant her absolution, for that when yet a little maid, in waiting on the Queen Regent's majesty, and called by the name of Tallard, she did lose her scissors while sewing of her seam, and did make a vow to St. Allivergot to perform the same, an if she found them. This she presently did, yet did never accomplish her vow, not knowing where the said Saint's body lay. The second petition was that he give her pardon forasmuch as, when Pope Clement came to Marseilles, she being still Mlle. Tallard, she did take one of the pillows of his Holiness' bed, and did wipe herself therewith in front and in rear, on the which his Holiness did afterward rest his noble head and face. The third was this, that the Sieur de Tays, because she did love the same, but he loved not her, and the man is accursed and should be excommunicated which loveth not again, if he be loved.

The Pope at first was sore astonished at these requests, but having enquired of the King who she was, did learn her witty ways, and laughed heartily over the matter with the King. Yet from that day forth all she did was found admirable, so good a grace did she display in all her ways and words.

Now never suppose this same great monarch was so strict and stern in his respect for ladies, as that he did not relish well enough any good stories told him concerning them, without however any scandal-mongering or decrying of their good name. Rather like the great and highly privileged King he was, he would not that every man, and all the vulgar herd, should enjoy like privileges with himself.

I have heard sundry relate how he was ever most anxious that the noble gentlemen of his Court should never be

[101]

without mistresses. If they won none such, he did deem them simpletons and empty fools; while many a time he would ask one Courtier or another the name of the lady of his choice, and promise to do them good service in that quarter, and speak well of their merits. So good-natured a Prince was he and an affable. Oftentimes too, when he did observe his gentlemen full of free discourse with their mistresses, he would come up and accost them, asking what merry and gallant words they were exchanging with their ladies, and if he found the same not to his liking, correcting them and teaching them better. With his most intimate friends, he was no wise shy or sparing to tell his stories and share his good things with them. One diverting tale I have heard him tell, which did happen to himself, and which he did later on repeat. This was of a certain young and pretty lady new come to Court, the which being little skilled in the ways of the world, did very readily yield to the persuasions of the great folks, and in especial those of the said monarch himself. One day when he was fain to erect his noble standard and plant the same in her fort, she having heard it said, and indeed begun to note that when one gave a thing to the King, or took aught from him and touched it, the person must first kiss the hand for to take and touch it withal, did herself without more ado fulfil the obligation and first very humbly kissing her hand did seize the King's standard and plant it in the fort with all due humbleness. Then did she ask him in cold blood, how he did prefer her to love him, as a respectable and modest lady, or as a wanton. No doubt he did ask her for the latter, for herein was she more able to show herself more agreeable than as a modest woman. And indeed he soon found out she had by no means wasted her time, both after the event and before it, and all. When all was done, she would drop him a deep curtsy, thanking him respectfully for the honour he had done her, whereof she was all unworthy, often suggesting to him at the same time some promotion for her husband. I have heard the lady's name, one which hath since grown much less simple than at first she was, and is nowadays cunning and experienced enough. The King made no ado about repeating the tale, which did reach the ears of not a few folks.

This monarch was exceeding curious to hear of the love of both men and women, and above all their amorous engagements, and in especial what fine airs the ladies did exhibit when at their gentle work, and what looks and attitudes they did display therein, and what words they said. On hearing all this, he would laugh frank and free, but after would forbid all publishing abroad thereof and any scandal making, always strongly recommending an honourable secrecy on these matters.

He had for his good follower herein that great, most magnificent and most generous nobleman, the Cardinal de Lorraine. Most generous I may well call him, for he had not his like in his day; his free expenditure, his many gracious gifts and kindnesses, did all bear witness thereof, and above all else his charity toward the poor. He would regularly bear with him a great game-bag, the which his valet of the bed-chamber, who did govern his petty cash, never failed to replenish, every morning, with three or four hundred crowns. And as many poor folk as he met, he would plunge his hand in the game-bag, and whatsoever he drew out therefrom, without a moment's thought, he gave away, and without any picking or choosing. 'Twas

of him a poor blind man, as the Cardinal was passing in
the streets of Rome and was asked for an alms, and so did
throw him according to wont a great handful of gold,
said thus, crying out aloud in the Italian tongue: *O tu
sei Christo, o veramente el cardinal di Lorrena,*—"Either
you are Christ, or the Cardinal de Lorraine." Moreover
if he was generous and charitable in this way, he was no
less liberal toward other folks as well, and chiefly where
fair ladies were concerned, whom he did easily attach to
him by this regale. For money was not so greatly abundant in those days as it hath nowadays become, and for
this cause women were more eager after the same, and
every sort of merry living and gay attire.

I have heard it said that ever on the arrival at Court of
any fair damsel or young wife that was handsome and
attractive, he would come instantly to greet the same, and
discoursing with her would presently offer to undertake
the training of her. A pretty trainer for sooth! I ween
the task was not so irksome an one as to train and break
some wild colt. Accordingly 'twas said at that time, was
scarce dame or damsel resident at Court or newly come
thither, but was caught and debauched by dint of her own
avariciousness and the largesse of the aforesaid Cardinal;
and few or none have come forth of that Court women
of chastity and virtue. Thus might their chests and big
wardrobes be seen for that time more full of gowns and
petticoats, of cloth of gold and silver and of silk, than
be nowadays those of our Queens and great Princesses of
the present time. I know this well, having seen the thing
with mine own eyes in two or three instances,—fair ladies
which had gotten all this gear by their dainty body; for

neither father, mother nor husband could have given them the same in anything like such wealth and abundance.

Nay! but I should have refrained me, some will say, from stating so much of the great Cardinal, in view of his honoured cloth and most reverend and high estate. Well! his King would have it so, and did find pleasure therein; and pleasure one's Sovereign, a man is dispensed of all scruple, whether in making love or other matters, provided always they be not dishonourable. Accordingly he did make no ado about going to the wars, and hunting and dancing, taking part in mascarades, and the like sports and pastimes. Moreover he was a man of like flesh and blood with other folk, and did possess many great merits and perfections of his own, enough surely to outweigh and cloak this small fault,—if fault it is to be called, to love fair ladies!

I have heard the following tale told of him in connection with the proper respect due to ladies. He was naturally most courteous toward them; yet did he once forget his usual practice, and not without reason enough, with the Duchess of Savoy, Donna Beatrix of Portugal. Travelling on one occasion through Piedmont, on his way to Rome on his Royal master's service, he did visit the Duke and Duchess. After having conversed a sufficient while with the Duke, he went to find the noble Duchess in her chamber for to pay his respects to her; arrived there and on his coming forward toward her, her Grace, who was haughtiness itself, if ever was such in the world, did offer him her hand to kiss. The Cardinal, loath to put up with this affront, did press forward to kiss her on the mouth, while she did draw back all she could. Then losing all patience and crowding up yet nearer to her, he takes her fairly by the head, and in spite of her struggles did kiss her two or three times over. And albeit she did protest sore with many cries and exclamations both in Portuguese and Spanish, yet had she to endure this treatment. "What!" the Cardinal cried out; "is it to me this sort of state and ceremony is to be used? I do kiss right enough the Queen of France my Mistress, which is the greatest Queen in all the world, and I am not to kiss you, a dirty little slip of a duchess! I would have you to know I have bedded with ladies as fair as you, and as good to boot, and of better birth than ever you be." And mayhap he spoke but the truth. Anyway the Princess was ill-advised to make this show of haughtiness toward a Prince of so high an house, and above all towards a Cardinal; for there is never one of this exalted rank in the Church, but doth liken himself with the greatest Princes of Christendom. The Cardinal too was in the wrong to take so harsh reprisals; but 'tis ever very irksome to a noble and generous spirit, of whatever estate and calling, to put up with an affront.

Another of the same rank, the Cardinal de Granvelle, did likewise well know how to make the Comte d'Egmont feel his displeasure on the same account, and others too whose names be at the tip of my pen, but whom I will pass over for fear of confusing my subject overmuch, though I may return again to them later. I do now confine myself to our late King Henri le Grand, which monarch was exceeding respectful to the ladies, whom he was used to treat with all reverence, and did alway hate gainsayers of their honour. And when so great King doth so serve fair ladies, a monarch of such puissance and repute, very loath for sure be all men of his Court to open mouth for to speak ill of the same. Beside, the Queen mother did exert a strong hand to guard her ladies and damsels, and make calumniators and satirists feel the weight of her resentment, when once they were found out, seeing how she had been as little spared by such as any of her ladies. Yet 'twas never herself she did take heed for so much as others, seeing, she was used to declare, how she did know her soul and conscience pure and void of offence, and could afford to laugh at these foul-mouthed writers and scandalmongers. "Why! let them say their worst," she would say, "and have their trouble for nothing"; yet whenever she did catch them at it, she knew how to make them smart soundly.

It befell the elder Mlle. de Limeuil, at her first coming to Court, to compose a satire or lampoon (for she had the gift of witty speech and writing) on the Court generally, not however so much scandalous in its matter as diverting in form. Be assured the King's mother did make her pay for this well and feel the whip smartly, as well as two of her comrades which were in the secret to her majesty, through the house of Turenne, which is allied to that of Boulogne, she would have been chastised with every ignominy, and this by express order of the King, who had the most particular and curious dislike of such writings.

I do remember me of an incident connected with the Sieur de Matha, a brave and gallant gentleman much loved of the King, and a kinsman of Madame de Valentinois, which did ever have some diverting quarrel and complaint against the damsels and dames of the Court, of so merry a complexion was he. One day having attacked one of the Queen's maids of honour, another,

known by the name of "big Méray," was for taking up the
cudgels for her companion. The only reply Matha did
vouchsafe her was this: "Go to! I'm not attacking you,
Méray; you're a great war-horse, and should be barded!"²
For insooth she was the very biggest woman, maid or
wife, I have ever seen. She did make complaint of the
speech to the Queen, saying the other had called her a
mare and a great war-horse to be barded. The Queen
was so sore angered that Matha had to quit the Court
for some days, spite of all the favour he had with his kinswoman Madame de Valentinois; and for a month after
his return durst not set foot in the apartment of the
Queen and her maids of honour.

The Sieur de Gersay did a much worse thing toward
one of the Queen's maids of honour, to whom he was ill-
disposed, for to avenge him upon her, albeit he was never
at a loss for ready words; for indeed he was as good as
most at saying a witty thing or telling a good story, and
above all when spreading a scandal, of which art and
mystery he was a past master; only scandal-mongering
was at that time strongly forbidden. One day when he
was present at the after dinner assembly of the Queen
along with the other ladies and gentlemen of her Court,
the custom then being that the company should not sit
except on the floor when the Queen was present, de Gersay
having taken from the pages and lackeys a ram's pizzle
they were playing with in the Office Court of the Palace,
sitting down beside her he did slip the same into the girl's
frock, and this so softly as that she did never notice it,—
that is not until the Queen did proceed to rise from her
chair to retire to her private apartment. The girl, whose
name I had better not give, did straight spring up, and as

she rose to her feet, right in front of the Queen, doth give
so lusty a push to the strange plaything she had about
her, as that it did make six or seven good bounces along
the floor, for all the world as though it were fain of its
own accord to give the company a free exhibition and
some gratuitous sport. Who more astonished than the
poor girl,—and the Queen to boot, for 'twas well in front
of her with naught to prevent her view? "Mother of
God!" cried the Queen, "and what is that, my child;
what would you be at with that thing?" The unhappy
maid of honour, blushing and half fainting with confusion, began to cry out she knew not what it was, that
some one who did wish her ill had played this horrid
trick on her, and how she thought 'twas none other
but de Gersay which had done it. The latter waiting
only to see the beginning of the sport and the first few
bounces, was through the door by now. They sent to
call him back, but he would never come, perceiving the
Queen to be so very wroth, yet stoutly denying the whole
thing all the while. So he was constrained for some days
to fly her resentment, and the King's too; and indeed had
he not been, along with Fontaine-Guérin, one of the Dauphin's prime favourites, he would assuredly have been in
sore straits, albeit naught could ever be proven against
him except by guess-work, and notwithstanding the fact
that the King and his courtiers and not a few ladies could
not refrain them from laughing at the incident, though
they durst not show their amusement in view of the
Queen's displeasure. For was never a lady in all the
world knew better than she how to startle folk with a
sudden and sore rebuke.

A certain honourable gentleman of the Court and a

maid of honour did one time, from the good affection they
erst had with one another, fall into hate and sore quarrel;
this went so far that one day the young lady said loud
out to him in the Queen's apartment, the twain being in
talk as to their difference: "Leave me alone, Sir, else I
will tell what you told me." The gentleman, who had informed her in strict confidence of something about a very
great lady, and fearing ill would befall him from it, and
at the least he would be banished the Court, without more
ado did answer back,—for he was ready enough of speech:
"If you do tell what I have told you, I will tell what I
have done to you." Who more astonished than the lady
at this? yet did she contrive to reply: "Why! what have
you done to me?" The other did reply: "Why! what
have I told you?" Thereupon doth the lady make answer: "Oh! I know very well what you told me." To
which the other: "Oh! and I know very well what I did
to you." The lady doth retort, "But I'll prove quite
clearly what you told me;" and the other: "And I'll
prove clearer still what I did to you." At long last, after
sticking a long while at this counterchange of reply and
retort in identical form and almost the same words, they
were parted by the gentlemen and ladies there present,
albeit these got much diversion from the dispute.

This disputation having come to the Queen's ears, the
latter was in great wrath thereanent, and was fain at
once to know the words of the one and the deeds of the
other, and did send to summon them. But the pair of
them, seeing 'twas to be made a serious matter, did consult and straight agree together to say, whenas they did
appear before the Queen, how that 'twas merely a game
their so disputing with each other, and that neither had

she been told aught by the gentleman, nor yet had he done aught to her. So did they balk the Queen, which did none the less chide and sore blame the courtier, on the ground that his words were over free and like to make scandal. The man sware to me twenty times over that, and if they had not so made it up and agreed in a tale, and the lady had actually revealed the secret he had told her, which might well have turned to his great injury, he would have resolutely maintained he had done his will on her, challenging them to examine her, and if she should not be found virgin, that 'twas himself had deflowered her. "Well and good!" I answered, "but an if they had examined her and found her a maid, for she was quite young and unmarried, you would have been undone, and 'twould have gone hard but you had lost your life.— "Body of me!" he did return, "that's just what I should have liked the best, that they should have examined the jade. I was well assured of my tale, for I knew quite well who had deflowered her, and that another man had been there right enough, though not I,—to my much regret. So being found already touched and soiled, she had been undone, and I avenged, and her good name ruined to boot. I should have got off with marrying her, and afterward ridding me of her, as I could." And these be the risks poor maids and wives have to run, whether they be in the right o't or the wrong!

3.

DID one time know a lady of very high rank which did actually find herself pregnant by the act of a very brave and gallant Prince;[1] 'twas said however the thing was done under promise of marriage, though later the contrary was ascertained to be the case. King Henri was the first to learn the facts, and was sore vexed thereat, for she was remotely connected with his Majesty. Any way, without making any further noise or scandal about the matter, he did the same evening at the Royal ball, chose her as his partner and lead her out to dance the torch-dance[2] with him; and afterward did make her dance with another the *galliard* and the rest of the "brawls," wherein she did display her readiness and dexterity better than ever, while her figure had all its old grace and was so well arranged for the occasion as that she gave no sign of her bigness. The end was that the King, who had kept his eyes fixed on her very strictly all the time, did perceive naught, no more than if she had not been with child at all, and did presently observe to a great nobleman, one of his chief familiars: "The folk were most ill-advised and spiteful to have gone about to invent the tale that yonder poor girl was big with child; never have I seen her in better grace. The spiteful authors of the calumny have told a most wicked falsehood." Thus this good King did shield the noble lady and poor girl, and did repeat the same thing to his Queen whenas he was to bed with her that night. But the latter, mistrusting the thing, did have her examined the next morning, herself being present, and she was found to be six months gone in preg-

[112]

nancy; after she did confess and avow the whole truth to
the Queen, saying 'twas done under pretence of marriage
to follow. Natheless the King, who was all good nature,
had the secret kept as close as ever possible, so as not to
bring shame and scandal on the damsel, though the Queen
for her part was very wrathful. Any way, they did send
her off very quietly to the home of her nearest kinsfolk,
where she was presently brought to bed of a fine boy.
Yet was the lad so unfortunate that he could never get
him recognized by his putative father; the trial of the
case did drag out to great length, but the mother could
never get aught decided in her favour.

Now good King Henri did love merry tales as well as
any of his predecessors, but he would never have scandal
brought on ladies therein nor their secrets divulged. In
fact, the King himself, who was of amorous complexion
enough, when he was away to visit the ladies, would ever
go thither stealthily and under cover all ever he could,
to the end they might be free of suspicion and ill-repute.
But an if there was any that was discovered, 'twas never
by his fault or with his consent, but rather by the fair
dame's doing. So have I heard of one lady of the sort,
of a good house, named Madame Flamin, a Scotswoman,
which being gotten with child by the King, did make no
sort of secret of it, but would say it out boldly in her
French Scotch thus: "I hae dune what I could, sae that
the noo, God be thankit, I am wi' bairn by the King,
whilk doth mak me an honoured and unco happy woman.
And I maun say the blude Royal hath in it something
of a more douce and tasty humour than the ordinar, I
do find myself in sic gude case,—no to speak of the fine
bits o' presents forthcoming."

[113]

Her son, that she had presently, was the late Grand
Prior of France, who was killed lately at Marseilles,—a
sore pity, for he was a very honourable, brave and gallant
nobleman, and did show the same clearly at his death.
Moreover he was a man of property and sense, and the
least tyrannical Governor of a District of his own day
or since. Provence could tell us that, and beside that he
was a right magnificent Seigneur and of a generous expenditure. He was indeed a man of means, good sense and
wise moderation.

The said lady, with others I have heard of, held the
opinion that to lie with one's Sovereign was no disgrace;
those be harlots indeed which do abandon their bodies to
petty folk, but not where great Kings and gallant gentlemen be in question. Like that Queen of the Amazons I
have named above, which came a journey of three hundred leagues for to be gotten with child by Alexander the
Great, to have good issue therefrom. Yet there be those
who say one man is as good as another for this!

After King Henri came Francis II., whose reign however was so short as that spiteful folks had no time even
to begin speaking ill of ladies. Not that we are to believe, if he had enjoyed a long reign, that he would have
suffered aught of the kind at his Court; for he was a
monarch naturally good-natured, frank, and not one to
take pleasure in scandal, as well as being most respectful
toward ladies and very ready to pay them all honour.
Beside he had the Queen his wife and the Queen his mother,
and his good uncles to boot, all of which were much for
checking these chatterers and loose-tongued gentry. I
remember me how once, the King being at Saint-Germain
en Laye, about the month of August or September, the

[114]

fancy took him one evening to go see the stags in their
rut in that noble forest of Saint-Germain, and he did
take with him certain princes, his chief familiars, and
some great ladies, both wives and maids, whose names I
could very well give, an if I chose. Nor was there lacking
one fain to make a talk of it, and say this did not smack
of his womankind being exactly virtuous or chaste, to be
going to see these lovemakings and wanton ruttings of
beasts, seeing how the appetite of Venus must heat them
more and more at sight of such doings. In fact, so sore
will they be longing to taste, that sure the water or saliva
will be coming to their mouth, in such wise that no other
remedy will there be thereafter for to get rid of the same
except only by some other discharge of saliva, or something else. The King heard of this speech, and the noblemen and ladies which had accompanied him thither. Be
well assured, an if the gentleman had not straightway
decamped, he had fared very ill; nor did he ever again
appear at Court till after that King's death and the end
of his reign. Many scandalous pamphlets there were put
forth against them which were then in direction of the
Government of the Kingdom; but there was never an one
that did so hurt and offend as a satire entitled *The Tiger*[3]
—modelled on the first invective of Cicero against Catiline,—especially as it spake freely of the amours of a
very great and fair lady, and a great nobleman, her kinsman. An if the gallant author had been caught, though
he had had an hundred thousand lives, he had surely lost
them every one; for the two great folks, lady and gentleman, were so exceeding vexed and angered as that they
did all but die of despair.

This King Francis II. was not subject to love like his

[115]

predecessors; and truly he would have been greatly to blame, seeing he had to wife the fairest woman in all the world and the most amiable. And when a man hath such a wife, he doth not go seeking fortune elsewhere as others use, else is he a wretch indeed. And not so going, little recks he to speak ill of ladies, or indeed to speak well either, or to speak at all about them, except always of his own good lady at home. 'Tis a doctrine I have heard a very honourable personage maintain: natheless have I known it prove false more than once.

King Charles came next to the throne, which by reason of the tenderness of his years, did pay no heed at the beginning of his reign to the ladies, but did rather give his thoughts to spending his time in youthful sports and exercises. Yet did the late deceased M. de Sipierre his Governour and Tutor, a man who was in my opinion and in that of every one else, the most honourable and most courteous gentleman of his time, and the most gentle and respectful toward women, did so well teach the same lesson to the King his master and pupil, as that he was as ready to honour ladies as any of the kings his predecessors. For never, whether as boy or man, did he see a woman, no matter how busied he was in other matters, whether he was hurrying on or standing still, on foot or on horse-back, but he would straight salute the same and most respectfully doff his cap. Whenas he came to an age for love, he did serve several very honourable dames and damsels I have known of, but all this with so great honour and respect as that he might have been the humblest gentleman of the Court.

In his reign the great lampoonists did first begin their vogue, and amongst them even some very gallant gentlemen of the Court, whose names I will not give, did strangely abuse the ladies, both in general and in particular, and even some of the greatest in the land. For this some of them have found themselves entangled in downright fierce quarrels, and have come off second best,—not indeed that they did avow the truth, for they did rather always deny they had aught to do with it. If they had confessed, they had had heavy payment to make, and the King would certainly have let them feel the weight of his displeasure, inasmuch as they did attack ladies of over high a rank. Others did show the best face they could, and did suffer the lie to be cast in their teeth a thousand times over, conditionally as we may say and vaguely, and had to swallow a thousand affronts, drinking the same in as sweetly as though they had been milk, without daring to retort one word, else had their lives been at risk. 'Tis a thing which hath oft given me great surprise that suchlike folks should set them to speak ill of their neighbours, yet suffer others to speak ill of themselves so sorely and to their very face. Yet had these men the repute of being gallant swordsmen; but in this matter they would aye endure all but the extremest insult bravely and without one word of protest.

I do remember me of a lampoon which was made against a very great lady, a widow, fair and of most honourable birth, which did desire to marry again with a very great Prince, a young and handsome man.[4] There were certain persons, (and I have accurate knowledge of the same), who disliking this marriage, and to dissuade the Prince therefrom, did concoct a lampoon on her, the most scandalous I have ever seen, in the which they did compare her to five or six of the chiefest harlots of Antiquity, and

[117]

the most notorious and wanton, declaring how that she did overtop them each and all. The actual authors of the said satire did present it to the Prince, professing however that it did emanate from others, and that themselves had merely been given it. The Prince, having looked at it, gave the lie to its statements and hurled a thousand vague and general insults at them which had writ it; yet did they pass all over in silence, brave and valiant men though they were. The incident however did give the Prince pause a while, seeing the lampoon did contain several definite revelations and point direct at some unpleasant facts; natheless after the lapse of two years more was the marriage accomplished.

The King was so great-hearted and kindly that he was never inclined to favour folks of this kidney. To pass a spicy word or two with them aside, this he did like well enough; but he was always most unwilling the common herd should be fed on such diet, declaring that his Court, which was the best ennobled and most illustrious by reason of great and noble ladies of any in all the world, should never, such being its high repute, be cheapened and foully aspersed by the mouth of suchlike reckless and insolent babblers. 'Twas well enough to speak so of the courtesans of Rome, or Venice, or other the like places, but not of the Court of France; it might be permitted to do the thing, it was not permitted to speak thereof.

Thus do we see how this Sovereign was ever respectful toward ladies, nay! so much so that in his later days when some I know of were fain to give him an evil impression of certain very great, as well as most fair and honourable dames, for that these had intermeddled in some highly important matters of his concern, yet would he never

credit aught against them; but did accord them as good
favour as ever, dying at the last in their very good graces
and with many a tear of their shedding to wet his corpse.
And they did find good cause to say so too, so soon as
ever King Henri III. came to succeed him, who by reason
of sundry ill reports he had been told of these ladies when
in Poland, did not make near so much of them as he had
done aforetime. Both over these and over some others
that I know of, he did exercise a very strict censorship,
and one we may be sure that made him not more liked; and
indeed I do believe they did him no little hurt, and con-
tributed in part to his evil fortune and final ruin. I
could allege sundry special facts in proof hereof, but I
had rather pass them over,—saying only this much, that
women generally are keen set on taking vengeance. It
may be long in coming, but they do execute it at the last.
On the contrary many men's revenge is just the opposite
in its nature, for ardent and hot enough at its first beginning to deceive all, yet by dint of temporising and putting
off and long delays it doth grow cool and come to naught.
And this is why 'tis meet to guard against the first attempt, and take time by the forelock in parrying the
blows; but with women the first fury and attempt, and the
temporising and delay, do both last out to the end,—that
is in some women, though hardly many.

Some have been for excusing the King for the war he
made on women in the way of crying them down, by saying 'twas in order to curb and correct vice,—as if the
curb were of any of the slightest use in these cases, seeing
woman is so conditioned of nature as that the more this
thing is forbid her, the more ardent is she after the same,
and to set a watch on her is just labour lost. So in actual

fact myself have seen how, for all he could do, they were never turned out of their natural road.

Several ladies that I wot well enough, did he love and serve with all due respect and very high honour,—and even a certain very great and fair Princess,[5] of whom he had fallen so deep in love before his going into Poland, that after he became King, he did resolve to wed the same, although she was already married to a great and gallant Prince, but one that was in rebellion against him and had fled to a foreign land to gather an army and make war upon him. But at the moment of his return to France, the lady died in child-birth. Her death alone did hinder the marriage, for he was firm set thereon. He would certainly have married her by favour and dispensation of the Pope, who would not have refused him his consent, being so great a Monarch as he was, and for sundry other reasons that may be readily imagined.

Others again he did make love to only for to bring the same into disparagement. Of such I wot of one, a great lady, in whose case, for the displeasures her husband had wrought him, and not able otherwise to get at him, the King did take his revenge on his wife, whom he did after publish abroad for what she was in the presence of a number of folk. Yet was this vengeance mild and merciful after all, for in lieu of death he did give her life.

Another I wot of, which for overmuch playing the wanton, as also for a displeasure she did the King, the latter did of set purpose pay court to. Anon without any vast deal of persuasion, she did grant him an assignation in a garden, the which he failed not to keep. But he would have naught else to do with her (so some folk say, but be sure he did find something to do with her right enough)

but only to have her so seen offering herself in open market, and then to banish her from the Court with ignominy.

He was anxious and exceeding inquisitive to know the
life of all and every fair lady of his Court, and to penetrate their secret wishes. 'Tis said he did sometimes reveal one or other of his successes with women to sundry
of his most privy intimates. Happy they! for sure the
leavings of suchlike great monarchs must needs be very
tasty morsels.

The ladies did fear him greatly, as I have myself seen.
He would either reprimand them personally, when needful, or else beg the Queen his mother so to do, who on her
part was ready enough at the work. 'Twas not however
that she did favour scandal-mongers, as I have shown
above in the little examples I have there given. And paying such heed as she did to these and showing so great
displeasure against them, what was she not bound to do
others which did actually compromise the good name and
honour of her ladies?

This monarch again was so well accustomed from his
earliest years, as myself have seen, to hear tales of ladies
and their gallantries (and truly myself have told him one
or two such), and to repeat them too,—yet alway in
secret, for fear the Queen his mother should learn thereof,
for she would never have him tell such stories to any
others than herself, that she might check the same,—so
well accustomed was he to all this, that coming to riper
years and full liberty, he did never lose the habit. And
in this wise he did know how they did all live at his Court
and in his Kingdom,—or at the least many of them, and
especially the great ladies of rank, as well as if he had
frequented them every one. And if any there were which

[121]

were new come to Court, accosting these most courteously and respectfully, yet would he tell them over such tales as that they would be utterly amazed at heart to know where he had gotten all his information, though all the while denying and protesting against the whole budget to his face. And if he did divert himself after this fashion, yet did he not fail, in other and more weighty matters, to apply his visit to such high purpose as that folk have counted him the greatest King which for an hundred years hath been in France, as I have writ elsewhere in a chapter composed expressly upon this Sovereign.[6]

Accordingly I do now say no more about him, albeit it may be objected to me that I have been but chary of examples of his character on this point, and that I should say more, an if I be so well informed. Yea! truly, I do know tales enough, and some of them high-spiced; but I wish not to be a mere chronicler of news whether of the Court or of the world at large. Beside, I could never cloak and cover up these my tales so featly but that folk would see through them, and scandal come therefrom.

Now these traducers of fair ladies be of divers sorts. Some do speak ill of women for some displeasure these have done them, though all the while they be as chaste as any in all the world, and instead of the pure and beauteous angel they really resemble do make out a picture of a devil all foul and ugly with wickedness. Thus an honourable gentleman I have both seen and known, did most abominably defame a very honourable and virtuous lady for a slight affront she had put upon him, and did sorely wreak his displeasure on her. He would say thus: "I know quite well I am in the wrong, and do not deny the lady to be really most chaste and virtuous. But be it who it may, the woman which shall have affronted me in the smallest degree, though she were as chaste and pure as the Blessed Virgin herself, seeing I can in no other way bring her to book, as I would with a man, I will say every evil gallows thing I can think of concerning her." Yet surely God will be angered at such a wretch.

Other traducers there be, which loving ladies and failing to overcome their virtue and get aught out of them, do of sheer despite proclaim them public wantons. Nay! they will do yet worse, saying openly they have had their will of them, but having known them and found them too exceeding lustful, have for this cause left them. Myself have known many gentlemen of this complexion at our French Kings' Courts. Then again there is the case of women quitting right out their pretty lovers and bed favourites, but who presently, following the dictates of their fickleness and inconstancy, grow sick again and enamoured of others in their stead; whereupon these same lovers, in despite and despair, do malign and traduce these poor women, there is no saying how bitterly, going so far even as to relate detail by detail their naughtinesses and wanton tricks which they have practised together, and to make known their blemishes which they have on their naked bodies, to win the better credence to their tale.

Other men there be which, in despite because ladies do give to others what they refuse to them, do malign them with might and main, and have them watched and spied upon and observed, to the end they may afford the world the greater signs and proofs of their true speaking.

Others again there be, which, fairly stung with jealousy, without other cause than this, do speak ill of those men whom women love the most, and of the very women whom they themselves love fondly until they see their faults fully revealed. And this is one of the chiefest effects of jealousy. Yet are such traducers not so sore to blame as one would at first say they were; for this their fault must be set down to love and jealousy; twin brother and sister of one and the same birth.

Other traducers there be which are so born and bred to backbiting, as that rather than not backbite some one or other, they will speak ill of their own selves. Now, think you 'tis likely ladies' honour will be spared in the mouth of folks of this kidney? Many suchlike have I seen at the Courts of our Kings, which being afeared to speak of men by reason of their sword play, would raise up scandal around the petticoats of poor weak women, which have no other means of reprisal but tears, regrets and empty words. Yet have I known not a few which have come off very ill at this game; for there have been kinsmen, brothers, friends, lovers of theirs, even husbands, which have made many repent of their spite, and eat and swallow down their foul words.

Finally, did I but tell of all the diverse sorts of detractors of ladies, I should never have done.

An opinion I have heard many maintain as to love is this: that a love kept secret is good for naught, an if it be not in some degrees manifest,—if not to all, at the least to a man's most privy friends. But an if it cannot be told to all, yet at the least must some show be made thereof, whether by display of favours, wearing of fair ladies' liveries and colours, or acts of knightly prowess, as tiltings at the ring, tourneys, mascarades, fights in the lists, even to fights in good earnest when at the wars.

Verily the content of a man is great at these satisfactions.

For to tell truth, what would it advantage a great Captain to have done a fine and signal exploit of war, if not a word were said and naught known thereof? I ween 'twould be a mortal vexation to him. The like would rightly seem to be the case with lovers which do love nobly,—as some at any rate maintain. And of this opinion was that prince of lovers, M. de Nemours, the paragon of all knighthood; for truly if ever Prince, great Lord or simple gentleman, hath been fortunate in love, 'twas he. He found no pleasure in hiding his successes from his most privy friends, albeit from the general he did keep the same so secret, as that only with much difficulty could folk form a judgment thereanent.

In good sooth, for married ladies is the revealing of such matters highly dangerous. On the other hand for maids and widows, which are to marry, 'tis of no account; for that the cloak and pretext of a future marriage doth cover up all sins.

I once knew a very honourable gentleman at Court, which being lover of a very great lady, and finding himself one day in company of a number of his comrades in discourse as to their mistresses, and agreeing together to reveal the favours received of them to each other, the said gentleman did all through refuse to declare his mistress, and did even feign quite another lady to be his dear, and so threw dust in their eyes,—and this although there was present in the group a great Prince, which did conjure him to tell the truth, having yet some suspicion of the secret intrigue he was engaged in. But neither he nor his companions could draw anything more out of him, al-

though in his inmost heart he did curse his fate an hundred
times over, which had so constrained him not to reveal,
like the rest of them, his success and triumph, ever more
sweet to tell of than defeat.

Another I once knew, and a right gallant gentleman,
by reason of his presumption and overmuch freedom of
speech in proclaiming of his mistress' name, the which he
should have held sacred, as much by signs and tokens as
by actual words, did come parlous near his death in a
murderous attack he but barely escaped from. Yet afterward on another count he did not so escape the assassins'
swords, but did presently die of the hurt they gave him.

Myself was at Court in the time of King Francis II.
when the Comte de Saint-Aignan did wed at Fontainebleau
with young Madame la Bourdaisière.⁷ Next day, the
bridegroom having come into the King's apartment, each
and all of the courtiers present did begin to vent their
japes on him. Amongst others a certain great Lord and
very gallant soldier did ask him how may stages he had
made. The husband replied five. As it fell out, there
was also there present an honourable gentleman, a Secretary, which was then in the very highest favour with a
very great Princess, whose name I will not give, who hereupon declared,—'twas nothing much, considering the fair
road he had travelled and the fine weather he had, for it
was summer-time. The great Lord then said to him,
"Ho! my fine fellow, you 'ld be for having birds enough
to your bag, it seems!"—"And prithee, why not?" retorted the Secretary. "By God! why! I have taken a
round dozen in four and twenty hours on the most fairest
meadow is in all this neighbourhood, or can be anywhere
in all France." Who more astounded than the said Lord,

who did learn by these words a thing he had longwhile suspected? And seeing that himself was deep in love with this same Princess, he was exceeding mortified to think how he had so long hunted in this quarter without ever getting aught, whereas the other had been so lucky in his sport. This the Lord did dissimulate for the moment; but later, after long brooding over his resentment, he had paid him back hot and strong in his own coin but for a certain consideration that I prefer not to mention. Yet did he ever after bear him a secret grudge. Indeed, an if the Secretary had been really well advised, he would never have so boasted of his bag, but would rather have kept the thing very secret, especially in so high and brilliant an adventure, whereof trouble and scandal were exceeding like to arise.

What should we say of a certain gentleman of the great world, which for some displeasure his mistress had done him, was so insolent as that he went and showed her husband the lady's portrait, which she had given him, and which he carried hung at his neck. The husband did exhibit no small astonishment, and thereafter showed him less loving toward his wife, who yet did contrive to gloze over the matter as well as she could.

Still more to blame was a great Lord I wot of, who disgusted at some trick his mistress had played on him, did stake her portrait at dice and lose it to one of his soldiers, for he was in command of a large company of infantry. Hearing thereof, the lady came nigh bursting with vexation, and was exceeding angered. The Queen Mother did presently hear of it, and did reprimand him for what he had done, on the ground that the scorn put on her was far too extreme, so to go and abandon to the chance of

[127]

the dice the portrait of a fair and honourable lady. But the Lord did soon set the matter in a better light, declaring how that in his hazard, he had kept back the parchment inside, and had staked only the box encasing the same, which was of gold and enriched with precious stones. Myself have many a time heard the tale discussed between the lady and the said Lord in right merry wise, and have whiles laughed my fill thereat.

Hereanent will I say one thing: to wit, that there be ladies,—and myself have known sundry such,—which in their loves do prefer to be defied, threatened, and eke bullied; and a man will in this fashion have his way with them better far than by gentle dealings and complacencies. Just as with fortresses, some be taken by sheer force of arms, others by gentler means. Yet will no women endure to be reviled and cried out upon as whores; for such words be more offensive to them than the things they do represent.

Sulla would never forgive the city of Athens, nor refrain from the utter overthrow of the same root and branch, not by reason of the obstinacy of its defence against him, but solely because from the top of the walls thereof the citizens had foully abused his wife Metella and touched her honour to the quick.

In certain quarters, the which I will not name, the soldiery in skirmishes and sieges of fortified places were used, the one side against the other, to cast reproach upon the virtue of two of their sovereign Princesses, going so far as to cry forth one to the other: "Your Princess doth play ninepins fine and well!"—"And yours is downright good at a main too!" By dint of these aspersions and bywords were the said Princesses cause of rousing them to do havoc and commit cruelties more than any other reason whatever, as I have myself seen.

I have heard it related how that the chiefest motive which did most animate the Queen of Hungary to light up those her fierce fires of rage about Picardy and other regions of France was to revenge sundry insolent and foul-mouthed gossips, which were forever telling of her amours, and singing aloud through all the countryside the refrain:

> Au, au Barbanson,
> Et la reine d'Ongrie,

—a coarse song at best, and in its loud-voiced ribaldry smacking strong of vagabond and rustic wit.

4.

ATO could never stomach Cæsar from that day when in the Senate, which was deliberating as to measures against Catiline and his conspiracy, Cæsar being much suspected of being privy to the plot, there was brought in to the latter under the rose a little packet, or more properly speaking a *billet doux*, the which Servilia, Cato's sister, did send for to fix an assignation and meeting place. Cato now no more doubting of the complicity of Cæsar with Catiline, did cry out loud that the Senate should order him to show the communication in question. Thus constrained, Cæsar made the said letter public, wherein the honour of the other's sister was brought into sore scandal and open disrepute. I leave you then to imagine if Cato, for all the fine airs he did affect of hating Cæsar

for the Republic's sake, could ever come to like him, in view of this most compromising incident. Yet was it no fault of Cæsar's, for he was bound to show the letter, and that on risk of his life. And I ween Servilia bare him no special ill-will for this; for in fact and deed they ceased not to carry on still their loving intercourse, whereof sprang Brutus, whose father Cæsar was commonly reputed to have been. If so, he did but ill requite his parent for having given him being.

True it is, ladies in giving of themselves to great men, do run many risks; and if they do win of the same favours, and high privileges and much wealth, yet do they buy all these at a great price.

I have heard tell of a very fair lady, honourable and of a good house, though not of so great an one as a certain great Lord, who was deep in love with her. One day having found the lady in her chamber alone with her women, and seated on her bed, after some converse betwixt them and sundry conceits concerning love, the Lord did proceed to kiss the lady and did by gentle constraint lay her down upon the bed. Anon coming to the main issue, and she enduring that same with quiet, civil firmness, she did say thus to him: " 'Tis a strange thing how you great Lords cannot refrain you from using your authority and privileges upon us your inferiors. At the least, if only silence were as common with you as is freedom of speech, you would be but too desirable and excusable. I do beg you therefore, Sir! to hold secret what you do, and keep mine honour safe."

Such be the words customarily employed by ladies of inferior station to their superiors. "Oh! my Lord," they cry, "think at any rate of mine honour." Others say,

"Ah! my dear Lord, an if you speak of this, I am undone; in Heaven's name safeguard mine honour." Others
again, "Why! my good Lord! if only you do say never a
word and mine honour be safe, I see no great objection,"
as if wishing to imply thereby a man may do what he
please, an if it be in secret. So other folk know naught
about it, they deem themselves in no wise dishonoured.

Ladies of higher rank and more proud station do say
to their gallants, if inferior to themselves: "Be you exceeding careful not to breathe one word of the thing, no
matter how small. Else it is a question of your life; I
will have you thrown in a sack into the water, or assassinated, or hamstrung;" such and suchlike language do
they hold. In fact there is never a lady, of what rank
soever she be, that will endure to be evil spoke of or her
good name discussed however slightly in the Palace or in
men's mouths. Yet are there some others which be so ill-
advised, or desperate, or entirely carried away of love,
as that without men bringing any charge against them,
they do traduce their own selves. Of such sort was, no
long while agone, a very fair and honourable lady, of a
good house, with the which a great Lord did fall deep in
love, and presently enjoying her favours, did give her a
very handsome and precious bracelet. This she was so
ill-advised as to wear commonly on her naked arm above
the elbow. But one day her husband, being to bed with
her, did chance to discover the same; and examining it,
found matter enough therein to cause him to rid him of
her by a violent death. A very foolish and ill-advised
woman truly!

I knew at another time a very great and sovereign
Prince who after keeping true to a mistress, one of the

fairest ladies of the Court, by the space of three years, at the end of that time was obliged to go forth on an expedition for to carry out some conquest. Before starting, he did of a sudden fall deep in love with a very fair and honourable Princess, if ever there was one. Then for to show her he had altogether quitted his former mistress for her sake, and wishing to honour and serve her in every way, without giving a second thought to the memory of his old love, he did give her before leaving all the favours, jewels, rings, portraits, bracelets and other such pretty things which his former mistress had given him. Some of these being seen and noted of her, she came nigh dying of vexation and despite; yet did she not refrain from divulging the matter; for if only she could bring ill repute on her rival, she was ready to suffer the same scandal herself. I do believe, had not the said Princess died some while after, that the Prince, on his coming back from abroad, would surely have married her.

I knew yet another Prince,[1] though not so great an one, which during his first wife's lifetime and during his widowhood, did come to love a very fair and honourable damsel of the great world, to whom he did make, in their courting and love time, most beautiful presents, neck-chains, rings, jewels and many other fine ornaments, and amongst others a very fine and richly framed mirror wherein was set his own portrait. Well! presently this same Prince came to wed a very fair and honourable Princess of the great world, who did make him lose all taste for his first mistress, albeit neither fell aught below the other for beauty. The Princess did then so work upon and strongly urge the Prince her husband, as that he did anon send to

demand back of his former mistress all he had ever given
her of fairest and most rich and rare.

This was a very sore chagrin to the lady; yet was she
of so great and high an heart, albeit she was no Princess,
though of one of the best houses in France, as that she
did send him back all that was most fair and exquisite,
wherein was a beautiful mirror with the picture of the
said Prince. But first, for to decorate the same still better, she did take a pen and ink, and did scrawl inside a
great pair of horns for him right in the mid of the forehead. Then handing the whole to the gentleman, the
Prince's messenger, she spake thuswise to him: "Here,
my friend, take this to your master, and tell him I do
hereby send him back all he ever gave me, and that I have
taken away nor added naught, unless it be something he
hath himself added thereto since. And tell yonder fair
Princess, his wife, which hath worked on him so strongly
to demand back all his presents of me, that if a certain
great Lord (naming him by name, and myself do know
who it was) had done the like by her mother, and had
asked back and taken from her what he had many a time
and oft given her for sleeping with him, by way of love
gifts and amorous presents, she would be as poor in gewgaws and jewels as ever a young maid at Court. Tell
her, that for her own head, the which is now so loaded at
the expense of this same Lord and her mother's belly, she
would then have to go scour the gardens every morning
for to pluck flowers to deck it withal, instead of jewelry.
Well! let her e'en make what show and use she will of
them; I do freely give them up to her." Any which hath
known this fair lady will readily understand she was such
an one as to have said as much; and herself did tell me

[133]

she did, and very free of speech she aye was. Yet could she not fail but feel it sore, whether from husband or wife, to be so ill treated and deceived. And the Princess was blamed of many folk, which said 'twas her own fault, to have so despitefully used and driven her to desperation the poor lady, the which had well earned such presents by the sweat of her body.

This lady, for that she was one of the most beautiful and agreeable women of her time, failed not, notwithstanding she had so sacrificed her virtue to this Prince, to make a good marriage with a very rich man, though not her equal in family. So one day, the twain being come to mutual reproaches as to the honour they had done each the other in marrying, and she making a point of the high estate she was of and yet had married him, he did retort, "Nay! but I have done more for you than you have done for me; for I have dishonoured myself for to recover your honour for you;" meaning to infer by this that, whereas she had lost hers when a girl, he had won it back for her, by taking her to wife.

I have heard tell, and I ween on good authority, how that, after King Francis I. had quitted Madame de Chasteaubriand, his most favourite mistress, to take Madame d'Etampes, Helly by her maiden name, whom the Queen Regent had chosen for one of her Maids of Honour and did bring to the King's notice on his return from Spain to Bordeaux,—and he did take her for his mistress, and left the aforesaid Madame de Chasteaubriand, as they say one nail doth drive out another,—his new mistress Madame d'Etampes, did beg the King to have back from the Chasteaubriand all the best jewels which he had given her. Now this was in no wise for the price or value of the same, for in those days pearls and precious stones had not the vogue they have since gotten, but for liking of the graceful mottoes which had been set, imprinted and engraven thereon, the which the Queen of Navarre, his sister, had made and composed; for she was a past mistress of this art. So King Francis did grant her prayer, and promising he would do this, was as good as his word. To this end he did send one of his gentlemen to her for to demand their return, but she on the instant did feign herself sick and appointed the gentleman to come again in three days' time, when he should have what he craved. Meantime, in her despite, she did send for a goldsmith, and had him melt down all the jewels, without any regard or thought of the dainty devices which were engraven thereon. Then anon, when the messenger was returned, she did give him all the ornaments converted and changed into gold ingots. "Go, carry this," she said, "to the King, and tell him that, as it hath pleased his Majesty to ask back what he did erst so generously give me, I do now return and send back the same in gold ingots. As for the mottoes and devices, these I have so well conned over and imprinted on my mind, and do hold them so dear, as that I could in no wise suffer any other should use or enjoy the same and have delight therein but myself."

When the King had received the whole, ingots and message and all, he made no other remark but only this, "Nay! give her back the whole. What I was for doing, 'twas not for the worth of the gold (for I would have gladly given her twice as much), but for liking of the devices and mottoes; but seeing she hath so destroyed these, I care not for the gold, and do return it her again.

[135]

Herein hath she shown more greatness and boldness of heart than ever I had dreamed could come of a woman." A noble-spirited lady's heart, chagrined so and scorned, is capable of great things.

These Princes which do so recall their presents act much otherwise than did once Madame de Nevers, of the house of Bourbon, daughter of M. de Montpensier. This same was in her day a very prudent, virtuous and beautiful Princess, and held for such both in France and Spain, in which latter country she had been brought up along with Queen Elisabeth of France, being her cup-bearer and giving her to drink; for it must be known this Queen was aye served by her gentlewomen, dames and damsels, and each had her rank and office, the same as we Courtiers in attendance on our Kings. This Princess was married to the Comte d'Eu, eldest son of M. de Nevers, she worthy of him as he was right well worthy of her, being one of the handsomest and most pleasing Princes of his time. For which cause was he much loved and sought after of many fair and noble ladies of the Court, amongst others of one which was both this, and a very adroit and clever woman to boot. Now it befell one day that the Prince did take a ring from off his wife's finger, a very fine one, a diamond worth fifteen hundred or mayhap two thousand crowns, the which the Queen of Spain had given her on her quitting her Court. This ring the Prince, seeing how his mistress did admire it greatly and did show signs of coveting its possession, being very free-handed and generous, did frankly offer her, giving her to understand he had won the same at tennis. Nor did she refuse the gift, but taking it as a great mark of affection, did always wear it on her finger for love of him. And thus Madame de Nevers,

[136]

who did understand from her good husband that he had lost the ring at tennis, or at any rate that it was lying pawned, came presently to see the same on the hand of her rival, whom she was quite well aware was her husband's mistress. Yet was she so wise and prudent and had such command of herself, as that, merely changing colour somewhat and quietly dissembling her chagrin, without any more ado she did turn her head another way, and did breathe never a word of the matter either to her husband or his mistress. Herein was she much to be commended, for that she did show no cross-grained, vixenish temper, nor anger, nor yet expose the younger lady to public scorn, as not a few others I wot of would have done, thus delighting the company and giving them occasion for gossip and scandal-mongering.

Thus we see how necessary is moderation in such matters and how excellent a thing, as also that here no less than elsewhere doth luck and ill-luck prevail. For some ladies there be which cannot take one step aside or make the very smallest stumble in the path of virtue, or taste of love but with the tip of their finger, but lo! they be instantly traduced, exposed and satirized right and left.

Others again there be which do sail full before the wind over the sea and pleasant waters of Venus, and with naked body and wide spread limbs do swim with wide strokes therein, wantoning in its waves, voyaging toward Cyprus and the Temple of Venus there and her gardens, and taking their fill of delight in love; yet deuce a word doth any say about them, no more than if they had never been born. Thus doth fortune favour some and mislike others in matter of scandal-making; myself have seen not a few examples thereof in my day, and some be found still.

[137]

In the time of King Charles was writ a lampoon at
Fontainbleau, most base and scurrilous, wherein the fellow
did spare neither the Royal Princesses nor the very greatest ladies nor any others. And verily, an if the true
author had been known, he would have found himself
in very ill case.

At Blois moreover, whenas the marriage of the Queen
of Navarre was arranged with the King, her husband, was
made yet another, against a very great and noble lady,
and a most scurrilous one, whereof the author was never
discovered. But there were really some very brave and
valiant gentlemen mixed up therein, which however did
carry it off very boldly and made many loud general denials. So many others beside were writ, as that naught
else was seen whether in this reign or in that of King
Henri III.—and above all one most scurrilous one in the
form of a song, and to the tune of a *coranto* which was
then commonly danced at Court, and hence came to be
sung among the pages and lackeys on every note, high and
low.

5.

N the days of our King Henri III. was a yet
worse thing done. A certain gentleman, whom
I have known both by name and person, did
one day make a present to his mistress of a
book of pictures, wherein were shown two and thirty ladies
of high or middling rank about the Court, painted in true
colours, a-bed and sporting with their lovers, who were
likewise represented and that in the most natural way.
Some had two or three lovers, some more, some less; and
these thirty-two ladies did figure forth more than seven

and twenty of the figures or *postures* of Aretino, and all
different. The actors were so well represented and so
naturally, as that they did seem actually to be speaking
and doing. While some were disrobed, other were shown
clad in the very same clothes, and with the same head-
dresses, ornaments and weeds as they were commonly
to be seen wearing. In a word, so cunningly was the book
wrought and painted that naught could be more curious;
and it had cost eight or nine hundred crowns, and was
illuminated throughout.

Now this lady did show it one day and lend it to another, her comrade and bosom friend, which latter was
much a favourite and familiar of a great Lady that was
in the book, and one of the most vividly and vigorously represented there; so seeing how much it concerned herself,
she did give her best attention. Then being curious of all
experience, she was fain to look it over with another, a
great lady, her cousin and chiefest friend, who had begged
her to afford her the enjoyment of the sight, and who was
likewise in the pictures, like the rest.

So the book was examined very curiously and with the
greatest care, leaf by leaf, without passing over a single
one lightly, so that they did spend two good hours of the
afternoon at the task. The fair ladies, far from being
annoyed or angered thereat, did find good cause for
mirth therein, seeing them to admire the pictures mightily,
and gaze at them fixedly.

These two dames were bolder and more valiant and
determined than one I have heard tell of, who one day
looking at this same book with two others of her friends, so
ravished with delight was she and did enter into such an
ecstasy of love and so burning a desire to imitate these

[139]

same luscious pictures, as that she cannot see out of her
eyes till the fourth page, and at the fifth did fall in a
dead faint. A terrible swoon truly! very different to that
of Octavia, sister of Cæsar Augustus, who one day hearing
Virgil recite the three verses he had writ on her dead son
Marcellus (for which she did give him three thousand
crowns for the three alone) did incontinently swoon right
away. That was love indeed, but of how different a
sort!

I have heard tell, in the days when I was at Court, of
a great Prince of the highest rank, old and well stricken
in years, and who ever since the loss of his wife had borne
him very continently in his widowhood, as indeed was but
consistent with his high repute for sanctity of life. At
last he was fain to marry again with a very fair, virtuous
and young Princess. But seeing how for the ten years he
had been a widower he had never so much as touched a
woman, and fearing to have forgot the way of it (as
though it were an art that a man may forget), and to
get a rebuff the first night of his wedlock, and perform
naught of his desire, was anxious to make a previous essay.
So by dint of money he did win over a fair young maid, a
virgin like the wife he was to marry; nay more, 'tis said
he had her chosen to resemble somewhat in features his
future wife. Fortune was so kind to him that he did
prove he had by no means forgot as yet his old skill; and
his essay was so successful that, bold and happy, he did
advance to his wife's fortress, and won good victory and
high repute.

This essay was more successful than that of another
gentleman whose name I have heard, whom his father,
although he was very young and much of a simpleton,

did desire should marry. Well! first of all he was for making an essay, to know if he would be a good mate with his
wife; so for this end, some months aforehand, he did get
him a pretty-faced harlot, whom he made to come every
afternoon to his father's warren, for 'twas summer-time,
where he did frisk and make sport with the damsel in the
freshness of the green trees and a gushing fountain in
such wise that he did perform wonders. Thus encouraged,
he feared no man, but was ready enough to play the like
bold part with his wife. But the worst of it was that when
the marriage night was come, and it was time to go with
his wife, lo! he cannot do a thing. Who so astonished
as the poor youth, and who so ready to cry out upon his
accursed recreant weapon, which had so missed fire in
the new spot where he now was. Finally plucking up his
courage, he said thus to his wife, "My pretty one, I cannot
tell what this doth mean, for every day I have done wonders in the warren," and so recounted over his deeds of
prowess to her. "Let us to sleep now, and my advice is,
to-morrow after dinner I will take you thither, and you
shall see very different sport." This he did, and his wife
found him as good as his word. Hence the saying current at Court, "Ha, ha! an if I had you in my father's
warren, you should see what I would do!" We can only
suppose that the god of gardens, Dan Priapus, and the
fauns and wanton satyrs which haunt the woods, do there
aid good fellows and favour their deeds of prowess.

Yet are not all essays alike, nor do all end favorably.
For in matter of love, I have both seen and heard tell of
not a few good champions which have failed to remember
their lessons and keep their engagements when they came
to the chief task of all. For while some be either too

hot or too cold, in such wise that these humours, of ice or of fire, do take them of a sudden, others be lost in an ecstasy to find so sovran a treat within their arms; others again grow over fearful, others get instantly and totally flaccid and impotent, without the least knowing the reason why, and yet others find themselves actually paralysed. In a word there be so many unexpected accidents which may occur just at the wrong moment, that if I were to tell them all, I should not have done for ages. I can only refer me to many married folk and other amateurs of love, who can say an hundred times more of all this than I. Now such essays be good for the men, but not for the women. Thus I have heard tell of a mother, a lady of quality, who holding very dear an only daughter she had, and having promised the same in marriage to an honourable gentleman, avant que de l'y faire entrer et craignant qu'elle ne pût souffrir ce premier et dur effort, à quoi on disait le gentilhomme être très rude et fort proportionné, elle la fit essayer premièrement par un jeune page qu'elle avait, assez grandet, une douzaine de fois, disant qu'il n'y avait que la première ouverture fâcheuse à faire et que, se faisant un peu douce et petite au commencement, qu'elle endurerait la grande plus aisément; comme il advint, et qu'il y put avoir de l'apparence. Cet essai est encore bien plus honnête et moins scandaleux qu'un qui me fut dit une fois, en Italie, d'un père qui avait marié son fils, qui était encore un jeune sot, avec une fort belle fille à laquelle, tant fat qu'il était, il n'avait rien pu faire ni la première ni la seconde nuit de ses noces; et comme il eut demandé et au fils et à la nore comme ils se trouvaient en mariage et s'ils avaient triomphé, ils répondirent l'un et l'autre: *"Niente.*—A

quoi a-t-il tenu?" demanda à son fils. Il répondit tout
follement qu'il ne savait comment il fallait faire. Sur
quoi il prit son fils par une main et la nore par une autre
et les mena tous deux en une chambre et leur dit: "Or
je vous veux donc montrer comme il faut faire." Et fit
coucher sa nore sur un bout de lit, et lui fait bien élargir
les jambes, et puis dit à son fils: "Or vois comment je
fais," et dit à sa nore: "Ne bougez, non importe, il n'y
a point de mal." Et en mettant son membre bien arboré
dedans, dit: "Avise bien comme je fais et comme je dis,
Dentro fuero, dentro fuero," et répliqua souvent ces deux
mots en s'avançant dedans et reculant, non pourtant tout
dehors. Et ainsi, après ces fréquentes agitations et
paroles, *dentro* et *fuero*, quand ce vint à la consommation,
il se mit à dire brusquement et vite: *Dentro, dentro,
dentro, dentro*, jusqu'à ce qu'il eût fait. Au diable le
mot de *fuero*. Et par ainsi, pensant faire du magister,
il fut tout à plat adultère de sa nore, laquelle, ou qu'elle
fit de la niaise ou, pour mieux dire, de la fine, s'en trouva
très bien pour ce coup, voire pour d'autres que lui donna
le fils et le père et tout, possible pour lui mieux apprendre
sa leçon, laquelle il ne uli voulut pas apprendre à demi
ni à moitié, mais à perfection. Aussi toute leçon ne vaut
rieu autrement.

I have heard many enterprising and successful Love-
laces declare how that they have often seen ladies in
these faints and swoonings, yet always readily coming
to again afterward. Many women, they said, do cry
out: "Alackaday! I am a-dying!"—but 'tis, I ween, a
mighty agreeable sort of death. Others there be which
do turn back their eyes in their head for excess of pleasure, as if about to expire outright, and let themselves

[143]

go absolutely motionless and insensible. Others I have been told do so stiffen and spasmodically contract their nerves, arteries and limbs, as that they do bring on cramp; as one lady I have heard speak of, which was so subject thereto she could never be cured.

Anent these same swoonings, I have heard tell of a fair lady, which was being embraced by her lover on top of a large chest or coffer. Very suddenly and unavoidably for herself, she did swoon right off in such wise that she did let herself slide behind the coffer with legs projected in the air, and getting so entangled betwixt the coffer and the tapestry of the wall, that while she was yet struggling to free herself and her cavalier helping her, there entered some company and so surprised her in this forked-radish attitude. These had time enough to see all she had,—which was all very pretty and dainty however, —and all the poor woman could do was to cover herself up as best she might, saying so and so had pushed her, as they were playing, behind the coffer, and declaring how that she would never like the fellow again for it.

Cette dame courut bien plus grande fortune qu'une que j'ai ouï dire, laquelle, alors que son ami la tenait embrassée et investie sur le bord de son lit, quand ce vint sur la douce fin qu'il eut achevé et que par trop il s'étendait, il avait par cas des escarpins neufs qui avaient la semelle glissante, et s'appuyant sur des carreaux plombés dont la chambre était pavée, qui sont fort sujets à faire glisser, il vint à se couler et glisser si bien sans se pouvoir arrêter que, du pourpoint qu'il avait, tout recouvert de clinquant, il en écorcha de telle façon le ventre, la motte le cas et les cuisses de sa maitresse que vous eussiez dit que les griffes d'un chat y avaient passé; ce qui cuisait si fort la dame qu'elle en fit un grand cri et ne s'en put garder ; mais le meilleur fut que la dame, parce que c'était en été et faisait grand chaud, s'était mise en appareil un peu plus lubrique que les autres fois, car elle n'avait que sa chemise bien blanche et un manteau de satin blanc dessus, et les caleçons à part e si bien que le gentilhomme.

The lady told the story to one of her female friends, and the gentleman to one of his comrades. So the thing came to be known, from being again repeated over to others ; for indeed 'twas a right good tale and very meet to provoke mirth.

And no doubt but the ladies, whenas they be alone, among their most privy bosom-friends, do repeat merry tales, everywhit as much as we men-folk do, and tell each other their amorous adventures and all their most secret tricks and turns, and afterward laugh long and loud over the same, making fine fun of their gallants, whenever these be guilty of some silly mistake or commit some ridiculous and foolish action.

Yea! and they do even better than this. For they do filch their lovers the one from the other, and this sometimes not so much for passion's sake, but rather for to draw from them all their secrets, the pretty games and naughty follies they have practised with them. These they do then turn to their own advantage, whether still further to stir their ardour, or by way of revenge, or to get the better one of the other in their privy debates and wranglings when they be met together.

In the days of this same King Henri III. was made that satire without words consisting of the book of pictures I have spoke of above, of sundry ladies in divers postures and connections with their gallants. 'Twas exceeding

[145]

base and scurrilous,—for the which see the above passage wherein I have described the same.

Well! enough said on this matter. I could wish from my heart that not a few evil tongues in this our land of France could be chastened and refrain them from their scandal-making, and comport them more after the Spanish fashion. For no man there durst, on peril of his life, to make so much as the smallest reflection on the honour of ladies of rank and reputation. Nay! so scrupulously are they respected that on meeting them in any place whatsoever, an if the faintest cry is raised of *lugar a las damas*, every man doth lout low and pay them all honour and reverence. Before them is all insolence straitly forbid on pain of death.

Whenas the Empress,[1] wife of the Emperor Charles, made his entry into Toledo, I have heard tell how that the Marquis de Villena, one of the great Lords of Spain, for having threatened an alguasil, which had forcibly hindered him from stepping forward, came nigh being sore punished, because the threat was uttered in presence of the Empress; whereas, had it been merely in the Emperor's, no such great ado would have been made.

The Duc de Feria being in Flanders, and the Queens Eleanor and Marie taking the air abroad, and their Court ladies following after them, it fell out that as he was walking beside them, he did come to words with an other Spanish knight. For this the pair of them came very nigh to losing their lives,—more for having made such a scandal before the Queen and Empress than for any other cause.

The same befell Don Carlos d'Avalos at Madrid, as Queen Isabelle of France was walking through the town;

and had he not sped instantly into a Church which doth there serve as sanctuary for poor unfortunate folk, he had been straightway put to death. The end was he had to fly in disguise, and leave Spain altogether; and was kept in banishment all his life long and confined in the most wretched islet of all Italy, Lipari to wit.

Court jesters even, which have usually full license of free speech, an if they do assail the ladies, do get somewhat to remember. It did so fall out one time to a Fool called Legat, whom I once knew myself. Queen Elizabeth of France once in conversation speaking of the houses at Madrid and Valladolid, how charming and agreeable these were, did declare she wished with all her heart the two places were so near she could e'en touch one with one foot and the other with the other, spreading her legs very wide open as she said the words. The Fool, who heard the remark, cried, "And I should dearly wish to be in betwixt, *con un carrajo de borrico, para encarguar y plantar la raya*,"—that is, "with a fool's cudgel to mark and fix the boundary withal." For this he was soundly whipped in the kitchens. Yet was he well justified in forming such a wish; for truly was she one of the fairest, most agreeable and honourable ladies was ever in all Spain, and well deserving to be desired in this fashion,— only of folk more honourable than he an hundred thousand times.

I ween these fine slanderers and traducers of ladies would dearly love to have and enjoy the same privilege and license the vintagers do possess in the country parts of Naples at vintage time. These be allowed, so long as the vintage dureth, to shout forth any sort of vile word and insult and ribaldry to all that pass that way, coming and going on the roads. Thus will you see them crying and screaming after all wayfarers and vilifying the same, without sparing any, whether great, middling or humble folk, of what estate soever they be. Nor do they spare, —and this is the merry part on't,—the ladies one whit neither, high-born dames or Princesses or any. Indeed in my day I did there hear of not a few fine ladies, and see them too, which would make a pretext to hie them to the fields on purpose, so as they might pass along the roads, and so hearken to this pretty talk and hear a thousand naughty conceits and lusty words. These the peasants would invent and roll off in plenty, casting up at the great ladies their naughtiness and the shameful ways they did use toward their husbands and lovers, going so far as to chide them for their shameful loves and intimacies with their own coachmen, pages, lackeys and apparitors, which were of their train. Going yet further, they would ask them right out for the courtesy of their company, saying they would assault them roundly and satisfy them better than all the others could. All this they would let out in words of a fine, natural frankness and bluntness, without any sort of glossing or disguising. The ladies had their good laugh and pastime out of the thing, and there an end, making their servants which were with them answer back in the like strain and give as good as they got. The vintage once done and over, there is truce of suchlike language till another year, else would they be brought to book and sore punished.

I am told the said custom doth still endure, and that many folk in France would fain have it observed there also at some season of the year or other, to enjoy in security the pleasure of their evil speaking, which they do love so well.

Well! to make an end of the subject, 'tis very meet all ladies be respected of all men, and the secret of their loves and favours duly kept. This is why Pietro Aretino said, that when lovers were come to it, the kisses that man and maid did give each other were not so much for their mutual delight as for to join connection of the mouths together and so make signal betwixt them that they do keep hid the secret of their merry doings. Nay, more! that some lustful and lascivious husbands do in their wantonness show them so free and extravagant in words, as that not content with committing sundry naughty profligacies with their wives, they do declare and publish the same to their boon-companions, and make fine tales out of them. So much so that I have myself known wives which did conceive a mortal repugnance to their husbands for this cause and would even very often refuse them the pleasures they had erst afforded them. They would not have such scandalous things said of them, albeit 'twas but betwixt husband and wife.

M. du Bellay, the poet, in his book of Latin epitaphs called *Les Tombeaux*, which he hath composed, and very fine it is, hath writ one on a dog, that methinks is well worth quoting here, for 'tis writ much in our own manner. It runneth thus:

> Latratu fures excepi, mutus amentes.
> Sic placui domino, sic placui dominæ.

(By my barking I did drive away thieves, with a quiet tongue I did greet lovers. Thus I did please my master, and thus my mistress.)

Well! if we are so to love animals for discreetness, how much more must we not value men for holding silence? And if we are to take advice on this matter of a courtesan which was one of the most celebrated of former days, and a past mistress in her art, to wit Lamia, here it is. Asked wherein a woman did find most satisfaction in her lover, she replied 'twas when he was discreet in talk and secret as to what he did. Above all else she said she did hate a boaster, one that was forever boasting of what he did not do, yet failing to accomplish what he promised,—two faults, each as bad as the other. She was used to say further: that a woman, albeit ready enough to be indiscreet, would never willingly be called harlot, nor published abroad for such. Moreover she said how that she did never make merry at a man's expense, nor any man at hers, nor did any ever miscall her. A fair dame of this sort, so experienced in love's mysteries, may well give lessons to other women.

Well, well! enough said on these points. Another man, more eloquent than I, might have embellished and ennobled the subject better far. To such I do pass on hereby mine arms and pen.

SEVENTH DISCOURSE

Concerning married women, widows and maids,—to wit, which of these same be better than the other to love.

INTRODUCTION

NE day when I was at the Court of Spain at Madrid, and conversing with a very honourable lady, as is the way at Kings' Courts, she did chance to ask me this question following: *Qual era mayor fuego d'amor, el de la biuda, el de la casada, o de la hija moça,*—"which of the three had the greater heat of love, widow, wife or maid?" After myself had told her mine opinion, she did in turn give me hers in some such terms as these: *Lo que me parece d' esta cosa es que, aunque las moças con el hervor de la sangre, se disponen á querer mucho, no deve ser tanto como lo que quieren las casadas y biudas, con la gran experiencia del negocio. Esta razon debe ser natural, como lo seria la del que, por haver nacido ciego de la perfeccion de la luz, no puede cobdiciar de ella con tanto deseo como el que vio, y fue privado de la vista.*—"What I think on the matter is this: that albeit maids, with all that heat of blood that is theirs, be right well disposed to love, yet do they not love so well as wives and widows. This is because of the great experience of the business the latter have, and the obvious fact that supposing a man born blind, and from

[151]

birth robbed of all power of vision, he can never desire
the gift so strongly as he that hath sweetly enjoyed the
same a while and then been deprived thereof." To which
she did presently add this further remark: *Con menos
pena se abstiene d' una cosa la persona que nunca supo,
que aquella que vive enamorada del gusto pasado*—"How
that one could with a lesser ado refrain from a thing
one had never tried, than from one already known and
loved." Such were the reasons this lady did adduce on
this moot point.

Again the respected and learned Boccaccio, among the
questions discussed in his *Filicopo*, doth in the ninth treat
of this same problem: Which of these three, wife, widow
or maid, a man should rather fall in love with, in order
the more happily to carry his desire into effect? The
author doth answer by the mouth of the Queen he doth
there introduce speaking, that although 'tis of course
very ill done and against God and one's own conscience
to covet a married woman, which is in no sense another's,
but subject to her husband, it is natheless far easier to
come to the point with her than ever with maid or widow,
albeit such love is dangerous,—seeing the more a man
doth blow the fire, the more he rouseth it, whereas otherwise it dieth down. Indeed all things do wane in the
using, except only wantonness, which doth rather wax.
But the widow, which hath been long without such exercise, doth scarce feel it at all, and doth take no more
account of love than if she had never been married, and
is more heated by memory of the past than by present
concupiscence. Also the maid, which hath no knowledge
nor experience of what it is, save by imagination, hath
but a lukewarm longing therefor. On the other hand

[152]

the married woman, heated more than the others, doth oft
desire to come to the point and enjoy this pleasure, in
spite of its sometimes bringing on her her husband's sore
displeasure manifested in words and eke blows. For all
this, fain to be revenged on him (for naught is so venge-
ful as a woman), as well as for sake of the thing itself,
doth the wife make him cuckold right out, and enjoy the
desire of her heart. Beside, folk do soon weary of eating ever of the same meat, and for this cause even great
Lords and Ladies do often leave good and delicate viands
for to take others instead. Moreover, with girls, 'tis a
matter of overmuch pains and consumption of time to
tame them and bring them round to the will of men; nay!
an if they *do* love, they know not that they do. But
with widows, the old fire doth readily recover its vigour,
very soon making them desire once more what by reason
of long discontinuance they had forgot the savour of.
Thus they be not slow to come back again to the old
delights, only regretting the time wasted and the weary
nights of widowhood passed all alone and uncomforted
in their cold beds.

In answer to these arguments of the Queen, a certain
gentleman named Faramond doth make reply. Leaving
married women aside altogether, as being so easy to get
the better of without a man's using any great reasoning
to persuade them to it, he doth consider the case of maids
and widows, maintaining the maid to be more steadfast
in love than the widow. For the widow, who hath experienced in the past the secrets of passion, doth never
love steadfastly, but always doubtfully and tentatively,
quickly changing and desiring now one, now another gallant, never knowing to which she should give herself for

[153]

her greater advantage and honour! Nay! sometimes so
vacillating is she in her long deliberations she doth choose
never an one at all, and her amorous passion can find no
steadfast hold whatever. Quite opposite is the maid, he
saith, and all such doubts and hesitations be foreign to
her. Her one desire is to have a lover true, and after
once choosing him well, to give all her soul to him and
please him in all things, deeming it the best honour she
can do him to be true and steadfast in her love. So being
only too ardent for the things which have never yet been
seen, heard or proven of her, she doth long far more than
other women which have had experience of life, to see,
hear and prove all such matters. Thus the keen desire
she hath to see new things doth strongly dominate her
heart; she doth make enquiries of them that know,—
which doth increase her flame yet more. Accordingly she
is very eager to be joined with him she hath made Lord
of her affections, whereas this same ardour is not in the
widow, seeing she hath passed that way already.

Well at the last the Queen in Boccaccio, taking up the
word again and wishing to give a final answer to the question, doth thus conclude: That the widow is more painstaking of the pleasure of love an hundred fold than the
virgin, seeing the latter is all for dearly guarding her
precious virginity and maidenhead. Further, virgins be
naturally timid, and above all in this matter, awkward
and inept to find the sweet artifices and pretty com-
plaisances required under divers circumstances in such
encounters. But this is not so with the widow, who is
already well practised, bold and ready in this art, having
long ago bestowed and given away what the virgin doth
make so much ado about giving. For this cause she hath

no fear of her person being looked at, or her virtue impugned by the discovery of any mark of lapse from honour; and in all respects she doth better know the secret ways for to arrive at her end. Beside all this, the maid doth dread this first assault of her virginity, which in many women is sometimes rather grievous and painful than soft and pleasant, whereas widows have no such fear, but do submit themselves very sweetly and gently, even when the assailant be of the roughest. Now this particular pleasure is quite different from many others, for with them a man is oft satisfied with the first experience and goeth lightly to others, whereas in this the longing to return once more to the same doth ever wax more and more. Accordingly the widow, which doth give least, but giveth it often, is an hundred times more liberal than the maid, when this last doth at length consent to abandon her most precious possession, to the which she doth direct a thousand thoughts and regrets. Wherefore, the Queen doth conclude, 'tis much better for a man to address himself to a widow than to a maid, as being far easier to gain over and corrupt.

ARTICLE I

OF THE LOVE OF MARRIED WOMEN

OW to take and further consider these arguments of Boccaccio, and expand them somewhat, and discuss the same, according to the words I have heard spoke of many honourable gentlefolk, both men and women, on these matters,—as the result of ample knowledge and experience, I declare there can be no doubt that any man wishing quickly to have fruition of love, must address him to married ladies, an if he would avoid great trouble and much consumption of time; for, as Boccaccio saith, the more a fire is stirred, the more ardent doth it grow. And 'tis the married woman which doth grow so hot with her husband, that an if he be lacking in the wherewithal to extinguish the fire he doth give his wife, she must needs borrow of another man, or burn up alive. I did once know myself a lady of good birth, of a great and high family, which did one day tell her lover, and he did repeat the tale to me, how that of her natural disposition she was in no wise keen for this pleasure so much as folk would think (and God wot this is keen enough), and was ready and willing many a time to go without, were it not that her husband stirring her up, while yet he was not strong or capable enough to properly assuage her heat, he did make her so fierce and hot she was bound to resort for succour in this pass to her lover. Nay! very often not

getting satisfaction enough of him even, she would withdraw her alone, to her closet or her bed, and there in secrecy would cure her passion as best she might. Why! she declared, had it not been for very shame, she would have given herself to the first she met in a ballroom, in any alcove, or on the very steps, so tormented was she with this terrible feeling. Herein was she for all the world like the mares on the borders of Andalusia, which getting so hot and not finding their stallions there to leap them and so unable to have satisfaction, do set their natural opening against the wind blowing in these plains, which doth so enter in and assuageth their heat and getteth them with foal. Hence spring those steeds of such fleetness we see from those regions, as though keeping some of the fleetness and natural swiftness of the wind their sire. I ween there be husbands enough would be right glad if their wives could find such a wind as this, to refresh them and assuage their heat, without their having to resort to their lovers and give their poor mates most unbecoming horns for their heads.

Truly a strange idiosyncrasy in a woman, the one I have just adduced,—not to burn, but when stirred of another. Yet need we be in no way astonished thereat, for as said a Spanish lady: *Que quanto mas me quiero sacar de la braza, tanto mas mi marido me abraza en el brazero*,—"The more I am for avoiding the embers, the more my husband doth burn me in my brazier." And truly women may well be kindled that way, seeing how by mere words, by touching and embracing alone, even by alluring looks, they do readily allow themselves to be drawn to it, when they find opportunity, without a thought of the consideration they owe their husbands.

[157]

For, to tell the real truth, what doth most hinder every woman, wife or maid, from taking of this pleasure again and again is the dread they feel of having their belly swell, without eating beans,—an event married ladies do not fear a whit. For an if they do so swell, why! 'tis the poor husband that hath done it all, and getteth all the credit. And as for the laws of honour which do forbid them so to do, why! Boccaccio doth plainly say the most part of women do laugh at these, alleging for reason and justification: that Nature's laws come first, which doth never aught in vain, and hath given them such excellent members to be used and set to work, and not to be left idle and unemployed. Nature neither forbiddeth the proper exercise of these nor imposeth disuse on these parts more than on any other; else would the spiders be building their webs there, as I have said in another place, unless they do find brushes meet to sweep them away withal. Beside, from keeping themselves unexercised do very oft spring sore complaints and even dangers to life, —and above all a choking of the womb, whereof so many women die as 'tis pitiful to see, and these right fair and honourable dames. All this for sake of this plaguey continence, whereof the best remedy, say the doctors, is just carnal connection, and especially with very vigorous and well provided husbands. They say further, at any rate some of our fair ones do, that this law of honour is only for them that love not and have got them no true and honourable lovers, in whom no doubt 'tis unbecoming and blameworthy to go sacrifice to the chastity of their body, as if they were no better than courtesans. But such as truly love, and have gotten them lovers well chosen and good, this law of honour doth in no wise forbid them to help these to assuage the fires that burn them, and give them wherewithal to extinguish the same. This is verily and indeed for women to give life to the suppliant asking it, showing themselves gentle-hearted benefactresses, not savage and cruel tyrants.

This is what Renaldo said, whom I have spoke of in a former discourse, when telling of the poor afflicted Ginevra. As to this, I did once know a very honourable lady and a great one, whom her lover did one day find in her closet, translating that famous stanza of the said Renaldo beginning, *Una donna deve dunque morire,*—"A lady fair was like to die," into French verse, as fair and fairly wrought, as ever I have seen,—for I did see the lines after. On his asking her what she had writ there, she replied: "See, a translation I have just made, which is at once mine own judgment by me delivered, and a sentence pronounced in your favour for to content you in that you desire,—and only the execution doth now remain;" and this last, the reading done, was promptly carried out. A better sentence i'faith than was ever given in the Bailey Court of the Paris Parliament![1] For of all the fine words and excellent arguments wherewith Ariosto hath adorned Renaldo's speech, I do assure you the lady forgat never an one to translate and reproduce them all well and thoroughly, so as the translation was as meet as ever the original to stir the heart. Thus did she let her lover plainly understand she was ready enough to save his life, and not inexorable to his supplication, while he was no less apt to seize his opportunity.

Why then shall a lady, when that Nature hath made her good and full of pity, not use freely the gifts given her, without ingratitude to the giver, and without resistance and contradiction to her laws? This was the view of a fair lady I have heard speak of, which watching her husband one day walking up and down in a great hall, cannot refrain her from turning to her lover and saying, "Just look at our good man pacing there; has not he the true build of a cuckold? Surely I should have gone sore against dame Nature, seeing she had created him and destined him for this, an if I had contradicted her intent and given her the lie!"

I have heard speak of another lady, which did thus complain of her husband, which did treat her ill and was ever jealously spying on her, suspecting she was making him a set of horns: "Nay! he is too good," she would cry to her lover; "he thinks his fire is a match for mine. Why! I do put his out in a turn of the hand, with four or five drops of water. But for mine, which hath a very different depth of furnace, I do need a flood. For we women be of our nature like dropsical folk or a sandy ditch, which the more water they swallow, the more they want."

Another said yet better, how that a woman was like chickens, which do get the pip and die thereof, if they be stinted of water and have not enough to drink. A woman is the same, which doth breed the pip and oft die thereof, if they are not frequently given to drink; only 'tis something else than spring water it must have. Another fair lady was used to say she was like a good garden, which not content with the rain of heaven only, doth ask water of the gardener as well, to be made more fruitful thereby. Another would say she would fain resemble those good economists and excellent managers which do never give out all their property to be guided and a profit

[160]

earned to one agent alone, but do divide it among several hands. One alone could not properly suffice to get good value. After a similar fashion was she for managing herself, to make the best thereof and for herself to reap the highest enjoyment.

I have heard of yet another lady which had a most ill-favoured lover, and a very handsome husband and of a good grace, the lady herself being likewise very well-looking. One of her chiefest lady friends and gossips remonstrating with her and asking why she did not choose a handsomer lover, "Know you not," she said, "that to cultivate well a piece of land more than one labourer is wanted, and as a rule the best-looking and most dainty be not the most meet workers, but the most rustical and hardy?" Another lady I knew, which had a very ill-favoured husband and of a very evil grace, did choose a lover as foul as he; and when one of her friends did ask her the reason why, " 'Tis the better," quoth she, "to accustom me to mine husband's ugliness."

Yet another lady, discoursing one day of love, as well her own as that of other fair ladies her companions, said: "An if women were alway chaste, why! they would never know but one side of life,"—herein basing on the doctrine of the Emperor Heliogabalus, who was used to declare, "that one half of a man's life should be employed in virtues, and the other half in vices; else being always in one condition, either wholly good or wholly bad, one could never judge of the opposite side at all, which yet doth oft serve the better to attemper the first." I have known great personages to approve this maxim, and especially where women were concerned. Again the wife of the Emperor Sigismund, who was called Barba, was used to

[161]

say that to be forever in one and the same condition of chastity was a fool woman's part, and did much reprove her ladies, wives or maids, which did persist in this foolish opinion, and most surely for her own part did very thoroughly repudiate the same. For indeed all her pleasure lay but in feasts, dances, balls and love-makings, and much mockery was for any which did not the like, or which did fast to mortify the flesh, and were for following a quiet life. I leave you to imagine if it went not well at the Court of this Emperor and Empress,—I mean for all such, men and women, as take joy in love's pleasures.

I have heard speak of a very honourable lady and of good repute, which did fairly fall ill of the love which she bare her lover, yet did never consent to risk the matter, because of this same high law of honour so much insisted on and preached up of husbands. But seeing how day by day she was more and more consumed away and burned up, in such wise that in a twinkling she did behold herself wax dry, lean, and languishing, and from being aforetime fresh, plump and in good case, now all changed and altered, as her mirror informed her, she did at length cry: "Nay! how shall it be said of me that in the flower of mine age, and at the prompting of a mere frivolous point of honour and silly scruple making me overmuch keep in my natural fire, I did thus come to dry up and waste away, and grow old and ugly before my time, and lose all the bloom of my beauty, which did erst make me valued and preferred and loved. Instead of a fair lady of good flesh and bone I am become a skeleton, a very anatomy, enough to make folk banish me and jeer at me in any good company, a laughing-stock to all and sundry. No! I will save me from such a fate; I will use the remedies I have in my power." And herewith, what she said, she did, and contenting her own and her love's desires, she soon gat back her flesh again and grew as fair as before,—without her husband's ever suspecting the remedy she had used, but attributing the cure to the doctors, whom he did greatly honour and warmly thank for having so restored his wife to health for his better profit and enjoyment.

I have heard speak of another great lady, one of a merry humour and a pretty wit, to whom, being sick, her physician did one day declare how that she would never be well, unless she changed her habits. Hereupon she answered straight, "Well then! let us do it." So the physician and she did take one with the other joy of heart and body. One day she said to him, "People all declare you do it for me; but there, 'tis all one, as I am so much better. And all ever I can, I will go on doing it,—as mine health doth depend on it."

These two dames last spoke of were quite unlike that honourable lady of Pampeluna in Spain, whom I have already mentioned in a previous passage, and who is described in the *Cent Nouvelles* of the Queen of Navarre. This lady, being madly in love with M. d'Avannes, did think it better to hide her flame, and keep hid in her bosom the passion that was consuming her, and die thereof, than lose her honour. But by what I have heard sundry honourable lords and ladies say in discussing the matter, she was a fool for her pains, and little regardful of her soul's salvation, seeing she did bring about her own death, it being in her power to avoid this extremity, and all for a trifle. For in very fact, as an old French proverb doth put it, "*D'une herbe de pré tondue et d'un c... f...,*

[163]

le dommage est bientôt rendu." And what is it, when all is done? The business, once done, is like any other; what sign is there of it to men's eyes? Doth the lady walk any the less upright? doth the world know aught? I mean of course when 'tis done in secret, with closed doors, and no man by to see. I would much like to know this, if many of the great ladies of mine own acquaintance, for 'tis with such love doth most take up abode (as this same lady of Pampeluna saith, 'tis at high portals that high winds do beat), if these do therefore cease to walk abroad with proudly lifted head, whether at this Court of France or elsewhere, and show them as unabashed as ever a Bradamant or Marfisa of them all. And pray, who would be so presumptuous as to ask them if they condescend to it? Even their husband (I tell you), the most of them at any rate, would never dare to charge them with it, so well do they understand the art of concealment and the keeping of a confident show and carriage. But an if these same husbands, any of them, do think to speak thereof and threaten them, or punish them with harsh words or deeds, why! they be undone; for then, even though before they had planned no ill against them, yet do they straightway plot revenge and give them back as good as they have gotten. For is there not an old proverb which saith, "When and so soon as a husband doth beat his wife, her body doth laugh for joy"? That is to say, it doth presently look for good times, knowing the natural bent of its mistress, who unable to avenge her wrongs by other weapons, will turn it to account as second and best ally, to pay her husband back with her lover's help, no matter what watch and ward the poor man keep over her.

For verily, to attain their end, the most sovran means they have is to make their complaints to one another, or to their women and maids of the chamber, and so win these over to get them new lovers, if they have none, or an if they have, to convey these privily to places of assignation; and 'tis they which do mount guard that neither husband nor any other surprise them at it. Thus then do these ladies gain over their maids and women, bribing them with presents and good promises. In certain cases beside they do make agreement and composition with these, on the terms that of all the lover may give their lady mistress, the servant shall have the half or at least the third part thereof. But the worst is, very often the mistresses do deceive their servants, taking the whole for themselves, making excuse that their lover hath given them no more than so small a share as that they have not enough to spare aught for others. Thus do they hoax these poor wenches and serving maids, albeit they stand sentinel and keep good watch. This is a sore injustice; and I ween, were the case to be tried with proper arguments pleaded on this side and that, 'twould afford occasion for much merriment and shrewd debate. For 'tis verily theft, no less, so to filch their benefices and emoluments duly agreed upon. Other ladies there be however who do keep faithfully their promise and compact, and hold back naught, for to be the better served and loyally helped, herein copying those honest shop-keepers, who do render a just proportion of the gain and profit of the talent their master or partner hath entrusted them withal. And truly such dames do deserve to be right well served, seeing they be duly grateful for the trouble, and good watch and ward of their inferiors. And these last do run many risks and perils,—as one I wot of, who keeping guard one day, the while her mistress was with her lover and having merry times, both the twain being right well occupied, was caught by the husband's house-steward. The man did chide her bitterly for what she was at, saying 'twere more becoming for her had she been with her mistress than to be playing procuress like this and standing sentinel outside her door. 'Twas a foul trick she was playing her mistress' husband, and he would go warn him. However the lady did win him over by means of another of her maids, of whom he was enamoured and who did promise him some favour at her mistress' prayers; beside, she did make him a present, and he was at last appeased. Natheless she did never like him afterward, and kept a shrewd eye on his doings; finally spying an opportunity and taking it on the hop, she did get him dismissed by her husband.

I wot of a fair and honourable lady, which did take a serving maid of hers into great intimacy and high favour and friendship, even allowing her much intimacy, having trained her well for such intercourse. So free was she with her mistress that sometimes when she did see this lady's husband longtime absent from his house, engaged either at Court or on some journey, oft would she gaze at her mistress as she was dressing her, (and she was one of the most beautiful and lovable women of her day), and presently remark: "Ah, me! is he not ill-starred, Madam, that husband of yours, to possess so fair a wife, and yet have to leave her thus all alone so long without ever setting eyes on her? Doth he not deserve you should cuckold him outright? You really ought; and if I were as handsome as you, I should do as much to mine hus-

band, if he tarried so much away." I leave you to judge
if the lady and mistress of this serving maid did find
this a tasty nut to crack, especially finding as she did
shoes all ready to her feet, whereof she did after make
good use, freely employing so handy an instrument.

Again, there be ladies which do make use of their serving maids to help them hide their amours and prevent
their husbands observing aught amiss, and do give them
charge of their lovers, to keep and hold them as their
own suitors, under this pretext to be able at any time to
say, if the husbands do find them in their wives' chambers,
that they be there as paying court to such or such an
one of their maids. So under this cloak hath the lady a
most excellent means of playing her game, and the husband know naught at all about it. I knew a very great
Prince indeed which did set him to pay court to a lady
of the wardrobe to a great Princess, solely to find out the
secret intrigues of her mistress, and so the better gain
success in that quarter.

I have seen plenty of these tricks played in my lifetime,
though not altogether in the fashion followed by a certain
honourable lady of the world I once knew, which was so
fortunate as to be loved of three brave and gallant gentlemen, one after the other. These on quitting her, did
presently after love and serve a very great lady, whereon
she did very pleasantly and good-humouredly deliver herself to this effect. 'Twas she, she said, who had so trained
and fashioned them by her excellent lessons, as that coming now into the service of the said great Princess, they
were exceeding well formed and educated. To rise so high,
she declared, 'twas very needful first to serve smaller folk,
in order not to fail with greater; for to arrive at any su-

preme degree of skill, a man must needs mount first by small and low degrees, as is seen in all arts and sciences.

This did her great honour. Yet more deserving still was another I have heard tell of, which was in the train of a great lady. This lady was married, and being surprised by her husband in her chamber receiving a little paper note or *billet doux* from her lover, was right well succoured by her subordinate. For this last, cleverly intercepting the note, did swallow down the same at one gulp without making any bones about it and without the husband perceiving aught, who would have treated his wife very ill indeed, if he had once seen the inside. This was a very noble piece of service, and one the great lady was always grateful for.

On the other hand I wot well of ladies which have found them in evil case for having overmuch trusted their serving maids, and others again for not having trusted them at all. I have heard speak of a fair and honourable lady, who had taken and chose out a gentleman, one of the bravest, most valiant and well accomplished of all France, to give the same pleasure and delight of herself. She would never trust any one of her women, and assignation being given in a friend's house, it was concerted and arranged there should be but one bed in the chamber, her women all sleeping in the antechamber. As settled, so done. And as there was a cat's-hole in the door, which they had not remembered or provided for till the moment, they bethought them to stop this with a thin board, to the end that if any pushed it down, it would make a rattle, which they would hear and could take measures accordingly. One of her women, suspecting a snake in the grass, and angry and hurt because her mistress had not con-

[168]

fided in her, whom she had ever made her chiefest confidante, and had given many proofs thereof, doth now make
up her mind, so soon as her mistress was to bed, to keep
a look out and listen at the door. She could hear quite
well a low murmuring, yet was sure 'twas not the reading
aloud her mistress had for some days indulged in in bed,
with a candle, the better to dissemble what she was going
to do. Just as she was on the tip-toe of curiosity, to
know more, an excellent occasion did present itself most
opportunely. For a kitten happening to come into the
room, she and her companions take the animal and push
it through the cat's-hole into her mistress' chamber, not
of course without knocking down the board that kept it
closed and making a clatter. At this the pair of lovers,
sore startled, did suddenly sit up in bed, and saw by the
light of their candle 'twas only a cat that had come in and
knocked down the board. Wherefore without troubling
more about it, they laid them down again, seeing 'twas
now late and everybody presumably asleep, but never shut
to again the cat's-hole, leaving the same open for the cat
to go out again by, as they did not care to have it shut
up in their room all night long. Seizing so good an opportunity, the said waiting maid and her companions had
a fine chance to see enough and to spare of their mistress'
doings. These they did after reveal to the husband,
whence came death for the lover, and shame and disgrace
for the lady.

This is what doth come of despite and want of confidence shown folk, which be often just as productive of ill
consequences as over-confidence. I have heard of a very
great nobleman which was moved one time to take all his
wife's waiting-maids (and she was a well-born and very

fair lady), and have them tortured to make them confess all their misdeeds and the services they had rendered her in her amours. However his first intent was carried no further, to avoid too horrible a scandal. The first suggestion came from a lady whose name I will not give, who had a grudge against the said great lady. For the which God did punish her later.

ARTICLE II

OF THE LOVE OF MAIDS

1.

SO now, following the order of Boccaccio, our guide in this discourse, I come next to maids. These, it must certainly be allowed, be of their nature exceeding timid at first beginning, and dare in no wise yield up what they hold so dear, spite of the constant persuasion and advice their fathers, mothers, kinsfolk and mistresses do give them, along with most moving threats. So it is that, though they should have all the good will thereto in the world, yet they do deny themselves all ever they can; beside they have ever before their eyes the terror lest their bodies do play them false and betray them, else would they try many a tasty morsel. Yet all have not this scrupulousness; for shutting their eyes to all reflection, some do rush boldly into it,—not indeed with head down, but rather thrown well back. Herein do they make a sore mistake, seeing how terrible is the scandal of a maid deflowered, and of a thousandfold more import than for married woman or widow. For a maid, this treasure of hers once lost, is made the object of endless scandal and abuse, is pointed at by all men, and doth lose many a good opportunity of marriage. For all this, I have known not a few cases where some rough fellow or other hath been found, either willingly, or of sudden caprice, knowingly or unwittingly, on compulsion, to go throw himself into the breach, and marry them, as I have described elsewhere, all tarnished as they were, but right glad to get them churched after all.

Many such of either sex have I known in my day, and in especial one maid which did most shamefully let herself be got with child by a great Prince, and that without an attempt at hiding or dissembling her condition. On being discovered, all she said was this: "What was I to do? 'tis not my frailty you must blame, nor my lustfulness, but only my over heedlessness and lack of foresight. For an if I had been as clever and knowing as the most part of my companions, which have done just as ill as I, or even worse, but have had wit enough to cure their pregnancy or conceal their lying-in, I should not now be in this strait, nor had any known a word about it." Her companions did for this word wish her mighty ill; and she was accordingly expelled the band by her mistress, albeit 'twas reported this same mistress had ordered her to yield to the wishes of the Prince, wishing to get an hold over him and win him to herself. For all this, however, the girl failed not some while after to make a good match and contract a rich marriage, and presently give birth to a noble offspring. Thus we see, an if the poor child had been as wily as her comrades and other girls, this luck had never been hers. And truly in my day I have seen mere girls as clever and expert in these matters as ever the oldest married woman, nay! going so far as to be most effective and experienced procuresses, and not content with their own satisfaction

[172]

only, to be after contriving the same delights for others
to boot.

'Twas a lady in waiting at the French Court which did
invent and have performed that fine Comedy entitled the
Paradis d'Amour (Paradise of Love) in the Salle de
Bourbon with closed doors, at which performance were
none but actors and actresses present, forming players
and audience both together. Such as do know the story
will know what I mean. The play had six characters,
three male and three female. Of these one was a Prince,
who had his fair one, a great lady, though not too great
neither, yet did he love her dearly; the second was a
Lord, who did intrigue with the great Lady, a lady very
liberal of her favours; the third was a simple gentleman,
who did carry on with the maid, whom he did marry later.
For the gallant authoress was fain to see her own character represented on the stage no less than the rest!
Indeed 'tis ever so with the author of a Comedy; he doth
put himself in the play, or else in the prologue. And so
did this one, and on my faith, girl as she was, did play
the part as well as the married women, if not better.
The fact is she had seen more of the world than just her
own country, and as the Spaniards say *rafinada en
Secobia*,—had had a Segovia polish or fining. This is a
proverb in Spain, Segovia being where the best cloths are
fined.

I have heard tales told of many maids, who while serving their lady mistresses as *Dariolettes*, or confidantes,
have been fain to taste and try the same dainties. Such
ladies moreover be often slaves in their own women's
hands, from dread of their discovering them and publishing abroad their amours, as I have noted above. 'Twas

[178]

a lady in waiting who did one day tell me her opinion,—
that 'twas a mighty piece of folly for maids to sacrifice
their honour to their passions, and while some silly creatures were restrained therefrom by their scruples, for
herself she would not deign to do it, the whole thing
ending in mere shame and disgrace. On the other hand
the trick of keeping one's affair privy and secret made
all right, and girls were mere fools and unfit for this
wicked world which cannot help themselves and manage
the thing quietly.

A Spanish lady, thinking her daughter was afraid of
the violence of the first wedding night, went to her and
began to encourage her and persuade her 'twas naught
at all and she would feel no pain, adding that herself
would be right glad to be in her place the better to show
her how to bear it. To this the girl replied, *Bezo las
manos, señora madre, de tal merced, que bien la tomaré
yo por mi*,—"Much thanks, my lady mother, for your
kind offer, but I will manage very well by myself."

I have heard a merry tale of a girl of very high birth,
who had contrived to afford herself much pleasure in her
life so far, and whom her family now spake of marrying
in Spain. One of her most special and privy friends said
one day to her, by way of jest, how surprised he was to
find that she, which had so dearly loved the *rising* quarter, was now about to travel toward the setting or western, because Spain lies to the westward. To this the
lady made answer, "Truly, I have heard mariners say,
men that have travelled far, how that the navigation of
the rising quarter is right pleasant and agreeable; and
indeed myself have steered many a time thither by the
compass I do alway carry on me. So I will take advan-

tage of this same instrument, when I am in the land of the setting sun, yet to hie away me straight to the rising." Judicious commentators will find it easy enough to interpret the allegory and make a shrewd guess at what I point to. I leave you to judge by these words whether the damsel had invariably limited her reading to the "hours" of Our Lady, and none other.

Another damsel I have heard of, and could give her name, who hearing of the wonders of the city of Venice, its singular beauties and the liberties there enjoyed of all, and especially of harlots and courtesans, did exclaim to one of her bosom friends, "I would to God we had despatched thither all our wealth by letter of credit, and were there arrived ourselves for to lead the gay and happy existence of its courtesans, a life none other can come near, even though we were Empresses of all the whole world!" Truly a good wish and an excellent! And in very deed I opine they that be fain of such a life could hardly dwell in a better spot.

No less do I admire another wish, expressed by a lady of former days. She was questioning a poor slave escaped from the Turks as to the tortures and sufferings these did inflict on him and other unhappy Christian captives, who did tell her enough and to spare of cruelties so inflicted of every sort and kind. Presently she did ask him what they did to women. "Alas and alas! Madam," said he, "they do it to them, and go on doing it, till they die."—"Well! I would to God," she cried, "I might die so, a martyr to the faith."

Three great Ladies, of whom one was a maid, being together one day, as I am told, did begin telling their wishes. One said, "I would fain have an apple-tree that should bear every year as many golden apples as it doth common fruit." The second, "I would have a meadow that should yield me jewels and precious stones as many as it doth flowers." The third, which was a maid, "And I would choose a dovecote, whereof the openings should be worth as much to me as such and such a lady's coop, such and such a great King's favourite, whose name I will not speak; only I should like mine to be visited of more pigeons than is hers."

These dames were of a different complexion from a certain Spanish lady, whose life is writ in the History of Spain, and who, one day when Alfonzo the Great, King of Aragon, made a state entry into Saragossa, threw herself on her knees before his Majesty to ask justice of him. The King signifying his willingness to hear her, she did ask to speak to him in private, and he did grant her this favour. Hereupon she laid a complaint against her husband, for that he would lie with her two and thirty times a month, by day no less than a-nights, in such wise that he gave her never a minute of rest or respite. So the King did send for the husband and learned of him 'twas true, the man deeming he could not be in the wrong seeing it was his own wife; then the King's council being summoned to deliberate on the matter, his Majesty did issue decree and ordered that he should touch her but six times,—not without expressing his much marvel at the exceeding heat and puissance of the fellow, and the extraordinary coldness and continence of the wife, so opposite to the natural bent of other women (so saith the story), which be ever ready to clasp hands and beseech their husbands or other men to give them enough of it, and do make sore complaint an if these do give to others what is their share by rights.

Very different from this last was another lady, a young girl of a good house, who the day after her wedding, recounting over to her companions her adventures in the night just done, "What!" cried she, "and is that all? For all I had heard some of you say, and other women, and men to boot, which do boast them so bold and gallant, and promise such mountains of wondrous deeds, why! o' my faith, friends and comrades mine, the man (meaning her husband), that made himself out so hot a lover and valiant a wight, and so fine a runner at the ring, did run but four all counted,—as it were the regular three for the ring and one for the ladies." We can but suppose, as she made such complaint of scanty measure, she would fain have had a round dozen to her share; but everyone is not like the Spanish gentleman of our last story.

This is how they do make mock of their husbands. So one, who when just wed on her first marriage night, did play the prude and was for obstinately resisting her husband. But he did bethink him to declare that, and if he had to take his big dagger, 'twould be another game altogether, and she would have something to cry out for; whereat the child, fearing the big weapon he did threaten her withal, did yield her instantly to his wishes. But next time, she was no longer afeared, and not content with the little one, did ask at first go off for the big one he had threatened her with the night before. To which the husband replied he had never a big one, and had said so but in jest; so she must e'en be satisfied with what little provision he had about him. Then she cried, "Nay! 'tis very ill done, so to make mock of poor, simple

[177]

maids!" I wot not whether we should call this damsel
simple and ignorant, and not rather knowing and artful,
as having tried the thing before. I do refer the question
to the learned for decision.

Bien plus estait simple une antre fille, laquelle s'estant
plaincte à la justice que un gallant l'ayant prise par
force, et lui enquis sur ce fait, il respondit: "Messieurs,
je m'en rapporte à elle s'il est orai, et si elle i'a pris mon
cas et l'a mis de sa main propre dans lie sien.—Ha! Messieurs, (dit la fille) il est bien orai cela, mais qu'il ne l'enst
fait? Car, amprés qu'il m'ent couchée et trousée, il me
mit sou cas roide et poinctu comme un baston contre la
ventre, et m'en domisit de si grands coups que j'ens peur
qu'il me le percast et m'y fist im trou. Dame! je lui
pris ahers et le mis dans le tron qui estoit tout fait." Si
cette fille estoit simplette, on le contrefaisoit, j m'en
rapporte.

I will now tell a couple of stories of two married
women, of as great a simplicity as the last,—or, if you
prefer it so, of as great artfulness. The first was a very
great lady of mine acquaintance, a very fine woman and
much sought after for this reason. One day a very great
Prince did make offers to her, pressing her right eagerly
and promising her very fine and most advantageous conditions, rank and riches without end for herself and her
husband, so much so that she did hearken at first and
give a willing ear to such seductive temptations. However she would not right off consent, but in her simplicity as a new made wife, knowing naught of the wicked
world, she did come and reveal the whole matter to her
husband, asking his advice whether she should do it or

[178]

no. The husband firing up instantly, cried, "Never, never, by God! little wife; what are you talking about, what would you be at? 'Tis a foul deed, an irreparable stain on both of us!"—"But, Sir," returned the lady, "we shall both be such grand folk, no one will have a word to say against us." In a word the husband did refuse absolutely; but the lady, beginning presently to pluck up a spirit and understand the world, was loath to lose the chance, and did take her fling with the said Prince and others beside, quite forgetting her erstwhile simpleness. I have heard the story told by one which had it of the Prince in question. The lady too had confided it to him; and he had chid her, counselling her that in such affairs one should never consult the husband, who was of necessity a prejudiced party.

Not less simple-minded, or very little, was another young married dame I have heard of, to whom one day an honourable gentleman did proffer his love, at the husband's very elbow, who for the moment was holding discourse with another lady. The suitor did suddenly put *son instrument entre les mains Elle le prit et, le serrant fort étroitement et se tournant vers son mari, lui dit: "Mon mari, voyez le beau présent que me fait ce gentilhomme; le recevraije? dites-le-moi." Le pauvre gentilhomme, étonné, retire à soi son épervier de si grande rudesse que, recontrant une pointe de diamant qu'elle avait au doigt, le lui esserta de telle façon d'un bout à l'autre qu'elle le crut perdre du tout,* and suffered very great pain and even came in danger of his life. He rushed frantically from the room, watering all the place with his gore which flowed in torrents. The husband

[179]

made no ado about running after him to utter any re-
criminations on the matter; all he did was to burst out
a-laughing heartily, at once at the simplicity of his poor
little wife, and because the fellow was so soundly punished.

Well! here is a village story I must needs tell, for
'tis not a bad one. A village wench, as they were leading
her to church on her wedding-day to the sound of tabor
and flute, and with much rustic ceremony, chancing to
catch sight of her girlhood's lover, did shout out these
words to him, "Farewell, Pierre, farewell! I've got . . .
You'll never give it me any more. My mother's married
me now,"—blurting the word right out. Her simplicity
was no less admirable than the soft regret she showed
for past days.

One more, as we are on village tales. A pretty young
girl took a load of wood to sell at the market town.
Asked how much, she kept continually raising her price
at each offer made her by the dealers. "You shall have
so much," they cried, "and something else into the bargain."—" 'Tis well said," she cried, "and thank you!
you're the very man."

Right simple-minded wenches these, and very different,
they and their like, (for there be plenty such), from a
whole host of others in this wicked world, which be far
more double-dealing and knowing than these, never asking
counsel of their husbands nor never showing them such
presents as they may get.

I heard an anecdote once in Spain of a young girl who
the first night after her marriage, as her husband was
struggling and sweating sore and hurting himself in his
attempts, did set up a laugh and tell him, *Señor, bien es*

razon que seays martyr, pues que io soy virgen; mas pues que io tomo la paciencia, bien la podeys tomar,—"Sir, 'tis but right you should be a martyr, since I am a virgin; but as I am so patient, you must be patient too." Thus in revenge of his making fun of his wife, did she make fine fun of him. And in good sooth many a girl hath good cause to make mock at such a time, especially when they have learned afore what it all is, or have been informed of others, or have themselves dreamed and pictured out this mighty moment of delight, which they do suppose so great and lasting.

Another Spanish bride, telling over next morning her husband's merits, found several to praise, "only" she added, "*que no era buen contador aritmetico, porque no sabia multiplicar,*—that he was not a good arithmetician at all, for he couldn't multiply."

Another young maid of good birth and family (one myself have known and talked with), on her wedding night, when all the company were listening outside the door according to custom, and the husband had just given her the first embrace, and as he did rest a while, though not yet asleep, asked her if she would like some more of the same, "An if it please you, Sir!" she said. Imagine the gallant bridegroom's astonishment at such an answer, and how he must have rubbed his ears.

Maids which do say such tricky things so readily and so soon after marriage, may well rouse strange suspicions in their poor husbands' breasts, and lead them to suppose they be not the first that have dropped anchor in their bay, nor will be the last so to do. For we cannot doubt, an if a man do not strive hard and nigh kill himself to work well his wife, she will soon bethink her of giving

[181]

him a pair of pretty horns, or as an old French proverb put it,

> Et qui ne la contente pas,
> Va ailleurs chercher son repas.

Yet when a woman doth get all ever she can out of a man, she doth knock him clean over, just doing him to death. 'Tis an old saying: A woman should not take of a lover all she would have, but must spare him what she can; not so with an husband, him she should drain to the very bones. And this is why, as the Spanish saw hath it, *que el primero pensamiento de la muger, luego que es casada, es de embiudarse.*—"A married woman's first thought is to contrive to make herself a widow." This saying is not universally true, as I do hope to show in another place; it doth only apply to some women, and not all.

Some girls there be which, when no longer able to restrain themselves, be ready to give themselves only to Princes and great Lords, folk very meet to stir their passion, both by reason of their gracious condescension and the fine presents they make, as well as for love of their good looks and pretty ways, for indeed all is fine and point-device, though they may be silly coxcombs and no more, as myself have seen some. Other girls again do not seek after such at all, but do rather avoid them all they can, because they have something of a repute for being scandal-mongers, great boasters, indiscreet and garrulous. They do prefer instead simple gentlemen of prudent and discreet complexion, but alas! the number of such is very small. Happy she who doth meet with such an one! To avoid all these inconveniences, girls do

[182]

choose, (at least some do) their men-servants, some being handsome men, some not,—and I have myself known ladies which have acted so. Nor doth it take much urgency to persuade the fellows; for putting them to bed and getting them up as they do, undressing them, putting their foot-gear on and off, and even changing their shifts, —and I have seen many young girls at Court and elsewhere which did make no sort of difficulty or scruple about all this,—seeing so many pretty sights as they must, they cannot but feel temptation. And I ween some of their mistresses do of set purpose let them see their charms freely. The end can only be that, when the eyes have done their office, other senses be presently called in to execute theirs.

I knew once a fair damsel of the great world, a beauty if ever there was one, which did make her man-servant share her with a great Prince, who kept her as his mistress and supposed he was the only happy possessor of her favours. But herein the valet marched step by step with him; and indeed she had made no ill choice, so handsome a man was he and of so fine a figure; indeed, no difference was to be noted. In fact the valet did have the advantage of the Prince in many beauties of person; and the latter knew never a word about the intimacy till he finally quitted the lady on his marriage. Nor did he for this treat the man any the worse, but was always glad to see him; and whenever he caught sight of him in passing, he would merely cry, "Is it possible now this fellow was my rival? Well, well! I can quite believe it, for barring my rank, he hath the better of me otherwise." He bore the same name as the Prince, and was a most excellent tailor, one of the most famous at Court. There was hardly a woman there, single or married, but he did dress them, when they were for exquisite costumes. I cannot tell whether he was used to dress them in the same fashion he dressed his mistress, but they were invariably well put on.

I knew once a young girl of a good house, which had a boy lackey of only fourteen, whom she had made her fool and plaything. Amid their plays and foolings, she did make no kind of difficulty whatever to let him kiss her, as privily as it had been only a woman,—and this very often before company, excusing it all by saying he was her pretty fool and little playmate. I wot not whether he went further, but I do know that afterward, as wife and widow, and wife once more, she was ever a most notable whore. Remember how she did kindle her match at this first fire, so that she did never after lack flame in any of her later and greater passions and escapades. I had tarried a good year before I saw this lady; but when I did behold her at home and with her mother, who had the repute of being one of the most accomplished of sham prudes of her day, laughing and making light of the whole thing, I did foresee in a moment how this little game would lead to a more serious one, and one played in downright earnest, and that the damsel would one day grow a very glutton at it, as was afterward the case.

I knew two sisters of a very good old family in Poitou, and both unmarried, of whom strange tales were told, and particularly with regard to a tall Basque footman of their father's. This fellow, under pretext of his fine dancing, (for he could dance not only his native *brawls*, but all the other dances as well), would commonly take

them out to dance and teach them the steps and be partner to them. Later he did teach them the harlot's reel,
and they gat themselves finely talked about. Still they
found no difficulty in getting husbands, for they were
very wealthy folk; and this word wealth covereth up all
defects, so as men will pick up anything, no matter how
hot and scalding. I knew the said Basque afterward as a
good soldier and brave man, and one that showed he had
had some training. He was dismissed his place, to avoid
scandal, and became a soldier in the Guard in M. d'Estrozze's regiment.

I knew likewise another great house, and a noble, the
lady mistress whereof did devote herself to bringing up
young maids of birth in her household, amongst others
sundry kinswomen of her husband's. Now the lady being
very sickly and a slave to doctors and apothecaries, there
was always plenty of these to be found thereabouts.
Moreover young girls be subject to frequent sicknesses,
such as pallors, anæmia, fevers and the like, and it so
happened two of them fell ill of a quartan ague, and
were put under the charge of an apothecary to cure them.
And he did dose them well with his usual drugs and medicines; but the best of all his remedies was this, that he
did sleep with one of them,—the presumptuous villain, for
he had to do with as fair and honourable a maid as any
in France, and one a great King had been well content
to enjoy; yet must Master Apothecary have his will of
her.

Myself knew the damsel, who did certainly deserve a
better lover. She was married later, and given out for
virgin,—and virgin she was found to be. Herein did she
show her cunning to some purpose; for *car, puisqu'elle*

*ne pouvait tenir son eau, elle s'adressa à celui qui donnait
les antidotes pour engarder d'engrosser, car c'est ce que
les filles craignent le plus: dont en cela il y en a de si
experts qui leur donnent des drogues qui les engardent
très bien d'engrosser; ou bien, si elles engrossent, leur font
écouler leur grossesse so subtilement et si sagement que
jamais on ne s'en aperçoit, et n'en sent-on rien que le vent.*

*Ainsi que j'en ai ouï parler d'une fille, laquelle avait
été autrefois nourrie fille de la feue reine de Navarre
Marguerite. Elle vint par cas fortunt, ou à engrosser
sans qu'elle y pensât pourtant. Elle rencontra un rusé
apothicaire, qui, lui ayant donné un breuvage, lui fit
évader son fruit, qui avait déjà six mois, pièce par pièce,
morceau par morceau, si aisément, qu'étant en ses affaires
jamais elle n'en sentit ni mal ni douleur; et puis après
se maria galamment, sans que le mari y connut aucune
trace; car on leur donne des remèdes pour se faire par-
aître vierges et pucelles comme auparavant, ainsi que
j'en ai allégué un au* Discoups des Cocus. *Et un que
j'en ouï dire à un empirique ces jours passés, qu'il faut
avoir des sangsues et les mettre à la nature, et faire par
là tirer et sucer le sang: lesquelles sangsues, en suçant,
laisent et engendrent de petites ampoules et fistules
pleines de sang; si bien que le galant mari, qui vient le
soir des noces les assaillir, leur crève ces ampoules d'où
le sang sort, et lui et elle s'ensanglantent, qui est une
grande joie à l'un et à l'autre; et par ainsi, l'honor della
citella è salva. Je trouve ce remède plus souverain que
l'autre, s'il est vrai; et s'ils ne sont bons tous deux, il
y en a cent autres qui sont meilleurs, ainsi que le savent
très bien ordonner, inventer et appliquer ces messieurs les
médecins savants et experts apothicaires. Violà pour-*

quoi ces messieurs ont ordinairement de très belles et bonnes fortunes, car ils savent blesser et remédier, ainsi qui fit la lance de Pélias.

Myself knew the Apothecary I spake of but now, as to whom I will add only one word more in passing,—how I saw him at Geneva the first time I did visit Italy, for at that time the common road for French travellers thither was by Switzerland and the Grisons, because of the wars then raging. He came to see me at my lodging. Of a sudden I did ask him what he was doing in that town, and whether he was there to medicine pretty girls, the same as he had done in France. He answered me he was there to repent of such misdoings. "What!" said I, "you have not such dainty bits to taste here as you had there?"—"Ah! Sir," he replied, "'tis because God hath called me, and I am enlightened of his spirit, and I have now knowledge of his Holy Word."—"Yes! yes!" I went on, "in those days too you were a pious Protestant, and did combine medicine for the body and for the soul, preaching to the girls and giving them some fine instruction."—"But, my dear Sir, I do know my God better these days," he returned again, "than then, and would fain sin no more." I need not repeat much other discourse we had on this subject, both seriously and in jest; but the impudent scamp did certainly enjoy that pretty bit of flesh, more meet for some gallant gentleman than for such as he. It was as well for him he did quit that house pretty smartly; else had he fared ill. However, enough of this. Cursed be the fellow, for the hate and envy I do bear him,—as did M. de Ronsard to a physician which was used to come night and morning rather to see the poet's mistress, and feel her breasts and bosom and

[187]

rounded arm, than to medicine her for the fever she had. He writ a very charming sonnet on the subject; 'tis in the second book of his *Amours*, and begins thus:

Hé que je porte et de hayne et d'envie
Au médecin qui vient et matin,
Sans nul propos, tastonner le tétin,
Le sein, le ventre et les flancs de ma mye.

I do bear a like fierce jealousy against a physician which did similarly toward a fair and noble lady I was enamoured of, and from whom I never gat any such privileges and familiarities, though I had loved them better than the winning of a little kingdom. These gentry are for sure exceeding agreeable to dames and damsels, and do have fine adventures with them, an if they seek after such. I have known two physicians at Court, one M. Castellan, physician to the Queen Mother, the other the Seigneur Cabrian, physician to M. de Nevers, and who had held the same office with Ferdinand de Gonzague. Both have enjoyed successes with women, by all one hears, that the greatest noblemen at Court would have sold their souls to the devil for to have gone shares with them.

We were discoursing one day, the late Baron de Vitaux and myself, with M. Le Grand, a famous physician of Paris, a man of agreeable manners and excellent counsel, he having come to visit the said Baron, who was ill of some amorous indiscretion. Both of us questioning him on sundry little ways and peculiarities of the ladies, he did entertain us finely, and told us a round dozen of tales that did verily take the prize. So engrossed did he grow

[188]

herewith, that, nine o'clock striking, he cried, getting up
from the chair where he was seated: "Truly, I am a greater
simpleton than you two, which have kept me here two
good hours chattering with you rascals, and all the while
I have been forgetting six or seven sick folk I am bound
to go visit." So with a word of farewell, he doth hie him
away, though not without a further last word in reply
to us, when we called after him: "Rascal yourself, Doctor! Oh! you doctors know some fine things and do 'em
too, and you especially, for you talk like a past master
of the art." He answered us, looking down, "True
enough, true enough! we both know and do some fine
doings, for we do possess sundry secrets not open to all
the world. But I'm an old man now, and have bid a long
farewell to Venus and her boy. Nowadays I leave all this
to you younger rascals."

2.

E read in the life of St. Louis, in the History of
Paulus Aemilius, of a certain Marguerite,
Countess of Flanders, sister of Jeanne, daughter of Baldwin I., Emperor of the Greeks, and
his successor, seeing she had no children,—so says History.
She was given in her early girlhood a teacher named Guillaume, a man esteemed of an holy life and who had already
taken minor orders. Yet did this in no wise hinder him to
get two children of his fair pupil, which were christened
Baldwin and John, and all so privily as that few folk knew
aught of the matter. The two boys were later declared
legitimate by the Pope. What fine teaching, and what a
teacher! So much for History.

[189]

I knew a great Lady at Court which had the repute of being over familiar with her reader and teacher,—so much so indeed that one day Chicot, the King's jester, did openly reproach her therewith in presence of his Majesty and many other personages of the Court, asking her if she were not ashamed to have herself loved (saying the word right out) of so ugly and base a loon as yonder fellow, and if she had not wit to choose a better man. The company hereon began to laugh uproariously and the lady to weep, supposing that the King had abetted the game; for strokes of the sort were quite in character with his usual play. Other very great ladies and high Princesses I have known, which every day would amuse themselves with making their Secretaries, whom I have likewise known, write, or rather pretend to write, and have fine games. Or if they did not call for them to write, having naught to say, then would they make them read aloud, for to give a better colour to the whole thing, declaring how reading themselves did weaken their sight.

Great ladies which do make choice of suchlike paramours be quite inexcusable and most blameworthy, seeing they have their liberty of action, and full freedom and opportunity to choose whom they will. But poor girls which be abject slaves of father and mother, kinsfolk and guardians and mistresses, and timid to boot, are constrained to pick up any stone they can find for their purpose, never thinking whether it be cold or hot, roast or boiled. And so, according as occasion offer, they do generally resort to their men-servants, to their school-master and teacher, to fellows of the artist craft, lute-players, fiddlers, dancing masters, painters, in a word their different instructors in knowledge and accomplishments, and even sometimes preachers of religion and holy monks, as Boccaccio doth describe and the Queen of Navarre in her *Nouvelles*. The like is done by pages, as myself have noted, lackeys, and especially stage-players, with whom I have known two maids of honour desperately in love and not scrupling to indulge the same. Poets too I have known in some cases to have debauched fair maids, wives and widows.

These do fondly love to be praised and worshipped, and with this bait are caught, as indeed by almost any they do find convenient and can attract to them. Lawyers again be very dangerous folk in these matters.

Now note why 'tis Boccaccio and other writers with him do find maids to be more constant in love and more steadfast than wives or widows. 'Tis because they do resemble persons afloat on a river in a sinking boat. They that cannot swim at all do spring at the first branches they can catch hold of, and do grasp these firmly and obstinately till they see help arrive. Others that can swim, do leap into the water and strike out boldly till they have reached the bank. Even so young maids, whenas they have gotten a lover, do hold and keep him steadfastly, the one they have first chose, and will in no wise let him go, but love him steadfastly. This cometh of the dread that, having no free choice and proper opportunity, they may not be able, an if they lose him, to get another such as they would wish. Whereas married women and widows, which do know the wiles of love and are well experienced, and have full liberty and all convenience to swim in all waters without danger, may choose what mate they please; and if they weary of one

[191]

lover or lose him, why! they can straight get another, or even take two. For with them 'tis ever a case of "one lost, two got back."

Beside, young girls have not the means, the money and crown-pieces, to win them new lovers every day; for all ever they can give their lovers is some small gift of a lock of hair, a little seed pearl or so, a bracelet, a small ring or a scarf, or other insignificant presents that cost almost naught. For high-born as a girl may be (I have seen it myself), and no matter of how great an house and how rich an heiress, she is kept so short of money, by father, mother, kinsfolk or guardians, as the case may be, that she simply hath not the means to give much to her lover, nor scarce ever to untie her purse widely,— unless it be her purse in front. Besides, girls be of them- selves miserly, if for no other reason, yet because they be forced to it, having scarce any means of extravagance; for generosity in giving doth rest and depend above all on the ability to gratify it. On the contrary wives and widows can dispose of their wealth very freely, when they have any; and above all, when they have fancied a man, and be taken with passion and caprice for him, there is naught they will not sell and give away to the very shift on their back, rather than not have enjoyment of him. Herein they are just like gluttons and folk that be slaves of their mouths, who taking a fancy to a tid-bit, must have the same, no matter what it cost them at the market. Poor maids be in quite other case; whatsoever they can get, be it good or bad, this must they stop and buy.

I could bring forward a whole host of their intrigues, and their divers appetites and curious preferences. But I should never get me done at that rate; beside what would such tales be worth, unless the subjects were given by name and surname. But this is a thing I will not do at any price, for I desire to bring shame on no woman; and I have made profession to avoid in this my book all evil-speaking whatsoever, so that none may have aught to reproach me with on the score of scandal-mongering. However to tell my tales, suppressing the names, in this can be no harm. I do leave my readers to guess the persons intended; and many a time they will suppose it to be one, though all the while 'tis quite another.

3.

OW just as we do see different sorts of wood of such different nature, that some will burn when quite green, as the ash and the beech, but others, be they as dry, old and well seasoned as you please, for instance the elm, the alder and others, do burn only as slowly and tediously as possible, while many others, following the general nature of all dry and old wood, do blaze up in their dryness and oldness so rapidly and suddenly 'tis rather a destroying and instant reducing to ashes than burning proper, so is the like true of women, whether maids, wives or widows. Some, so soon as ever they be come to the first greenness of their age, do burn so easily and well, you would say from their very mother's womb they do draw thence an amorousness; as did the fair Laïs from her fair mother Tymandra, that most famous harlot, and an hundred thousand others which herein do take after the good whores their mothers. Nay! sometimes they do not so much as wait for the age of maturity, that may be put

at twelve or thirteen, to begin loving, but are at it
sooner yet. This happened not twelve years agone at
Paris to a pastry-cook's child, which was discovered to
be pregnant at nine years of age.[1] The girl being very
sick with her pregnancy, and her father having taken a
specimen of her urine to a physician, the latter said at
once she had no other sickness but only that she was
with child. "What!" cried the father; "Why, Sir! my
daughter is only nine years old." Who so astonished as
the doctor? " 'Tis all one," said he; "of a surety, she
is with child." And after examining her more closely,
he did indeed find her so. The child afterward confessing
with whom she had had to do, her gallant was condemned
to death by the judges, for having gone with her at so
very tender an age. I much regret I have come to give
this example and mention the thing here, seeing I had
made up my mind not to sully my paper with suchlike
mean folk, but to deal only with great and well-born
persons.

Herein I have somewhat gone wide of my purpose, but
the story being so rare and uncommon, I must e'en be
excused.

This doth remind me of a tale of a brave and gallant
Lord if ever there was one, since dead, which was one day
making complaint of the amplitude of women's affairs
with whom he had had to do, as well maids as married
ladies. He declared 'twould come to his having to look
for mere children, just come from the cradle so to speak,
so as not to find so wide a space of open sea as he had done
with the rest, but get better pleasure by swimming in a
narrow strait. An if he had addressed these words to a
certain great and honourable dame I do know, she would

have made him the same answer she did to another gentleman of the great world, to whom, on his making a like
complaint, she did retort thus: "I wot not which hath
better cause of complaint, you men of our width and over
amplitude, or we women of your tenuity and over small-
ness, or rather your tiny, tiny littleness; truly we have
as much to lament in you as ever you in us."

The lady was right enough in what she said. Similarly
another great lady, one day at Court looking curiously
at the great bronze Hercules in the fountain at Fontainebleau, as she was a-walking with an honourable gentleman
which did escort her, his hand beneath her arm, did complain that the said Hercules, albeit excellently well
wrought and figured otherwise, was not so well proportioned in all his members as should be, forasmuch as his
middle parts were far too small and out of proper measure, in no wise corresponding to his huge colossus of a
body. The gentleman replied he did not agree with what
she said, for 'twas to be supposed that in those days
ladies were not so wide as at the present.

A very great lady and noble Princess[2] learning how
that certain folk had given her name to a huge great cul-
verin, did ask the reason why. Whereupon one present
answered: " 'Tis for this, Madam, because it hath a calibre
greater and wider than all the rest."

*Si est-ce pourtant qu'elles y ont trouvé assez de remède,
et en trouvent tous les jours assez pour rendre leurs portes
plus étroites, carrées et plus malaisées d'entrée; dont au-
cunes en usent, et d'autres non; mais nonobstant, quand
le chemin y est bien battu et frayé souvent par continu-
elle habitation et fréquentation, ou passages d'enfants,
les ouvertures de plusieurs en sont toujours plus grandes*

*et plus larges. Je me suis là un peu perdu et dévoyé;
mais puisque ç'a été à propos il n'y a point de mal, et je
retourne à mon chemin.*

Many other young girls there be which let safely pass
this early, tender, sappy time of life, waiting a greater
maturity and dryness, whether because they be naturally
cold at first beginning and start, or that they be kept
close guarded, as is very needful with some. Others there
be so steadfast, the winds and tempests of winter would
avail naught to shake or stir them. Others again be so
foolish and simple-minded, so raw and ignorant, as that
they would not so much as hear the name of love. So
have I heard of a woman which did affect the virtuous
prude, that an if she did hear the word harlot mentioned,
she would instantly faint. A friend telling this story to
a certain great Lord in presence of his wife, the latter did
exclaim: "She'd better not come here, that woman; for
if she doth faint to hear speak of whores, she'll die right
out to see one."

On the other hand there be some girls which from the
first moment they begin to feel they have a heart, grow
so tame they will eat from the hand at once. Others be
so devout and scrupulous, fearing so sore the commandments of the Lord our God, that they do quite neglect that
of love. Yet have I seen many of these same devout pat-
terers of prayers, these women that be forever a-kissing
of images and all but living in churches, which did under
this hypocritical veil cover and conceal the fire of their
passions, to the end that by such false and feigned semblance the world might perceive never a trace of them,
but deem them perfect prudes, or even half way to being
saints like St. Catherine of Sienna, by the which profes-

[196]

sions they have often succeeded in deceiving all mankind. Thus have I heard it related of a very great Princess, a Queen indeed, now dead, who when she was fain to make love to any man, (for she was exceeding given that way), would invariably begin her conversation with the love we do owe to God, and then suddenly bring it round to carnal love, and what she did want of her interlocutor, whereof she did before long come to the practice or quintessential part. This is how these devotees, or bigots rather, do cajole us men; such of us that is as be not well versed in wiles of the sort and know not life.

I have heard a tale, though I wot not if it be true. Anyway of late years, on occasion of a general procession at a certain city, was seen a woman, well born or not, barefooted and in great contrition, playing the penitent with might and main,—and it was in Lent. Straight from there she hied her away to dine with her lover on a quarter of kid and a ham. The savour did penetrate to the street, and going up to her chamber, folk found her in the midst of this glorious feast. She was arrested and condemned to be led through the town with the joint on a spit over her shoulder and the ham hanging at her neck. Was not this a meet and proper punishment?

Other ladies there be so proud and haughty they do scorn heaven and earth in a way of speaking, and utterly snub and reject men and all their offers. But for such all that is need is to wait and have patience and perseverance, for with these and time you do surely subdue them and find them humble enough at last, for 'tis the property of highmindedness and pride, after much swelling and exaltation, presently to come down and bate its lofty claims. And with these same proud dames, I have seen many instances where after scorning love and all that spake to them thereof, they have given in and loved like any others, or have even wedded husbands of mean estate and in no way their equals. Thus doth Love make mock of them and punish them for their hard-heartedness, taking especial delight in attacking them more than other folk, forasmuch as the victory is then a prouder one, as vanquishing pride.

I knew erstwhile a Court damsel, so proud and scornful that when some gallant man of the world would come to address her and speak of love, she would ever answer him so haughtily and with so great contempt, in words so fierce and arrogant (for she had a gift of speech as good as any), that presently they did cease altogether. But an if any did chance now and again still to try and vanquish her pride, 'twas a sight how she would snub them and send them packing with words and looks and scornful gestures; for she was very clever at this game. In the end Love did surprise and sore punish her, for she gave in to one which did get her with child some score of days only before her marriage; yet was this lover in no wise to be compared with many other honourable gentlemen which had aforetime been fain to be her suitors. Herein we can only say with Horace, *sic placet Veneri,* "such is Venus' pleasure,"—for these be miracles.

'Twas my humour once while at Court to be lover to a fair and honorable damsel, accomplished and expert if ever woman was, and of a very good house, but proud and highhanded; and I was very much smit with her indeed. I did make up my mind to court her, but alway to deal with her in the same arrogant spirit she did use in her words and answers to me,—as the proverb saith,

"When Greek meets Greek." Yet did she show no resentment for all this, for indeed, all the while I was treating her so cavalierly, I was used to praise her exceedingly, seeing there is naught doth more soften a woman's heart than commendation whether of her beauty and charms or of her proud spirit, even declaring how that her port did much become her, forasmuch as she kept her from all common familiarity, and that any woman, damsel or dame, which did make her too common and familiar, not maintaining a haughty port and high repute, was not worthy to be so courted. For all which I did but respect her the more, and would never call her by any other name but *my lady Disdain.* Whereat she was so well pleased she did herself likewise choose to call me always *Master Arrogance.*

So ever continuing, I did court her long and faithfully; and I may boast me I had as large a share of her good graces as any great Lord at Court which did care to court her, or larger. However a chief favourite of the King, a brave and gallant gentleman without a doubt, did take her from me, and by favour of his King did win and marry her. Natheless, so long as she did live, the connection was ever kept up betwixt us, and I have always honoured her well. I know not an if I shall be blamed for having told this tale, for 'tis a common saying that all tales about a man's self be bad. Anyway I have let it out this time; as indeed throughout my book I have related not a few stories of myself in divers relations, though I do generally suppress the name.

Other girls there be again of so merry a complexion and so lighthearted, so devoted to amusement and enjoyment, they never have another thought in their heads

[199]

but to laugh, and make sport and pastime, and never time
to hear or dream of anything else but only their little
amusements. I have known many such which had rather
hear a fiddle play, or dance or leap or run, than hearken
to any love discourse whatsoever; while other some do
so adore the chase they should better be called servants
of Diana than of Venus. I did once know a brave and
valiant Lord, since dead, which fell so deep in love with
a maid, and a great lady to boot, that he was like to die;
"for whenas I am fain," he used to say, "to declare my
passion, she doth answer me never a word but about her
dogs and her hunting. I would to heaven I were meta-
morphosed into a hunting-dog or greyhound, and my
soul entered in their body, according to Pythagoras'
opinion, to the end she might give some heed to my love,
and I be healed of my wound." Yet afterward did he leave
her, for he was not good lackey or huntsman enough to
go everywhere a-following her about, wherever her lusty
humours, her pleasures and amusements might lead her.

Yet must we note one fact. Maids of this sort, after
leaving their chickenhood behind and outgrowing the pip,
(as we say of poultry), having taken their fill of these
childish amusements, do always come, at long last, to essay a woman's pleasures too. Such young girls do resemble little wolf-cubs, which be so pretty, engaging and
playful in their downy youth; yet being come to maturity,
they do ever take to evil courses and ravening and killing. The sort of girls I am speaking of do ever the like,
who after much sport and youthful merriment, after
pleasures of all kinds, hunting, dancing, leaping, skip-
ping and jigging, do always, I ween, indulge at last in
dame Venus' gentle sport. In a word, to put it briefly,

scarce ever a one of the sex is seen, maid, wife or widow, but sooner or later she and all her sisters do burn, in season or out of season,—as do all woods, excepting only one, yclept the *larix*, the which they do in no wise resemble.

Now this Larix is a wood which will never burn, and maketh neither fire, flame nor ash, as Julius Cæsar did find. On his return back from Gaul, he had ordered the inhabitants of Piedmont to furnish him vivers, and establish magazines on his main line of march. He was duly obeyed, except by the garrison of a castle called *Larignum*, whither had withdrawn certain ill-disposed rascals, recusants and rebels, the result being Cæsar had to turn back and besiege the place. Coming nigh the fortress, he saw its defences were only of wood, whereat he did straightway make mock, deeming they would immediately take the same. Wherefore he did give orders at once to collect large plenty of fagots and straw to set fire to the bulwarks, and soon was there so huge a conflagration and mass of flame that all hoped soon to see the ruin and destruction of the fort. But lo! whenas the fire was burned out and the flame disappeared, all were exceeding astonished, for they beheld the stronghold in the same state as before and quite unhurt, neither burned nor ruined one whit. This did compel Cæsar to resort to other means, mining to wit, which did at last bring those within to come to terms and render up the place. From this Cæsar did learn the virtues of this larix-wood, from the which the castle had its name of *Larignum*, because it was built and defended of the same.

I ween there be many fathers, mothers, kinsmen and husbands, that would dearly like their daughters and

[201]

wives should share the properties of this wood, that they should burn fiercely without its leaving mark or effect behind. They would have a far more unruffled mind and not so many suspicions a-buzzing in their heads, nor would there be so many whores on show nor cuckolds before the world. But 'tis not really desirable in any shape or form, for the world would be clean depopulated, and folk would live therein like blocks of stone, without pleasure or satisfaction. So many persons I wot of, of either sex, would say; and indeed Nature would be left imperfect, instead of very perfect as she is. Following her kindly lead as our best captain, we need never fear to lose the right path.

ARTICLE III

1.

ELL! enough said of maids; 'tis but right we now proceed to speak of widows in their turn. The love of widows is good, easy and advantageous, seeing they be in full liberty of action, and in no sense slaves of fathers, mothers, brothers, kinsmen and husbands, nor yet of any legal bar, a still more important point. A man may make love and lie with a widow as much as ever he please, he is liable to no penalty, as he is with maids or married women. In fact the Romans, which people hath given us the most of the laws we have, did never make this act punishable, either in person or property. I have this from a great lawyer, who did cite Papinian for confirmation of the point, that great Roman jurisconsult, who treating of adultery declares: if occasionally under this term adultery hath been inadvertently included lawless intercourse with maid or widow, 'tis a misuse of words. In another passage the same authority saith: the heir hath no right of reproach or concern with the character of the deceased man's widow, except only if the deceased had in his lifetime brought action against his wife on this ground; then could the said heir take up and carry on the prosecution,

[203]

but not otherwise. And as a fact in all the whole of
Roman law is no penalty ordained for the widow, except
only for one that did marry again within the year of her
mourning, or who without re-marrying had borne a child
subsequently to the eleventh month of her first year of
widowhood, this first year being deemed sacred to the
honour of her former husband. There was likewise a law
made by Heliogabalus, that no widow must marry again
for one year after the death of her husband, to the end
she might have due leisure to bewail his loss and deliberate carefully on the choice of a successor. A truly pater-
nal law, and an excellent reason i' faith! As for a widow's
original dowry, the heir could not in any case rob her
thereof, even though she should have given her person
to every possible form of naughtiness. And for this my
authority did allege a very good reason; for the heir
having no other thought but only the property, if once
a door were opened to him to accuse the widow in hope of
making her forfeit this and so rob her of her dowry, she
would be exposed at once to every calumny his malignity
could invent. So there would be never a widow, no matter
how virtuous and unoffending, could safeguard her from
slanderous actions on the part of enterprising heirs.

All this would seem to show, I think, that the Roman
ladies did have good opportunities and occasion for self-
indulgence. No need then to be astonished if one of them,
in the reign of Marcus Aurelius, (as is found writ in that
Emperor's life), as she was walking in her husband's
funeral procession, and in the midst of all her cries, sobs,
sighs, tears and lamentations, did so strictly press the
hand of the gentleman which was her escort, as to surely
signify thereby her willingness for another taste of love

and marriage. Accordingly at the end of a year,—for he could not marry her before, without a special dispensation, as was done for Pompey whenas he did wed Cæsar's daughter, but this was scarce ever given but to the greatest personages,—he did marry the lady, having meantime enjoyed some dainty foretastes, and picked many an early loaf out of the batch, as the saying goes. Mighty fain was this good lady to lose naught by procrastination, but take her measures in good time; yet for all this, she did lose never a doit of her property and original dowry.

Thus fortunate were Roman widows,—as are still in the main their French sisters, which for giving heart and fair body satisfaction, do lose naught of their rights; albeit several cases hereanent have been pleaded before our parliaments. Thus I wot of a great and wealthy French Lord, which did carry on a long process against his sister-in-law concerning her dowry, charging her that her life had been lascivious and with another crime of a less gay sort to boot. Natheless did she win her case; and the brother-in-law was obliged to dower her handsomely and give her all that did belong to her. Yet was the governance of her son and daughter taken from her, seeing she had married again. This the judges and noble councillors of the parliaments do look to, forbidding widows that re-marry to have guardianship of their children. In spite of this I do know of widows which within the last few years have successfully asserted their rights, though re-married, over their daughters being under age, against their brothers-in-law and other kinsmen; but then they were greatly helped by the influence of the Prince which was their protector. Indeed there is never a law a fine *motte* cannot traverse. Of these subjects I do now

[205]

refrain me from speaking more, seeing 'tis not my trade; so thinking to say something mighty clever, 'tis very like I may say what is quite from the point. I do refer me to our great men of the law.

Now of our widows some be alway glad to try marriage once again and run its risks, like mariners that twice, thrice and four times saved from shipwreck do again and again go back to the sea, and as married women do, which in the pains of motherhood do swear and protest they will never, never go back to it again, and no man shall ever be aught to them, yet no sooner be they sound and clean again, but they take to the same old dance once more. So a Spanish lady, being in her pangs, had a candle lighted in honour of Our Lady of Mont-Sarrat, who much succours women in child-birth. Yet did she fail not to have sore pain and swear right earnestly she would never go back to it any more. She was no sooner delivered but turning to her woman who held the candle still alight, she said, *Serra esto cabillo de candela para otra vez*, "Put away that bit of candle for another time."

Other ladies do prefer not to marry; and of these are always some, and always have been, which coming to be widows in the flower of their age, be content to stay so. Ourselves have seen the Queen Mother, which did become a widow at the age of seven or eight and thirty years, and did ever after keep that state; and fair, pleasant and agreeable as she was, did never so much as think of any man to be her second husband. No doubt it may be said on the other side,—Whom could she have wedded suitable to her lofty estate and comparable with the great King Henri, her late lord and master; beside she would thereby have lost the government of the Kingdom, which was

[206]

better worth than an hundred husbands, and its enjoyment more desirable and pleasant? Yet is there no advantage Love doth not make women forget; wherefore she is the more to be commended and worthy to be recorded in the temple of fame and immortality. For she did master and command her passions,—not like another Queen, which unable to restrain herself, did wed her own steward of the household, by name the Sieur de Rabodanges. This the King, her son, did at first beginning find exceeding strange and bitter; but yet, because she was his mother, he did excuse and pardon the said Rabodanges for having married her; and it was arranged that by day, before the world, he should serve her alway as steward, not to deprive her, being the King's mother, of her proper state and dignity, but by night she should make of him what pleased her, using him either as servant or master at her choice, this being left to their own discretion and good pleasure. We may readily imagine who was master then; for every woman, be she as high-born as she may, coming to this point, is ever subject to the superior male, according to the law of nature and humanity in this matter. I have the tale from the late Grand Cardinal de Lorraine, second of the name and title, which did tell it at Poissy to King Francis II., the time he did institute the eighteen knights of the Order of Saint Michael,—a very great number, and one never seen or heard of before then. Among others was the Seigneur de Rabodanges, a very old man, that had not been seen for years at Court, except on occasion of some of our warlike expeditions, he having withdrawn soon after the death of M. de Lautrec out of disappointment and despite, a common enough case, having lost his good master, the Captain of whose Guard he was, on his journey to the Kingdom of Naples, where he died. And the Cardinal did further say he did believe this M. de Rabodanges was descended of the marriage in question.—Some while agone a lady of France did marry her page, so soon as ever his pagehood was expired and he his own master, thinking she had worn her widow's weeds quite long enough.

Well, to leave this sort of widows, and say somewhat of more high-minded and prudent dames.

We have had our Queen of France, Donna Isabelle of Austria, which was wife to the late King Charles IX., whom we may in all ways declare to have been one of the best, gentlest, wisest and most virtuous Queens that ever reigned of all the Kings and Queens that ever were. This I may confidently affirm, and every one that hath ever seen her or heard her speak will say the same, and this without disparaging others and with the most perfect truth. She was a very beautiful Princess, with features and face as fair and delicate as any lady at the Court, and most affable. Her figure too was very fine, albeit she did scarce reach the middle height. She was very sensible and prudent moreover, most virtuous and good-natured, and one that did never hurt or displeasure any, or give offence by so much as the smallest word. And indeed she was very careful of her speech, saying but very little and alway in her native Spanish.

She was truly pious, but no wise bigoted, not overmuch manifesting her religion by outward acts and shows, and an extremeity of devotion, such as I have seen some of our prayer-patterers display, but rather without missing any of the regular hour for supplication to God, she did employ these well and sufficiently, without going out of

her way to borrow other extraordinary ones. 'Tis very
true, as I have heard some of her ladies declare, that
whenas she was to bed apart and hid, and her curtains
close drawn, she would kneel there devoutly in her shift
and make prayer to God by the space of an hour and a
half, beating and tormenting her breast in her zeal of
devotion.

This habit had never been noted at all till after the
death of King Charles her husband. But one night after
she had gone to bed and all her women were retired,
one of those which did sleep in her chamber, hearing her
sighing, did bethink her to peep between the curtains, and
saw her in the posture described, so praying and beseeching God, which practice she did continue well nigh every
evening. At length the said bedchamber-woman, who was
on very familiar terms with her, did venture to remonstrate one day with her on the ground she was hurting
her health. The Queen was angered against the woman
for her discovery and advice, and fain almost to deny the
thing, and did straitly charge her to breathe never a word
about it. Wherefore for that evening she did desist; but
in the night she did fully make up for it, supposing her
women would not observe it. But they saw her, and found
how it was, by the reflexion of her chamber-light of wax,
the which she did keep burning by her bedside next the
wall, for to read in her Book of Hours and pray God
at whiles, using for this pious purpose the same space
where other Queens and Princesses do keep their table of
refection. Suchlike prayers do little resemble those of
hypocrites, which wishing to appear religious before the
world, do make their orisons and devotions publicly, and

[209]

aye with mumbling of the lips, to the end folk may deem them exceeding devout and sanctified.

Thus would our good Queen pray for the soul of the King, her husband, whom she did sorely grieve for, yet all the whole making her moan and lamentation not like a wild and desperate woman, screaming, and tearing her cheeks and hair, nor yet merely counterfeiting one that is commended for her tears, but sorrowing gently, dropping her fair and precious tears so tenderly, sighing so soft and low, as that 'twas plain to see she was restraining her grief all she could, to the end people might not think her desirous of making a fine seeming and grand impression (a thing I have seen many ladies do in such case), yet failing not at all to convince all of the deep anguish of her heart. Even so a torrent is ever more violent whose course is stayed than when it hath free space to run in. I do well remember me how, all through the King's malady, her dear lord and husband, he lying in his bed and she coming to visit him, she would quick sit her down by his side, not close to his bed's-head, as is usual, but a little withdrawn, yet within his sight, where remaining without speaking scarce at all to him, or he to her, she would keep her eyes all the while so fixed upon him, that never taking them from off his face she did verily seem to be warming him in her heart with the heat of all the love she bare him. Presently she might be seen dropping tears so soft and secret, that any which had not chanced to note them, would have never known her grief. There would she sit, drying her wet eyes under pretence of using her handkerchief, that 'twas downright pity to every soul there (I saw the thing myself) to see her so troubled to hide her grief and love, and prevent the King from seeing the signs of her sorrow. Such was ever

her practise in her husband's sickness; whereafter she
would rise and hie her to her prayers for his restoration
to health. She did truly love and honour him exceedingly, albeit she knew him of amorous complexion and that
he had mistresses, whether for his renown or for his
pleasure. But yet was she never a whit less kind, nor ever
said an ill word to him, patiently bearing her little load
of jealousy and the wrong he did her. She was a very
meet and proper mate for him; for 'twas indeed fire
and water come together in one, the King being naturally
quick, hot and stirring, she cool and temperate in all
things.

I have been told on good authority, how that after her
widowhood, among certain of her more privy ladies, which
were for giving her such consolation as they could suggest,
was one (for, as you may suppose, among so great a band
there will alway be one more maladroit than the rest),
which, thinking to please highly, did address her thus:
"At least, Madam, an if instead of a daughter he had but
left you a son, you would at this moment be the King's
Queen Mother, and your dignity by so much increased and
strengthened."—But her answer was: "Alas! alas! say
not such a thing. As if France had not misfortunes
enough already, without my having caused yet another to
be her utter ruin. For had I had a son, this would only
have mean more factions, troubles and seditions for to get
the care and guardianship of the young King during his
infancy and minority. Hence would have sprung more
war and strife than ever, each striving to make his profit
and draw advantage by plundering the poor child, as they
were fain to do to the late King, my husband, and would
have done but for the Queen, his mother, and his good

[211]

servants which did oppose such doings. But an if I had had a son, I should have but found unhappiness in the thought of having borne him, and gotten a thousand maledictions of the people, whose voice is the voice of God. Wherefore I tell you I do praise my God, and am right thankful for the fruit he hath vouchsafed me, be it for better or for worse to me in the end." Such was the kindness of this good-hearted Princess toward the country of her adoption.

I have likewise heard tell how at the massacre of the Saint Bartholomew, the Queen, knowing naught of it and having never the least suspicion in the world of what was plotting, did get her to bed in her usual fashion. On her waking in the morning, she was first thing informed of the fine mystery that was a-playing. "Woe is me!" she did cry out instantly, "the King, my husband, doth he know of it?"—"Of a surety, Madam," came the answer; " 'tis he that doth order it."—"Great God," she cried in horror, "what thing is this? and what counsellors be they which have given him this advice? Oh, God! I do beseech and pray thee to pardon this sin, for an if Thou be not piti- ful, this offence, I fear me sore, is beyond all pardon." Then she did quick ask for her Book of Hours, and so to prayers and supplication to the Almighty, the tears dropping from her eyes.

Prithee consider the wisdom and goodness the said Queen did manifest in not approving of such a merrymaking and the cruel game that was played thereat, and this although she had much cause to desire the utter extermination of the Admiral (Coligny) and his fellow religionists, seeing they were absolutely opposed in every way to her own faith, the which she did adore and honour more than aught else in all

the world, and on the other hand because she could plainly
see how they did trouble the Kingdom of her gracious lord
and husband. Moreover the Emperor her father had
actually said to her, as she was setting forth with him on
her way to France: "My daughter," he said, "you are
going as Queen to a Kingdom the fairest, strongest and
most puissant in the world, and so far I do hold you a very
happy woman. Yet would you be happier still, an if you
could but find it at peace within its borders and as flourishing as erstwhile it was used to be. But you will actually
find it sorely torn, dismembered, divided and weakened,
for albeit the King, your future husband, is on the right
side, yet the Princes and Lords of the Protestant faith do
much hurt and injury on the other." And indeed she did
find it even as he said.

Being now a widow, many of the most clear-sighted folk
I wot of at Court, both men and women, did deem the new
King, on his arrival back from Poland, would marry her,
in spite of the fact she was his sister-in-law. But then
he could well do so by virtue of the Pope's dispensation,
who can do much in this respect, and especially where
great personages be concerned, in view of the public
advantage involved. And there were many reasons for
concluding the said marriage, the which I have left to
more authoritative writers than myself to deduce, without
my alleging them here. But amongst others one of the
chiefest was to recognise by the marriage the great
obligations the King lay under to the Emperor on the
occasion of his quitting Poland for to return to France.
For there can be no reasonable doubt, an if the Emperor
had chose to put the smallest obstacle in his path, he
would never have been able to get away and cross the

[213]

frontier and make his way to France. The Poles were anxious to keep him, only he did leave them without ever a farewell; while the Germans were on the watch on every side to capture him (as was done to the gallant King Richard of England, on his return from the Holy Land, as we read in our Chronicles), and would have certainly held him prisoner and made him pay ransom, or maybe worse. For they were exceeding sore with him, for the sake of the Feast of Saint Bartholomew,—or at any rate the Protestant Princes were. However, he did voluntarily and without ceremony throw himself suddenly on the protection of the Emperor, which did receive him very graciously and lovingly, and with great honour and much gracious familiarity, as if the twain had been brothers. Then presently, after he had tarried with him some days, he did in person convoy him a day or two's journey on his way, and give him a perfectly safe passage through his dominions, so by his favour he did eventually win to Carinthia, the Venetian territories, Venice itself, and presently his own kingdom.

Such was the obligation the King of France lay under to the Emperor, one which many persons, as I have said, did suppose the former would have paid back by binding yet firmer his alliance with him. But at the time he went into Poland, he had seen at Blamont in Lorraine, the fair Louise de Lorraine, Mademoiselle de Vaudémont, one of the most beautiful, virtuous and accomplished Princess in all Christendom. On her he did cast such ardent eyes as that being presently inflamed with deepest love, and keeping his passion warm all the while he was away, he did straightway on his return to Lyons despatch M. du Gua, one of his chiefest favourites (as truly he did in every way

deserve to be), to Lorraine. Arrived there, he did settle
and conclude the match betwixt him and her very easily and
with no great disputing, as you may well imagine, such
good fortune being beyond the utmost hopes of him and
his daughter,—the one to be father-in-law of the King of
France, the other to be Queen of that Realm. Of this
Princess I do propose to speak elsewhere.

2.

O return once more to our little Queen. Wearied
of a longer tarrying in France for sundry
reasons, and in especial because she was not
properly respected and appreciated there as
she did deserve to be, she did resolve to go finish out the
remainder of her virtuous days with the Emperor, her
father, and the Empress, her mother. During her residence at their Court, the Catholic King was widowed of
his Queen, Anne of Austria, own sister of the said French
Queen Elisabeth. The latter he would fain have married
and did send to beg the Empress, who was sister of the said
Catholic King, to open the first proposals to that effect.
But she would never hearken, once, twice or three times
that her mother spake to her of the matter, appealing to
the ashes of the late King, her husband, the which she
declared she would never insult by a second marriage,
and likewise alleging the over close consanguinity and
near relationship which was betwixt the two, whereby the
marriage might well anger God sorely. Whereupon the
Empress and the King her brother did bethink them to
have a Jesuit Father, a very learned and very eloquent
man, speak with her, who did exhort and sermonize her

[215]

all ever he could, not forgetting to quote all the most telling passages of Holy Scripture of every sort that might advance his object. But the Queen did straight confound him with other as good and more appropriate quotations, for since her widowhood she had applied her earnestly to the study of God's Word, alleging moreover her fixed determination, which was her chiefest bulwark, never to forget her husband in a second marriage. The end was the Jesuit came back with naught accomplished. However, being strongly urged there by letters from the King of Spain, he did return once again to the attack, not content with the firm answer he had already had of the said Princess. The latter, unwilling to waste more time in vain contest with him, did treat him to some strong words and actual menaces, cutting him short with the warning that if he would persist in deafening her any more with the matter, she would make him repent his interference, even threatening she would have him whipped in her kitchen. I have further heard tell,—I know not with how much truth,—that, the man having attacked her for the third time, she went beyond threats, and had him chastised for his insolence. But this I do not believe, seeing she did too well love folk of holy life, such as these men be.

Such was the constancy and noble firmness of this virtuous Queen,—a constancy she did keep unbroken to the end of her days, ever honouring the sacred ashes of her husband. Faithfully did she water these with her mournful tears, whose fountain at the last drying up, she did succumb to her sorrow and die very young. She could not have been more than five and thirty at her decease,— truly a quite inestimable loss, for she might long have been a mirror of virtue to all honourable ladies throughout Christendom.

And verily, showing as she did the love she bare the King, her husband, by her constancy, virtuous continence and unceasing plaints, she did manifest the same even more finely toward the Queen of Navarre, her sister-in-law. For knowing her to be in great extremity of distress, and reduced to live in a remote Castle of Auvergne, all but deserted of all her friends and followers and by the most part of those she had erstwhile obliged, she did send to greet her and offer her every assistance. In fact she did presently give her one-half of all her jointure which she did enjoy in France, sharing with her as if she had been her own proper sister. They say indeed this high-born Queen would have had no little hardship to endure but for this great liberality of her good and gentle kinswoman. Accordingly she did pay her great respect, loving and honouring her so well she had all the difficulty in the world to bear her death with proper patience. Indeed, for twenty days running she did keep her bed, weeping and crying and making continual moan; and ever after did naught but regret and deplore her loss, devoting to her memory the noblest words, such that there could be no need to borrow better to praise her withal and keep her remembrance immortally green. I have been told further that Queen Elisabeth too did compose and endite a work of such beauty it cometh near God's own word, as also one containing the history of all that did hap in France while she was in that country. I know not if this be true, but I have been assured the book was seen in the hands of the Queen of Navarre, as though it had been sent her as a last present before the other's death.

[217]

'Twas most highly thought on of her, and pronounced a most admirable production. At the word of so noble and divine an oracle, what can we do but believe 'twas verily so?

Such then is the summary account I have been able to give of our good Queen Elisabeth, of her kindness, virtue, constancy and faithfulness, and her true and loyal love toward the King, her husband. And 'twas but her nature to be so good and virtuous (I have heard M. de Lansac, who was in Spain when she died, tell how the Empress said to him on that occasion, *El mejor de nosotros es muerto,*—"The best of us all is dead"), and we may well believe how in such actions this Queen was but for imitating her own mother, her great aunts and aunts. For the Empress, her mother, albeit she was left a widow when still quite young and very handsome, would never marry again, but did ever after continue in her widowhood, right wisely and steadfastly, having quitted Austria and Germany, the scene of her rule, after the death of the Emperor, her husband. She went to join her brother in Spain, having been summoned of him and besought to go thither to help him in the heavy burden of his affairs. This she did, for indeed she was a very prudent and well-counselled Princess. I have heard the late King Henri III., who was more skilled in reading character than any other man in all his Kingdom, declare she was in his opinion one of the most honourable, wise and accomplished Princesses in the world.

On this, her journey to Spain, after passing through the divers States of Germany, she did presently arrive at Genoa in Italy, where she embarked. But seeing 'twas in winter, in the month of December, that she took ship, a storm did overtake her at Marseilles, at which port she was forced to cast anchor in the roads. Yet would she never come within the harbour, she or her galleys, for fear of giving any ground for umbrage or suspicion; nor did herself enter the town but only once, to see the sights. Off this port she did tarry seven or eight days, a-waiting for fair weather. Her most favourite course was every morning to leave her galley (for she did usually sleep a-board), and so during the day to go hear the service of mass at the Church of St. Victor with very devout attention. Then presently, her dinner having been brought and made ready in the Abbey, she would there dine; after which she would indulge in discourse with her ladies, or her folk generally, or else with divers gentlemen of Marseilles, which did show her all the honour and respect due to so noble a Princess, the King of France indeed having bid them specially to receive her as it were his own kingly person in recompense for the good welcome and excellent cheer she had given him at Vienna. This she did readily enough perceive; and for that reason would converse very intimately with them and show herself exceeding condescending, treating them more after the German and French fashion than the Spanish. In fact they were no less delighted with her than she with them, and did write a most courteous letter to the King, thanking him and informing him they were as worthy and honourable folk as ever she had seen in any place. Moreover she did make separate mention by name of some score or so of them, among whom was M. Castellan, known as the Seigneur Altyvity, Captain of the King's Galleys, a man much renowned for having wedded the fair Chasteauneuf, a Court lady, and for having killed the Grand Prior,

[219]

himself falling along with him, as I do hope to relate in another place. It was none other than his wife which did relate to me what I here set down, and did tell me of all the perfections of this noble Princess, and how pleasant she did find her enforced stay at Marseilles, and how she admired and enjoyed the place in her walks abroad. But evening once come, she did never fail to return to sleep on board her galley, to the end, the moment fine weather and a favourable wind should come, she might straight make sail, or mayhap because she was anxious to give no cause of umbrage. I was at Court at the time these facts were reported to the King concerning her passing visit, who was most anxious to know if she had been well received, and how she was, and did wish her well in all respects. The said Princess is yet alive, and doth continue in her good and virtuous behaviour, having done her brother excellent service, by all I am told. She did later retire for her final abode and dwelling-place to a Convent of religious women, called the *descalçadas* (unshod), because they do wear neither shoes nor stockings. This house was founded by her sister, the Princess of Spain.

This same Princess of Spain was a very beautiful lady in her day, and of a most courtly dignity. Else truly she would not have been a Spanish Princess; for of a surety, fine bearing and becoming grace do ever go along with Royalty, and above all with Spanish Royalty. Myself have had the honour of seeing her and speaking with her on terms of some intimacy, whenas I was in Spain after my return from Portugal. The first time I went to pay my duty to our Queen Elisabeth of France, and was discoursing with her, answering her many questions as to the news from France and Portugal, they came to inform the Queen that the Princess of Spain was coming in. Instantly she said to me: "Nay! do not retire, Monsieur de Bourdeille; you will see a very fair and noble Princess, and will find pleasure in so doing. She will be very glad to see you and to ask you news of the King, her son, as you have just lately seen him." Hereupon cometh the Princess herself, whom I thought exceeding handsome, and in my opinion very becomingly attired, on her head a Spanish cap of white crêpe, coming low down in a point over the face, but not otherwise in widow's weeds, according to the Spanish fashion, for indeed her almost constant wear was silk. At first I did gaze long at her and admire her beauty, till just as I was growing quite enthralled, the Queen did call me up, and told me the Princess was fain to hear news of me concerning the King her son; for I had already overheard the Queen informing her how she had but now been conversing with a gentleman of the King's, late come from Portugal. At this, I came forward, and did kiss her gown in the Spanish mode, whereupon she did greet me very graciously and familiarly, and began asking me news of the King, her son, his behaviour, and what I thought of him. For at the time a proposed match was being talked of betwixt him and the noble Princess Marguerite of France, the King's sister and now Queen of Navarre. I did give her abundance of information; for in those days I did speak Spanish as well as my native French, or even better. Among other questions, she did ask me, "Was her son handsome, and who was he most like?" I told her he was one of the handsomest Princes in Christendom, as truly he was, and that he was like her in every way, and the living image of her

[221]

beauty, whereat she gave a little smile and blush, plainly showing her pleasure at what I had said.

After we had conversed a long while together, the Queen's attendants came to summon her to supper, and so the two sisters separated. Then did the Queen say to me (she had been amusing herself at the window, yet had heard most of what we said), with a laugh: "You did please her mightily by what you said as to the likeness betwixt her son and her." Presently she asked what I thought of her, and if I did not think her a noble lady, and such as she had described her, and anon remarked: "I imagine she would be right glad to wed the King, my brother, and I should dearly love it." All this I did duly report later to the Queen Mother, when I was returned back to the French Court, which was at the time at Arles in Provence. But she did declare the Princess was too old for him, old enough to be his mother. I informed her moreover of what I had been told in Spain, and did consider of good authority, to wit that she was firm resolved never to marry again, an it were not to wed the King of France, or failing this to withdraw from the world altogether.

And truly she did grow so enamoured of this high match and fair prospect, for she was of high heart and ambition, and she did firmly believe she was approaching its accomplishment, or failing this, was resolved to end her days in the convent I have spoken of, where already she was having buildings constructed against her possible retirement from the world. Accordingly she did long cling to this hope and belief, ever wisely maintaining her widowhood, till she did learn of the King's marriage with her niece. Then, all her hopes frustrated, she did pronounce these words expressive of despite or something like it, as I have been told: *Aunque la nieta sea por su verano mas moza, y menos cargada de años que la tia, la hermosura de la tia, ya en su estio toda hecha y formada por sus gentiles y fructiferos años, vale mas que todos los frutos que su edad florescida da esperanza à venir; porque la menor desdicha humana los harà caer y perder ni mas nï menos que alguinos arboles, los quales, en el verano, por sus lindas y blancos flores nos prometen linda fruta en el estio, y el menor viento que acade los lleva y abate, no quedando que las hojas. Ea! dunque pasase todo con la voluntad de Dios, con el qual desde agora me voy, no con otro, para siempre jamas, me casar,*—"True the niece is younger and in her first prime, and less advanced in years than the aunt, yet is the beauty of the latter, already in its summer glory, fully grown and formed by the gracious years, and bearing fruit, better worth than all the fruits that the other's age, now but beginning to bloom, doth give expectation of. For the smallest human accident will destroy the same, withering and ruining them, just like trees in the spring-time, which by their fair white blossoms do promise us fair and excellent fruits in summer. But let only a little blast of wind arise, and lo! they be broken off and beaten down and spoiled, and naught left but only leaves. Well! God's will be done, with whom I am about to wed for all eternity, and with no human bridegroom at all." So said, so done; and thereafter she did lead a life so good and holy, altogether removed from the wicked world, as that she hath left behind to all ladies, great and small, a noble example for their imitation.

Some folks might possibly say, "Well! God be thanked she could not marry King Charles; for be sure, and if this

[223]

could have been brought about, she would have sent far
enough the hard life of a widow, and been right glad to
take up again the soft and pleasant one of a wife." This
may well be allowed; but this likewise it must be granted
on the other hand, that the great wish she did display to
wed this puissant Monarch was but a manifestation of her
proud and ambitious Spanish heart, for to show her high
spirit, and prove she would in no wise take a lowly place;
but seeing her sister an Empress, not able to be one too,
yet fain to rival her, she did therefore aspire to be Queen
of the realm of France, which is as good as any Empire, or
better, and, if not in actual fact, yet in will and desire to
be on an equal footing with her. Such motives do well
accord with her character, as I have heard it described.
To make an end, she was in mine opinion one of the most
noble and high-bred foreign Princesses I have ever seen,
albeit she may perhaps be reproached with her retirement
from the world, due rather to despite than to genuine
devotion. Yet she did thus piously withdraw her; and
her good life and holy have sufficiently made manifest the
true sanctity of her character.

3.

 ER aunt, Queen Mary of Hungary, did the like,
but at a very advanced age, and this no less
from her own desire to retire from the world
than in order to help her brother the Emperor
to serve God well and piously. This same Queen was
widowed at a very early age, having lost King Louis, her
husband, which fell very young in a battle he fought with
the Turks,—a battle he should never of rights have lost,

but for the obstinacy of a Cardinal, which had much influence over him and did over-persuade him against his
better judgement, declaring 'twas not meet to distrust
God's power and a righteous cause. Though he should
have but ten thousand Hungarians, more or less, on his
side, yet these being all good Christians and fighting in
God's quarrel, he should easily rout ten thousand Turks.
In fine he did so incite and push him to recklessness, as
that he did lose the battle; and presently attempting to
retreat was entangled in a marsh and there choked.

The same fate befell the last King of Portugal, Don
Sebastian, which did perish miserably, having risked battle
with too weak a force against the Moors, that were three
times as strong as himself. This was done through the
advice, preaching and obstinacy of sundry Jesuits, which
were forever alleging the power of Almighty God, who
with a look could strike a whole host dead, above all when
this was banded together against him. An excellent and
a true doctrine doubtless; yet must we not be over confident and abuse God's promises, for His secret purpose
will alway be past our finding out. Some say the Jesuit
Fathers gave the counsel they did in all good faith, as is
quite credible; others that they were traitors and had been
gained over by the King of Spain, to the end they might
so bring about the undoing of the young and gallant King
of Portugal, courageous and fiery as he was, and himself
be the better able to lay his hands on that he did after
seize. Be this as it may, 'tis certain both these disasters
befell through these folk, which be fain to manage armies,
yet have never learned the trade of war.

And this is why the great Duc de Guise, after he had
been sore deceived in his Italian expedition, was often used

to say, "I do love God's Church, yet will I never undertake a conquest on the word and faith of any Priest." By this he was for chiding the Pope, Caraffa, known as Paul IV., which had not kept his promises made to him in the most impressive and solemn words, or mayhap the Cardinal, his brother, who had gone all the way to Rome to discuss the matter and see how the land lay, after which he did recklessly urge his brother to the enterprise. It may well be the aforesaid Duc de Guise had in his mind both Pope and Cardinal; for undoubtedly, as I have been informed, whenever the Duke did repeat this saying, as oft he did, before his brother, the latter deeming it a stone pitched into his garden, would be secretly much enraged and furiously angry. This is a digression, but my subject seemed to warrant it.

To return now to our good Queen Mary of Hungary. After this disaster to her husband, she was left a very young and beautiful widow, as I have heard many persons say which have seen her, as also according to the portraits of her I have seen, which do all represent her as very fair, giving her never an ugly or censurable feature, except only her heavy, projecting mouth, or "Austrian lip." However this doth not really come from the House of Austria, but from that of Burgundy, as I have heard a lady of the Court at that time relate. She said how once when Queen Eleanor was passing by way of Dijon on her way to pay her devotions at the Monastery of the Chartreuse in that region, and to visit the reverend sepulchres of her ancestors, the Dukes of Burgundy, she was curious to have these opened, as many monarchs have done with theirs. Some of the bodies she did find so whole and well preserved she did recognise many of their features, and amongst others the mouth. Whereupon she did suddenly cry: "Ah! I thought we did take our mouths from them of Austria; but by what I see here, we seem rather to get them from Mary of Burgundy, our ancestress, and the Dukes of Burgundy, our ancestors. If ever I see the Emperor, my brother, I will tell him; nay! I will write him at once." The lady which was then present told me she did herself hear these words, declaring further the Queen did pronounce them as if pleased at her discovery. And in this she was very right, for truly the House of Burgundy was every whit as good as that of Austria, springing as it did from a son of France, Philip le Hardi, from whom they had inherited much wealth and courage and high spirit. Indeed I imagine there were never four greater Dukes, one after the other, than were these four Dukes of Burgundy. Truly I may be charged with everlastingly wandering from my subject; but 'tis an easy matter to excuse me, I think, seeing I have never been taught the art of careful and correct writing.

Our Queen Mary of Hungary then was a most fair and agreeable Princess, and a very amiable, albeit she did show herself somewhat over masculine. But for that she was none the worse for love, nor yet for war, which she did take for her chiefest exercise. The Emperor, her brother, seeing her meet for this work and very apt therein, did send to summon her and beg her to come to him, for to give her the charge of her aunt Marguerite of Flanders had held, which was a very wise Princess and one that did govern his Province of the Low Countries with as much gentleness as the other had used severity. Wherefore so long as she lived, King Francis did never direct his arms toward that quarter, saying he would fain avoid giving displeasure to so noble a Princess, which did show her so well disposed to France, and so wise and virtuous to boot. Unhappy too beyond her deserts in her marriages, whereof the first was with King Charles VIII., by whom she was while still quite a girl sent back to her father's house; the second with the King of Aragon's son, John by name, of whom she had a posthumous son that died soon after its birth. The third was with the handsome Duke Philibert of Savoy, of whom she had no offspring, and for that cause did bear the device, *Fortune infortune, fors une.* She doth lie with her husband in the beautiful and most splendid Cloister of Brou, near the town of Bourg en Bresse, a Church I have myself visited.

This same Queen of Hungary then did greatly help the Emperor, seeing how isolated he was. 'Twas true he had Ferdinand, King of the Romans, his brother; yet was it all he could do to make head against that great conqueror, the Sultan Soliman. The Emperor had moreover on his hands the affairs of Italy, which was at that time all a-fire; while Germany was little better by reason of the Grand Turk, and he was harassed to boot with Hungary, Spain at the time of its rebellion under M. de Chièvres, the Indies, the Low Countries, Barbary, and France, which last was the most sore burden of all, in a word with the business of nigh half the world, in a manner of speaking. He did make his sister Governess General of all the Netherlands, where by the space of two or three and twenty years she did him such excellent service I really cannot tell what he would have done without her. So he did entrust her with entire charge of the government of those districts, and even when himself was in Flanders, did leave all the management of his provinces in that quarter in her hands. The council was held under her direction and in her apartments even when the Emperor was present and did attend, as I have been told he often did. 'Tis true she was very able and did manage it all for him, reporting to him all that had taken place at the meeting when he was not there, in all which he did find the utmost pleasure. She did carry out some very successful wars too, whether by her generals or in person, always riding a-horse, like a noble-hearted Amazon-queen.

She it was which did first begin those burnings of strongholds in our land of France, destroying thus some of the finest houses and castles, and in especial that of Folembray, a beautiful and agreeable residence our Kings had built them for the delight and pleasure of the chase. At this the King did feel so sore despite and displeasure as that no long while after she did get of him as good as she gave, for he took his revenge on her noble house of Bains, the which was held for one of the marvels of the world, shaming so to speak all other beautiful buildings of the earth, and I have heard those say that had seen it in its perfection, comparable even to the seven wonders of the world, so renowned in Antiquity. 'Twas there she did entertain the Emperor Charles and all his Court, the time when his son, King Philip, came from Spain to Flanders for to visit his father, such excellence and perfection of magnificence being then displayed that naught else was spoke of at the time save only *las fiestas de Bains*, as the Spaniards said. Moreover I do remember on the journey to Bayonne, when some very splendid shows were given, tilting at the ring, combats, masquerades and games, 'twas all naught to be compared with these famous *fiestas de Bains*,—as sundry old Spanish noblemen which had witnessed them did declare, and as I have seen myself in a Work writ in Spanish on purpose to celebrate them. And it may be certainly said there hath never aught been done or seen finer, equalling even the splendours of Roman days, and copying their old-time sports, always excepting the fights of Gladiators and wild beasts. But with this only exception, the feasts of Bains were finer, more agreeable, as well as more varied and general.

These fêtes I would most dearly love to describe here, according to the particulars I have gleaned from this Spanish work, as well as learned from sundry eye-witnesses, and in especial from Madame de Fontaine, surnamed Torcy, acting as sister for the time being to Queen Eleanor; but I should be blamed as too continually digressing from my subject. So I must e'en keep it for a tid-bit some other time, the matter really meriting full description. Amongst the most splendid of the shows, I will name but this. She had a great fortress of brick, which was assaulted, defended, and relieved by a body of six thousand foot-men of veteran regiments, bombarded by thirty pieces of ordnance, whether in the trenches or on the walls, with all identical methods and ceremonies as in actual war. The siege did last three days and an half, and so fine a sight was never seen; for assaults were delivered, relief brought up, the besieged beaten back, both cavalry and infantry participating in the manœuvres, under charge of the Prince of Piedmont, the place being eventually surrendered on terms, in part favourable, in part rather hard, the garrison being granted their lives and withdrawing under escort. In a word no detail of real war was forgot,—all to the singular gratification of the Emperor.

Rest assured, if the Queen was lavish on that occasion, 'twas but to show her brother that what he had had of him, estates, pensions, benefits, share of his conquests, all was vowed to the further heightening of his glory and pleasure. Wherefore the said Emperor was greatly pleased and did highly commend and approve the great expenditure, and especially that lavished on his own chamber. This was hung with tapestry of a raised warp, all of gold, silver and silk, where were figured and represented in their true colours all the famous conquests, high emprises, warlike expeditions and battles, he had ever made and won, above all not forgetting the defeat of Soliman before Vienna, and the taking prisoner of King Francis I. In fact there was naught therein that was not of the best and most highly wrought.

But truly the unfortunate mansion did lose all its splendour later, forasmuch as it was utterly devastated, pillaged, ruined and overthrown. I have heard say how its mistress, on learning this ruin, did fall in such distress, despite and fury, that 'twas many days ere she could be appeased. Subsequently, when one day passing near the spot, she was fain to see the remains, and gazing very sadly at these, did swear, the tears in her eyes, that all France should repent the deed and be right sorry for these conflagrations, and that she would never be content till yonder proud Castle of Fontainebleau, whereof folk did make so much, was levelled with the earth and not one stone left on another. And in very deed she did spew out her anger right fiercely over the unhappy land of Picardy, which felt the sore effects of her wrath and the fires she kindled there; and I ween, if truce had not interfered, her vengeance would have been startling. For she was of a proud and hard heart, and slow to be appeased, and was generally held, of her own people as well as ours, somewhat over cruel; but such is ever the bent of women, especially of high-born women, which be very ready to take vengeance for any offence done them. The Emperor, by all they say, did only love her the more for this.

I have heard tell how, when the Emperor did abdicate at Brussels and strip him of his power, the ceremony being held in a great Hall wherein he had called together an assembly of his Estates, after he had made a set speech and said all he wished to his son, and had likewise humbly thanked his sister, Queen Mary, which was seated by the side of the Emperor her brother, the latter presently rising from her seat, and with a deep reverence to her brother, did address the people with a grave and dignified port and much confidence and grace, and said as follows: "Gentlemen, for these three and twenty years past that my brother, the Emperor, hath been pleased to grant me the charge and government of these Low Countries, I have ever employed in the said task all the means and abilities that God, Nature and Fortune have bestowed on me, for to perform the same to the utmost of my powers. But an if in aught I have made failure, I am surely to be excused, for I think I have never forgot my duty nor spared the proper pains. Yet, and if I *have* lacked in anything, I do beg you to forgive me. However, if there be any one of you will not so do, but is ill content with me and my government, why! 'tis the smallest of my cares, seeing the Emperor, my brother, is well content, and to please him, and him alone, hath ever been the chiefest of my desires and cares." With these words and another

[232]

deep reverence to the Emperor, she did resume her seat.
I have heard some say this speech was found of many
somewhat over proud and haughty, more especially on
occasion her giving up her charge and bidding farewell
to a people she was about to leave. 'Twould surely have
been more natural, had she desired to leave a good savour
in their mouth and some grief behind her on her departure.
But for all this she had never a thought, seeing her sole
end was to please and content her brother, and from
henceforth to take no heed of the world but keep her
brother company in his retirement and life of prayer.

This account I had of a gentleman of my brother's
suite, which was at the time at Brussels, whither he had
gone to treat of the ransom of my brother aforesaid, he
having been taken prisoner in Hedin, and having spent five
years in confinement at Lille in Flanders. The said
gentleman was present throughout this assembly and
mournful abdication of the Emperor; and did tell me how
not a few persons were something scandalized in secret
at this haughty pronouncement of the Queen's, yet did
never dare say a word or let their opinion appear, seeing
plainly they had to do with a masterful dame, which, if
angered, would surely before her final departure have
done something startling for a last stroke.

Presently freed of all her charge and responsibility, she
doth accompany her brother to Spain; which land she
did never after quit, either she or her sister Queen Eleanor,
till the day of death. Of the three, each did survive the
other by one year; the Emperor died first, the Queen of
France next, being the eldest, then the Queen of Hungary
after the two others, her brother and sister. Both sisters
did behave them wisely and well in widowhood; the Queen

of Hungary was a longer time widow than her sister, and did never marry again, while her sister did so twice, partly to be Queen of France, a dainty morsel, partly by the prayers and persuasion of the Emperor, to the end she might be a sure pledge of peace and public quietness. Not that the said pledge did avail for long while, for War brake out again presently, as cruel as ever. However this was no fault of the poor Princess, who did all she could. Yet for all that did King Francis, her husband, treat her but scurvily, hating and abominating the connection, as I have been told.

4.

FTER the departure of the Queen of Hungary there was left no great Princess with King Philip (now Sovereign Lord invested with his domains in the Netherlands and elsewhere), but only the Duchesse de Lorraine, Christina of Denmark, his cousin german, later entitled Her Highness, which did always hold him good company, so long as he tarried in these parts. She did add much to the brilliance of his Court, for truly no Court, whether of King, Prince, Emperor or Monarch, no matter how magnificent it be, is of much account, if it be not accompanied and seconded by a Queen's or Empress's Court, or at least a great Princess's, and thereat a good abundance of noble dames and damsels, as both myself have observed and have heard pronouncement to the same effect in the highest quarters.

This said Princess was in mine opinion one of the most beauteous and most well accomplished Princesses I have ever seen,—in face very fair and pleasing, her figure very tall and fine, her conversation agreeable, and above all her dress most excellent. In fact all her life she was the pattern and model of fashion to all the ladies of France. This mode of dressing head and hair and arranging the veil was known as the Lorraine way, and 'twas a pretty sight to see our Court ladies so attired. These were ever a-making grand fêtes and splendid shows, the better thereat to show off their dainty adornments, all being *à la Lorraine* and copied after Her Highness. In especial she had one of the prettiest hands ever seen; and I have heard the Queen Mother herself praise the same, and liken it to her own for perfection. She had an excellent seat on horseback, and rode with no little grace, always using the stirrup attached to the saddle, the mode whereof she had learned of the Queen Marie, her aunt, and the Queen Mother, so I have heard say of her; for previously she had ridden with help of the old-fashioned "planchette," [1] which was far from properly showing off her grace and her elegant seat like the stirrup. In all this she was for imitating the Queen her aunt, never mounting any but Spanish horses, Turks, Barbs and the very best jennets, which could go well at the amble. Of such I have seen a dozen capital mounts at one time in her stable, all so excellent, 'twere impossible to say one was better than another. The said aunt did love her dearly, as well for the exercises they both were fond of, hunting, riding and the like, as for her virtues, the which she did observe in her. Accordingly, after her marriage, she did often go to visit her in Flanders, as I have heard Madame de Fontaines relate; and indeed after she became a widow, and especially after her son had been taken from her, she did quit Lorraine altogether in despite, so proud and high of heart was she. She did thereafter take up her abode with the Emperor her uncle and the Queens her aunts, all which great personages did receive her with no small pleasure.

She did bear exceeding hardly the loss and absence of her son, and this in spite of all possible excuses which King Henri did make her, and his declared intention of adopting him as his son. But presently, finding no assuagement, and seeing how they were giving him one M. de La Brousse as tutor, instead of the one he now had, namely M. de Montbardon, a very wise and honourable gentleman the Emperor himself had assigned to that office, having long known him for a worthy man, for he had been in the service of M. de Bourbon, and was a French refugee, the Princess, thinking all desperate, did seek out King Henri one Holy Thursday in the great Gallery at Nancy, where all his Court was assembled. Thus, with an assured grace and that great beauty which did make her yet more admirable, she did advance, with no undue awe or any sort of abasement at his grandeur, albeit bowing low in reverence before him; and in suppliant wise, with tears in her eyes, the which did but make her more fair and more delightsome to look upon, did remonstrate with the King as to the wrong he was doing her in taking away her son,—the dearest possession she had in all the world. Little did she deserve, she added, so harsh treatment, seeing the high station she was born in and the fact she had never dreamed of doing aught to his disservice. All this she said so well and with so excellent a grace, with reasoning so cogent and complaint so pitiful, as that the King, always very courteous toward ladies, was deeply stirred with compassion,—and not he alone, but all the Lords and Princes, great and small, which were present at the sight.

The King, who was the most respectful monarch toward ladies hath ever been in France, did answer her in very honourable terms, albeit with no rigmarole of words nor by way of set harangue, as Paradin doth represent the matter in his *History of France;* for indeed of his nature this monarch was not so prolix, nor copious in reasons and fine speeches, nor a mighty orator. Neither had he any need to be, nor is it becoming that a King should play the philosopher and rhetorician, the shortest replies and briefest questions being more meet for him and more becoming. This I have heard argued by not a few great men, amongst others by M. de Pibrac, whose judgment was much to be relied on by reason of the competence of knowledge he did possess. Moreover any one that shall read the speech as given by Paradin, as supposed by him to have been delivered in this place by King Henri, will credit never a word of it; besides which, I have heard positively from a number of great folk which were there present that he did not make any such lengthy harangue as the historian saith.

'Tis quite true at the same time that he did condole with her in very honourable and proper phrase on her alleged grievance, saying she had no real reason to be troubled thereat, for that 'twas to assure the lad's estate, and not out of any selfish hostility toward him, he was fain to have her son by his side, and to keep him along with his own son and heir, to share his bringing up and fashion of life and fortune. Further that himself being French, and the boy of French extraction, he could scarce be better off than to be reared at the French Court and

[237]

among French folk, where he had so many kinsmen and
friends. In especial he forgat not to add how the house
of Lorraine did lie under greater obligation to that of
France than to any other in all Christendom, alleging the
countenance given by France to the Duke of Lorraine as
against Duke Charles of Burgundy, that was slain before
Nancy. For that 'twas an undoubted truth to say that
but for that Country's help, the said Duke would have
utterly undone the Duke of Lorraine and his Duchy to
boot, and made him the most unhappy Prince in the world.
He did further allege the gratitude they of the House of
Lorraine did owe to the French, for the great assistance
rendered them by the latter in their successes in the Holy
Wars and conquests of Jerusalem, and the Kingdom of
Naples and Sicily. Further he did declare how neither his
natural bent nor true interests were like to set him on
ruining and undoing Princes, but rather to help the same
in all ways, when in danger and difficulty,—as he had
actually done to the little Queen of Scots, a near kinswoman of his son, to the Duke of Parma, as well as to
Germany, that was so sore pressed it was nigh coming to
utter ruin without such help. The same kindness and
generosity, he said, was his motive for taking the young
Prince of Lorraine under his protection, for to bring him
up to an higher estate than else he could aspire to, and
make him his son by marrying him eventually to one of
his own daughters; in fine that she had no sort of call to
be afflicted at his action.

Yet could not all these fine words and excellent reasons
in any wise calm her grief, neither enable her to bear her
loss one whit more patiently. So presently with another
deep reverence, and still shedding many pathetic tears,

she did withdraw her to her own chamber, the King himself conducting her to the door thereof. Next day, before quitting the place, he did visit her in her chamber to bid her farewell, but without her winning any concession as to her petition. Accordingly having thus seen her beloved son torn from her and carried away to France, she did resolve for her part to leave Lorraine altogether and retire to Flanders to the side of her uncle the Emperor (oh! the fine sound of that word) and to the company of her cousin King Philip and the Queens her aunts—a noble alliance and a great! This she did; and did never leave Flanders more, till after conclusion of the peace betwixt the two Kings, when he of Spain took ship and sailed away for that country.

To the making of the said peace she did no little avail, my! rather was the chiefest contributor thereto. For the delegates of the one side and the other, by what I have heard said, after having laboured and sweated all in vain at Cercan for several days, without arranging or settling aught, were still at fault and off the scent, as we say in hunting, when she, whether inspired by wisdom from on high or urged thereto by Christian zeal and her own kind heart, did take up the chase, and carry this important negotiation to a good end and one so fortunate to all Christian peoples. And of a truth 'twas said no other could have been found so meet to move and set in place this great corner stone, seeing she was a lady of skill and experience if ever there was one, as well as of high and weighty authority,—and there can be never a doubt but petty, low-born folk are not so apt for the like business as great personages be. For this and many other reasons the King her cousin did feel much trust and

[239]

confidence in her, well knowing her good qualities. He did ever love her well, bearing her much affection and esteem; and indeed she did help him much and contribute greatly to the splendour and renown of his Court, the which without her would have sorely lacked brilliancy. Yet afterward, I have been told, he did show her but poor gratitude and treated her scurvily with regard to her lands which did fall to her for jointure in the Duchy of Milan, where she had been married in first wedlock with the Duke Sforza; for by what I have been informed, he did rob her and bring her short of some portion of these.

I have heard it said that after the loss of her son, she did remain very ill content with the Duc de Guise and the great Cardinal her brother, holding them to blame for having advised the King to that course, by reason of their ambition, both because they were fain to see their near cousin adopted as son and married within the House of France, and because she had some while before refused M. de Guise in marriage, which had sent to her to make such offer. She being one of the proudest of womankind, made answer she would never wed the younger son of the house whereof she had been wife of the eldest. For this rebuff the Duke did ever after bear her a grudge, and this although he did lose naught in his subsequent marriage, his wife being of a most illustrious house and granddaughter of a King, Louis XII., one of the best and bravest monarchs have ever sat on the French throne,— and what is more, being one of the most beautiful women in Christendom.

Hereanent I have heard tell how the first time these two beauteous Princesses met, both were so curious to mark one the other, whether directing their gaze straight in the face, or askance or sideways, as that neither could look long enough, so set were they and eager to examine each other's charms. I leave you to fancy all the divers thoughts must have traversed these fair ladies' minds. Just so we do read how a little before the great battle was fought in Africa betwixt Scipio and Hannibal, which did put a final end to the War of Rome and Carthage, how previous to its beginning, they did come together in a short truce of some two hours' duration. Whenas they were approached near each other, there the twain of them stood some little while wrapped in contemplation one of the other, each thinking of the valour of the other, so renowned by their exploits and so well represented in their gallant visages, their persons, and their fine, warlike ways and bearing. Then after so tarrying entranced in these noble dreams the one of the other, they did presently set them to negotiation after the fashion Livy hath so well described. Thus valour doth make itself esteemed in the midst of enmity and hate, as doth beauty in the midst of mutual jealousy,—as proven in the case of the two fair Princesses I have spoke of.

Truly the beauty and charming grace of these twain might well be pronounced equal, only that Madame de Guise mayhap did in some ways bear the bell. But she was well content to surpass her rival in these qualities only, never a whit in pride and high bearing; for indeed she was the most gentle, good, condescending and affable Princess ever known, albeit she could show herself at need high-spirited and gallant. Nature had framed her so, no less by reason of her tall and noble figure than of her dignified port and stately carriage, so that to look at her a man might well fear and think twice about address-

ing her in speech, yet having plucked up courage so to
accost her, naught would he find in her but all sweetness,
candour and good-nature,—these pleasant qualities being
inherited from her grandfather, the good father of his
people, and the kindly French habit. 'Tis true enough
however she knew very well how to keep her dignity and
show her pride, when need was. I do hope to further
speak of her specially in another place.

Her Highness of Lorraine on the contrary was exceeding proud and somewhat overweening. This myself did
note on sundry occasions in her bearing toward the Queen
of Scots, who after she was a widow, did make a journey
to Lorraine, where I then was. Not seldom you would
have thought the aforesaid proud Princess was eager to
take advantage and encroach somewhat upon the unhappy
Queen's majesty. Yet the latter, who was a woman of
the world and of a high spirit, did never give her occasion
to glory over her or in any wise encroach on her dignity,
albeit her bearing was always gentleness itself. Indeed the
Cardinal her brother had duly warned her and given her
an inkling of the haughty humour of the said Princess.

Never could this latter entirely rid her of her pride,
yet was she fain to modify the same somewhat toward the
Queen Mother (Catherine de Medici), when they met.
Verily 'twas pride against pride; for the Queen Mother
was the very proudest woman in all the world, when need
was, as I have myself seen, and heard the same character
given her of many great personages,—and above all if
it were necessary to lower the pride of some presumptuous
person, for she would ever contrive to abase such to the
very bowels of the earth. Yet did she always bear herself
courteously toward her Highness, treating her with suf-

ficient deference and respect, yet ever keeping a tight
rein, hand high or hand low as occasion did demand, for
fear she should mayhap forget herself and presume on
some liberty; and myself did hear her twice or thrice declare, "Yonder is the proudest woman I ever saw!" This
was at the time she came to the coronation of our late
King Charles IX. at Reims, whither she was invited. On
her entry into that city, she would not ride a-horseback,
fearing thereby to derogate something of her dignity and
rank, but did arrive in a coach magnificently furnished,
all covered with black velvet, by reason of her widowhood,
and drawn by four white barbs, the finest could anywhere
be chosen, harnessed four abreast, as it had been a triumphal chariot. Herself was at the carriage door,
splendidly attired, though all in black, in a velvet robe,
but her head dress all of white, magnificently arranged
and set off. At the other door was one of her daughters,
which was after Duchess of Bavaria; and within, her
maid of honour, the Princess of Macedonia. The Queen
Mother, desiring to see her enter the outer court in this
triumphant guise, did set her at a window, exclaiming in
an undertone, "Oh! the haughty dame it is!" Presently
when she had stepped down from her carriage and
mounted to the great hall above, the Queen did go forward to meet her only so far as the midmost of the hall,
or mayhap a little farther and somewhat nearer the entrance door than the upper end. Yet did she receive her
very graciously, and showed her great honour; for at the
time she was ruler in all things, in view of the youth of
the King her son, and did govern him and make him
entirely conform to her good pleasure. All the Court,
great and small alike, did esteem and much admire the

[243]

said Princess, and much appreciate her beauty, albeit she was coming nigh the decline of her years, which might then be something over forty; yet was no sign of change or decay in her, her Autumn altogether surpassing other women's Summer. None can do other than think highly of this fair Princess, seeing how beautiful she was, and yet did safeguard her widowhood to the tomb, and so inviolably and chastely, indulging in no third marriage, keep her faith to the manes of her husband.

She did die within a year after hearing the news of her being Queen of Denmark, whence she did spring, and the Kingdom of which had fallen to her. In this wise before her death she did see her title of Highness, the which she had borne so long, changed to that of Majesty, which yet was hers but a short while, less than six months in all. I ween she would gladly enough have borne the old title still, an if she could have kept therewith her erstwhile bloom of youth and beauty, for truly all empires and kingdoms be as nothing compared with youth. Natheless was it an honour and consolation to her before her death to bear this name of Queen; but for all this, by what I have heard say, she was firm resolved not to go to her kingdom, but to finish out the rest of her days on her jointure lands in Italy, at Tortona. And the folk of that country did call her naught else but the Lady of Tortona—not a very grand title and quite unworthy of her. Thither she had retired a good while before her decease, as well for sake of certain vows she had sworn to perform at the holy places of that region, as to be nearer the baths of those parts; for she had fallen into bad health and grown exceeding gouty.

Her life was spent in very pious, holy and honourable

exercises,—praying God and giving much alms and charity toward the poor, and above all toward widows, among whom she did not forget the unfortunate Madame Castellane of Milan, the which we have seen at Court dragging out a miserable existence, had it not been for the help of the Queen Mother, which did always provide her somewhat to live on. She was daughter of the Princess of Macedonia, being a scion of that great house. Myself have seen her a venerable and aged dame; and she had been governess to her Highness. The latter, learning the extreme poverty wherein the poor lady did live, sent to seek her out, and had her brought to her side and did treat her so well she never more felt the sore distress she had endured in France.

Such is the summary account I have been able to give of ths great and noble Princess, and how, a widow and a very beautiful woman, she lived a most wise and prudent life. True, it may be said she was married previously to the Duke Sforza. Well and good! but he did die immediately after, and they were married less than a year, and she was made a widow at fifteen or sixteen. Whereupon her uncle the Emperor did wed her to the Duke of Lorraine, the better to strengthen himself in his divers alliances. But once again she was widowed in the flower of her age, having enjoyed her fine marriage but a very few years. The days which were left her, the best of her life and those most highly to be valued and most delightfully to be enjoyed, these she did deliberately spend in a retired and chaste widowhood.

Well! seeing I am on the subject, I must e'en speak of some other fair widows in briefest phrase,—and first of one of former days, that noble widow, Blanche de Montferrat, one of the great and ancient houses of Italy, which was Duchess of Savoy and the most beauteous and most perfect Princess of her time, and one of the most prudent and well advised. So well and wisely did she govern her son's minority and his lands, that never was seen so prudent a dame and so excellent a mother, left a widow as she was at three and twenty.

She it was which did receive so honourably the young King Charles VIII., on his way to his Kingdom of Naples, in all her lands, and above all in her good town of Turin, where she did afford him a very stately entry. Herself was pleased to be present, and did walk in the progress very sumptuously attired, showing she well understood her dignity as a great lady; for she was in imposing array, clad in a long robe of cloth of gold fretted, and all bordered with great diamonds, rubies, sapphires, emeralds, and other rich jewels. Her head likewise was encircled with the like precious stones, while at her neck she wore a necklace or collar of huge Oriental pearls of priceless worth, and on her arms bracelets of the same. She was mounted on a fine white hackney, very magnificently caparisoned and led by six tall lackeys, dressed in figured cloth of gold. Following her came a large company of damsels, very richly, neatly and charmingly dressed in the Piedmontese fashion, that 'twas a pleasure to see them, and after these a very strong body of gentlemen and knights of the country. Then after her train did enter and march into the city King Charles himself under a rich canopy of state, lighting down at length at the Castle, where he was lodged. There at the Gate, before entering in, the Duchess of Savoy did present her son to him, which was yet a mere boy; after which she did make

him a very excellent speech of welcome, putting at his
service all her lands and goods, both her own and those
of her son. This courtesy the King did accept with gratitude, thanking her heartily and expressing great obligation to her. Through all the city were to be seen the
scutcheons of France and of Savoy, bound together with
a true lovers' knot, uniting the two scutcheons and the
two blazons, with these words, *Sanguinis arctus amor*
(Close the tie of blood), as described in the *Chronicle of
Savoy.*

I have heard sundry of our fathers and mothers, which
had it of their own parents as eye-witnesses, and in especial of the noble lady, the Séneschale de Poitou, my grandmother, who was then a maid of honour at the Court, declare how in those days naught else was talked of but the
beauty, wisdom and prudence of this same Princess, and
how all the Courtiers and gallants of the King's suite,
when they were returned back to France from their journey thither, were forever discoursing of her and entertaining the dames and damsels of the Court with praises
of her beauty and virtue, and the King more than any,
which did show every sign of being smit to the heart with
love for so beautiful a lady.

Yet apart from her beauty altogether, he had much
occasion to love her well; for she did help him by every
means she could, and did even strip her of all her precious
stones, pearls and jewelry, to lend them him to raise
money on in whatsoever way seemed good to him. This
was indeed a great obligation and sacrifice, seeing what
great attachment women do always have for their precious
stones, rings and jewelry, so as they would almost rather
lend and put in pawn some precious part of their own

body than their wealth of such things; I mean some would, though not of course all. At any rate the kindness done was a very great one; for but for this generosity, and likewise that of the Marquise de Montferrat, another very noble and very fair lady, he would have come to downright shame in no long time, and must have returned from his expedition before it was half done, having undertaken the same without money. Herein he was in the like sorry case with a certain French Bishop that went to the Council of Trent without money and without Latin. Verily a putting to sea without biscuit! Yet is there a difference 'twixt the two; for what the one did was of his fine, high spirit and noble ambition, the which did close his eyes to all inconveniences, finding naught impossible to a brave heart, whereas the other was in lack both of mother wit and proper experience, offending out of sheer ignorance and stupidity, unless indeed it were that he hoped to send round the bag when he got to his destination.

In the description given of this magnificent entry I have spoke of just above, is to be noted the splendour of the attire and adornments of this same Princess, which were more in accord (some will say) with what is becoming a wife than a widow. On this the ladies did say at the time that, to welcome so great a King, she might well be excused so far, albeit he did hardly claim so great expenditure; and further that great folk, men and women, be a law to themselves, and that in those days widows, so they said, were not so straitlaced and exact in their dress as they have been for the last forty years. The fact is a certain great lady I wot of, being in high favour with a King, indeed his mistress, did dress her somewhat in more quiet and modest garb than most, yet always in silk, to the end she might the better conceal and hide her game; wherefore the widows then at Court, being fain to imitate her, did adopt the same fashion. Natheless was she by no means so strict with herself, nor so stern in her moderation, but that she dressed both prettily and richly, only all in black and white, displaying more worldliness therein than did exactly accord with strict widow's weeds, and in especial ever making a point of showing her beautiful bosom.

Myself did hear the Queen, mother of King Henri III., on occasion of the coronation and marriage of that monarch, say the same: how that widows in days gone by had not the same carefulness as to their attire, modest bearing and strict life, as nowadays. She had seen this in the time of King Francis, who did love an easy-going Court in all respects. Widows did even dance thereat, and were taken as partners as readily as maids or wives. In fact she did once command and beg M. de Vaudemont, by way of honouring the occasion, to lead out the Dowager Princess of Condé to the dance. This he did, and danced a full round with her, as they which were present for the coronation, as I was myself, did see and well remember. Such the freedom widows did then enjoy. Nowadays all this is forbid them as if 'twere a sacrilege, as also the wearing of colours, for none now dare wear aught but black and white; though as for underskirts and petticoats, these as well as their stockings, may be grey, drab, violet or blue. Some indeed I have seen which have so far indulged them as to adopt red, scarlet and chamois-yellow, as in former days; for they could then wear any colour

[249]

for bodices and stockings, though not for robes, by what I am told.

Moreover this same Duchess we have been speaking of might well enough wear such a robe of cloth of gold, seeing 'twas her proper ducal habit and state costume, and therefore becoming and lawful, for to display the sovranty and high dignity of her exalted rank. And this is even now done by our Countesses and Duchesses, the which can and do wear the robes belonging to their several orders on state occasions. Only our widows of to-day dare under no circumstances wear jewelry, except only in rings, and on mirrors and *Books of Hours* and the like, and set in handsome belts, but not on neck or arms, or even any great display of pearls in necklaces and bracelets. Yet I do declare solemnly I have seen widows as becomingly attired in their white and black, and every whit as attractively, as some of our tawdrily dressed wives and maids.

5.

OWEVER enough said concerning this foreign Princess. 'Tis time to say somewhat of our French Princesses, and I would wish first to deal with our fair and unsullied Queen, Louise de Lorraine, wife of King Henri III., late deceased. This Princess can and ought to be commended on many grounds. In her marriage she did bear her towards the King her husband so wisely, modestly and loyally, as that the knot wherewith she was bound in wedlock with him did always remain so firm and indissoluble, no breaking or slackness of the same was ever found, and this although

[250]

the King did sometimes wander elsewhither to satisfy his passions, as great folks will, the which have a special freedom accorded them. Beside this, quite at the very beginning of their married life, in fact within ten days of their union, he did give her no slight cause for displeasure, for that he did deprive her of her women of the chamber and maids of honour, which had ever been with her and in her service, when still a girl, whereat she was exceeding sorry. 'Twas a heavy blow to her affection, in especial for Mlle. de Changy, a very fair and most honourable damsel, and one little deserving to be banished the company of her mistress and expelled the Court. Indeed 'tis ever a sore despite to lose a trusty companion and confidante. I have heard how one day a lady, one of her most privy friends, was presuming enough to chide her and urge, by way of jest and half-serious flaunt, that, seeing she could never have children by the King, for many reasons then commonly alleged, she would do well to borrow secret aid of some third person, for to have offspring, to the end she might not be left without authority, supposing her husband did chance to die, but might some day very like be Queen Mother of a King of France, and hold the same rank and high estate as the Queen mother-in-law. But the lady did long regret her counsel, semi-burlesque as it was; for the Queen took the same exceeding ill, and did never after like her worthy adviser, preferring to base her dignity on her chastity and virtuous life rather than on a lineage sprung of evil-doing. Still the advice, in a worldly point of view and according to Macchiavelli's doctrine, was not to be despised.

Very different was the behaviour, so 'tis said, of Queen Mary of England, third wife of King Louis XII. Being

[251]

but ill-content and distrustful of the feebleness of the
King her husband, she was fain to sound these waters for
herself, taking for guide in crossing the ford the noble
Comte d'Angoulême, the same which was afterward King
Francis, then a young, handsome and charming Prince,
to whom she did show much favour, always addressing
him as "My excellent son-in-law;" as indeed he was, having already married Madame Claude, daughter of King
Louis. The fact is she was smit with love for him; and
he on seeing her was in much the same case. The end
was the pair were very nigh coming together, the which
they would surely have done but for the late M. de Grignaux, a nobleman of honour and good birth from Périgord, a prudent and well advised man, who had been
gentleman in waiting to the Queen Anne, as we have above
said, and was so still to Queen Mary. He seeing the play
was very like to come off, did chide the aforesaid Comte
d'Angoulême for the fault he was about to commit, saying
with an angry energy: "Nay! by the Risen God (this
was his favourite oath), what would you be at? See you
not this woman, keen and cunning as she is, is fain to draw
you to her, to the end you may get her with child? But
an if she come to have a son, what of you? You are still
plain Comte d'Angoulême, and never King of France, as
you do hope to be. The King her husband is old, and
cannot now make her children. You must needs meddle
and go with her, you with your young hot blood, and she
the same, and by the Risen Lord! the end will be she will
just catch on like a limed bird, conceive you a child, and
there you are! After that you've only to say, 'Good-
bye! my chance of the fair Kingdom of France!' Wherefore I say, reflect."

In fact the said Queen was for practising and proving true the Spanish saw or proverb, which saith, *munca muger aguda murio sin herederos,* "no clever woman ever died without heirs;" or in other words, an if her husband make her none, she will call in other help to get her end. Now M. d'Angoulême *did* reflect and sware he was going to be wise and refrain; yet tried and tempted again and again with the wiles and advances of the fair Englishwoman, did presently throw him more fiercely than ever into the pursuit of her. Such the effects of love and passion! such the power of a mere bit of flesh and blood, that for its sake men will surrender kingdoms and empires, and altogether lose the same, as we find over and over again in History. Eventually M. de Grignaux, seeing the young man was bent on his own undoing and the carrying further of his amour, told Madame d'Angoulême, his mother, of the matter, which did so reprove and smartly chide him, as that he gave up the sport once and for all.

None the less 'tis said the Queen did all she could to live and reign as Queen Mother for some little while before and after the death of the King her husband. However she lost him too soon, and had no sufficient time to carry through her purpose. Yet even so, she did spread the report, after the King's death, that she was pregnant. Accordingly, albeit naught really inside her belly, 'tis said she would swell out the outside thereof by means of linen wrappages gradually more and more every day, and that when her full time was come, she did propose to have ready a supposititious child of another woman, and produce this at the instant of her pretended delivery. But the Queen Regent, which was from Savoy and knew somewhat about child-bearing and the like, seeing things were going somewhat too fast for her and her son, had her so well watched and examined of physicians and midwives, that her wrappages and clouts being noted, she was found out and baulked in her design, and instead of being Queen Mother was incontinently sent back to her own country.

See the difference betwixt this Princess Mary and our good Queen Louise, which was so wise, chaste and virtuous, she did never desire, whether by true or false pretence, to be Queen Mother. But an if she had wished to play the like game as other, there would have been little difficulty, for there was none to watch her with any care, —and 'twould have sore surprised not a few. And for her behaviour our present King doth owe her much thanks, and should love and honour her greatly; for an if she had played this game, and had brought forward an infant, her own or another's, the King instead of being what he is, would have been but a Regent of France, mayhap not even that. And this feeble title would ill have guarded him from many more wars and troubles than he hath actually had.

I have heard some, both men of religion and of the world, hold and maintain this opinion: that our Queen would have done better to have played this part, and that in that case France would never have endured so much wretchedness, poverty and ruin as she hath now, and is like to have, and the True Faith better supported into the bargain. As to this I can but refer me to those gallant and curious questioners which do debate these points (but myself do believe never a word of it, for we be all right well satisfied with our King, God save him!) for them to pronounce judgment thereon; for they have a fine subject, and one admitting wide discussion as to the

State's best interests, though not as to God's, as seemeth
me. To Him our Queen hath always been deeply devoted,
loving and adoring Him so well, that to serve Him, she
would e'en forget herself and her high estate. For being
a very beauteous Princess (the King indeed did choose her
for her beauty and high virtues), and young, tender and
most charming, she did give up herself to naught else but
only to serve God, do her devotions, visit constantly the
hospitals, heal the sick and bury the dead, forgetting nor
omitting any of the good and holy works which in this
province the holy devout and righteous ladies, Princesses
and Queens of days of yore, did practise in the early
Church. After the death of her husband, she did ever
lead the same life, spending her time in weeping and
mourning for him, beseeching God for his soul; and in
fact her life as a widow was of the same holy character
as her married life had been.

'Tis true she was supposed, during her husband's lifetime, to have leaned somewhat to the side of the party of
the *Union*, because, being so good a Christian and Catholic as she was, she did naturally prefer them which were
fighting and contending for her Faith and Religion; yet
did she never more favour them, but quitted their faction
altogether, after their assassination of her husband,
though claiming no other vengeance of punishment as a
right but what it should please God to inflict, not that
she did not duly petition men, and above all our King,
with whom lieth the performing of justice for this monstrous deed of a man of religion.[1] Thus both in married
life and widowhood, did this excellent Princess live blame-
less. Eventually she died in the enjoyment of a most
noble and worthy repute, having long languished in sick-

ness and grown hectic and parched,—'twas said owing to her overmuch indulgence in sorrow. She made a very excellent and pious end. Just before her death, she had her crown placed at the head of her bed close beside her, and would never have it removed from there so long as she yet lived, directing that after her death she should be crowned and so remain till her body was laid beneath the ground.

She did leave behind her a sister, Madame de Joyeuse, which was her counterpart in her chaste and modest life, and did make great mourning and lamentation for her husband; and verily he was a brave, valiant and well accomplished Lord. Beside, I have heard say, how when our present King was in such straits, and shut up and imprisoned as in a bag in Dieppe, which the Duc du Maine held invested with forty thousand men, that an if she had been in the place of the Commander of the town De Chastes, she would have had revenge of the death of her husband in a very different fashion from the said worthy Commander, who for the obligations he lay under to M. de Joyeuse, ought never to have surrendered, in her opinion. Nor did she ever like the man afterward, but did hate him worse than the plague, being unable to excuse a fault as he had committed, albeit others deem him to have kept faith and loyalty according to his promises. But then an angry woman, be the original cause of offence just or unjust, will take no satisfaction; and this was the way with this Princess, who could never bring herself to like our reigning monarch, though she did sore regret the late King and wore mourning for him, and this although she did belong to the *League;* for she always declared both her husband and she did lie under many obligations to

him. In fine, she is a good and a wise Princess, and one
that is honoured by the grief and respect she did show to
the ashes of her husband,—for some while that is, for
eventually she did marry again with M. de Luxembourg.
So young as she was, was she to consume away in vain
regrets forever?

6.

HE Duchesse de Guise, Catherine of Clèves,
one of the three daughters of the house of
Nevers (all three Princesses that can surely
never be enough commended, no less for their
beauty than for their virtue and on whom I have writ a
separate chapter in another place), hath celebrated and
doth celebrate all her days in right worthy fashion the
irreparable loss of her noble husband; but indeed what a
husband was he! He was truly the nonpareil of the world,
and this and no less she did call him in sundry of her letters, the which she writ to some of her most familiar
friends and lady companions, which myself also did see
after her bereavement, showing them plainly therein by
the sad and mournful words she used with what sore regrets her soul was wounded.

Her noble sister-in-law, Madame de Montpensier, of
whom I do hope to speak further elsewhere, did also bewail her husband bitterly. Albeit she did lose him when
still very young, and beautiful and charming for many
perfections both of mind and body, she did never think
of marrying again,—and this although she had wedded
him when a mere child in years, and he might have been
her grandfather, so that she had tasted but sparely with

[257]

him of the fruits of wedlock. Yet would she never consent
to indulge a second taste of the same and make up her
defect and arrears in that kind by another marriage.

I have heard not a few noblemen, gentlemen and great
ladies oftentimes express their wonder that the Princesse
de Condé, the Dowager Princess I mean, of the house of
Longueville, did always refuse to marry again, seeing
how she was one of the most beautiful ladies in all France,
and one of the most desirable. But she did remain satisfied with her condition of widowhood, and would never take
a second husband, and this though left a widow very
young.

The Marquise de Rothelin, her mother, did the like, who
beautiful woman as she was, died a widow. Verily mother
and daughter both might well have set afire a whole kingdom with their lovely eyes and sweet looks, the which were
renowned at Court and through France for the most
charming and alluring ever seen. And doubtless they did
fire many hearts; yet never a word was ever to be spoke
of love or marriage, both having loyally kept the faith
once pledged to their dead husbands, and never married
again.

I should never have done if I were to name all the Princesses of our Kings' Courts in similar case. I must e'en
defer their panegyric to another place. So I will leave
them now, and say somewhat of sundry other ladies,
which though no Princesses, be yet of as illustrious race
and generous heart as they.

Fulvia Mirandola, Madame de Randan, of the noble
house of Admirande, did remain unwed, though left a
widow in the flower of her age and her exquisite beauty.
So great mourning did she make over her loss, that never

more would she deign to look at herself in her mirror, but
refused the sight of her lovely face to the pellucid crystal
that was so fain to see the same. Her act though not her
words were like those of an ancient dame, which breaking
her mirror and dedicating the fragments to Venus, spake
these words to the Goddess:

> Dico tibi Veneri speculum, quai cernere talem
> Qualis sum nolo, qualis eram nequeo.

(To thee, Venus, I do dedicate my mirror, for such as I am
now, I care not to see myself, and such as I was, I cannot
more.)

Not that Madame de Randam did scorn her mirror for
this reason, for indeed she was very beautiful, but by
reason of a vow she had made to her husband's shade, who
was one of the best and noblest gentlemen of all France.
For his sake she did altogether leave the world and its
vanities, dressing her always very soberly. She wore a
veil habitually, never showing her hair; yet spite of careless head-dress and her neglect of appearances, her great
beauty was none the less manifest. The late M. de Guise,
late deceased, was used always to call her naught but *the
nun;* for she was attired and put on like a religious. This
he would say by way of jest and merriment with her; for
he did admire and honour her greatly, seeing how well
affectioned and attached she was to his service and all his
house.

Madame de Carnavalet, twice a widow, did refuse to wed
for the third time with M. d'Espernon, then known as M.
de la Valette the younger, and at the commencement of his

[259]

high favour at Court. So deep was he in love with her, that unable to get of her what he would so fain have had, for truly she was a very lovely widow and very charming, he did follow her up persistently and press her sore to marry him, inducing the King three or four times over to speak to her in his favour. Yet would she never put herself again under a husband's yoke. She had been married twice, her first husband being the Comte de Montravel, the second M. de Carnavalet. And when her most privy friends, myself first and foremost, who was much her admirer, did chide her for her fault she was committing in refusing so high a match, one that would place her in the very midmost and focus of greatness, wealth, riches, favour and every dignity, seeing how M. de la Valette was chiefest favourite of the King, and deemed of him only second to himself, she would answer: that her delight lay not at all in these things, but in her own free-will and the perfect liberty and satisfaction.

Madame de Bourdeille, sprung of the illustrious and ancient house of Montbron and of the Counts of Périgord and Viscounts of Aunay, being left a widow at the age of seven or eight and thirty, a very beautiful woman (and I do think that in all Guienne, of which province she was, was never another that in her day did surpass her in beauty, charm and good looks, for indeed she had one of the finest, tallest and most gracious figures could anywhere be seen, and if the body was fair the mind was to match), being so desirable and now widowed, was wooed and sought after in marriage by three great and wealthy Lords. To them all she made reply as follows: "I will not say, as many dames do, that they will never, never marry again, adding such asseverations you can in no wise doubt their firm intention. But I am ready to declare that, unless God and my carnal being give me not very different desire to what I feel at this present, and change me utterly, I have very surely said farewell forever to matrimony." Then when another did further object: "Nay! Madam, but would you wish to burn away in the flower of your age?" she added: "I wot not what you mean by burning away; but I do assure you that up to the present hour, it hath never yet been possible for me to warm me even, all alone in my bed which is widowed and cold as ice. Yet in the company of a second husband, I say not but that, coming nigh his fire, I might not mayhap burn as you say. But forasmuch as cold is more easy to endure than heat, I am resolved to continue in my present condition, and abstain from a second marriage." And this resolve she did so express, she hath kept to this day, having remained a widow twelve years, without losing aught of her beauty, ever maintaining and holding sacred one fixed determination. This is truly a great obligation to her husband's ashes, and a testimony how well she loved him, as well as an exceeding binding claim on her children to honour her memory forever, seeing how she did end her days a widow.

The late M. d'Estrozze was one of the aspirants to her hand, and had had his wishes conveyed to her. But great, noble and allied with the Queen Mother as he was, she did refuse the match, excusing herself in seemly terms. Yet what a strange humour, after all, to be beautiful, honourable and a very rich heiress, and finish out one's days over a pen or a solitary seam, lone and cold as ice, and spend so many widowed nights! Oh! how many dames there be of a very different complexion,—though not a few also of the like! But an if I were for citing all these, I should never have ended; and especially if I should include among our Christian ladies those of pagan times. Of these was that right fair, and good and gentle Roman lady of yore, Martia, second daughter of Cato of Utica, sister to Portia, who after losing her husband incessantly bewailing the said loss, being asked when would be the last day of her mourning, did make answer 'twould be only when the last day of her life should come. Moreover being both very beautiful and very rich, she was more than once asked when she would marry again, to which she replied: " 'Twill be when I can find a man that will marry me rather for my merits than for my wealth." And God knoweth she was both rich and beautiful, and no less virtuous, than either, nay! far more so; else had she not been Cato's daughter nor Portia's sister. Yet did she pass this rebuff on her lovers and suitors, and would have it they did seek her for her wealth and not for her merits and virtues, albeit she was as well furnished with these as any. Thus did she readily rid her of these importunate gallants.

Saint Jerome in a letter he wrote to one Principia, a virgin, doth celebrate the praises of a gentle Roman lady of his time, which was named Marcella, of a good and noble house, and sprung from a countless line of consuls, pro-consuls, Praetors, and one that had been left a widow very young. She was much sought after, both for her youth and for the antiquity of her house, as well as for her lovely figure, the which did singularly entrance the will of men (so saith Saint Jerome, using these very words; note his observation), and her seemly mien and virtuous character. Among other suitors was a rich and

high-born Roman Lord, likewise of Consular rank, and
by name Cerealis, which did eagerly seek to persuade her
to give him her hand in second marriage. Being something far stricken in years, he did promise her great
wealth and superb gifts as chiefest advantage in the
match. Above all her mother, Albina by name, did
strongly urge her to the marriage, thinking it an excellent offer and one not lightly to be refused. But she
made answer: "An if I had any wish to throw myself in
the water and entangle me in the bonds of a second marriage, and not rather vow me to a second chastity, yet
would I fain prefer to get me an husband rather an inheritance." Then, the lover deeming she had said this
with an eye to his advanced age, he made reply: that old
folk might very well live long, and young ones die early.
But she retorted: "True, the young may die early, but an
old man cannot live long." At which word he did take
umbrage, and so left her. I find this fair lady's saying
admirable and her resolve most commendable.

Not less so was that of Martia, named above, whose
behaviour was not so open to reproof as that of her
sister Portia. For the latter, after the death of her
husband, did determine to live no longer, but kill herself.
Then all instruments of iron being removed, wherewith
she might have taken her life, she did swallow live coals,
and so burned all her inwards, declaring that for a brave
woman means can never be lacking whereby to contrive
her death. This hath been well told by Martial in one
of his Epigrams, writ expressly on this lady's fate, and
a fine poem it is. Yet did she not, according to certain
philosophers, and in especial Aristotle in his Ethics,
(speaking of courage or fortitude) show herein any high

degree of courage or magnanimity in killing herself, as many others have done, and her own husband; for that, to avoid a greater ill, they do throw themselves upon the less. On this point I have writ a discourse elsewhere.

Be this as it may, 'twould surely have been better, had this same Portia rather devoted her days to mourning her husband and avenging his death than in contriving her own. For this did serve no good end whatsoever, except mayhap a gratification of her own pique, as I have heard some women say in blame of her action. Natheless for myself, I cannot enough commend her, and all other widows, which do show their love for their dead husbands as lively as in their lifetime. And this is why Saint Paul hath so highly praised and commended them, holding this doctrine of his great Master. Yet have I been taught of some of the most clear sighted and most eloquent persons I know, that beautiful young widows which do remain in that condition in the very flower of their sweet age and heyday of their life, do exercise an over great cruelty upon themselves and nature, so to conspire against their own selves, and refuse to taste again the gentle joys of a second marriage. This much doth divine law no less than human allow them, as well as nature, youth and beauty; yet must they needs abstain in obedience to some vow and obstinate resolve, the which they have fantastically determined in their silly heads to keep to the vain and empty simulacra of their husbands, that standing like sentinels forgot in the other world, and dwelling yonder in the Elysian fields, be either altogether careless of them and their doings or mayhap do but deride the same. On this question generally all such dames should refer them to the eloquent remonstrances and excellent arguments the which Anna doth bring forward to her sister Dido, in the Fourth Book of the Aeneid. These be most excellent for to teach a fair young widow not over sternly to swear a vow of never altering her condition, rather out of bigotry than real religion. An if after their husbands' death, they should be crowned with fair chaplets of flowers or herbs, as was the custom of yore, and as is still done with young maids in our day, this triumph would be good and creditable while it lasted, and not of over long duration. But now all that may be given them, is a few words of admiration, the which do vanish into air so soon as spoken and perish as quick as the dead man's corse. Well then, let all fair young widows recognise the world and its claims, since they be of it still, and leave religion to old women and the strait rule to perpetual widowhood.

7.

ELL! enough said of widows which go fasting. 'Tis time now to speak of another sort, to wit those which detesting all vows and abnegations against second marriages, do wed again and once more claim the aid of the gentle and agreeable God Hymen. Of such there be some which, over fond of their admirers during their husband's life, be already dreaming of another match before these be well dead, planning afore-hand betwixt them and their lovers the sort of life they will lead together: "Ah, me! an if mine husband were but dead," they say, "we would do this, we would do that; we would live after this pleasant fashion, we would arrange it after that,—and all so discreetly none should

ever suspect our bygone loves. A right merry life we would have of it then; we would go to Paris, to Court, and bear us so wisely naught should ever do us hurt. You would pay court to such and such a great lady, I to such and such a great nobleman; we would get this from the King, and that. We would get our children provided with tutors and guardians, and have never a care for their property and governance. Rather would we be making our fortunes, or else enjoying theirs, pending their coming of age. We would have plenishing enough, with that of mine husband to boot; the last for sure we could not lack, for I wot well where be the title deeds and good crown pieces. In a word, who so happy as we should be?"—and so on and so on.

Such the fine words and pleasant plans these wives do indulge in to their lovers by anticipation. Some of them do only kill their husbands in wishes, words, hopes and longings; but others there be that do actually haste them on the way to the tomb, if they be over laggard. Cases of this sort have been, and are yet to-day, more plenty before our Courts of Law and Parliaments than any would suppose. But verily 'tis better and more agreeable they do not as did a certain Spanish dame. For being ill treated of her husband, she did kill him, and afterward herself, having first writ this epitaph following, which she left on the table in her closet, indited in her own hand:

Aqui yaze qui a buscado una muger,
Y con ella casado, no l'ha podido hazer muger,
A las otras, no a mi, cerca mi, dava contentamiento,
Y pore este, y su flaqueza y atrevimiento,
     Yo lo he matado,

Por le dar pena de su pecado:
Ya my tan bien, por falta de my juyzio,
Y por dar fin à la mal-adventura qu'yo aviô.

(Here lieth one which did seek a wife, yet could not satisfy
a wife; to other women, but not me, though near me, he would
give contentment. And for this, and for his cowardice and
insolence, I have killed him, to punish him for his sins. Myself likewise I have done to death, for lack of understanding,
and to make an end of the unhappy life I had.)

This lady was named Donna Madallena de Soria, the
which, in the judgment of some, did a fine thing to kill
her husband for the wrong he had done her; but did no
less foolishly to slay herself,—and indeed she doth admit
as much, saying "for lack of understanding she did herself
to death." She had done better to have led a merry life
afterward, were it not, mayhap, she did fear the law and
dread to get within its clutches, wherefore she did prefer
to triumph over herself rather than trust her repute to
the authority of the Judges. I can assure you, there have
always been, and are yet women more astute than this; for
they do play their game so cunningly and covertly, that
lo! you have the husband gone to another world, and themselves living a merry life and getting their complaisant
gallants to give 'em no mere artificial joys with *godemiches*
and the like, but the good, sound, real article.

Other widows there be which do show more wisdom,
virtue and love toward their late husbands, with never a
suspicion of cruelty toward these. Rather they do mourn,
lament and bewail them with such extremity of sorrow
you would think they would not live one hour more.
"Alackaday!" they cry, "am not I the most unhappy

[267]

woman in all the world, and the most ill-starred to have
lost so precious a possession? Gracious God! why dost
not kill me straight, that I may follow him presently to
the tomb? Nay! I care not to live on after him; for
what is left me in this world or can ever come to me, to
give me solace? An it were not for these babes he hath left
me in pledge, and that they do yet need some stay, verily
I would kill myself this very minute. Cursed be the hour
ever I was born! If only I might see his ghost, or behold
him in a vision or dream, or by some magic art, how
blessed should I be e'en now! Oh! sweetheart, sweet soul!
can I in no way follow thee in death? Yea! I will follow
thee, so soon as, free from all human hindrance, I may
be alone and do myself to death. What could make my
life worth living, now I have had so irreparable a loss?
With thee alive I could have no other wish but to live; with
thee dead, no wish but only to die! Well, well! is't not
better for me to die now in thy love and favour and mine
own good repute and satisfaction, than to drag on so
sorrowful and unhappy a life, wherein is never a scrap
of credit to be gotten? Great God! what ills and torments
I endure by thine absence! what a sweet deliverance, an
if I might but see thee soon again, what a crown of bliss!
Alas! he was so handsome, he was so lovable! He was
another Mars, another Adonis! and more than all, he was
so kind, and loved me so true, and treated me so fondly!
In one word, in losing him, I have lost all mine happiness."

Such and an infinity of the like words do our heart-
broken widows indulge in after the death of their husbands.
Some will make their moan in one way, others in another,
but always something to the effect of what I have set
down. Some do cry out on heaven, others curse this earth

of ours; some do blaspheme God, others vent their spleen
on the world. Some again do feign to swoon, while others
counterfeit death; some faint away, and others pretend
to be mad and desperate and out of their wits, knowing
no one and refusing to speak. In a word, I should never
have done, if I were to try to specify all the false, feigned,
affected tricks they do use for to prove their grief and
mourning to the world. Of course I speak not of all, but
of some, and a fine few these be and a good round number.

Good folk of either sex that would console suchlike dole-
ful widows, thinking no ill and supposing their grief genuine, do but lose their pains and none is a whit the better.
Others again of these comforters, when they see the poor
suffering object of their solicitude failing to keep up
the farce and make the proper grimaces, do instruct them
in their part, like a certain great lady I wot of, which
would tell her daughter, "Now faint, my pet; you don't
show near enough concern."

Then presently, after all these wondrous rites performed, just like a torrent that after dashing headlong
down its course, doth anon subside again and quietly
return to its bed, or like a river that hath overflowed its
banks, so you will see these widows recover them and
return to their former complexion, gradually get back
their spirits, begin to be merry once again and dream of
worldly vanities. Instead of the death's-heads they were
used to wear, whether painted, engraven or in relief,
instead of dead men's bones set crosswise or enclosed in
coffins, instead of tears, whether of jet or of enamelled
gold, or simply painted, you will see them now adopt
portraits of their husbands worn round the neck, though
still adorned with death's-heads and tears painted in

[269]

scrolls and the like, in fact sundry little gewgaws, yet all so prettily set off that spectators suppose they do use and wear the same rather by way of mourning for their deceased husbands than for worldly show. Then presently, just as we see young birds, whenas they quit the parental nest, do not at the very first make very long flights, but fluttering from branch to branch do little by little learn the use of their wings, so these widows, quitting their mourning habits and desperate grief, do not appear in public at once, but taking greater and greater freedom by degrees, do at last throw off their mourning altogether, and toss their widows' weeds and flowing veil to the dogs, as the saying is, and letting love more than ever fill their heads, do dream of naught else but only a second marriage or other return to wanton living. So we find their great and violent sorrow hath no long duration. It had been better far to have exercised more moderation in their sorrow.

I knew once a very fair lady, which after her husband's death was so woebegone and utterly cast down that she would tear her hair, and disfigure her cheeks and bosom, pulling the longest face ever she could. And when folk did chide her for doing such wrong to her lovely countenance, "My God!" she would cry, "what would you have? What use is my pretty face to me now? Who should I safeguard it for, seeing mine husband is no more?" Yet some eight months later, who but she is making up her face with Spanish white and rouge and besprinkling her locks with powder,—a marvellous change truly?

Hereof I will cite an excellent example, for to prove my contention, that of a fair and honourable lady of Ephesus, which having lost her husband could find no consolation

whatever in spite of all efforts of kinsmen and friends.
Accordingly following her husband's funeral, with endless
grief and sorrow, with sobs, cries, tears and lamentations,
after he was duly put away in the charnel-house where his
body was to rest, she did throw herself therein in spite of
all that could be done to hinder, swearing and protesting
stoutly she would never leave that place, but would there
tarry to the end and finish her days beside her husband's
corpse and never, never abandon the same. This resolution she did hold to, and did actually so live by the space
of two or three days. Meantime, as fortune would have
it, a man of those parts was executed for some crime and
hanged in the city, and afterward carried forth the walls
to the gibbets there situate to the end of the bodies of
malefactors so hanged and put to death should there
remain for an example to others, carefully watched by a
band of officers and soldiers to prevent their being carried
off. So it fell out that a soldier that was guarding the
body, and was standing sentry, did hear near by a very
lamentable voice crying and approaching perceived 'twas
in the charnel-house. Having gone down therein, he beheld
the said lady, as fair and beautiful as day, all bathed in
tears and lamenting sore; and accosting her, set him to
enquiring the reason of her pitiful state, the which she
told him gently enough. Thereupon doing his endeavours
to console her grief, but naught succeeding for the first
time, he did return again and once again. Finally he was
enabled to gain his point, and did little by little comfort
her and got her to dry her eyes; till at length hearkening
to reason, she did yield so far as that he had her twice
over, holding her on her back on the very coffin of her
husband, which did serve as their couch. This done,

[271]

they did swear marriage, one with the other; after which
happy consummation, the soldier did return to his duty,
to guard the gibbet,—for 'twas a matter of life and death
to him. But fortunate as he had been in this fine enterprise of his and its carrying out, his misfortune now was
such that while he was so inordinately taking his pleasure,
lo! the kinsfolk of the poor dangling criminal did steal up,
for to cut the body down, an if they should find it unguarded. So finding no guard there, they did cut it down
with all speed, and carried the corpse away with them
swiftly, to bury it where they might, to the end they might
rid them of so great dishonour and a sight so foul and
hateful to the dead man's kindred. The soldier coming
up and finding the body a-missing, hied him in despair to
his mistress, to tell her his calamity and how he was ruined
and undone; for the law of that country was that any
soldier which should sleep on guard and suffer the body
to be carried off, should he put in its place and hanged
instead, which risk he did thus run. The lady, who had
but now been consoled of him, and had felt sore need of
comfort for herself, did quick find the like for him, and
said as follows: "Be not afeared; only come help me to
lift mine husband from his tomb, and we will hang him
and set him up in place of the other; so they will take
him for the other." No sooner said than done. Moreover
'tis said the first occupant of the gibbet had had an ear
cut off; so she did the same to the second, the better to
preserve the likeness. Next day the officers of justice did
visit the place, but found naught amiss. Thus did she save
her gallant by a most abominable deed and wicked act
toward her husband,—the very same woman, I would have
you note, which had so grievously deplored and lamented

his loss, so that no man would ever have expected so shameful an issue.

The first time ever I heard this history, 'twas told by M. d'Aurat, which did relate it to the gallant M. du Gua and sundry that were dining with him. M. du Gua was not one to fail to appreciate such a tale and to profit thereby, no man in all the world loving better a good anecdote or better able to turn the same to account. Accordingly soon after, being come into the Queen's chamber, he saw there a young, new-made widow, but just bereaved and all disconsolate, her veil drawn half way down her face, sad and pitiful, with scarce a word for any man. Of a sudden M. du Gua said to me: "Dost see yonder widow? well! before a year be out, she will one day be doing as the lady of Ephesus did." And so she did, though not altogether so shamefully; but she did marry a man of base condition, even as M. du Gua had foretold.

The same story I had also of M. de Beau-Joyeux, valet of the chamber to the Queen Mother, and the best violin player in Christendom. Not only was he perfect in his art and music generally, but he was likewise of an amiable disposition, and well instructed, above all in excellent tales and fine stories, little known and of rare quality. Of these he was by no means niggardly with his more intimate friends, and beside could relate sundry from his own experience, for in his day he had both seen many good love adventures and had not a few of his own; for what with his noble gift of music and his good, bold spirit, two weapons very meet for love, he could carry far. The Maréchal de Brissac had given him to the Queen Mother, having sent him to her from Piedmont with his company of violins, the whole most exquisite and complete. He was

then called Baltazarin, but did after change his name.
Of his composition were those pretty ballets that be always
danced at Court.   He was a great friend of M. du Gua and
myself; and we would often converse together.   On these
occasions he had always some good tale ready to tell,
especially of love and ladies' wiles.   Among such he did
tell us that of the lady of Ephesus, already heard from
M. d'Aurat, as I have mentioned, who said he had it
from Lampridius.   Since then I have read it also in the
Book of Obsequies (des Funérailles), a right excellent
work, dedicated to the late M. de Savoie.

The author might surely have spared us this digression,
some may object.   Yea!—but then I was fain to make
mention of my friend hereanent, which did oft bring the
story to my mind, whenever he beheld any of our woe-be-
gone widows.   "Look!" he would exclaim, "see yonder
one that will some day play the part of our lady of
Ephesus, or else mayhap she hath played it already."
And by my faith, 'twas a mighty strange tragi-comedy, an
act full of heartlessness, so cruelly to insult her dead
husband.

At the massacre of the Saint Bartholomew was slain
the Seigneur de Pleuviau, who in his time had been a right
gallant soldier, without a doubt, in the War of Tuscany
under M. de Soubise, as well as in the Civil War, as he did
plainly show at the battle of Jarnac, being in command
of a regiment there, and in the siege of Niort.   Some
while after the soldier which had killed him did inform
his late wife, all distraught with grief and tears,—she
was both beautiful and wealthy,—that an if she would
not marry him, he would kill her and make her go the
same way as her husband; for at that merry time, 'twas

all fighting and cut-throat work. The unhappy woman accordingly, which was still both young and fair, was constrained, for to save her life, to celebrate wedding and funeral all in one. Yet was she very excusable; for indeed what could a poor fragile, feeble woman have done else, unless it had been to kill herself, or give her tender bosom to the murderous steel? But verily

Le temps n'est plus, belle bergeronnette,
(Those days be done, fair shepherdess;)

and these fond fanatics of yore exist no more. Beside, doth not our holy Christian faith forbid it? This is a grand excuse for all widows nowadays, who always say,— and if 'twere not forbid of God, they would kill themselves. Thus do they mask their inaction.

At this same massacre was made another widow, a lady of very good family and most beauteous and charming. The same, while, yet in the first desolation of widowhood, was forced by a gentleman that I know well enough by name; whereat was she so bewildered and disconsolate she did well nigh lose her senses for some while. Yet presently after she did recover her wits and making the best of her widowhood and going back little by little to worldly vanities and regaining her natural lively spirits, did forget her wrongs and make a new match, gallant and high-born. And in this I ween she did well.

I will tell yet another story of this massacre. Another lady which was there made a widow by the death of her husband, murdered like the rest, was in such sorrow and despair thereat, that whenever she did set eyes on a poor unoffending Catholic, even though he had not

[275]

taken part in the celebration at all, she would either faint away altogether, or would gaze at him with as much horror and detestation as though he were the plague. To enter Paris, nay! to look at it from anywhere in the neighbourhood within two miles, was not to be thought of, for neither eyes nor heart could bear the sight. To see it, say I?—why! she could not bear so much as to hear it named. At the end of two years, however, she did think better, and hies her away willingly enough to greet the good town, and visit the same, and drive to the Palace in her coach. Yet rather than pass by the Rue de la Huchette, where her husband had been killed, she would have thrown herself headlong into fire and destruction rather than into the said street,—being herein like the serpent, which according to Pliny, doth so abhor the shade of the ash as that 'twill rather adventure into the most blazing fire than under this tree so hateful is it to the creature.

In fact, the late King, the then reigning King's brother, was used to declare he had never seen a woman so desperate and haggard at her loss and grief as this lady, and that 'twould end by their having to bring her down and hood her, as they do with haggard falcons. But after some while he found she was prettily enough tamed of her own accord, in such sort she would suffer herself to be hooded quite quietly and privily, without any bringing down but her own will. Then after some while more, what must she be at but embrace her Paris with open arms and regard its pleasures with a very favourable eye, parading hither and thither through its streets, traversing the city up and down, and measuring its length and breadth this way and that, without ever a thought of any vow to the contrary. Mighty surprised was I myself one day, on returning from a journey, after an absence of eight months from Court, when after making my bow to the King, I did suddenly behold this same widow entering the great Hall of the Louvre, all tricked out and bedecked, accompanied by her kinswomen and friends, and there appearing before the King and Queen, the Royal personages and all the Court, and there receiving the first orders of marriage, affiancing to wit, at the hands of a Prelate, the Bishop of Digne, Grand Almoner of the Queen of Navarre. Who so astonished as I? Yet by what she did tell me after, she was even more astounded, whenas thinking me far away, she saw me among the noble company present at her affiancing, standing there gazing at her and challenging her with mine eyes. Neither of us could forget the oaths and affirmations made betwixt us, for I had been her admirer and suitor for her hand and indeed she thought I had come thither of set purpose to appear on the appointed day to be witness against her and judge of her faithlessness, and condemn her false behaviour. She told me further, how that she would liever have given ten thousand crowns of her wealth than that I should have appeared as I did, and so helped to raise up her conscience against her.

I once knew a very great lady, a widowed Countess, of the highest family, which did the like. For being a Huguenot of the most rigorous sort, she did agree to a match with a very honourable Catholic gentleman. But the sad thing was that before the completion of the marriage, a pestilential fever that was epidemic at Paris did seize her so sore as to bring her to her end. In her anguish, she did give way to many and bitter regrets, crying:

"Alas! can it be that in a great city like Paris, where all learning doth abound, never a doctor can be found to cure me! Nay! let him never stop for money; I will give him enough and to spare. At any rate 'twere not so bitter, an if my death had but come after my marriage, and my husband had learned first how well I loved and honoured him!" (Sophonisba said differently, for she did repent her of having wedded before drinking the poison.) Saying these and other words of like tenour the poor Countess did turn her to the other side of the bed, and so died. Truly this is the very fervour of love, so to go about to remember, in midst of the Stygian passage to oblivion, the pleasures and fruits of passion she would so fain have tasted of, before quitting the garden!

I have heard speak of another lady, which being sick unto death, overhearing one of her kinsfolk abusing another (yet are they very worthy folk really), and upbraiding her with the enormous size of her parts, she did start a-laughing and cried out, "You pair of fools, you!" and so turning o' the other side, she did pass away with the laugh on her lips.

Well! an if these Huguenot dames have made such matches, I have likewise known plenty of Catholic ladies that have done the same, and wedded Huguenot husbands, and that after using every hang-dog expression of them and their religion. If I were to put them all down, I should never have done. And this is why your widow should always be prudent, and not make so much noise at the first beginning of her widowhood, screaming and crying, making storms of thunder and lightning, with tears for rain, only afterward to give up her shield of defence and get well laughed at for her pains. Better far it

[278]

were to say less, and do more. But themselves do say to
this: "Nay! nay! at the first beginning we must needs
steel our hearts like a murderer, and put on a bold front,
resolved to swallow every shame. This doth last a while,
but only a while; then presently, after being chief dish
on the table and most observed of all, we be left alone and
another takes our place."

I have read in a little Spanish work how Vittoria
Colonna, daughter of the great Fabrice Colonna, and
wife to the great and famous Marquis de Pescaïre, the
nonpareil of his time, after losing her husband,—and God
alone knoweth how good an one he was,—did fall into such
despair and grief 'twas impossible to give or afford her
any consolation whatever. When any did offer any form
of comfort, old or new, she would answer them: "For
what would you give me consolation?—for my husband
that is dead? Nay! you deceive yourselves; he is not
dead. He is yet alive, I tell you, and stirring within mine
heart. I do feel him, every day and every night, come to
life and move and be born again in me." Very noble
words indeed these had been, if only after some while,
having taken farewell of him and sent him on his way
over Acheron, she had not married again with the Abbé
de Farfe,— an ill match to the noble Pescaïre. I mean
not in family, for he was of the noble house of the Des
Ursins, the which is as good, and eke as ancient, as that
of Avalos,—or more so. But the merits of the one did far
outweight those of the other, for truly those of Pescaïre
were inestimable, and his valour beyond compare, while the
said Abbé, albeit he gave much proof of his bravery, and
did work very faithfully and doughtily in the service of
King Francis, was yet employed only in small, obscure and

[279]

light emprises, far different from those of the other,
which had wrought great and conspicuous deeds, and won
right famous victories. Moreover the profession of arms
followed by the Marquis, begun and regularly pursued
from his youth up, could not but be finer far than that
of a churchman, which had but late in life taken up the
hardier calling.

Saying this, I mean not to imply thereby think ill of
any which after being vowed to God and the service of
his Church, have broke the vow and left the profession of
religion for to set hands to weapons of war; else should
I be wronging many and many a great Captain that hath
been a priest first and gone through this experience.

8.

ÆSAR BORGIA, Duc de Valentinois, was
he not first of all a Cardinal, the same
which afterward was so great a Captain that
Macchiavelli, the venerable instructor of
Princes and great folk, doth set him down for example
and mirror to all his fellows, to follow after and mould
them on him? Then we have had the famous Maréchal
de Foix, which was first a Churchman and known as the
Protonotary de Foix, but afterward became a great Captain. The Maréchal Strozzi likewise was first vowed to
holy Church; but for a red hat which was refused him,
did quit the cassock and take to arms. M. de Salvoison,
of whom I have spoke before (which did follow close at
the former's heels, and was as fit as he to bear the title
of great Captain,—and indeed would have marched side
by side with him, an if he had been of as great a house,

and kinsman of the Queen), was, by original profession,
a wearer of the long robe; yet what a soldier was he!
Truly he would have been beyond compare, if only he had
lived longer. Then the Maréchal de Bellegarde, did he
not carry the lawyer cap, being long named the Provost
of Ours? The late M. d'Enghien, the same that fell at
the battle of St. Quentin, had been a Bishop; the Chevalier
de Bonnivet the same. Likewise that gallant soldier M. de
Martigues had been of the Church; and, in brief, an host
of others, whose names I cannot spare paper to fill in. I
must say a word too of mine own people, and not without
good cause. Captain Bourdeille, mine own brother, erst
the Rodomont of Piedmont in all ways, was first dedicate
to the Church. But not finding that to be his natural
bent, he did change his cassock for a soldier's jacket, and
in a turn of the hand did make him one of the best and
most valiant captains in all Piedmont. He would for
sure have become a great and famous man, had he not
died, alas! at only five and twenty years of age.

In our own day and at our own Court of France, we
have seen many such, and above all our little friend, the
noble Clermont-Tallard, whom I had seen as Abbé of Bon-
Port, but who afterward leaving his Abbey, was seen in
our army and at Court, one of the bravest, most valiant
and worthy men of the time. This he did show right well
by his glorious death at La Rochelle, the very first time
we did enter the fosse of that fortress. I could name
a thousand such, only I should never have done. M. de
Soleillas,[1] known as the young Oraison, had been Bishop
of Riez and after had a regiment, serving his King right
faithfully and valiantly in Guienne, under the Maréchal
de Matignon.

In short I should never have done, an if I were for
enumerating all such cases. Wherefore I do stop, both
for brevity's sake, and also for fear I be reproached for
that I indulge overmuch in digressions. Yet is this one
not inopportune I have made, when speaking of Vittoria
Colonna which did marry the Abbé. An if she had not
married again with him, she had better deserved her name
and title of Vittoria, by being victorious over herself.
Seeing she could not find a second husband to match the
first, she should have refrained her altogether.

I have known many ladies which have copied her however. One I knew did marry one of mine uncles, the
most brave, valiant and perfect gentleman of his time.
After his death, she did marry another as much like him
as an ass to a Spanish charger; but 'twas mine uncle
was the Spanish steed. Another lady I knew once, which
had wedded a Marshal of France, a handsome, honourable
gentleman and a valiant; in second wedlock she did take
one in every way his opposite, and one that had been a
Churchman too. What was yet more blameworthy in her
was this, that on going to Court, where she had not appeared for twenty years, not indeed since her second marriage, she did re-adopt the name and title of her first
husband. This is a matter our courts of law and parliament should look into and legislate against; for I have
seen an host of others which have done the like, herein
unduly scorning their later husbands, and showing them
unwilling to bear their name after their death. For having committed the fault, why! they should drink the cup
to the dregs and feel themselves bound by what they have
done.

Another widow I once knew, on her husband's dying,

did make such sore lamentation and so despairing by the space of a whole year, that 'twas hourly expected to see her dead right off. At the end of a year, when she was to leave off her heavy mourning and take to the lighter, she said to one of her women: "Prithee, pull me in that crêpe becomingly; for mayhap I may make another conquest." But immediately she did interrupt herself: "Nay! what am I talking about? I am dreaming. Better die than have anything more to do with such follies." Yet after her mourning was complete, she did marry again to a husband very unequal to the first. "But,"— and this is what these women always say,—"he was of as good family as the other." Yes! I admit it; but then, what of virtue and worth? are not these more worth counting than all else? The best I find in it all is this, that the match once made, their joy therein is far from long; for God doth allow them to be properly ill-treated of their new lords and bullied. Soon you will see them all repentance,—when it is too late.

These dames which do thus re-marry have some opinion or fancy in their heads we wot not of. So have I heard speak of a Spanish lady, which desiring to marry again, when they did remonstrate with her, asking what was to become of the fond love her husband had borne her, did make answer: *La muerte del marido y nuevo casamiento no han de romper el amor d' una casta muger,* —"The death of husband and a new marriage should in no wise break up the love of a good woman." Well! so much shall be granted, an if you please. Another Spanish dame said better, when they were for marrying her again: *Si hallo un marido bueno, no quiero tener el temor de perderlo; y si malo, que necessidad he del,*—"An if I find

[283]

a good husband, I wish not to be exposed to the fear of losing him; but if a bad, what need to have one at all?"

Valeria, a Roman lady, having lost her husband, whenas some of her companions were condoling with her on his loss and death, said thus to them: " 'Tis too true he is dead for you all, but he liveth in me for ever." The fair Marquise I have spoke of a little above, had borrowed a like phrase from her. These expressions of these noble ladies do differ much from what a Spanish ill-wisher of the sex declared, to wit: *que la jornada de la biudez d' una muger es d' un dia,*—"that the day of a woman's widowhood is one day long." A lady I must now tell of did much worse. This was Madame de Moneins, whose husband was King's lieutenant, and was massacred at Bordeaux, by the common folk in a salt-excise riot. So soon as ever news was brought her that her husband had been killed and had met the fate he did, she did straight cry out: "Alas! my diamond, what hath become of it?" This she had given him by way of marriage present, being worth ten to twelve hundred crowns of the money of the day, and he was used to wear it always on his finger. By this exclamation she did let folk plainly see which grief she did bear the more hardly, the loss of her husband or that of the diamond.

Madame d'Estampes was a high favourite with King Francis, and for that cause little loved of her husband. Once when some widow or other came to her asking her pity for her widowed state, "Why! dear heart," said she, "you are only too happy in your condition, for I tell you, one cannot be a widow by wishing for't,"—as if implying she would love to be one. Some women be so situate, others not.

But what are we to say of widows which do keep their marriage hid, and will not have it published? One such I knew, which did keep hers under press for more than seven or eight years, without ever consenting to get it printed and put in circulation. 'Twas said she did so out of terror of her son, as yet only a youth, but afterward one of the bravest and most honourable men in all the world, lest he should play the deuce with her and her man, albeit he was of very high rank. But so soon as ever her son fell in a warlike engagement, dying so as to win a crown of glory, she did at once have her marriage printed off and published abroad.

I have heard of another widow, a great lady, which was married to a very great nobleman and Prince, more than fifteen years agone. Yet doth the world know nor hear aught thereof, so secret and discreet is it kept. Report saith the Prince was afeared of his mother-in-law, which was very imperious with him, and was most unwilling he should marry again because of his young children.

I knew another very great lady, which died but a short while agone, having been married to a simple gentleman for more than twenty years, without its being known at all, except by mere gossip and hearsay. Ho! but there be some queer cases of the sort!

I have heard it stated by a lady of a great and ancient house, how that the late Cardinal du Bellay was wedded, being then Bishop and Cardinal, to Madame de Chastillon, and did die a married man. This she did declare in a conversation she held with M. de Mane, a Provençal, of the house of Senjal and Bishop of Fréjus, which had served the said Cardinal for fifteen years at the Court of

[285]

Rome, and had been one of his privy protonotaries. Well! happening to speak of the Cardinal, she did ask M. de Mane if he had ever told him or confessed to him that he was married. Who so astounded as M. de Mane at such a question? He is yet alive and can contradict me, if I lie; for I was present. He made answer he had never heard him speak of it, either to him or to others. "Well, then! I am the first to tell you," she replied; "for nothing is more true than that he was so married; and he died actually the husband of the said Madame de Chastillon, before a widow." I can assure you I had a fine laugh, seeing the astonished face of poor M. de Mane, who was a very careful and religious man, and thought he knew every secret of his late master; but he was out of court for this one. And indeed 'twas a scandalous license on the Cardinal's part, considering the sacred office he held.

This Madame de Chastillon was the widow of the late M. de Chastillon, the same which was said to chiefly govern the young King Charles VIII. along with Bourdillon, Galiot and Bonneval, the guardians of the blood royal. He died at Ferrara, having been wounded at the siege of Ravenna, and carried thither to be healed. She became a widow when very young, being both fair and also wise and virtuous,—albeit but in appearance, as witness this marriage of hers,—and so was chosen maid of honour to the late Queen of Navarre. She it was that did tender the excellent advice to this noble lady and great Princess, which is writ in the *Cent Nouvelles* of the said Queen. The tale is of her and a certain gentleman which had slipped by night into her bed by a little trap-door in the wainscot beside her bed, and was fain to enjoy the reward

[286]

of his address; yet did win naught but some fine scratches on his pretty face. The Queen being purposed to make complaint of the matter to her brother, he did remonstrate with her very judiciously, as may be read in the *Nouvelle* or Tale in question, and did give her the excellent advice referred to, as good and judicious and as well adapted to avoid scandal as could possibly be devised. Indeed it might have been a First President of the Parliament of Paris that gave the advice, which did show plainly, however, the lady to be no less skilled and experienced in such mysteries than wise and judicious; wherefore there can be little doubt she did keep her affair with the Cardinal right well hidden.

My grandmother, the Séneschale de Poitou, had her place after her death, by choice of King Francis himself, which did name and elect her to the post, sending all the way to her home to summon her. Then he did give her over with his own hand to the Queen his sister, forasmuch as he knew her to be a very prudent and very virtuous lady,—indeed he was used to call her *my knight without reproach*,—albeit not so experienced, adroit and cunning in suchlike matters as her predecessor, nor one that had contracted a second marriage under the rose. But an if you would know who are intended in the Tale, 'twas writ of the Queen of Navarre herself and the Admiral de Bonnivet, as I have been assured by my grandmother. Yet doth it appear to me the Queen need never have been at pains to conceal her name, seeing the other could get no hold over her virtue, but did leave her all in confusion. Indeed she was only too wishful to make the facts public, had it not been for the good and wise advice given her by that same maid of honour, Madame de Chas-

[287]

tillon. Anyone that hath read the Tale will find it as I have represented it. And I do believe that the Cardinal, her husband as aforesaid, which was one of the cleverest and wisest, most eloquent, learned and well-advised men of his day, had instilled this discreetness in her mind, to make her speak so well and give such excellent counsel. The tale might mayhap be thought somewhat over scandalous by some in view of the sacred and priestly profession of the Cardinal; but, an if any be fain to repeat the same, well! he must e'en suppress the name.

Well! if this marriage was kept secret, 'twas by no means so with that of the last Cardinal de Chastillon. For indeed he did divulge and make it public quite enough himself, without need to borrow any trumpet; and did die a married man, without ever having quitted his gown and red hat. On the one hand he did excuse himself by alleging the reformed faith, whereof he was a firm adherent; on the other by the contention that he was desirous of still retaining his rank and not giving up the same (a thing he would most surely never have done in any case), so as he might continue of the council, whereof being a member he could well serve his faith and party. For 'tis very true he was a most able, influential and very powerful personage.

I do imagine the aforenamed noble Cardinal du Bellay may have done the like for like reasons. For at that time he was no little inclined to the faith and doctrine of Luther, and indeed the Court of France generally was somewhat affected by the taint. The fact is, all novelties be pleasing at first, and beside, the said doctrine did open an agreeable license to all men, and especially to ecclesiastics, to enter the married state.

9.

OWEVER let us say no more of these dignified folk, in view of the deep respect we do owe their order and holy rank. We must now something put through their paces those old widows we wot of that have not six teeth left in their chops, and yet do marry again. 'Tis no long while agone that a lady of Guienne, already widowed of three husbands, did marry for a fourth a gentleman of some position in that province, she being then eighty. I know not why she did it, seeing she was very rich and had crowns in plenty,—indeed 'twas for this the gentleman did run after her,—unless it were that she was fain not to surrender just yet, but to win more amorous laurels to add to her old ones, as Mademoiselle Sevin, the Queen of Navarre's jester, was used to say.

Another great lady I knew, which did remarry at the age of seventy-six, wedding a gentleman of a lower rank than her previous husband, and did live to an hundred. Yet did she continue beautiful to the last, having been one of the finest women of her time, and one that had gotten every sort of delight out of her young body, both as wife and widow, so 'twas said.

Truly a formidable pair of women, and of a right hot complexion! And indeed I have heard experienced bakers declare how that an old oven is far easier to heat than a new one, and when once heated, doth better keep its heat and make better bread.

I wot not what savoury appetites they be which do stir

[289]

husbands and lovers to prefer these hot-loaf dainties; but I have seen many gallant and brave gentlemen no less eager in love, nay! more eager, for old women than for young. They tell me 'twas to get worldly profit of them; but some I have seen also, which did love such with most ardent passion, without winning aught from their purse at all, except that of their person. So have we all seen erstwhile a very great and sovran Prince,[1] which did so ardently love a great dame, a widow and advanced in years, that he did desert his wife and all other women, no matter how young and lovely, for to sleep with her only. Yet herein was he well advised, seeing she was one of the fairest and most delightsome women could ever be seen, and for sure her winter was better worth than the spring-tide, summer and autumn of the rest. Men which have had dealings with the courtesans of Italy have seen, and do still see, not a few cases where lovers do choose the most famous and long experienced in preference, and those that have most shaken their skirts, hoping with them to find something more alluring in body or in wit. And this is why the beauteous Cleopatra, being summoned of Mark Antony to come see him, was moved with no apprehension, being well assured that, inasmuch as she had known how to captivate Julius Cæsar and Cnæus Pompeius, the son of Pompey the Great, when she was yet but a slip of a girl, and knew not thoroughly the ways and wiles of her trade, she could manage better still her new lover, a very fleshly and coarse soldier of a man, now that she was in the full fruition of her experience and ripe age. Nor did she fail. In fact, the truth is that, while youth is most meet to attract the love of some men, with others 'tis maturity, a sufficient age, a practised wit, a long experience, a well-hung tongue and a well trained hand, that do best serve to seduce them.

There is one doubtful point as to which I did one time ask doctors' opinion,—a question suggested by one who asked why his health was not better, seeing all his life long he had never known nor touched old women, according to the physicians' aphorism which saith: *vetulam non cognovi,* "I have known never an old woman." Among many other quaint matters, be sure of this,—these doctors did tell me an old proverb which saith: "In an old barn is fine threshing, but an old flail is good for naught." Others say: "Never mind how old a beast be, so it will bear." I was told moreover that in their practice they had known old women which were so ardent and hot-blooded, that cohabiting with a young man, they do draw all ever they can from him, taking whatever he hath of substance, the better to moisten their own drouth; I speak of such as by reason of age be dried up and lack proper humours. The same medical authorities did give me other reasons to boot; but an if readers be still curious, I leave them to ask further for themselves.

I have seen an aged widow, and a great lady too, which did put under her tooth in less than four years a third husband and a young nobleman she had taken for lover; and did send the pair of them under the sod, not by violence or poison, but by mere enfeeblement and distillation of their substance. Yet to look at this lady, none had ever supposed her capable of aught of the sort; for indeed, before folk she did rather play the prude and poor-spirited hypocrite, actually refusing to change her shift in presence of her women for fear of their seeing her naked. But as one of her kinswomen declared, these objections

[291]

were all for her women, not for her lovers and admirers.

But come, what is the difference in merit and repute betwixt a woman which hath had several husbands in her life,—and there be plenty that have had as many as three, four or even five, and another which in her life shall have had but her husband and a lover, or two or three,—and I have actually known some women continent and faithful to that degree? As to this, I have heard a noble lady of the great world say she found naught to choose betwixt a lady who had had several husbands, and one that had had but a lover or so, along with her husband,—unless it be that the marriage veil doth cover a multitude of sins. But in point of sensuality and naughtiness, she said there was not a doit of difference. Herein do they but illustrate the Spanish proverb, which saith that *algunas mugeres son de natura de anguilas en retener, y de lobas en excoger,*—"some women are like eels to hold, and she-wolves to choose," for that the eel is mighty slippery and ill to hold, and the she-wolf doth alway choose the ugliest wolf for mate.

It befell me once at Court, as I have described elsewhere, that a lady of a sufficiently exalted rank, which had been four times married, did happen to tell me she had just been dining with her brother-in-law, and I must guess who 'twas. This she said quite simply, without any thought of roguishness; and I answered with a touch of waggery, yet laughing the while: "Am I a diviner to guess such a riddle? You have been married four times: I leave to the imagination how many brothers-in-law you may have." To this she retorted: "Nay! but you speak knavishly," and named me the particular brother-in-law.

"Now you do talk sense," I said then; "before you were talking all at large."

There was in old days at Rome [2] a lady which had had two and twenty husbands one after other, and similarly a man which had had one and twenty wives. The pair did hereupon bethink them to make a suitable match by re-marrying once more to each other. Eventually the husband did outlive the wife; and was so highly honoured and esteemed at Rome of all the people for this his noble victory, that like a successful General, he was prom-enaded up and down in a triumphal car, crowned with laurel and palm in hand. A splendid victory truly, and a well deserved triumph!

In the days of King Henri II., there was at his Court a certain Seigneur de Barbazan, Saint-Amand by sur-name, which did marry thrice—three wives one after other. His third was daughter of Madame de Monchy, governess to the Duchesse de Lorraine, who more doughty than the other two, did quite surpass them, for he died under her. Now whenas folk were mourning his loss at Court, and she in like wise was inordinately afflicted at her bereavement, M. de Montpezat, a very witty man, did rebuke all this demonstration, saying: that instead of compassionating her, they should commend and extol her to the skies for the victory she had gotten over her man, who was said to have been so vigorous a wight and so strong and well provided that he had killed his two first wives by dint of doing his devoir on them. But this lady, for that she had not succumbed in the contest but had remained victorious, should be highly praised and admired of all the Court for so glorious a success,—a victory won over so valiant and robust a champion; and that for the

[293]

same cause herself had every reason to be proud. What a victory, and what a source of pride, pardy!

I have heard the same doctrine cited a little above maintained also by a great nobleman of France, who said: that he did find no difference 'twixt a woman that had had four or five husbands, as some have had, and a whore which hath had three or four lovers one after other. Similarly a gallant gentleman I wot of, having wedded a wife that had been three times married already, one I also know by name, a man of ready tongue and wit, did exclaim: "He hath married at last a whore from the brothel of good name." I'faith, women which do thus marry again and again be like grasping surgeons, that will not at once bind up the wounds of a poor wounded man, so as to prolong the cure and the better to be gaining all the while their bits of fees. Nay! one dame of this sort was used actually to say outright: " 'Tis a poor thing to stop dead in the very middle of one's career; one is bound to finish, and go on to the end!"

I do wonder that these women which be so hot and keen to marry again, and at the same time so stricken in years, do not for their credit's sake make some use of cooling remedies and antiphlogistic potions, so as to drive out all these heated humours. Yet so far be they from any wish to use the like, as that they do employ the very opposite treatment, declaring suchlike cooling boluses would ruin their stomach. I have seen and read a little old-fashioned tract in Italian, but a silly book withal, which did undertake to give recipes against lasciviousness, and cited some two and thirty. But these be all so silly I recommend not women to use them, nor to submit themselves to any such annoying regimen. And so I have

not thought good to copy them in here. Pliny doth
adduce one, which in former days the Vestal virgins were
used to employ; the Athenian dames did resort to the
same remedy during the festivals of the goddess Ceres,
known as the *Thesmophoria,* to cool their humours thereby and take away all hot appetite of concupiscence. 'Twas
to sleep on mattresses of the leaves of a tree called the
agnus castus. But be sure, an if during the feast they
did mortify themselves in this wise, after the same was
over, they did very soon pitch their mattresses to the
winds.

I have seen a tree of the sort at a house in Guienne
belonging to a very high-born, honourable and beautiful
lady. She would oft times show the tree to strangers
which came thither as a great rarity, and tell them its
peculiar property. But devil take me if ever I have seen
or heard tell of woman or dame that hath sent to gather
one single branch, or made the smallest scrap of mattress
from its leaves. Certainly not the lady that owned the
said tree, who might have made what use she pleased
thereof. Truly, it had been a pity an if she had, and her
husband had not been best pleased; for so fair and charming a dame was she, 'twas only right nature should be
allowed her way, and she hath borne to boot a noble line
of offspring.

10.

ND to speak truth, suchlike harsh, chill medicines should be left to poor nuns and prescribed to them only, which for all their fasting and mortifying of the flesh, be oft times sore assailed, poor creatures, with temptations of the flesh. An if only they had their freedom, they would be ready enough, at least some would, to take like refreshment with their more worldly sisters, and not seldom do they repent them of their repentance. This is seen with the Roman courtesans, as to one of whom I must tell a diverting tale. She was vowed to take the veil, but before her going finally to the nunnery, a former lover of hers, a gentleman of France, doth come to bid her farewell, ere she entered the cloister forever. But before leaving her, he did ask one more gratification of his passion, and she did grant the same, with these words: *Fate dunque presto; ch' adesso mi veranno cercar per far mi monaca, e menare al monasterio,*—"Do it quick then, for they be coming directly to make me a nun and carry me off to cloister." We must suppose she was fain to do it this once as a final treat, and say with the Roman poet: *Tandem hæc olim meminisse juvabit,*—" 'Twill be good to remember in future days this last delight." A strange repentance insooth and a quaint novitiate! But truly when once they be professed, at any rate the good-looking ones, (though of course there be exceptions), I do believe they live more on the bitter herb of repentance than any other bodily or spiritual sustenance.

Some however there be which do contrive a remedy for this state of things, whether by dispensation or by sheer license they do take for themselves. For in our lands they have no such dire treatment to fear as the Romans in old days did mete out to their Vestal virgins which had gone astray. This was verily hateful and abominable in its cruelty; but then they were pagans and abounding in horrors and cruelties. On the contrary we Christians, which do follow after the gentleness of our Lord Christ, should be tender-hearted as he was, and forgiving as he was forgiving. I would dsecribe here in writing the fashion of their punishment; but for very horror my pen doth refuse to indite the same.

Let us now leave these poor recluses, which I do verily believe, once they be shut up in their nunneries, do endure no small hardship. So a Spanish lady one time, seeing them setting to the religious life a very fair and honourable damsel, did thus exclaim: *O tristezilla, y en que pecasteis, que tan presto vienes à penitencia, y seis metida en sepultura viva!*—"Poor creature, what so mighty sin have you done, that you be so soon brought to penitence and thus buried alive!" And seeing the nuns offering her every complaisance, compliment and welcome, she said: *que todo le hedia, hasta el encienso de la yglesia,*—"that it all stank in her nostrils, to the very incense in the church."

Now as to these vows of virginity, Heliogabalus did promulgate a law to the effect that no Roman maid, not even a Vestal virgin, was bound to perpetual virginity, saying how that the female sex was over weak for women to be bound to a pact they could never be sure of keeping. And for this reason they that have founded hospitals for the nourishing, rescuing and marrying poor girls, have done a very charitable work, no less

[297]

to enable these to taste the sweet fruit of marriage than to turn them from naughtiness. So Panurge in Rabelais, did give much wealth of his to make such marriages, and especially in the case of old and ugly women, for with such was need of more expenditure of money than for the pretty ones.

One question there is I would fain have resolved in all sincerity and without concealment of any kind by some good lady that hath made the journey,—to wit, when women be married a second time, how they be affected toward the memory of their first husband. 'Tis a general maxim hereanent, that later friendships and enmities do always make the earlier ones forgot; in like wise will a second marriage bury the thought of the first. As to this I will now give a diverting example, though from an humble source,—not that it should therefore be void of authority and to be rejected, if it be as they say, that albeit in an obscure and common quarter, yet may wisdom and good intelligence be hid there. A great lady of Poitou one day asking a peasant woman, a tenant of hers, how many husbands she had had, and how she found them, the latter, bobbing her little country curtsey, did coolly answer: "I'll tell you, Madam; I've had two husbands, praise the Lord! One was called Guillaume, he was the first; and the second was called Collas. Guillaume was a good man, easy in his circumstances, and did treat me very well; but there, God have good mercy on Collas' soul, for Collas did his duty right well by me." But she did actually say the word straight out without any glozing or disguise such as I have thrown over it. Prithee, consider how the naughty wench did pray God for the dead man which was so good a mate and so lusty,

[298]

and for what benefit, to wit that he had covered her so
doughtily; but of the first, never a word of the sort. I
should suppose many dames that do wed a second time
and a third do the same; for after all this is their chiefest
reason for marrying again, and he that doth play this
game the best, is best loved. Indeed they do always
imagine the second husband must need be a fierce performer,—though very oft they be sore deceived, not finding in the shop the goods they did there think to find. Or
else, if there be some provision, 'tis oft so puny, wasted
and worn, so slack, battered, drooping and dilapidated,
they do repent them ever they invested their money in the
bargain. Of this myself have seen many examples, that
I had rather not adduce.

We read in Plutarch how Cleomenes, having wedded the
fair Agiatis, wife of Agis, after the death of the latter,
did grow fondly enamoured of the same by reason of her
surpassing beauty. He did not fail to note the great
sadness she lay under for her first husband's loss; and
felt so great compassion for her, as that he made no
grievance of the love she still bare her former husband,
and the affectionate memory she did cherish of him. In
fact, himself would often turn the discourse to her earlier
life, asking her facts and details as to the pleasures that
had erstwhile passed betwixt them twain. He had her not
for long however, for she soon died, to his extreme sorrow. 'Tis a thing not a few worthy husbands do in the
case of fair widows they have married.

But 'tis time now surely, methinks, to be making an
end, if ever end is to be made.

Other ladies there be which declare they do much better
love their second husbands than their first. "For as to

[299]

our first husbands," some of these have told me, "these we do more often than not take at the orders of our King or the Queen our mistress, or at the command of our fathers, mothers, kinsmen, or guardians, not by our own unbiassed wish. On the other hand, once widowed and thus free and emancipated, we do exercise such choice as seemeth us good, and take new mates solely for our own good will and pleasure, for delight of love and the satisfaction of our heart's desire." Of a surety there would seem to be good reason here, were it not that very oft, as the old-time proverb saith,—"Love that begins with a ring, oft ends with a halter." So every day do we see instances and examples where women thinking to be well treated of their husbands, the which they have in some cases rescued from justice and the gibbet, from poverty and misery and the hangman, and saved alive, have been sore beaten, bullied, cruelly entreated and often done to death of the same,—a just punishment of heaven for their base ingratitude toward their former husbands, that were only too good to them, and of whom they had never a good word to say.

These were in no way like one I have heard tell of, who the first night of her marriage, when now her husband was beginning his assault, did start sobbing and sighing very sore, so that at one and the same time she was in two quite opposite states, cold and hot, winter and summer, both at once. Her husband asking her what cause she had to be so sad, and if he were not doing his devoir well, "Alas! too well, good sir!" she made answer; "but I am thinking of mine other husband, which did so earnestly pray me again and again never to marry afresh after his death, but to bear in mind and have compassion on his young children. Alackaday! I see plainly I shall have the like ado with you. Woe's me! what *shall* I do? I do think, an if he can see me from the place he now is in, he will be cursing me finely." What an idea, never to have thought on this afore, nor to have felt remorse but when 'twas all too late! But the husband did soon appease her, and expel this fancy by the best method possible; then next morning throwing wide the chamber window, he did cast forth all memory of the former husband. For is there not an old proverb which saith, "A woman that burieth one husband, will think little of burying another," and another, "There's more grimace than grief, when a woman loseth her husband."

I knew another widow, a great lady, which was quite the opposite of the last, and did not weep one whit the first night. For then, and the second to boot, she did go so lustily to work with her second husband as that they did break down and burst the bedstead, and this albeit she had a kind of cancer on one breast. Yet notwithstanding her affliction, she did miss never a point of amorous delight; and often afterward would divert him with tales of the folly and ineptitude of her former mate. And truly, by what I have heard sundry of either sex tell me, the very last thing a second husband doth desire of his wife is to be entertained with the merits and worth of her first, as though jealous of the poor departed wight, who would like naught so well as to return to earth again; but as for abuse of him, as much of that as ever you please! Natheless there be not a few that will ask their wives about their former lords, as did Cleomenes; but this they do, as feeling themselves to be strong and vigorous; and so delighting to institute comparisons, do

[301]

cross-question them concerning the other's sturdiness and vigour in these sweet encounters. In like wise have I heard of some which to put their bedfellows in better case, do lead them to think their former mates were prentice hands compared with them, a device that doth oft times answer their purpose well. Others again will say just the opposite, and declare their first husbands were perfect giants, so as to spur on their new mates to work like very pack mules.

11.

IDOWS of the sort just described would be in good case in the island of Chios, the fairest, sweetest and most pleasant of the Levant, formerly possessed by the Genoese, but now for five and thirty years usurped by the Turks,—a crying shame and loss for Christendom. Now in this isle, as I am informed of sundry Genoese traders, 'tis the custom that every woman desiring to continue a widow, without any intent to marry again, is constrained to pay to the Seigneurie of the island a certain fixed sum of money, which they call *argomoniatiquo*, which is the same as saying (with all respect to the ladies), *an idle spot is useless.* So likewise at Sparta, as Plutarch saith in his *Life of Lysander,* was a fine established by law against such as would not marry, or did marry over late, or ill. To return to Scio (Chios), I have enquired of certain natives of that island, what might be the aim and object of the said custom, which told me 'twas to the end the isle might always be well peopled. I can vouch for this, that our land of France will surely never be left desert or infertile

by fault of our widows' not marrying again; for I ween
there be more which do re-marry than not, and will pay
never a doit of tribute for idle and useless females. And
if not by marriage, at any rate in other ways, these
Chiotes do make that same organ work and fructify, as
I will presently show. 'Tis well too for our maids of
France they need not to pay the tax their sisters of Chios
be liable to; for these, whether in country or town, if
they do come to lose their maidenhead before marriage,
and be fain after to continue the trade, be bound to pay
once for all a ducat (and surely 'tis a good bargain to
compound for all their life after at this price) to the
Captain of the Night Watch, so as they may pursue their
business as they please, without let or hindrance. And
herein doth lie the chiefest and most certain profit this
worthy Captain doth come by in his office.

These dames and damsels of this Isle be much different
from those of olden days in the same land, which, by
what Plutarch saith in his *Opuscula*, were so chaste for
seven hundred years, that never a case was remembered
where a married woman had done adultery, or a maid
had been deflowered unwed. A miracle! 'twill be said, a
mythic tale worthy of old Homer! At any rate be sure
they be much other nowadays!

Never was a time when the Greeks had not always some
device or other making for wantonness. So in old times
we read of a custom in the isle of Cyprus, which 'tis said
the kindly goddess Venus, the patroness of that land, did
introduce. This was that the maids of that island should
go forth and wander along the banks, shores and cliffs
of the sea, for to earn their marriage portions by the
generous giving of their bodies to mariners, sailors and

[303]

seafarers along that coast. These would put in to shore
on purpose, very often indeed turning aside from their
straight course by compass to land there; and so taking
their pleasant refreshment with them, would pay handsomely, and presently hie them away again to sea, for
their part only too sorry to leave such good entertainment behind. Thus would these fair maids win their
marriage dowers, some more, some less, some high, some
low, some grand, some lowly, according to the beauty,
gifts and carnal attractions of each damsel.

Nowadays 'tis different. No maids in any Christian
nation do thus go wandering forth, to expose them to
wind and rain, cold and heat, sun and moon, and so win
their dower, for that the task is too laborious for their
delicate and tender skins and white complexions. Rather
do they have their lovers come to them under rich pa-
vilions and gorgeous hangings, and do there draw their
amorous profit from their paramours, without ever a
tax to pay. I speak not now of the courtesans of Rome,
who do pay tax, but of women of higher place than
they. In fact for the most part for such damsels their
fathers, mothers and brothers, be not at much pains to
gather money for their portion on marriage; but on the
contrary many of them be found able to give handsomely
to their kinsfolk, and advance the same in goods and
offices, ranks and dignities, as myself have seen in many
instances.

For this cause did Lycurgus ordain in his Laws that
virgins should be wedded without money dowry, to the
end men might marry them for their merits, and not from
greed. But, what kind of virtue was it? Why! on their
solemn feast-days the Spartan maids were used to sing

and dance in public stark naked with the lads, and even wrestle in the open market-place,—the which however was done in all honesty and good faith, so History saith. But what sort of honesty and purity was this, we may well ask, to look on at these pretty maids so performing publicly? Honesty was it never a whit, but pleasure in the sight of them, and especially of their bodily movements and dancing postures, and above all in their wrestling; and chiefest of all when they came to fall one atop of the other, as they say in Latin, *illa sub, ille super; ille sub et illa super,*—"she underneath, he atop; he underneath, she atop." You will never persuade me, 'twas all honesty and purity herein with these Spartan maidens. I ween there is never chastity so chaste that would not have been shaken thereby, or that, so making in public and by day these feint assaults, they did not presently in privity and by night and on assignation proceed to greater combats and night-attacks. And no doubt all this might well be done, seeing how the said Lycurgus did suffer such men as were handsome and well grown to borrow other citizens' wives to sow seed therein as in a good and fruitful soil. So was it in no wise blameworthy for an old outwearied husband to lend his young and beautiful wife to some gallant youth he did choose therefor. Nay! the lawgiver did pronounce it permissible for the wife herself to choose for to help her procreation the next kinsman of her husband, then an if he pleased her fancy, to couple with him, to the end the children they might engender should at least be of the blood and race of the husband. Indeed there is some sense in the practice, and had not the Jews likewise the same law of license betwixt sister-in-law and brother-in-law? On the other hand our

Christian law hath reformed all this, albeit our Holy
Father hath in divers cases granted dispensations founded
on divers reasons. In Spain 'tis a practice much adopted,
but never without dispensation.

Well! to say something more, and as soberly as we may,
of some other sorts of widows,—and then an end.

One sort there is, widows which do absolutely refuse
to marry again, hating wedlock like the plague. So one,
a lady of a great house and a witty woman withal, when
that I asked her if she were not minded to make her vow
once again to the god Hymen, did reply: "Tell me this,
by'r lady; suppose a galley-slave or captive to have tug-
ged years long at the oar, tied to the chain, and at last
to have got back his freedom, would he not be a fool and
a very imbecile, an if he did not hie him away with a good
heart, determined never more to be subject to the orders
of a savage corsair? So I, after being in slavery to an
husband, an if I should take a fresh master, what should
I deserve to get, prithee, since without resorting to that
extreme, and with no risk at all, I can have the best of
good times?" Another great lady, and a kinswoman of
mine own, on my asking her if she had no wish to wed
again, replied: "Never a bit, coz, but only to bed again,"
playing on the words *wed* and *bed*, and signifying she
would be glad enough to give herself some treat, but
without intervention of any second husband,—according
to the old proverb which saith, "A safer fling unwed than
wed." Another saying hath it, that women be always
good hostesses, in love as elsewhere; and a right saying
'tis, for they be mistresses of the situation, and queens
wherever they be,—that is the pretty ones be so.

I have heard tell of another, which was asked of a

gentleman which was fain to try his ground as a suitor
for her hand, an if she would not like an husband. "Nay!
sir," she answered, "never talk to me of an husband, I'll
have no more of them; but for a lover, I'm not so sure."—
"Then, Madame, prithee, let me be that lover, since husband I may not be." Her reply was, "Court me well,
and persevere; mayhap you will succeed."

A fair and honourable widow lady, of some thirty summers, one day wishing to break a jest with an honourable
gentleman, or to tell truth, to provoke him to love-making,
and having as she was about to mount her horse caught
the front of her mantle on something and torn it somewhat in detaching it, taking it up said to him: "Look
you, what you have done, so and so" (accosting him by
his name); "you have ripped my front."

"I should be right sorry to hurt it, Madam; 'tis too
sweet and pretty for that."

"Why! what know you of it?" she replied; "you have
never seen it."

"What! can you deny," retorted the other, "that I
have seen it an hundred times over, when you were a little
lassie?"

"Ah! but," said she, "I was then but a stripling, and
knew not yet what was what."

"Still, I suppose 'tis yet in the same place as of old,
and hath not changed position. I ween I could even now
find it in the same spot."

"Oh, yes! 'tis there still, albeit mine husband hath
rolled it and turned it about, more than ever did Diogenes
with his tub."

"Yes! and nowadays how doth it do without movement?"

[307]

" 'Tis for all the world like a clock that is left un-wound."

"Then take you heed, lest that befall you that doth happen to clocks when they be not wound up, and continue so for long; their springs do rust by lapse of time, and they be good for naught after."

" 'Tis not a fair comparison," said she, "for that the springs of the clock you mean be not liable to rust at all, but keep in good order, wound or unwound, always ready to be set a-going at any time."

"Please God," cried the gentleman, "whenas the time for winding come, I might be the watchmaker to wind it up!"

"Well, well!" returned the lady, "when that day and festive hour shall arrive, we will not be idle, but will do a right good day's work. So God guard from ill him I love not as well as you."

After this keen and heart pricking interchange of wit, the lady did mount her horse, after kissing the gentleman with much good-will, adding as she rode away, "Good-bye, till we meet again, and enjoy our little treat!"

But alas! as ill fate would have it, the fair lady did die within six weeks whereat her lover did well nigh die of chagrin. For these enticing words, with others she had said afore, had so heartened him with good hope that he was assured of her conquest, as indeed she was ready enough to be his. A malison on her untimely end, for verily she was one of the best and fairest dames you could see anywhere, and well worth a venial fault to possess,—or even a mortal sin!

Another fair young widow was asked by an honourable gentleman if she did keep Lent, and abstain from eating

meat, as folks do then. "No!" she said, I do not."—"So
I have observed," returned the gentleman; "I have noted
you made no scruple, but did eat meat at that season
just as at any other, both raw and cooked."—"That was
at the time mine husband was alive; now I am a widow,
I have reformed and regulated my living more seemly."—
"Nay! beware," then said the other, "of fasting so strictly,
for it doth readily happen to such as go fasting and anhungered, that anon, when the desire of meat cometh on
them, they do find their vessels so narrow and contracted,
as that they do thereby suffer much incommodity."—
"Nay! that vessel of my body," said the lady, "that you
mean, is by no means so narrow or hunger-pinched, but
that, when mine appetite shall revive, I may not afford
it good and sufficient refreshment."

I knew another great lady, which all through her unmarried and married life was in all men's mouths by
reason of her exceeding stoutness. Afterward she came
to lose her husband, and did mourn him with so extreme
a sorrow that she grew as dry as wood.[1] Yet did she
never cease to indulge her in the joys of former days,
even going so far as to borrow the aid of a certain Secretary she had, and of other such to boot, and even of her
cook, so 'twas reported. For all that, she did not win
back her flesh, albeit the said cook, who was all fat and
greasy, ought surely, I ween, to have made her fat. So
she went on, taking now one, now another of her serving-
men, all the while playing the part of the most prudish
and virtuous dame in all the Court, with pious phrases
ever on her lips, and naught but scandal against all other
women, and never a word of good for any of them. Of
like sort was that noble woman of Dauphiné, in the *Cent*

Nouvelles of the Queen of Navarre, which was found lying
flat on the grass with her groom or muleteer by a certain
gentleman, that was ready to die of love for her but this
sight did quick cure his love sickness for him.

I have heard speak of a very beautiful woman at
Naples, which had the repute of going in like manner
with a Moor, the ugliest fellow in the world, who was
her slave and groom, but something made her love him.

12.

 HAVE read in an old Romance, *Jehan de
Saintré*, printed in black letter, how the late
King John of France did rear the hero Jehan
as his page. Now by custom of former days,
great folk were used to send their pages to carry messages, as is done likewise to-day. But then they were
wont to go everywhere, and up and down the countryside, a-horseback; I have even heard our fathers say
they were not seldom sent on minor embassies, for by
despatching a page and horse and a broad piece, the
thing was done and so much expense well spared. This
same little Jehan de Saintré (for so he did long continue
to be called) was very much loved of his master the King,
for that he was full of wit and intelligence, and was often
sent to carry trifling messages to his sister, who was
at the time a widow,—though the book saith not whose
widow. This great lady did fall enamoured of the lad,
after he had been several times on errands to her; so one
day, finding a good opportunity and no one nigh, she did
question him, asking him an if he did not love some lady
or other at Court, and which of them all liked him best.

This is a way a great many ladies have, whenas they be fain to score the first point and deliver their first attack on one they fancy, as myself have seen done. Well! little Jehan de Saintré, who had never so much as dreamed of love, told her, "No! not yet," going on to describe several Court ladies, and what he thought of them. Then did she hold forth to him on the beauties and delights of love, but he only answered, "Nay! I care less than ever for't." For in those old days, even as to-day, some of our greatest ladies were slaves to love and much subject to detraction; for indeed folk so adroit as they have grown since, and 'twas only the cleverest that had the good fortune to impose on their husbands and pass as good women by virtue of their hypocrisies and little wiles. The lady then, seeing the lad to be well-favoured, goes on to tell him how she would give him a mistress that would love him well, provided he was a true lover to her, making him promise under pain of instant shame and disgrace, that above all he should be sure and secret. Eventually she did make her avowal to him, and tell him herself would fain be his lady and darling,—for in those days the word *mistress* was not as yet in vogue. At this the young page was sore astonished, thinking she did but make a mock of him, or wished to trap him and get him a whipping.

However she did very soon show so many unequivocal signs of fire and heat of love and such tender familiarities, as that he perceived 'twas no mockery; while she kept on telling him she would train and form him and make him a great man. The end was their loves and mutual joys did last a long while, during his pagehood and after he was no more a page, till at the last he had to depart on a distant journey,—when she did change him for a great, fat Abbé. This is the tale we find in the *Nouvelles du monde advantureux*, writ by a gentleman of the chamber to the Queen of Navarre, wherein we see the Abbé put an affront on the said Jehan de Saintré, that was so brave and valiant; yet did he in no long while pay the worthy Abbé back in good coin and three times over. 'Tis an excellent Tale, and cometh from the book I have named.

Here we see how 'tis not only of to-day that fair ladies do love pages, above all when they be gay and speckled like partridges. And verily, what creatures women be!— that be ready enough to have lovers galore, but husbands not! This they do for the love of freedom, which is indeed a noble thing. For they think, when once they be out of their husband's rule, they are in Paradise, having their fine dower and spending it themselves, managing all the household, and handling the coin. All goeth through their hands; and instead of being servants, they be now mistresses, and do make free choice of their pleasures, and such as do best minister to the same.

Others again there be, which do surely hate the notion of making a second marriage, from distaste to lose their rank and dignity, their goods, riches and honours, their soft and luxurious living, and for this cause do restrain their passions. So have I known and heard speak of not a few great dames and Princesses, which from mere dread of their failing to find again the grandeurs of their first match, and so losing rank, would never marry again. Not that they did cease therefor one whit to follow after love and turn the same to their joy and delight,—yet all the while never losing their rank and dignity, their

[312]

stools of state and honourable seats in Queens' chambers
and elsewhere. Lucky women, to enjoy their grandeur
and mount high, yet abase them low, at one and the
same time! But to say a word of reproach or remonstrance to them, never dream no such thing! Else no
end would there be of anger and annoyance, denials and
protestations, contradiction and revenge.

I have heard a tale told of a widow lady, and indeed I
knew her myself, which had long enjoyed the love of an
honourable gentleman, under pretext she would marry
him; but he did in no wise make himself obtrusive. A
great Princess, the lady's mistress, was for reproaching
her for her conduct. But she, wily and corrupt, did
answer her: "Nay! Madam, but should it be denied us
to love with an honourable love? surely that were too
cruel." Only God knoweth, this love she called honourable, was really a most lecherous passion. And verily all
loves be so; they be born all pure, chaste and honourable,
but anon do lose their maidenhead, so to speak, and by
magic influence of some philosopher's stone, be trans-
formed into base metal, and grow dishonourable and
lecherous.

The late M. de Bussy, who was one of the wittiest
talkers of his time, and no less pleasing as a story-teller,
one day at Court seeing a great lady, a widow, and of
ripe years, who did still persist in her amorous doings,
did exclaim: "What! doth this hackney yet frequent the
stallion?" The word was repeated to the lady, which
did vow mortal hate against the offender. On M. de
Bussy's learning this, "Well, well!" he said, "I know how
to make my peace, and put this all right. Prithee, go
tell her I said not so, but that this is what I really said,

[313]

'Doth this *filly*[1] yet go to be mounted? For sure I am
she is not wroth because I take her for a light o' love,
but for an old woman; and when she hears I called her
filly, that is to say a young mare, she will suppose I do
still esteem her a young woman.' " And so it was; for the
lady, on hearing this change and improvement in the
wording, did relax her anger and made it up with M.
de Bussy; whereat we did all have a good laugh. Yet for
all she might do, she was always deemed an old, half-
foundered jade, that aged as she was, still went whinnying
after the male.

This last was quite unlike another lady I have also
heard tell of, who having been a merry wench in her
earlier days, but getting well on in years, did set her to
serve God with fast and prayer. An honourable gentleman remonstrating and asking her wherefore she did
make such long vigils at Church and such severe fasts
at table, and if it were not to vanquish and deaden the
stings of the flesh, "Alas!" said she, "these be all over
and done with for me." These words she did pronounce
as piteously as ever spake Milo of Croton, that strong
and stalwart wrestler of old, (I have told the tale elsewhere, methinks), who having one day gone down into
the arena, or wrestlers' ring, but only for to view the
game, for he was now grown very old, one of the band
coming up to him did ask, an if he would not try yet a
fall of the old sort. But he, baring his arms and right
sadly turning back his sleeves, said only, gazing the
while at his muscles and sinews: "Alas! they be dead
now."

Another like incident did happen to a gentleman I
wot of, similar to the tale I have just told of M. de Bussy.

Coming to Court, after an absence of six months, he there beheld a lady which was used to attend the academy, lately introduced at Court by the late King. "Why!" saith he, "doth the academy then still exist? I was told it had been abolished."—"Can you doubt," a courtier answered him, "her attendance? Why! her master is teaching her philosophy, which doth speak and treat of perpetual motion." And in good sooth, for all the beating of brains these same philosophers do undergo, to discover perpetual motion, yet is there none more surely so than the motion Venus doth teach in *her* school.

A lady of the great world did give even a better answer of another, whose beauty they were extolling highly, only that her eyes did ever remain motionless, she never turning the same one way or the other. "We must suppose," she said, "all her care doth go to move other portions of her body, and so hath she none to spare for her eyes."

However, an if I would put down in writing all the witty words and good stories I know, to fill out my matter, I should never get me done. And so, seeing I have other subjects to attack, I will desist, and finish with this saying of Boccaccio, already cited above, namely, that women, maids, wives and widows alike, at least the most part of them, be one and all inclined to love. I have no thought to speak of common folk, whether in country or in town, for such was never mine intention in writing, but only of well-born persons, in whose service my pen is aye ready to run nimbly. But for mine own part, if I were asked my true opinion, I should say emphatically there is naught like married women, all risk and peril on their husbands' side apart, for to win good enjoyment

[315]

of love withal, and to taste quick the very essence of its delights. The fact is their husbands do heat them so, they be like a furnace, continually poked and stirred, that asks naught but fuel, water and wood or charcoal to keep up its heat for ever. And truly he that would have a good light, must always be putting more oil in the lamp. At the same time let him beware of a foul stroke, and those ambushes of jealous husbands wherein the wiliest be oft times caught!

Yet is a man bound to go as circumspectly as he may, and as boldly to boot, and do like the great King Henri, who was much devoted to love, but at the same time exceeding respectful toward ladies, and discreet, and for these reasons much loved and well received of them. Now whenever it fell out that this monarch was changing night quarters and going to sleep in the bed of a new mistress, which expecting him, he would never go thither (as I learn on very good authority) but by the secret galleries of Saint-Germain, Blois or Fontainebleau, and the little stealthy back-stairs, recesses and garrets of his castles. First went his favourite valet of the chamber, Griffon by name, which did carry his boar-spear before him along with the torch, and the King next, his great cloak held before his face or else his night-gown, and his sword under his arm. Presently, being to bed with the lady, he would aye have his spear and sword put by the bed's-head, the door well shut, and Griffon guarding it, watching and sleeping by turns. Now I leave it to you, an if a great King did give such heed to his safety (for indeed there have been some caught, both kings and great princes,—for instance the Duc de Fleurance Alexandre in our day), what smaller folks should do, following the

[316]

example of this powerful monarch. Yet there are to be found proud souls which do disdain all precaution; and of a truth they be often trapped for their pains.

I have heard a tale related of King Francis, how having a fair lady as mistress, a connection that had long subsisted betwixt them, and going one day unexpectedly to see the said lady, and to sleep with her at an unusual hour, 'gan knock loudly on the door, as he had both right and might to do, being the master. She, who was at the moment in company of the Sieur de Bonnivet, durst not give the reply usual with the Roman courtesans under like circumstances, *Non si puo, la signora è accompagnata*,—"You cannot come in; Madam has company with her." In this case the only thing to do was to devise quick where her gallant could be most securely hid. By good luck 'twas summer time, so they had put an heap of branches and leaves in the fire-place, as the custom is in France. Accordingly she did counsel and advise him to make at once for the fire-place, and there hide him among the leafage, all in his shirt as he was,—and 'twas a fortunate thing for him it was not winter. After the King had done his business with the lady, he was fain to make water; so getting up from the bed, he went to the fire-place to do so, for lack of other convenience. And so sore did he want to, that he did drown the poor lover worse than if a bucket of water had been emptied over him, for he did water him thoroughly, as with a garden watering-pot, all round and about, and even over the face, eyes, nose, mouth and everywhere; albeit by tight shut lips he may have escaped all but a drop or so in his chops. I leave you to fancy what a sorry state the poor gentleman was in, for he durst not move, and what a picture of patience and grim endurance he did present! The King having done, withdrew, and bidding his mistress farewell, left the chamber. The lady had the door immediately shut behind him, and calling her lover into her, did warm the poor man, giving him a clean shift to put on. Nor was it without some fun and laughter, after the fright they had had; for an if he had been discovered, both he and she had been in very serious peril.

'Twas the same lady, which being deep in love with this M. de Bonnivet, and desiring to convince the King of the contrary, for that he had conceived some touch of jealousy on the subject, would say thus to him: "Oh! but he's diverting, that Sieur de Bonnivet, who thinks himself so handsome! and the more I tell him he is a pretty fellow, the more he doth believe it. 'Tis my great pastime, making fun of the man, for he's really witty and ready-tongued, and no one can help laughing in his company, such clever retorts doth he make." By these words she was for persuading the King that her common discourse with Bonnivet had naught to do with love and alliance, or playing his Majesty false in any wise. How many fair dames there be which do practise the like wiles, and to cloak the intrigues they are pursuing with some lover, do speak ill of him, and make fun of him before the world, though in private they soon drop this fine pretense; and this is what they call cunning and contrivance in love.

I knew a very great lady, who one day seeing her daughter, which was one of the fairest of women, grieving for the love of a certain gentleman, with whom her brother was sore angered, did say this to her amongst other things: "Nay! my child, never love that man. His

manners and form be so bad, and he's such an ugly
fellow. He's for all the world like a village pastry cook!"
At this the daughter burst out a-laughing, making merry
at his expense and applauding her mother's description,
allowing his likeness to a pastry-cook, red cap and all.
For all that, she had her way; but some while after, in
another six months that is, she did leave him for another
man.

I have known not a few ladies which had no words
bad enough to cast at women that loved inferiors,—their
secretaries, serving-men and the like low-born persons,
declaring publicly they did loathe such intrigues worse
than poison. Yet would these very same ladies be giving
themselves up to these base pleasures as much as any.
Such be the cunning ways of women; before the world
they do show fierce indignation against these offenders,
and do threaten and abuse them; but all the while behind
backs they do readily enough indulge the same vice themselves. So full of wiles are they! for as the Spanish
proverb saith, *Mucho sabe la zorra; mas sabe mas la
dama enamorada,*—"The fox knoweth much, but a woman
in love knoweth more."

13.

OWEVER, for all this fair lady of the tale
told above did to lull King Francis' anxiety,
yet did she not drive forth every grain of
suspicion from out his head, as I have reason
to know. I do remember me how once, making a visit
to Chambord to see the castle, an old porter that was
there, who had been body servant to King Francis, did

receive me very obligingly. For in his earlier days he
had known some of my people both at Court and in the
field, and was of his own wish anxious to show me everything. So having led me to the King's bed-chamber, he
did show me a phrase of writing by the side of the window
on the left hand. "Look, Sir!" he cried, "read yonder
words. If you have never seen the hand-writing of the
King, mine old master, there it is." And reading it, we
found this phrase, "*Toute femme varie,*" writ there in
large letters. I had with me a very honourable and very
able gentleman of Périgord, my friend, by name M. des
Roches, to whom I turned and said quickly: " 'Tis to be
supposed, some of the ladies he did love best, and of
whose fidelity he was most assured, had been found of him
to *vary* and play him false. Doubtless he had discovered
some change in them that was scarce to his liking, and
so, in despite, did write these words." The porter overhearing us, put in: "Why! surely, surely! make no mistake, for of all the fair dames I have seen and known,
never a one but did cry off on a false scent worse than
ever his hunting pack did in chasing the stag; yet 'twas
with a very subdued voice, for an if he had noted it,
he would have brought 'em to the scent again pretty
smartly."

They were, 'twould seem, of those women, which can
never be content with either their husbands or their
lovers, Kings though they be, and Princes and great
Lords; but must be ever chopping and changing. Such
this good King had found them by experience to be,
having himself first debauched the same and taken them
from the charge of their husbands or their mothers,
tempting them from their maiden or widowed estate.

I have both known and heard speak of a lady, so fondly
loved of her Prince, as that for the mighty affection he
bare her, he did plunge her to the neck in all sorts of
favours, benefits and honours, and never another woman
was to be compared with her for good fortune. Natheless
was she so enamoured of a certain Lord, she would never
quit him. Then whenas he would remonstrate and declare to her how the Prince would ruin both of them,
"Nay! 'tis all one," she would answer; "an if you leave
me, I shall ruin myself, for to ruin you along with me.
I had rather be called your concubine than this Prince's
mistress." Here you have woman's caprice surely, and
wanton naughtiness to boot! Another very great lady
I have known, a widow, did much the same; for albeit
she was all but adored of a very great nobleman, yet
must she needs have sundry other humbler lovers, so as
never to lose an hour of her time or ever be idle. For
indeed one man only cannot be always at work and afford
enough in these matters; and the rule of love is this, that
a passionate woman is not for one stated time, nor yet
for one stated person alone, nor will confine her to one
passion,—reminding me of that dame in the *Cent Nouvelles* of the Queen of Navarre, which had three lovers
all at once, and was so clever she did contrive to manage
them all three most adroitly.

The beautiful Agnes Sorel, the adored mistress of King
Charles VII., was suspected by him of having borne a
daughter that he thought not to be his, nor was he ever
able to recognize her. And indeed, like mother, like
daughter, was the word, as our Chroniclers do all agree.
The same again did Anne Boleyn, wife of King Henry
VIII. of England, whom he did behead for not being

[321]

content with him, but giving herself to adultery. Yet
had he chose her for her beauty, and did adore her fondly.

I knew another lady which had been loved by a very
honourable gentleman, but after some while left by him;
and one day it happened that these twain fell to discussing their former loves. The gentleman, who was for
posing as a dashing blade, cried, "Ha! ha! and think
you, you were my only mistress in those days? You will
be much surprised to hear, I had two others all the while,
would you not?" To this she answered on the instant,
"You would be yet more surprised, would you not? to
learn you were anything but mine only lover then, for I
had actually three beside you to fall back on." Thus
you see how a good ship will always have two or three
anchors for to ensure its safety thoroughly.

To conclude,—love is all in all for women, and so it
should be! I will only add how once I found in the tablets
of a very fair and honourable lady which did stammer a
little Spanish, but did understand the same language well
enough, this little maxim writ with her own hand, for I
did recognize it quite easily: *Hembra o dama sin com-
pagnero, esperanza sin trabajo, y navio sin timon; nunca
pueden hazer cost que sea buena,*—"Man or woman without companion, hope without work, or ship without rud-
der, will never do aught good for much." 'Tis a saying
equally true for wife, widow and maid; neither one nor
the other can do aught good without the company of a
man, while the hope a lover hath of winning them is not
by itself near so like to gain them over readily as with
something of pains and hard work added, and some strife
and struggle. Yet doth not either wife or widow give
so much as a maid must, for 'tis allowed of all to be an

easier and simpler thing to conquer and bring under one
that hath already been conquered, subdued and overthrown, than one that hath never yet been vanquished,—
and that far less toil and pains is spent in travelling a
road already well worn and beaten than one that hath
never been made and traced out,—and for the truth
of these two instances I do refer me to travellers and men
of war. And so it is with maids; indeed there be even
some so capricious as that they have always refused to
marry, choosing rather to live ever in maidenly estate.
But an if you ask them the reason, " 'Tis so, because my
humour is to have it so," they declare. Cybelé, Juno,
Venus, Thetis, Ceres and other heavenly goddesses, did
all scorn this name of virgin,—excepting only Pallas,
which did spring from her father Jupiter's brain, hereby
showing that virginity is naught but a notion conceived
in the brain. So, ask our maids, which will never marry,
or an if they do, do so as late as ever they can, and at
an over ripe age, why they marry not, " 'Tis because I
do not wish," they say; "such is my humour and my
notion."

Several such we have seen at the Court of our Princes
in the days of King Francis. The Queen Regent had a
very fair and noble maid of honour, named Poupincourt,
which did never marry, but died a maid at the age of
sixty, as chaste as when she was born, for she was most
discreet. La Brelandière again died a maid and virgin at
the ripe age of eighty, the same which was governess of
Madame d'Angoulême as a girl.

I knew another maid of honour of very great and exalted family, and at the time seventy years of age, which
would never marry,—albeit she was no wise averse to

love without marriage. Some that would fain excuse her
for that she would not marry, used to aver she was meet
to be no husband's wife, seeing she had no affair at all.
God knoweth the truth! but at any rate she did find a
good enough one to have good fun elsewhere withal. A
pretty excuse truly!

Mademoiselle de Charansonnet, of Savoy, died at
Tours lately, a maid, and was interred with her hat and
her white virginal robe, very solemnly, with much pomp,
stateliness and good company, at the age of forty-five
or over. Nor must we doubt in her case, 'twas any defect
which stood in the way, for she was one of the fairest,
most honourable and most discreet ladies of the Court,
and myself have known her to refuse very excellent and
very high-born suitors.

Mine own sister, Mademoiselle de Bourdeille, which is
at Court maid of honour of the present Queen, hath in
like wise refused very excellent offers, and hath never
consented to marry, nor never will. So firm resolved is
she and obstinate to live and die a maid, no matter to
what age she may attain; and indeed so far she hath
kept steady to her purpose, and is already well advanced
in years.

Mademoiselle de Certan, another of the Queen's maids
of honour, is of the same humour, as also Mademoiselle
de Surgières, the most learned lady of the Court, and
therefore known as *Minerva*,—and not a few others.

The Infanta of Portugal, daughter of the late Queen
Eleanor, I have seen of the same resolved mind; and she
did die a maid and virgin at the age of sixty or over.
This was sure from no want of high birth, for she was
well born in every way, nor of wealth, for she had plenty,

and above all in France, where General Gourgues did
manage her affairs to much advantage, nor yet of natural
gifts, for I did see her at Lisbon, at the age of five and
forty, a very handsome and charming woman, of good
and graceful appearance, gentle, agreeable, and well deserving an husband her match in all things, in courtesy
and the qualities we French do most possess. I can affirm
this, from having had the honour of speaking with this
Princess often and familiarly.

The late Grand Prior of Lorraine, when he did bring
his galleys from East to West of the Mediterranean
Sea on his voyage to Scotland, in the time of the minority
of King Francis II., passing by Lisbon and tarrying
there some days, did visit and see her every day. She
did receive him most courteously and took great delight
in his company, loading him with fine presents. Amongst
others, she gave him a chain to suspend his cross withal,
all of diamonds and rubies and great pearls, well and
richly worked; and it might be worth from four to five
thousand crowns, going thrice round his neck. I think
it might well be worth that sum, for he could always
pawn it for three thousand crowns, as he did one time
in London, when we were on our way back from Scotland.
But no sooner was he returned to France than he did
send to get it out again, for he did love it for the sake of
the lady, with whom he was no little captivated and taken.
And I do believe she was no less fond of him, and would
willingly have unloosed her maiden knot for him,—that
is by way of marriage, for she was a most discreet and
virtuous Princess. I will say more, and that is, that
but for the early troubles that did arise in France, into
the which his brothers did draw him and kept him engaged

therein, he would himself have brought his galleys back and returned the same road, for to visit this Princess again and speak of wedlock with her. And I ween he would in that case have hardly been shown the door, for he was of as good an house as she, and descended of great Kings no less than she, and above all was one of the handsomest, most agreeable, honourable and best Princes of Christendom. Now for his brothers, in particular the two eldest, for these were the oracles of the rest and captains of the ship, I did one day behold them and him conversing of the matter, the Cardinal telling them of his voyage and the pleasures and favours he had received at Lisbon. They were much in favour of his making the voyage once more and going back thither again, advising him to pursue his advantage in that quarter, as the Pope would at once have given him dispensation of his religious orders. And but for those accursed troubles I have spoke of, he would have gone, and in mine opinion the emprise had turned out to his honour and satisfaction. The said Princess did like him well, and spake to me of him very fondly, asking me as to his death,—quite like a woman in love, a thing easily enough perceived in such circumstances by a man of a little penetration.

I have heard yet another reason alleged by a very clever person, I say not whether maid or wife,—and she had mayhap had experience of the truth thereof,—why some women be so slow to marry. They declare this tardiness cometh *propter mollitiem*, "by reason of luxuriousness." Now this word *mollities* doth mean, they be so luxurious, that is to say so much lovers of their own selves and so careful to have tender delight and pleasure by themselves and in themselves, or mayhap with their bosom friends, after the Lesbian fashion, and do find such gratification in female society alone, as that they be convinced and firmly persuaded that with men they would never win such satisfaction. Wherefore they be content to go without these altogether in their joys and toothsome pleasures, without ever a thought of masculine acquaintance or marriage.

Maids and virgins would seem in old days at Rome to have been highly honoured and privileged, so much so that the law had no jurisdiction over them to sentence them to death. Hence the story we read of a Roman Senator in the time of the Triumvirate, which was condemned to die among other victims of the Proscription, and not he alone, but all the offspring of his loins. So when a daughter of his house did appear on the scaffold, a very fair and lovely girl, but of unripe years and yet virgin, 'twas needful for the executioner to deflower her himself and take her maidenhead on the scaffold, and only then when she was so polluted, could he ply his knife upon her. The Emperor Tiberius did delight in having fair virgins thus publicly deflowered, and then put to death,—a right villainous piece of cruelty, pardy!

The Vestal Virgins in like manner were greatly honoured and respected, no less for their virginity than for their religious character; for indeed, an if they did show any the smallest frailty of bodily purity, they were an hundred times more rigorously punished than when they had failed to take good heed of the sacred fire, and were buried alive under the most pitiful and terrible circumstances. 'Tis writ of one Albinus, a Roman gentleman, that having met outside Rome some Vestals that were going somewhither a-foot, he did command his wife and

[327]

children to descend from her chariot, to set them in it and so complete their journey. Moreover they had such weight and authority, as that very often they were trusted as umpires to make peace betwixt the Roman people and the Knights, when troubles did sometimes arise affecting the two orders. The Emperor Theodosius did expel them from Rome under advice of the Christians; but in opposition to the said Emperor the Romans did presently depute one Symmachus, to beseech him to restore them again, with all their wealth, incomings and privileges as before. These were exceedingly great, and indeed every day they were used to distribute so great a store of alms, as that neither native Roman nor stranger, coming or going, was ever suffered to ask an alms, so copious was their pious charity toward all poor folk. Yet would Theodosius never agree to bring them back again.

They were named Vestals from the Latin word *vesta*, signifying fire, the which may well turn and twist, shoot and sparkle, yet doth it never cast seed, nor receive the same,—and so 'tis with a virgin. They were bound so to remain virgins for thirty years, after which they might marry; but few of them were fortunate in so leaving their first estate, just like our own nuns which have cast off the veil and quitted the religious habit. They kept much state and went very sumptuously dressed,—of all which the poet Prudentius doth give a pleasing description, being apparently much in the condition of our present Lady Canonesses of Mons in Hainault and Réaumond in Lorraine, which be permitted to marry after. Moreover this same Prudentius doth greatly blame them because they were used to go abroad in the city in most magnificent coaches, correspondingly attired, and to the Amphi-

[328]

theatres to see the games of the Gladiators and combats to the death betwixt men and men, and men and wild beasts, as though finding much delight in seeing folk thus kill each other and shed blood. Wherefore he doth pray the Emperor to abolish these sanguinary contests and pitiful spectacles altogether. The Vestals at any rate should never behold suchlike barbarous sports; though indeed they might say for their part: "For lack of other more agreeable sports, the which other women do see and practise, we must needs content us with these."

As for the estate of widows in many cases, there be many which do love just as soberly as these Vestals, and myself have known several such; but others again would far fainer take their joy in secret with men, and in the fullness of complete liberty, rather than subject to them in the bonds of marriage. For this reason, when we do see women long preserve their widowhood, 'tis best not over much to praise them as we might be inclined to do, till we do know their mode of life, and then only, according to what we have learned thereof, either to extol them most highly or scorn them. For a woman, when she is fain to unbend her severity, as the phrase is, is terribly wily, and will bring her man to a pretty market, an if he take not good heed. And being so full of guile, she doth well understand how to bewitch and bedazzle the eyes and wits of men in such wise they can scarce possibly recognize the real life they lead. For such or such an one they will mistake for a perfect prude and model of virtue, which all the while is a downright harlot, but doth play her game so cunningly and furtively none can ever discover aught.

I have known a great Lady in my time, which did

remain a widow more than forty years, so acting all the while as to be esteemed the most respectable woman in country or Court, yet was she *sotto coverto* (under the rose) a regular, downright harlot. So featly had she followed the trade by the space of five and fifty years, as maid, wife and widow, that scarce a suspicion had she roused against her at the age of seventy, when she died. She did get full value of her privileges as a woman; one time, when a young widow, she fell in love with a certain young nobleman, and not able otherwise to get him, she did come one Holy Innocents' day into his bed-chamber, to give him the usual greetings. But the young man gave her these readily enough, and with something else than the customary instrument. She had her dose,—and many another like it afterward.

Another widow I have known, which did keep her widowed estate for fifty years, all the while wantoning it right gallantly, but always with the most prudish modesty of mien, and many lovers at divers times. At the last, coming to die, one she had loved for twelve long years, and had had a son of him in secret, of this man she did make so small account she disowned him completely. Is not this a case where my word is illustrated, that we should never commend widows over much, unless we know thoroughly their life and life's end?

But at this rate I should never end; and an end we must have. I am well aware sundry will tell me I have left out many a witty word and merry tale which might have still better embellished and ennobled this my subject. I do well believe it; but an if I had gone on so from now to the end of the world, I should never have made an end; however if any be willing to take the trouble to do better, I shall be under great obligation to the same.

Well! dear ladies, I must e'en draw to an end; and I do beg you pardon me, an if I have said aught to offend you. 'Tis very far from my nature, whether inborn or gotten by education, to offend or displeasure you in any wise. In what I say of women, I do speak of some, not of all; and of these, I do use only false names and garbled descriptions. I do keep their identity so carefully hid, none may discover it, and never a breath of scandal can come on them but by mere conjecture and vague suspicion, never by certain inference.

I fear me 'tis only too likely I have here repeated a second time sundry witty sayings and diverting tales I have already told before in my other Discourses. Herein I pray such as shall be so obliging as to read all my works, to forgive me, seeing I make no pretence to being a great Writer or to possess the retentive memory needful to bear all in mind. The great Plutarch himself doth in his divers Works repeat several matters twice over. But truly, they that shall have the task of printing my books, will only need a good corrector to set all this matter right.

NOTES

NOTES

P. 3: At first this discourse was the last; it is outlined in the manuscript 608 as follows: "Discourse on why beautiful and faithful women love valiant men, and why worthy men love courageous women."

P. 4: Virgil, in his Æneid (Bk. I), makes Penthesileia appear only after Hector's death. For these accounts on the Amazons, consult *Traité historique sur les Amazones,* by Pierre Petit, Leyde, 1718.

P. 5: See Boccaccio, *De Claris Mulieribus.*

P. 6: Æneid, IV., 10-13.

P. 8: A Latin work of Boccaccio in nine books.

P. 8: Bk. IX., Chap. 3.

P. 9: *Nouvelle,* 1554-1574.

P. 9: Bandello, t. III., p. 1 (Venice, 1558).

P. 11: The Duc d'Anjou, afterwards Henri III. of France, is meant. He was the third son of Henri II. and Catherine de Medici, and was born at Fontainebleau 1551. On the death of his brother Charles IX. in 1574 he succeeded to the throne. Died 1589. The victories referred to are those of Jarnac and Montcontour.

P. 12: Ronsard, *Œuvres,* liv. 1, 174th sonnet.

P. 13: "Petit-Lit" is Leith,—the port of Edinburgh, on the Firth of Forth. The English army under Lord Grey of Wilton invaded Scotland in 1560, and laid siege to Leith, then occupied by the French. The place was stubbornly defended, but must soon have fallen, when envoys were sent by Francis II. from France to conclude a peace. These were Monluc, Bishop of Valence, and the

Sieur de Rendan mentioned in the text; the negotiators appointed to meet them on the English side were the Queen's great minister Cecil and Wotton, Dean of Canterbury. The French troops were withdrawn.

P. 13: The little Leith. (Cf. Jean de Beaugué, *Histoire de la guerre d'Ecosse,* reprinted by Montalembert in 1862, Bordeaux.)

P. 13: Jacques de Savoie, Duke de Nemours, died in 1585.

P. 13: Charles de La Rochefoucauld, Count de Randan, was sent to England in 1559, where he arranged peace with Scotland.

P. 14: An imaginary king without authority.

P. 14: Philibert le Voyer, lord of Lignerolles and of Bellefille, was frequently employed as a diplomatic agent. He was in Scotland in 1567. He was assassinated at Bourgueil in 1571, because he was suspected of betraying Charles IX.'s avowal regarding Saint Bartholomew.

P. 15: Brantôme knew quite well that the woman the handsome and alluring Duke de Nemours truly loved was no other than Mme. de Guise, Anne d'Este, whom he later married.

P. 15: XVIth Tale. Guillaume Gouffier, lord of Bonnivet.

P. 16: Marguerite de Valois took Bussy d'Amboise partly because of his reputation as a duellist.

P. 17: Jacques de Lorge, lord of Montgomerie, captain of Francis I.'s Scotch Guard and father of Henri II.'s involuntary murderer.

P. 18: Claude de Clermont, Viscount de Tallard.

P. 18: François de Hangest, lord of Genlis, captain of the Louvre, who died of hydrophobia at Strassburg in 1569.

P. 19: It is undoubtedly Louise de Halwin, surnamed Mlle. de Piennes the Elder, who later married Cipier of the Marcilly family.

P. 20: It is to this feminine stimulation that King Francis I. alluded in the famous quatrain in the Album of Aix, which is rightly or wrongly attributed to him.

P. 20: Agnès Sorel, or Soreau, the famous mistress of Charles VII., was daughter of the Seigneur de St. Gérard, and was born at the village of Fromenteau in Touraine in 1409. From a very early age she was one of the maids of honour of Isabeau de Lorraine, Duchess of Anjou, and received every advantage of education. Her wit and accomplishments were no less admired than her beauty.

She first visited the Court of France in the train of this latter Princess in 1431, where she was known by the name of the *Demoiselle* de Fromenteau, and at once captivated the young King's heart. She appeared at Paris in the Queen's train in 1437, but was intensely unpopular with the citizens, who attributed the wasteful expenditure of the Court and the misfortunes of the Kingdom to her. Whatever may be the truth of Brantôme's tale of the astrologer, there is no doubt as to her having exerted her influence to rouse the King from the listless apathy he had fallen into, and the idle, luxurious life he was leading in his Castle of Chinon, while the English were still masters of half his dominions.

She was granted many titles and estates by her Royal lover,— amongst others the castle of Beauté, on the Marne, whence her title of La Dame de Beauté, and that of Loches, in the Abbey Church of which she was buried on her sudden death in 1450, and where her tomb existed down to 1792.

P. 20.   Charles VII., son of the mad Charles VI., born 1403, crowned at Poitiers 1422, but only consecrated at Reims in 1429, after the capture of Orleans and the victories due to Jeanne d'Arc.   The adversary of the Burgundians and the English under the Duke of Bedford and Henry V. of England.   Died 1461.

P. 20:   Henry V. of England, reigned, 1413-1422.

P. 20: Bertrand du Guesclin, Constable of France, the most famous warrior of the XIVth Century, and one of the greatest Captains of any age, was born about 1314 near Rennes of an ancient and distinguished family of Brittany.   He was the great champion of France in the wars with the English, and the tales of his prowess are endless.   Died 1380.

P. 21: Béatrix, fourth daughter of Raymond-Béranger IV., Count de Provence.

P. 22: Isabeau de Lorraine, daughter of Charles II., married René d'Anjou.

P. 24: He called himself René de La Platière, lord of Les Bordes, and was ensign in Field Marshal de Bourdillon's company; he was killed at Dreux. He was the son of François de La Platière and Catherine Motier de La Fayette.

P. 24: Brantôme, in his eulogy of Bussy d'Amboise, relates that he reprimanded that young man for his mania of killing. The woman whom he compares here to Angélique was Marguerite de Valois.

P. 27: Brantôme is unquestionably referring again in this paragraph to Marguerite de Valois and Bussy d'Amboise.

P. 28: *Orlando furioso,* canto V.

P. 30: That is why Marguerite de Valois turned away "that big disgusting Viscount de Turenne." She compared him "to the empty clouds which look well only from without." (*Divorce satyrique.*)

P. 30: This is very likely an adventure that happened to Brantôme, and he had occasion to play the rôle of the "gentilhomme content."

P. 32: According to Lalanne, the two gentlemen are Le Balafré and Mayenne. If the "grande dame" was Marguerite, she bore Mayenne no grudge, whom she described as "a good companion, big and fat, and voluptuous like herself."

P. 37: It is Madeleine de Saint-Nectaire or Senneterre, married to the lord of Miramont, Guy de Saint-Exupéry; she supported the Huguenots. She defeated Montal in Auvergne, and according to Mézeray, killed him herself in 1574. (See Anselme, t. IV., p. 890.) In 1569, Mme. de Barbancon had also fought herself; she, too, was formerly an Italian, Ipolita Fioramonti.

P. 39: On the large square with the tower, in the centre of Sienna.

P. 40: Livy, Bk. XXVII., Chap. XXXVII.

P. 42: *Orlando furioso,* cantos XXII. and XXV.

P. 42: Christophe Jouvenel des Ursins, lord of La Chapelle, died in 1588.

P. 42: Henri II.

P. 44: Ipolita Fioramonti, married to Luigi di Malaspina, of the Padua branch; she was general of the Duke of Milan's armies. (Litta, Malaspina di Pavia, t. VIII., tav. xx.)

P. 44: Famous fortified city and seaport on the Atlantic coast of France; 300 miles S. W. of Paris, capital of the modern Department of Charente-Inférieure.

P. 45: The interview between François de La Noue, surnamed Bras-de-Fer (iron arm), and the representatives of Monsieur, François, Duke d'Alencon, took place February 21, 1573. The scene that Brantôme describes happened Sunday, February 22.

P. 46: What Brantôme advances here is to be found in Jacques de Bourbon's *La grande et merveilleuse oppugnation de la noble cité de Rhodes*, 1527.

P. 46: The siege took place in 1536.

P. 47: August 14, 1536. Count de Nassau besieged Péronne at the head of 60,000 men; the population defended itself with the uttermost energy. Marie Fouré, according to some, was the principal heroine of this famous siege; according to others, all the honor should go to Mme. Catherine de Foix. (Cf. *Pièces et documents relatifs au siège de Péronne, en 1536*. Paris, 1864.)

P. 47: The siege of Sancerre began January 3, 1573; but the rôle of the women was more pacific than at Péronne; they nursed the wounded and fed the combatants. The energetic Joanneau governed the city. (Poupard, *Histoire de Sancerre*, 1777.)

P. 47: Vitré was besieged by the Duke de Mercœuer in 1589. This passage of Brantôme's is quoted in the *Histoire de Vitré* by Louis Dubois (1839, pp. 87-88).

P. 47: Péronne, a small fortified town of N. W. France, on the Somme and in the Department of same name. It was bombarded by the Prussians in 1870, and the fine belfry of the XIVth Century destroyed. Its siege by the Comte de Nassau was in 1536.

P. 47: Sancerre, a small town on the left bank of the Loire, modern Department of the Cher, 27 miles from Bourges. The Huguenots of Sancerre endured two terrible sieges in 1569 and 1573.

P. 47: Vitré, a town of Brittany, modern Department Ille-et-Vilaine, of about 10,000 inhabitants. Retains its medieval aspect and town walls to the present day.

P. 48: Collenuccio, Bk. V.

P. 49: Boccaccio has arranged this story in his *De claries muli-eribus*, cap. CI. Vopiscus, *Aurelius*, XXVI-XXX, relates this fact more coolly.

P. 49: Zenobia, the famous Queen of Palmyra, widow of Odena-thus, who had been allowed by the weak Emperor Gallienus to participate in the title of Augustus, and had extended his empire over a great part of Asia Minor, Syria and Egypt. She was eventually defeated by Aurelian in a great battle on the Orontes not far from Antioch. Palmyra was destroyed, and its inhabitants massacred; and Zenobia brought in chains to Rome.

P. 49: The Emperor Aurelian was born about 212 A. D., and was of very humble origin. He served as a soldier in almost every part of the Roman Empire, and rose at last to the purple by dint of his prowess and address in arms, succeeding Claudius in 270 A. D. Almost the whole of his short reign of four years and a half was occupied in constant fighting. Killed in a conspiracy 275 A. D.

P. 53: Perseus, the last King of Macedon, son of Philip V., came to the throne 179 B. C. His struggle with the Roman power lasted from 171 to 165, when he was finally defeated at the battle of Pydna by the consul L. Aemilius Paulus. He was carried to Rome and adorned the triumph of his conqueror in 167 B. C., and afterwards thrown into a dungeon. He was subsequently released, however, on the intercession of Aemilius Paulus, and died in honourable captivity at Alba.

P. 53: Maria of Austria, sister of Charles V., widow of Louis II. of Hungary, and ruler over the Netherlands; she died in 1558. It was against her rule that John of Leyden struggled.

P. 53: Brantôme has in mind Aurelia Victorina, mother of Victorinus, according to Trebillius Pollio, *Thirty Tyrants*, XXX.

P. 54: In Froissart, liv. I, chap. 174.

NOTES

P. 54: Henri I., Prince de Condé, died in 1588 (January 5), poisoned, says the *Journal de Henri*, by his wife Catherine Charlotte de la Trémolle.

P. 54: Isabella of Austria, daughter of Philip II.

P. 54: Jeanne de Flandres.

P. 55: Jacquette de Montberon, Brantôme's sister-in-law.

P. 55: Macchiavelli, Dell'arte della guerre, Bk. V., ii.

P. 56: Paule de Penthièvre, the second wife of Jean II. de Bourgogne, Count de Nevers.

P. 57: Richilde, Countess de Hainaut, who died in 1091.

P. 57: Hugues Spencer, or le Dépensier.

P. 57: Jean de Hainaut, brother of Count de Hainaut.

P. 57: Cassel and Broqueron.

P. 57: Edward II. of Caernarvon, King of England, was the fourth son of Edward I. and Queen Eleanor. Ascended the throne 1307, and married Isabel of France the following year. A cowardly and worthless Prince, and the tool of scandalous favourites, such as Piers Gaveston. Isabel and Mortimer landed at Orwell, in Suffolk, in 1326, and deposed the King, who was murdered at Berkeley Castle, 1307.

P. 58: Eleonore d'Acquitaine.

P. 59: Thevet wrote the *Cosmographie;* Nauclerus wrote a *Chronographie.*

P. 60: Vittoria Colonna, daughter of Fabrizio Colonna and of Agnes de Montefeltro, born in 1490, and affianced at the age of four to Ferdinand d'Avalos, who became her husband. The letter of which Brantôme speaks is famous; he found it in Vallès, fol. 205. As for Mouron, he was the great Chancellor Hieronimo Morone.

P. 61: Plutarch, *Anthony,* Chap. xiv.

[341]

NOTES

P. 62: Catherine Marie de Lorraine, wife of Louis de Bourbon, Duke De Montpensier.

P. 62: Henri III., assassinated at Paris, 1589.

P. 65: The *other man* was Mayenne.

P. 67: Poltrot de Méré was tortured and quartered (March 18, 1563). As regards the admiral, he was massacred August 24, 1572.

P. 68: Philibert de Marcilly, lord of Cipierre, tutor of Charles IX.

P. 71: On this adventure, consult the Additions au Journal de Henri III., note 2.

P. 72: Louis de Correa, *Historia de la conquista del reino de Navarra*.

P. 76: Louise de Savoie.

P. 77: Charlotte de Roye, married to Francis III. de La Roche-foucauld in 1557; she died in 1559.

P. 78: Marguerite de Foix-Candale, married to Jean Louis de Nogaret, Duke d'Eperon.

P. 79: Renée de Bourdeille, daughter of André and Jacquette Montberon. She married, in 1579, David Bouchard, Viscount d'Aube-terre, who was killed in Périgord in 1593. She died in 1596. The daughter of whom Brantôme is about to speak was Hippolyte Bouchard, who was married to François d'Esparbez de Lussan. The three daughters whom he later mentions were: Jeanne, Countess de Duretal, Isabelle, Baroness d'Ambleville, and Adrienne, lady of Saint-Bonnet.

P. 80: Married subsequently to François d'Esparbez de Lusan, Maréchal d'Aubeterre.

P. 83: Renée de Clermont, daughter of Jacques de Clermont-d'Amboise, lord of Bussy; she was married to the incompetent Jean de Montluc-Balagny (bastard of the Bishop de Valence), created Field Marshal of France in 1594.

P. 84:   Gabrielle d'Estrées.

P. 85:   Popular song of the day; Musée de Janequin.   See *Recueil* of Pierre Atteignant.

P. 89:   Renée Taveau, married to Baron Mortemart.   François de Rochechouart.

P. 91:   There is a copy of this sixth discourse in the MS. 4783, *du fonds français*, at the Bibliothèque Nationale: this copy is from the end of the sixteenth century.

P. 92:   Charlotte de Savoie, second wife of Louis XI., daughter of Louis, Duke de Savoie.

P. 92:   Louis XI. is generally supposed not only to have bandied many such stories with all the young bloods at the Court of Philippe le Bon, Duke of Burgundy, where he had taken refuge when Dauphin, but actually to have taken pains to have a collection of them made and afterwards published in the same order in which we have them, in the Work entitled *"Cent Nouvelles nouvelles," lequel en soy contient cent chapitres ou histoires, composées ou récitées par nouvelles gens depuis naguères,*—"An Hundred New Romances,—a Work containing in itself an hundred chapters or tales, composed or recited by divers folk in these last years."   This is confirmed by the words of the original preface or notice, which would appear to have been written in his life-time: "And observe that throughout the *Nouvelles,* wherever 'tis said by *Monseigneur,* Monseigneur the Dauphin is meant, which hath since succeeded to the crown and is now King Louis XI.; for in those days he was in the Duke of Burgundy's country."   But as it is absolutely certain this Prince only withdrew into Brabant at the end of the year 1456, and only returned to France in August 1461, it is quite impossible the Collection can have appeared in France about the year 1455, as is stated without sufficient consideration in the preface of the latest editions of this work.   Two ancient editions are known, one,— Paris 1486, folio; the other also published at Paris, by the widow of Johan Treperre, N. D., also folio.   Besides this, two modern editions, with badly executed cuts, printed at Cologne, by Pierre Gaillard, 1701 and 1736 respectively, 2 vols. 8vo.

P. 93:   By *Bourguignonne* the King meant *étrangère* (foreigner).

[343]

NOTES

P. 94: See the sojourn of Charles VIII. at Lyons: *Séjours de Charles VIII. et Louis XII. à Lyon sur le Rosne jouxte la copie des faicts, gestes et victoires des roys Charles VIII. et Louis XII.*, Lyon, 1841.

P. 94: Louis XII. had really been a "good fellow," without mentioning the laundress of the court, who was rumored to be the mother of Cardinal de Bucy, he had known at Genoa Thomasina Spinola, with whom, according to Jean d'Authon, his relations were purely moral.

P. 97: Francis I. forbade by the decree of December 23, 1523, that any farces be played at the colleges of the University of Paris "Wherein scandalous remarks are made about the King or the princes or about the people of the King's entourage." (Clairambault, 324, fol. 8747, at the Bibilothèque Nationale.) This king maintained, as Brantôme says, that women are very fickle and inconstant; he wrote to Montmorency of his own sister Marguerite de Valois, November 8, 1537: "We may be sure that when we wish women to stop they are dying to trot along; but when we wish them to go they refuse to budge from their place." (Clairambault, 336, fol. 6230, v°.)

P. 98: Paul Farnese, Paul III.—1468-1549.

P. 98: The queen arrived at Nice, June 8, 1538, where the king and Pope Paul III. were. The ladies of whom Brantôme speaks should be the Queen of Navarre, Mme. de Vendôme, the Duchess d'Etampes, the Marquess de Rothelin—that beautiful Rohan of whom it was said that her husband would get with child and not she—and thirty-eight gentlewomen. (Clair., 336, fol. 6549.)

P. 98: John Stuart, Duke of Albany, grandson of James II., King of Scotland. He was born in France in 1482 and died in 1536. The anecdote that Brantôme relates is connected with the journey of Clement VI. to Marseilles at the time of the marriage of Henri II., then Duke d'Orléans, with the niece of the pope, Catherine de Medici. The marriage took place at Marseilles in 1533.

P. 100: Louise de Clermont Tallard, who married as her second husband the Duc d'Uzes. Jean de Taix was the grand master of artillery.

P. 107: He was called Pierre de La Mare, lord of Matha, master of the horse to Marguerite, sister of the king. (Bib. Nat., Cabinet des Titres, art. Matha.)   Aimée de Méré was at the court from 1560 to 1564.   Hence this adventure took place during that time.   (Bib. Nat. ms. français 7856, fol. 1136, v°.)

P. 108: Provided with "bards," plate-armour used to protect a horse's breast and flanks.

P. 109: This Fontaine-Guérin was in all likelihood Honorat de Bueil, lord of Fontaine-Guérin, gentleman of the king's bed-chamber, councillor of State, who died in 1590.   He was a great favorite of Charles IX.

P. 112: The lady in question was Françoise de Rohan, dame de La Garnache, if we are to believe Bayle in the *Dict. Critique,* p. 1317, 2nd. ed., though there would seem to be some doubt about it.   The "very brave and gallant Prince" was the Duc de Nemours.

P. 112: A German dance, the *Facheltanz.*

P. 113: Marie de Flamin.

P. 114: The son of this lady was Henri d'Angoulème, who killed Altoviti and was killed by him at Aix, and not at Marseilles, June 2, 1586.   Philippe Altoviti was the Baron of Castellane; he had married the beautiful Renée de Rieux-Châteauneuf.

P. 115: *Le Tigre*—a pamphlet by François Hotman directed against the Cardinal de Lorraine and the Duchesse de Guise, 1560.

P. 116: Philibert de Marcilly, lord of Cipierre.

P. 117: That pamphlet was aimed at Anne d'Este, Duchess de Guise, at the time of her marriage with the Duc de Nemours.

P. 119: Brantôme alludes to the hatred of the Duchess de Montpensier.

P. 120: Marie de Clèves, who died during her lying-in in 1574.

P. 120: Catherine Charlotte de La Trémolle, Princess de Condé.

P. 122: Not found anywhere in Brantôme's extant works.

[345]

P. 125: Du Guast or Lignerolles. However, it may refer to Bussy d'Amboise.

P. 126: Marie Babou de la Bourdaisière, who married Claude de Beauvillier Saint-Aignan in 1560.

P. 128: Plutarch, *Sylla,* cap. XXX.

P. 129: Queen Maria of Hungary, ruler of the Netherlands, and sister of Charles V.

P. 129: Plutarch, *Cato of Utica,* cap. XXXV.

P. 132: The personages in question are Henri III., Renée de Rieux-Châteauneuf, then Mme. de Castellane, and Marie de Clèves, wife of the Prince de Condé.

P. 132: Louis de Condé, who deserted Isabeau de La Tour de Limeuil to marry Françoise d'Orléans. The beauty of which Brantôme speaks can scarcely be seen in the portrait in crayon of Isabeau de Limeuil who became Mme. de Sardini.

P. 135: Mottoes were constantly used at that time.

P. 136: Anne de Bourbon, married in 1561 to François de Clèves, Duke de Nevers and Count d'Eu.

P. 146: The empress was Elizabeth of Portugal; the Marquis de Villena, M. de Villena; the Duke de Feria, Gomez Suarez de Figueroa, Duke de Feria; Eleonor, the Queen of Portugal, later married to François Iᵉʳ; Queen Marie, the Queen of Hungary.

P. 147: Elizabeth, daughter of Henri II.

P. 151: The MS. of this discourse is at the Bibliothèque Nationale (Ms. fr. 3273); it is written in a good hand of the end of the sixteenth century. It is dedicated to the Duke d'Alençon.

P. 152: *Opere* di G. Boccaccio, *Il Filicopo,* Firenze, 1723, t. II., p. 73.

P. 159: *La Tournelle* in the original. This was the name given to the Criminal Court of the Parliament of Paris.

P. 161: Barbe de Cilley; she died in 1415.

P. 166: Brantôme is undoubtedly referring to Mme. de Villequier.

P. 172: This is again Isabeau de La Tour Limeuil.

P. 178: See XXVth Tale in *Cent Nouvelles nouvelles.*

P. 188: Honoré Castellan.

P. 188. Baron de Vitteau was this member of the Du Prat family; he killed Louis de Béranger du Guast.

P. 190: Chicot was Henri III.'s jester who killed M. de La Rochefoucauld on Saint Bartholomew's Day.

P. 194: *Alberic de Rosate,* under the word "Matrimonium" in his *Dictionary* reports an exactly similar instance. *Barbatias* has something even more extraordinary, how a boy of seven got his nurse with child.

P. 195: The Queen Mother Catherine de Medici. The author gives her name in his book of the *Dames Illustres,* where he tells the same story.

P. 207: Jean de Rabodanges, who married Marie de Clèves, mother of Louis XII. She was *reine blanche,* that is, she was in mourning; at that time the women of the nobility wore white when in mourning.

P. 207: These eighteen chevaliers, who were elevated in one batch, caused a good deal of gossip at the court.

P. 214: Louis de Béranger du Guast.

P. 216: She was thirty-five; she died three years later.

P. 217: It is the Château d'Usson in Auvergne.

P. 218: Louis de Saint-gelais-Lansac.

P. 220: Jeanne, married to Jean, Prince of Portugal. She died in 1578.

[347]

P. 225: Sébastien, died in 1578. This passage in Brantôme is not one of the least irreverent of this hardened sceptic.

P. 226: The portraits of Marie disclose a protruding mouth. She is generally represented with a cap over her forehead. This feature is to be found in a marked degree in Queen Eleanore; and her brother Charles V. also had a protruding mouth. The drooping lip was likewise characteristic of all the later Dukes de Bourgogne.

P. 228: The entanglements of which Brantôme speaks were: the revolt of the Germanats, in Spain, in 1522; of Tunis or Barbarie, 1535; the troubles in Italy, also in 1535; the revolt in the Netherlands, provoked by the taxes imposed by Maria, in 1540. M. de Chièvres was Guillaume de Croy.

P. 229: Folembray, the royal residence occupied by François Ier and later by Henri II. Henri IV. negotiated there with Mayenne during the Ligue.

P. 229: Bains en Hainaut.

P. 230: Claude Blosset, surnamed Torcy, lady of Fontaine Chalandray.

P. 234: Christine of Denmark, daughter of Christian II., first married to Francesco Maria Sforza, Duke of Milan. In 1540, five years after her husband's death, she married Francis I. of Lorraine. Her son was Charles II. of Lorraine.

P. 235: N. de La Brosse-Mailly.

P. 235: A small plank attached to the saddle of a lady's horse, and serving to support the rider's feet. Superseded by the single stirrup and pommel.

P. 236: Guy du Faur de Pybrac.

P. 243: Renée, wife of Guillaume V., Duke de Bavière.

P. 246: Blanche de Montferrat, wife of Charles Ier, Duke de Savoie; she died in 1509.

P. 247: Paradin, *Chronique de Savoye*, III, 85.

P. 247: The seneschal's lady of Poitou was Mme. de Vivonne.

P. 249: Nicolas de Lorraine-Vaudemont, father-in-law of Henri III.

P. 249:—Françoise d'Orléans, widow of Louis, Prince de Condé.

P. 250: Louise, daughter of Nicolas de Lorraine-Vaudemont, married in 1575; she died in 1601.

P. 252: Jean de Talleyrand, former ambassador at Rome.

P. 256: Marguerite de Lorraine, whose second marriage was with François de Luxembourg, Duke de Piney.

P. 256: Mayenne, Duke du Maine.

P. 256: Aymard de Chastes.

P. 256: Refers of course to the assassination of Henri III., by the monk Clément (1589).

P. 257: Catherine de Lorraine.

P. 273: Jean Dorat, died in 1588. Louis de Béranger du Guast.

P. 280: Cæsar Borgia, son of Pope Alexander VI.

P. 280: Thomas de Foix, lord of Lescun, brother of Mme. de Châteaubriant.

P. 280: Piero Strozzi, Field Marshal of France.

P. 281: Jean de Bourdeille, brother of Brantôme. He died at the age of twenty-five at the siege of Hesdin. It was from him that the joint title of Brantôme passed on to our author.

P. 281: Henri de Clermont, Viscount de Tallard.

P. 281: André de Soleillas, Bishop of Riez in Provence, in 1576. He had a mistress who was given to playing the prude, but whose hypocrisy did not deceive King Henri IV. That Prince, one day rebuking this lady for her love affairs, said her only delight was in *le jeune et l'oraison,*—fast and prayer.

P. 282: This widow of a Field Marshal of France was very likely the lady of Field Marshal de Saint-André. She wedded as a second husband Geoffroi de Caumont, abbé de Clairac. She called herself Marguerite de Lustrac. As for Brantôme's aunt, it should be Philippe de Beaupoil; she married La Chasteignerie, and as a second husband François de Caumont d'Aymé.

P. 285: Anne d'Anglure de Givry, son of Jeanne Chabot and René d'Anglure de Givry. Jeanne married as a second husband Field Marshal de La Chastre.

P. 285: Jean du Bellay and Blanche de Tournon.

P. 288: Odet de Coligny, Cardinal de Chastillon, married to Elizabeth de Hauteville.

P. 290: Henri II., who neglected his wife, the Queen, for the Duchesse de Valentinois (Diane de Poitiers), who was already quite an old woman and had been his father, the preceding King's, mistress.

P. 293: About the year 400 of the Christian era, St. Jerome witnessed the woman's funeral, and he it is reports the fact mentioned in the text. *Epist. ad Ageruchiam, De Monogamia.*

P. 293: Charles de Rochechouart.

P. 302: Scio was taken in 1566 by the Turks.

P. 309: It was to her that King Henri IV. said at a court ball by way of amusing the company, that she had used green wood and dry wood both. This jest he made at her expense, because the said lady did never spare any other woman's good name.

P. 310: L'histoire et Plaisante cronique du Petit Jehan de Saintré, par Antoine de La Salle. Paris, 1517.

P. 312: XLVth Tale.

P. 316: An allusion to the affair of Jarnac, who killed La Chasteignerie, Brantôme's uncle, in a duel (1547) with an unexpected and decisive thrust of the sword.

NOTES

P. 316: Alesandro de Medici, killed, in 1537, by his cousin Loren-
zino.

P. 314: According to Rabelais, *poultre* (filly) is the name given to
a mare that has never been leapt. So Bussy was not speaking with
strict accuracy in using the term in this case.

P. 317: Mme. de Chateaubriant.

P. 318: Perhaps Marguerite de Valois and the ugly Martigues.

P. 321: The one-eyed Princess d'Eboli and the famous Antonio
Perez.

P. 323: Jeanne de Poupincourt.

P. 324: Anne de Berri, Lady de Certeau, at the court in 1583.
Hélène de Fonsèques.

P. 324: This princess was very ugly.

P. 330: In the sixteenth century it was customary to whip lazy
people in bed. See Marot's epigram: Du Jour des Innocens.